RAJ, SECRETS, REVOLUTION

A life of Subhas Chandra Bose

Mihir Bose

Grice Chapman
PUBLISHING

LONDON | SYDNEY | NEW YORK

First published worldwide in 2004
Grice Chapman Publishing
The Shire House
Burgh-next-Aylsham
Norwich NR11 6TP

www.gricechapman.com

ISBN 0-9545726-4-5

British Library Cataloguing in Publication Data
A catalogue record of this book is available in the British Library and the National Library of Australia

Printed & designed in England by
Barnwell's Print Ltd
Printing Works, Aylsham, Norfolk,
NR11 6ET, UK
Tel: +44 (0)1263 732767
www.barnwellprint.co.uk

Grice Chapman Publishing is part of the
Evergreen Media Group
LONDON | SYDNEY | NEW YORK

Acknowledgements

As recently as 20 years ago Subhas Chandra Bose was virtually unknown outside India. Inside the country the debate was almost wholly about whether he was still alive. But since then interest in Bose has grown, partly because of epic films like Richard Attenborough's *Gandhi* and the television series *Jewel in the Crown*, and also as a result of works by various historians and other writers, including myself.

In the last few years much fascinating new information about Bose has come to light, which reveals not only why he is now celebrated as a hero in contemporary India, but also places him as a significant figure in the history of the sub continent.

Indeed, the Subhas Bose industry has mushroomed. There have been two more television documentaries in Britain about him, and now Shyam Benegal has made a film about his life. The Netaji Research Bhavan, published nine volumes of Bose's *Collected Works*. They bring to light much new material not previously known, such as the intimate letters between Bose and his 'secret' Austrian wife Emilie. Major Iwaichi Fujiwara, the idealist Japanese intelligence officer who was the father of the first Indian National Army, published his memoirs. The British government has completed the mammoth task of completing and publishing the Transfer of Power Papers. Milan Hauner, whose epic study of Axis strategy during the Second World War was consulted by me as an unpublished manuscript, has since published it and it remains the last word on the Axis view of the Indian freedom movement.

Crucial in my decision to write a new study of Bose has been the release in the last few years of hitherto classified material. Most valuable are the files of the Indian Political Intelligence, the Raj's MI5, whose classified papers were released just as India was celebrating 50 years of freedom. I have been the first author to examine the IPI's Bose files in detail and they throw new and fascinating light on the Raj's allegation that he was a revolutionary and leader of the Indian terrorist movement. They also demonstrate how much the Raj feared him. It shadowed Bose right from the start of his political career to his end. Indeed it is the refusal of the British to release a letter from these files which has much exercised the latest judicial enquiry into Bose's death.

In addition there has been release of other classified documents by the Public Record Office in London relating to Bose and the Second World War, in particular, the confession to the Raj's police by people like Bhagat Ram Talwar and other Bose associates. They throw a most vivid light on the war years and require us to revise our accepted version of that period.

Finally, a few documents have begun to emerge from the Soviet archives which are tantalising and indicate the intricate web between the British, the Russians and the Axis powers during the Second World War. The result is a new biography, which adds considerably to our picture of the man and the period prior to Indian independence. Bose emerges as an even more substantial figure.

I owe a great debt to Milan Hauner and cannot thank him enough for his insights and kindness with which he has shared them with me. I have also been privileged to come to know Hugh Toye who must have the greatest treasure trove of material relating to Bose and the Second World War in his Wheatley home. Hugh has been kind enough to say publicly that he thinks my biography on Bose is the best, that shows the great generosity of his spirit and his unfailing courtesy to my many demands on his time. His absolute mastery of facts and details, even at the age of 87, demonstrate what a remarkable man he is. As a young boy in Bombay I read his *Springing Tiger*, his study of Bose's war-time activities, and I hope his revised edition will soon be published.

Despite my surname, I am not in any way related to Subhas Bose. My family comes from east Bengal, his from west. However I grew up in Bombay very aware of him, for my father was in business with his youngest brother Sailesh, whose wife remains my mother's best friend. while their son was at college with me. So I was always aware of the Bose lore. It was through them that I first met Anita Bose, Subhas's daughter, who came to our Bombay house when she visited India in 1961. In the course of the research for this edition I have renewed my acquaintance and also met her husband, Martin, both of whom have been very helpful. I am as every grateful to archivists and librarians all over the world for, once again, helping me find material I can never forget the kindness of my uncle Dhiren, whose MP's flat in Delhi proved such a home away from home when I did my research there.

I am grateful to Phillip Knightley, not only for writing the foreword, but introducing me to Susan Grice and Colin Chapman, who were brave enough to take on the book. Ashok Kumar's encouragement and advice was always a spur and Daljit Sebhai was ever helpful. Anthony MacDougall has been a shrewed and perceptive editor, and I think Karen Fuller's splendid cover has captured the spirit of the book.

Nicky Braganza and Alyson Hazelwood were extremely helpful and my brother-in-law Tapan enterprisingly found material, which shed new light on Bose. Above all I owe a debt I cannot repay to my wife Caroline who has had to revise all her ideas of Raj history to come to terms with Subhas Bose. The fact that she has managed it with such good humour is a testimony both to her ability to assimilate new information and her intrinsic grasp of diverse subjects.

I would like to dedicate this book to Baba and Ma - my parents.

Mihir Bose
London, Autumn 2004

Contents

Dramatis Personae

Aga Khan III. Was the spiritual head of the Ismaili Muslims and active in Indian politics until 1947. He was the Muslim leader the British most liked and he repaid them with active support for their rule in India, except during the Second World War which he spent in Switzerland. His Nazi contacts made the British debate whether they should try him for treason but they decided against it.

Amanullah Khan. King of Afghanistan who during the 1920s sought to modernise Afghanistan but was forced into exile in Italy where he died in 1960.

Leopold Charles Amery. A Conservative MP between 1911 and 1945, held various cabinet posts ending up as Secretary of State for India in Churchill's war Cabinet of 1940-45. His son John joined the Nazis and was hanged for treason after the war.

Kemal Ataturk led the Turkish armies to victory over the Allies in Gallipoli and then after the First World War transformed Turkey into a secular republic.

Clement Richard Attlee was a relatively unknown Labour MP when, as part of the all white commission of British politicians, he served on the Indian Statutory (Simon) Commission in 1927-30 deciding whether the Indians were capable of ruling themselves. In 1947, as the first Labour Prime Minister with a Commons majority, he granted India independence.

Sir Claude John Eyre Auchinleck. Commander-in-Chief of the British Army in India from June 1943 until 1947 who decided to hold the trial of Indian soldiers who had joined Subhas Bose's INA.

Aung San. Burmese political and military leader. Commander Burma Independence Army 1942, Minister for Defence 1943-45, President Anti Fascist People's Freedom, assassinated in 1947.

Aurobindo Ghose, born in 1872, was educated in England by a father who wanted his children to be English. But Aurobindo abandoned his training for the Indian Civil Service to become a fighter for India's freedom. But in 1910, pursued by the British. he took shelter in French controlled Pondicherry where he renounced politics to become a guru.

S.A. Ayer. A Reuters journalist who during the second world war became Minister of Information in Subhas Bose's Provisional Government of Free India.

Maulana Abdul Kalam Azad. The name "Maulana" was given to him by Gandhi in recognition of his scholarly abilities. He was one of the few leading Muslims to be part of the Congress and served long terms in prison. President of the Congress in 1923 and again between 1940-1946, he was Minister for Education in free India from 1947 until his death in 1958.

Satya Ranjan Bakshi. A Bengali revolutionary who was one of Subhas Bose's most devoted followers and refused to believe he had died in the air crash.

Frederick Edwin-Smith, the first Lord Birkenhead, was a prominent Conservative politician in the first part of the 20th century. Lord Chancellor and then Secretary of State for India between 1924 and 1928, he believed Indians were incapable of ruling themselves.

Ghanshyam Das Birla, one of India's leading industrialists who financed Mahatma Gandhi and was on friendly terms with many Congress leaders.

Asoke Bose, eldest son of Sarat who while studying in Europe in the 1930s often accompanied Subhas on his travels. It was in his house in Bararee that Subhas stopped for a night during his escape from India.

Dwijendranath Bose, son of another of Subhas's brothers who was actively involved in Subhas Bose's political movements during the late 1930s and early 1940s.

Rash Behari Bose, no relation of Subhas but a Bengali revolutionary who had sought to kill the Viceroy and foment rebellion before and during the First World War. He then fled India to Japan where he married a Japanese woman and settled down.

Sarat Bose. Mejda, the term of respect Subhas used for him, meant second brother and Subhas was closest to him. Sarat, who qualified as a barrister in London, was both a very successful lawyer in Calcutta and active in politics. When he was not in a British jail his large income financed Subhas and his large house in Calcutta provided Subhas a home.

Sisir Bose, one of Sarat's son who helped Subhas escape from India in 1941. Only 19 and a medical student, he drove the car that took Subhas on a midnight journey from his Calcutta home to Bararee on the first leg of a trip that landed him in Berlin. Later Sisir founded the Netaji Research Bhavan in memory of his uncle.

Dr Sunil Bose, a brother of Subhas who often examined him in Raj jails.

Nirad Chaudhuri, perhaps the greatest writer produced by the cultural clash between India and England. Worked as a secretary for Sarat and has left behind some vivid personal memories of the Bose brothers.

Achhar Singh Cheena was a member of the Kirti Party, the Punjab communist party. He was approached by Bose to help his escape to the Soviet Union but when Bose postponed the trip he went to Moscow himself.

Chiang Kai-shek. For two decades between the 1920s and the late 1940s he was the most important leader of war-torn China, the Generalissimo of China, first fighting the communists, then joining them to fight the Japanese. He fled the mainland for Taiwan following Mao's victory in 1949. During the Second World War he and his wife the American-educated Meiling were much courted by the Allies and heavily promoted as the ideal Asian political couple.

Nirmal Chunder Chunder, a Bengal Congress leader.

Count Galeazzo Ciano a career diplomat he married Mussolini's daughter and became Foreign Minister of Italy He was executed by the Germans on Mussolini's orders in 1943.

Miles John Clauson an official in the India Office in London who held various positions including Private Secretary to the Secretary of State for India.

Sir James Crerar, a member of the ICS he was Home Secretary of the Government of India, 1922-1927 and then Home Member 1927-1932.

Sir Stafford Cripps, a prominent left-wing Labour politician, he developed close links with Indian politicians visiting India in 1939.In 1942, having been British ambassador in Moscow, he entered the War Cabinet and was sent to India in a bid to try and make a deal with the Indian nationalists. He was also a member of Cabinet mission to India 1946. He was Chancellor of the Exchequer 1947-1950.

Basanti Devi Das, wife of Chitta Ranjan Das and a woman Subhas treated as his mother.

Beni Madhav Das, Subhas Bose's headmaster at Ravenshaw Collegiate School in Cuttack and a man Subhas adored.

Chitta Ranjan Das, in the Indian style of honouring great men with new names was given the title Desbandhu (friend of the people) by Gandhi. Born into a family of lawyers and educated in Calcutta's Presidency College he, like many children of the Bengali renaissance, had a love for literature, especially Bengali poetry. Encouraged by his father, Das went to London to prepare for the ICS, but failed twice and turned to law instead, qualifying as a barrister in1893. In London, he made speeches on Indian reform during the 1892 election campaign. On his return to India, he had to struggle as a lawyer, working in small town courts as he paid off his father's debts. He first became prominent before the First World War as a legal defender of the Extremists nationalists fighting the Raj during the Swadeshi movement. In 1917, he became President of the Bengal Provincial Congress marking his entry into formal politics and by 1920 he was the most prominent leader of Bengal and a major national figure. After Gandhi's first civil disobedience campaign had failed, he urged a new tactic to oppose the Raj. This was to fight the elections under the limited franchise given to the Indians, but then to obstruct the work of the councils the Raj had created. His aim was to prove that these councils and the reforms were meaningless.. He was elected Mayor of Calcutta in 1924, but within a year died, aged only 55.

Bhulabhai Desai, a lawyer who opposed Bose during his fight with Gandhi in 1939 but made a forceful advocate defending the INA at the Red Fort trials six years later.

Eamon De Valera, the Irish revolutionary who became *Taoiseach* (Prime Minister) and minister for external affairs of Eire and kept Ireland neutral during the Second World War.

Sir Herbert Emerson, a member of the ICS, he was Home Secretary 1930-1933 and Governor of the Punjab 1933-8.

Arthur Greenwood, Labour MP who became Lord Privy Seal in Attlee's government in 1945.

Sir Harry Haig, a member of the ICS he was private secretary to Viceroy 1925; Home Secretary 1926-30; Home Member 1932-4 and Governor of U.P. 1934-9.

Sir Maurice Hallett, an ICS, he was Chief Secretary Bihar and Orissa 1930-32; Home Secretary 1932-6; Governor of Bihar 1937-9 and Governor of U.P. 1939-45.

Lt General Iwaichi Fujiwara. He headed the F Kikan. (F stood for Fujiwara, freedom and friendship), and helped organise the First INA and then worked with Bose on the second. He was the Japanese Lawrence of Arabia, a rare breed of an idealistic Japanese officer who did believe that Japan's war against the European powers would also mean the liberation of fellow Asiatics.

Fazlul Huq, a Muslim lawyer and politician from east Bengal, he became Chief Minister of Bengal in 1937 following the elections held under the 1935 Act. He was in office until 1943.

Heinrich Himmler was not only head of Hitler's SS police, but also in charge of the death camps in eastern Europe.

Adolf Hitler, former Chancellor of Germany, and leader of the Third Reich.

Sir Samuel Hoare held various Cabinet positions in British Conservative governments and was Secretary of State for India 1931-5; Foreign Secretary 1935; Home Secretary 1937-9.

Lord Irwin, later Earl Halifax, landowner, was Minister for Agriculture 1924-5 when he was chosen to became Viceroy of India. He served there between 1926-31; later Foreign Secretary 1938-40 and then British ambassador in Washington 1941-6.

Faquir of Ipi (Mirza Ali Khan). Born about 1897, a religious leader active among the tribes in North Wazirstan.

M.A.H Ispahani, businessman of Calcutta and member of Working Committee of Muslim League who was Pakistan's ambassador in the United States 1947-52.

Muhammad Ali Jinnah was a barrister, and a nationalist but later successfully campaigned for the creation of Pakistan, of which he was Governor-General 1947-8.

Lt-General Masakazu Kawabe was appointed commander of Japan's Burma Area Army in 1943. After the debacle at Imphal he was transferred to command the Central District Army and 15th Area Army in Japan and following the suicide of Field Marshal Sugiyama after Japan's surrender he became Commander-in-Chief of Japan's 1st General Army.

Wilhelm Keppler, Hitler's financial adviser who was appointed to various jobs in the German Foreign Office and eventually head of the India Department

Abdul Gaffoor Khan, Congress leader of the NWFP who founded the 'Red Shirt' volunteer organisation in 1929.

Sahib Khan, brother of Gaffar Khan. Chief Minister of Congress ministries in NWFP 1937-9 and 1945-7.

Shah Nawaz Khan, a captain in the 1/14th Punjab regiment of the British Indian Army he surrendered to the Japanese at Singapore's Farrer Park. He later joined Subhas Bose's INA and was after the war was put on trial by the British. He was the only INA officer to gain political prominence in free India becoming a Cabinet minister.

Major-General Mohammed Zaman Kiani, an officer of the British Indian Army who joined the INA and in August 1945, following Japan's surrender, was left behind by Bose in Singapore as the representative of his Provisional Government to complete the surrender formalities.

JB Kripalani. A devoted follower of Gandhi he was general Secretary of the Congress between 1934-46, a period that covered Subhas Bose 's Presidency. President in 1946; he later resigned from Congress.

Kitty Kurti, a German Jewess who was friendly with Subhas Bose during the 1930s.

Harold Laski, prominent Labour party member whose economic views influenced an entire generation of students of the London School of Economics.

Dr Vladmir Lesny, a Czech Orientalist who was friendly with Bose.

Lord Linlithgow, 2nd Marquis (Victor Alexander John Hope). Chairman of Royal Commission on Indian Agriculture 1926-8; chairman of Joint Select Committee on Indian Constitutional Reform 1933; Viceroy of India 1936-43.

Major-General A.D.Loganadhan, a member of Bose's government who Bose appointed as commissioner for the Andamans.

Lord Lytton, Governor of Bengal in the 1920s who wrote a memoir of his time, *Pundits and Elephants* which is a classic study in imperial spin doctoring.

Madan Mohan Malaviya. President of the Congress 1909 and 1918; later developed a Hindu outlook in politics; founder of the Banaras Hindu University.

Uttam Chand Malhotra, an Indian shopkeeper in Kabul, who in 1941 sheltered Subhas Bose during his escape from the Raj. He later exploited this claim to fame and until well into the 1970s floated stories saying Subhas was about to return. They all proved false.

Ba Maw Burmese politician who became leader of the government the Japanese set up in Burma after their conquest.

VK Krishna Menon, spent much of his life in London campaigning for India's freedom. He was Secretary, India league in London 1929-47; borough councillor St Pancras 1934-47 and after independence became India's first High Commissioner in London.

Sir Frank Walter Messervy, GOC 7th Indian Division 1944, GOC IV Corps (Lt-General) Burma to Rangoon 1944-45. GOC Malaya Command 1945. GOC-in-C Northern Command, India 1946, Commander-in-Chief Pakistan Army 1947.

Sir AN Moberley, Home Member of the Governor's Executive Council of Bengal in the 1920s.

Edwin Stanley Montagu, Secretary of State for India 1917-22. He was one of the few prominent British politicians to visit India and with the Viceroy, Lord Chelmsford, made proposals which formed the basis of the reforms of 1919.

Girija Mookerjee, an Indian nationalist who lived in Europe during the 30s and joined Subhas Bose in Germany during the second world war.

Balkrishna Sheoram Moonje, eye surgeon and medical practitioner of Nagpur, he became a leader of the Hindu Mahasabha.

Sir David Taylor Monteath, an official in the India Office who was Permanent Under-Secretary of State for India and Burma from 1942

Lord Louis Mountbatten, (1st Earl Mountbatten) Chief of Combined Operations 1942-3; Supreme Allied Commander South-East Asia 1943-6; Viceroy of India March-August 1947; Governor-General of India August 1947 - June 1948.

Sir Alexander Muddiman, Home Member of the Viceroy's Executive Council in the 1920s.

Sir Robert Francis Mudie, member of the ICS who was Home Member of the Viceroy's Executive Council 1944-45.

KM Munshi, a right-wing Congress politician he was Home Minister of Bombay 1937-9.

Lt General Renya Mutaguchi was involved in the so-called Marco Polo incident on the night of 7 July 1937 which launched Japan's war with China. Appointed Commander of the 15th Army in March 1943, he was placed on reserve following his failure to take Imphal and ended his days Director of the Junior Course at the Military Academy in Tokyo.

Sarojini Naidoo, Poet and politician; President of the Congress in 1925; Governor of Uttar Pradesh 1947-9.

A.C.N Nambiar who married Sarojini's sister was a journalist who lived in Europe through the 1930s and 40s. He worked for Bose during the war taking over the running of the Free India Centre when Bose left for the east.

Jaya Prakash Narayan a left-wing Congress politician.

Khwaja Nazimuddin, a Muslim League leader in Bengal who became Home Minister in the Muslim dominated government of Bengal formed in 1937.

Motilal Nehru, father of Jawaharlal. Lawyer of Allahabad and President of the Congress in 1919 and 1928; founder with Das of the Swaraj Party within the Congress and leader of that Party in the Central Assembly 1924-6.

P.N Oak, ADC to Major General Bhonsle in Subhas Bose's INA he later became notorious in India for setting up the Historical Institute which claimed that the Hindus had had an empire including England and Taj Mahal was really a Hindu palace.

Edward Farley Oaten, a lecturer in Presidency College Calcutta who Subhas Bose is said to have struck. After Bose's death he wrote a poem on the affair.

Sir Michael O'Dwyer, Lieutenant-Governor of the Punjab 1913-19; in 1919 he authorised the imposition of martial law, which made possible the Amritsar massacre; assassinated in 1940.

First Baron Oliver, a civil servant in Colonial Office he was secretary of the Fabian Society and Secretary of State for India in 1924.

Govind Ballabh Pant a lawyer of Allahabad, he was a devoted follower of Gandhi and Nehru. Severely beaten along with Jawaharlal Nehru at Lucknow in the demonstration against the Simon Commission, 1928, he became Chief Minister of U.P. 1937-39 and 1946-55, later Indian Home Minister.

Nathalal Parekh, a Bombay friend of Subhas Bose.

Vallabhbhai Patel, a lawyer, he ran Gandhi's Congress machine who gave him the title Sardar, leader. As member of the Interim government in 1946-47 he prevented the Balkanisation of India by making sure the 560-odd princely states became part of India. Deputy Prime Minister of Free India 1947-50.

Vithalbhai Patel, also a lawyer and older brother ofVallabhai who was one of the first Indian leaders to realise the need for overseas propaganda in support of Indian freedom. He died in Geneva and left money in his will for Bose.

Dr Hans Pilger the German minister in Kabul while Bose was fleeing India.

Colonel Habib-ur Rahman, an officer of the British Indian Army , the 1/14th Punjab, he joined the INA, becoming deputy chief of staff. He survived the flight that killed Subhas Bose.

Rajendra Prasad, a Calcutta trained lawyer from Bihar, he was a prominent supporter of Ghandi helping him in his seminal Champaran campaign and became the first President of the Indian Republic.

Chakravarti Rajagopalachari, a lawyer from Salem in Madras, he was close to Mahatma Gandhi. His daughter married one of Gandhi's sons. But in the late 30s he pushed for a compromise with the British and in 1942 left the Congress, returning in 1946 to become the first Indian Governor-General of India in 1948.

Marquis of Reading went from being Lord Chief Justice of England to Viceroy of India 1921-26.

Joachim von Ribbentrop, Foreign Minister of Germany 1938-45.

Bidhan Chandra Roy, a physician and prominent Congress leader of Bengal.

Kiran Shankar Roy, one of the so-called Big Five Congress politicians of Bengal prominent during the two decades between 1920s and 1940s.

Manabendra Nath Roy left India in 1915 to organise revolutionary movements in Mexico and Europe, attended the Second World Congress of the Comintern in 1920, represented the Comintern in China in 1928, but then began his long march away from communism. On his return to India in 1930 he was jailed by the Raj for six years. Supported the British during the Second World War.

Gopinath Saha, an Indian revolutionary who while trying to kill Charles Tegart the Commissioner of Police in Calcutta killed Ernest Day, a businessman by mistake and was hanged.

Lt Colonel Prem Kumar Sahgal an officer in the 2/10th Baluch regiment of the British Indian Army, he surrendered to the Japanese in Singapore's Farrer Park. He later joined Bose's INA.

Nalini Ranjan Sarkar, one of the few successful Bengali businessmen and politician who formed part of Huq's ministry in 1937.

V.S Srinivasa Sastri, a Madras politician, became a member of the Viceroy's Executive Council and was the first agent of the Government of India in South Africa 1927-29.

Mian Akbar Shah, active in the political movement in the North West Frontier Province, he had been to the Soviet Union, was jailed by the British and became a member of the Forward Bloc Working Committee.

Lala Shankarlal, a businessman whom Bose used to try to contact the Japanese before Japan's entry into the Second World War.

Lt-General Shidei, a Japanese expert on the Soviet Union who was on Bose's last flight and died instantly when the plane crashed.

Abdul Rahman Siddiqi, a prominent Muslim League politician elected Mayor of Calcutta in 1940 with the support of Bose.

First Viscount Simon, prominent Liberal politician who chaired the all white eponymous Simon Commission to judge how qualified Indians were to rule themselves. Lord Chancellor in Churchill's War Cabinet.

Mohan Singh, a captain in the 1/14 Punjab Regiment of the British Indian Army who, with the help of the Japanese intelligence officer Major Fujiwara, formed the first Indian National Army. He fell out with the Japanese, the army was disbanded and he was jailed.

Sodhi Mohinder (also known as Harminder) Singh, a member of the Kirti, the Punjab Communist party, who was desperate to get to the Soviet Union and accompanied Bhagat Ram Talwar to Kabul. He was later arrested by the British and made a full confession.

A.N Sarkar, a Bengali lawyer who found himself in east Asia when Japan entered the war and became Legal Adviser to Bose's provisional government of Free India.

Pattabhi Sitaramayya, Congress Leader in Andhra who was defeated by Bose in the presidential fight of 1939. Famous for his two-volume history of the Congress.

M Sivaram, an Indian journalist working Bangkok as editor of the *Bangkok Chronicle*, he was recruited by Bose as part of his propaganda team. Later wrote a colourful book of his experiences called *The Road to Delhi.*

Field Marshal Sir William Slim, (First Viscount), Commander of the 14th Army which defeated the Japanese at Imphal and later became Commander-in-Chief Allied Land Forces South East Asia in 1945.

Ian Stephens, editor of *The Statesman,* Calcutta, during the war.

Hajime Sugiyama, an army officer, he was War Minister in 1937 during the first year of the war with China, army chief of staff between 1940-44 and from July 1944 to April 1945 he was again War Minister. In August 1945, he and his wife committed hari kiri following Japan's surrender.

Charles Tegart, Commissioner of Police in Calcutta in the 1920s, unsuccessful object of assassination attempts by Indian revolutionaries.

Field Marshal Count Hisaichi Terauchi, presided from Saigon as Commander-in-Chief of all Japanese armies in the Southwest Pacific area from 1941-45.

Bal Gahandhar Tilak, a Brahmin from Pune, he was an extremist who claimed "freedom is my birthright" and was deported to Mandalay for six years.

General Hideki Tojo, an army officer, he became Prime Minister of Japan in October 1941, taking responsibility for leading Japan into the war and resigned in July 1944. Hanged as a war criminal.

First Marquis of Willingdon, Liberal MP, Governor of Bombay 1913-19 and Viceroy of India 1931-36.

Admiral Isoroku Yamamoto conceived the Pearl Harbour attack and promised his Emperor six months of victory. In April 1943, as Bose travelled from Germany to Japan in a submarine, the Americans ambushed and shot down Yamamoto's plane near the Solomon Islands.

Colonel Yamamoto Bin, Japanese military attaché in Berlin in 1941-42 who became close to Bose; on their return to the east Yamamoto acted as Bose's liaison officer with the Japanese.

Marquis of Zetland, Governor of Bengal 1917-1922, Secretary of State for India 1935-40.

Mohammed Ziauddin, the name that Bose took when he was escaping from India in 1941.

Foreword by Phillip Knightley

The major architects of the struggle for Indian independence are household names not only in India but also in the West - Mahatma Gandhi, Pandit Nehru and the Congress Party. But there was another freedom fighter, Netaji Subhas Chandra Bose, who was just as influential.Yet he is either unknown to Westerners or, for those who have heard of him, reviled as a traitor who sided with Germany and Japan against Britain in the dark days of the Second World War.

Mihir Bose, like Netaji, a Bengali (but no relation) sets out to separate the myth and prejudice about Netaji from his real role and to show that he was a great visionary, a true Indian patriot who sacrificed his life for his nation's cause. He differed from Mahatma Gandhi and Pandit Nehru in that he worked for Indian independence there and then, not at some unspecified date in the future. He recognised and was alarmed by the genius of the British in mobilising Indians to fight for Britain against each other and then persuading them to collaborate with its imperial rule. He wanted Indians to "stand on our own two legs" and stop being dependent on others. He scorned passive resistance and believed that only military service would bring Indians the strength and decisiveness to win their freedom.

The British recognised the danger he posed - he was jailed eleven times between 1920 and 1941 for periods varying from six months to three years. He was not deterred. When the authorities tried to silence him by expelling him from his own country, he defied the ban and came back, only to be imprisoned again. As war loomed in Europe in 1939, he warned Indians that Britain would try to drag India into a European war. Just as he predicted, when war broke out in September 1939 the Governor-General, without even consulting Indian leaders, declared that India was at war with Germany too.

Netaji immediately started a mass movement against the use of Indian troops, arguing it made no sense to lose Indian lives for the sake of a colonial and imperial power. There was wide support for his actions and the British promptly imprisoned him once more. He was under house arrest early in 1941 when he suddenly disappeared, only to turn up in Kabul, Afghanistan, and then to vanish again.

In November that year, Netaji made his position crystal clear. In a broadcast on German radio, he revealed that he had struck a deal with Germany for help to fight the British. How this plan would work was revealed in 1943 - after Japan had entered the war - when Netaji was warmly welcomed in Tokyo. There he was declared head of the Indian National Army (INA), which consisted largely of 40,000 Indian soldiers who had been taken prisoner after Singapore fell to the Japanese in 1942.

Netaji planned to free India by invading from the Eastern front. Under solely Indian command, the INA marched through Burma and occupied Coxtown on the Burma-India border. INA soldiers kissed the soil of Mother India and shouted, "Delhi chalo" ("Onward to Delhi").

But the campaign got bogged down and the bombing of Hiroshima and Nagasaki and the imminent end to the war sent Netaji hurrying from Singapore to Tokyo to decide what to do next. His plane crashed near Taipei and he died in hospital of severe burns, aged only 48. But his influence did not die with him.

Britain decided to put a representative group of INA officers and men on trial for treachery. The court martial was to be held in the Red Fort in Delhi with all the ceremony the Raj could muster. But there was a countrywide protest. Ordinary Indians, even those who had fought for Britain, refused to countenance any punishment for fellow Indians who had fought for India's freedom. Britain was in no position to face open rebellion and declared a general amnesty for all INA soldiers.

Subhas Chandra Bose and his militant stance for India's independence made him a controversial figure in his lifetime and a legend after his death. For many he has the status of an Indian mythological hero. They insist that he did not die in the plane crash and will re-appear when his country again needs him.

Mihir Bose tells the story of this dedicated nationalist leader and the earth-shaking events of the independence struggle with a verve and passion that will inspire a new generation in India and Britain, two great countries inextricably linked by their common history.

Phillip Knightley
London, August 2004

Prologue:

JOURNEY INTO THE *UNKNOWN*

At 10 pm on the night of 15 August 1945, just hours after Japan's surrender to the Allies brought the Second World War to a close, and six months after the end of hostilities in Europe, a small group of Indians gathered on the first floor verandah of a house in the Kallong area of Singapore.

A few minutes before - in the dining room just below - the group had enjoyed a very good Indian dinner of fish curry, rice, dal, soft little pooris, Indian bread, followed by sweets. As they settled on the cane chairs dotted round the verandah, nothing could have seemed better. For the first time in years there were no bombers or blackouts to worry about. Nature that moonlit night looked serene and wonderful. The house itself was a lovely bungalow, and from the sumptuous first floor verandah the men could look down on a very well kept manicured lawn bordered with roses and yellow cannas, which in turn adjoined a white sandy beach and the Indian Ocean. But this peaceful scene was deceptive and misleading. The men were in turmoil, as they wrestled with an immense decision: what should their leader do now that Japan had given up.

For him Japan's surrender did not mean the end of their war. The war he was fighting was against the British for the freedom of India. Although he had allied himself with the Japanese to fight Britain he was not ready to accept that just because Japan had surrendered his war was over.

This Indian leader was, of course, Subhas Chandra Bose. A charismatic 48 year old, he had spent his entire adult life fighting the Raj. He could so easily have lived a comfortable life collaborating with British rule in India, as had many of his contemporaries. A product of British education, both in India and England, where he was a graduate of Cambridge, he had rejected the advice of his father, whose collaboration with the British had earned him a title, and spurned employment in the Indian Civil Service, the awesome administrative arm that ruled British India. Bose saw such service as compromising with the people who had enslaved India. Such was his opposition to the Raj that the British had long ago dubbed him as "an implacable foe of British rule in India" and had often imprisoned him.

Two years after the start of the Second World War Bose had escaped from India via Kabul and Moscow to Berlin to seek Adolf Hitler's help, and then traveled by German and Japanese submarines to Japan. For him the Second World War and Britain's peril was India's moment of liberation. In Japan he had organized an Indian National Army from the Indian prisoners the British had surrendered to the Japanese, seeking to convert mercenaries who had fought to preserve the British Empire into freedom fighters. But now his army and that of his Japanese ally had been routed in Burma. Bose, on that Singapore verandah chain-smoking and sipping coffee, was only too painfully aware that the British would soon arrive in the city to retake their old imperial stronghold. Just to add to the mental anguish there was the physical pain of a tooth extraction.

Bose's colleagues bombarded him with conflicting advice as to what he should so. The discussions went on far into the night, and it was not until three the next morning that a decision was reached. While the INA would surrender as it stood in Singapore, Bose, along with a small group of his most trusted lieutenants, would flee, flying east to seek new allies to continue their fight for India's freedom. They would not meekly wait for the British to arrive in Singapore and take them prisoners. Bose knew the inside of British Raj prisons, and had no intention of sitting around waiting for inevitable capture.

Bose quickly choose the men who would join him. They included Habib-ur-Rehman, a former soldier of the British Indian Army who had been made a colonel in the Indian National Army, another INA colonel Pritam Singh and S.A Ayer, a pre-war Reuters correspondent in east Asia, whom Bose had made minister of propaganda in the Provisional Government of Free India he had established in Singapore.

At 9.30 am on 16 August Bose, having bid farewell to the men he was leaving behind, and accompanied by Ayer, Habib-ur Rehman, Pritam Singh, and T Nigeshi, Bose's long standing Japanese interpreter, took off in a Japanese bomber for Bangkok. That morning the Japanese surrender had officially come into effect and on the same day three Imperial princes set out from Tokyo for the headquarters of the main Japanese forces spread around east Asia and the Pacific. Their brief was to make sure that Emperor Hirohito's edict of a total surrender would be obeyed. The Japanese had major worries that having prepared their people to fight the Americans and their allies to the last island and the last man, many of their men would refuse to lay down their arms. For Bose Japan's intentions did not matter, so he pushed the surrender to the back of his mind. As he prepared for his journey he was in a carefree, almost jovial, mood. He told Ayer that he saw this as an "adventure in to the unknown", perhaps even a "wild goose chase".

But even on that initial flight out of Singapore there were problems. The plane taxied for about five minutes, but returned for a defect in the brake of the landing gear to be fixed. Then, after the bomber took off, Ayer noticed that every time the plane jerked he was being splashed by petrol drenching the sleeve of his tunic and the left leg of his breeches. Bose was sitting in the front just behind the pilot, and Ayer realised with alarm that on Japanese bombers there were no restrictions on smoking. Grim visions of one of Bose's cigarettes setting the plane alight filled Ayer's mind, but the Japanese were unfazed. The pilot said the nuts joining the pipe attached to the tank had got loose. Nigeshi, the interpreter, tightened the nuts.

In mid-afternoon Bose and his men arrived in Bangkok. Nobody knew he was coming, and the party had to wait two hours before Major General Jaganathrao Krishnarao Bhonsle, chief of staff of the INA, rushed up to the airport with transport. News of his arrival soon spread and many of the local Indians gathered to meet Bose in his Bangkok residence. There were so many administrative matters to handle and so many Indians wanted to talk to him that the house was soon very overcrowded, with standing room only. It was midnight before he or his men could sit down and eat.

After dinner Bose gathered about thirty officers of the INA on the verandah of the Bangkok house. Chain-smoking once more and drinking endless cups of coffee, he talked to them until five in the morning. "Although we have to surrender now," he said, "we carry on the fight for India's freedom. Think not of defeat but of your achievements. Maintain your dignity and go on preaching the cause The INA has inculcated in the Indian masses a unity and spirit that will never die."

The men had only to see the select group Bose had chosen to travel with him to realize how even in this very limited sphere he had demolished the British myth that Indians could never unite because of multiple religions. Although Bose was a devout Hindu, religion for him was a private matter, and as a truly secular Indian leader his chosen companions on this adventure into the unknown was a Muslim in Habib-ur-Rehman, a Christian in Ayer and a Sikh in Pritam Singh. In Bangkok he added three more to the group, including one more Sikh officer, and Abid Hassan, who had been his secretary in Germany, and had travelled with him on the German submarine to east Asia, and was, of course, a Muslim.

Just as dawn was breaking over Bangkok they returned to the airport and at 8 am on August 17, Bose and his group, now numbering ten, left in two planes for Saigon, each of them carrying a light suitcase, but with revolvers in their belts. By 10 am they were in the Vietnamese city. In Saigon there was no one to meet them, and no aircraft for an onward journey. By now two days had passed since Japan had surrendered, and Bose and his companions did not know whether under international law Japanese planes were allowed to fly. As Bose stepped out on to the empty tarmac at Saigon airport he saw a solitary Indian in the distance. Bose summoned the man, who turned out to be Chandra Mal, secretary of the local Indian Independence League. Chandra Mal had heard of Bose's arrival, and had come to the airport to help. He hurriedly arranged for two cars, and Bose was driven to the house of another local Indian on the outskirts of Saigon.

Saigon was a city Bose had come to know well. Indeed three months earlier, as Bose and the INA had retreated from Burma back to Malaya, the Southern Army of Japan had suggested that he move his headquarters to Saigon. But Bose had told the Japanese he wanted to move his armies to mainland China. He gave orders to have the Indian Independence League in Shanghai, and other places in China, strengthened. It was from there that he planned to contact the Russians Bose's thoughts had been turning towards Russia, and he had tried to contact Kremlin leaders without success.

On the morning of 17 August, one week after the Soviet Union declared war on Japan, the Saigon that Bose drove through was not a place prepared to welcome him, let alone allow him to make his headquarters there. It was a city preparing for a change of masters. The streets were deserted, there was hardly another car on the road, and all the shops were shut, with their windows shuttered. There was an air of menace, and Indians felt in peril. With the Japanese occupiers on their way out, the talk concerned what the returning French colonialists would do to the Indians that had allied themselves with Japan. There was hardly an Indian to be seen and, apart from Chandra Mal, most of the officers of the Indian Independence League had disappeared, fearing retribution by the French. Within weeks there would be a terrible massacre of civilians before the returning French imposed order.

Not that Bose wanted to stay in Saigon long. He wanted rest, and a flight to take him and his group nearer the Russians. No sooner had he arrived in Saigon then Bose sent an appeal to the Japanese, "Along with the trusted persons of my cabinet I would like to go to the Soviet Union. If it is necessary I shall enter the Soviet Union alone. In that case I request the Japanese Government to allow any of my cabinet members to take charge".

Bose's request pained the Imperial general headquarters. Just one week before Japan's surrender the Russians had entered the war against it, seizing Japanese territory with alacrity. Now the Japanese told Bose, "after all they we have done for you, how can you want to go to Russia now? Please do not write Japan off yet".

Subhas turned to the two Japanese officials who had travelled with him from Bangkok to Saigon. In Bangkok he had already discussed with them the question of going to Russia. The two officials were Lt Gen Saburo Isoda, head of the Hikari Kikan, the Japanese Liaison office established to work with the INA and Teruo Hachiya, ambassador designate to the Provisional Government of Free India. After hurried consultations on the tarmac at Saigon airport they travelled to Dalat, 150 miles away, where Field Marshal Count Terauchi Hisaichi, the commander-in-chief of the Southern Army had his summer headquarters. The mission was to see if Terauchi could be persuaded to provide a plane for Bose to travel further, and possibly to contact the Russians.

Terauchi, a foxy old commander, had never much cared for the INA, but he liked Bose personally and is once reported to have said, "Ah, the fat-headed staff in Tokyo seem to regard Bose as a Japanese subject! Tell Tokyo that I respect the free will of my friend who fought for his country." However that day Terauchi was too preoccupied to see Isoda, and his staff told him he was wasting precious hours: Japan was living on borrowed time. No safe conduct had been arranged, and the Americans might at any time ground all Japanese flights - the surrender, after all, was already two days old. Japan and its leadership was in turmoil, preoccupied with arranging a smooth surrender, worried about the deteriorating situation in Thailand, where anti-Japanese guerrillas were active.

While Isoda was pleading, a Japanese liaison officer arrived at Bose's temporary home in Saigon. Bose, who had just got to sleep, having had a shave and a bath, was woken up to be told that the Japanese could provide him only one seat on a plane leaving Saigon. "Where is it going?" Bose asked. The Japanese could not explain, and Bose refused to budge, saying. "I am not going until I know the destination of the plane. I am not going to be rushed off like this." The Japanese official was asked to get out more details, and Bose told his colleagues that he would rather wait for information from Isoda or Hachiya before making a decision top go on alone.

It turned out that the solitary seat on the aircraft would be on a flight carrying Lt-Col. Shidei to Dairen in Manchuria. Fluent in English, French and German, and a Japanese expert on Russia he had been assigned to the Manchurian Army to facilitate the surrender there to the Soviets.

Half an hour after Bose had sent him packing, the liaison officer returned, accompanied by Isoda, Hachiya and a senior staff officer of Terauchi. Bose and Rahman met them behind closed doors. It is not clear exactly what happened at this meeting, but it seems that it was then that Isoda conveyed to Bose the offer he had negotiated in Dalat. But while Isoda could now tell Bose where the plane was headed he could not offer him more than a single seat. Moreover, Bose was told, the plane was already revving its engines at Saigon airport, and Bose had to decide immediately whether he would accept the offer. Bose is said to have replied, "In that case, I won't go." But Isoda was helpless.

Bose faced a tricky situation. Having decided not to surrender to the British in Singapore, it made even less sense to do so to the French in Saigon, where the situation was even more unpredictable. Bose asked the Japanese to wait, and called a hurried conference with Ayer and the rest of his group. For the first time since he had come to East Asia to lead an army to fight the British, he seemed rattled.

In the two years he had worked with Bose, Ayer had always found him cool and collected. Ayer had been with him on many difficult missions, including the retreat from Burma to Bangkok, where Bose and his men had kept ahead of the pursing British troops by only a day or so. On that retreat Bose had walked miles, despite blisters on his feet, and had repeatedly risked being killed several times by straffing planes from the Royal Air Force. Throughout this he had remained calm, reading a book on the Irish fight for freedom against the British. Ayer had been struck by how often at times Bose seemed almost deliberately to court danger from British bombers. But now, on the afternoon of 17 August in Saigon, Subhas was impatient, nervous, and on edge. Ayer had never seen him like that.

As the doors were shut for the meeting Bose noticed two of his group were not there. They had gone to a neighbouring house to change. Bose shouted, "Tell them not to bother about their dress, but to come at once. I have no time to lose. We have to take important decisions and that without a moment's delay. Come along, hurry up".

As soon as the group was assembled Bose told them, "Look here, there is a plane ready to take off in the next few minutes and we have got to decide something important right now. The Japanese say there is only one seat to spare, and what we have got to decide now in a few seconds, is whether I should go even if I have to go alone. I have tried my best to get at least one more seat, but there is little hope. Shall we take that one seat and shall I go alone?"

For a few moments there was no answer. The men were devoted to Bose, but hated having to make such a decision. They pleaded with him to go back to the Japanese, and get more seats. Some of them were angry with the Japanese, maintaining that a bomber could easily carry half a dozen passengers in addition to a crew. Bose cut in, saying he needed a categorical answer from them, "If the Japanese can give only one seat in that plane, shall I or shall I not go alone?"

The men were agreed that whatever happened Bose should not be taken prisoner in Saigon. Bose went back to the Japanese to try and haggle for more seats, and returned to say, "We are getting one more seat. Let Habib come with me. I am sure they won't spare any more seats in this plane. But let us try our luck". He asked Ayer and Gulzara Singh, another Sikh Colonel of the INA, to pack a light bag and come to the airport.

In two cars, the group rushed to the airport. As the first car carrying Bose neared the airport they heard the deafening roar of the plane. The engines had been running for nearly an hour and the Japanese were becoming very impatient.

A bomber of type 97-2, known as Sallys by the Allies, had been trundled out of its bombproof shelter, and made ready for the flight. The journey could hardly have begun in less auspicious circumstances. The machine was old and had not been well maintained, and the crew was inexperienced. The captain and another crewmember were not even qualified pilots, while the pilot was a non-commissioned officer: but in Saigon at that time this was the best crew Japan could muster. They were appalled when told that they would be expected to fly a bomber designed to carry a maximum of thirteen people with Bose and six colleagues as extra passengers. They reluctantly agreed to take two, Bose and Rahman, and refused to consider any more. Bose pleaded, but made no headway. Japanese irritation turned to anger when Bose and Rahman started clambering aboard with about ten pieces of luggage. Bose was persuaded to discard some of the luggage.

There was then another problem. Just as the plane was about to taxi on to the runway, an Indian officer rushed up and asked the pilot to stop. The second car carrying some of Bose's men had not yet arrived. Ayer says it contained "an important piece of luggage". In reality the car had made a detour to pick up boxes containing precious jewellery and gold. Within days a British spy would describe the important luggage in graphic detail telling London that it amounted to "four boxes of varying sizes". There was also, the spy told London, an additional quantity of gold purchased on the way to Moulmein during the retreat from Burma to the value of 700,000 rupees, or £70,000 drawn by Bose from the Yokohama Specie Bank, Moulmein Branch. This was actually part of the gold reserve from the Azad Hind (Free India) Bank which Bose had set up and which was funded by donations from Indians in east Asia. Bose refused to board the plane without this gold and jewellery and, while a stiff breeze blowing across Saigon airport threw up dust into everyone nostrils and the Japanese fumed, the Indians scoured the road leading away from the airport for this second car. About half an hour later the car with the "important luggage" arrived. Despite the crew's protests it was loaded on to the aircraft, and at last Bose and Habib-ur Rahman were ready to leave.

The events of the previous few days had been bewildering, and now there was a sudden and confused parting. Bose said goodbye to Ayer and to each of the men he was leaving behind, giving them each a vigorous handshake "Well, *Jai Hind (Hail India),* I will meet you later." Ayer was still not sure what was happening, and tried hard to control his tears. But Bose had promised his men that he would not rest content till the Japanese provided transport for them to join him, and, although there were no other bombers or transport planes on that airport, Ayer and his companions soon began anticipating the moment of reunion. After all, thought Ayer, could not a Japanese pilot just turn the propellers, start the engine and take off? Bose had not told his men where he was going, and they had not asked him but Ayer knew he was headed for Manchuria. At about 5 p.m. on 17 August 1945 the Sally, dreadfully overloaded, left Saigon.

As it did so Isoda, who had stayed behind in Saigon, signalled his headquarters in Bangkok, that Bose had left for Tokyo via Taiwan and Darien. Isoda's reference to Tokyo adds a touch of confusion. Was Bose planning to go to the Japanese capital after all? Habib-ur Rahman would later maintain Bose wanted to go to Tokyo to consult the leadership about the surrender formalities, as did Hachiya. He had told Bose that, once in Tokyo Japan would help in "shifting him to a safe area".

The Sally headed for Tourane, a Japanese airport midway between Saigon and Hanoi, later to become famous as the American airbase of Da Nang. The plane arrived at about seven on the evening of 17 August. Because it was so overloaded the pilot refused to undertake a night flight. The passengers were put up in a hotel which had been converted into barracks, while the crew got rid of about 600 pounds of excess weight by dismantling the six machine-guns and also some ammunition and unwanted baggage. At 5 am the next morning the aircraft took off again, destination Formosa, arriving at Taihoku (the Japanese name for Taipei) airport at noon. While the passengers ate a light lunch of sandwiches and bananas in a tent quickly pitched for them at the airstrip, the crew checked the bomber. They were not happy about the portside engine, but during the test run it stood up well, and two hours the Sally was airborne again. Darien was another thousand nautical miles away, and the pilot wanted to get there before dark.

At Taipei Rahman had changed into warm clothes and asked Bose if he would like to do the same, but Bose laughed off the idea, although he did accept a sweater from Rahman which, after checking whether the plane would fly at high altitudes, he put on. It was rather tight fitting, a feature that was soon to acquire enormous significance.

The plane was still climbing from the runway when Rahman heard a terrific noise. He thought the aircraft was being attacked, but in fact the propeller of the port engine had sheared off. Only the starboard engine was operating and the plane was wobbling. Almost immediately it caught fire, dived steeply, hit a mud dyke on the edge of the airstrip, and snapped in two. Six passengers were killed instantly: three engineers, a Japanese major and Colonel Shidei, whose neck was severed by a wildly swinging petrol-tank.

Bose was sitting on cushions next to the petrol tank, and the crash splashed petrol all over his cotton khaki military uniform. He was injured, but still able to attempt to get out of the aircraft. At first he tried to get out of the back, where Rahman was seated. But Rahman, who had lost consciousness on impact, was buried under luggage that had piled on top of him. A fire had started in front of him. There was no way out through the rear. As Rahman regained consciousness he spotted Bose trying to escape through the rear, and told him to go forward, even though this meant walking through fire. Bose took his advice, but as he struggled out through the nose of the plane, by then a burning inferno, his clothes caught fire.

Habib-ur Rahman whose injuries were superficial, helped by another passenger Lt Colonel Nonogaki, tried to undo Bose's uniform by trying in desperation to unbuckle the belt. Another Japanese, unable to explain in English, mimicked a roll on the ground, as a means of dousing the flames. Nonogaki found the tight fitting sweater difficult to remove, while Habib burnt his hands in the process of trying to remove Bose's belt. As he was doing so Habib looked up,"and my heart nearly stopped when I saw his face, battered by iron and burnt by fire. A few minutes later he collapsed and lay on the ground of the Taihoku aerodrome."

Between them Habib and Nonogaki eventually succeeded in beating out the flames, and Bose was removed to a nearby emergency dressing station where the burnt clothing was cut away from his body. By this time he was virtually naked, and his body was a crisp, burnt mass of flesh. He also had terrible head injuries. He and the other injured, including Habib, were put in a Japanese Army truck, and immediately rushed to the Taihoku Military hospital. Bose got there shortly after 3 pm.

Tsuruta Toyoshi, a probationary medical officer, was on duty at Nammon Ward. He had been told that a VIP suffering from severe injuries had been brought to the hospital in a truck. He found Bose lying naked on a stretcher, and supervised Bose's admittance to the ward. Subhas was still conscious, but suffering from terrible third degree burns on his face and all over his body. For the next few hours doctors struggled to save his life. Tanyeoshi Yoshimi was the main doctor involved:

> One of the Japanese, a Staff Officer with the rank Lt-Col whose name I cannot properly recall, but believe was Ishii-something, informed me that one of the Indians, pointing him out, was Chandra Bose and that I was not to spare myself and must give him the very best of treatment. I immediately gave instructions for some medical orderlies to go and prepare a bed, and for others to carry in the injured men. When he was laid on the bed, I personally cleaned his injuries with oils and dressed them. He was suffering from extensive burns over the whole of his body, though most serious were those on his head, chest and thighs. There was very little left on his head in the way of hair or other identification marks. During the first four hours he was semi-conscious, and practically normal, speaking quite a good deal. The first words I remember him

> speaking were in Japanese, when he made a request for water, which had to be fed to him through a hospital cup with a spout. As most of his speaking was in English, a request for an interpreter was made, and one was sent from the Civil Government Offices named Nakamura. He informed me that he had very often interpreted for Chandra Bose and had many conversations with him. He appeared to have no doubt that the man he was speaking with was Chandra Bose. During the treating of his injuries, I twice inquired of Chandra Bose if he was in any pain, and neither time did he make any answer.

Habib was lying on the next bed and after a time Bose spoke to him, alternating in Hindi and English. He dictated a message of thanks to Terauchi and asked, "What happened to Colonel Shidei? My blood is rushing to the head. Please give me treatment for that." He was occasionally delirious, and at one stage confused Habib with Hassan. Habib said in Hindi, "Hassan yahan nahi hain, Sab, main hun Habib (Hassan is not here, Sir, I am here, Habib) Bose knew he was not going to make it and told Habib, "Habib, my end is coming very soon. I have fought all my life for my country's freedom. I am dying for my country's freedom. Go and tell my countrymen to continue the fight for India's freedom. India will be free, and before long.

By this time, at about 6 pm Tsuruta returned to the ward after his evening meal and Bose asked him in English if he would sit with him. But there was little chance of Bose making it through the night. An hour later, at around 7 pm he had a relapse. Yoshimi once again gave him some camphor injections. "I inquired whether there was any statement, will, or such matter he wished to make. He answered, "Nothing". After the fourth hour he appeared to be sinking into unconsciousness. He murmured, and muttered in his state of coma.

As he did so he struggled to get his words out. Habib reached forward to hear them, there was a groan and the words became fainter. A nurse, who had been watching over Bose, heard mumbled words that sounded like "quiet death. I am dying peacefully."

And then he was gone. Like the fighter he was he had accepted death bravely, enduring the most unbearable pain for hours with great courage.

The next morning, 19 August 1945, Colonel Miyata, staff officer of General Ando came to the hospital to express mourning on behalf of the general and his staff, and as is the Japanese custom bought gifts of flowers, fruits and cakes for the deceased.

Rahman was very keen that Bose's body should be taken to Tokyo so that there would be no doubt about his death. In order to prepare the body for the journey Yoshimi injected formalin into the corpse, and also had the coffin partly filled with lime. The whole thing was put in a box, and on 20 August, taken to Taihoku airport for transporting to Japan, in charge of a warrant officer. However, recalls Yoshimi, " W.O.Nishi returned later and informed me that the body could for some unknown reason not be taken to Japan, and was to be sent to the crematorium for cremation. I therefore made out a death certificate, stating that causes of death to be extensive burning and shock. The orders for this change of plans came from the Adjutant's Department, Taiwan Army." Rahman says:

> They told me there were practical difficulties in getting Netaji's [leader, the name given to Bose by his followers] coffin into the plane. They told me then it was impossible to carry Netaji's remains out of Taihoku (Taipei) and cremation had to be arranged as early as possible. They wanted my consent to it. I had no other alternative but to agree to the cremation in Taihoku. The funeral service with full military honours was held in the shrine attached to the hospital and the cremation took place on the 20th. They placed Netaji's ashes in an urn and kept it in the shrine.

However, for the moment, the Japanese did not want anyone to know Bose was dead and Yoshimi was told that news of Bose's death must be kept a secret, "and my staff and I were warned not to divulge that we knew who it was that had died.

It would be easy to read into this a huge conspiracy, but given the state of Japan, it was understandable. Bose's death could not have come at a worse moment for Japan. It had surrendered, but the Americans were yet to arrive on Japanese soil; the first time the foreign devils would actually step on to their homeland. In this unprecedented situation - with the Japanese struggling to come to terms with something they had never before experienced or anticipated, let alone planned - the delay in announcing Bose's death was more a mistake due to the unwillingness of anyone to take responsibility for the announcement, than a well planned conspiracy.

In any event an announcement was not long delayed; no more than a few hours, in fact. What made it seem a conspiracy was the way the Japanese hinted at it before making the announcement. On 19 August, the next day, Ayer and his group, unaware of the fate of Bose, and besieging the Japanese for a plane to follow their leader, were given a hint that Bose was no more, but in such a cryptic fashion that they thought it was the indifferent interpretation of the Japanese translator. Then on 20 August, as Ayer finally secured a seat on a bomber to take him to Japan, he was told Bose was dead, although it was not until much later that he learned the details. The same day Isoda signaled Bangkok with news of Bose's death. This signalled also meant that London knew their great enemy was dead.

For some months the British had a spy very high up in Bose's camp. He was codenamed B 1189. Isoda spoke to him, and the next day, 21 August, the spy informed London of the last movements of Bose. B1189 had requested Isoda to keep photographs of Bose's funeral and other rites as well as his remains, sensing that without such proof there may be questions raised about the authenticity of the death.

It was B 1189 who had informed London of the gold and jewelry Bose was carrying. Now he said:

> B1189 has no direct information regarding the gold mentioned above. His own impression is that a major portion of the gold was taken by S. C. Bose while the remainder was left with the rest of his party.

Meanwhile the gold and the jewelry that Bose insisted be carried on the fatal flight were still strewn across the tarmac at Taipei airport. When the Sally bomber had crashed, the cases spilled their treasure on the tarmac, with enough of value to fill a five-gallon oil can near the wreckage. They remained there for almost a week, and then the treasure was collected and handed over to the Indian League in Japan, and later to the Indian government.

Many years afterwards when British records were declassified it emerged that B 1189 was none other than Bhonsle, the man who had turned up late to receive Bose in Bangkok. Although chief of staff of the INA, Bhonsle never went to the front, which provoked criticism. He often disagreed with Bose, and his decision to turn traitor was a moment of some significance. A Sandhurst graduate, he was like most Indian officers in the British Indian Army, merely a captain, but when he joined the INA he was promoted to major general, and then head of the War Council in Bangkok. However, as the war turned against Japan and the INA, he clearly reverted to his old loyalties. He regularly reported back to the British, and provided enough details for a note entitled *The Last Movement of S.C. Bose (April- August 1945)* to be prepared.

The news of Bose's death finally became public on 23 August. A couple of nights before this Subhas's older brother, Sarat Bose, who had been jailed by the British in Coonoor jail in southern India, had a dream that Subhas had come to visit him. He saw him standing on the verandah of the bungalow in which Sarat was jailed, and looked very tall. Sarat jumped up to see his face, but almost immediately he disappeared.

On 6 September, after Rahman had recovered from his own injuries, he took Bose's ashes to Tokyo, travelling on an ambulance plane. There he, Ayer and Rama Murti, a long-time resident of Tokyo, arranged a final resting place for him. Unable to believe that their leader was dead, unsure of how the Americans occupying Japan would react, they took the ashes furtively to a Japanese Buddhist temple near Rama Murti's house. There, on 14 September 1945, in the presence of some of the young boys Bose had sent to Tokyo for training and representatives of the Japanese Foreign Office and War Office, a simple memorial service was performed. The urn was entrusted to Reverend Mochizuki. In a temple dedicated to the militantly nationalist Nichiren Buddhist sect, Subhas Bose had found his final resting-place.

As he looked on, Ayer thought back to what Bose had said as they were leaving Singapore on his journey into the unknown. When Ayer wondered about the risk of a flight in a Japanese plane following Japan's surrender, Bose said, "Oh, I am a fatalist."

Some months later, when Ayer returned to India, he heard a story from a friend of Bose. Many years before this friend and Bose were walking very late one night along Bombay's Marine Drive, a promenade that fronts the Arabian Sea. Suddenly Bose halted, looked up at the moonlit sky, and, after a few minutes of silence, said, "Do you know what kind of death I would wish for myself? I should be flying very high, and then I must suddenly crash down to earth and die. That'll be wonderful."

Ayer returned to India, and soon India was free and he hoped that his leader's ashes would be brought back with ceremony. That never happened. Today 60 years after that ceremony in September 1945, and more than half a century after India's freedom, Bose's ashes still lie in that obscure Tokyo temple. Indian dignitaries on their visits to Tokyo always make a point of visiting this temple. The visitors' book of the temple shows that both Nehru and his daughter Indira , both Prime Ministers of Free India visited that temple, as did visiting Indian presidents, but to the utter bewilderment of the Japanese, they refuse to take home the remains of one of India's most illustrious sons.

One reason perhaps is that a whole industry has been built seeking to prove that not only did the air crash not take place, but also that Bose was never on the plane. No single aspect of Bose's life has been so meticulously investigated as his death, and each investigator has dwelt deeply and lovingly on various inconsistencies. This has resulted in three government inquiries producing a copious flow of distorted, poorly researched, books speculating on his whereabouts, and periodic demands that the Indian government summon the intelligence chiefs and secret files of all the major powers - the United States., Russia, China, France and Britain - to ascertain finally exactly what happened to Bose.

Bose's death has generated a curious Indian game. Every few years another government commission is announced to inquire into the circumstances of his death, with much speculation that he escaped to Russia, and is probably still there or died in the Gulag. As this book is being published the third such inquiry headed by a former Justice of the Indian Supreme Court is holding another inquiry which has seen him visit various parts of the world and take evidence from all sorts of people - many of whom did not know Bose when he was alive but have very definite views as to how he died.

Bose, who so wanted to bring the story of India's freedom struggle to a glorious conclusion, is now in that awful historical limbo, where his own life story, 60 years after his death, has no end, and no finality.

Let us now turn to Cuttack and the closing years of the 19th century to see how his story began.

Part One

THE REBEL AND THE *BHADRALOKS*

Those who are considered good boys in the society are in fact nothing but eunuchs. Neither in this world nor in any other has any great work been achieved or will any great work be done by these people. These boys somehow or other reduced their burden of sin and they follow the track of the most orthodox people like a herd of sheep. Throughout their most prosaic life there is no taste of anything new or novel, there is no outburst of full-hearted laughter, there is no inspired self-sacrifice. . . . One has to love new things, one has to grow mad for the unknown, one has to express himself in the free mind and under the open sky by breaking through all the barriers of life and by razing them to the ground.

Subhas Bose, *Prison Notebook III,*
Mandalay 1925-7

1

Muscular Hinduism

Subhas Chandra Bose was bom in Oriya Bazar, Cuttack, south of Calcutta in what is now modern Orissa at midday on Saturday 23 January 1897. It was the height of the Empire: Queen Victoria was celebrating her Diamond Jubilee, Indians who mattered vied with one another to pay homage 'to her gracious Majesty'.

The sub-continent of India and its 380 million people was the 'Jewel in the Crown' of the British Empire, and the authority of British rule – the Raj – seemed to outsiders unchallenged. This was not altogether true. In Poona the first stirrings of a violent struggle against the Raj had been efficiently crushed, its leader Tilak exiled on charges of sedition. Swami Vivekananda, the Hindu monk whose influence moulded Subhas' s early life, returned from America a hero.

Bengal at the end of the nineteenth century saw the first attempts (the 1857 revolt and subsequent armed uprisings notwithstanding) to organise revolution against the British Raj. The nature of the Raj and the overwhelming superiority of the British dictated that these should take the form of small secret societies – and not all of them were revolutionary, nor at first even overtly hostile to the Raj. Their stress was on drill, exercises with the *lathi* , perhaps swordplay, a high moral tone, and generous readings about the activities of revolutionaries abroad. Later, as muscular Hinduism took hold, the ideology shaped itself: the *Gita,* in which the Lord Krishna had preached the Hindu philosophy of life to Arjuna, was a constant source of reference; the motherland conveniently became the mother goddess Durga, and the goddess Kali the symbol of strength. All this, laced with a sort of socialism, produced a strong, if confused, driving force. Its limitations were that the stress on Hindu myths alienated the Muslims (though some of them did join during the early stages) and that it was never a mass movement. But the few thousands it attracted were devoted, dedicated and sincere. In Bengal, Maharashtra and Punjab it exerted a remarkable influence, though it was always in Bengal that it was most potent.

Subhas' s birth created no stir in the large Bose family, though his mother Prabhabati had a difficult delivery. "Thank God she somehow got through", recorded Subhas' s father Janakinath in his diary. For him it was an event of no great importance. "Not much to note, things as usual", he had written the day before the birth. This was, after all, their sixth son and ninth child (several more had died soon after birth) in a Hindu family, and a large family was part of the life-style of a man who had established a reputation and a practice at the Cuttack Bar.

If proof was required, people only had to see the house where Janakinath lived. It would have been prominent anywhere; in Oriya Bazar it was a sensation: a characteristically flamboyant piece of Bengali architecture in a very drab setting. Oriya Bazar is like any other Cuttack lane, narrow, meandering and messy; the houses are dreary, unremarkable and mostly inhabited by poor Muslims. They have no numbers and few names except for Janakinath's.

An imposing gate opens on to a large *ootan,* the obligatory Bengali courtyard formed by the U-shaped building, which leads to a narrow flight of stone stairs, a large verandah and a long line of rooms. In the middle of this is one room with a high ceiling and many windows. This caters to the Bengali fetish for open air, and has three doors, one of which faces south. It contains a built-in wooden *almirah* (safe) and an iron bed. It was in this room that Subhas was born.

Today Oriya Bazar and the house itself are fully part of the growing quantity of 'Subhasiana'. While a small group of poor Muslims play cards on the verandah, the official guide takes pains to recreate — perhaps create — history. He points out the spot on the stairs where toddler Subhas often fell; the middle room now cluttered up with pictures of Subhas in every conceivable corner; an adjoining room crammed with indistinguishable pieces of what are described as Subhas' s toys; his first *charka* (spinning-wheel); and the terrace from where he could see much of Cuttack as well as the three service privies in the backyard for servants. On the wall outside the house, a stone plaque announces the event of his birth. It is white and shiny and only a few years old.

Janakinath was an immigrant to Cuttack from Kodalia, a village that in recent years has become part of the ever-widening boundaries of Calcutta. Legend has it that when matchmakers first proposed marriage between Janakinath – then a college teacher in Calcutta – and Prabhabati, her father Ganganarayan Dutt was not particularly enthusiastic. Prabhabati was the eldest, and a great favourite; a poor teacher would hardly fit in a family whose other sons-in-law included a district and session judge, a subordinate judge and a Rai Bahadur (one of the high titles the British Raj conferred on the prominent Indian middle-class professionals who served its interests). Ganganarayan Dutt, it is said, had one look at his prospective son-in-law and refused to agree to the marriage, "Go and make money and come back, and then perhaps we can consider you." So Janakinath went off to Cuttack, and returned years later flushed with money to claim the hand of Prabhabati. Like all the best stories, this is probably apocryphal; but Bengali myth was definitely against the marriage. There is a very old Bengali saying:

> Ghosh Bangsho boro bongsha Bose Bongsho Datta
> Mitra kutil jat
> Dutta sala haram jadha.

It means:

> The Ghoshes are high caste,
> The Boses are generous,
> The Mitras are cunning,
> The Dutts are scoundrels.

In the case of the Boses, contemporary history had provided an economic edge to the argument. Janakinath belonged to the older Hindu elite which had had power and influence in pre-British India; Muslim rulers of Bengal had had Bose ministers, and the family had had titles, land and various privileges conferred on them. However by August 1879, at the age of 19, when he moved to Cuttack Janakinath was a poor immigrant trying to make his way in the world.

The Hathkola Dutts were the new elite - the first to realise the benefits of collaboration with the British. Soon after British rule was established they started working in British commercial firms, pleading in British courts and even presiding over them; they eagerly accepted British titles and honours. Interestingly, when Subhas wrote his autobiography at the age of forty he glossed over the close collaboration of his mother's family with the British, but stressed the pre-British eminence of his father's family. In fact, both were Kayasthas, one of the numerous castes of the fantastic Hindu caste system. Though they like to describe themselves as Kshatriyas – the second of the four legendary Hindu castes - Brahmans (priests), Kshatriyas (warriors), Vaishyas (traders), Sudras (Untouchables) – little definite is known about the origin of the Kayasthas. They were probably low-caste Sudras who, by their opportunism and cleverness during Muslim rule, rose to positions of eminence and power. Long before Subhas was born the Kayasthas had acquired a status in Bengal second only to that of the Brahmans.

Janakinath was the product of the renaissance that had swept Bengal at the time of the Indo-British honeymoon: at no time before or after it did the British connection look so fruitful or collaboration prove so profitable. For a whole generation of Indians it was the most glorious period of Indian history. It was a time of iconoclasm, a time of change, a time when the decadent, dying Indian culture was suddenly confronted with a vibrant, confident Western one which would revive it, and whose reforming evangelism would cure Hinduism of its barbaric practices.

Michael Madhusudan Dutt renounced the English language and introduced blank verse to Bengalis, while Bankim Chandra Chatterjee's Hindu heroes, after expelling the alien Muslim, paid homage to the British. This new force was helping India discover its own history and culture. Astonished Indians learnt that the hoary Indian past had been rich, eventful and interesting. Western learning investigated and unearthed Hindu knowledge. Hindus yearned to go back to the blissful days of the Vedas where it was all gold. As so often in religious masonic movements, the past shone without any blemish – if buttressed by Western learning and scholarship.

Janakinath was a good example of the sort of Indian collaborator the Raj had produced. It was more than a hundred years after Clive established British rule in Bengal, and nearly 30 years after what the British called the 1857 Mutiny, and what his son Subhas would later call the First War of Independence. Janakinath took the view that British rule was necessary and that it would bring Indians progress. Most educated Indians thought like that and indeed the embryo Indian political movement, the Congress, which was founded in 1884 by the Scot Allan Octavian Hume, proudly broadcast its loyalty to the Raj. The Raj cleverly promoted the idea that Indians who supported them were not collaborating with them but being loyal to the best thing that had happened to India. Janakinath Bose essentially accepted this view, and he profited splendidly. He became a government pleader, was appointed to the Bengal Legislative Council in in 1912, and finally made a Rai Bahadur.

There was a brief moment of tension between the Raj and Janakinath of which we know little. Subhas in his autobiography makes a cryptic reference to it saying, "In 1917 owing to some disagreement with the District Magistrate, he gave up the post of Government Pleader".

A possible explanation came many years later when a former judge, Thomas Macpherson, in a letter to the India Office, made damaging allegations against Janakinath. Macpherson described how he had met Subhas and his younger brother in 1910 when he was a Judge in Cuttack, Janakinath having brought his sons to meet this English sahib. This is Macpherson's version of why Janakinath gave up his job as Government pleader:

> At the beginning of 1917 when I was Legal Remembrancer of Bihar and Orissa, it fell to me to deal with the case of the Rai Bahadur. According to the Sessions Judge, he had funked prosecuting in a Sessions trial at Cuttack in the bad weather of 1916 where a prominent local man (Assistant Surgeon in charge of the Medical School) was to be tried at the Sessions, with some of his students, for rape of a Muslim girl, and had taken leave, with the result that Government was at the expense of sending the Assitant Government Advocate at the Patna High Court to do the work which the local Government Pleader ought to have done. Under orders of government the District Magistrate was directed to intimate to the Rai Bahadur that he should resign. He did so, resentfully, it is said.

Macpherson had his own motives for making the allegations. The letter was written in 1938 just after Subhas Bose had made his second and last visit to England and was clearly meant to provide propaganda against him. It inferred that Bose's father, educated in the British system, had ran away from responsibility, a common feeling against the Raj educated Indians at the time. All we know is that if he felt resentful towards the Raj he certainly concealed it very well.

Essentially Janakinath remained a quiet, simple man. He presided over the Cuttack Theosophical Lodge, supported the Victoria School and started the Union Club. Every evening at five he and his wife would climb into their *fitton gari* (horse-drawn carriage), the hood would be pulled down and they would drive to the Union Club. In the British-established courts he dressed in the European style, and like many Bengalis of his generation was well read in English literature, almost considering Shakespeare as a Bengali writer. Having been brought up in Bengali-medium schools he was determined that his sons should go to schools taught in the English language, and learn to speak the language of the Raj properly. Plain living and high thinking formed part of his constant advice to his sons and grandchildren. Outside the courts he dressed simply: tennis shoes, *dhoti,* a shirt. Even when Subhas was already a national figure, he would go thus attired for walks round Calcutta's Maidan. Like the mythical Boses he was generous. Every Sunday he would distribute grain to his servants and dependents. For nearly all his life he maintained his immediate family and a whole host of relatives, and just before his death provided for them. Today older Cuttack residents still talk of his generosity.

For his host of grandchildren he was *dadabhai:* kind, loving, affectionate. But for his sons, and Subhas in particular, Baba (as the father is called in Bengali) was distant, reserved. Whenever he entered the room Subhas would stand to indicate respect, and he was always *apni* (the more formal application of the personal pronoun 'you'). *Ma* (mother), however, was *tumi* – a little more approachable, more intimate. With her there could be discussion, argument, even differences, though Prabhabati was stubborn. Her word was law. She had never been to school, could not speak a word of English, had been married at an early age, eleven, and started producing the first of her fourteen children from the age of fourteen. Between 1884 and 1905 she produced a child almost every other year, first two daughters, then five sons, followed by a daughter, then Subhas, then three daughters, and, finally, two more sons. Yet she guided the education of her children and other relatives and effectively ran the family. She also possessed a deep and abiding devotion to the Hindu religion.

It is interesting to note that in a certain limited sense Subhas's early life was quite similar to that of Jawaharlal Nehru who was eight years older. Nehru also had a father who was a lawyer and a Raj loyalist, and a mother who did not speak English and who tried to make Jawaharlal a good Hindu. Unlike Subhas's parents Motilal encouraged his son to rebel against the Hindu rituals his mother tried to foist on him.

Subhas's closest associate was a simple servant girl called Sarada who called him Raja (king) and doted on him. He was a lonely child, spending entire days in study and prayer in the little prayer-room on the terrace, or hoarding his share of bread in a cupboard meant for books, for subsequent distribution to the poor of the neighbourhood.

The first school Subhas attended, in 1902 at the age of five, reinforced this sense of alienation. From a wholly Bengali setting he found himself at the Protestant European School run by the Baptist Church. The headmaster, despite twenty years in India, could not speak the local dialect; the great majority of Anglo-Indian students (always more English than the genuine product) detested the minority Indians; and Subhas was wretched in sports, which formed an important part of the school curriculum. In his autobiography *The Indian Pilgrim*, published after his death, Subhas the nationalist expressed his distaste for this English environment, but while he was at the Protestant European School he tried to be a model pupil. Anglicised Indians were his heroes and he knew British history better than Indian. This was to change at his next school.

In 1909, much to Subhas's relief, he was transferred to Ravenshaw Collegiate School. Bengali was a compulsory subject in the important matriculation examination, and in this

Indian setting he was soon an outstanding student. His command of the English language distinguished him from most Bengali students, sports meant a few hours' ineffectual drill, and he had soon come to terms with the intricacies of the Bengali language (though he spoke Bengali at home he had received little formal instruction in it). His father's immense reputation had preceded his arrival at Ravenshaw and soon Subhas stories were circulating widely. A Sanskrit teacher questioned why he had awarded Subhas 100 per cent for an exam paper is said to have replied, "Because I am not allowed to give him 110 per cent".

Beni Madhav Das, the head master, was the first idol of Subhas's adolescent life. Das's characteristics seemed to make him the morally perfect man. The head master, too, was much taken by the "glow" around Subhas, and was soon guiding this "young budding rose" through the wonderfully mysterious Hindu epics and legends. A keen naturalist, he advised Subhas to explore nature. For some years afterwards the adolescent searched out river banks, secluded hills and isolated meadows to commune with the elements. Best of all he loved to wander along the banks of the rivers round Cuttack devouring Washington Irving's *Sketchbook,* Mazzini's *Duties of Men,* Smiles' *The Secret of Success* and Gibbon's *Decline and Fall of the Roman Empire.* If the scenic atmosphere matched the natural setting, he would recite poetry: Wordsworth, the fifth-century Sanskrit poet Kalidasa and the Hindu epics *Ramayana* and *Mahabharata.*

When Das was transferred, Subhas wept unashamedly. Years later he remembered it as one of the most traumatic moments of his adolescence. Simultaneously sex reared its head. This was the start of what he would later describe as "one of the stormiest periods in my physical life which was to last five or six years ... a period of acute mental conflict causing untold suffering and agony." Solace came from an unexpected source. One day while visiting a neighbour's home he chanced upon some books by a Hindu monk.

As with Das, Subhas underwent an immediate conversion. Just turned fifteen, he discovered Narandranath Datta, known to worshipping Indians as Swami Vivekananda, who had returned to India after achieving fame in the United States. He explained India's colonial status; his sexual balm quietened the demon that was disturbing Subhas. Borrowing Western terms, Vivekananda explained India's subjugation at the hands of the British as a recent spiritual and ideological failure. There had been a Hindu Eden but it had been corrupted. It could only be regained if Hindus would revive Vedanta (literally the last of the Vedas, Hindu India's most revered books). Hinduism was scientific, it was rational, it was a religion for all men, it was the salvation for a world desperate to find a magic cure for its problems. India might be materially poor and technologically backward, but she was spiritually rich, capable with her scientific Hinduism and her rational Yoga to save the "sick" West. Vivekananda argued that India also had to learn much from the West: self-confidence, viability, skills, above all power. He advised his followers to play football as diligently as they read the Vedas. Subhas considered Vivekananda "saintly" and writing to his mother in 1913 would say, "There stands he, with his angelic appearance, his large piercing eyes and his sacred dress to preach to the whole world, the sacred truths lying embedded in Hinduism". He now collected as much of Vivekananda as he could.

Like all good Hindus Subhas also developed an affinity for the mountains. In 1907 he had been taken to Darjeeling, one of the hill stations developed by the British to provide relief for them from the summer heat of Calcutta. In October 1915 he travelled to Kurseong and from there released a stream of consciousness about the Himalayas, Aryans and the need to regenerate the impure Aryan blood. In a letter to a friend he wrote that the blood of the Hindus had become impure as a result of the "slavery of ages" and much adulteration:

> As I wander about the hills, I think of this very often. The sense of power must permeate our entire being. We again have to leap across mountains- it was only when the Aryans did such things that they were able to produce the Vedas. The

> Hindu race no longer has that pristine freshness - that youthful vigour and those unmatched human qualities. If we want to get them back we must begin from the land of birth-the sacred Himalayas. If India has something priceless, something noble - something to be proud of - the memory of all that is linked up with the Himalayas.

Though in later years Subhas would involve himself with the more universal ideas of nationalism and socialism, something of Vivekananda's philosophy would always remain with him. In the prison notebook he was to keep later in Mandalay Jail he would sketch out plans to spread Hinduism to Africa as a crusading, proselytising religion with a zest and influence to match that of Islam and Christianity. This, he noted, was how Christianity and Islam had created empires and converted millions, and it could be the key to India's greatness. Vivekananda's work displayed an interesting mixture of two great Bengali religious traditions, *vaishnava* (roughly 'love') *and shakti* (roughly 'strength'), and Bose would always remain wedded to both.

The sexual balm was more immediately relevant. Hindu ambivalence about sex is well known. Explicitly erotic inscriptions and paintings co-exist quite happily with sustained attempts to deny that sex exists. In the land of the *Kama Sutra* people furtively read *Fanny Hill.*

Scholars and historians have suggested the ambivalence lies in the wreckage of Hindu history and the numerous defeats suffered by the Hindus over the centuries. Reforming Hinduism, responding perhaps to the prudery of the Victorians (who were horrified by ancient Hindu eroticism), added a new and unexpected twist. The young Ramakrishna (Vivekananda's guru) had spied on women bathing at his village pond; the grown Ramakrishna, married to a young girl, found sexual cohabitation impossible. Often convulsed by hallucinations and fits, he could only come to terms with his wife by treating her as a mother, a representation of the great goddess of strength Kali. Vivekananda, developing Ramakrishna, saw in celibacy the answer to sex: every young man was encouraged to think of every woman as his mother, or, failing that, as his sister.

This was the balm Subhas was looking for, and he decided that he too would become a celibate. But the demon was not that easily frustrated. In *The Indian Pilgrim* Subhas would write,

> Ramakrishna's example of renunciation and purity entailed a battle royal with all the forces of the lower self. And Vivekananda's ideal brought me into conflict with existing family and social order. I was weak, the fight was a long-drawn one in which success was not easy to obtain, hence tension and unhappiness with occasional fits of depression.

Years later, during his exile in Europe and enjoying the company of European women, he would doubt whether the whole exercise had been worthwhile.

Vivekananda had preached a bastard socialism: help the poor, the poor are God. Subhas, with about ten friends, formed at school a Sechaa Seva Sangh (Volunteer Service Corps) that looked after smallpox and cholera victims in Cuttack and every Sunday distributed free rice to poor students. Social work on this scale in India was limited to missionaries, and when Subhas and his volunteers visited villages near the city they encountered hostility: affluent young men were not supposed to do such things, though some villagers rationalised it by suggesting that it was all part of the accepted Hindu practice of accumulating religious 'merit'.

These activities were soon formalised. Through a school friend Subhas met Hemanta Sarkar, a boy of about his age who lived in Calcutta. At this stage Hemanta's ideas were more developed than Subhas's, and he belonged to a formal Calcutta group which had a *dada* (literally 'older brother', but used as a term of respect in Bengali). Soon Subhas became part of this group. Hemanta Sarkar has provided an interesting, if overly sentimental, recollection of his first meeting with Subhas. It is one of the few first-hand descriptions of the young adolescent:

> I was sitting in the drawing room of Gopal Chandra Ganguly. At that time a fair, thin, spectacled boy arrived. As soon as I saw him, I felt I was looking at the boy who would bring freedom to India. His face showed that he had a firm determination. He told me: "Beni Madhav Das wrote to me that you will stay in our house." I replied: "Brother, you all are rich. A poor man like me can't stay there." His eyes instantly filled with tears, and he said: "You have insulted me by saying that I was born with a silver spoon, but have I personally committed any crime?" Then we started talking.

Subhas's life was dominated by two great friendships. His friendship with Hemanta lasted till 1924, when there was a breach. By that time another friend, Dilip Roy, had emerged, and he would remain close to Subhas until the end of his life. To Dilip and Hemanta, Subhas would deny nothing. They would be his confidants, sounding-boards and confessors.
Thirty-one of the letters he wrote in his late teens to Hemanta between 1914 and1919 have been preserved, and reveal the deep bond between these two, an adolescent love that is striking. In one letter Subhas wrote, "You are forever mine, I am forever yours, don't forget this...that you are my Lord...don't you know you have always been my Krishna?" Subhas sometimes addressed Hemanta as "sentimentalist" and "poet", while signing himself as "rationalist" or "western philosopher."

The times were revolutionary. Curzon's decision to partition Bengal had sparked the first nationalist agitation in India, ranging from boycott of British goods to the growth of secret revolutionary societies. Subhas was unaffected. He had enthusiastically joined in the celebrations marking George V's Durbar in Delhi in 1911, but knew little of wider political movements and rarely discussed politics at home. Under Vivekananda's influence he had turned to religion and to his mother. In an extraordinary series of letters, probably written during the winter of 1912-13 when aged 15, he expressed his bewilderment and anguish. He wrote of vegetarianism, of the proof of God's existence, of the difference between humans and animals, of the wretched state of India ("God's country"), of the depressing prevalence of sin, and of his own personal failure to do anything:

> Mother, how much longer shall we sleep? How much longer shall we go on playing with non-essentials? Shall we continue to turn a deaf ear to the wailings of our nation? Our ancient religion is suffering the pangs of near death — does that not stir our hearts? How long can one sit with folded arms and watch this state of our country and religion? One cannot wait any more - one cannot sleep any more - we must now shake off our stupor and lethargy and plunge into action. But, alas! How many selfless sons of the Mother are prepared, in this selfish age, to completely give up their personal interests and take the plunge for the Mother? Mother, is this son of yours yet ready?

We do not know how his mother reacted, but Vivekananda's influence had begun to take its toll: his studies had been affected and *bhadralok* society was outraged. *Bhadralok* literally means gentle people, and its nearest English equivalent would perhaps be 'gentry'. In Bengal it defined a whole cluster of higher castes — Brahmans, Kayasthas, Viaydas – who shunned manual labour and created for themselves bastions of privilege, power and status from which they could look down upon *abadra,* or *chotolok* - literally small people.(In colloquial Bengali the term has a more abusive meaning: it is equivalent to 'bastard'.) The two *loks* (groups of people) represented the deeper divisions within the Bengali Hindu caste system; and, though the Raj would later blame its political problems on the revolt by the *bhadraloks,* the latter were most comfortable during British rule in Bengal. They formed a middle-class dedicated to success yet unwilling to sacrifice security, eager to accept the benefits of British rule but keen to maintain ancient privileges - a class that practised, with remarkable success, the Hindu work ethic:

> *Porasuno kora jey Gari*
> *gora chorey shey*
> (Those who study hard
> Get to ride in carriages).

Whatever the distractions, his performance at school was good. Subhas, who always liked competitive examinations and invariably did well, came second, and his parents decided he must continue his studies for a degree at Presidency College in Calcutta, one of British India's most prestigious colleges. He started there in the monsoon of 1913, aged 16. At this juncture Subhas had no particular idea of a future career.

Calcutta brought new influences. One in particular was Aurobindo – in British eyes the leader of the revolutionary movement that had ravaged Bengal a few years earlier. He was another of that generation of Indians whose parents, convinced that everything good must come from England, sought to make him an Englishman. The experiment misfired and Aurbindo emerged as an advocate of Indian nationalism. Sent to England at the age of seven he spent 14 years in Britain, passed the Indian civil service examinations, and returned home to work for the Gaekwar of Baroda. There, developing Vivekananda's ideas, he recycled myths into his own concept of nationalism. Like Vivekananda he argued that India needed strength: physical, mental and moral, but above all spiritual. Aurobindo's political heyday was in the early years of the twentieth century, when he became part of the extremist wing of the Congress party. The Congress was still far from a rebel organisation. Its loyalty to the Raj was unquestioned, it merely sought more Indian representation under British tutelage. Aurobindo called for resistance, passive at first but violent if necessary. In 1910, three years before Subhas went to Calcutta, Aurobindo, fearing arrest by the British, exiled himself to the French-ruled enclave Pondicherry in south India and openly renounced politics. But when Subhas started at Presidency College Aurobindo was still a potent figure and his writings were avidly collected and read in Calcutta. Inevitably, legends grew that he would return and liberate India.

One story Subhas heard often: On the day of reckoning there would be a "march of blanketeers" - fakirs with blankets would march on Fort William in Calcutta, the British soldiers there would freeze and power would pass to the Indians. Subhas, was possibly more interested in Aurobindo's abstruse philosophical writings on yoga and the gathering of the "inner cosmic forces". As he delved further into them, he became convinced that he needed a guru. He had searched for spiritual mentors in Cuttack, but they had proved unsatisfactory, and those in Calcutta were either mercenary or bureaucrats. So in the summer of 1914, soon after the end of his first academic year at Presidency, he borrowed money from a friend and, accompanied by Hemanta, went on on a religious pilgrimage to northern India, that great supermarket of Indian gurus. The pair made a grand tour of Hinduism's holy places; and, while his family searched frantically for him, Subhas encountered the unacceptable face of Hinduism.

Some *sadhus* suspected them of being Bengali revolutionaries disguising themselves as mystics; at a Hardwar eating house they were not served because, as Bengalis, they were considered dirty. At another food was eaten separately by the different castes, and the village well from which the Brahmans drew water could not be touched by non-Brahmans. By the time he arrived at Benares Subhas was thoroughly disillusioned. He was easily persuaded by Swami Brahmananda, a friend of the family, to return home.

There followed emotional scenes which Subhas would later recount to Hemanta. Halfway up the stairs at Oriya Bazaar he met his mother. As he touched her feet she wept and said: "It seems you have come into this world to kill me. I would not have waited so long before drowning myelf in the Ganges; only for the sake of my daughters have I not done so."

Subhas smiled inwardly at this very Indian, very Bengali mother's lamentation. His father embraced him and led him to his room. But, "on the way he broke down and in the room he wept for quite some time holding on to me. Then he lay down and I massaged his feet – it appeared as if he was feeling some heavenly pleasure."

Then, probably weakened by his journey, Subhas fell ill with typhoid; the First World War broke out and the debate about a spiritual guru came to an end. Years later, in his autobiography, he would call this the moment of change. A nation's life could not be divided into watertight religious and political compartments.

Probably he simplified things. The search for a guru went on. But it would be many years before he found one, and then that person would be a full-fledged politician.

2
The Rebellion

Subhas returned to his studies in Calcutta determined to be the good *bhadralok*. He was keen to get a first in philosophy in the BA (Hons) course. Yet Western rationalism had begun to dent the *papier-mâché* facade of Vedic beliefs and Vivekanandian rationalisations. If the mystic had produced one revolution, Western logic was to produce another and far-reaching one. Subhas took an active part in flood-relief programmes, produced a college magazine and was soon organising debates as a method of promoting Indian self-reliance.

"We Indians are too dependent on others for actions, views, initiative, everything. So I have decided that debating classes have got to stimulate us to stand on our own legs". The words were said to Dilip Roy, son of the famous Bengali literary figure Dwijendralal Roy, who Subhas had met as he tried to recruit debaters. Within a few years Dilip would supplant Hemanta as his great friend.

By August 1915 Subhas was confident that "I have a definite mission to fulfil in life for which I have been born and I am not to drift in the current of popular opinion." Within a few months these ambitions were thrown into relief by an incident of distinct political significance, one that Subhas would later call the turning-point of his life.

It involved Edward Farley Oaten, Professor of History at Presidency College. In the Indian reconstruction of the event, Oaten has become the great rogue. Indian nationalist historians have no doubt that Oaten represented all that was obnoxious in British rule. A year before the incident, talking to some students he had said, "As the Greeks had Hellenised the barbarian people with whom they came in contact, so the mission of the English is to civilise the Indians."

On 10 January 1916 some students in Subhas's class were involved in a corridor altercation with Oaten, who claimed they were wilfully disrupting his teaching by making noise as they passed. Subhas, as the representative of his class on the newly elected students' consultative committee, took up the matter with the principal, Henry R. James. James suggested the two sides make up; but the time had long since passed for such a simple solution. Presidency College, of course, was still devoted to the Empire. Europe was in the middle of a World War and the college magazine ran articles in praise of Britannia, describing it as the good, the free, the sublime. The British view of the excesses of German nationalism was uncritically accepted. However, the streets of Calcutta were also witness to the first stirrings of an Indian nationalism. Outside the college, blows were being exchanged in Calcutta tram-cars, and Indians ejected from reserved seats in trains were fighting back against the racial discrimination practiced by the British in India.

The students at Presidency College went on strike. James imposed a fine and the strike was called off. Despite a meeting between Oaten and the students, the situation remained explosive. On 15 February there was a repetition of the corridor incident. This time one of the students alleged that Oaten had called him a rascal and boxed his ears. That afternoon at about three, as Oaten came down to the ground floor to pin up a cricket notice, he was quickly surrounded by some boys and beaten: "brutally assaulted" said the government committee which investigated the matter. Oaten, 55 years later, recalled only "a few bruises" The whole thing was over in less than a minute.

Subhas probably master-minded the attack, but did he actually take part himself? And, if he did, was he the one who attacked Oaten from behind? In his autobiography Subhas claimed only to be an "eyewitness". Years later, asked by his nephew Amiya whether he actually assaulted Oaten, he smiled enigmatically. (The argument is itself revealing about attitudes towards Bose. That Subhas took a leading part in avenging a British insult ties in neatly with his subsequent role as *Netaji* – putative liberator of India. But if it was he who hit Oaten from behind, it would not help foster the image of Subhas the chivalrous hero and fighter.)

The head master had no doubts about Subhas' role. When a witness identified Subhas as the main culprit James said: "Bose, you are the most troublesome man in the college. I suspend you." The governing body quickly confirmed the suspension.

Subhas banked on his reputation as a good student, and on his acquaintance with important figures in the Calcutta educational hierarchy, in particular his family's friendship with Sir Ashutosh Mookerje, the vice chancellor of Calcutta University. He thought Bansilal's "weak evidence" could be overturned. A committee of inquiry was set up to investigate the affair and the wider issue of the relationship between Presidency College and its students. But the committee was more concerned with the issue of student discipline and education politics, and approved the college's action. The university refused him permission to study at any other college. Subhas had held up well under the strain, but now he confessed to a friend: "I do not know if I shall survive this."

Writing his autobiography 20 years later he had forgotten these youthful doubts, and saw this as the moment when he had a foretaste of leadership and of the martyrdom it involved. "In short, I had acquired character and could face the future with equanimity."

Calcutta was clearly not a safe place for students; many had been arrested, including some from Presidency College. His elder brother Sarat (or 'Mejdada', the Bengali term that Subhas used to denote him), decided Subhas would be better off in Cuttack. *Bhadralok* society had finally extracted a price for rebellion.

Subhas spent a year undertaking community work in exile in Oriya Bazaar while efforts were made to enable him to return to college. After a year the university authorities indicated they would with draw his suspension provided he could secure a place at a college. Subhas decided to try his luck at Scottish Church College. He found the principal, Dr Urquhart, a likeable man, and Dr Urquhart in turn was impressed by Subhas. In July 1917 Subhas resumed his studies.

Scottish Church was a world removed from Presidency. Urquhart was a man of philosophy, his Bible classes were excellent and Subhas, quieter and more reflective, took his studies very seriously. The only luxury he permitted himself was military training. He had applied to join the recently formed 49th Bengalees but failed the eye test. Some Indians had successfully petitioned the government to allow a University Corps, and the university provided a military unit as part of the territorial army. This supplied a deeply felt Subhas need; it was the answer to the British slander that Bengalis could not fight. Bose implictly accepted the British view of the Bengali but was determined to provide a remedy. This could only come, he was convinced, through military service: there lay strength, decisiveness and the final answer to Macaulay's jibe about the effete *babus.* India's special role could then be wedded to modern European organisation.

There is an early photograph taken while he was training, possibly at Belghoria where the unit had set up a temporary camp. It shows a young man in military shorts reclining on the grass with his rifle across his shoulders: there is an unmistakable look of childish pleasure and naive happiness on the bespectacled face. On the first day of training Bose marched into Fort William, the fort built by the East India Company overlooking the Calcutta Maidan and the symbol of British military power in India. As he did so he "experienced a queer feeling of satisfaction, as if we were taking possession of something to which we had an inherent right but of which we had been unjustly deprived." Bose even took to the officer commanding:

Captain Gray a gruff Scotsman, who always wore a scowl but had a "heart of gold".

"When he joined our Company," he would recall years later, " the staff officers in Fort William were of the opinion that we would be utter failure as soldiers. The captain showed that their estimate was wrong".

For Subhas this military training was essential. "This training gave me something which I needed or which I lacked. The feeling of strength and self-confidence grew still further. As soldiers we had certain rights which as Indians we did not possess." In April 1919 he sat for his final graduation exams. He had worked hard, selected likely questions from previous papers and discussed matters with his friend Bholanath Roy, who already knew what the exam was all about. Though he did very well in two of his favourite subjects, History of Philosophy and Essay, he was not happy with his performance in others. This probably cost him the first place, and he had to be content with the second place in the overall university rankings. He had hardly reconciled himself to this when suddenly his father, who was in Calcutta, summoned him. He found Sarat with him. The pair had decided that Subhas should sit for the Indian Civil Service exam in England, known as the ICS. For a son of Janakinath to go and study in England was not new. Sarat had been the first and returned from England a barrister five years earlier. At the time Satish, the eldest brother, was living in London's Belsize Park taking the bar examinations. But Subhas was being asked to serve the Raj more directly and given only twenty-four hours in which to make up his mind. He was presented with a terrible dilemma. The ICS was the greatest examination of the Raj. It attracted the best talents and was considered to be the toughest; success meant entry to the "heaven-born" service that ruled for the Raj and promised a lifetime of power, glory and luxurious security. Faced with his father's demand Subhas's carefully laid plans collapsed. He did not want to serve the British, certainly not as an instrument of their rule in India, and while he wanted to go to England, he had set his heart on the Tripos, which would help him in his intended educational career. As it was late August, he had already left it late to get into a Cambridge college, perhaps too late. But if the only way he could get to England for his Tripos was to sit for the ICS, then he had to bite the bullet. He convinced himself he would not be able to pass the ICS examination, so the crisis would never arise. He agreed to sail for England.

There was some problem in getting a passport (the police knew about him), but on 15 September 1919 he left Kidderpore Docks for England aboard the SS *City of Calcutta.* He arrived at Tilbury on a cold, wet, dark winter day made more depressing by the news from the universities. There was, said the adviser of Indian students, no hope; none of his relations had been to Oxbridge, and it was late in the academic year to apply. Fortunately for him, Dilip was already at Fitzwilliam, then a non-collegiate body affiliated to Cambridge, and by early November Subhas was able to settle down. Within three weeks of his arrival, he wrote to Hemanta:

> Whether one wills it or not, the climate of this country makes people energetic. The activity you see is most heartening. Every man is conscious of the value of time and there is a method in all that goes on. Nothing makes me happier than to be served by the whites and to watch them clean my shoes. Students here have a status and the way the professors treat them is different. One could see here how man should treat his fellow man. They have many faults - but in many matters you have to respect them for their virtues.

There was much to learn from the English:

> The natives of this country have certain qualities which have made them so great. First they can work strictly to time with clock-work precision, secondly, they have a robust optimism -we think more of the sorrows of life, they think

> more of the happy and bright things of life. Then they have a strong common sense - they appreciate national interest very well!

Simple things delighted him. There were no police to watch students, he could buy books on credit at Cambridge bookshops, and witness the excitement of debate, both at the university and in Parliament. But he could never forget that the English were the masters of his country. Leonard Gordon, the American scholar, in his book *Bengal, the Nationalist Movement, 1876-1940*, has sought to explain this ambivalence in terms of the "good-boy-bad-boy"syndrome: Subhas Bose wanted to rebel against authority yet win its approval. This would explain everything: the revolt against parental authority, against *bhadralok* society, against the British, and later even against Gandhi. There may well be psychological explanations, but his ambivalence towards the British was also the classical result of the distortions of colonial rule. Living in this alien world, his nationalism deepened. No Indian weaknesses were to be exhibited. The English must be made to realise that Indians, too, had all the desired English qualities: morality, sense of values, dedication. "We must prove it to them that we are their superiors. We must beard the lion in his den," he told Dilip. When he discovered Dilip sitting cross-legged in his rooms wrapped in a *dhoti,* he was furious. What would the English think of this strange Indian custom? Subhas, of course, was always upright, dedicated, sincere: and made even the most hackneyed of clichés sound like newly discovered *mots.* He was also, of course, terribly priggish. His books were always in place, his clothes neat and pressed, and he was terrified of sex. In England's more sexually liberated society all his Vivekananda fears were aroused.

One woman managed to break through his anxiety. Mrs Dharmavir was the English wife of a Punjabi doctor practising in Lancashire. She was some years older, and in need of some diversion from her nationalist husband's provocative taunts about the British. She became 'Didi', older sister. The balm worked. With her Subhas would form a deep, affectionate, platonic relationship and he would later act as an older brother to her two daughters. At the Dharmvir's house, as Dilip Roy has recounted, there would be many evenings spent in song and poetry recitals. Dilip was already a fine singer, Subhas loved reciting poetry.

It was to this Englishwoman that Subhas opened his heart, even more than to Dilip. His letters to her show his intense sentimental side and how easily moved he was. On one occasion as he was about to leave her house, she gave him some nuts and fruits, and Subhas wrote, "There was something characteristically Oriental in the whole incident. My mind at once travelled home and I was reminded of what an Indian mother would do under similar circumstances."

When he left England he would write and explain to her his shyness with women and confess to her that he could never feel comfortable in her land:

> Looking back upon my stay in England, may I say that I was never happy during my residence there. Our political relations with England are such that happiness is impossible. A sensitive Indian is reminded every moment of his stay in England about his position in the world. The reminder is of the most galling sort. I do not think I shall be happy merely by returning to India. The same reminder will be haunting me even in India. But while I am there, I shall have the assurance and the consolation of trying to do my little bit for the creation of a new India. The consolation I could not find when I was in England.

In his letters to Didi, Subhas also revealed his distrust of Western materialism and heaped praise on what he described as the superior Indian civilisation:

> You will find in India a people highly unconventional in many ways a people for whom civilisation does not consist in the accumulation of factories, sky-scrapers and beautiful clothes, but for whom civilisation consists in the elevation of human spirit to the Divine. You will find there a people who respect most - not the politician or the millionaire or the businessman - but the penniless ascetic whose only wealth is God.

Years later, when the Dharmavirs returned to India, Didi's house in the Himalayas would be a convenient retreat and it was there that he would finally begin to express his love for another European woman. Subhas felt close to only one other person in England. This was a Mr Bates at whose Leigh-on-Sea house in Essex, Subhas went to stay in September 1920, as he deliberated on what to do with his life. From there wrote to Sarat:

> Mr Bates represents English character at its very best. He is cultured and liberal in his views and cosmopolitan in his sentiments, He is altogether unlike the ordinary run of Englishmen - who are proud, haughty, and conceited and to whom everything that is non-English is bad. Mr Bates counts among his friends Russians, Poles, Lithuanians, Irishmen and members of other nationalities. He takes a great interest in Russian, Irish and Indian literature and admires the writings of Romesh Dutt and Tagore.

Subhas was so taken by him he wanted to present him with a miniature model of the Taj Mahal and asked Sarat whether he could send one from Calcutta provided it did not cost more than twenty or thirty rupees. His experiences were in sharp contrast to Sarat's, who appears to have had a richer exposure to English life. In 1912 Sarat had been the first of the Boses to travel to England, qualifying as a barrister. At that time, even in Western-educated Hindu homes, the idea of a son travelling abroad was seen as disturbing, not least because of the prospect of him getting involved with an English woman. So Sarat had only been allowed to leave after getting married, an arranged marriage which was meant to keep him away from the temptations of Western women. But once in London Sarat revelled in going to the theatre and even enjoyed the friendship of English women, albeit platonic ones. The experiences were rich enough for him to come to some pretty definite conclusions about the difference between Eastern and Western love. In a letter to his wife, Sarat would say that the love a Bengali woman has for her husband was of less value than the one a Western woman had for hers. Sarat reasoned that a Bengali woman's love for her husband was a duty, while a Western woman first fell in love with a man and then got married, which placed a higher value on the love she gave him.

> Love of a woman of good character is more praiseworthy than love of a woman of good character in our country because she has liberty here and must have strength of character. The men here live correct lives, but when our boys come here they become libertines, so don't you think they are more praiseworthy?

Unlike Sarat, Subhas distrusted the theatre and anything frivolous. Five years earlier Subhas had gone one evening to a Calcutta function to honour Jagadish Chandra Bose, the great scientist. Subhas was horrified that the students had decided to honour him with songs, the playing of instruments, poetry reading and an English drama which ended with a rendition of *God Save the King*.

> When I found acting was on the programme I at once thought of leaving. But in fond expectation of hearing him speak, I tried to have a nap for the duration

> of the drama. Amongst a gathering of boisterous young men, I sat with my eyes closed like a stern puritan. I returned broken-hearted and thought to myself that until we learnt to honour our great men properly, there could be no deliverance for us Bengalis or for that matter of India. Honouring the great with a theatrical performance! What a shame! Poor India! O Bengalis to what depth you have descended.

In July 1920 Subhas sat for the ICS examination. He had nine subjects to take and the one he clearly enjoyed most was Modern European History.

> Before I studied this subject, I did not have a clear idea of politics of continental Europe. We Indians are taught to regard Europe as a magnified edition of Great Britain. Consequently we have a tendency to look at the Continent through the eyes of England. This, of course, is a gross mistake, but not having been to the Continent I did not realise it till I studied Modern European History and some of the original sources like Bismarck's autobiography, Metternich's memoirs, Cavour's letters etc. These original sources, more than anything else I studied at Cambridge helped me foster my understanding of the inner currents of international politics.

Despite his hard work he went into the exam with misgivings. But when the results were announced in mid-September he discovered to his great joy that he had come fourth. Subhas had scored 2284 marks out of a maximum 6000. Six of the first seven that year were Indians. However, having done so well, he was now faced with the crucial choice of his *bhadralok* life: should he continue into the ICS? Subhas turned to the one person he knew: his elder bother Sarat. In the years to come Sarat would be his banker, guide, friend and confessor. His family would not understand nor approve his rejection of the ICS. Janakinath was aghast and for seven months letters went backwards and forwards between England and India, as Subhas took the first major decision of his life. On 22 September 1920 he wrote a long letter to Sarat in which he outlined why he could not possibly join an alien civil service. "The civil service can bring all kinds of worldly comfort but are not these acquisitions made at the expense of one's soul?" Subhas wrote that "father is sure to be hostile to the idea of my not joining the civil service. He would like to see me settled down in life as soon as possible. Moreover if I have to qualify for another career it will add considerably to the financial burden which is already on your shoulders."

"I am not going to marry", he wrote, "hence considerations of worldly prudence will not deter me from taking a particular line of action if I believe that to be intrinsically right."

Janakinath, supported by his sons Sarat and Satish, suggested a compromise,"Why not give the ICS a chance for a few years, and then if you do not like it you can always leave?"But for Subhas this would mean pledging allegiance to a foreign power and that he could not do. Yet the pain he was causing his father distressed him and in one of his letters to Sarat he confessed he could not summon up the courage to write to his father directly.

By mid-January Subhas had edged towards a decision. Suddenly he had found a man who stirred his imagination. That man was Chitta Ranjan Das.

Das had been one of the greatest lawyers in Calcutta, able to command briefs and fees of his own choosing. But then he came up against the repressive Rowlatt Acts, which allowed special trials without juries and powers to restrict and imprison suspects. When Gandhi made his call for non-co-operation, Das followed. He sacrificed his practice and his fine Western clothes, and took to Gandhi's ordained *khadi,* leading the non-co-operation movement in Bengal. This was the example Subhas was looking for. He wrote to Sarat:

> If C.R. Das at his age can give up everything and face the uncertainties of life — I am sure a young man like myself who has no worldly cares to trouble him is much more capable of doing so. .. A life of sacrifice to start with, plain living and high thinking, whole-hearted devotion to the country's cause , all these are highly enchanting to my imagination and inclination. Further, the very principle of serving under an alien bureaucracy is intensely repugnant to me.

On 16 February 1921 Subhas wrote to Das offering his services: he could be a journalist on a nationalist paper, a village worker or even a teacher in the national schools being set up, and he precociously offered his own ideas on what the Congress, already the main nationalist party in India, should do. It should have a permanent house, announce policies for native states (those ruled by Indian princes) and depressed Hindu castes, maintain a permanent bureau with its own research and study wings and set up an intelligence department for collecting information and organising publicity and propaganda. Das, realising Subhas's value, accepted with alacrity, and so on April 1921 Bose wrote to Edwin Montagu, then secretary of state for India, formally telling him he could not serve the British Raj. The Raj government, determined not to lose him, asked Satish to go to Cambridge to try and persuade Subhas to change his mind. It was a lost cause.. Bose had taken eight months to make his decision and he was sticking to it.

Subhas completed his Tripos in June, borrowed £90 from Dilip and later that month sailed for India. Travelling on the boat with him was the revered writer RabindranathTagore. The two discussed the new political movements sweeping India. Their main talking point was Mohandas Gandhi, and what seemed to them his remarkable tactic of achieving change through non-violence. Subhas was uncertain what his role in this movement would be. He could join the Ramakrishna Mission, or teach at Tagore's university. But whatever it was, his life had irrevocably changed. On the day he turned down a career in the ICS he wrote to his friend Charu Ganguly:

> You are aware that once before I sailed on the sea of life at the call of duty. The ship has now reached a port offering great allurement - where power, property and wealth are at my command. But, the response from the innermost corner of my heart is, "You will not find happiness in this. The way to your happiness lies in your dancing around with the surging waves of the ocean." Today, in response to that call, I am sailing forth again with the helm in His Hands. Only He knows where the ship will land. Let us see what happens.

The revolt was complete.

Part Two

THE MYSTICAL *HERO*

There is nothing that lures me more than a life of adventure away from the beaten track, and in search of the unknown. In this life there may be suffering, but there is joy as well; there may be hours of darkness but there are also hours of dawn. To this path I call my countrymen.

- Subhas Bose's inscription on an
autograph given at Vithalnagar,
Haripura, on 23 February 1938, and
quoted in Dilip Roy's *The Subhas I Knew*

3

At Last: The Guru

"The career of Netaji Subhas Chandra Bose", writes Christopher Sykes in *Troubled Loyalty,* his biography of the German resistance hero Adam von Trott, "is most easily seen as a cautionary tale about the dangers of a narrow mind, of dedicating life to one obsessional hatred, of the blindness induced by fanaticism and irrational self-confidence." This is one expression of an old-established view of English conservatism. Here, as Subhas Bose prepares to enter the political field, let us pause to consider an example of extreme English nationalism, which would have a far-reaching effect on Indian nationalism. The event in question is the Jallianwalla Bagh massacre – the Amritsar massacre of 1919. Like Lidice or Sharpeville, it defines a certain moment in time and explains a whole range of historical events. Before Jallianwalla Indian collaborators could live in peace with their consciences. After Jallianwalla Bagh there could be no compromise on basic issues.

Curiously, the massacre occurred in the middle of the Raj's search for more reliable collaborators. The Raj had always depended on collaborators. It was physically and economically impossible to run India without them. In the eighteenth and nineteenth centuries shrewd alliances with Indian princes, local satraps and prominent village, district and religious strong men had produced reliable, efficient collaborators who saw in British rule a guarantee for their own increasingly archaic feudalism. But by the beginning of the twentieth century the collaborators were themselves becoming archaic. A new class of educated people had emerged from the Macaulay-inspired educational system, quoting John Stuart Mill and believing in English liberal capitalism. A more sophisticated approach to collaboration was required.

The First World War made this need urgent, and India responded magnificently to the British cause. The origins of the war were mysterious to most Indians, the war itself was remote, but, apart from a few revolutionary groups most Indians rallied to the Empire. India supplied 800,000 troops in all theatres of the war, 50,000 of them on the battlefields of Europe. A quarter of a million Indians fought in extending the British Empire into Mesopotamia, Persia and the Trans-Caspian and Caucasian regions south of Russia. Indian troops were decisive in the battles of the Middle East in helping defeat the Turks. Iraq was conquered with the help of Indian troops, and Allenby took Palestine with an army of which two-thirds of the infantry and one third of the cavalry were Indian. The picture of India's loyalty to the Raj was summed up in the *Punch* cartoon of the turbaned Indian atop a horse saluting John Bull and saying: "There are 165,000 of us, sir, ready and waiting." Gandhi won the Kaisar-e-Hind award for "loyally" encouraging Indians to enlist. More than 60,000 Indian soldiers died.

On 20 August 1917, Edwin Montagu announced in the House of Commons that Britain's goal was to make India self-governing and work for " a progressive realisation of responsible government in India as an integral part of the British Empire". Apologists of the Raj, masquerading as historians, have since claimed that the Montague Declaration meant that this marked the moment when the British agreed to set India free, and that after this the only debate was about setting the date for freedom. This is historical nonsense. The declaration spoke of Indians still being "part of the British Empire". In British thinking there was no question of an independent life outside the Empire.

The most vivid illustration of how differently the white dominions and India were treated comes when you examine the battle of Gallipoli during the First World War. At Gallipoli the Australians, New Zealanders and the Indians all fought under a common British flag and British command. For the white ANZAC troops this was the moment that marked the emergence of their nation on the world stage. Although it was a terrible British defeat, today Australians and New Zealanders take great pride in preserving the memory of the campaign.

Indians of all castes fought with exemplary bravery, indeed in one battle they achieved greater success than any of the other Allied troops, but one has to search very hard around the battlefields of Gallipoli to find any mention of their role. On memorial stones the occasional Indian name is to be found tucked away after all the British, Australian and New Zealanders names of those who died fighting for the Empire. The Anzacs were part of the great all white British family, although to this day the Australians blame the defeat on the British leadership. The Indians were regarded as mercenaries. They were certainly not treated as part of the family. Indeed Australians who had not previously met Indians thought they were Turks.

As R.J. Moore, the eminent historian, has shown, the Montague Declaration was both a compromise and a mistake. It emerged from an overstressed war cabinet, unsure of final victory over Germany, and was a result of its own propaganda that the war was being fought for liberty, democracy and national self-government. These aims were not intended to apply to India. Educated Indians did not realise this, and it was to cause them much grief. In fact the very phrase "responsible government" which was to lead to so much trouble over the next few decades was an alternative to Montague's original phrase "self-government". Both Curzon and Balfour feared that the use of the words "self government" with respect to India meant Parliamentary government, and believed that Indians, however well-educated, would never be able to sustain parliamentary government. Curzon feared that self government in India would mean government in India by the educated classes and he had total contempt for them. Curzon thought Indians might conceivably be ready for "self government" in about 500 years time, and it was he who substituted the words "responsible government" for "self government" in the documents. Lloyd George, the war-time prime minister, did not care for Curzon, but accepted him as the expert on India. In fact Lloyd George had little time at all for Indians, let alone educated Indians. He had once described them as "niggers". It is interesting that the two British prime ministers of the two World Wars, Lloyd George and Winston Churchill, had broadly similar views on India.

In 1919 the Montagu-Chelmsford reforms, which provided for elections to provincial councils with some local powers, were introduced. A growing revolutionary movement taking hold in the years between 1910 and 1915 was particularly strong in the Punjab and Bengal, and was curbed only with the free use of the notorious wartime Defence of India Act. With the war over and the act about to be repealed, the Raj decided to retain it under a new name: the Rowlatt Acts, named after the judge whose committee had recommended this ingenious remedy. All the repressive powers of the war remained intact: press censorship, power to ban meetings, arrests without warrants. For many Indians ready to believe in the Montagu-Chelmsford reforms the Rowlatt Acts revealed the deeper imperial purpose. Gandhi called for *Satyagraha* or civil disobedience against the Rowlatt Acts, shrewdly aligning himself with a cause dear to many Indian Muslims. This curious but strong alliance between Hindu and Muslim produced the beginnings of a mass movement in India. By April 1919 the Raj was facing its gravest crisis since the revolt of 1857.

In Amritsar, key to the vital Punjab, which supplied the best soldiers and the most efficient collaborators, a nervous Deputy Commissioner named Miles Irving panicked. There had been *hartals* (the hartal was a brilliantly effective Indian form of strike in which almost everything in a particular place would come to a halt), marches and demonstrations; but no violence. Irving nevertheless, instructed by the Punjab government, spirited away two of the Punjab's best-loved leaders.

Violence resulted, and on 13 April 1919 Amritsar was handed over to Brigadier-General Reginald Dyer, commander of the Jullunder Brigade. He immediately imposed martial law, which banned any public assemblies, but, even as his soldiers went round the city drumming the news, he heard of a massive meeting being held at Jallianwalla Bagh. He hurried there with troops and armoured cars. Jallianwalla Bagh was (and is) a large open space with a single very narrow entrance. When Dyer arrived he found more than 20,000 men, women and children assembled there.

How many of the crowd were there for the politics is debatable. April 13 also marked Baishaki, a joyous spring celebration that in some parts of India also marks New Year's Day.(Indians do not have a uniform New Year's Day). It made little or no impression on Dyer that the crowd was unarmed and contained many women and children. He found the entrance too narrow for his armoured cars, so he abandoned them there, ordered his troops to block the entrance and, without warning, to open fire. "I made up my mind I would do all the men to death if they were going to continue the meeting", he later told the Hunter Commission of Enquiry. After 337 men, 41 women and a baby of seven weeks had been killed, and 1,500 people injured, his troops ran out of ammunition and the firing ceased. (The Congress would later assert that over 1,000 were killed.). Dyer went on to inflict some remarkable punishments: Indian suspects were flogged. Indians passing through a certain street where an English missionary woman had been beaten were made to crawl on their hands and knees in what became known as the crawling order.

The Hunter Committee found that Dyer's deeds were "inhuman and un-British'" Churchill, secretary of state for war, condemned Dyer's action, in a stormy House of Commons debate, as a "monstrous event." Montague, as secretary of state for India, faced removal from office. In fact, ugly overtones of anti-Indian sentiments fused with anti-Semitic ones (Montagu was a Jew). Although Montagu survived, 129 members of the Commons supported Dyer. In the House of Lords a motion deploring the government's action against Dyer was passed by 129 to 86. During the debate Lord Sinha, who was under secretary of state for India, and one of the highest ranking Indian collaborators, made a moderate and sensible speech. One peer was heard to say, "If they are all like him the more they massacre the better." Dyer was eventually forced to leave the Army. But such was the approval of Dyer's actions that the editor of the *Morning Post* collected a fund of £28,000 for the general, and many Britons in India and England acclaimed him as a hero.

Jawaharlal Nehru, then cutting his teeth in nationalist politics, went to Amritsar when travel became possible and collected evidence on the atrocities Dyer had inflicted. He recorded in his diary, "Visited the lane (Durga Koti Lane) where people were made to crawl on their bellies. Told that one respectable woman raped in a neighbouring house. General misbehaviour of Tommies." Later, in 1919, Nehru travelled from Amritsar to Delhi by the night train. In the morning he found his compartment was full of British military officers, one of them was Dyer. He was telling his fellow Britons what a heroic job he had done in Amritsar to save the Raj. Nehru recorded:

> He pointed out how he had the whole town at his mercy and he had felt like reducing the rebellious city to a heap of ashes, but he took pity on it and refrained. He was evidently coming back from Lahore after giving evidence before the Hunter Committee of Inquiry. I was greatly shocked to hear his conversation and to observe his callous manner. He descended at Delhi station in pyjamas with bright pink stripes and a dressing gown.

All Indians felt Jawaharlal's shock. Dyer's atrocities were bad enough but what really shook Indians leaders was that English opinion saw him as their great hero. Dyer was presented with a sword inscribed "Saviour of Punjab", the European Association in India protested that he had not been reinstated in the Army and English ladies in India started a "Dyer Appreciation Fund." As Gandhi would say in his historic trial in front of Justice Bloomfield in 1922, "The Punjab crime was whitewashed and most culprits were not only unpunished but remained in service and some continued to draw pensions from the Indian revenue and, in some cases were even rewarded."

After the Amritsar Massacre there could be no going back for Gandhi, Nehrus (both Motilal and Jawaharlal), Das and a host of others. Such was the backdrop as Bose took his first steps onto the Indian political scene.

Bose's ship arrived in Bombay on 16 July 1921. On the same afternoon he presented himself at Gandhi's headquarters at Mani Bhawan in the posh locality of Bombay's Chowpati. He felt distinctly awkward. In a sea of homemade *khadi* (or *khaddar*— the words are interchangeable) he was the only one in a Western suit. Imbued with revolutionary lore he eagerly sought answers to questions that were worrying him. Gandhi easily explained how his campaign would finally lead to the non-payment of taxes. (As the government took action against his boycott of foreign cloth, the time would come for disobeying the government and ending up in prison. The prisons would overflow, and non-payment of taxes would result.) But Bose was less satisfied by the explanation as to how India would get freedom "within a year". He had expected Gandhi to ensure that his boycott would cause distress in Lancashire, thereby putting pressure on the British Parliament and the Cabinet. But Gandhi seemed to believe in some sort of change of heart. Bose was disappointed, and went to Calcutta.

> Though I tried to persuade myself at that time there must have been a lack of understanding on my part, my reason told me clearly again and again that there was a deplorable lack of clarity in the plan which the Mahatma had formulated and that he himself did not have a clear idea of the successive stages of the campaign which would bring India to her cherished goal of freedom.

Too much should not to be read into this estimate of Gandhi, which was written years later in 1934 when his differences with Gandhi were already sharp. But the fact remains that Gandhi's magic had not worked with Bose. Subhas would refer to Gandhi as "*Gandhiji*" or "*Mahatmaji*" ("ji" is a term of respect) but never "*Bapu*"(Father), the expression almost obligatory for Gandhians, and popularised by Jawaharlal Nehru. Bose respected Gandhi, but did not worship him. His reverence was reserved for the guru he had so long sought, C.R. Das. Bose's friend Hemanta was well established as Das' private secretary, and soon after arriving back at his Calcutta home in Elgin Road Bose was taken to meet him. His first acquaintance was with Basanti Devi, Das's wife, of whom we shall hear more later. When he finally met Das, he was captivated. He saw in him all the qualities he had long searched for. He was a man of intellect and reason who was also emotional; a lawyer who was also a poet and a man of letters; and, above all, a man of total commitment: an Indian patriot who felt deeply about Bengal.

In some ways Das remains a curious choice of guru. Gandhi was a social revolutionary, like Bose. But Bose's estrangement from Gandhi was part of the wider quarrel that the children of the Bengali renaissance had with the Mahatma. Gandhi could not be accommodated in the vision of Bengal that Bose had long cherished, and which Das also held. Though Das ended his life as a politician, he was essentially a man of the establishment who disagreed with it on certain issues and used mass campaigns in limited spells to achieve his aims. A product of the Raj, he turned his civilised fury against it, but he always hoped that there could be a middle way. Like all shrewd political operators Das was a broker of men. His achievement was to bring together people of conflictingly different views, get them to agree on a common minimum programme and weld them together in a coalition that was as remarkable for its diversity as for its strength. The coalition would not long outlive Das, but, while it did, it provided a wonderful sight and in retrospect a golden age of strength and unity. Men who would dominate Bengal politics till the end of the 1950s, well after the Raj had disappeared, all grew up under him.

Gandhi's field was different. He was the first leader to appeal to all Indians. Before him there had only been regional leaders: Gandhi changed all that. He broke through regional, linguistic and caste barriers: after his rise no regional caucus could be sure of its hold, no satrap confidant that his men would not break. Shrewdly sensing that a continental organisation was necessary to fight the Raj, he modelled the Congress on the Indian government's structure. Offices in villages, towns, wards and cities led upwards to district committees; they in turn led to provincial ones, until finally, at the apex, sat the All-India Congress Committee (AICC), the Congress Parliament that met at regular intervals and made policy. Implementation was in the hands of the Congress executive, known as the Working Committee, which, because of the power it exercised, was soon christened the Congress High Command. At the same time Gandhi drafted almost every clause of the Congress constitution, set out the qualifications for membership, and sought to bring in the masses by keeping the membership levy down to four annas and by holding the annual sessions in a semi-rustic setting. The first proper Indian political party had been formed: a model that survives intact even today.

But the regional satraps of Bengal were among the principal obstructions. During Bose's childhood the Bengali politician had been able to boast: "What Bengal thinks today India thinks tomorrow." Bengal had created Indian nationalism and taught it to the rest of India; now Gandhi's takeover jeopardised all that. Das had watched it warily, and though he did join Gandhi he would always remain a critic and finally break with him. Gandhi would never completely control Bengal, and this partly explains the precarious post-Independence hold Congress had over the province, and the rise of Bengali Marxists who have exercised power in the province for more than a quarter of a century.

The argument was not just about power. Ideology was also involved. The Bengali definition of Indian nationalism was based on trying to use Western methods to reform Indian systems. It sought a synthesis between East and West. Gandhi preferred to use religion to further nationalism. Recycling Hindu myths, he sought to recreate Ramrajya. This was a mythical Hindu Eden: a land of peace, prosperity and primitive agricultural bliss where there were no modern inventions and no worries about equality. The poor would trust the rich; the rich would be kind and benevolent towards the poor. A few simple things would govern the Eden like *charka* – spinning cloth on a little hand spinning wheel; *Satyagraha; khadi.*

But, for all the apparent humility with which these ideas were propounded, there was a strong element of totalitarian force, as in any movement based on myths. Gandhi wanted complete, unquestioning obedience to his creed. That, he said, was essential if *Swaraj* (independence) was to be obtained; and Gandhiji's Swaraj seemed rigidly ascetic, intolerantly puritanical and quite opposed to the sensual, culturally more liberal Bengali version that was part of Bose's heritage.

Tagore, returning to India at the same time, wrote: "Today in the atmosphere of the country there is a spirit of persecution, which is not that of armed force, but something still more alarming because it is invisible". Bose, although he agreed with Gandhi that a national movement against the British in India was inevitable, shared Tagore's doubts about the final value of Gandhism.

Das was greatly taken by the earnest, totally dedicated young man, and within a week of their meeting he appointed Bose secretary of his publicity board. One of Bose's first tasks was to organise a national college in opposition to the Raj's educational institutions. This was just the sort of work he was looking for and he took up the job of setting up and running the college earnestly. He arranged lectures by his old Presidency and Scottish Church contacts. He mapped out courses, planned timetables, and set out detailed guidelines for the benefit of the lecturers.

His friend Upendra Nath Banerjee, later to be jailed for articles arguing for Indian freedom, recalls that Bose organised everything from the benches, chairs, and tables in the classrooms to teaching the boys and even keeping the books of account. His dedication, even when students had lost interest and stopped coming to the class, meant he could often be found sitting in empty classrooms. Banerjee recalls:

> Once I went to the National College to find out whether Subhas was there. I saw my friend Kiran Shankar Roy sitting in a room downstairs reading the newspapers. I asked him, "Where is Subhas?" Laughingly Kiran Babu said, "Subhas, he is in the classroom teaching the benches". I went upstairs and found the classroom empty, Subhas sitting on a chair engaged in writing, Well, the students might be absent, but he must be present in the classroom; that was his duty and he must do it.

Just as he had told Dilip in England that the Indians there must not show any weakness to the people who ruled over them so now in India he displayed what became known as the "bulldog tenacity". That is how his friend Banerjee described it:

> He never gave up something in the middle and once a job was started by him it had to be finished. A must for him. And hardship was no problem for him; he was ready to go without food, rest or sleep to finish the job. So he was also not ready to tolerate the laxity of others working with him and any sign of it in others made him mad, though he often did not express his anger outwardly; rather used to suffer inwardly from suppressed anger and disappointment. Sometimes he wept like a child.

Bose's role as publicity secretary meant a battle with the government's awesome machinery, much of the established press and a great many collaborators increasingly worried about the sweep of Gandhi's campaign. Soon Bose was organising picketing of shops selling foreign goods in south Calcutta. He and his volunteers, marching through such well-known Bengali middle-class localities as Jogoo Babu's Bazar, Russa Theatre (now Purna Theatre) and Russa Road, became a regular - and, for some shopkeepers an unwelcome - sight. The climax of this frenetic activity came on 17 November 1921, the day the Prince of Wales, emulating his father, arrived in Bombay.

Ostensibly, the Prince's visit was to thank India for its generous support during the war; privately the Raj hoped that once again the anodyne of British monarchy and its supposed benevolent paternalism would turn Indians away from Gandhi and his movement. The Congress was determined to resist, and on the day of his arrival in India, Gandhi declared a complete *hartal*. In Calcutta, Bose acted as Das' chief of staff. He arranged for the transportation of volunteers from Howrah and Sealdah, Calcutta's two main railway stations, to the place of the demonstration, and saw to it that the whole city had a holiday. The government, hitherto relaxed, now acted swiftly: the Congress and allied volunteer organisations were banned and meetings were prohibited. Das, reacting slowly, decided to offer selective *Satyagraha*. Groups of Congressmen would go out in the streets, try to sell *khaddar and* if arrested offer no resistance. If this worked, the jails would be full and the government paralysed.

The Prince was due to visit Calcutta on 24 December. Das decided that six volunteers – two Bengalis, two Marwaris and two Muslims, representing nearly all the major communities of Calcutta – would sell *khaddar* and call for *hartal* that day; Bose was asked to organise the volunteers. But the police refused to rise to the bait. Every evening a grim Subhas would report to Das.

"Well, Subhas, how many are arrested?"
"None yet, sir."

Das decided to send first his son, then his wife Basanti and finally his sister Urmilla to jail. Bose was horrified. Women were meant to be protected, looked after, succoured, and Basanti Devi was well on her way to becoming a substitute mother for him. For long hours he argued, but Das held firm. The plan worked brilliantly, but even after Basanti had been released and had returned home Bose was not appeased. She recalled:

> His face was black with anger. I could see that Subhas had not yet calmed down. I laughed and told him, 'It is all right now. I have come back - so do be quiet.' Subhas slowly quietened down and then started weeping profusely. He wept like a child and I could gauge some of the endless love he had for me.

Now volunteers poured into Congress offices everywhere, demanding *Satyagraha* opportunities, and three days later the government took steps to crush the movement. Das and most of his lieutenants were arrested. The police also enquired about Bose. In the evening he rang up the Commissioner of Police, Lalbazar. "I am told you enquired of me. Do you mean to arrest me? I am now ready." Bose was taken away and quickly sentenced by the Chief Presidency Magistrate of Calcutta to six months in jail. As he was led away he is said to have asked - in what has become a famous remark – "Only six months? Have I then robbed a fowl?"

In jail an old Chinese convict was bewildered by the new inmate, and by others like him. Jail was a place for criminals, the dregs of society. But here were educated, well-off people, who ordinarily should never see the inside of a prison. For a long time the old Chinese wondered. At last he approached Bose and his group. He knew little English and asked haltingly, "Opium? Opium? Opium?"

"No," replied the young Congressmen.

"Cocaine? Cocaine? Cocaine?" persisted the Chinaman.

No again.

At last light dawned. "Gandhi? Gandhi? Gandhi?"

Yes, nodded the Congressmen.

This was the first of Bose's eleven terms in British prisons and no other would be so enjoyable. Frequent, unhindered interviews were allowed, and relations with the Raj were quite cordial. Bose revelled in it. He was given a cell next to Das and was listed as his cook; Hemanta acted as Das' servant. Bose took his tasks seriously. Basanti Das visited Alipore Central Jail daily and Subhas was forever adding items to her shopping-list. His culinary variations were endless and he exchanged eager notes on cooking with her. For the first time he got close to the guru he had chosen and the more he got to know Das the more he appreciated him and was struck by his knowledge of both Bengali and English literature.
While in prison he heard that Gandhi had decided to call off the campaign following violence in Chauri Chaura, a village in the United Provinces where angry villagers had set fire to the police station and killed some policemen. Though Gandhi's official reason was that it proved people were not ready for his type of non-violence, Bose concluded that this was a typical Gandhian way of presenting failure. Das felt that while Gandhi could begin a campaign brilliantly, and lead it with great skill to its height, once at the zenith he would lose his nerve and begin to falter. Bose agreed with that assessment.

The government, delighted at this unexpected reprieve, took full advantage of it, arrested Gandhi, jailed him for six years and put an end to the first nationalist movement for Indian independence.

Das seized the opportunity to fashion a new programme. The Congress had so far completely boycotted the reformed councils set up under the Montagu-Chelmsford Act. But this boycott was under increasing strain, and Das argued that more could be achieved by getting elected to the councils and then wrecking the reforms.

For Gandhi nothing could have been more unnecessary and damaging. Non-co-operation could only succeed if it was total and all-embracing. But the quarrel between the two men has been pictured simply as a fight about how best to achieve *Swaraj*, the accepted creed of the Congress. The truth is that neither Gandhi nor Das defined *Swaraj*. Gandhi was more interested in his alternative vision of India, and would have accepted a constitutional link with Britain short of complete freedom, or even home rule. Das, for his part, used political movements to wrest concessions from the Raj, not destroy it. Though the reforms of 1919 were thoroughly inadequate in terms of broader Indian national aspirations, in local terms they provided rich pickings for collaborators. The Congress boycott of council meant that other politicians could use these local powers. As in any national coalition of diverse groups, some had joined Congress more for immediate gain than for the long-term goal. Non-co-operation strained their loyalty. Das shrewdly understood these strains within the organisation. Non-co-operation was dead. Gandhi was reduced to the spinning wheel and the outer reaches of Hindu asceticism. Council entry, Das argued, would replace non-co-operation and hold the Congress together.

The fight with Gandhi meant a proper organisation, and as he prepared for his release Bose was assigned a crucial role. In addition to publicity he was to organise labour and a youth movement. The existing organisations were no more than debating chambers: something truly vigorous was required.

Bose was released on 4 August 1922 and immediately set about his tasks. Two days later he organised a meeting of young people, and by the middle of September had made enough progress for the first All-Bengal Young Men's Conference to be held. He made a very effective speech and the conference unanimously adopted a reformist resolution urging the removal of "untouchability", the abolition of dowry and the prevention of early marriage.

Within a week the young men had an opportunity to put their enthusiasm into practice. Devastating floods ravaged four large Bengal districts. The Congress sent Bose to organise relief there, and in little over six weeks he set up the entire relief machinery. Living in tents pitched on the only available patches of dry highland, he organised the provision of food and shelter for the marooned thousands and fodder for the cattle capable of being rescued. Congress efforts had collected 400,000 rupees, and Bose and his volunteer army provided the only succour available. Such was Subhas's dedication that when Janakinath came to visit him on his way to celebrate Durga Puja, Subhas refused to go with him saying, "No, father, no, you all go to worship Durga at home and I will go to worship my real mother Durga with the helpless."

He only came back to Calcutta when ordered by Das to do so and then accompanied his chief to the annual session of the Congress. Das tried to get the Congress to adopt his council-entry plan. But although the Gandhians could not call on Gandhi, who was still in jail, they defeated Das by 1,748 votes to 890. When Das analysed the results he found he was in a minority even in his own province of Bengal. He immediately resigned as president, and on 31 December 1922 he, Motilal, Nehru and a few others formed the Swaraj Party. Das vowed the Congress would accept his policies within a year and returned to Calcutta to wage war against the Congress establishment.

The first problem was the press. With the nationalist press now mostly pro-Gandhian, Das shrewdly used his power to influence rich people to start his own paper. Bose became editor of a four-page Bengali paper, *Banglar Katha,* and when efforts to buy *The Servant* floundered (Bose had been a negotiator on Das' behalf), *Forward* was launched, with Bose as manager.

Bose had already begun to debate with those who uncritically accepted Gandhi as saviour (this had reached such ludicrous proportions that during Bose's spell in jail the warders there had told him Gandhi could never be arrested because of his magical powers, among them the ability to take the shape of a bird and fly away). During the Bengal Provincial Conference in April 1923, Bose argued that the Congress must aim for a political freedom that would ensure individual liberty and material prosperity: the amorphous Gandhian ideal of Swaraj was not adequate. A month later, at the Bombay AICC, he argued the case for contesting the council elections. This meeting also saw the first of many tortuous steps towards the eventual compromise between Das and the Gandhians, which allowed Das's party to contest the elections.

The elections produced a great victory for Das and his men – at least in Bengal with Bose running the political machine during the campaign. The Calcutta Corporation elections that took place in March 1924 saw both Sarat and Subhas elected to the Corporation and the Swarajists won two-thirds of the seats. This was Das's chance to prove to the Raj, and to Gandhi, that he could put into effect a constructive programme. Das was elected Mayor, and choose Subhas as the Chief Executive Officer. Bose himself was not entirely pleased about this. He asked, Das, "Have I given up the ICS to be Chief Executive Officer of the Calcutta Corporation". But Das insisted he accept the job. Some of Das's followers were also opposed to Bose becoming chief executive officer, and opponents of the Swaraj Party in the Corporation, including the British members (who called themselves Europeans) expressed opposition in the chamber when the proposed appointment was discussed. Some of this opposition centred on the fact that Subhas was also councillor, a post from which he had to resign. But in general the choice met with approval, most significantly from the Muslims, in whose eyes Subhas was already established as their second favourite Hindu politician, second only to Das.

At 27 years of age he was in effective charge of the corporation of the second city in the Empire. He was entitled to a salary of Rupees 3,000 but decided he would take only half, 1,500 rupees per month. He had the use of a car and a contract for three years. Subhas Bose's love affair with the corporation had begun. Wherever he went, whichever city he visited, he would first go to its municipality and city corporation. Many years later, in exile in Vienna, he would plan a book about the Vienna municipality.

In Calcutta in 1924 the municipality had almost to be built from scratch. Khadi was made the official uniform for its employees, an education department was started, dispensaries were opened and the weekly *Calcutta Municipal Gazette* was launched. Soon stories about Bose began to circulate. When a Mr Coates the chief engineer, first met Subhas, the Englishman sauntered in calmly smoking a cigarette. Bose smiled and gently enquired: "Is it proper, Mr Coates, to smoke before a superior officer?" Coates mumbled his apology and crushed his cigarette in the ashtray. He was soon a reformed man and never smoked again without permission. Such, possibly apocryphal, stories added to the growing legend of the young man who was an organisational genius and an administrative miracle. He was now the constructive arm of the Swaraj Party. Visitors recounted with awe how they had seen him hard at work till ten or eleven at night.

But, in a narrow, congested lane a mile from where Bose worked, and just a few minutes' walk from 38/2 Elgin Road, another group of people were taking an interest in him. At 14 Elysium Row (now Lord Sinha Road) was located the headquarters of the Special Branch, or political police. Bose was aware they had been watching him for a long time, but he may not have known that almost every day an agent had reported on his activities and that the dossier was now complete. It only required action from Writers' Building, the home of the Bengal government. The agents' hard work and Writers' Building's worries were centred on the alternative arm of Indian nationalism, the revolutionaries, and on Bose's relationship with them.

There was one other effect of his becoming Chief Executive Officer. When Subhas was about to accept the post, Hemanta wrote advising him to turn it down. It would, he said, be a betrayal of their youthful idealism. Subhas and Hemanta had worked on the magazine *Atma Katha*, which means the "voice of the heart", set up in 1921. Subhas had taken up its editorship after the original editor had been jailed by the Raj under the dreaded Regulation III of 1918, which allowed the authorities to imprison people without charging them with any offence. While the Raj considered Bose the managing director of the paper, many of the most radical editorials in the paper was written by Hemanta who was arguing that the middle class leaders of the nationalist struggle did not represent the majority of the people in the country, who were peasants and labourers. Many of these labourers working on the land did not have any property rights. There could be no real *Swaraj* unless their wishes were accommodated.

Subhas shared some of these views but disagreed on the tactics to be followed. Working for the Corporation at this stage was a step in the process of forming a national movement to unseat the Raj. The two friends parted. Hemanta went back to his village, Nalin, turned increasingly towards homespun socialism, and vanishes from our story. The first great friendship of his life was over. Subhas was saddened by Hemanta's departure but he had marked out his political course and could not be deflected.

Was Bose wrong to devote so much time to the Calcutta Corporation and its affairs? There is certainly a dichotomy here: Subhas Bose, the revolutionary, seeking to destroy the British, yet glorying in using one of their most characteristic institutions. The Corporation was useful because it provided a taste of power in a limited but effective sphere, and there was undoubtedly the attraction of patronage. Besides, the Congress civil-disobedience campaigns meant that none of the Raj's institutions were available, and the Corporation provided an honourable exception — as British intelligence agents were quick to note. Subhas Bose saw it as a way to demonstrate that Indians could do good as well. But such a course had its dangers, and at least one critic, the writer Nirad Chaudhuri , has argued that the Corporation fatally attracted Subhas, diverting him from real power in the Congress Working Committee to the ways of the "hard-boiled and worldly middle-class of Calcutta, to whom civic welfare meant welfare of their class". Worse still, argued Chaudhuri it damaged Bose's political career as over the years Bose's obsession with the Calcutta Corporation made him neglect wider all-India politics. Chaudhuri wrote:

> Yet Bose would not give up his obsession, because it arose out of his very concept of revolutionary politics. His knowledge of the French and the Russian Revolution made him regard a big city and its proletariat and student population as the most effective instrument of a revolution. Calcutta was the first corporate body in British India to pass under complete Indian control, and in point of wealth and population was almost like a small Indian province. In giving more attention to the Calcutta Corporation than to Congress affairs, Bose was in theory preferring practical power to agitational. But the Calcutta Corporation itself had nothing revolutionary about it, and, as I have shown, it was not even an efficient or honest civic body. This justified the complaints of Gandhi and his followers. But Bose, as long as he remained in India, allowed this Old Man of the Sea with all his abominations to sit on his shoulders.

The Calcutta Corporation has become a byword of corruption and inefficiency and certainly Bose's devotion to it does raise questions. There is the obvious question as to why he choose to work with a system that the British had instituted, the very rulers he wanted to throw out of India. It must also be said that the Municipal Act of 1923 which had Indianised the Corporation had just been passed and, as Chadhuri, himself, acknowledges, Bose and his guru Das were driven by the best motives. These were finally to have a civic body in Calcutta that looked after the overwhelming population of the city who were Indians as opposed to the very small minority of the English. If they failed it was because of events out of their control as Chaudhuri admitted:

> The new dispensation had begun with high hopes for us natives in 1924 when C.R. Das became its first Mayor, and Subhas Chandra Bose its first Executive Officer. We thought at last we should have the same amenities as the European quarters and we did. Within a year asphalt began to be put on the streets of Bengali Calcutta and, we did not have to be splattered with mud during the rainy season. But C. R. Das, the only man who could have made the self-governing Calcutta Corporation serve the public interest as part of an enlightened policy of promoting self interest died in 1925 and young Subhas Bose, who as its Chief Executive Officer had shown energy in putting through some reforms, was put in jail for his association with the revolutionary movement.

So even this fierce critic of Bose admits that in one case death, in the other the Raj, deprived Calcutta of developing the sort of corporate body it needed. It seems excessively harsh to blame Bose for being jailed by the British, which prevented him from fulfilling in a limited sphere what he set out to achieve.

4
The Man

With Subhas settling into his first and only job, this is a good moment to dispose of the idea that he wanted at heart to be a mystic and was only reluctantly an activist. A whole generation of Indians has grown up believing this exaggerated picture.

It is true that he was a man of intellect who had read many philosophers. He was personally drawn to Hegel and Bergson, and attracted by Marx's intellectual rigour, though not to his stress on atheism and complete rejection of the spiritual. Writing in 1940, he saw philosophy as a missed vocation, unexplored because of his hectic political career. But although certain reclusive traits, such as secretiveness and ability to withdraw, were in him from the beginning, he was essentially a vigorous person who used words to further action and whose philosophy was an aid to his politics, never a substitute for them. Throughout his endless debates with Dilip he never failed to resist his friends' calls to renounce the world and take to the guru and the *ashram*.

His present life-style, too, was far removed from that of the a mystic. His political involvements had already revealed the inadequacy of the family home of 38/2 Elgin Road, and a new house, 38/1, rented by Sarat would from now on become his home. In effect he moved in with Mejda and his family. In 1927 Sarat, by now a very successful barrister, built a house for himself at Woodburn Park, a road that intersected Elgin Road. After that, whenever he was out of jail or in India, Subhas lived on the top floor of this three-storey house. For an Indian nationalist seeking to gain the country's freedom there could never be a settled home life. There was no knowing when there would be a knock on the door from the police. As we shall see, Bose spent more time as an unwilling guest of the Raj than any other major Indian politician. But while Nehru had Anand Bhavan, the house built by his father, which was then given to the nation and became the Congress headquarters, Bose had to rely on Sarat. Often he set up something like a household in jail with his fellow political "guests", but to an extent the only time he acquired homes of his own were when he was abroad, in Vienna in the 1930s, in Berlin in the 1940s and then in Singapore between 1943-45. This is one of the many ironies of Subhas Bose's life.

In the 1930s Nirad Chaudhuri worked as a secretary for Sarat Bose and has described the tyranny that visitors can impose in India:

> Like all men in India who had power, which also meant some sort of patronage, he had visitors coming to see him at all hours of the day, insisting on seeing him, and doing so. Thus it happened that he took many of his decisions late at night when he was tired. In his desperation he tried to protect himself from intrusion by making a pathetic appeal to the visitors, One morning going to his house, I saw a large board hung up near the front door. On it, painted in large white letters on a black background, was a notice couched in the most persuasive and gentle terms.
>
> In it he said to his visitors that whether they saw him or not, he was always engaged in their service, but trying to see him at all hours simply came in the way of that service; so would they consider that had more to lose than gain by disturbing him, and kindly leave him alone so far as they could. The

visitors were such a plague to all nationalist leaders that they really had peace only when sent to prison by the kindly British authorities. Forced imprisonment was for them what self-imposed retreats were for devout Christians.

Over the years Subhas' life would become more hurried, but its basic contours would not change. He generally got up late after a night of work and reading; then, after a leisurely breakfast, would plunge into his ceaseless day. Lunch, dinner and brief moments of rest would be improvised. We have two pictures of Subhas Bose's domestic life. In the 1930s Chaudhuri's job as Sarat's secretary meant he worked in Sarat's house in Woodburn Park shared with Subhas. He has provided the most vivid picture of life there:

> The house was large and with its three storeys quite high. It was placed back from the street, and was separated from it by a largish lawn, with flowering shrubs on the far side, and low beds of English annuals by the house. There was an iron gate, which had by its side a small lodge for the gate-man. The entrance hall was furnished with ornate tables and chairs... The staircase was hung with large photographs instead of pictures, and one of the photographs showed Sarat Babu in impeccably tailored morning dress complete with top hat. All the rooms were high, fairly large and of good proportions. In the middle was a very large waiting hall, with a large table and chairs in the Queen Anne style all around, and the table top, not less than twelve by five feet, was covered by a single sheet of plate glass. All the rooms were provided with lavatories and some even with bathroom. Fitted with basins, toilets etc, in gleaming porcelain and chromium plate all imported from England. One specialty of the household was the attention and care bestowed on maintenance. Even the wealthiest Indian houses were notoriously careless about this. But neither Sarat Babu nor his wife tolerated that. An architect's firm regularly sent inspectors to examine the house for damp and deposits of saltpetre, and also for any loosening of marble slabs. The leading Indian firm of sanitary engineers in Calcutta sent plumbers every week to see to the taps, cisterns and baths. Sarat Babu had clocks in very room and in those days they needed winding. So, a man came every Saturday to wind and regulate them. The furniture was of the best quality and was supplied by the leading Bengali cabinetmaker of Calcutta, the Chatterjees. All the pieces were of solid teak and very well finished. There was a large staff of servants, maids, cooks, gardeners, sweepers, along with a chauffer and one lodge keeper.

Sarat also maintained two kitchens, one that provided English style food and the other Bengali style food. Chaudhuri continued:

> The European kitchen, run on gas, was in the main house, under a Bawarchi i.e. Muslim cook who knew English cuisine, a Khansma or waiter who was also called boy irrespective of age, and a kitchen boy. Food cooked in this kitchen was taken in the dining room in the European manner. The Bengali kitchen run on coal occupied a separate building under the Thakur or Brahmin cook and a number of maids.

Sarat was a big eater. He started with an English breakfast, then before going to court ate a five course Bengali meal at around 11. For lunch, which was sent from his home to the bar library, he reverted to English food, he returned in the evening for Bengali sweets and snacks and then ended the day with an English dinner with lots of pudding, on which he considered himself something of an expert. Not surprisingly Sarat developed health problems and had to go on a diet.

Whether Subhas ate quite as much we do not know but whenever he was jailed the Raj officials delighted in making malicious remarks about his weight and how jail might act as a sort of weight watchers and reduce his bulk. Interestingly Chaudhuri says Sarat dined alone in his English style dining room while his wife and children preferred the Bengali cooking of the Thakur.

The only other intimate portrayal of Subhas Bose's domestic life comes a decade later. S.A Ayer, who worked with him in East Asia during the period 1943-45 described life in the Bose household in Japanese-occupied Singapore. In Singapore Bose's personal habits were to change somewhat. He lived in a seaside bungalow, a more beautiful setting than Woodburn Park, but less opulent and much more frugal. Yet the house had grounds where he could play badminton and did so most evenings. His personal physician Colonel Raju kept pets, which Bose grew quite fond of: two monkeys, two goats, two rabbits and three or four ducks, and geese and a tonga pony. One of the monkeys was called Ramu, the other Sita, and Ramu was Bose's favourite. The moment he would see Bose he would climb on his shoulder and check out the few strands of hair he had by then. There were also cats, which Subhas hated.

But, back to 1924, at the beginning of his political career, we see a man surrounded by his family and the comforts prosperous Indian society can bring, who was also clearly one of Bengal's most eligible bachelors. Bose's tall, well-built figure always inclined towards plumpness (he normally weighed about 182 pounds) and his pleasant, rotund, Mongolian features added an element of attraction to the opposite sex.

Marriage offers came frequently. Once a rich Bengali offered to bankroll Das if Subhas agreed to marry his daughter, but Subhas indignantly refused the offer. Although Subhas never formally renounced marriage, he did write to Sarat from England, as he prepared to resign from the ICS, saying that he was not going to marry. Finance may have been the reason. For most of his life he was dependent on Sarat. Living in a joint family, too, created constraints for as long as he lived in India. This, together with Ramakrishna's and Vivekananda's views on sex, also determined his relationship with women. This is seen in the bond that developed between Bose and Basanti Das. It had been instinctive, and within weeks of his becoming Das' lieutenant it was firmly established. In time the two would become so close that Subhas would wish Bashanti had been his mother, and Basanti Devi, looking back, would lovingly remember Prabhavati's words, "I gave birth to Subhas but you are his real mother." Her house became Subhas's second home and he would spend some of his happiest moments there. Basanti Devi would be subject to his every *abdar.* 'Capricious demand' is an inadequate translation of this rich Bengali word, which conveys a whole Indian world of relationships between favourite child and loving guardian, in which no wish of the child is too burdensome (though the wish is almost invariably domestic). The relationship has, in fact, formed the basis for a succession of highly emotional Indian films.

Subhas was in and out of the Das household, often returning late at night, tired and hungry, and demanding food. Patient, loving Basanti would explain that dinner was long over, there was no cooked food, and the servants had retired for the night. Subhas would insist on something hot. Basanti, cursing gently, headed for the kitchen, and another late night. Another wet night Subhas turned up, tired, hungry and shadowed by the ubiquitous Bengali police detective. Basanti suggested he went home, wouldn't Subhas' mother be getting anxious, and wasn't the poor detective getting drenched in the rain? Subhas was totally unmoved. "Let the bastard suffer – who asked him to spy on me?", he said. These stories, and others like them, convey the essence of this very Bengali, very *bhadralok* relationship.

Nirad Chaudhuri has tried to analyse Bose's attachment to matrons rather than women of his age. His analysis is certainly very original. Chaudhuri says that Bose was frustrated by the fact that while he was passionately opposed to British rule and was convinced it would end he could also see that there were no signs of the Raj departing. "He could not have helped the feeling that he was up against a wall. I believe that kept him in fits of rage like a caged beast of prey, and made him emotionally tense and unstable beneath a cold mask." A close friend of Subhas, who had also been at college with Chaudhuri suggested that this was due to sexual repression and one day he said to Chaudhuri "The madcap is becoming more and more mad everyday, Is there no frenzied beautiful hussy in Calcutta who could shut herself with him in a room and rape him, so that he would feel honour bound to marry her? Then the mad cap would become normal."

Chaudhuri rejected this Freudian view as the clue to Bose. He concluded that Bose's attitude to women could be explained by:

> The psychological situation in Bengal from the end of the nineteenth century to my young days in the twentieth...What I had observed was Subhas Bose's indifference to women, I knew why at this age he would avoid being in any kind of intimate or confidential relationship with young women, and would rather seek female companionship among matrons, who could quiz him about becoming an old bachelor. This was quite common in our social life on the part of matronly acquaintances. But he would keep aloof from young women because with his delicate sense of honour he would feel that with his looks and position he would have an overwhelming advantage over any young woman, and would never be able to meet her even half-way. In fact after seeing both the brothers (Subhas and Sarat) I used to express the very decided opinion, certainly doing great injustice to others, that of all the men I had been around the two Boses were the only ones I would trust with money or a woman.

Despite his views on marriage, Subhas could always attend wedding feasts, and his presence at a Bengali wedding became a must. He would refuse nobody, though this often produced absurd results. Once he had promised to be present at a wedding on a day when he was due to attend a political meeting at Howrah, near Calcutta. By the time Subhas and his friends returned it was the small hours of the morning. Satya Bakshi was keen to go home and get some sleep, but Subhas insisted they keep his promise, and at 2 am they arrived at the bride's place. The sleepy family were woken up and, after Subhas had made his apologies, he demanded the bridal feast. Nothing was left of it, or very little, but the surprised family managed to conjure up some sweets and tea.

Tea was his constant drink. During a hectic working day Subhas would probably drink about twenty cups, and many years later he told Hari Vishnu Kamath that without tea there could be no politics. He never drank a great deal of hard liquor, and was not choosy about food — he certainly never developed the fastidious habits that drove Gandhi into more and more bizarre culinary experiments. But, as we have seen, he loved cooking and eating.

Subhas never developed a light, self-deprecatory sense of humour. During his 93-day submarine trip from Germany to Japan in 1943, Bose, sketching out his plans for the liberation of India, even began to discuss how he would assign diplomatic posts. At some stage during this fantasy, he turned to his companion Abid Hasan and asked him what job he would like in a free India. Hasan, who has a delightful sense of impish fun, kept a straight face and said,

> 'Could you kindly send me out as Minister to Honduras?'
> Bose, genuinely puzzled, enquired: "Why?"
> Hasan replied, "Well, sir, there will be such a scramble for jobs when you reach India that I don't wish to be in the running except for something few others might ask for." Bose was not amused.

Once during his wartime stay in Germany Bose, suffering from a headache, turned to a companion and asked him to tell him a joke. He told him the one about a man who goes out wearing one yellow and one green shoe. When somebody pointed this out to him he replied "I have another pair just like this at home." Bose heard the joke in silence, and then asked, "Is this the new fashion in Germany?" But then his sense of fun was very Bengali and Indian.

S.A Ayer, who was later to become his minister of propaganda in his Provisional Government of Free India in 1943, and who often lunched and dined with him in his bungalow in Singapore once said that "Netaji always relaxed and radiated cheer, laughter, wit and humour". In his memoirs, Ayer sought hard to prove that Bose had a wonderful sense of humour. However, his example of the daily banana joke that Subhas bandied with Kali, the house boy, a joke that centred round how much Kali had paid for bananas that day, must have sounded funnier in the Singapore war-time setting than in the retelling. Ayer's other examples of Bose's wit indicate a man more used to the bludgeon than a rapier. He could laugh uproariously, but he often flushed, reminding Dilip of a schoolgirl caught making love. And he could be surprisingly gentle in personal relationships. Political associates and even enemies recall the warmth of his friendship and contrast it with the intellectual austerity that Nehru carried into personal relationships. V.B Karnik recalled that "Bose was much more likeable than Nehru. He was warm-hearted. He would try and establish contact with you."

To a whole generation of the Bose family, numerous nephews and nieces, he was special: "Rangakaka Babu", literally "Colourful Uncle", but the term is more often used to denote a favourite younger brother. He would play hide-and-seek with the children, running down the Elgin Road stairs and searching furiously in the various nooks and corners of the vast house to locate yet another hidden nephew or niece. He would lead them in instructional, devotional hymns, and be their guide in the fulsome patriotic songs that were one of Bengal's contributions to the nationalist movement. In illness, too, he was there to nurse them. Subhas genuinely loved nursing, and although he never trained as a nurse he acquired sufficient experience to act as one.

Something of his childhood reserve always clung to him, however, and for all his revolutionary zeal the code of the gentleman remained part of his character. In 1939, in the middle of his epic conflict with Gandhi, he wrote: "You have remarked in one letter that you hope that whatever happens, "our private relations will not suffer. I cherish this hope with all my heart. If there is anything in life on which I can pride myself, it is that I am a son of a gentleman and as such I am a gentleman."

5

Enter Revolutionaries

In the years after 1919 the Indian government identified two major revolutionary groups: Anushilan and Jugantar. In fact, there were many more small secret organisations often bitterly divided by personal feuds but sharing a belief in armed revolution and a free India. Anushilan was probably the best organised of them. There is still some doubt about when it was started; none about its effectiveness. It was tightly knit and had one leader. It laid down precise rules for recruitment, elaborate duties for its members and various vows at different stages of training. Anushilan revolutionaries went forward to do battle reciting the *Gita* and shouting "Vande Mataram!", meaning "Hail to the Mother!" . Jugantar, on the other hand, remained, even at its height, a loose federation. They never managed to combine, and except for brief periods during 1914-17 and 1925-8, the two groups opposed each other with almost as much energy as they opposed the British.

The peak of revolutionary violence occurred between 1910 and 1915. The Raj used all its awesome machinery to crush it, and it was only in December 1919 that it felt secure enough to proclaim a royal amnesty. The revolutionary survivors who slowly emerged into the sunlight found a very different world: the reign of Gandhi. In Bengal Das, quickly realising their potential, attempted to bring together those prepared to renounce violence, or at least not carry out open acts against the Congress. But, according to a secret government report of March 1924, the police had learnt that:

> Swarajya (another name for the Swaraj Party) . . . had agreed to co-operate with revolutionists as soon as the latter abstained from overt acts and that as soon as revolutionary methods were adopted the Swarajya Party would stand aside and would not interfere.

Das, in the Bengal government's view, was a weak, opportunistic man forever seeking alliances to prop up his power; the revolutionaries were using the new Gandhi-led movement to further their own violent ends, and in time some of Das's men were converted to the revolutionary cause. Bose, of course, was now easily recognised as Das's principal lieutenant. His past, his flamboyant resignation from the ICS, his refusal to condemn violence *per se* all seemed proof that he must be in league with the revolutionaries. From there, it was a short step to seeing him as a dangerous revolutionary, a step made effortless by the diligent, anonymous work of the numerous informants in the nationalist movement.

The early months of 1923 had witnessed a revival of violence in Bengal, including some murders. On 23 August 1923, the chief secretary to the government of Bengal addressed a long letter to the Indian government, and asked for power to arrest suspects without a warrant, power to intern, and all the powers of the Defence of India Act and the notorious Rowlatt Acts. The police had intercepted a letter to Bose written by M.N. Roy, an old Jugantar hand now in Moscow, inviting Bose and Chiranjan, son of C.R. Das, to be delegates from India to the Comintern Conference (it is not clear whether Bose actually received the letter). The government of India declined to approve naked repression. Not that Simla (its summer retreat) was any more liberal than Delhi. But repression on this scale would be out of place at a time when the government was keen to "touch the heart of India". As a concession it unleashed the hoary and tested Regulation III of 1818, first used against recalcitrant *nawabs* and princes. It was this that abruptly removed many Swarajists, including the designated assistant editor of *Forward,* for whom Bose was ordered to deputise.

On 12 January 1924 Gopinath Saha, a young revolutionary, shot a man he was convinced was Charles Tegart, the red haired Irishman who was Police Commissioner of Calcutta. Charles Augustus Tegart, to give his full name, had come to Calcutta to take up this position only in the previous year and his arrival indicated how seriously the Raj took the revolutionaries. He had come straight from the London headquarters of the Indian Political Intelligence, the MI5 of the Raj. Set up after consultation with Scotland Yard as a result of Indian anarchist activities in England in 1909, IPI was housed in the same offices in London as MI 5. It was by the very nature of its work a very secretive organisation. It accumulated dossiers on the Raj's opponents, was the only Imperial or Dominion intelligence agency allowed to operate out of London and always had senior officers deputed from Indian Police Intelligence working for it in London. Tegart had worked in London from 1918 to 1923.

The problem for Saha was he did not know what Tegart looked like and mistook Ernest Day, an innocent British businessman, for Tegart and killed him. Saha was promptly arrested, tried and sentenced to death. When, he heard the judge pronounce the death sentence he declared: "May every drop of blood of mine sow the seed of liberty in every Indian home." The Bengal Provincial Congress Conference in May 1924 passed a resolution in Bengali whose original translation was given as:

> While adhering to the policy of non-violence this Conference pays its respectful homage to the patriotism of Gopinath Saha who suffered capital punishment in connection with Mr Day's murder.

Gandhi was appalled. He replied that, if Gopinath Saha's patriotism was to be mentioned, it should be qualified by the word "misleading". Das replied that the translation from Bengali was incorrect and that the qualifying word had, in fact, been used. After the session the Bengal Provincial Congress Committee met and confirmed Das' translation. This read (complete with brackets):

> This Conference, while denouncing (or 'dissociating itself from') violence (every kind of *himsa*)* and adhering to the principle of non-violence, appreciates Gopinath Saha's ideal of self-sacrifice, misguided though that is in respect of the best interests of the country, and expresses its respect for his self-sacrifice. (**Hinsa* means violence)

Government agents, desperately keen to prove that Das had modified his stand in response to Gandhi, spent hours agonising over the translation. They became convinced that, intricate grammatical arguments aside, Subhas Bose had tried and failed to remove the epithet "misleading" from the resolution when it was re-adopted by the committee.

Saha was cremated in Calutta's Presidency Jail and Bose and a few others tried to get permission to enter the jail to perform the funeral rites. But the authorities would not allow that. However they released Saha's clothes after his cremation and according to one source Subhas touched the clothes and was very much moved. This did not mean Subha sympathised with terrorism, but the spirit of sacrifice filled him with admiration.

The indictment against Bose was slowly, steadily getting stronger. A further letter from Bengal to the Indian government declared:

> It has been shown that Subhas Bose is a leader of the Jugantar Party [reading government documents it is not exactly clear when this was shown], and since

> he is the Chief Lieutenant of Mr C.R. Das, it is impossible to believe that Mr Das is not fully aware of his activities . . . . There was considerable competition for the post of Chief Executive Officer of the Corporation, and the support given to Subhas by his revolutionary followers helped to weigh down the scales in his favour. He promised to employ a number of revolutionists in the Corporation, and there is excellent reason to believe that he has not overlooked the importance of the control of the Corporation by the revolutionists, in the event of an armed rising

Having made Bose leader, the government saw him everywhere:

> Information obtained from an exceedingly reliable source showed that Satyen Mitra ... in conjunction with . . . Subhas Bose, was planning a spectacular outrage, viz., the throwing of a bomb in the Council Chamber. In pursuance of this plot they succeeded in obtaining an official plan of the building and in introducing fellow revolutionists into the visitors' gallery of the Council House to arrange details.

Soon the agents were able to provide the clinching argument: Bose himself was directing the conspiracy to kill Tegart. Bengal spent much of 1924 in detailed correspondence with Delhi, pleading for special powers and drafting a bill that provided for draconian measures. Realising that the Swarajist-dominated Council of Bengal would never pass such measures, it asked the Viceroy to issue an ordinance. Though the Home Secretary of the Government of India, Crerar, was impressed, his superior, the Home member Alexander Muddiman, felt that the idea of the mayor of Calcutta wanting to kill the commissioner of police suggested "Ruritanian opera" (In the Raj a secretary was the permanent ICS official who reported to a member of the Executive Council which advised the Viceroy, or in the case of the provinces, the Governor. The Executive Council was a sort of Cabinet, though in fact the Viceroy was more of an absolute monarch, answerable only to the secretary of state for India in London.)

When the Viceroy's Executive Council continued to baulk at the measures, Lord Lytton, Governor of Bengal, travelled to Simla personally to plead for them, arguing that unless something was done the future would be grim, and might even require the imposition of martial law. On 23 August, Bengal applied by cipher telegram for warrants for the arrest of Bose and 21 other leaders, under Regulation III of 1818, backing the requests up with all kinds of miscellaneous intelligence information.

Now C.R. Das, eager to get results, quite unwittingly played into the Bengal government's hands. In an interview with the *The Statesman* on 30 August 1924 he said that the anarchist movement was much more serious than the government thought, and if "the Swarajist movement fails ... anarchy is sure to raise its head". Tegart immediately summoned a representative of *The Statesman* and, after "incessant heckling", wheedled out of him that, in an off-the-record chat, Das had gone even further: he knew that a consignment of 200 small arms had arrived. This prompted a flurry of telegrams from Bengal, and at last the government of India relented. The secretary of state for India in London had been kept fully informed. By now all that was required was his formal consent, and that was quickly obtained. On 25 October 1924 the ordinance was promulgated.

The government story was a strange mixture of hearsay evidence and conjecture; but, if even some of the details were true, it was and is devastating. We have, unfortunately, no means of checking. The government in Delhi and Simla was never told precisely who Bengal's agents were or how they obtained their information. These details were kept by the Bengal government's Special Branch, and secrecy in the West Bengal archives, even those at Writers'

Building, was an obsession. As for Elysium Row, no scholar has ever been allowed to examine its records; even to this day the archive is not available.

In the mid-1990s the British government released the files of the Indian Political Intelligence. The most voluminous are those on Bose. The material relating to his alleged revolutionary activities shows how misleading were many of the Raj statements. The note on the file made by J.W.Hose, the official in charge of the criminal proceedings in India Office, put it succinctly:

> The story against him is derived from 10 different informers of 4 different police officers; from 5 intercepted letters; from information given by the Director of the Intelligence Bureau at Simla, based partly on news which he received from this country (meaning England) and from a notice published in the newspapers.

The case against Bose is summarised in a 25-page document entitled the *History Sheet of Subhas Chandra Bose*. The document dated 30 April 1924 was the work of J.E. Armstrong, deputy director general of police intelligence branch, CID. He did not identify the various agents. They only have initials, some of which may well have been false. One was identified as KGS, which could have been the initials of a real person and he did most of the spying on Bose. The others seem false names picked at random: XY,C-8, C-10, C-15, C-20 M-12, M-16, and ASP.

Much of what they report on Bose was clearly false and somewhat sensational, but with no proof. The picture painted was that there was not one Subhas Bose but two: the public politician and the private revolutionary. Bose had been spied on from the moment he decided to resign the ICS and join the civil disobedience movement. One of the first bits of "information" on him came from a spy who claimed that Subhas Bose was none other than Dr S Basu who "had been induced to resign his appointment and proceed to Bengal to form a Communist Group. This information leaves little doubt that Dr S. Basu and Subhas Basu are identical."

By November 1921, as Bose organised protests against the visit of the Prince of Wales the Raj was convinced:

> A revolutionary party had been organised in Bengal chiefly by Subhas, and that the members of the party proposed to prepare themselves with arms and ammunition, in order to be ready to take advantage of the first opportunity which might arise in the chaos which was expected to result from the non-coperation movement. One Ashoke Chaterji, son of Ramananda Chatarji, who was then at Cambridge was reported to have received a letter from Subhas in which he was requested to find out the best methods of introducing communism into India, since this, in the opinion of the writer, was the only means of India's salvation at that time.

In December, agent KGS again reported that Santosh Mitter, then in custody for alleged revolutionary activities, had written to Subhas advising him to avoid any outward demonstrations as his arrest would harm the secret organisation. By September of 1922 KGS had met a certain Muzaffar Ahmad who had told him that "Subhas's conversation indicated that he was connected with enemies of England beyond India who promised to assist Indians as soon they were in a position to start an armed rebellion against the British. The agent added that Subhas was said to be have no faith that "non-violent non-cooperation would ever bring about Swaraj".

The fact that Bose had proved adept at organising flood relief and was involved in setting up a young men's association which encouraged the young to learn lathi play was also part of the charge sheet. When the Young Men's Association started organizing schools to provide moral and literary training, one Raj spy reported, "He was convinced that Subhas's object in this organising activity was to prepare on a wide scale to embark on an effective campaign for revolutionary activity".

On 17 March 1923 a Dacca district intelligence officer saw Subhas walking with some revolutionaries sought by the police. By April 23 KGS was reporting that Bose had presided over a conference of revolutionaries. But, in contrast to the earlier report that saw Bose as seeking outside help, he was now accused of saying that outside help would not help India.

On 16 June 1923 an Intelligence Branch officer reported that proposals had been made for the marriage of Subhas to the sister of Kiran Shankar Roy (another Bengali Congress leader) "who would then send him to England to qualify for the Bar." This is a classic piece of informer gossip, for no evidence has ever emerged to support the claim, and the idea that having left the ICS Bose would return to England to follow in the footsteps of Sarat and Satish was ludicrous.

On 1 July 23, C-8 said that the Cherry Press was the haunt of the revolutionaries and that Subhas visited it often. Three weeks later C-8 appears to have worked out that the address of the Cherry Press was also the headquarters of the Swaraj Party and it would have been strange if Bose had not been there.

But KGS's great "find" came on 21 January 1924:

> On the same day this agent informed us that Subhas was very probably privy to the plot to bomb the Council Chamber on the opening day of the Bengal Legislative Council. The ticket of admission, which had been given to the member who was deputed to effect the preliminary reconnaissance necessary before the commission of the outrage had been supplied by Subhas. Two days later, the same agent reported that he was now confident that Subhas was concerned in the plot. The latter had been making enquiries regarding what had happened in the Council Chamber and had declared that the plan, would, in all probability, not succeed since Bengalies were fertile in ideas which failed to attain success. The agent stated that Subhas was then busy in organizing a strong standing corps of volunteers, properly unformed and officered.

On 27 January 1924 the agent reported that Subhas and other associates had decided that Tegart should be assassinated. This would be followed by an attack on Bhowanipore Barrack, the residence of the deputy superintendent of Police of the intelligence branch.

On 5 February 1924 the same agent reported that Subhas believed his former friend Hemanta to be a spy. One of his reasons was that the police had not received prior information of the attempted assassination of Tegart, which had culminated in the murder of Day, of which Hemanta knew nothing, and he had therefore made arrangement for watching Hemanta's movements. He desired that all plans of outrages should be suspended until he arrived at a definite finding regarding Hemanta. Agents then reported that there was a difference in the ranks of the revolutionaries. Some of them had wanted to assassinate Tegart as it would demoralise the police, but Bose wanted to target the governor with his executive councillors, on the grounds that this would create a worldwide sensation. Bose had also warned one of his party members to destroy anything incriminating as he feared his house would be searched by the police.

Agents portrayed Bose as an international communist. They reported that he was in cahoots with Somesh Bose, a mathematician, who had returned from England with important messages from revolutionaries abroad. He had come back via Paris, where he had stayed with a French woman who was a Bolshevik. According to these agents, Somesh Bose arrived in

Calcutta with an invitation for Das to visit England and liaise with a group there which included Colonel Josiah Wedgwood, a Liberal MP, who had defected to Labour. Back in 1919 Wedgwood had incurred the wrath of the British in India for making a brave speech in the House of Commons denouncing Dyer and the Amritsar massacre. The agents alleged that Wedgewood's party, a reference to the Labour party which then was on the verge of taking power in Britain for the first time, was controlled by the communists.

Soon agents were reporting on plans to blow up the train taking the Bengal governor to Darjeeling. Bose, said KGS, was against th idea. But the Raj took the warning seriously enough for the Governor to abandon the trip.

On the 13th April 1924, the agent XY confirmed the information previously received that Subhas intended to give "preference to political sufferers" in his appointments to posts under the Calcutta Corporation, with the object of relieving the economic distress of members of the revolutionary party. He stated that Subhas had said that their ultimate object could only be attained through revolution, but the time was not yet ripe, and the party should restrain its hot-headed youths from acts of violence.

Bose, described as the architect of the plot to kill Tegart, was the subject of more reports by these agents. On 16 April 1924, KGS reported that three days earlier Subhas had said that the murder of Mr Tegart "was difficult". A plan had been made to blow up a train in which he was travelling near Santahar, but one of the would-be assassins thought that they were being watched and it was abandoned. In reply to a suggestion that heavy loss of life (mainly Indian) would have resulted if the plot had been successful, Subhas stated that he did not mind this if only Tegart could be put out of the way, and quoted slokas(Sanskrit verses) to justify his actions. A week later the same agent was to report that Subhas sought information on graduates who would be prepared to emigrate to islands and countries to the east of India, which were not in British possession, in order that arms and ammunition might be stored there and sent to India when necessary for a revolution.

There is no connecting thread in this plethora of agents' reports. But Armstrong, reviewing the file, had no doubts about Bose the revolutionary:

> Subhas Basu is a young man of considerable ability and is believed to exercise not a little influence over Mr C R Das. For some years past he has been acquainted with a number of known revolutionists – chief among whom are Upendra Banarji, Amarendra Chatarji, Bhupati Majumdar, Antosh Mitra, Satyen Mitra, Satish Chakravarty and Purna Das, and there is little doubt that he enjoyed a good deal of their confidence.
>
> But, for a long time, it was believed – and it is probable, that he confined himself almost exclusively to Congress work and that, though cognisant of most of the revolutionary activity, he was not a party thereto.
>
> Recent events, however, have clearly demonstrated that he has now (if never before) definitely joined hands with the revolutionists and that, at the present moment, he occupies and important place in their councils. He is now firmly of the opinion that no measures save violence will suffice to bring about Swaraj and his complicity in the plot to bomb the Legislative Council proves beyond all doubt that he is prepared to stick at nothing. He has already acquired considerable authority in the revolutionary ranks and it is probable with the most active spirits of the organisation and their implicit trust in him, will, on the arrest of the former leaders, combine to bring the reins of the leadership more completely within his grasp.

There are two very interesting features of this spy dossier.. The spy reports lack any assessment as to their validity. Bose was not the only public figure mentioned in this dossier, but he was to be the only one against whom action was taken.

On 18 February 1924 the ubiquitous GS reported that Bose along with Kiran Shakar Roy and others "held a secret meeting from 5 am to 7.30 am during which period Bepin (a revolutionary) had arranged for two men to mount guard on the stairs with revolutionaries." Again on 19 April 1923 agent XY reported that another meeting had taken place at the home of J. M. Sengupta, another prominent Congress leader and a man who would become, as we shall see, a rival of Bose, where "it was discussed how far the Swarajya Party would co-operate with the revolutionaries." However neither Roy nor Sengupta was tracked with the ferocity with which the Raj spied on Bose. The Raj had shrewdly identified him as the real danger man to its rule in India, and were determined to neutralise him by whatever means they could. The British also knew the falsity of much of what the agents reported. As a note by J.W Hose put it:

> It is not necessary to claim that everything in these statements is true. They are simply a collection of information received from informers and from other sources and tabulated against the person mentioned by the Police Intelligence Officer. If it were desired to prosecute any person against whom similar material existed, no doubt only a portion of the story as contained here would be found suitable for production in Court.

The document was considered so secret that it seems to have been delivered in person to the India Office, neither telegram nor post being considered safe enough. On 16 June 1924, four months before the police knocked on Bose's door, Sir Hugh Stephenson, a government spokesman in the Bengal Legislative Council, while in London went to the India Office. After being briefed by J.W. Hose, he met the secretary of state, Lord Oliver, and provided him with the history sheet. Hose noted that the India secretary would like to see statements "which show men who are ostensibly public politicians are closely associated with criminals." Whether he saw this history sheet is not known. One of the alleged facts reported by KGS was that the Communists had "captured" a party in England, the party in question being the one to which Oliver belonged. Another alleged that Das was soon to visit London for a conference, which would seek the release those imprisoned under Regulation III. C-20, another spy, then "corroborated" this by saying that the invitation had come from Colonel Josiah Wedgwood, a Cabinet colleague of Lord Oliver. Wedgwood had indeed invited Das to come to London, but the police in Bengal had intercepted the letter.

As it happens Colonel Wedgwood was privately making comments on the events in Bengal. Had the same standards been applied to him as the Raj applied to Bose, it would not have required much more evidence for him to be jailed.

In the summer of 1924 the Labour Cabinet debated the repressive measures proposed by the Bengal government in order to thwart Bose. It was in this connection that Colonel Wedgwood had written to a fellow Cabinet minister, Sir Charles Trevelyan: "What does it matter if a few Englishmen are murdered? As millions were killed in the war- all as it were for the good name of England. If we could keep it off for two months all might be well." But unlike Wedgwood, Lord Oliver was an old colonial hand, and while he had doubts about the reliability of the spies' reports, he followed Kipling's advice to the Raj: when it comes to India *v* Britain, always support your local Britons.

For the Raj the police reports were a much prized document, but the evidence shows that officials in London not only did not understand, but also knew little of what was really happening in India.

Two years later this was to introduce a comical element in this story. In assessing whether Bose was a revolutionary, the old Bengali revolutionaries who survived into the 1980s should have been helpful, but I found their memories confusing. Occasionally they were very obdurate. Some still nurtured the illusion that they were fighting the British, and refused to discuss their past. Others dropped tantalising hints that Bose was still alive, which led nowhere, while others believed the investigation was futile. When I approached Satya Ranjan Bakshi, Bose's closest lieutenant, in June 1978, he said, "But Netaji is going to be in the field in two months. That will change everything."

In 1964 Bakshi, probably less sure that Netaji would return, told Leonard Gordon, an American scholar, that Bose knew what was going on at the time in question but was not actively involved. Surendra Mohan Ghosh, who was close to Das and a Jugantar leader, confirmed this view.

Bose did not believe in Gandhian non-violence. He viewed it as just a technique useful in certain circumstances. Violence could also have its uses. Faced early on with Dilip's revulsion at terrorism, he told him: " admit it is regrettable, even ugly if you will, though it also has a terrible beauty of its own. But maybe that beauty does not unveil her face except to her devotees. But what would you have?"

The question is, however, whether Bose in 1924 decided the time had come for violence. He himself stoutly denied that he was involved. And indeed, the idea of Bose the revolutionary planning to bomb the council, smuggle in arms, and kill Tegart is absurd. He was just making his political mark, proving his organisational worth; he had much to lose by going to prison. He had possibly heard of the revolutionaries, and had certainly helped them on a personal basis. In the Corporation people who had suffered in the national cause were given preference in employment, and that meant jobs for a lot of revolutionaries and ex-revolutionaries. But it is doubtful if Bose did anything more than that. Also, the government had strong reasons for acting as they did, not only to crush the revolutionaries but also to deal with the Swarajists. The latter had the government by the throat, as the Bengal Secretary's crucial letter of 1 September 1924 to the government of India acknowledged:

> The Swarajists have now practically achieved their object as far as the Bengal Legislative Council is concerned...at present government can command no support for any of their actions.

Even as the proclamation was issued, police were on their way to 38/2 Elgin Road. In the small hours of Saturday 25 October Subhas was woken up and told by the deputy commissioner of police, "Mr Bose, I have a very unpleasant duty to perform. I have a warrant for your arrest under Regulation III of 1818." His house was thoroughly searched, some papers and correspondence were seized and he was taken again to Alipore Central Jail, that vast collection of barracks between the Calcutta Zoo and the race-course. This was to be a very different experience from his first time in prison with Das.

Bose was never presented with the charges in writing, though several times during his period in jail police officers visited him and read out a list of them. Bose, shocked and somewhat bemused, replied that he was wholly innocent and demanded to be tried in a court of law. When the *Catholic Herald* alleged that Subhas' father was glad his son's Corporation work kept him away from revolutionary activities, and *The Englishman* and *The Statesman* repeated this statement, Subhas immediately instructed Sarat to file libel suits against the papers. The cases dragged on for a long time. Eventually Justice Gregory of the High Court found the *Catholic Herald* guilty of "very serious libel" and awarded Bose 4,000 rupees. Father Gille, the editor, fled the country and the paper ceased publication. Bose obtained 2,000 rupees from *The Englishman* but could not win against *The Statesman* for Justice Buckland came to the conclusion that the newspaper had not asserted any facts. No public proof has ever been presented either way. Bose himself was convinced that the allegation was "the result of personal malice against me on the part of high police officials"

There were constant efforts to get Bose released, and two years later an intervention in

London by some Labour MPs produced an amusing result. By now the Conservatives had replaced Labour and Lord Birkenhead had became secretary of state for India. In March 1926 a deputation of Labour MPs lead by Tom Johnston and James Thomas visited him to ask for Bose's release. They apparently did not know much about Bose. For a start neither Thomas nor Johnston seemed to know Bose's name. Even had they known it they would not have been able to spell his name for the transcript of the meeting spelled Bose as Bhose.

During their interview with Birkenhead, they did not mention his name, referring to him as the Town Clerk of Calcutta, which is how they saw the chief executive. They had heard he had been jailed for sending some money to an Indian in Germany, who had then used it to buy guns and ammunition. Birkenhead, who knew even less about India, and had at that stage not read the police reports, got even more confused and thought Bose had sent money to a German.

At this point Thomas interjected to say, " He is an Indian" and went on to say Bose had sent it to an Indian student "on his uppers who wrote to this town clerk, and the town clerk sent money". Thomas added that the student was "probably a "scoundrel using the money to buy pistols". Nothing came of this interview, although Birkenhead subsequently read the police reports and then wrote to Thomas. He described how the case against Bose was "derived from 15 or 16 different sources , some of them documents". As we have seen, most of the information was from police informers. There were only two documents, one of then a newspaper clipping.

Birkenhead had formed the impression Bose was a dangerous anarchist which would later cause problems with British officials in India when they wanted to exile him to Europe. The secretary of state was thought to be one of the greatest minds in England at the time, and the police files, wretchedly written and argued, must have bored him. His job required him to meet with Indians but, as one biographer says, he did not much care for this and to them was often rude. Although he had condemned the Amritsar massacre he did not believe Indians could ever govern themselves. In 1930 his name appeared as author of a futuristic book called *The World in 2030* in which he made many predictions which have since come true, such as the automation of industry, cheap air travel, synthetic food, and the atom bomb.

He was also sure that the Indians would never progress enough to be able to govern themselves, and even in 2030 would still be part of the British Empire, ruled by the British. If he thought of Bose at all, he would have felt that it was a good thing for this formidable opponent of the Raj to be locked up. Birkenhead's intervention, however, was crucial in another way. His name was successfully invoked by the London barrister consulted by *The Statesman* in its defense against Bose's libel action. The barrister was a A.M. Dunne, an old India hand, and at one time a leading figure in the Calcutta bar. By this time he had returned to London and was a counsel for the Judicial Committee of the Privy Counsel.

Dunne condemned Das for saying Bose had been arrested merely because he belonged to the Swarj party. Dunne wrote: "It is sheer chicanery to pretend the arrests were made because the persons arrested were members of the Swarajya(sic) Party. They are in confinement today because there was evidence sufficient to convince such a skilled assessor of the value of evidence as the former Lord Chief Justice of England that they were planning or aiding and abetting in crimes of violence." [Birkenhead in a previous ministerial incarnation had been Lord Chancellor]

Nobody knew what Birkenhead had assessed, and, in 1926, for the purposes of a libel action, invoking his name and prestige as a former Lord Chancellor was extremely useful.

There is one other legal by-product of this whole affair that is revealing about British-Indian relations. J.A. Jones, *The Statesman's* man in London, who had obtained the legal advice from Dunne, wrote a letter to the Calcutta firm of Knight & Sons, which was handling the action there. Jones expressed his relief that this case would not come before an Indian jury, but then added: "But some Indian judges are scarcely to be trusted more than Indian jurors".

As part of the legal process this letter had to be disclosed to Bose and he immediately seized on it as it showed the British had not moved forward from the Ilbert controversy of nearly half a century before. Then the idea of an Indian judge sitting in judgement on a Briton had thrown the British in India into a fit of collective hysteria.

However, in that letter, Jones also mentioned the names of the legal counsels who would act for *The Statesman* and two of the three were Indians: N.N.Sircar and B.C. Mitter, the same Mitter who in his schooldays Subhas had admired. Apparently, some Indians, like Sircar and Mitter, " made the grade" as long as they were fighting for the English against the Indians.

6
Guru Lost

With Bose's arrest Das had lost the one man he could always rely upon. Das summoned Gandhi, Motilal Nehru and other leaders to Calcutta, and between 26 and 31 October 1924 five public meetings were held, ending with a mammoth meeting on the 31st where over 150,000 joined them in condemning the "lawless laws". In November an all-party conference condemned the laws, and at the annual Congress session, with Gandhi in the chair, a motion "congratulated the Swarajists and others arrested under the new Ordinance of Regulation III of 1818."

The history of the independence movement in India is the history of the prison shuttle: a leader would be arrested, perhaps put on trial; then, after he refused to defend himself, he would spend some time in jail in moderate comfort. This would be a time for studying and writing, to be followed by a spell of freedom and then prison again. All the prominent nationalist leaders endured this, though Bose's experiences were somewhat different. He was generally held under laws that did not require trials, his spells in jail were longer than most of the others, and the conditions were sufficiently poor to damage his health. The British were to release Bose three times on health grounds.

After a little over a month and a half at Alipore, where he continued to do his work as chief executive, receiving both files and officials, including English officials, he was transferred to Berhampur in the heart of the Bengal countryside. Then, on 25 January 1925, he was informed that he was no longer a prisoner under Regulation III of 1818 but under the Ordinance of 1925, and was quickly taken back to Calcutta. Here, after a night in a veritable hell-hole, Calcutta's Lalbazar police station, crawling with vermin and mosquitoes and with filthy sanitary arrangements, he was bundled into a van and then on board a boat cruising the river Hooghly. Soon he was transferred to a ship, and only then realised that he and other detainees were bound for Mandalay in Burma. Armed guards stood outside their cabins, and a large police escort accompanied them from Rangoon to Mandalay. Burma, then part of the British administration in India, was a convenient repository for political prisoners, particularly the more obdurate ones. Bose lived in the same yard where Tilak, a militant nationalist, had lived twenty years before. He could gaze on the lemon trees Tilak had planted, and found that life in Mandalay Jail had changed little since those days. The buildings were of wooden palisading and offered no resistance to heat, rain or cold. He had arrived in the middle of the worst season, just three months before the monsoon rains, and found Mandalay, as he told Sarat, to be the kingdom of dust. Dust was in food, clothes and furniture, indeed everywhere.

There was a household of sorts in the jail consisting of fellow prisoners and servants, a cook, a cook's mate, a cleaner, a sweeper, making 20 in all. Bose lived in a jail within a jail and was not allowed to mix with other prisoners. Apart from living quarters, the small jail consisted of a kitchen, a water tank and a tennis court. There was a garden, but it was in a very poor state and when Bose and his fellow inmates planted some flowering seeds these were soon eaten up by ants, insects and chickens. To run this jailhouse Bose and his fellow prisoners appointed as manager another prisoner who also did not know why he was in prison. He acted like a housewife, and kept accounts and made shopping lists. Bose mockingly called the place a hotel and in a letter to Bivabati, Sarat's wife, wrote:

> Anything is available in our hotel. The other day the manager fed us with hot jilebis. and we blessed him wholeheartedly praying he may ever remain in prison. Sometime ago he entertained us with rosogollas; although the balls were floating in the syrup alright, they had no syrup inside and if you threw them at anybody there was the risk of his head getting fractured. The manager has come to the conclusion that in this world, papaya is the queen of vegetables, and therefore papaya is everywhere, in the stew, in the curry, in pickles or anything else. And as the manager is a half-doctor, he has given the verdict that the more you eat papaya, the better will be your digestion.

Subhas was glad he ate mutton and chicken for otherwise it would have been an endless diet of papaya. He complained that good tea was not available. Despite the fact that Burma was close to Assam, tea had to come all the way from England, a reflection of how imperial trade worked. Bose was keen to have physical exercise, for he feared he might otherwise get arthritis. He took to tennis and badminton, overcoming his initial prejudice against the latter. Before being jailed he had thought of badminton as a ladies game. There was little else to distract him, and no sooner had he arrived in Mandalay than he was unwell: first he had indigestion, then a weakening dyspepsia-cum-flu. The government had yet to supply him with any books, and they told him he could not even have his favourite paper *The Forward,* which the authorities thought would prevent him from reforming his ways.

But prison can be a great educator, and Subhas used his time well. He managed to read widely, he wrote innumerable letters and articles, classified his ideas, and planned for the future. His two and a half years in Burma were a turning-point in his life. He entered prison as a 28-year-old activist full of dedication but without properly developed political ideas. He left as a hardened, sceptical man of 31, brimming with ideas and plans. He made great efforts to get to know Burma and although the climate did not agree with him he was full of admiration for the Burmese. As he wrote to Dilip:

> I consider the Burmese, like the Chinese, to be considerably advanced from a social point of view. What they do lack most of all is initiative - what Bergson would call '*elan vital*' - that vital impulse to overcome all obstacles and march along the road to progress. They have developed a perfect social democracy. Women, by the way are more powerful here than in any European country-but alas! The enervating climate seems to have robbed them of all initiative.

Bose admired the Burmese educational system where priests undertook the primary education and every boy was required for a time to don the robes of a priest. It was not only educational but egalitarian, bringing the rich and poor together. "There is thus an extensive system of primary education which hardly costs anything," he wrote to Dilip.

At this stage Subhas was still trying to control all lustful feelings and in an undated letter to Haricharan Bagchi, which the editors of his collected papers think was probably written in 1926, he returned to the Vivekananda theme of sex:

> The best means of conquering lust are to visualise the mother-image in all women, to invest women with that halo and to worship God in the mother-form, such as Durga and Kali. When man contemplated God or Guru in the form of the mother, he learns to see divinity in all women; when he reaches this state he has overcome lust. That is why our forefathers, in order to create an image of Divine Power, thought in terms of the form of women.

Subhas had always felt keenly about what he thought of as a defect in his education, an ignorance of Bengali literature. Prison helped him correct that but he was also reading a great deal of western literature and books. He was constantly petitioning Sarat and Dilip for books: Dostoievsky's *The Brothers Karamazov,* Turgenev's *Smoke* and lots of Russell: *The Prospects of Industrial Civilization, Icarus or the Future of Science, Free Thought and Official Propaganda.*

He made detailed notes on books he read. These were books such as *Ireland a Nation* by Robert Lynd, *Voices of New Ireland* by P.H. Pease, *The History of Civilisation in Europe* by Francois Guizot and by the same author *The Revolution of Civilisation*; Kaiser Wilhelm's *Memoirs(1878-1918)*, *Asia and Europe* by Meredith Townsend, *The Criminal Mind* by Maurice de Fluery, *Physical Efficiency* by James Cantlie and *National Welfare and National Decay* by W. M. McDougall. His notes when published in his *Collected Works* ran to 151 printed pages.

Subhas made revealing comments as he read McDougall's book, which dealt with race and eugenics. McDougall, a Professor of Psychology at Harvard Unviersity, expounded the race-based ideas then common in the western world and argued that Britain's leading position was due to the predominance of Nordic blood in Britons, while the "docility of the German people under an autocracy or bureaucracy was due to alpine blood, which was somewhat less represented in the French people. It is this which inspite of his lack of subtlety and sympathy and intellectuality has enabled him to subdue and govern the 300 million of India."

Subhas noted in the margins: "Why have not all Nordic races been equally advanced? If the Nordic blood gives a Briton his restless wandering habit, why does it not give the same to the other Nordic races?"

Townsend's *Asia and Europe* predicted how British rule in India would end: "If we are to take the history of Asia for our guide, the British dominion in India should be overthrown by external violence exerted by some Asiatic people; just as the Alexandrine Empire was overthrown." Subhas did not make any comments on this prediction. Less than 20 years later, he was to be a central player when Japan became the Asiatic power that swept away the white man's dominance in the continent.

Dilip hesitated to send him Russell's *What I Believe.* The book was fine, he wrote, "but his sincere views on morality must needs shock you'" Dilip was already established as his philosophical sparring partner, and they exchanged lengthy letters which provide a fascinating insight into Bose's mind as he underwent his first real personal and political test. Since their Cambridge days the two had spent little time together. While Subhas was active in politics, Dilip, affected by Subhas' resignation from the ICS, had abandoned his own desire for a career, and turned to his first love: music. He would soon draw further away, renouncing the world for Aurobindo's ashram at Pondicherry, and in the years to come he would try to lure Subhas away from what he saw as the wasteful world of politics to the infinitely more satisfying one of mysticism, divine glory and Utopian wonder.

Subhas also wrote down his thoughts and developing ideas in a book, *Pebbles on the Sea-shore,* in an essay entitled *The Failure of Buddhism*, and in eight prison notebooks. These covered, as always, a remarkably catholic range. He developed his ideas on the necessity for revolt; on the modernisation of Hinduism; and above all on the role of Bengal. Bengali literature must break away from 'foreign' (English) influence and develop "an intimate relationship with the heart of the Society". Above all, Bengal must realise her heritage, her mission.

Once upon a time Bengal too had been great. Medieval Gaur had been a centre of learning and scholarship, a meeting-place for the different strands of Hindu and Buddhist thought. Culture had flourished; everyone had been happy. But then had come the fall: he did not specify his cause, though one main reason for it had been the coming of the British. Bengal had betrayed India. Now:

> The people of Bengal must not forget that she occupies a distinctive place not

only in India but also in the whole world, that she will have duties to perform peculiar to the position she holds . . . The new India will be created by Bengal's genius through a revival of her literature, science, art and music coupled with a renewed interest in physical culture and social service. The Bengalees alone are capable of bringing about a cultural synthesis and effecting comprehensive development of our national life.

Then he learned that C.R. Das was dead.

Das had fought the Raj almost to a standstill. The Indian budget had been upset. The Viceroy, Lord Lytton, had prorogued the council and taken over the administration himself, proving dyarchy to be the farce it was: puppet assemblies assuming grandeur via the pretence of power. But the process had taken its toll on Das's health, and, in June 1925, he suddenly died in Darjeeling.

Bose was desolate. Now, in the middle of their first period of separation, Das, his guru, was gone. Four years later, he would write to Basanti: "He who was at once my friend, philosopher and guide in my life's mission is no more. Today I am utterly destitute." He urged Basanti to take her husband's place; and on his release, nearly two years later, pleaded, "Please give some thought to the duties and tasks awaiting me ... I do not wish to take up any work now without consulting you." But Basanti did not seek a public role, and this deepened the pain of Das' death.

There was much of the emotional Bengali in Bose's reaction, but with the death of Das an important political prop had vanished: the older, more experienced politician who shrewdly smoothes the way for his protégé. Bose's great rival Jawaharlal Nehru enjoyed the benefits of a guru well into his late middle-age. Nehru's initial political prominence had been due almost entirely to the fact that he was the son of Motilal, a contemporary of Das and Gandhi. Gandhi had quickly realised the worth of Nehru and during the crucial 1920s and 1930s, he promoted him as his successor, getting him elected as Congress president in 1930 and, despite their much-trumpeted philosophical and ideological differences, readily succouring and guiding him. Das' premature death meant that, at a very crucial time in Bose's political life, there was nobody experienced or weighty enough to guide him through the often-factional waters of Indian politics.

Bose thought of writing a biography of Das but soon became involved in the first of his many battles in prison. Bose had always chafed at the strict prison regime. Things came to a head in early 1926 when the authorities refused to allow money to Bose and his friends to celebrate the festival of Saraswati Puja. Bose argued that the laws under which he had been detained did not permit any 'hardship savouring of punishment', and, in fact, entitled him to treatment 'in keeping with my rank and station in life', Bose wrote several letters to the Chief Secretary of the Burmese government, attacking its 'arbitrary infringement of religious rights'. The letters and petition were marked by characteristically extravagant religious and nationalistic sentiments extolling ancient Indian civilisations and declaring: "The materialistic organisation of the West of today is sitting like a nightmare on India's bosom."

On 18 February 1926 Subhas led his fellow-prisoners at Mandalay on a hunger strike. Four days later they were joined by the inmates of Insein Jail. By the eighth day the strikers were being force-fed, and nationalist India was getting increasingly concerned. Finally Maulana Shaukat Ali, a prominent leader of the Congress, arrived at Mandalay to reason with Subhas. His visit looked like proving fruitless until he produced his trump card: Subhas' friends in Bengal wanted him to give up the strike; even Sarat was of that view. Shocked, the strikers decided to call off their action, and this caused a rare strain between Subhas and Sarat which lead to Sarat spending some time explaining himself to Subhas.

Soon, however, the two brothers were in harness contesting seats for the Legislative Council. Subhas was initially not inclined to stand. Sarat was very keen and after much effort

Subhas gave in saying: "I have had my say. I depend entirely on your decision, whatever that may be." Sarat contested the Calcutta University seat, Subhas the north Calcutta non-Muslim seat.

This provided one of the most curious phenomena of the Raj. Subhas Bose was so dangerous – an anarchist, Bolshevist and revolutionary, according to Raj intelligence assessments – that he had to be jailed outside India. Yet he could stand for election to a state assembly! Sarat had to campaign for him but Subhas took a great interest in the election and in several detailed letters to Sarat advised shrewdly on election tactics. In one letter to Sarat he told him that his campaign should be concentrated on the libraries and Associations throughout the province. "Each bar library is a place where you can get so many solid votes…next in importance to the pleaders are the teachers." In another letter, he analysed the votes of his own constituency which showed Ward 1 as being the most important. His opponent was one Jatin Basu, and Subhas told Sarat that it was very important to hold meetings and processions: "It is more desirable to hold meetings in Ward I than in any other part of the constituency. After you hold half a dozen successful meetings you will find Mr Basu's organisation has gone to pieces."

His brother Sailesh came to Burma to get him to sign the nomination papers and on 17 November1926 Subhas and Sarat were elected comfortably. But if this was meant to create public pressure to release Subhas Bose it did not work. By now his health was a major concern.

Mandalay had never agreed with him, but now his health grew progressively worse. Every afternoon his temperature rose; he had pain in his spine and night sweats. A week after the election Subhas was preparing to go to Rangoon for a medical examination. He travelled there early in December where the civil surgeon examined him. The stomach and chest were fine but Kelsall wanted to keep him under observation for a fortnight to check his temperature and take urine and sputum samples. Before the end of the year he was back in Mandalay. He could have stayed in Rangoon but the jail there was even more uncomfortable; his temperature rose even higher. Although Sarat was planning to visit him with his family, Subhas decided he would be better off in Mandalay.

He took up tennis but gave it up as the strain was too much. When his fever got worse the government consented to a joint medical examination by Colonel Kelsall, and an older brother of Subhas, Dr Sunil Bose. Subhas left for Rangoon Central jail on the evening of 8 February, and the doctors examined him on 12 February. They decided he was probably suffering from tuberculosis, which could only be cured by rest and medical attention outside jail. Sunil Bose even recommended a prolonged stay in a sanatorium in Switzerland. Although Sunil had given a medical opinion and not a brother's view it provided a way for the Raj to get Bose out of India. Subhas later wrote to Sarat of his anger at the recommendation.

A fascinating debate began among Raj officials on how to deal with Subhas. Bose was too dangerous free, but in jail he might die. For Raj officials there was no escape from this dilemma. The Bengal government at first suggested that Bose be moved to a more suitable Indian jail. But Delhi found nobody willing to risk having Bose in custody. Burma, never happy about taking Bose, was now getting increasingly alarmed about Bengal's dilatoriness, as were top civil servants. Haig, the home secretary, thought acceptance of Sunil Bose's proposal would have been a humane answer to the release of Bose, as it was a problem "for which Bengal see no solution". Muddiman felt Bengal were behaving like the Stuarts: weak when they ought to be strong, and vice versa.

During a debate in the Bengal Council the home member of the Bengal Executive Council, Sir A.N.Moberley offered to release Bose provided he went straight to Switzerland from Rangoon, and gave his word to exile himself from India. The Bengal government hoped he would refuse, and thus absolve them of guilt. When Lord Birkenhead in London heard about Moberley's proposals in *The Times,* he furiously cabled Delhi: "Most improper to permit notorious anarchist to go to European country which is refuge of anarchists and focus of anarchical conspiracy without permission of His Majesty's Government with whom would rest responsibility of watching him there."

The Bengal government was now hoist with its own petard, having depicted Bose as a dangerous revolutionary. But the Viceroy did manage to pacify Birkenhead by declaring that, though Bose was a national hero in Bengal, he was likely to be less effective outside India than within. Subhas, in any case, rejected the proposals and was particularly upset about not being allowed to see his family *en route.*

On 25 March 1927 he was moved to Insein jail, and it was from here that he wrote some of his most thunderous letters against the Raj. In an 8-page letter dated 4 April 1927 he explained why he rejected exile to Switzerland. It would mean he would be endlessly followed by spies, and end up in permanent exile. He had no desire to be a nomadic Bolshevik agent, "the gay band who trot about from Paris to Leningrad talking of world revolution and emitting blood and thunder in their utterances." Bose was astonished to hear that he would have to promise not to return to India, Burma and Ceylon. "Am I so dangerous to the existence of British rule in India that a deportation from Bengal is not considered as an adequate safeguard or is all this but a hoax?" But his real anger emerged when he castigated the "callous" disregard of feeling for his family:

> There is one aspect of the Hon'ble Member's proposal which struck me as particularly callous. Government know that I have been away from home for nearly two years and I have not met any of my relations, including parents, during this period. They nevertheless propose that I should go abroad for a period which will be at least two or three years without having an opportunity of meeting them. This is hard for me - but much more for those who love me - and whose number I think is very large. It is not easy for a Westerner to appreciate the deep attachment which Oriental people have for their kith and kin and I hope it is this ignorance-rather than wilfulness-which is responsible for what I cannot but regard as a heartless feature of the Government offer. It would be typical only of a Western mind to presume that because I have not married – therefore I have no family - taking the word in its large sense and no attachment for anyone"

Subhas wrote to Sarat again from Insein, on 11 April 1927:

> My conception of honour, my duty as a political sufferer and my position in public life preclude me from accepting the conditions with which the Government have been pleased to qualify their proposal. It is too late in the day to talk of conditions, when I have already been in jail for nearly two years ...

The letters went back and forth between Subhas, Sarat and the government, with Subhas's own family playing an increasingly important role in an effort to get him out of jail. Eventually it was Satish, the eldest brother whom he called Bardada, who was the first to see him in April in Insein jail. Six years earlier he had tried to dissuade him from resigning from the ICS; now he sought a formula whereby Subhas could leave jail without making any concessions to the government.

Eventually a compromise was negotiated between the Bengal government and Sarat. It was agreed that the family would take a house in Almora, and that Subhas would stay there for three months with only family as company, and then proceed to Switzerland. After a great deal of pressure from Sarat, who did not always relay to Subhas what he had agreed with Moberley, Subhas agreed to go to Almora; but without promising to go on to Switzerland.

Subhas agreed that while he was at Almora the government could prevent him from receiving people on political grounds, but relations and Basanti Devi would be allowed to meet him. There would be no censorship of letters between him and his relations but correspondence with persons other than near relations would be censored. However Sarat added that as Subhas was not well no final decision could be taken.

On 7 May Bose was put on a steamer for Almora. Just before the steamer entered Calcutta it was intercepted by the Bengal government, whose doctors examined Bose. They pronounced his condition "serious" and the government decided to cut its losses. On16 May 1927 Bose was handed an unconditional release order. After two years and six months he returned to his bedroom at 38/2 Elgin Road, sick in body but quite clear about his intentions. In the middle of the negotiations with the Bengal government, Subhas had written to a colleague, "My mind and spirit now yearns for absolute achievement and absolute sacrifice" He was shortly to find out what that meant.

7

The Reluctant Heir

Through the summer of 1927 Bose recuperated at Kelsall Lodge in Shillong, a pleasant Assam hill station. What he observed of political events appalled him, for the world he had returned to was very different from the one he had left. The coalition put together by Das had all but disintegrated, and his would-be heirs were busy scrambling for power. The most important of them, Jatindra Mohan Sengupta, had already assumed Das's mantle: the triple crown of the presidency of the Swaraj Party and of the Bengal Congress Party and the mayoralty of Calcutta. To add to the completeness of his joy, Gandhi – in Calcutta to mourn Das – had himself anointed Sengupta as Das's successor. Afterwards a peeved Sarat asked him: "What have you left for Subhas?'"Gandhi smiled his toothless smile and replied: "For Subhas there is the whole of India." Sarat was not amused.

Sengupta, in fact, represented only one of the many factions that composed Das' coalition. There were also the revolutionaries of the Karmisangha (Workers' Society); there were provincials trying to break into the Calcutta-controlled Congress world. Sarat Bose had also formed his his own caucus, which was soon dubbed The Big Five: Sarat himself, Nirmal Chunder Chunder, Nalini Ranjan Sarkar, Bidhan Chandra Roy and Tulsi Charan Goswami. Though the latter were not as formally organised as the Karmisangha, they were united by identical interests and similar backgrounds. They all came from the Bengali high-caste elite.

All these groups were struggling with the impossible inheritance left by Das: here a concession to a regional interest, there an alliance with important caste groups, and towards the end of his life an attempt to solve the Hindu-Muslim problem at the elite level. Sengupta, the Big Five and the revolutionaries did not by themselves have the skill to hold all this together. News of their factional in-fighting had reached Bose in Mandalay and left him depressed. Sometime in 1926 he wrote to a friend: "Is there no such worker in Bengal today who can offer silent self-immolation in disregard of the quarrels of the power-hungry politicians?"

Before Bose was well enough to resume his political career he had one ceremonial function to peform, and one that was curious. He was an member of the Bengal Legislative Council, elected from jail, but who had never taken his seat . Now, though far from well and against medical advice, he made a short rail trip to Calcutta from Kelsall Lodge on 21 August 1927 to complete the formalites. On 23 August he took his oath of allegiance to the Crown. As he made his way to the council chambers, providing the first public glimpse of Bose for nearly three years, there were cheers. However the council was never his real arena and his doctors insisted he return to the hills, Kelsall Lodge having been rented until October 15, and Subhas travelled back to Shillong within a few weeks.

It was not until October, five months after his release, that he descended from Shillong to the now cool plains of Calcutta. Certified medically fit by his doctors he decided to resume politics. Almost immediately he was elected president of the Bengal Congress Committee, and for the moment peace reigned among the factions. His first task was to deal with mounting communal problems. Throughout 1926 and 1927 Hindus and Muslims had clashed in ugly riots all over the country. The causes were the familiar ones – Mulsims killing cows, Hindus playing music in front of mosques.

When Bengal had been re-united in 1911, undoing the 1905 Curzon partition,

Muslims formed a small majority in the province. They were wretchedly poor, largely illiterate and terribly oppressed, particularly in East Bengal, by heartless, absentee Hindu landlords. This situation contained the seeds of a great explosion, and Das had earlier tried, in his civilised way, to combat it. He got the Bengal Swaraj Party to agree that, when the Congress came to power, 60 per cent of all new jobs would be reserved for Muslims, and in the Calcutta Corporation as much as 80 per cent; but the party only accepted this after a relentless struggle. The upper-caste Hindus, who dominated the revolutionaries, were not convinced of the need for such a pact. Das was even less successful outside Bengal: the annual Congress session in 1923 rejected the idea.

For the Raj the pact was a disaster. Its whole policy was based on the theory, assiduously cultivated, that Hindu was Hindu and Muslim was Muslim and that never the twain should meet. Any attempt to bring them together, on however fragile a basis, was unnatural. The official announcement of the Bengal Pact had been made under Bose's signature as secretary of the Congress, and he was determined to preserve communal amity. After the Hindu-Muslim riots that racked Calcutta the leaders were sufficiently concerned to call for a unity conference in November 1927. Bose took up the theme at a large gathering at Calcutta's Shraddhananda Park:

> There may be Hindus who in a corner of their hearts felt elated at the shooting of unarmed Muslims at Kulkati. If that be so it is a pity and a shame. I beg of you to remember that those who can shoot down unarmed Muslims today can shoot down unarmed Hindus tomorrow.

How could freedom, he asked, be achieved if Hindus could not live together with Muslims? This was one of few occasions when Bose made a long public statement on the Hindu-Muslim problem. Like all Indian nationalists, he saw communalism almost wholly as a British creation. In *The Indian Struggle,* written seven years after this speech, he dealt briefly with the Muslim problem and how the Raj had helped set up the Muslim League in order to undermine the Indian nationalists. The Raj may not have created the Hindu-Muslim problem but it did nothing to solve it. It wanted the Hindus and Muslims to be separate as this provided one of the great justifications for continued British rule. This was plainly stated by Birkenhead two years before Bose made his speech in Shraddhananda Park. In a private letter to Lord Reading, then Viceroy of India, he revealed , as his biographer admits, the deeply cynical basis of British policy: Reading had just made a speech deploring Hindu-Muslim violence and Birkenhead wrote:

> In a latter passage, you lamented the recent renewal of outbreaks between Hindu and Mahomedan. Both you and I must of course speak of these outbreaks in terms you used... but surely the complete breakdown of a Hindu-Mahomedan anti-reform unity looked at very broadly, spells a death blow to Das and the whole of the Hindu campaign...His task is absolutely hopeless when the fundamental strength of our position is advertised to all India by the resolute determination of the powerful and virile Mahomedan community that they cannot and will not accept any form of Home Rule on terms which are acceptable to Das and Nehru. The more it is made obvious that these antagonisms are profound, and affect immense and irreconcilable sections of the population, the more conspicously is the fact illustrated that we and we alone, can pay the part of composers.

A few months later he was to write, "I have always placed my highest and most permanent hopes upon the eternity of the Communal situation."

Birkenhead was franker than most British politicians, but all of them shared his views. Lord Lamington, a governor of Bombay, had written to John Morley, the then secretary of state for India: "The real guarantees of our stay in India are as strong as ever over the caste system, the diversity of nationalities and creed and the lack of confidence and trust of one native for another."

Divide & Rule

Divide and rule has long been the secret of empires. The British did not invent the strategy, but they applied it ruthlessly in India.

Bose was right to draw attention to the Raj's role in the formation of the Muslim League in 1906. This started with discussions between Nawab Mehti Ali Khan, who preferred to be called Moshin ul Mulk, and W.A.J. Archibold, principal of Aligarh College. Archibold, like many Raj officials was convinced that India could never be ready for English-style parliamentary government. Moshin ul Mulk was alarmed that even the limited concessions the Liberal Government was making to the Congress on some form of Indian representation would prove seductive to Muslims. With Archibold's assistance and other Raj contacts, including Harcourt Butler, the father of 'Rab' Butler, who was then commissioner of Lucknow, he organised a Muslim deputation of Nawabs and landlords to present a petition to the Viceroy, Lord Minto.

The deputation was led by Aga Khan III, who was India's most fervent collaborator of the Raj,and prided himself on being its most devoted servant. On 1 October he led his party to Simla, the summer capital of the Raj. In the ballroom of the five-storey high Vice-regal Lodge, while the bossy Mary Minto and her three daughters, known as the Destroying Angels, looked on, he presented the deputation's respects to the Englishman who ruled India.

Seventy Muslims gathered in an elaborate ballroom that could actually accommodate 800. While his family watched, Lord Minto, dressed in his vice-regal robes and, accompanied by his staff, took his seat on the dais. In front and below him stood the Aga.

The Muslim League's petition affirmed its loyalty to the Raj, and it's guiding principle was its belief that European institutions, offering democracy and individual rights, could prove highly dangerous for India. Those institutions were new, said the petitioners, and had to be applied with care in order to protect the rights and privileges of the Muslims. The Muslims, said the Muslim's Memorial, were a significant minority. They numbered 62 million and while this meant they were only one fifth of the total population of India, they were more numerous than the entire population of any first class European power except Russia. The memorialists, however, were not just intent on securing a proper minority status in terms of number:

> We venture, indeed with your Excellency's permission, to go a step further and urge that the position accorded to the Mohammedan Community in any kind representation, direct or indirect, and in all other ways affecting their status and influence, should be commensurate not merely with their numerical strength but also with their political importance and the value of the contribution which they make to the defence of the Empire; we also know that your excellency will in this connection be pleased to give due consideration to the position which they occupied in India a little more than 100 years ago and of which the traditions have actually not faded from their minds.

This was not so much an argument for minority status as an argument for a separate nation. These upper class, feudal Muslims were saying that whatever democratic institutions were introduced in India by the British, they must always remember that the Hindus and Muslims had separate identities and should be treated separately; sentiments that the Raj heartily endorsed and found very useful. The rest of the petition was taken up with a plea for more 'Jobs for the Boys' . The Muslims wanted jobs in the Civil Service. Hindus, they felt, were getting the lion's share. There had, for instance, been Hindu judges in various High Courts in India, but no Muslims.

All this should have been anathema to Britain in 1906 which was advertising the wonders of British democracy. That year saw a reforming Liberal government headed by Asquith, who was elected with a massive majority. *The Times* saw this hotch-potch of a feudal petition as "the only piece of original political thought which has emanated from modern times" In the long history of that newspaper it is doubtful if a more ridiculous comment has been made.

The Raj's help and encouragement for separatist Muslim feeling was only one of several factors that ultimately divided the sub-continent between India and Pakistan.

The divisions were real enough. Most of the educated Indians were either Hindus or Parsees. The Parsees were the remnants of the old pre-Islamic inhabitants of Persia. Twelve hundred years ago, as Islam swept through Persia, some of the Persians, followers of the ancient prophet Zoroaster, had taken sanctuary in India. Their existence in India for such a long period as a separate community, allowed the freedom to practise their religion and culture, is testament to the tolerance of the Hindus. A small tight community , and somewhat inbred, it had not only survived but prospered and was ideally suited to take advantage of British education and influence. Nothing is known of their existence in India between their arrival as refugees in the sixth century, until the eighteenth century. When the British took power the Parsees emerged as if out of the undergrowth to be their intermediaries with the other Indians. They were the Indians who first took to cricket and provided the early leadership of the Congress party.

The Muslims, on the other hand, had reason to feel ambivalent about the British and, initially the British were vary of them. The Hindus or the Parsees, were subject races – and, as such, could be scorned or patronised. The British were always aware that they had succeeded the Muslims as rulers of India. Before the traumatic Indian Revolt of 1857, British rule in India – between 1757 and 1857 – was a most curious form of leasehold tenancy. Though the British actually ruled India from their headquarters in Calcutta, the Moghul Emperor still resided in Delhi, despite his powers being almost totally fictional.

The revolt of 1857 changed all that. Though the old Hindu aristocracy was deeply involved with the Muslims in the rebellion, the British saw it as a Muslim, Moghul attempt to win back what they had lost the previous century. Before 1857 British historical writing on India had coupled respect for Moghul achievements with a certain piety about its sad end. Now the ideologists of the Raj argued that the fanaticism that was inherent in Islam, with its call for *jihad* (holy war) against the Infidels, meant that all Muslim subjects would be rebellious.

As the Muslims fell, the Hindus rediscovered themselves. The advent of British rule had benefited certain Hindu upper classes. The British helped them rediscover ancient Hindu learning, and in Bengal educated Hindus made it the leading province of the Raj. However, this rediscovery of Hinduism with British help also revived the old hatreds of the Hindu upper classes and castes for the Muslims. It was one the British were happy to inflame. The Hindu upper classes and castes had carefully nurtured memories of the manner in which the invading Muslims had deprived them of their power, robbed them of their wealth and humiliated their women. They feared the crusading spirit of Islam, and dreaded even the allegedly greater sexual potency of the Muslims (a dread that remains to this day). Against an Islam that offered a system that was both simple and apparently, at least for the male, equal, all the Hindus had to offer was a caste system, and a tremendously confused and decayed system of values and duties. This selective Hindu memory was emphasised by Islamic rulers of India who stressed that they had spread Islam through the sword, killing infidels who did not submit. The reality was the great majority of Muslim converts had come from the wretchedly oppressed lower Hindu castes.

While this undoubtedly helped their self-esteem, it did little to improve their economic plight. The Muslim upper classes lived well, and their life-style was soon copied by their Hindu counterparts eager to serve their new masters, but the poor Hindus became the poorer Muslims and remained at the mercy of the more rapacious Hindu castes. By the 1920s both Hindus and Muslims were led by men eager to obscure uncomfortable economic facts by selective historial memory feeding religious fanaticism and the two communties were to slide slowly and steadily into communal tension and a cycle of hatred.

Subhas never had the time, nor perhaps the inclination, to examine the deeper problems of India's religious divisions. He always sought and worked for Hindu-Muslim unity based on respect for each other's religious rights. To an extent he was successful and in 1928, with communal passions riding high and the leaders unable to agree, Bose was one of the few Hindu politicians to earn praise from the Muslims. Abdul Karim, a Muslim leader from Burdwan in a speech in the Bengal Legislative Council said, "I should not omit to mention the earnest efforts that are being made by my young friend Mr Subhas Chandra Bose and others of his way of thinking, to bring about a relation of amity and cordiality between the two communities."

Bose was to prove more successful in his unity efforts in the Calcutta Corporation in 1940 and quite spectacularly so in the Indian National Army during the war. Years later M.A.H Ispahani, a Calcutta Muslim League businessman who barely concealed his hatred for the Congress, would recall the warmth of Subhas' friendship and his efforts to promote unity: "Had Bose remained in India, he may well have boldly struck out for Muslim friendship."

The question was: how could he strike out for such a friendship? There is only one known instance of a truly Hindu-Muslim alliance aimed at the Raj. It happened in 1919 when Gandhi, fashioning his first civil disobedience campaign, allied the Congress to the Khilafat movement. The Muslims in India had long been worried about how the west was treating Turkey, the only independent Muslim power. They were devastated by the terms the victorious Allies dictated to defeated Turkey after the First World War. This, they feared, would dismember Turkey, despite pledges to the contrary by Lloyd George. Turkey was not only to lose many of its prized possessions but the Sultan of Turkey was to be shorn of his powers. For Muslims worldwide he was not only ruler of the Turks but Caliph, the titular head of the Muslim world. So an attack on the Sultan and Turkey was an attack on all Muslims, and it was in defence of their faith that the Khilafat movement was launched. Gandhi shrewdly capitalised on this classic case of Islam in danger .

It is hard to disagree with Nirad Chaudhuri's conclusion that this was an "opportunistic" alliance on Gandhi's part; and it did not work. But to be fair to Gandhi he had little to work with as he sought Muslim allies. At this time some Muslims in India gave the impression that they saw India as a foreign land.

By the time Bose emerged from prison in 1927 with the Bengal Pact dead, attempts to forge a Hindu-Muslim alliance depended upon the success or otherwise of the Raj's plan to keep the different communities apart through separate electorates. The Raj had always divided Indians into separate races. The Indian Army had classified Indians into martial and non-martial races. For the limited elections to provincial assemblies, it now introduced divisions either by race, colour or caste. Each was given a certain number of seats. This was an early insight into the sort of mentality that was to later develop into the full-blown apartheid system in South Africa.

Through the late 1920s this issue dominated politics, particularly in Bengal where the Muslim leadership favoured separate electorates while the Swarajists, dominated by Hindus, stood for joint electorates. Bose, not surprisingly, was always opposed to separate electorates, and his decisive role on this question came when he sat on the committee formed by Motilal Nehru, which produced what was called the Nehru Report. It was meant to formulate a constitution for India and the whole exercise was an answer to Birkenhead's taunt that Indians were incapable of producing their own constitution. Indian political leaders spent much of 1928 making strenuous efforts to prove him wrong. In February and March of that year an all-party convention was held at Delhi, bringing together nearly every shade of political opinion. Throughout the summer Bose worked with Motilal Nehru, Tej Bahadur Sapru, a leading Indian liberal, and others in framing the report. The question of what kind of electorate a free India would have was obviously crucial.

Bose gathered information on elections to district boards in Bengal, although not all districts supplied him with the necessary facts, and some of the information was two years old. In his crucial letter to Motilal Nehru on 12 July 1928, he tried to show that when Muslims were in a majority, as they often were in many east Bengal districts, they could easily win elections defeating Hindus. So why did they need separate electorates? Bose's evidence formed Appendix C of the Nehru Report which concluded that there would be joint electorates everywhere, reservations of seats for Muslims only in Muslim-minority provinces and at the centre. This did not go down well with the Muslim leadership. Jinnah of the Muslim League, still a conciliator, tried to mediate between the Congress and the Muslim leadership but failed. The bulk of the Muslim leadership rejected the Nehru Report. This, says R.J. Moore, marked a decisive turning point. An agreed solution to the communal problem had been lost.

The historian Mushirul Hasan, in his study of the Nehru Report, has argued that secular politicians like Bose, Nehru and Gandhi were far too much influenced by Hindu communal leaders. These people moved back and forth from the Congress to unabashed communal organisations like the Hindu Mahasaba. Certainly on at least one issue Bose took the line of least resistance. Sometime earlier there had been lengthy debates in the Bengal Legislative Council about granting more rights to tenants who farmed the land Most of the landlords in Bengal were Hindus, most of the tenants Muslims, and the debate split along communal lines with the Muslims in the Council arguing for the tenants. Subhas Bose did not take part in the debate but he voted with his Swaraj party which, despite claiming to be neutral, came down in favour of the landlords.

On the Hindu-Muslim problem Bose had all the right instincts, but like Nehru, Gandhi and the others, was caught in a historical bind from which he could not escape. As the British were doing all they could to ensure the communities were kept divided, Bose, like all other Indian nationalists, was trapped.

For the moment the Hindu-Muslim problem was overshadowed by the wider political one: nationalist India had exhausted itself and the Congress was in a deep morass. Gandhi was still in one of his periodic retirements, and the Swaraj Party was in desperate trouble. Dyarchy, that much-trumpeted Raj experiment for educating Indians in parliamentary government, was dead; in fact it was, as Maurice Collins, a chief secretary of Burma, noted, a term of abuse. (He overheard one assistant township officer saying to another, "You are a dyarchy.') But in killing it the Swaraj Party had very nearly killed itself. Their tactics worked brilliantly in the short term but were impossible as a viable long-term strategy. As Gandhi had feared, many of their members were finding obstruction in council wearing and corrupting, and by mid-1926 the Swaraj Party of Das had split almost irretrievably into those who stayed in the assemblies and called themselves the Responsivist Party, and those following Motilal, who decided to walk out.

It was the Raj which provided the nationalists with unexpected assistance. The reforms of 1919 required that a review of the Indian political scene be made every ten years. The first was not due till 1929, but with the Conservatives in Britain uncertain of retaining power and Labour already a credible alternative, it was decided to send a commission from London long before the ten years were up.

On 8 November 1927 a seven-man team was announced; in an incredible act of racial arrogance the British government had decided that all seven would be whites. Lord Irwin, who by this time had replaced Reading as Viceroy, insisted that no Indians could be involved in deciding their own fates The seven wise white men were: Sir John Simon, Viscount Burnham, Lord Strathcona, Edward Cadogan, Stephen Walsh, Clement Attlee and Colonel George Lane-Fox. But after the names were announced Walsh resigned due to illness and was replaced by Vernon Hartshorn. Simon, a dry, humourless man who found it difficult to relate to people, was appointed chairman. A Liberal who had held high office, and would hold it again, he was at that time out of favour. Birkenhead offered the job to him while playing golf, and Simon jumped at the chance. The previous year Simon had come back from a visit to India and told Leo Amery that he was "very much impressed with the fact that the Oriental is not really adapted to our English scheme of Parliamentary Government." The other members were mostly nonentities. Burnham was a newspaper proprietor, Lane-Fox, a very unsuccessful Conservative minister of mines. Attlee, who had been a under-secretary to Walsh the secretary of state for war in the first Labour government was unknown, but the only one of the Simon seven to go on to greater things. India may have been the "jewel in the crown" and the basis of British power but for over a century, barring minor exceptions, mediocre British politicians presided over India's fortunes. Irwin's appointment illustrated this perfectly. Before he went to India he was known as Edward Wood, a large Yorkshire landowner and churchgoer who had become minister of agriculture. He was a close friend of the Conservative prime minister Stanley Baldwin, which secured him this prize job. To make sure he had the right status as Viceroy he was made a peer, taking the title Baron Irwin before he went to India.

Every shade of nationalist opinion in India opposed Simon and his men. Even the Indian Liberals described the commission as "a deliberate insult to the people of India". For Bose, the situation revealed a wider truth: He said:

> Our society affords numerous examples where a parent treats a 40-year-old son as a baby. No wonder it needs a Simon Commission to come from across the seas to shape the destinies of such a people.

On 3 February 1928 Sir John Simon and his colleagues arrived in India. The Congress had called for *hartal* on that day: strikes, demonstrations and effective closure of all shops and establishments. Bose had wanted a stronger demonstration, similar to the one during the Prince of Wales' visit seven years before. He was convinced that such a movement had tremendous possibilities, and in Calcutta he set out to prove it. That day Bengal witnessed massive demonstrations, a boycott of British goods and, inevitably, clashes with the police. By the time the commission returned for their second and more comprehensive visit in October 1928, political India was in turmoil. The lethargy and inertia of the earlier years had vanished.

But Gandhi was not impressed. He acknowledged the fervour aroused by Bose in Calcutta, but he still preferred to wait for the mysterious 'light' to guide him into action. He was aware of the very different feelings being voiced by Bose and Jawaharlal Nehru. In the Congress sessions of 1927 they had even passed a resolution for complete independence, although this was not yet established Congress policy. But the Mahatma was determined to prevent them from proceeding too rapidly. This was the first of the significant differences between the two men that came to dominate Indian politics in the ensuing years.

8

The Many Fronted War

On Christmas Day 1928, two days before the Congress met for its annual session in Calcutta, Bose welcomed the delegates to the third All-India Youth Congress. He was, he said, a pragmatist, and it was in this role that he wanted to analyse the effects of the two philosophies ruling in India at that moment, the school of Sabarmati, where Gandhi lived and preached; and the Pondicherry school of Aurobindo.

> The actual effect of the propaganda carried on by the Sabarmati school is to create a feeling and impression that modernism is bad, large scale production is evil, wants should not be increased and the standard of living should not be raised, that we must endeavour to the best of our ability to go back to the days of the bullock cart and that the soul is so important that physical culture and military training could well be ignored. The actual effect of the propaganda carried on by the Pondicherry school of thought is to create a feeling and an impression that there is nothing higher or nobler than peaceful contemplation. ... It is the passivism, not philosophic but actual, inculcated by these schools of thought against which I protest....In India we want today a philosophy of activism. We must be inspired by robust optimism. We have to live in the present and to adapt ourselves to modern conditions. We can no longer live in an isolated corner of the world.
>
> When India is free, she will have to fight her modern enemies with modern methods, both in the economic and in the political spheres. The days of the bullock cart are gone and gone forever. Free India must arm herself for any eventuality as long as the whole world does not accept wholeheartedly the policy of disarmament.

Verbal attacks on Gandhi were not uncommon. The majority of British officials saw him as a subversive (the shrewder ones thought he was a useful bulwark against a greater, more violently efficient movement), and many Indian collaborators feared his influence. Apart from M.N. Roy and the communists, nobody had so far attacked him from within the Congress. (Nehru's calls for socialism avoided any direct attacks on Gandhi, and when he occasionally erred he always apologised promptly.) Bose was the first openly to challenge him. He had moved a long way from muscular Hinduism, and would now steadily articulate the radical, activist alternative to Gandhi, long before it had become fashionable or even prudent. As Gandhi was later to acknowledge, "Subhas Babu will never pardon the loin cloth...He cannot help himself. He believes in himself and his mission.He must work it out as we must ours."

Two days after Bose had roused the young, Gandhi responded by clamping down the older, more seasoned Congressmen at the annual session. The subject of the debate was the Nehru Report. As we have seen, the final version provided for common electorates for all communities, retained the basically unitary form of government, and, most controversially, defined the goal of the Congress as "dominion status". Although Bose had gone along with the Nehru Report on this point he had made it clear that his goal was complete independence.

Even before Calcutta, Bose had strenuously opposed this back-sliding from the Madras Congress resolution favouring complete independence. In deference to his arguments, and to the feelings of the younger radicals, the statement of aims was qualified so that it would be adopted "without restricting the liberty of action of those political parties whose goal was complete independence". But when the report was presented to another session of the all-party convention at Lucknow in August 1928 Bose, Jawaharlal Nehru and the others seriously thought of opposing it. Finally they decided to record their feelings but not actually vote against the report. To emphasise their disagreement further, they decided to set up an Independence for India League. This, it appears, achieved little, largely because Jawaharlal could never galvanise it into action.

It is important to stress how revolutionary this demand for independence was for the Indian nationalists. Bose's guru Das did not mean independence when he called for Swaraj. In his declaration made in the spring of 1925, some months after Bose had been arrested and where Das had condemned violence, he had said, " We are determined to secure Swaraj and the poltical equality of India in terms of equality and honourable partnership in the Empire."

At the Calcutta Congress Das's old friend Motilal Nehru, fearing his report would be rejected, appealed to Gandhi. On Boxing Day 1928 Gandhi moved a resolution in the Subjects Committee to adopt the Nehru Report, with a warning to the British that if they did not respond by 31 December 1930 Congress would re-start non-cooperation, refuse to pay taxes and non-violently hinder the government. Bose and Jawaharlal Nehru argued strongly against him, and two days later Gandhi brought the deadline forward by a year. But even this was inadequate. Deciding on dominion status tather than independence, Bose was convinced, would be disastrous for the Congress, the national mood, international opinion and the younger, increasingly radical nationalists. What was worse, the resolution again contained no programme, and no plan of action. It was more of the search for the undefined Gandhi light. However, Gandhi had the numbers, and the Subjects Committee passed the resolution by 118 votes to 45. He also got Bose and Nehru to agree to support the motion in the open session.

But Bose was under intense pressure from his supporters to reverse this decision. The Bengal Provincial Congress of which he was President had called for complete independence and through the night preceding the open session many on the Congress Left, including revolutionaries, gathered support. Finally they confronted Bose. When he appeared reluctant to go back on his agreement with Gandhi, one of the delegates, in an emotional appeal, warned him of the consequences. Bengal's leader must speak for Bengal. Did he not realise the fervour for independence? If he failed Bengal now he would lose her. Bose relented, and in the open session moved an amendment to Gandhi's resolution. "Can you lay your hands on your breasts and say that there is a reasonable chance of getting dominion status within the period [of a year]? " As the delegates cried out, he continued:

> You can say, what do we gain by this resolution of independence? I say we develop a new mentality. . . . If you want to overcome the slave mentality you will do so by encouraging our countrymen to stand for complete independence.

There was prolonged applause after the speech, but Gandhi had the delegates firmly in control. His most potent weapon, as always, was personal. His supporters had asked him when he would return to politics, and in the Subjects Committee a few days earlier he had warned that if he did not get his way he would once again retire. The threat was an old Gandhi tactic: if you are not with me, you are against me. The Congress knew that without Gandhi there could be no successful movement against the British. Bose's amendment was lost by 973 votes to 1,350, with 48 abstentions. The arid green Park Circus *maidan* in Calcutta's teeming Muslim ghetto resounded with cries of "Mahatma Gandhi *ki jai!"* — "Long live the great-souled one!"'- and Gandhi was suitably scathing about Bose's *volte-face.*

But a different, wider-ranging expression of Bose's militancy had already found expression at the Park Circus *maidan.* At Congress sessions volunteers traditionally were organised to keep order and provide a guard of honour during the ceremonial functions. This time there was some dispute as to who would organise them. The East Bengal Jugantar group had a candidate, the Anushilan wanted their leader and the Calcutta-based Jugantar wanted their man. Eventually it was decided to ask Bose to do the job. Characteristically, he gave the operation a thoroughly military look. 2,000 volunteers were organised; all of them received a certain amount of military training and half of them wore uniforms, with specially designed steel-chain epaulettes for the officers. Nirad Chaudhuri was in Calcutta at that time and continues the story:

> Bose designated himself as its General-Officer-Commanding, G.O.C. for short, and his uniform was made by a firm of British tailors in Calcutta, Harman's. A telegram addressed to him as G.O.C. was delivered to the British General in Fort William and this was the subject of a good deal of malicious comment in the Anglo-Indian Press. Mahatma Gandhi, being a sincere pacifist, vowed to non-violence, did not like the strutting, clicking of boots and saluting, and he afterwards described the Calcutta session of the Congress as a Bertram Mills circus, which caused great indignation among the Bengalis

Some of the Bengalis were amused, too. As Bose discussed arrangements for the session and allocated jobs to the officers, Kiran Shankar Roy piped up with: "If we're all getting titles, can I be an admiral? After all, I come from East Bengal." The idea of an East Bengal navy, lost in the region's myriad waterways, was an old Bengali joke. For Bose, however, the volunteers were an expression of a certain side of his personality and a contemporary photograph captures this well. Bose is standing next to Motilal Nehru, who, as president, is taking the salute at the march-past. In his Harman-tailored uniform Bose looks like a thick-set, well-built Japanese general, stern and forbidding, but with a surprisingly mellow face. Next to him Motilal Nehru, in crumpled *shirwani* and *kurta,* looks bewildered and distinctly uncomfortable.

The volunteers were investigated by the intelligence department at the Viceroy's request; for once the Raj failed to penetrate their revolutionary origins, but in fact the Congress marked the birth of one of the most successful of the revolutionary groups in Bengal during the 1930s.

Bose was convinced that the key to a new India was the growing consciousness among the young. Those coming out of schools and colleges were full of worthy liberal ideas, but then had to face the realities of the Raj. Throughout 1928 and 1929 Bose travelled to various parts of the country to arouse and harness their enthusiasm and prepare them for the battle he knew was inevitable. He used such occasions to argue, to discuss and to organise his developing political ideas. He spoke of the recreation of a glorious Indian past, on the need for social restructuring, on the problem of harnessing mass consciousness, and on the economic reconstruction of India, always stressing his belief that democracy was as Indian as the Himalayas.

Bose's tour of the country had begun before the Calcutta Congress. In April and May 1928 he toured Bombay Presidency, a vast state then including present day Maharastra and Gujarat. He was eager to stress the links between Bengal and Maharashtra and after enthusiastic receptions in Nagpur and Bombay he headed for Poona where he was elected president of the Maharastra Provincial Congress. There he made one of the major and longest speeches of his career, setting out his philosophy on a wide variety of issues.

Bose pictured the beginnings of the coming struggle: the strikes, the *hartals,* the boycott of British cloth, goods and institutions, the flooding of British jails and, finally, the supplanting of the Raj by the Congress, whose offices and committees in districts, villages and city wards would become the parallel government of a free, sovereign, democratic India. Freedom, of course, was to him an end in itself:

> Freedom is as necessary for the human soul as oxygen is for the human lungs. . . . Freedom is the real *amrita*, the real nectar on this side of the grave.

He was not in favour of liberalised social behaviour. While he wanted, to sweep away all privileges and caste restrictions, and raise the status of women, Bose also said:

> I do not want the feminist movement of Europe and America to be reproduced in India. I have no love for bobbed hair and short skirts, on the other hand, I firmly believe that the women's movement in India will be inspired by our national ideals and traditions, and will follow its own distinctive course.

How this social reconstruction would come about was a question he had not yet considered. There were contradictions in his approach not least with regard to labour. Labour was organising itself with the help of the developing Indian and British communist movements. 1928 saw more strikes and man-hours lost than at any other period, exceeded only by 1946-47. Bose agreed that the Congress should ally itself with labour, but he argued:

> It would be disastrous in the highest degree if we were to launch on a class war while we are all bed fellows in slavery in order that we may afford amusement to the common enemy.

Only with class collaboration could freedom be won.

Bose played a role in the three significant strikes that took place in Bengal in 1928. Each one had its own characteristic and Bose played a different part in each of them. Eduard Lavelle in his study of Bose and the 1928 strikes has suggested that Bose had an elitist view of the uneducated worker and strived for too cosy an accommodation between labour and capital. This opinion seems excessively harsh. Trying to mobilise labour, yet keeping the nationalist movement together was not easy. The Raj took a very dim view of Bose's activities in the labour front and one secret report suggested that the trade union work in the Calcutta area "obviously represents a scheme to control oil and petrol supplies and road transport to Calcutta".

Bose could portray two of the strikes, concerning railway workers and jute workers, as a fight against the Raj and against foreign capital. This was easy as most of the jute mills were owned by Scots. When he addressed 6000 railway workers in Kharagpur he said that " those who were engaged in the sacred task of effecting the political emancipation of the country were also working for labour disputes because in disputes between workers and employees the latter had all the resources of the state behind them, while the Government in its efforts to put down the movement for freedom (was) aided by the employers".

The strike by the steel workers in Jamshedpur posed different problems. Here the employers were the Tata Iron and Steel Corporation, owned by Tata, the first Indian industrialist group, and now India's largest private corporation. However the top management of Tata was wholly European, employed at very high salaries.

The dispute concerned the recognition and status of the union. Some years earlier Bose's guru Das and Motilal Nehru had got the Tatas to agree to a union in return for help in trying to persuade the Raj to provide Tata with tariff protection against foreign competition. At Tata the clerks were often Bengalis, but the production workers came from other parts of India, usually Bihar and Orrisa. So the union's members were mainly clerks, and Bengali dominated. In 1928 a former Tata employee Manek Homi, like the owners was a Parsi, was brought in by some workers to represent them more effectively. Bose came to sort it out and was helped by management in this endeavour.

Bose's settlement did not please the workers. Homi, unhappy with the terms, formed a rival union and when Bose returned he was met with the workers' universal disapproval. As he tried to address them there were shouts of "maro" (hit him) and the deputy commissioner advised him not to speak. Bose refused to be intimidated. Flanked by police he calmed the workers. Later he would clash with the Tata chiefs for their failure to replace European managers with Indians.

It is clear that at this stage Bose was still some years from fully developing his economic views, but he was already far ahead of his political contemporaries. None of these, apart from Nehru and the small group of communists, were prepared to go beyond Gandhi's ideas, and his weekly missives in *Young India*.

But Bose's ideas were maturing fast, mirroring his ceaseless travel, described in a letter to Basanti Devi, "I am rushing along like a storm." He used his long journeys, often by train, criss-crossing the country, to develop and articulate his ideas.

In February 1929 Bose spoke at the Pabna Youth Conference in Bengal; in March in Rangpur, where he called for the abolition of the entire caste system or converting all castes into Sudras or Brahmins; in April in Assam; in June in Jessore and Khulna (both in Bengal); in July at Hooghly in Calcutta's twin city; in October in Lahore; and in December at Midnapore in Bengal and at Amraoti.

In October 1929, on his way back to Calcutta from his trip to Punjab, Bose wrote to Kalyani Devi:

> I have been shy by nature since my boyhood - and I continue to be so till today - in spite of the fact that I go about making speeches at public meetings. Whatever I may be - I am not a vain person - because I have nothing to be vain about. Where I surrender, I do with all my heart.

Just as his Bombay presidency tour the previous year had broken new ground, so this trip to Punjab in October 1929 confirmed his growing status as a national leader. As he had done in Maharashtra, when addressing the Punjab students, he linked Bengal to Punjab. The link, said Bose, was not merely through literature but also through the growing tide of revolution.

In April Bhagat Singh and Batukeshwar Dutt had thrown a bomb in the Legislative Assembly Hall in Delhi. No one was injured and Singh and Dutt were arrested. Bhagat Singh had been to Calcutta and worked on bomb making with Jatin Das, a Bengali Bose had known for years. Das was also arrested, and jailed with Singh and Dutt in the same Lahore prison. By the time Das joined them, Singh and Dutt were already on hunger strike, and Das refused to eat. In September Das died in jail. When his body was brought back to Calcutta, Bose, along with other Congress workers, kept an all-night vigil beside his coffin, and the next day led a funeral procession that was one of the biggest seen since the death of C.R.Das. In his address to Punjabi students, Bose spoke of the martial traditions of Punjab, of the heroic self-immolation of Das and the sacrifices of Bhagat Singh.

The Raj had started two court actions – one against the revolutionaries, known as The Lahore Conspiracy Case, the other against the Communists. The Meerut Conspiracy Case, directed against the Communists, was meant to stop the radicalisation of labour and went on for years. During his tour of Punjab Bose in addition to giving speeches in Lahore, Amritsar, Meerut and Delhi asked the Raj permision to visit both the Lahore conspiracy case prisoners and the jailed communists in Meerut. The Raj refused to let him meet the Lahore revolutionaries although he spent a few hours with the Meerut prisoners in what was to be the first of many visits. There was something ironic in this. The communists had been extremely critical of the Congress as a bourgeois organisation and scathing of both Jawaharlal Nehru and Bose. They said Nehru was a "tepid reformist", while "Mr Subhas Bose is a bourgeois and a ludicrous careerist." In his opening address in the Meerut case, the Raj's prosecutor made use of these words to try and create a rift between the communists and Bose and Nehru. This did not work. Whatever the communists had said of him, Bose was determined to show that they were part of the struggle to free India.

In the two years since his release from prison Bose had become a major figure across India. To audiences Bose was already a hero. The round cherub face, the horn-rimmed glasses, the Gandhi cap which covered encroaching baldness, the *chaddar* (a sort of wrap) just covering the *kurta,* all became a photographers' delight and almost a visible definition of nationalism. Unlike Gandhi, who could be strangely mystifying and full of esoteric advice, and Nehru, who was often cool and Olympian, Subhas was direct, clear and always practical.

The Raj witnessed the rise of Bose and Nehru with alarm. On 4 January 1929 Harry Haig, the home secretary, expressed his department's feelings in a note to the home member:

> When the idea of independence first emerged, the Home Department considered there was a reasonable prospect that it would be generally recognised as either visionary or dangerous and that it would not be br.ought forward as a practical issue. In the last few months, however, independence has ceased to be an academic ideal. We are faced now with a party who, it would seem, mean to translate it into a definite policy and to organise themselves with a view to attaining their object by force. Active steps are already being taken to develop organisations with this end in view. Youth movements and volunteer organisations are being discussed and started. I think there is no doubt that Jawaharlal Nehru and Subhas Chandra Bose do not mean to stop at words; they are preparing for action

The Raj had no intention of responding to Gandhi's call at the Calcutta Congress or of accepting the Nehru Report. Instead, in the great Raj tradition of selective but effective repression, Haig spelled out a solution:

> It would...probably be necessary in the first instance only to proceed against Jawaharlal Nehru and Subhas Chandra Bose. These two men are the undoubted leaders of the new movement. Successful prosecution of these two followed by adequate sentences may do a good deal to disorganise the movement, and would act as a warning to many who are at present somewhat half-heartedly dabbling with these ideas.

On 8 January 1929 it was decided to request Bengal to report on Subhas Bose and provide grounds for prosecution. Bengal itself soon concluded:

> The appeal of Subhas *Babu* and his other revolutionary associates was not made in vain and they are getting active support from the youth association in carrying out all the items of their programme - both open and secret. The All-Bengal Youth Association has introduced a form of vow for the boycott of foreign goods, particularly clothes, which its members must take and induce others to subscribe to, while repeated exciting and inflammatory speeches and constant secret propaganda have so changed the outlook of the minds of the youth of Bengal that they are no longer afraid to give vent to seditious and bloodthirsty feelings and to declare openly their demand for complete independence.

However, as one secret Bengal government note put it:

> [The] weakness of the whole revolutionary movement lies in the jealousies that

> permeate all the various branches. There is strong dissension among the political leaders. The attempt to amalgamate the two principal parties of revolution, the Jugantar and the Anushilan, have failed, and in every district the efforts of the group leaders are largely spent in trying to keep together and increase their own personal following.

The long-simmering fight between Bose and Sengupta had at last burst into the open. It was, of course, a reflection of the wider fight between Bose and Gandhi. Gandhi, as we have seen, never really controlled Bengal. The genuine Gandhians, the *khadi* crowd, were a small though tight minority in the Bengal Congress, living in their Gandhi-inspired *ashrams,* spinning yarn and fruitlessly trying to win the Bengal Congress. Sengupta, never a classical Gandhian, was by late 1929 their best bet. They enthusiastically took him up.

The quarrel also contained certain characteristic Bengali features, and in particular the regional factor. While Subhas' ancestral town of Kodalia was in West Bengal, Sengupta's Chittagong was the heart of East Bengal. Bengalis from the two sides of the state (now respectively part of India, and the separate nation of Bangladesh) have always maintained a steady but fierce rivalry. The subject of many inferior comedies, it has often prevented marriages or at least made them uncomfortable, and it is even enshrined in the soccer rivalry between Mohun Bagan and East Bengal, two of Calcutta's greatest football clubs, whose matches provide moments of collective Bengali hysteria. The West thinks the East is insensitive, brutish, ignorant, a collection of country rustics forever in need of education; the East thinks the West is sly, effeminate, shifty and living offf the dubious glories of Calcutta. Bose had general support all over Bengal, both in the East and in parts of the politically more conscious West, while Sengupta had strong support in Calcutta.

Predictably, Jugantar and Anushilan took opposite sides. As Sengupta prepared to fight Bose, he found ready allies among the Anushilan revolutionaries. If Bose, as the government claimed, was a leader of Jugantar, its support for him was natural. Besides, he was Das' natural heir, and Jugantar had worked happily with Das, while Anushilan had opposed Das and non-co-operation.

Perhaps, as some have suggested, the quarrel was fuelled by a personal quest for power by both men. No major policy differences seem to have marked the initial break. Until 1928 Bose and Sengupta had worked together. Bose had been president of the Bengal Congress, and Sengupta was busy with the Bengal Legislative Council and his practice at the Bar. That year Bose stood for mayor of Calcutta, but although the entire Congress united behind him he was not elected.

As the 1929 Bengal Congress elections approached, Bose's campaign was masterminded by Kiran Shankar Roy, an astute 'machine man' who lacked Bose's personal ambition but was his adroit supporter behind the scenes, particularly when it came to the enrolment of loyal party members. With his help, Bose gained a convincing majority, and was elected president. Sengupta alleged ballot rigging. The upshot was that the Bengal Congress split into two separate groups, both for the annual session in Lahore and during the civil-disobedience movementof the following year. Bose, snubbed at Lahore by Gandhi, announced (along with another outcast) the formation of the Congress Democratic Party. This breakaway group was, however, short-lived. Just before the Lahore Congress Bose wrote to Motilal Nehru, then Congress president, and announced his resignation, describing the Congress Working Committee as acting in " an illegal and unconstitutional manner". But after other Congressmen intervened Bose wrote to Motilal apologising, and saying he was like a father to him.

This whole episode provides interesting evidence of Subhas' discomfiture in factional politics. Meanwhile on the wider political front, the older Congress warriors were becoming tired and apprehensive of the radicals' activities. Through 1929 various Indian moderates, including Motilal, shuttled between the Raj and Gandhi to achieve a compromise. The Viceroy, Lord Irwin, a sincere Christian, was keen (as he later put it) to apply "the touch that carries with it healing and health". The whole debate revolved round the definition of dominion status. Birkenhead had declared "India was not the case of a daughter nation of our own creed and of our own blood." It is interesting to note that even within this racial parameter, Gandhi's *Ramrajya* could be comfortably reconciled with British ideas, since he sought a moral transformation. However the older Congressmen were now looking for ways that could somehow, produce a constitutional compromise the Raj could accept. Some months after the Calcutta Congress, on 24 March 1929, there was a meeting at the home of Tej Bahadur Sapru in Allahabad. Motilal Nehru met Sir Grimwood Mears, chief justice of the Allahabad High Court. Mears would later report to Irwin:

> The Pandit said to me: "Assume Dominion Status to consist of 1,2,3,4,5,6,7,8,9,10 ingredients. If in the discussion the least objection is taken to our having 2,5 and 7 we shall acquiesce readily. Once we get dominion status of any quality - in however limited a degree - we shall be content to prove ourselves responsible, and, then, readily, and without argument, be given other and wider powers as with the passing of time we prove ourselves capable.

Today it reads like such a modest demand, with Moital accepting that child India had still to prove itself to papa England that it was capable of taking charge. But even this was too much for the Raj in the 1920s. Irwin quickly saw that domestic British politics, with the ousting of the Tories and Birkenhead, had given him his chance, and on 31 October 1929 made his famous statement:

> It is implicit in the Declaration of 1917 that the natural issue of India's constitutional progress, as here contemplated, is the attainment of dominion status.

After the Simon Commission had reported, he promised a round-table conference to discuss its findings. This was not quite as revolutionary as the Raj made it out to be, or as its apologists have claimed. For Irwin dominion status was a remote prospect. His statement was a declaration of an ultimate policy - like, as he noted, a child being promised full family rights on adulthood. Paternalism and dependency were still part of the Raj's programme. The galaxy of Indian moderates – Gandhi , Motilal, Sapru, Malaviya, Vallabhbhai Patel, Moonje, Ansari, Sastri, Mrs Besant, Mrs Naidu – issued a joint declaration thanking the Viceroy for his sincerity, and promising all help in forming a dominion constitution for India.

But Bose and the younger elements of the Congress saw Irwin's declaration in a different light. The day after Irwin's statement Bose and 30 other Indian leaders met at Vallabhbhai Patel's Delhi house for a two-day conference. The meeting was attended by Jawaharlal Nehru who, at first, had indignantly refused to follow his father. But he could not overcome Gandhi, who had just made Jawaharlal president of the forthcoming Lahore Congress. Nehru accepted Gandhi's policy and then lamented to whoever would listen how broken-hearted he was.

For Bose all this was infuriating. He refused to sign this declaration, resigned from the CongressWorking Committee and issued a counter-manifesto. Dominion status, he said, was a myth, and a round-table conference would only be meaningful if it wwere a free meeting between representatives of India and Britain to discuss terms of British withdrawal.Bose's militancy undoubtedly had an effect on Gandhi, who began to see that independence could not be diluted. Though he had supported moderate positions, he had kept a sharp eye on the Congress organisation. Gandhi spoke to Jawaharlal Nehru about the need to keep it in good shape, and tried, as in 1920, to get the Muslim leaders behind him. He was concerned to do something to appease the increasingly restless young led by Subhas and Jawaharlal. Gandhi had realised that if he weaned Jawaharlal away he would weaken this youth axis. They were the future. He was 61, Motilal Nehru was 69 and fast fading, and none of the liberals had a mass following. If the young Nehru was aligned to him, he could be sure of half of that future; and Nehru, as Irwin shrewdly observed, knew that "his material interest and his political future depend, for the present at any rate, on his alliance with Mr Gandhi."

Just before the Lahore Congress convened Gandhi met Irwin. The Viceroy failed to give him any assurance about dominion status, and thus committed Gandhi to become an "independencewallah."When the Congress met in Lahore, Gandhi himself moved the resolution calling for complete independence.

Bose took malicious delight from the fact that he had urged this in Calcutta a year ago; but he was still unhappy because Gandhi had no plans to back up a civil-disobedience movement by setting up a parallel government. It seemed to be a case of "Leave it to the Mahatma - his inner light will come up with the right answer." In his amendment speech Bose argued that the Congress aim should be a parallel government and that it should start immediately with intensive mobilisation of youth, workers, and peasants. Swaraj must mean complete severance of the British connection and a harnessing of all the have-nots of India in a final struggle against alien rule.

"Hear, hear!" shouted his listeners (and the police spies dutifully made a note), but when the votes were taken the hands went up for Gandhi. Several other amendments were also defeated, and before the evening was over the air was rent with the usual cry of"Mahatma Gandhi *ki jai.*" As Sengupta had asked, "Do you have in India today any other leader who can lead the country to victory than Mahatma Gandhi?"

Bose's speech kept S.L.Sale busy. As legal remembrancer (law officer) of the Punjab, he had examined some of the conference speeches and come to the conclusion that Bose could be prosecuted. Nehru's speech was a rambling one about world movements and world co-operation, but Bose's object, he said, was to paralyse government and compel it to abdicate in favour of their complete independence. "Anything constitutional is abhorrent to Mr. Bose. In talking of a round table conference he makes it clear that his main objection is to the implication that the British Parliament has any right to interfere." He had, concluded Sale, violated several sections of the penal code. But when this opinion reached Delhi, Harry Haig wrote that it was "by this time rather ancient history".

In any case the Raj had at last dealt with Bose in a court of law, for only the second time in his life. On 23 January 1930 the Calcutta High Court had sentenced Bose and others to one year's rigorous imprisonment for the procession Bose had led in Calcutta in August 1929 in protest against government repression of revolutionaries and political prisoners. It had been a characteristic Bose-led demonstration: volunteers wearing uniforms, and Bose himself leading a whole contingent of marching, singing, placard-carrying volunteers. He had been arrested immediately afterwards and released on bail. Even after sentencing him, the magistrate was prepared to grant bail if Bose and the others would promise on their honour "to lead ordinary lives of private citizens". Bose contemptuously refused the offer.

At Lahore, the Congress had decided to celebrate 26 January as 'Independence Day' to mark its conversion to the goal of full independence. That was only three days away . There were were bound to be celebrations, and such promises were foreign to Bose anyway. Watched by a large crowd, Bose, Kiran Shankar, Roy and ten others were taken away from the court compound in police vans, amidst resounding cries of "Long live revolution", to the Alipore Central Jail. (Subsequently, after an appeal filed in the High Court, the sentences were reduced to nine months.)

Jail was a relief after the political intrigues, the bitter quarrels and the factional disputes of the last two years, and Bose soon settled down to a routine. He tried to keep fit, read voraciously and was the centre of the inevitable political debates and discussions with colleagues. He also tried to organise political education for the non-political prisoners; and he partitioned off a corner of his cell for prayer and meditation.

Gandhi now commenced the movement Bose had long argued and pleaded for; civil disobedience. It was the second of the three great national movements launched by the Mahatma. The first, as we have seen, had encouraged Bose to reject the ICS and to join Das and the freedom struggle. The third, the "Quit India" movement, would be launched when Bose was in Germany. The second was undoubtedly Gandhi's most spectacular. It came close to unnerving the government. Years later British officials and businessmen would recollect with anger "the reprehensible administrative breakdown"; and at its height even Bose would wonder and reflect on Gandhi's political genius.

Like everybody else, Bose was confused by the Mahatma's first moves. Gandhi first wrote to the Viceroy promising not to start his civil disobedience campaign if he carried out certain social reforms such as total prohibition and the abolition of the tax on the making of salt. There was no mention of dominion status, let alone independence. How, Bose wondered, could social reform achieve that? But Gandhi had shrewdly seized on a subject that he knew could bridge the elitist preoccupation with independence and the mass of the poor's struggle to survive. For centuries Indians had panned sea-water to make salt. Now the alien British government had taxed it and restricted manufacture to salt-works. This for the poor was the true meaning of alien rule. As Irwin contemptuously rejected Gandhi's letter, the old man set out on his historic march to Dandi on the sea, 240 miles from his *ashram* near Sabarmati. It was a carefully organised route and all along the way Gandhi attracted support. On 6 April 1930 Gandhi took up a lump of mud and salt from the beach near Dandi, and nationalist Indians were swept up into the civil-disobedience movement. Before the year was out 60,000, possibly 90,000, had been jailed, and the government had to make do with temporary huts to house inmates. There was a desperate response by the police, including firing on unarmed crowds, and, as correspondents reported, sickening use of clubs (*lathis*). By the summer Irwin was forced to concede that he was in difficulties.

Bose was to experience some of this violence. He always suffered in prison, but so far there had been no intimidation or torture. Now, for the first and only time in a British jail, he was the subject of an assault. It is still not clear how or why it took place. It may have been the eccentricity of the superintendent or, more likely, the inevitable result of repressive machinery at full throttle. The superintendent, Major Som Dutt, was fond of using Pathans from the north-west frontier to straighten out the young rebels crowding his jail. On the 22 April 1930 the Pathans, notorious for their ferocity, suddenly encountered spirited resistance. Dutt decided on a show of force, and got the Anglo-Indian prisoners to attack the "politicals". Bose and the others rushed out of their cells to find out what the commotion was all about. There was a struggle, and Bose was knocked unconscious. The news quickly spread through Calcutta, and a crowd surrounded Alipore Central. Though the government would not concede an inquiry, Dutt was transferred.

Bose was still president of the Bengal Provincial Congress, and tried to exercise his position from prison. The jailer had become a friend, and allowed Bose to smuggle out messages and letters through three Anglo-Indian youths, who passed them to Asoke, Sarat's eldest son. But while there was unprecedented enthusiasm for the civil disobedience movement, the Bengal Congress was still split. In April Sengupta was arrested and brought to Alipore Central. He was given a cell next to Bose. Attempts at a reconciliation were ruined by the rivalry between the groups in the Calcutta Corporation and what Bose saw as Sengupta's determination to cling to office.

While the two men were in jail their supporters fought for the job of mayor. Having served five terms Sengupta did not stand again, and Bose was nominated. Election as mayor was the crowning point of Subhas' love for the Calcutta Corporation. Bose was released from prison on 23 September 1930 and sworn in as mayor the next day. It was a moment of celebration with garlands, flowers and an inaugural speech noteworthy for one passage in particular:

> I would say that we have here in this policy and programme a synthesis of what modern Europe calls socialism and fascism. We have here the justice, the equality, the love which is the basis of socialism, and combined with that we have the efficiency and the discipline of fascism as it stands in Europe today.

Bose's power for good as mayor was limited. The corporation was hemmed in by the wider administration of the Raj. And leading a faction-ridden Congress was not easy. But Bose did try to improve the working of the Corporation and also to break the economic stranglehold British business had in the city. This was through the Swadeshi League, which tried to encourage more Indians to consume Indian-made products. Bose also enjoyed the ceremonial occasions which involved hosting receptions.During his time as mayor there were also moments when he and the British came together and he implicitly acknowledged western help in awakening India. This came in December 1930 when his old Alma Mater Scottish Church College celebrated its centenary. His former principal introduced him as one of the most famous students of the college. Bose responded with a speech in which he said:

> Twenty two centuries have gone by since Asoka, the greatest missionary-monarch known to history, sent forth to the western world India's inspiring message of Dharma. In the days that followed the flow of ideas changed channel. Then, when missionaries of an Oriental religion brought from the West, along with the message of Christ, the message of Intellectual Emancipation, an Era of Renaissance dawned on our ancient land, a spirit of enquiry permeated our intellect and vitalised our minds.

Once elected, Bose did not forget the wider needs of the Congress, and he toured Bengal incessantly. The Raj, as ever, tried to make life as difficult as possible. He once was arrested and jailed for seven days for trying to enter Malda in south Bengal.

Bose was keen to prepare for a resumption of the civil-disobedience movement, which had not so much stopped as slowly wound down, for Gandhi's incarceration had led to renewed attempts at a compromise between the Congress and the Raj. As the peace efforts gathered momentum Bose set about celebrating Independence Day on 26 January 1931.

Charles Tegart, the police commissioner, had been sent intercepted copies of Congress Party instructions regarding the celebrations. He was horrified that resolutions recording the suffering and sacrifice of the freedom fighters, cataloguing the police brutalities and re-affirming the goal of independence should be heard on the central *maidan* in Calcutta, virtually within earshot of Government House. He was determined not to allow the demonstration, for thousands would have flocked to the *maidan,* traffic would have been blocked and the control of the city would have been handed over to the Congress. But he feared the consequences of a clash with Bose, and on the morning of the 26th sent one of his officers, Pulin Chatterjee, to try and dissuade him. Bose replied, "Tell your boss I will break the law," and strode off.

Tegart's massive police arrangements deterred the crowds until mid afternoon when Subhas led 500 men out of the town hall on to Corporation Street. This led directly to that part of Chowringhee which was opposite the Octroleny monument. Singing and shouting lustily, Bose marched his followers to their goal. Just as they reached Chowringhee they were stopped, and Bose was shown a copy of an order by the commissioner. Bose brushed aside the policeman and, gripping the Indian national flag even more tightly, kept on marching towards the monument. The police attempted to snatch the flag. Bose resisted, and he was *lathi (charged)* and badly bruised, suffering contusion over the right side of the forehead and the back of the head; his right arm and clothes were liberally splattered with his own blood. The following day, having been provided with neither food or medical attention, he appeared before the Chief Presidency Magistrate. As a non-co-operator he refused to plead or take part in the proceedings, and was quickly found guilty and sentenced to six months' rigorous imprisonment.

Subhas had watched the launch of the civil-disobedience struggle from jail. He now watched from jail its denouement. A meeting between Gandhi and Irwin led to the Delhi Pact, in which Gandhi promised to call off the civil disobedience movement and take part in a round-table conference, while Irwin agreed to release all political prisoners arrested in connection with the movement, to withdraw the emergency ordinances, to allow people who lived within a certain distance of the sea to make salt, and to permit peaceful propaganda in favour of prohibition and against foreign cloth. But there was no mention of *Purna Swaraj* (independence) the great issue over which they had fought.

Bose saw the pact as a betrayal, and believed that Gandhi had acted under pressure from his rich backers, who had panicked, and the increasingly powerful Congress Right. In March, after his release from jail, he visited Gandhi in Bombay and was further depressed to find that the inquiry on police atrocities that had been a central plank in the Congress demands, had been voluntarily thrown away by the Mahatma. But what could Bose do? Gandhi was a hero, a saintly man who had discussed, debated and signed an agreement with the Viceroy on seemingly equal terms. The Congress session which followed the signing of the Delhi Pact re-affirmed Gandhi's power, and the Left just disappeared. The Viceroy gleefully reported: "Later opposition of Subhas absolutely collapsed".

Bose's subsequent speech to the militant socialist Punjab youth organisation Naw Jawan Bharat Sabha is interesting as one of his first specifically detailed references to a socialist India. Freedom was an absolute necessity, but it must include freedom from social, economic and political bondage: a full-fledged socialist republic. Class collaboration was no longer sufficient.

Bose was still out in the cold. During his talks with Irwin, Gandhi had said to the Viceroy that Bose, then in prison, should be in the talks, "He is my opponent and will denounce me; still if he wants to attend, we must give him a chance to do so." Yet Gandhi once again kept him off the Working Committee. This was an astonishing situation for the president of a powerful provincial Congress committee to be in; and the messy fight with Sengupta reached its unsatisfactory climax. On his return to Calcutta from the session at Karachi, Bose made an appeal for peace. He declared that he was prepared to give up the post of mayor and hoped everybody would now unite behind a single Congress committee. Sengupta was unconvinced and continued to organise his own rival Congress.

By June 1931, when the outlying districts started voting for the delegates who would represent them on the provincial executive and the AICC, Sengupta was convinced that he would not win without central support, and he appealed to his patron Gandhi. Bose and Sengupta met at least once but only succeeded in worsening the situation, and the Congress president, Vallabhbhai Patel, deputed M.S. Aney to examine and report on the situation in the province. When he arrived in mid-July there followed a flurry of meetings, talks about settlement, talks about the talks, and yet more conflict (even at times, violent disruption of rival meetings). The struggle affected everything, including organising relief from the floods that were then devastating Bengal.

W.S. Hoskyns, Chief Secretary of the Bengal government, noted with pleasure:

> The Corporation is in bad odour; the rows organised by the followers of Mr Sengupta and Mr Subhas Bose in the Council Chambers of the Corporation have disgusted all decent opinion...Moderate Indian opinion is perhaps

stronger now against the party responsible for civil disobedience than it has been for a long time.

Hoskyns' satisfaction increased as he watched the reaction to the Hijli firings. The Hijli detention camps housed some 2,000 of the most resolute of the freedom fighters of Midnapore, where civil disobedience had been especially strong. On the night of 16 September some fracas had developed and the jail police had shot two men dead. The news convulsed Bengal, and for Bose it was yet another illustration of the failure of the Delhi Pact. He rushed to Hijli, brought the dead bodies back to Calcutta and led nearly 100,000 mourners to the burning *ghat* for the cremation.

The provincial Congress committee had arranged a condolence meeting after the funeral. As Bose was about to leave for it he heard that Sengupta was going to address a rival meeting at the same time. In one of the quick, emotional gestures that characterised his politics, Bose telephoned Sengupta, and cancelled his own meeting. He also announced his resignation from the presidency of the Bengal Provincial Congress Committee. This was a moment for unity, he declared. Unity through negotiations had failed; his own reconciliation efforts had got nowhere. He had done no wrong - he had run the Congress according to the rules. He had been thinking of resigning for some time, and Hijli had convinced him. Then, in a typically extravagant statement, he concluded, "If Bengal can be saved as a result of my self effacement I shall be happy to pay that price and I shall feel more than amply rewarded if my countrymen will in exchange give me a corner in their hearts."

Sick since his civil-disobedience imprisonment, Sengupta now went off to Europe to recover his health and possibly consult Gandhi, who had just left for a round-table conference in London. He had spent the last few years either in jail or trying to recover. On his return from England he was again jailed and died in a Ranchi jail in July 1933. Bose remained the *de facto* leader of the Bengal Congress, the winner by default.

Gandhi's insistence on travelling alone to Europe had disturbed Bose. He would have preferred a proper delegation and, of course, a genuine round-table conference concerning independence negotiations. Gandhi's behaviour in England appalled him: there was too much of the naked fakir – living in the East End, being photographed with Chaplin – and not enough of the insurrectionary leader. In Bose's view the only good thing about Gandhi's visit was his meeting on the way back with Mussolini, who Bose thought was "a man who really counts in the politics of modern Europe"

What worried Bose even more was that these fruitless months of negotiations had dulled the Congress appetite for mass action and provided time for the government to prepare counter measures. The government was not serious about the Delhi Pact. The flamboyant Red Shirt movement of the North-West Frontier Province, led by Khan Abdul Gaffar Khan, was still being ruthlessly suppressed and, in Bengal, Chittagong was under virtual martial law. Bose was arrested for trying to investigate events in Dacca, where, on 28 October 1931, the district magistrate had been shot and wounded. Unable to find the culprits, the police laid siege to a considerable area of Dacca. Houses were raided, valuables and documents seized, and anybody who was remotely a nationalist was apprehended or harassed. Bose presided over a huge public meeting at Calcutta's Albert Hall to protest at this display of police *zoolum* (repression) and set off with two companions to make an on-the-spot survey. As his steamer arrived at Narayangunge, a sub-divisional town on the way to Dacca, he was met by police who refused to allow him to disembark. When he eventually did leave the boat, he was taken to the police station, Ellison, the police superintendent, protesting all the time that he was not arresting him but merely restraining him. Ellison incensed Bose by referring to him as Subhas – a familiarity that was allowed only to friends, and certainly not to the officials of the Raj. "Do you mind? I am Subhas Babu or Mr Bose to you." Ellison gracelessly yielded, but would not allow him to enter Dacca, and put him on a Calcutta-bound steamer.

Bose tried again to enter Dacca, this time from the north. At Tejgaon he was arrested under section 144 of the Criminal Police Code, an order promulgated at times of civil disorder. He was taken to Dacca Jail. Vallabhbhai Patel had begged him not to get arrested, but Bose had been unable to see how to avoid it. "Self-respect, manhood and the rights of the people have been trampled underfoot," he declared as he was led away, "and it is the duty of the people to vindicate them." He was no longer head of the Congress, and, if the Congress did not act, the people would have to organise themselves.

In the past, Bose's remarks had got him into trouble with the Congress High Command. In October he had told the Bengal Provincial Students' Conference that the Congress leaders did not seem interested in helping Bengal fight government repression. Patel had written to Jawaharlal Nehru protesting his innocence, and Nehru came to Calcutta and lectured Bengal rather superciliously on the need for party unity. For Subhas nothing could have been more galling, and he issued a statement rebutting Nehru. It was the first public indication of the growing tension between the two. Bengal had done much, he said, who was Nehru to lecture the provinces? Bengal had led India in the past, and it would do so again in the future. Though he spoke at the annual Bengal provincial conference as an ordinary Congressman, his definition of the problems as "to check the progress of repressive policy and to organise the scattered national forces" was quickly accepted. The provincial Congress decided that the "government had practically ended the Gandhi-Irwin pact", and that it was now time to resume the *satyagraha* campaign. Until the Congress officially accepted this there should be an intensification of the boycott of foreign goods and proper no-rent campaign.

However, Bose needed time. He did not think any of the Bengal districts were ready for civil disobedience; in another three or four months things might be looking up. But time was the one thing the Raj was determined not to give the national movement. Bengal was already under Ordinance Raj, as the Indians liked to put it. On 30 November the provincial government had secured the Viceroy's permission to promulgate yet another ordinance that allowed it extraordinary powers to deal with the growing revolutionary movement: trial by special tribunals, imposition of collective fines, internment. Bose and his activities had weighed on the government mind. The Viceroy had read with alarm Bose's speech to the Bengal provincial conference, and referred to it in his telegram to the secretary of state on 19 December 1931, in which he confessed the total lack of support for government policies.

But the Bengal ordinances were only the visible teeth of a policy that had been in preparation since the Gandhi-Irwin pact. It would soon lead to a second civil-disobedience movement, attracting even greater repression. The common historical view is that this was due to the change of Viceroy. Irwin had retired and had been replaced by the Marquess of Willingdon, an old India hand who had been previously been governor in Bombay and Madras. Though this undoubtedly played a part, Willingdon was also responding to pressures from the British officials and the expatriate community in India. Long before Willingdon moved into Irwin's vice regal palace, his officials had decided that if another civil disobedience movement arose, they should have the means to crush it. The 1930 movement had scared them badly, and they were determined not to be caught napping.

9

Re-enter Revolution

The revolutionary movement had always closely paralleled the Gandhian one, and in early 1930 it underwent a remarkable revival. As Gandhi reached Dandi and the sea it had, in what the government called "an amazing coup", very nearly succeeded in liberating one of British India's most important centres: Chittagong. There, on the night of 18 April 1930, 62 young Indians seized the police and auxiliary forces' armouries and set up a provisional revolutionary government. Although the British moved swiftly to recapture the city, this marked the start of a remarkable wave of revolutionary violence. No police officer, whether Indian or British, was immune from attack; bombs exploded in government offices, and on 8 December 1930 three men coolly entered Writers' Building and shot and killed the inspector general of police.

Occasionally plans misfired. On 25 August 1930 two young revolutionaries, Amiya Sen and Dinesh Chandra Mazumdar, stood exactly opposite each other across Calcutta's Dalhousie Square and lobbed bombs at a car carrying Tegart. Mazumdar's bomb hit Sen, killing him instantly; Sen's bomb hit Mazumdar, wounding him severely. Tegart drove past unhurt. But by the end of 1930 British officials were horrified at their losses: eleven killed, twelve injured, with ten non-officials killed and fourteen injured. The revolutionaries' losses were greater, with 26 fatalities and four injured.

There is no evidence that Bose was directly involved in the Chittagong uprising, but there is little doubt he was the hero to the men who planned it. The volunteer force he had used in Calcutta was the model used to provide the cover to recruit and train the India Republican Army.

After the uprising the judiciary were uneasy. One judge trying some revolutionaries warned that immediately after giving judgement he would leave "the country without leave", and Nirad Chaudhuri, walking the streets of Calcutta, felt a wave of what he called "'unbelievable hysteria" sweeping the British community in Bengal. Anglican clergymen slept with revolvers under their pillows, Englishwomen were terrified of contracting venereal disease from suspicious-looking handkerchiefs left in tramcars, and police officers thought they were seeing the beginnings of an Irish-type revolutionary movement. By mid-1931 intelligence officials were asking for "a freer hand" if "disaster" were to be averted. By the end of the year this free hand was, perhaps inevitably, translated into the need to arrest Bose. On 7 December 1931 W.S. Hoskyns forwarded to the Home department in Delhi a 75-page document about Subhas. This was an alleged record of almost all Bose's words and deeds between January 1930 and October 1931, as reported by government moles in the nationalist groups. It portrayed Bose as financier (though the government believed this was more the work of Sarat), as friend, as confessor and as father-figure.

The authorities in Bengal, fearful of the consequences of arresting Bose within its own borders, insisted he be arrested outside. This meant he would have to be detained under Regulation III of 1818, which required that the evidence of the moles be reviewed by two judges. After much deliberation Delhi thought the evidence would prevail, a decision helped by the fact that it had its own mole in the Congress Working Committee, 'SS', who reported that "Subhas Bose . . . pleaded the cause of terrorism", at one meeting at least. On 22 December 1931, after joint discussions between the Viceroy's Executive Council and the Bengal government, Delhi posted the warrant of arrest to the Bengal government. It now waited for Bose to leave Bengal and activate the carefully constructed machinery.

In early December Bose travelled to Bombay for a session of the Working Committee scheduled for Gandhi's return. The young, he told Gandhi, would no longer tolerate useless talk and dilatory tactics, and he urged him to take careful note of what was happening in Bengal, where the coming shape of the Raj's repression was clear. His militant urgings were given an unexpected edge by Willingdon's refusal to see Gandhi except on unacceptable conditions. By the morning of New Year 1932 Bose had at last persuaded Gandhi to declare that, if the Viceroy could not go back on this, the Delhi Pact would be over and civil disobedience resumed. Willingdon telegraphed that he could not see Gandhi under the threat of civil disobedience, and the Congress was at last made to realise that the phoney peace was over.

The next day Bose, eagerly anticipating the coming war, started on his way back to Calcutta. As the train stopped at Kalyan the Bengal police, already on board, entered his compartment, served him with a warrant. Two days later he was taken to Seoni Jail.

Seoni was a sub-jail with no electricity and few amenities, and it was hardly surprising that within a few weeks Subhas fell ill. His state of mind was not helped by the government's arrest of Sarat on 4 February on the grounds that he provided Subhas' finance. Sarat, too, was brought to Seoni. By mid-April Subhas' health had so alarmed the superintendent of Seoni that he asked for Subhas to be transferred. Bose had pains round his waist, digestive problems, and had lost weight, perhaps because of a diet of Horlicks and chicken soup.

Calcutta would have been the logical place for some medical treatment, but the Bengal government would not hear of it, and on 30 May Subhas was transferred to Jubbalpore Military Hospital. But this could only be a stop-gap and, as in 1927, the government of India began to shop around for a suitable jail. No government, however, seemed prepared to risk him, with the Punjab government frankly acknowledging that "Subhas Chandra Bose has always had a disturbing effect on Lahore students, who always turn out in large numbers whenever he visits the Punjab", and that, if brought to the Punjab, "his stay in Lahore should be as short as possible".

Finally, after a great deal of arm-twisting from the government of India, the Madras government accepted him. On 16 July Subhas was transferred to Madras. Medical examinations by August showed that he was suffering from tuberculosis, which could only be completely cured in Switzerland. But Delhi, remembering the turmoil such a suggestion had caused during Bose's previous period in jail, decided upon a sanatorium in Bhowali. But the sanatorium closed down for winter, and so he was moved to Lucknow.

At this point yet another medical board recommended a stay in Calcutta's prestigious Medical College, on the way to Switzerland. Though the Bengal government reacted with predictable hostility to any stay in Calcutta, it was prepared to agree to Switzerland without asking for any pre-conditions. On 12 January 1933 a passport was issued for Bose's travel to Europe. It was endorsed only for France, Switzerland, Italy, Austria and Denmark. Travel to Britain and Germany was expressly excluded.

It was another month before Bose left India, the time taken up by wrangles with the government. He unsuccessfully sought time to settle his affairs before leaving. He wanted to visit his parents, but the Bengal government declined to allow him to visit Calcutta, and they were too old and sick to travel to him. With Sarat in jail, it was Sarat's wife, Bibavati, who was really managing affairs, and Subhas thought it only reasonable that he should be allowed to meet her frequently. With the government ready to exile him without paying for his exile he had to raise the cash for going to Europe, estimated at 15,000 rupees (£1,200). But the government limited the interviews and insisted all conversation between Subhas and his relations had to be in English, in the hearing of police officers. Subhas was outraged, and in several thunderous letters to the Home Department in Delhi he said the government, by "kicking him about like a football", had ruined his health, and that he "scented trouble" in the way the government was restricting his passport. Finally, just before he left for Europe, he was allowed to meet Sarat and some relations in Jubbalpore Jail without humiliating restrictions. He was still not allowed to see his aged parents.

Bose was still under custody on 23 February 1933 as the Bombay police escorted him to his ship, the *Gange.* Bose was carried on board on a stretcher, and only released from custody when the ship left Indian waters. This produced a final angry letter to the government. His mood of anguish and suffering was more accurately reflected in a statement that defensively acknowledged help from friends who had enabled him to put the money together. He was doubtful if even Europe would restore his health. As the boat neared Venice he wrote to Dilip confessing that he had taken to *tantra*, an esoteric Indian philosophic system, in order to rekindle his spirits.

Part Three

EXILE

In international economics and international politics the Indian question is allowed to be treated as a domestic question between England and India in which the world at large has no right to interfere. But India should not take this position lying down. . . . India is entitled to bring her case before the bar of world opinion. ... In this connection I desire to urge upon my countrymen the dire necessity of appointing accredited representatives of India in foreign countries. . . . Even if representatives cannot be sent out from India owing to lack of funds there are Indians abroad who would be prepared to work even for love. The more one lives in Europe, the more one realises the great want of propaganda on behalf of India in foreign countries. And without international propaganda, India cannot possibly establish herself in the eyes of the world.

Subhas Bose, *in a letter from Vienna,*
7 June 1933

10

Ambassador With A Cause

In March 1931 M.N. Roy, one of the great romantic figures of the Indian political scene, had met Bose and had a long political talk with him. At the end of it Roy returned to his friends and said of Bose, "He is full of *Bharat Mata* [Mother India] nothing else."

It is a damning anecdote, and for many the most revealing insight into Bose's character: that of an ultra-nationalist who had no time for anything else, and who despite all his years in Europe never developed a proper world outlook. Bose's eclecticism, or what one of his more uncritical supporters has called his rejection of monotheism (the one path to salvation), made him pursue any movement that would help the cause of Indian freedom. Making the Indian peninsula into a goddess, as Dilip Roy puts it, led him into strange pathways, and occasional dead ends. Although consideration of *Bharat Mata* always remained the final arbiter, he was constantly aware of what he was doing and where he was going. He was clear, for instance, about the dangers of Nazism, and his analysis of Hitler's movement was more penetrating than that voiced by some of its more celebrated enemies. He believed, however, that a slave India could not afford the luxury of choosing friends. India had to make do with what was offered. This certainly made him blind to the fact that Nazism would have been an even greater scourge of India than the Raj. His pragmatism ran close to opportunism.

Bose had always stressed the need to get away from colonial attachments to Britain. He felt the English sedulously cultivated these attachments. He felt too few Indians visited Berlin, Paris or Rome – they always went to London.

His present trip on the Italian ship *Gange* did much to erase the starchy memory of the P&O liner on which he had sailed previously. The Italians fussed over him. The Italian government had given special instructions to the agents of Lloyd Treistino to make sure Bose was well received. In Venice, where he arrived on March 6, there was a large press contingent to interview him. On the jetty he was met by his nephew Asoke, Sarat's eldest son, who had been in Munich for the previous year and a half studying medicine. Although it was wet and foggy he enjoyed the ride in the motorboat that brought him to the Royal Daneli Hotel.

Bose knew he needed to make sure his name was not forgotten. He was determined to make his views known to the media. This meant the news agencies. The very next day he was writing to a friend in India assessing the different news agencies and how they treated him. Reuters, the British agency, had interviewed him only once, and could be expected to shun him. Bose debated the rival merits of the Associated Press and the Free Press.

By March 8 1931 he was in Vienna where he gave more interviews. Soon after he had settled in at Dr Fuerth's sanatorium, his room became the centre of Indian activity as students and visitors constantly dropped in. And there were Nilima and her friends, whose presence marked perhaps the most significant change that Dilip had wrought in Subhas.

Before his departure for Europe, Bose had requested letters of introduction from several people. Gandhi had informed him, just as his ship was to sail, that he could not provide him with one, Tagore had given him a very cursory one. Only Dilip had recognised his need to widen his contacts, particularly with desirable female company. One of the many westerners who, dissatisfied with their own culture, turn to the east, Nilima had been born Heddy Fullop-Muller, and was a distinguished opera singer. The wife of a well-known Austrian writer, she had fallen under the spell of Aurobindo. After meeting Bose she was soon writing to Dilip about this *wunderbar* friend of his, about Bose's *Seelensgrosse* (greatness of soul), his humility and his unspoilt, child-like innocence. Nilima guided Subhas into the right social and literary circles of Vienna. Although the relationship was strictly platonic, Subhas' armour was breached. The result was that, despite his travels in Europe over the next three years, Vienna remained his headquarters. It was the city he came to know well, Austrian politics became something of a speciality for him, and it was the place that was to provide the one and only true love of his life.

Bose recognised that exile had ended a chapter of his life. But he was not a natural exile. He missed India deeply, and although Vienna and the workings of city governments in Europe fascinated him, he pined for home. As he wrote to Satyendra Nath Majumdar:

> Today I am living in a foreign land across the seas in the city of Vienna, but my mind and entire being are with you... Where I have taken my stand today, I am alone, friendless ..I am walking along, that vast expanse, like a lonely traveller singing only that song: "If nobody harkens to your call, march ahead alone".

Bose's spirits were further lowered because he was not happy with Dr Fuerth's diagnosis that the main problem lay not in the lungs but in the abdomen, particularly the gall-bladder and the duodenum. When, by the first week of March 1933, there had not been much progress, he wrote to the secretary of state for India requesting extension of his passport facilities to Germany and England. He had other reasons for wanting to visit England as well. The India Office had expected his request. Their position was admirably minuted by WJ. Clauson on 25 March:

> On the whole, therefore, it might be best to say straightaway that Bose can go to Germany and leave it at that. If subsequently he insists on coming to England, it is, in fact, quite impossible to prevent him, as a British subject, from landing: but we must not encourage him.

On 8 May the India Office authorised the grant of passport facilities to Germany. But the chief passport officer was told to instruct the British consul in Vienna to take "special care ... to add an endorsement for Germany only. It is particularly desired to prevent Mr. Bose from coming to this country." Although, as one official noted, "the withholding of an endorsement for the UK is nothing but bluff. Any holder of a British passport is admitted to this country." Would Bose call the bluff? He seemed to be prepared to do so when, in June 1933, he was invited to preside over the third Indian Political Conference, to be held in Blackfriars Hall, London. Bose accepted and got James Maxton, a Scottish Communist friend of India, to plead his case. The India Office had watched his increasingly frequent political announcements from Vienna with alarm, and Maxton's letter merely confirmed Clausen's suspicion that an application was due:

> It is abundantly clear, therefore, that Bose does not want to come to London on grounds of health but for a political purpose. Last month, on the certificate of a Vienna doctor we gave him passport facilities for Germany - a sanatorium in the Black Forest. His health could not possibly demand a visit to London.

To Clausen's and the government's relief Bose did not call the bluff and took the secretary of state's reply to Maxton as a refusal. His speech was read out to a packed, cheering Blackfriars Hall. It was a milestone in his developing political philosophy. Ever since the civil-disobedience movement had been crushed, he had been thinking of a new approach. Now he had arrived at some conclusions. There could, he said, be no compromise with the British, because nothing united Britain and India. Everything divided them: social and cultural factors, and above all economic ones; India was a raw-material producer, Britain a raw-material consumer. Britain in India was a well-fortified alien fortress surrounded by the great mass of Indian people. The fortress could not survive if the people turned hostile. This had happened to a great extent; now the final push was required: economic blockage and armed assault. The Congress creed ruled out armed assault, but it had not even applied economic blockage.

Something new was required. Bose proposed the formation of a party of socialism and revolution: the *Samyavadi Sangha.* This would be a centralised and well-disciplined all-India party, with representatives in the Indian National Congress and the All-India Trade Union Congress, in the peasants', women's and youth organisations and also in the sectarian and communal organisations if necessary. It would first fight the British, then fight to establish a caste-free, privilege-free India, equal in all respects. In Delhi the Raj debated what it should do about the speech. One official wrote:

> The question for consideration now is whether it might be preferable to take this opportunity of allowing Bose to proclaim himself an advocate of armed revolution, or whether it is better to stamp on him and his new organisation with both feet at this and every other opportunity. Personally, I think it will be better not to do what Bose himself would prefer that we should do. Safe in a foreign country, he obviously wishes to advertise himself as the Lenin of the coming Indian revolution and with this purpose he has had the temerity publicly to condemn Gandhi. I think that if government were to allow a publication of this presidential address, its action would appear inexplicable to all those who have been made acquainted with Bose's designs and intentions in connection with the formation of the *Samyavadi Sangha.* In all the above circumstances, I recommend that the presidential address be banned under the Sea Customs Act.

The home secretary agreed:

> Looked at superficially the split between Gandhi and Subhas is satisfactory and it might be held that it would pay us to widen the gap; temporarily there might be some tactical advantage. But any such slight tactical advantage would be playing into the hands of Subhas and the extremists.

The speech was duly banned. However the Raj could not reach him in Austria, and on the very day he had planned to be in London he spoke at the English club in Vienna. This speech, in front of about 50 people, was probably, one of Bose's first public speeches outside India. We have the Indian police spies to thank for a very detailed account. In 1927 one reason Bose had given for not wanting to be exiled from India was the thought that in Europe he would be endlessly spied on by the British. Bose was well aware of this. In fascist countries, he explained, British agents portrayed him as a communist, in socialist or democratic countries as a fascist. The IPI spy's notes of this meeting, in a letter to Clauson dated 26 June 1933, give a graphic description of the Vienna meeting:

> It was meant to be a debate between Bose and a Miss Levetus, an elderly English teacher presenting the British case. But she did not turn up and Bose had the field to himself. As was his style he spoke extemporaneously, although he had made notes. Bose described how the mutiny of 1857 was the beginning of India's struggle for freedom, predicted that Gandhi's movement would fail and the British would never give up India.

The IPI spy quoted Bose as saying:

> All classes in England from capitalist to workers had too many material interests in exploiting India. India for her part would never agree to a compromise with the English. Such a thing was now impossible on account of the superior and haughty attitude of the English towards Indians and India and the reign of suppression and bribery which they had systematically carried on throughout the years; only this had made it possible for them to maintain their hold over India for so long. The younger generation realised that nothing could be obtained by non-violence and similar movements and that they must now take quite different measures.

Bose emphasised the need for propaganda, saying this was something the Indians had learnt from the British. Much, he said, was being made of German cruelties in the British press, including book burning. [The Nazi leader Adolf Hitler had become German Chancellor in January 1933] Bose thought what was happening in Germany was nothing compared to what the British had been doing in India for a long time. "Never a day passes without some book or pamphlet being seized or forbidden." He went on to say that of India's revenues 60 per cent went on the upkeep of the Army in India, 20 per cent on administration, chiefly the salaries of high British officials, and 20 per cent for education and social work.

For the Indian government this speech was confirmation of how their most determined enemy would seek to undermine its rule. Their spies acknowledged that within a short time Bose had made his presence in Vienna felt. The IPI note to Clauson said that Bose has "made a considerable impression in Vienna where he met a number of people prominent in political circles and successfully canvassed their support for the Hindusthan Academical Association for the city." As a result the body which had been "comparatively innocuous" changed character and took on a more nationalist and and anti British hue.

The immediate impact was on the Raj's Indian collaborators, particularly those used by the British to convince the world that Indians were slowly being taught how to rule themselves. Although India was not a free country the British had allowed India to acquire certain trappings that free countries have. Today these may seem ridiculous and spurious but in the 1930s they helped the Raj spin the story its way. So in 1930 India House was established in London with an Indian high commissioner.

In May 1933 Vienna hosted a conference of the International Chamber of Commerce. The Indian delegation was led by the Bombay businessman Walchand Hirachand. On May 29, the British Legation in Vienna gave a reception for all the British delegates including the Indians. Influenced by Bose, the Indians did not attend the British reception. Among Bose's most useful Viennese contacts were the Vetters. Herr Vetter was an Austrian government official who was prominent in Vienna's operatic and theatrical world. Bose developed a close friendship with his wife Naomi. Within two months of his arrival in Vienna he was presenting Naomi with mangoes from India. She translated his speeches into German and he used the Vetters as a sounding board, asking their advice on whether he should associate himself with Otto Faltis, an Austrian businessman with whom Bose worked to bring Austria and India closer together.

Bose would open himself up in his letters to Naomi. In one early letter he said:

> We are, as a people, exceedingly emotional, though personally I am supposed to have an impassive exterior. At least this is what some my friends criticise me for. The fact that you have been interested in our country has given me infinite pleasure and has increased my gratitude for you.

In Vienna Bose also established a close rapport with Vithalbhai Patel, Vallabhbhai's brother. Without the patronage of an older politician since Das's death, he immediately took to Vithalbhai, who had been a colleague of Das. It helped that the older man shared the passion of the younger one. In May 1933 he and Bose issued a strong statement condemning Gandhi. The Mahatma had watched helplessly from jail as the government had crushed the 1932 civil-disobedience campaign, and, seeking almost any issue to reactivate the moribund Congress, he had seized on the thorny question of communal electorates and reserved seats for Hindus, Muslims and Untouchables to launch a fast. Bose and Patel had met at the Hotel de France in Vienna, which was to become the headquarters of the Hindusthan Academical, and issued a warlike declaration. Bose thought Gandhi was a useless piece of furniture, and had fully convinced the aged Patel that he spoke for the young. The pair asserted: "The time has...come for a radical reorganisation of the Congress on a new principle and with a new method. For bringing about this reorganisation a change of leadership is necessary."

Bose made sure the statement got wide publicity, contacting Alfred Tyrnaeur who wrote it up in the *Saturday Evening Post* and distributed it to international news agencies. But Patel was a very ill man, with only a few months to live. A tour of the United States, arguing the Indian cause for freedom, had proved so exhausting that he had suffered a breakdown, and had been admitted to a Vienna sanatorium. This not only increased the burden on Bose but meant that for the second time in his political career Bose had found a mentor, and then lost him.

Bose was also unwell. He was still under treatment and had to follow a strict diet. This helped him lose weight and soon he looked almost ten years younger. Some people thought he could not be more than 28 when in fact he was 36. He was very conscious he should not put on weight.

When Bose's passport had been issued at Allahabad on 13 February 1933, under the column "Observations" had been written in red ink, "Not valid for entry into Germany or the United Kingdom." On 25 March 1933 Bose approached the British consul in Vienna, who had a close look at the passport, checked to see that Bose did not appear on the warning list, and endorsed it for Hungary and Czechoslovakia. On 24 April he added Yugoslavia, Rumania, Bulgaria, Greece, Turkey, Spain, Portugal, Sweden, Norway and Denmark; and on 30 June J.W. Taylor, the British vice-consul in Prague, added Belgium, Holland and Poland.

However, these consular officials had overlooked the red ink. That was the India Office's own bureaucratic shorthand for saying that, leaving aside Germany and the U.K., no endorsements for other countries should be given without India Office permission. Clauson commented sourly, "This is amusing. While we ponderously debated here about Germany, the consul at Vienna endorsed a passport for most other countries in the world. But no doubt it does not matter. The more he travels, the more he may die, presumably."

Bose used the next year to make up for his lack of European education. As he would put it to Naomi, he had decided to became " a rolling stone". All the endorsements except those for the Scandinavian countries were used: Prague, Berlin, Warsaw, Geneva, Rome, Milan, the Italian and French Rivieras, the Balkans, even Istanbul. Bose visited many of these places more than once. Wherever he went he tried to learn about the political systems, the social values and, of course, the municipalities concerned. And , in turn, he told these countries about India. In letters, newspaper interviews, and articles, he argued the case for Indian freedom and the need for propaganda on its behalf. His basic message was: India should organise itself free from British control, it should learn from the British and the other Europeans on how to utilise international gatherings. Soon after his arrival in Vienna he had carried on a spirited exchange of letters in the *Manchester Guardian* about political prisoners. As he began his travels he sought to link the Indian nationalist movement with the wider movement for freedom in central Europe.

His first foray outside Vienna was to Prague where he arrived on 29 June. With the

Czech government arranging the programme he was received by the mayor. He also met Dr Eduard Benes, the foreign minister. Prague had a peculiar charm for Bose, he often returned to the city, and formed a close liaison with a Dr Vladmir Lesny of the Oriental Institute there. But much as he liked Prague nothing could displace Vienna in his affections.

From Prague Bose visited Warsaw. He was much taken by the progress Warsaw had made in the 14 years since Poland had secured its independence from Russia. As he walked along the streets of Warsaw he could feel the "throb of a new life". As ever in his travels the *minutiae* of civil life fascinated him such as who owned the public utilities and how they were run.

From Warsaw he tried to get to Moscow, but the Soviets, who never showed much enthusiasm for him, were not keen, So, with some m isgivings, he caught a train to Berlin, arriving there on 18 July. Germany should have been ideal for Bose. Here was a country whose leading intellectuals had enjoyed a long and fruitful love affair with the idealised Indian past. It was German scholars who, in the nineteenth century, rediscovered ancient Indian scholarship and ironically served as gurus for a generation of Indians who had forgotten the deeds of their ancestors. Politically, Indians fighting the British had looked, since the turn of the century, to Germany for sympathy and help. But with Hitler in power everything had changed.

Hitler was a great admirer of the British and their Empire. In Flanders during the First World War , as he recorded in *Mein Kampf*, he had come face to face with the 'Tommies' and discarded his German prejudice that the British were cowards, admiring their grit and the determination. He repudiated the theory that the British had acquired their Empire by fraud, a view that Bose took, and saw their subjugation of India as the model for the German empire he wanted to create in eastern Europe. As for Indian nationalists wandering about seeking to organise against the British he could not be more contemptuous, writing in *Mein Kampf*:

> As early as 1920-21 ... the Party was approached from various quarters in an attempt to bring it into definite connection with the liberationist movements in other countries. This was in line with the plans of the ' League of Oppressed Nations' which had been advertised in many quarters and was composed, principally of representatives of the Balkan states and also of Eqypt and India. These always impressed me as charlatans who gave themselves big airs but had no real background at all. Not a few Germans, however, especially in the nationalist camp, allowed themselves to be taken in by these pompous Orientals, and in the person of some wandering Indian or Egyptian student, they believed at once that they were face to face with a representative of India or Egypt. They did not realise that in most cases they were dealing with persons who had no backing whatsoever, who were not authorised by anybody to conclude any sort of agreement whatsoever; so that the practical result of every negotiation with such individuals was negative and the time spent in such dealings had to be reckoned to be utterly lost. I was always on my guard against these attempts....
> ..I remember well the childish and incomprehensible hopes which arose suddenly in nationalist circles in the years 1920-21 to the effect that England was just nearing its downfall in India. A few Asiatic mountebanks who put themselves forward as 'the champions of Indian Freedom' then began to peregrinate throughout Europe and succeeded in inspiring otherwise reasonable people with the fixed notion that the British World Empire which had its pivot in India was just about to collapse there........England will never lose India unless she admits racial disruption in the machinery of her administration (which at present is entirely out of question in India) or unless she is overcome by the sword of some powerful enemy. But Indian risings will never bring this about. We Germans have had sufficient evidence to know how hard it is to coerce England. And, apart from all this, I as a German would far rather see India under British domination than under that of any other nation.

India was firmly excluded from civilisation by Nazi racial philosophy. Alfred Rosenberg, Nazi Germany's philosopher, who was credited with great insight into Indian culture, could find little virtue in these "poor bastards" and was convinced that from the "Nordic as well as German point of view the British rule in India must be supported". Bose, nevertheless, was convinced that something could be salvaged if only he could meet Hitler. Despite his persistence he failed. In his years of exile, Rosenberg was the only significant Nazi official he appears to have met.

It was not as though he had not been briefed on the new Germany. One of his most important meetings in Prague was with Arathil Candeth Nambiar, an Indian who was to became one of his principal assistants in Europe. Nambiar had arrived in Prague less than two months earlier, not by choice but because he was expelled from Germany. Nambiar was one of those Indians termed by the IPI "suspect civilian Indians on the continent of Europe". Born a year before Bose he had left India at about the same time as Bose for his further studies. After getting an educational diploma from London he went back to India but then moved to Berlin in 1922. He was in the Raj black book as a result of his association with Virendra Chattopadhyay, who the Raj dubbed "the notorious anti-British revolutionary and Comintern agent". He was divorced from his Indian wife, and had a German mistress called Eva Geissler, who had been a typist in the office of the German Communist party and helped Nambiar run the India Information Bureau.

On the evening of 28 February1933 six Nazi SA thugs, young boys of between 16 and 17, entered Nambiar's flat and at gun point drove him to a small Nazi office not far from his flat. They also ransacked his flat, taking away his typewriter, gramophone and some records. As he climbed the stairs of the Nazi office Nambiar was whipped on his back and shoulders. His passport was seized and he was taken to a police station where he was jailed. On the afternoon of March 2 he was locked in solitary confinement. Three weeks later, on 25 March at 8.30 am, he was served with a deportation order. He had been classified as an "undesirable alien" and given eight days to leave the Reich.

Nambiar was not the only Indian of whose mistreatment Bose would have heard. The stories must have disturbed Bose and contributed to his misgivings about visiting Germany. It did not help that he arrived in Berlin exhausted by his travels to Prague and Warsaw. He felt ill and feverish, and his first few days were spent in bed. He had refused German government hospitality at Harnack House, prefering to stay in the Grand-Hotel-am-Knie in Charlottenburg. When he was better he did meet some German officials including the Oberburgermeister, mayor of Berlin and some leaders of industry .

He also established contacts with the so-called Nazi left wing. For this he had to thank Lothar Frank. Frank, who was on the teaching staff of the *Technische Hochschule* (Technical High School) in Berlin and had also been a secretary of the Indo-German society, had been attracted to Nazism by Hitler's vague populism, and his talk of the radical changes necessary to remake the world. This was a fashionable concept in the beer-hall days.

With Lothar Frank as his guide, Bose keenly studied this party within a party, and compared it with the revolutionary organisations he had known in Bengal. He also arranged for material help for the Bengal revolutionaries: arms, ammunition and technical equipment. A secret code was devised using four tiny German-English dictionaries, and it was planned that these messages, and the arms, would be carried by merchant ships. But the words of the dictionaries carried no coded messages and, though German merchant ships called at Indian ports, they delivered no arms. It is not clear what exactly went wrong; possibly the trouble was that the Nazi 'radical' wing was, within a year, decimated in Hitler's bloody massacre of the SA. When Frank met Bose during the war, he did so in great secrecy. The contacts provided Bose with some idea of the Nazi intra-party struggles and, when Asoke drew his attention to Rosenberg's writings, he consoled him with the thought, "The rank and file, however, do not hold the views of the leaders."

With Frank's help Bose met Dr Curt Pruefer, head of the British Empire section of the German Foreign Office. Pruefer promised to see what he could do to help with the Indo-German Society but felt this was not an opportune moment to start anything new. He also saw Herr Schumann of the eastern section of the shadow cabinet of the NSDAP and the chief of the political police, one Dr Diehls. With him Bose raised the issue of getting the expulsion order of Nambiar cancelled. The Germans allowed Nambiar to visit Berlin for a few days at the end of November, and eventually gave him compensation.

Bose wanted Nambiar back in Germany because he knew he would not follow the Nazi line. He also saw him as a unifier of the Indians. Like all exile movements, the Indians in Germany were hopelessly split. British agents or informers had infiltrated their ranks. Chempakaram Pillai had tried hard to persuade Bose not to come, believing that he may not be well received. Two of Pillai's assistants, Benoy Kumar Sarkar and a Dr. Sinha, not only propagated the Nazi line but, as IPI admitted, "enjoy to some extent the approval of the British authorities." Pillai's great rival was Debendra Nath Bannerjea, who had been an adviser to the German government on Indian affairs and who had initially been lukewarm to Bose.

Bose eventually decided the only solution was a new Indian Students' Association, managed entirely by students with the older men joining only as associates. The Raj's spies faithfully reported on Bose's efforts to achieve unity, "Notwithstanding the fact that his health was not particularly good and that he had not made the progress for which his Vienna doctors had hoped, he set himself the task of reducing the various warring factions of the Indian community in Berlin to some sort of common denominator." Some of the Indians continued to act as moles for the British and reported back unfavourable comments. One IPI note recorded: "Debendra Nath Bannerjea rather doubts the impression Bose made in official German circles and the extent to which he succeeded in enlisting sympathy. He complains that Bose was suspicious and unresponsive towards offers of hospitality from various Germans... Bannerjea describes him as 'a fish out of water in Europe' and that possibly his nerves have been affected by his long imprisonment."

Despite this poor health Bose was active in Berlin. On 28 July he presided at a meeting which was attended by German offcials and some Indians. There were further meetings on 8 and 16 August, the latter at the American-German Church in Berlin, attended by both Germans and Americans. The Raj spies noted how in his speeches Bose emphasised that no country had won independence without bloodshed and recommended the Irish example, the strongest form of non-cooperation combined with military activities.

Towards the end of August Bose went to Franzesbad in Czechoslovakia to meet up with Vithalbhai. From there they returned to Vienna together where they consulted their respective doctors.

Patel was still making optimistic noises of returning to India but by early September he was at the Clinique La Ligniere in Gland, an hour by train from Geneva. Bose set off to be by his bedside, in his first trip across the Alps to Switzerland. The journey from Vienna to Zurich enchanted him. Bose attended the Conference of the International Committee for India in Geneva, speaking at a crowded evening gathering, said to be largest meeting on India ever held in Geneva, then hurried to Patel's side. For a time Bose himself entered the clinic. His abdominal pain had returned, he walked with a stick, and did not take much food. It was in the clinic that he learnt of his rival Sengupta's death in a British gaol, news which stunned him. He would later write to Nellie Sengupta to urge her to take up her husband's burden. Although she did not reply, she did follow his advice.

Soon Bose was also mourning Patel. Patel had a heart attack at the end of September 1933 and then a slight relapse in the first week of October. Bose was by his bedside as he breathed his last. Despite malicious gossip to the contrary by some IPI spies, the two men had become very close. Patel wanted to be cremated in India and Bose travelled to Marseilles to put the body on a boat. In his will, Patel left Bose money to spread the message of India and its struggle for freedom. Bose never received a penny, and, almost a year after Patel's death, he had to issue a public statement about the will and its provisions. The will was contested by Patel's relations, including Vallabhbhai, and like many an Indian court battle it became a Dickensian affair with little gain for anybody.

Bose could certainly have used the money. With his brother Sarat, his main financier, in gaol, Subhas was always aware that money would be tight, and so it proved throughout his three years in Europe. He had to borrow money from friends and became an expert in cheap rail travel. Within a week of arriving in Europe, on 15 March, he had written to Kantilal Parekh in India worrying about money, "Living here is more expensive than I thought, particularly when you stay in a sanatorium." An IPI note of 19 October 1933 said, "The financial aspect of his affairs is causing anxiety. Of the sum collected for him in Calcutta only Rs 1,000 remain."

By now Bose was thinking of writing a book; IPI was convinced that he was driven to writing by his need for money. From as early as 20 September, 1933 IPI had been carefully monitoring Bose's book writing efforts and its spies were reading Bose's proposals almost as soon as they left his typewriter. Bose had contacted Pulin Behari Seal, an Indian journalist in London, to ask him to try and find him a publisher. By 29 September, IPI had obtained a copy of the synopsis which had started circulating in London publishing houses. It ran to ten pages and was entitled *The Indian Problem*.

Bose planned sixteen chapters. They covered the geography of India, its natural resources, the problems of race, religion, Indian womanhood, the nature of the state and the ruling princes. The synopsis provides a fascinating insight into Bose's thinking. In the proposed chapter on Indian womanhood he mentioned the comparative freedom of Hindu women when Muslim influence was not strong, but also the high culture of Noor Jehan and the high ideal of chastity of the Rani of Jhansi.In the chapter on education he set out to demonstrate that English education in India was too literary and there was great need of more "sport and gymnastics and military training" as part of education.

As far as the princes were concerned he had no doubts of their fate:

> The Princes will go as soon as English rule ends - no possibility that any Prince will have a role emancipating India as the House of Savoy did in Italy - there is the bare possibility that some Princes may remain if they democratise their administration and sympathise with the Nationalist Movement -but signs of this possibility are very few - with the disappearance of Princes the provinces will have to be reorganised on a linguistic basis.

This is exactly what Patel and Nehru did when India became independent. In the light of what was to happen a decade later the most fascinating chapter was the last, "The Conflict between India and England". Bose planned to analyse how the First World War had caught the Indians by surprise, the attempts at revolutionary propaganda in the Indian Army and the short-lived mutiny by a Muslim regiment in Singapore in 1915.

Seal approached Gollancz, then the leading left wing publisher in England. While they were prepared to look at the manuscript once it was ready, and publish if their lawyers approved, they would not give Bose an advance based on a "partial synopsis."

Bose would never write *The Indian Problem* but some of his ideas formed part of a later book. Bose wrote another synopsis, a copy of which by March 1934 also found it way to the IPI. This was his proposed autobiography. He planned sixteen chapters beginning with his Cambridge days through to "Search for a Leader" and "First Prison Experience" to a final chapter on "Living In Europe" which would have taken his story up to December 1933. Bose told Seal that he would also be prepared to write his impressions of Das and Patel and a book on his own socio-political views. This, too, failed to find a publisher.

While he sought a publisher, Bose also considered and rejected the thought of returning to India, well aware he would be arrested the moment he reached Bombay. He decided to make the most of his freedom in Europe.In Geneva Bose explored the possibility of going to Ireland or the United States. He met the American consul and asked about securing a visa.The American writer J.T. Sutherland had presented him with a signed copy of his book *India in Bondage.* The American consul told him that British objections were not likely to influence the Americans in allowing him into their country, information which alarmed the Raj.

In Berlin Bose had made another effort to get to Moscow, this time using Eva Geissler, but the Russians did not respond. The Comintern continued to criticise him for his Congress and capitalist affiliations. Nambiar was not surprised as he thought Bose, unlike Nehru, had a fundamental dislike of communism.

That autumn Bose, following the treatment prescribed by Professor Neumann of Vienna had sought sunshine in the south of France. He was preparing to spend Christmas in the Hotel de Luxembourg in Nice when, quite unexpectedly, he received an invitation to attend a students' conference in Italy, and to address the Oriental Institute that Mussolini was inaugurating.The Italians also organised an Asiatic Students' Congress, inviting 600 students from various parts of Europe, including 90 Indians and 150 Chinese . All travelled free on the Italian railways and were given free accommodation in Rome for a week.

Unlike the Germans, the Italians were eager to welcome Bose.This was due largely to groundwork laid by Dr Gino Scarpa, who, as Italian consul-general in Calcutta, had developed close contacts with Bose and other Congress leaders. With Dr Scarpa now ensconced in the Foreign Office, Bose's stay was much more pleasant than his stay in Germany. He was put up in the Excelsior Hotel in Rome and had no problems in getting to see Mussolini, who he called the "Big Boss" in a letter to Asoke. He met him three times on this visit and twice subsequently, and had long discussions with him about India.

"Do you really and firmly believe that India will be free soon?" asked Mussolini.

"Yes", replied Bose.

Mussolini pressed further,"Are you for reformist or revolutionary methods for achieving Indian independence?"

Mussolini was impressed with Bose's belief in revolutionary methods: "Then indeed you have a chance." But he advised, "You must immediately prepare a plan for such a revolution and you must work continuously for its realisation." Bose would take this advice to heart and repeat it to friends later.

Mussolini courted foreign visitors and many in the 1920s formed favourable impressions of him. Winston Churchill made flattering comments and planned to write an article comparing him to Henry VIII. Many other leading Indians visited him including Gandhi and Tagore; the only exception was Nehru, who refused Mussolini's invitation. Tagore did not like him and denounced fascism. Gandhi found him a "riddle", admitted he had made attractive changes but did not like the compulsion and violence involved in fascism.

Bose saw fascism as a useful means of transforming a sleepy society into a vibrant one. The attention that Mussolini paid him had an effect, but Bose was aware of the reservations many had about the dictator. Writing to Naomi, he praised Mussolini's speech as " a fine one" but added,"whatever we might think of the speaker". After the conference Bose stayed on for a fortnight in Rome, where Asoke joined him for a week, then went to Milan where he spoke at a glittering gathering of the Cicolo Filologio Society on the new India and its problems. He also inaugurated an Association of Indian Students in Milan. Italians had little knowledge of India, but they were eager to learn and Bose wrote articles for various Italian newspapers.

"Socially", Bose wrote to Mrs Vetter, "Italians are generally inclined to keep aloof. They do not invite foreigners to their homes until they know them very intimately. But this, of course is in contrast to what I have seen among the German-speaking people in different parts of Europe."

The success of the Rome conference confirmed the India Office's worst fears. It warned the Foreign Office of other attempts by Bose to "impose" on those "ignorant of his record", prepared a note describing him as an "implacable foe" and warned foreign intelligence and police officials to watch out for him.

In early February Bose was back in Geneva where he stayed in a flat occupied by a Mrs Horup, a rich woman much interested in India. Bose helped her produce a publication called *The Indian Press* in which cuttings from various Indian newspapers such as the *Forward* and *The Free Press* figured prominently. Two other ladies also helped: a Mrs Ganguly and Madame Rolland, wife of Romain Rolland. Twelve hundred copies in English, French and German were cyclostyled and distributed free throughout Europe.

Bose felt that Geneva would be the ideal city from which he could make India's voice heard in Europe. It was the headquarters of the League of Nations, set up under the Treaty of Versailles. India was a founding member of the League and Indian revenues funded the expensive costs of membership. The cricketer Ranji was one of India's representatives at the League, while an English cricketer Charles Fry acted as Ranji's ghost writer. Bose thought the Indian nationalists could use the League as a forum for the nationalist case. Bose worked hard at this, raising questions with League officials about the paltry number of Indians employed, but in the end he had to concede defeat. In October 1933 the IPI, after assessing the reports of its various spies, had concluded:

> It would seem that Bose's main objective is to establish a chain of Indian propaganda centres throughout Europe. ...He estimates that a war is certain in Europe within the next three years and that such a war will spell the end of British domination in India.

By early spring 1934, IPI agents reported that Bose was not getting on with Horup. One report said she and her friends were followers of Gandhi. An agent reported:

> Bose's plans are much less definite than they were, owing to the two fold handicap of shortage of funds and ill health. .. he has undoubtedly lost a great deal of vitality, which is possibly the reason why he does not display the same degree of hostility towards Gandhi or even against the British, and finds it difficult to accomplish the amount of writing he has been contemplating.

Bose was certainly at a low ebb. But then suddenly he confounded his enemies and perhaps surprised himself by entering his most intense and active period in Europe. For a man short of money and not expected to recover his strength, in the spring and early summer of 1934 he showed uncommon energy. His health had improved and and he had a definite project. Seal had finally secured him a book contract. Wishart, later Lawrence and Wishart, a publishing firm in London, had advanced him £75 to write about his political experiences. *The Indian Problem* had now became *The Indian Struggle.* What Bose had envisaged as a history of India became a history of Indian politics since Gandhi had begun his non-co-operation movement. The publishers told Bose that they wanted a commentary on the political struggle in India in the last 13 years. The inspiration for this change was Maurice Dobbs, the Cambridge Marxist, with whom Seal had been in touch. His advice was that the synopsis had to be modified and simplified to appeal to the British public.

There was marvellous irony in this. The British spies were reporting on their enemy Bose when Dobbs was, totally unknown to them, acting as a "spotter" for the Soviets, helping them recruit what came to be known as the "Cambridge spies". The publishers wanted no fewer than 75,000 words, delivered by 30 August 1934. Bose would get a 10 percent royalty on the first 2,500 copies sold and, if the publishers sold the rights in America or Europe, Bose could make the deals himself.

Bose was not happy with the terms, but Seal told him it was difficult to get an advance before a line of the book had been written. The only Indians who had done so had been Gandhi and Tagore. Seal had only succeeded by means of introductions to Wishart and what he called judicious outlays of "douceurs" although what these sweeteners were Seal did not specify. Seal had also put Bose in touch with H.N Brailsford, a noted left-wing journalist, and there was talk of getting H.G.Wells to write a preface.

Before Bose set down to write, he visited Germany between March and April 1934. He started in Munich, and then went to Berlin, basing himself at the Eden Hotel. From there he visited various places including Dresden. This German visit made Bose aware of the increasingly strident racist campaign launched by the Nazis. Walking the streets of Munich Bose was called a "Neger" by school children, which shocked him. Indian students told him this was a common experience for them, and some said they had been pelted with stones. Children, far from being rebuked by their elders, were encouraged in this behaviour. From the Eden Hotel Bose wrote a memorandum to Pruffer protesting against this and the proposed legislation against Jews, Negroes and coloured people. If this became law, said Bose, " a mark of racial inferiority will be permanently put on India as a nation." He urged anti-Indian propaganda in the German press be stopped, that a statement friendly to India be made, and that the legislation against Indians be dropped.

Was Bose myopic in only calling on anti-Indian Nazi racist legislation to be dropped? What about the infinitely greater evil the Nazis were inflicting on the Jews, which was to result in the massacre of almost an entire race? He had enough evidence to see what the Nazis were doing to the Jews, but felt it was none of his business.

He got to know a German Jewish couple in Berlin well, Kitty and Alex Kurti. They attended one of his Berlin lectures and later invited him for lunch. When Kitty asked him how he could possibly want to work with the horrible Nazis, Bose admitted they were dreadful, and would later advise the Kurtis to leave Germany. But as far as India's freedom was concerned he felt that there was no choice but to work with them. Bose saw Europe as rotten to the core, the Nazi rottenness being matched by the British one. There were good people in Germany, as there were in England, but could Kitty imagine the despair, misery, humiliation, suffering and indignation of India? "British imperialism there can be just as intolerable as your Nazism here, I assure you", he said.

Bose's stress on India was similar to Gandhi who had started his great campaign in South Africa to remove the racist laws as they applied to Indians. Nehru was different. When Nehru came to Europe in 1937, not only did he go out of his way to buy from Jewish shops to show his sympathy for them, but in 1938 when Bose was Congress president, Nehru proposed that India take in Jewish refugees. The Congress rejected this idea. Bose was astounded when Nehru proposed the resolution, saying "frothy sentiments and pious platitudes do not make foreign policy". In a letter to Naomi in May 1937, referring to the visit of B.C Roy to Vienna, he wrote, "I want Dr Roy to see something of the real Vienna, and he should therefore get into the right hands. I am afraid that Jewish doctors may try to exploit him, if he is not forewarned."

Not that Bose was anti-semitic. Responding to something his future wife wrote about Jews, Bose in August 1937 would write, "Are they also not created by God, just like other people?" In his three years in Europe he made many Jewish friends. Apart from the Kurtis he got to know Mrs Helen Ashkanazy who as president of several women's clubs in Vienna often asked him to speak on India. Like the Kurtis, she too had to flee Europe before 1939.

Bose of course was not alone in linking Nazisim and British imperalism. In his *Discovery of India*, written in 1944 during one of his many spells in Raj gaols, Nehru wrote:

> Since Hitler emerged from obscurity and became the Fuehrer of Germany, we have heard a great deal about racialism and the Nazi theory of the *herrenvolk*. That doctrine has been condemned and is today condemned by the leaders of the United Nations. Biologists tell us that racialism is a myth and there is no such thing as a master race. But we in India have known racialism in all its forms ever since the commencement of British rule. The whole ideology of this rule was that of the *herrenvolk* and the master race and the structure of government was based upon it; indeed the idea of a master race is inherent in imperialism.

Where Bose differed from Nehru was that he sometimes did not realise the contradictory nature of what he was saying. This is vividly illustrated in another memorandum on German-Indian relations he wrote 18 months later to Dr. Franz Thierfelder, director of the German Academy in Munich. According to Lothar Frank, Bose was unable to make much headway with Nazis in Berlin and was pushed in the direction of the good doctor. On 7 November 1935, after another visit to Munich, Bose wrote to Frank about the problems Indians were having in Nazi Germany both with regard to the race campaign against them and what he perceived as the the increasingly pro-British attitude of the Hitler regime.

Ever the intensely practical man, as opposed to the idealistic Nehru, Bose wrote:

> I do not demand that you give up your race theory; no matter how much scientific reason we might offer against it. We only want it to be modified so that it, wittingly or unwittingly, does not provoke any bad opinion about Indians. Moreover, we also do not wish for once that you write in favour of Indians in the German press if you do not want to - we only ask that you do not write against India.

Here Bose unwittingly went on to highlight an important difference between Nazi rule in Germany and British rule in India. "The press in India was not under the strict control of the British government, nor under the thumb of any party. But in Germany, it is impossible at present to publish an article as refutation in the German newspapers, a refutation to all the anti-Indian articles. I say this from experience."

After Germany Bose's visits to cities in other central European countries came as a relief. In April 1934 he went to Prague for the opening of the Indo-Czech Institute, which drew support from companies like Bata and Skoda who were keen for an Indian market. As a result, the Czech authorities agreed to open an overseas section of the Czech Technical University for the special benefit of Indian, Chinese and Persian students. Bose also went to Rome, and on 3 May was back in Vienna for the opening of the Indo-Central European Society. Based on the plans Faltis had outlined some months earlier, its aim was to promote cultural and commercial relations between Austria and India. In front of 150 people Bose spoke about the youth movement in India and on the British lack of encouragement, seeing all young people as revolutionaries and imprisoning them on the first suspicion of potential rebellion.

In early summer, accompanied by Nilima, Bose left on a tour of the Balkans. In little over a month, he visited five cities. In Bucharest he was much taken by Dr Narsing Mulgund, a lieutenant-colonel in the medical department of the Romanian army. Mulgund, a Maharashtrian by birth, had studied at Bose's Scottish Church College before joining one of the Indian medical missions to Turkey during the Balkan wars, eventually arriving in Romania in 1913. There he joined the medical corps of the Romanian army, and settled in Bucharest. When Subhas arrived he was well established as the country's best eye surgeon, with a Romanian wife who had given him two daughters. Bose devoted one of his articles in *The Modern Review* to him.

But when he reached Belgrade, Bose's attempts to get into print were less successful. Soon after his arrival, the prestigious Belgrade paper *Politika* interviewed him and agreed to publish an article stating the nationalist cause. But later *Politika* rang Bose to say the interview had been held up by the Foreign Office. Some time afterwards Reuters spread the story that the state censor had killed the story, implying that Bose had offended the Yugoslavs. The interview was never published. The truth was that the India Office had intervened. As D.J. Gowan, His Majesty's minister in Belgrade, reported to London:

> On hearing that Bose had arrived I took an opportunity of mentioning his history to the political director of the Ministry of Foreign Affairs with the result that the press were instructed to confine their reports to the mere fact of his presence in Belgrade. I understand that Bose left Yugoslavia bitterly disappointed at the lack of publicity given to his visit.

Istanbul also proved disappointing. He had gone there with "glorious expectations," but found neither the romance of the east nor the material prosperity of the west. The state seemed to be collapsing. From Istanbul Bose moved to Sofia. Close co-operation between the British and the Greeks had already scotched his plans to visit Athens, and in Sofia Bose was closely shadowed by the Bulgarian police.

He returned to Vienna in mid-June and, for the first time since he had arrived in Europe, settled down into something like home life. He acquired a flat in a street in a quiet upper middle class suburb, Peter Jordan Strausse, It was here, despite occasional abdominal pain for which he received short wave therapy, that he settled down to write *The Indian Struggle.*

His first need was a secretary. The choice Subhas made was to prove momentous. An Indian called Mathur ran a discussion group in English, attended by two young Austrian women. When Subhas asked Mathur if he knew anybody who might help him, Mathur turned to them. Subhas was not impressed with the first woman, so asked to see the second. She was Emilie Schenkl, six months short of her twenty fifth birthday.

There was something in Emilie that impressed Subhas. She would later tell her daughter that as a young woman she was far too fat. But pictures of her at that time show an attractive woman with a fine face, though not a great beauty. Appearance apart, she was discreet (she had considered then rejected the idea of becoming a nun), her English was good and she could take shorthand. To Subhas, she was ideal.

Emilie certainly needed the money. This was the height of depression. Unemployment in Austria was very high. Her father was nervous about her working for a foreigner, but was reassured to find the flat was not far from where the Schenkls lived, a fifteen-minute walk away and in a prosperous neighbourhood.

The Schenkls were a lower middle class Catholic family. While her mother's father had been a burgher of Vienna in the nineteenth century, at a time when the city was still developing and burgher meant a man of some position, her paternal grandfather was a German immigrant from Sudetenland, whose large German population would soon provide Hitler with a ready excuse to dismember Czechslovakia.

Emilie came every day to take Subhas's dictation. This would last for three or four hours. She then typed it up for him to correct. Every now and again he wrote in long hand which she retyped. For much of that summer he worked hard. By July Bose had written 40,000 words, but he was not entirely happy with them. The August deadline was clearly impossible to meet, and was extended to the end of September. There were also photographs needed.

Bose wanted a preface by a leading writer or thinker and asked Tagore if he would approach George Bernard Shaw, H.G. Wells or Romain Rolland. Such requests are not uncommon, but what was unusual was the frank and less than diplomatic tone in which Bose worded his letters. He bluntly told Tagore that his book would be critical of Gandhi. Wells, Shaw and Rolland were all admirers of Gandhi. His letter was so tactless that even as he asked a favour he accused Tagore of being a "blind admirer" of Gandhi, which provoked a lecture from the great poet on Indian politics. The result was the book had no foreword. In September the book was still unfinished. In ailing health, Bose went to Karlsbad to take the spa waters. He returned to Vienna late that month with his autumn plans very much up in the air. He longed for sunshine and India, and worked on issuing a manifesto for India. He even fleetingly considered standing for the Assembly elections, but was deterred by the prospect of another spell in prison. He made one last unsuccessful effort to set up a central publicity bureau in Geneva. He was unable to get the Patel legacy money, his relationship with Mrs Horup was not good and Nambiar was unwilling to move from Prague. Bose had been providing Nambiar with £5 a month, and had helped him get 1200 marks in compensation for damage done when Nazi thugs raided his flat. Nambiar was now established as a journalist in Prague working for several Indian papers, and had been joined by his girlfriend, Eva Geissler.

Bose busied himself correcting the proofs from Wishart until, on 26 November 1934, he received a cable from Prabhabati telling him that his father Janakinath was seriously ill. His father had suffered a heart attack a month before, and now the doctors held out little hope.

Subhas booked a seat on a KLM flight from Rome. It would take four days with nightly stopovers to reach Calcutta. He spent all night correcting proofs, and departed for Rome on the morning of 29 November. This was his first long flight and he waxed lyrical to his western friends about the "variegated colours of an Oriental sunrise ... unknown in the west". Despite his problems with the India Office he had no fears about being allowed back into India.

The Raj saw things differently. The prospect of a Bose return had long exercised various departments of the governments in Delhi and Calcutta. Before Bose had been allowed to leave India in March 1933 the Bengal government had advised Delhi to warn him that he would be arrested if he returned. Delhi had not done so, either because of bureaucratic bungling or through fear that if he had known that permanent exile awaited, he would not have left. To complete the confusion, the government of India was not even sure whether his passport carried the all-important endorsement, "Valid for re-entry into India." During the familiar fierce intra-governmental debate, Bengal insisted:

> He has maintained touch throughout the period with terrorists in Bengal and secret information shows that he is working steadily towards his declared intention of a mass revolution. Ground at present moment is favourable for his plan. He will come back as long lost leader and will put fresh heart into terrorists, correspondingly discouraging our own servants and, among public generally breaking that confidence in government's determination to crush terrorism which has been slowly extending, but even now is far from universal.

Delhi issued a warrant for Subhas' detention. On the Sunday before Subhas arrived Jankinath Bose died. Subhas heard the news of his father's death as he landed at Karachi. His grief was compounded when customs officials seized proofs of his book. When he landed at Calcutta the same afternoon he learned of the Bengal government's decision. The government had originally decided to arrest him and take him straight from the airport to Presidency gaol. But hints of this action had been aired in the press, and there were concerns about the possible reaction. The authorities decided to confine him at 38/2 Elgin Road for seven days, with visitors allowed only with government approval. Then he would face a simple choice: to fly back to Europe on the next plane or be arrested. Bose, anxious to be home, agreed and indicated that he planned to return to Vienna for his operation.

But things were not straightforward. There was the matter, still unresolved, of the cause of his ill health. Bose wanted to consult doctors in India before agreeing to the operation recommended in Vienna. In addition, his finances demanded attention. With Sarat in his third year of captivity, the family had been deprived of its principal breadwinner and Subhas of an ever-willing patron. The book advance of £75 had been spent, and Subhas needed to make sure that the friends and well-wishers who had arranged finance in 1933 would still support him. Most importantly, he now realised that the government wanted to exile him permanently. He had rejected exile in 1927 and was reluctant to accept it now. He wrote to the government for permission to have his visit extended till the complicated Hindu funeral ceremonies were over (the normal period of mourning is twenty-one days).

The government set up a medical board to examine his case, and Delhi once again started to search for a suitable gaol. The doctors solved the problem by recommending Europe. On 11 January 1934 Subhas sailed back to Europe. In contrast to his earlier journey, he was allowed to bid farewell to his friends, and even to meet the press.

Three days before his thirty-eighth birthday, on 20 January 1935, Bose arrived in Naples, where a surprise package awaited him. *The Indian Struggle, 1920-34* had been published in mid-December, and Seal had sent him some copies. In London the British government was ready with plans for the book. It had closely monitored its progress toward publication.

On 18 October 1934, Peel had secured a 16-page summary of the contents and warned, "The book will be troublesome because Bose is much more skilful at distorting facts than are most Congress propagandists. Enclosure A on terrorism is a monstrous perversion of the facts."

While the rest of the book was summarised, the remarks on terrorism were given in full. Bose's references to the terrorist movement occupied no more than four pages in a book of over 350 printed pages and could not have presented a more reasonable explanation of why there was revolutionary violence in Bengal and other parts of India. The behaviour of the British in India, he argued, had encouraged the Indians to believe that Britain only respected physical force. Bengalees had been denounced as cowards and kept out of the Army on the grounds they were not warlike, and peaceful protests were put down by force. "In sheer despair, young men took to the bomb and the revolver. The effect was immediate. The behaviour of the Britisher began to improve."

Bose's remedy for revolution was for the British to demonstrate that it was possible to win freedom through peaceful means. This was hardly the language of the *jihadi*. But Peel was trying to find any excuse to prevent the book from reaching India . The Raj view was that while carefully worded, Bose's book was really expressing his deeply felt sympathy with terrorist acts of "retaliation". While the book could circulate in England it was banned in India. The ban did not surprise Bose although it meant financial loss. The 500 copies Gopal Sanyal had ordered for India could not be delivered. There was some consolation in the good reviews not only in the European press but also in the English papers, which pleased Bose greatly. He wrote to Curt Pruefer about publishing a German edition and thought of an American one as well.

Although it was not quite what was sketched out in the synopsis, the book was a very comprehensive and up to date history of the Indian freedom struggle from 1920 to 1934. Like everything Bose wrote it was written in a clear, distinct style. If much of it pleaded the standard nationalist case for Indian freedom, it included a fascinating chapter on Gandhi which was not the usual hagiography, and Bose's vision of free India.

Bose declared, "The logic of history will....follow its inevitable course. The political struggle and the social struggle will have to be conducted simultaneously. The party that will win political freedom for India will also be the party that will win social and economic freedom for the masses." Continuing with this analysis, one which bore unmistakable traces of Marxist influence, Bose now set out the programme for *Samyavadi Sangha*. The party would be for the peasants and workers, and emphasise a strong federal government, economic planning, industrialisation, regeneration of village industries and abolition of social differentiation. It would be anti-landlord and opposed to pussy-footing mid-Victorian parliamentary democracy.

Above all, *Samyavadi Sangha*, would provide the key. India had absorbed much from her numerous conquerors and the varied cultures they had brought with them. The new influences were fascism and communism. In spite of the antithesis between communism and fascism there are certain traits common to both. Both communism and fascism believe in the supremacy of the state over the individual. Both denounce parliamentarian democracy. Both believe in party rule. Both believe in the dictatorship of the party and in the ruthless suppression of dissenting minorities. Both believe in a planned industrial reorganisation of the country. These common traits will form the basis of the new synthesis. That synthesis is called by the writer *Samyavada* – an Indian word which means literally "the doctrine of synthesis or equality'. It will be India's task to work out this synthesis.

Subhas had arrived at an important turning point in his life. His criticisms of Gandhi would create for him life-long enemies; his belief in an Indian world role through synthesis has provoked many accusations of naivety and fascism. Let us examine the latter, the remarkable doctrine that he would occasionally modify but never abandon. For the next 11 years it would form the basis of his political belief, and nine months before his death he would re-state it to students at Tokyo University. For both the friends and enemies of Subhas Bose, it is his contribution to the fundamental problem of Indian revolution.

Bose was no fascist. Even the British recognised this. At the Bombay press conference on the eve of his departure in 1935, he was asked about his admiration for Hitler. He replied:

> It is entirely news to me. However, there is much in his organisation worth studying. But as far as his principles are concerned, I do not see how they can appeal to India. On the economic side he is more or less in the hands of big capitalists and politically he is pro-British. I earnestly deplore the tendency to reproduce in India the fascist and communist systems blindly.

Later he admitted he may have been wrong in equating fascism and communism. In November 1937, interviewed by R.P Dutt and Ben Bradley, he said:

> What I really meant was that we in India wanted our national freedom and having won it, we wanted to move in the direction of socialism. ... I should like to point out that when I was writing the book, fascism had not started on its imperialistic expedition, and it appeared to me merely as an aggressive form of nationalism. I should also point out that communism as it appeared to be demonstrated by many of those who were supposed to stand for it in India, seemed to me to be anti-national, and this impression was further strengthened in view of the hostile attitude which several among them exhibited towards the Indian National Congress.

Seven long years later, at Tokyo University in 1944 he would state:

> You cannot have a so-called democratic system, if that system has to put through economic reforms on a socialistic basis. Therefore, we must have a political system - a state - of an authoritarian character. . . . To repeat once again, our political philosophy should be a synthesis between National Socialism and communism. The conflict between thesis and antithesis has to be resolved in a higher synthesis. This is what the Law of Dialectic demands. If this is not done,

> then human progress will come to an end. India will, therefore, try to move on to the next stage of political and social evolution.

Bose's eclecticism had finally produced this absurd theory. Subhas recognised that there was no theory of thought or belief behind fascism, no philosophy that gave it sustenance. What attracted him were its organisational methods. He was clearly fascinated by the role the party played in the Italian state. "The party take charge of every individual in the state regardless of age or sex. No individual is isolated from the state, and it is the function of the party to train citizens for the state." Bose believed, unlike Gandhi, that the party of freedom must be the party of reconstruction, and he was eager to look at all possible models. The philosophy must be Indian but the methods could be borrowed from anywhere, however tainted their sources might be.

He rejected Nehru's clear and unambiguous choice in favour of communism because that would mean, "we are at the end of the process of evolution . . . there is no reason to hold that our choice is restricted to two alternatives." To accept Nehru would be to limit India's role: evolution was the law of nature, and synthesis was the great Indian gift. The idea is best summed up in the London speech that Bose was not allowed to read:

> India will be called upon to play an important role in world history in the near future. We all know that in the seventeenth century England made a remarkable contribution to world civilisation through her ideas of constitutional and democratic government. Similarly, in the eighteenth century, France made the most wonderful contribution to the culture of the world through her ideas of "liberty, equality and fraternity". During the nineteenth century Germany made the most remarkable gift through her Marxian philosophy. During the twentieth century Russia has enriched the culture and civilisation of the world through her achievements in proletarian revolution, proletarian government and proletarian culture. The next remarkable contribution to the culture and civilisation of the world, India will be called upon to make.

It was this belief that drove him forward, that he repeated in one form or another in all his speeches and writings, and that finally made him find a synthesis where there was none.

From Naples. Bose hurried to Rome to present a copy personally to Mussolini. While there he visited the Fascist Hall of Martyrs which gave him an idea, which many years later was to became Calcutta's Mahajati Sadan. In another unsuccessful attempt to get to the Soviet Union, he met Maxim Litvinoff, commissioner of foreign affairs of the USSR at the Russian Embassy in Rome.

With his book published, Bose's priority was to recover his health. In Geneva he met Romain Rolland, a figure of awe for Indians of Bose's generation, and one of the foremost European thinkers who was drawn to India. He had also written biographies of Ramakrishna and Virekanamda. When Bose had sent him a copy of his book, Rolland ordered two more for his wife and sister. Their meeting took place on 3 April 1935, and Bose wrote a gushing piece about it. When he arrived at Rolland's home in Villa Olga in Villeneuve, the door was opened by Rolland's wife and then:

> There emerged a tall figure with a pale countenance and with wonderful penetrating eyes. Yes, this was the face I had seen in many a picture before, a face that seemed to be burdened with the sorrows of humanity. There was something exquisitely sad in that pallid face - but it was not an expression of defeatism. For no sooner did he begin to speak than colour rushed to his white cheeks - the eyes glowed with a light that was uncommon - and the words that he poured forth were pregnant with life and hope.

As Bose was not fluent in French and Rolland was not an English speaker, there was need for an interpreter.

Rolland told Bose he had been guided in his life by four principles. These were that all races were equal, there should be justice for exploited workers, freedom for all suppressed nationalities and equal rights for women. Today these principles would sound very commonplace, in 1935 they were revolutionary.

Bose returned to Vienna for surgery. On 24 April 1935 his much-postponed operation took place at the Sanatorium Rudofinerhaus, where his gall-bladder "with a big stone inside" was removed. He spent much of the summer in Karlsbad, recuperating. With improving health and finances came news of the release of Sarat on 26 July 1935. Sarat quickly re-established his considerable practice at the Bar, and was soon leading the Congress in Bengal.

The excellent reviews of *The Indian Struggle* made Bose think of writing another book on the Indian national movement for foreigners interested in India. 1936 marked the fiftieth birthday of the Congress and Bose, for all his status as a rebellious Congressman, was keen to join in the celebrations. He still wanted to visit the Soviet Union but was unable to obtain a visa. In a letter to Naomi he speculated whether Dr Vetter could tell the Soviets that the impression in India was that Bose was being denied a visa because the Soviets wanted to get close to the British. "This is rather damaging to the reputation of the Soviet government in India.

This latest rebuff by the Soviets had come just after another trip to Germany, this time to Munich in the autumn of 1935. It was his third visit to Germany since his arrival in Europe in 1933 and led to a memo to Thierfelder on the "anti Indian propaganda" of the Nazis. He went to Berlin again in February 1936, meeting Prufer and Dychoff. But while they were cordial he was later to tell Thierfelder, " the results of the interview was practically nil"

By this tme Bose was also involved with the Nehrus on a personal level. Nehru had been released from gaol the previous autumn on the news that his wife Kamala was seriously ill in Europe. Nehru rushed to her side and when she improved a little he went to London with his daughter Indira. No concern had been expressed by the India Office.

While the British drew a very sharp distinction between Nehru and Bose, Nehru's arrival in Europe had renewed his personal links with Bose. For the first and only time the two men grew close. Bose was at the station at nine on the morning of June 4, 1935 when the train carrying Kamala and Indira had arrived in Vienna. He took them to the Hotel Bristol and as Kamala lay dying he was often by her bedside. He also introduced Nambiar to the Nehrus and they took to calling him "Nanu".

In September 1935 when Jawaharlal, freed from gaol, arrived in Basel, Subhas met and drove him to Badenwelier in the Black Forest where Kamala was being treated.

Jawaharlal, despite past differences, was like an older brother, and these European meetings marked the start of a short warm friendship between the two men. In contrast to his earlier criticisms of Nehru, repeated *in The Indian Struggle*, Bose even accepted being reproved by Nehru. When Nehru wrote to him pointing out errors in the book Bose apologised, hoping that they were not major. He might, he said, have got some dates wrong but he had relied on memory.

The British watched the two young Indian leaders in Europe with great interest. An IPI note commented:

> Ever since the arrival of Nehru in Europe, his attitude towards his own prospects, despite his marked improvement in his health, might be described as one of defeatism. There is evidence that he is prepared to work with Nehru, whom he professes to meet again in Lausanne in the latter part of February, and he most certainly intends to be back in India for the opening of the Lucknow Congress. But Nehru, whether willingly or not, has stolen his thunder and it

remains to be seen how far he will be willing to play satellite to Nehru's Jove.

After three years of Nazi rule Indians in Germany were under severe restrictions. The authorities had banned a meeting called by the Islamic Association to protest against an anti-Indian film called *Bengali*. However, Bose did speak to the Indian Students Association in Berlin on February 4 1936 and made his views very clear: "Since the new regime has come into power in Germany, the position of Indians had considerably worsened."

In Berlin Bose got the impression that the economic situation was deteriorating and that more people were criticising the regime. "The Haus-Frau as a class were discontented because butter, eggs, etc were difficult to get. And the government cannot put the women into prisons so easily!" he wrote to Naomi. Stormtroopers no longer marched through the streets, as he had witnessed in 1933 and 1934, and while he felt the government was pro-British, the people wanted peace.

Shortly afterwards Hitler made anti-Indian, anti-Asian remarks. Bose, who was in Geneva issued a statement which suggested he had given up all hopes of ever doing business with Hitler:

> During the last few weeks my mind has been greatly disturbed at the insulting remarks made by the German Fuehrer about the Indian People. This is not the first time that India has been insulted by the outstanding leaders of Nazi Germany. It is quite clear that Germany today is determined to curry favour with England by insulting India. I can have no objections if the Germans desire to lick the boots of the Britishers, but if they think that in the year 1936 an insult hurled at India will be quietly pocketed by us, they are sadly mistaken. I am glad to find indications that public opinion in India has already been aroused on this question, and I hope that we shall be able to demonstrate that the Indian people can no longer be insulted with impunity.

Bose had realised that the Hitler regime in Germany worshipped strength, and urged Indian students in Europe to protest strongly and boycott German goods in India. Germany sold more to India than she bought and while Bose could not see the Hitler regime falling except through war, "if as a result of our boycott Germany's trade suffers, then German businessmen will put pressure on Hitler."

The only consolation for Bose was that not all European countries were like Germany. Bose had arrived in Berlin on the night train from Prague accompanied by Nambiar. In four visits to Germany no prominent Nazi had seen him. In Prague he met Benes, now President of Czechslovakia, with Nambiar acting as his interpreter. Despite Benes's busy schedule, Bose's was squeezed in between calls by the French and the Austrian ambassadors and this pleased him greatly.

Bose used this trip to visit parts of northern Europe. From Berlin he went to Cologne, Brussels and then Antwerp, where there was a thriving Indian business community dealing in diamonds and precious stones. Nathalal Parikh was one of these businessman. Bose had met him at Patel's bedside; now the friendship deepened as Parikh took him around Belgium. Bose went to the battlefield at Waterloo; in Spa he was denied entry to a casino because he refused to remove his Indian cap; but was enchanted by the Grotto-de-Han caves. He was also interviewed by *Le Matin* and then set off for his first visit to Paris, staying at the Hotel Ambassador in Boulevarde Haussmann. He met Andre Gide and planned to visit Ireland.

For radical Indians, particularly Bengalis, Ireland was a magic country. It had done the impossible - proved that even the mighty British Empire was vulnerable. Indians had absorbed Irish history, and the lives of Irish heroes had through endless re-telling acquired the status of ancient Hindu myths. Bose himself could recall the tremendous enthusiasm when Terence

McSwiney's family sent a message of condolence on Jatin Das' death. He had been long planning to go to Ireland and in 1934, the Irish Free State legation at Berlin had granted him a visa. But Bose had then still been hoping to visit England, and was convinced that a visit to Ireland would spoil his chances. Now this constraint had vanished.

Bose planned to sail to Ireland from France. On 30 January he boarded the US Lines S.S. *Washington* at Le Havre for Cobh, arriving on 1 February 1936. From Cobh he went to Cork where he called on Miss Mary McSwiney, a well known Republican, and later took the train to Dublin.

The Irish had planned a grand welcome for him. Present were Republican stalwarts led by Maud Gonne Macbride as well as Indian students. An Indian girl garlanded him. He was accorded a reception by the Indian-Irish Independence League, attended by virtually the entire Republican old guard. And in one of the many ironies of his life in Dublin, he also by chance met Colonel J.H. Smith who had been the officer in charge of Mandalay when he was in prison there.

His ten days in Dublin became a mini-state-visit. He had discussions with government ministers and the Lord Mayor of Dublin and listened to Dail debates from the Strangers' Gallery.

The high points of his visit, and the events that pleased him immensely, were his three meetings with Eamon De Valera. The first meeting on 3 February with De Valera as Ireland's foreign minister, was at Government Buildings. Then on 7 February there was a tea party by the ruling *Fianna Fail* and finally dinner at De Valera's home. De Valera, who had himself left Ireland for America during its freedom struggle, warned Bose not to be an exile for too long and cautioned him that it was difficult to confront the British. Before he left Dublin, Bose gave a reception at his hotel, the Shelbourne, then considered the best in Dublin, and emphasised the ties that linked India with Ireland. The Irish trip made a great impression on Bose. He would often think of it and feel it was like a dream that had gone rather too quickly.

Nowadays such visits have become so common as to be unremarkable. But in 1936, Bose's activities created a sensation. His visit dominated the news in both Ireland and India, and inevitably British intelligence kept track on his movements.

Interestingly, when Bose was asked in Dublin about being followed by British spies, he brushed the question aside. He was more concerned that the interviewer called him a Bengal leader: "Why do you call me a Bengal leader? I am not provincial."

The British had to accept that "much was made of Bose's visit in the Irish papers" and one IPI note said, "Subhas Bose showed great skill in adapting himself to the mentality of his audience."

They consoled themselves by arguing that this was their old enemy up to his publicity tricks and in any case Irish ministers were always keen to court anyone who was *persona non grata* with the British government. The only crumb of comfort they had was that Bose was not given a civic reception or an honorary degree.

The British worried that Bose would use Ireland to come to England. On 9 December 1935 the question of why Bose was not allowed into Britain had been raised in Parliament. The Under Secretary of State for India had informed the House of Commons that Lord Zetland, the Secretary of State, considered that Bose's presence in Britain would be undesirable. This had led to some controversy in the left-wing British papers.

The British government was concerned that if Bose reached London he might succeed in uniting the divided Indian community in England. IPI agents kept careful watch on Indians who might go to Dublin to meet Bose. They had no fears about Nehru visiting the capital of their empire. A few months previously he had been in London and received a great reception. His daughter Indira was about to enter Somerville College, Oxford. The IPI now took pity on Bose. He had not quite succeeded in getting Indian propaganda together in Europe:

> ... It might be argued that he has been singularly unfortunate in the combination of circumstances against him. His efforts to establish propaganda centres in Europe was frustrated first by the action of the trustees in declining up to the present to allow him the handling of the Patel legacy; secondly by the lack of faith shown by the leading Congress personalities in the efficacy of foreign propaganda and, lastly, by the international crisis. The European situation occasioned dissension in the ranks of his followers in Continental circles; it vitiated his bids for simultaneous patronage of Nazis and Fascist semi-government Departments and the final outbreak of war between Italy and Abyssinia relegated the whole question of his Indian activities in Europe to insignificance.

For Bose, India beckoned again. He had never liked the life of an exile, and the thought of permanent separation from his homeland was unbearable. He knew that return to India meant prison but it was infinitely preferable even to Vienna. In February 1936, he had more reason to return home. Jawaharlal Nehru was going to be the next president of the Congress and Subhas Bose was determined that the Left should unite behind him.

Bose was aware of Nehru's vacillation when confronting Gandhi, and in private discussions and letters tried to build up his confidence and urge him to lead the Left.

In an affectionate "dear Jawahar" letter he told him that his position was so unique that not even Gandhi could "take a stand which will alienate you". But was there more to the Bose-Nehru discussions than recorded in their letters?

On 25 May 1936 the Foreign Office in London would write a secret letter to a Mr. Dibdin in the India Office enclosing a copy of a memorandum from a Mr. Hadow at the British Legation in Prague.

The two-page memo said that when Bose and Nehru had met at Badenweiler, Bose had asked for Nehru's support for violent terrorist attacks on as many British officials as possible, and that Nehru had refused. It then went on to say how Bose had received a rebuff from the Germans, but had received encouragement from Mussolini, the Irish and the Japanese, all of whom promised support including arms.

Hadow said the information had come from a violent opponent of the German regime who in turn had got it from an Indian supporter of Bose. The Foreign Office said the supporter was an anti-British journalist in Prague, but that the revelations were so sensitive that they should not be passed to the Government of India.

IPI studied the report and concluded that while the source was Nambiar much of the information was rubbish. True, Bose had been in Berlin with Nambiar and received a rebuff from the Germans, but "Bose has not seen Mussolini this year, and it is by no means obvious why Ireland should come into any attempt to smuggle arms for terrorists." Another IPI official said "I suspect Nambiar was exaggerating possibly in order to increase his own importance."

The memo may be dismissed as one of those pieces of pointless information intelligence agencies get from time to time. But it shows how bizarre were some of the stories Bose generated. Bose wanted to be in India for the Lucknow Congress in April 1936. On his way back from Ireland he visited Paris, returning to the Hotel Ambassador for a longer stay. This time he met Andre Malraux, Victor Basch, and Guernut, the minister of education. The Vetter's introductions proved useful in Paris. Bose also spoke to the French section of the League Against Imperialism, stressing the need for a worldwide anti-imperialist front. Subhas had watched with dismay the rape of Abyssinia by Italy in 1935 and the continuing Japanese aggression against China. But it was about Japan that he felt most strongly: "It is necessary for us to think of the means of preventing the growth of Japanese imperialism in Asia. If tomorrow China could be strong and unified; if tomorrow India could be free, I am sure it would influence the balance of power in Asia and serve to check the spread of Japanese imperialism."

He had condemned the Italian invasion of Abyssinia in a long article for *The Modern Review,* stating that it proved that " a nation can hope to be free only if it is strong, from a physical and military point of view, and is able to acquire all the knowledge which modern science can impart."

The wider lesson he drew was that imperialism could only come to an end if it was overthrown by an anti-imperialist agency or "through an internecine struggle amongst the imperialists themselves. If the second course is furthered by growth of Italian Imperialism, then Abyssinia will not have suffered in vain."

Bose was with Nehru when Kamala Nehru died in Lausanne, at 5 am on 28 February, 1936. Bose helped Nehru in arranging for her cremation. There followed another visit to Romain Rolland and then Bad Gastein. The British, meanwhile, wondered about how and when Bose would get back to India. The Bengal government was worried that Bose, who had bought a return ticket, might arrive at any moment and catch them unawares. One of the Delhi officials calmed these fears: "My opinion is that it is extremely unlikely that Subhas Chandra Bose will attempt to come to India like a thief in the night. He thrives almost entirely on publicity and will, in my opinion, continue to do so."

Bose had planned to leave for India from Marseilles on the *Viceroy of India* on 20 March. The Bengal government persuaded Delhi to get the India Office to issue a warning. This was a remarkable testimony to Bose's power. 1936 in India was a year of peace. The Congress was inching towards accepting ministries in the provinces, and had decided to contest elections under the new Government of India Act of 1935. For the first time in many years nearly all its prominent leaders were sleeping in their own homes. In Bengal Sarat Bose had been released and the government had declared that terrorism was defeated.

The India Office sent a long telegram to the Government of India which summarised the familiar case against Bose and then concluded: "We trust this account will enable you to satisfy critics that Bose is a dangerous revolutionary; the more so because of his great ability and influence in Bengal." On 12 March the British Consul in Vienna warned Bose that if he returned he could not be expected to remain at liberty.

Bose wrote to a number of people including Nehru asking for advice. Should he return or should he not go? Rolland advised him not to.

But Bose was fed up with exile. He decided he would return but not on a British ship. On 27 March 1936 he sailed from Naples on an Italian ship *Counte Verde,* for Bombay. The ship was full of Italians, "some of whom are probably going to their doom in the wilds of Abyssinia. There are a few Indians and no Englishmen." As the ship arrived at Port Said, the long arm of the English caught up with Bose. Police officers came aboard, seized his passport and mounted a guard over him. Only as the *Counte Verde* was about to sail were they withdrawn. As soon as he reached Bombay on the morning of 8 April, Bose was whisked off to Arthur Road prison and, a few days later, to Poona where he was put into the same gaol and same yard in Yeravada where Gandhi had been interned a few years earlier.

Bose's first letter from his Bombay gaol, written on the very afternoon of his imprisonment, was to a young lady in Vienna. He had written to her quite often but now there would be many more letters as he once again experienced life inside a Raj gaol. We now come to the most intriguing personal relationship in the life of Subhas Bose.

Part Four

THE EMBATTLED *LEADER*

Your eyes are filled with tender light
For those whose eyes are dimmed with tears
They see your brow is crowned and bright
But not its ring of wounding spears.

George Russell
(one of Bose's favourite poets)

11
Subhas In Love

Bose's first letter from gaol was written to Emilie Schenkl. This was not the first letter to her nor the last. Subhas was to write many hundreds to her between 1934 and 1942, 180 of which survive, and form part of the *Collected Works of Subhas Bose*. Only a few of Emilie's letters have been traced.

Sisir Bose, his nephew who co-edited the works, has argued that the letters show the human and emotional aspects of Bose and that the relationship made him a more complete human being. What they reveal is a man struggling to come to terms with love; the love of a woman, a foreign woman, totally different from the women he had known in his earlier life. Emilie's few preserved letters were found in an old cigar box in Calcutta in 1980. They give the impression of two very private and intensely reserved individuals slowly finding themselves.

In all his letters, Emilie was always "Dear Fraulein Schenkl", and Emilie always started her letters "Dear Mr Bose". And this form of address did not change between the first letter in November 1934 to the last in December 1942, by which time Schenkl should have become a Frau, as they were said to have married and also produced a child. The most Subhas would unburden himself was to address Emilie as "a gracious lady" in a couple of letters and write them in block capitals as if to convey how deeply he felt for her. If the letters add to our knowledge about a certain aspect of Subhas's life they also show how mysterious the private man could be, in sharp contrast to the public figure. While the letters add greatly to our knowledge of Bose, we are still left in the dark about many aspects of him.

It was Janakinath's death, which had made Bose hurry back to India in the winter of 1934, that prompted the letters. Emilie, of course, had typed the manuscript of his book and had given him a letter as he headed home. That letter has not survived but Subhas's reply, "The kind letter you gave me I read with pleasure," indicated how welcome it was.

Subhas, interned at his parents' Elgin Road home, and mourning the loss of his father, did not write to anybody else but Emilie. He wrote 14 letters between 30 November 1934 and 26 January 1935. There was clearly a bond. Emilie sent him a present and later Subhas on his way back to Europe took *Dhup*, incense, and a book about Vivekananda for her.
Occasionally there was even a touch of playfulness from Subhas. When he landed back in Europe in January 1935, and was on his way to Emilie's home town of Vienna, he wrote to her from Rome asking, "Do you think I have forgotten your telephone number?" The letter was written two days after his birthday, and after Emilie had written to him wishing him happy birthday. Subhas wrote:

> Thanks very much for your kind message for my birthday. As a matter of fact, I had forgotten about it! I am awful, am I not? ... I am sorry for your old cough - *mien kopf! Mein kopf!...Auf wiedersehen.*

Emilie clearly meant a lot to him. When the letters resumed in January 1936, after Subhas had left Vienna, they indicated how much he had begun to miss her when he was away. From the Hotel Ambassador in Paris, just before his trip to Ireland he asked, "But why don't you write to me?" and sent her £2 for stamps. By this time Subhas was also becoming possessive. In March 1936, while in Bad Gastein, he wrote:

> You must be very careful before deciding to give lessons to Indians. Generally they want some lady who will flirt with them and also teach them dancing perhaps. There are such girls already and I am afraid that you may be taken as one among them. How is Dr Sen [who Subhas has recommended she consult about her cough and cold] behaving towards you?

One problem was that Emilie had no job, and Subhas wanted to make her financially independent. He decided to help her become a journalist. It was a bizarre decision since Emilie neither had the aptitude for journalism nor the interest in world affairs that Subhas wanted her to cultivate. The result was that Subhas, far from coming over as the tender lover, often seemed more like a well meaning but strict headmaster teaching, at times severely disciplining, a pupil much in need of education.

Subhas first thought of making Emilie a journalist as he sailed to Ireland on the *Washington* in January 1936. He advised her what newspapers to read, suggested she visit the cafes of Vienna and pick up old copies of French newspapers and *The Times* at a cheap rate. He sent her his own copy of *The Times*, gave her detailed guidance on preparing a business card and contacting the press attaches of the embassies in Vienna. He even instructed her on how to address them.

Subhas thought Emilie could be a special correspondent of *The Hindu*, one of India's leading daily newspapers, and so keen was he on this he acted as her agent. He corresponded with *The Hindu* on her behalf and got them to agree to take two articles from her every month for a fee of £2. In Vienna in 1936 this would have been a very useful income.

Subhas told her she should write about the Balkans and the Near East and some of his letters were a history tutorial on what various terms such as Little Entente and Locarno Treaty meant. But Emilie's first article for *The Hindu* proved a disaster. Subhas wanted to vet the article before Emilie sent it off and when he received it he was furious:

> Your article is unsatisfactory. Firstly you have altogether forgotten that you are not a Vienna correspondent but a correspondent of the Balkans and the Near East. Secondly, there are serious mistakes in it, which an Austrian should be ashamed of. The article is rejected (But I have corrected your article to show you your mistakes.)

The letter had an appendix entitled "Remarks" in which Subhas numbered the mistakes. The first was "bad English". The Remarks concluded in italics, in case Emilie missed the significance, *Very bad! Very disappointing! English also is bad!* So keen was he to see Emilie become a journalist that Subhas Bose became a ghostwriter and rewrote the article for Emilie. He was not happy about his ghosted effort and rewrote it again a few days later before allowing Emilie to post it to *The Hindu* as her first journalistic effort.

Nambiar suggested that *The Hindu* might welcome articles on women and the cinema. Subhas did not veto the idea but said that Emilie should first write on Balkan politics. At this stage the relationship was fragile, and Subhas was often annoyed with Emilie. When, against his wishes, she sent his winter clothes to him, he was angry:

> I cannot tell you how greatly annoyed I feel with you. I do not know under whose instructions you have sent them. They are quite useless as there is no snow here … Please let me know how much money you have spent over this. I am sure you are always spending a lot of money in similar foolish ways. I thought you had intelligence but I find that you are very foolish. I am very, very sorry.

He saw the parcel had been marked "express" and this angered him even more. He added a PS, "What was the urgency I wonder! So you have spent a good bit over this meaningless thing!"This letter was written on 12 March 1936 and two weeks later, even as he was on the high seas and his letters were describing the voyage back to India – the excessive food, musical concerts, film shows, and deck sports – some of the anger remained. On 30 March 1936 he wrote:

> I want you to realise how you bungle things where you do not obey my instructions faithfully. The last example is your telling Dr Sen about my postponing my departure for India. The difficulty is that you never think before acting. You must now cultivate this habit before you do anything. Think thrice before you act. If you do this, you will seldom make any mistakes.

The transition from head master to a tender lover appears to have started the nearer Subhas Bose got to India, and more particularly, as he went up to the Himalayas. When Bose once again fell ill in jail, he was transferred to his brother Sarat's house and kept under the same "relaxed" detention laws that had restricted Sarat. Though Subhas never formally accepted what he felt were humiliating conditions, he did not violate them, preferring to get re-acquainted with his family after nearly four years in jail and exile, and to assimilate the European experience.

From time to time, Bose corrected Emilie's English. When she wrote about drinking *Kaffee*, Subhas pointed out that if she meant the drink it should be coffee, and that a café was the place where you had the drink. But he was no longer the stern head master he had been when trying to turn her into a journalist. Now he added, "I hope you will not mind me correcting you in this manner." Emilie replied: "You would oblige me if you would correct my mistakes".

Bose's years in Europe had made him fond of European music, and he wanted Emilie's help in getting the names of good records. In June 1936 he had been allowed to have a gramophone, but warned Emilie that he found classical European music difficult, his taste was more for the Vienna waltz. Emilie was delighted to hear this. She could not abide heavy music such as Wagner's opera, for she too liked light music like Viennese songs or jazz.

Emilie told Subhas of her love for matters spiritual. In her early teens she had been inspired by a German author, Hans Sterneder, who argued that the way to salvation lay in withdrawing from active life and living like a nun. Emilie was not prepared to do this; she believed in living life to the full.

> First I think it would do no good to give up the world, because in active life one can fulfil a mission, while as a monk or so, one does not fulfil a useful mission. The world as a whole is not yet ripe to penetrate into a more spiritual sphere.

Emilie had all but given up her Catholic faith, had not been to church for years,and wrote caustically about Roman Catholic priests who were worldly men sitting night after night in the inns and cafes of Central Europe, drinking and dancing with the girls. Both of them had their mutual illnesses to talk about. Subhas, while in Kurseong, caught flu, Emilie had what she called her two "faithful friends", cough and cold, which were always with her in winter. Emilie also seemed to develop an illness in sympathy with Subhas. She started getting pains in her gall bladder after meals, and gave up meat and, for a time, alcohol. This must have pleased Subhas who did not drink, did not eat beef, and was, like all Bengalis, a big fish eater. Emilie and Subhas also discussed taking photographs. Subhas had a camera, but was not very good at using it. Emilie was much better.

As the summer of 1936 progressed the two of them were absorbed in two very different events. For Emilie it was the Olympics, for Subhas it was one of the most sensational court cases to grip India at that time. In that summer Berlin staged what became known as the Nazi Olympics, which provided Hitler with a showcase for his new Germany. It did not work quite according to plan. The black American, Jesse Owens, won four athletics gold medals, still a record to this day, creating consternation for the Nazis. They were furious that the Americans allowed their blacks, whom the Nazis considered sub-human, to take part and undermine Nazi propaganda of the blond, blue eyed Aryan master race. When Owens won, Hitler walked out of the stadium refusing to shake his hand.

Emilie followed the Olympics Games closely on the radio and noted with pleasure how the Austrian athletes were greeted as they entered the stadium. There is no record of her making any reference to the issue of the black Americans. On a trip to the mountains she took part in what she called "Olympic sessions", forming an Olympic Committee which organised long mountains walks.

Subhas followed the Olympics in the papers, noting that the Indians had as usual done badly except for hockey where the team was led by the greatest player in the game's history, Dyan Chand. Bose who, unusually for Indian politicians, had an interest in sports observed: "You can see there is hardly any scientific training in India for this – and lack of funds is an important factor."

In a letter to Emilie Subhas wrote a detailed account of an Indian court case, so as to explain words with which she would be unfamiliar. He sent her cuttings from newspapers, marking extracts. Despite the vast distances that separated them, their bond was growing stronger. Emilie sent Subhas a four-leaf clover known as *Glucsklee*: "Put it your purse, it shall bring you luck". Subhas wrote back: "We in India have heaps and heaps of superstitions with the result that I do not believe in any of them. In fact I sometimes think there are no superstitions outside India, because we have bagged the lot." Realising Emilie might be hurt he added: "Pardon my being so rude if I hurt your feelings but I cannot help saying what I feel."

In September 1936 Emilie wrote of her struggle to find a job. Her mother blamed her for not trying hard enough and she was under severe nervous strain. Although the trip to the mountains had helped, she was back in Vienna. Eventually she found work as a nanny to a young Indian child, a job that left her exhausted. All this correspondence was read by the authorities, censored and passed by the police superintendent in Darjeeling. The two lovers had to be discreet but occasionally they let slip something that clearly carried a deeper meaning.

In 1936 came the first elections following the much-trumpeted Government of India Act of 1935. This was the new "charter of liberty" born after an eight-year pregnancy through the Simon Commission, round-table conferences and innumerable debates in Parliament. It was dyarchy – government by two dependent bodies – by more sophisticated means. As R.J. Moore says, "It aimed at the representation of interest, not of numbers." All the groups on whom the Raj could rely were catered for: upper class Muslims, dependable Hindus, other minorities, and princes. Existing separate electoral arrangements for Hindus, Muslims and other minorities were strengthened; the provinces were given more power, but the British governors held wide reserve powers. A federal centre was created, but it was left weak and ineffectual, its very existence subject to the agreement of the princes. (Encouraged by Churchill and the Conservative Right, the princes refused to agree to this part of the act and it was never implemented.)

On the larger questions of national independence and freedom the 1935 Act provided the same answers as ever: India was still the fief of the secretary of state and would be run from the well-fortified corridors of the India Office in Whitehall. The Act remains one of history's most sophisticated attempts at spin, an occupying power seeking to perpetuate its rule while not appearing to do so. In the end it failed, but it is a reflection of the strength of imperialist propaganda that, even today, the historians of the Raj can see it as the latter's crowning glory.

Subhas Bose, like all other Left nationalists, had no illusions about the Act. He had condemned the White Paper as soon as it was issued, and he was convinced that the Congress would have to fight the Act in every possible way. The only question was how. Although total opposition was theoretically the easiest way, it was not necessarily the best. In fact, it could turn out to be dangerous. It would leave the British free to organise collaborators to win the election and prove its popular support. So Bose wanted the Congress to contest the elections, then reject the Act.

It was this that the government feared, though their public justification for Bose's continued arrest (when all the other prominent leaders were free) was his connection with revolutionary violence. They stuck to this line despite considerable public protest which included a one-day country-wide *hartal,* launched on 20 May 1936, to secure his release.

Through the summer and autumn of 1936 public protests about Bose's detention had continued. There were motions in the Delhi assembly, angry demands by Nehru, and questions in the House of Commons. But the government always gave the same answer: that he was a man of great ability, but dedicated towards revolutionary violence, and had been imprisoned for that reason. In December, his intestinal troubles flared up again, and he was admitted to the Medical College Hospital in Calcutta. He had lost 10 kilos in weight but the doctors assured him that nothing was wrong with his lungs and that he should soon regain his weight.

With the elections just a month away, the Indian government had successfully prevented Bose from organising the Congress during a crucial period; but now even the Bengal government could afford to accommodate him. He was allotted a separate room, a special day bearer was appointed, extra diet was sanctioned and he was thoroughly examined and X-rayed. When he was a little better, relatives were allowed to visit him. Later, under police escort, he was driven every afternoon to spend a few hours with Prabhabati at 38/2 Elgin Road and allowed to go for a drive around Calcutta.

Subhas was glad to be back in the noise and bustle of Calcutta, although his years in Europe had affected him sufficiently for him to envy Emilie the snow in Vienna. He wrote to Emilie:

> This hospital is one of the biggest in India and the biggest in Calcutta. It is also the oldest in India and is in the centre of the town. The rooms are not properly separated from the general ward, and that is how I get the noise whenever any patient nearby is in pain. However, after a long period of isolation the proximity (nearness) of human beings even when they are noisy is welcome.

The government still had no intention of letting him free. The question was what the Congress would do if it won the election, and whether or not to accept office. A free Bose would strengthen the Left and complicate matters. While the government waited for the election results, it decided that once Bose had recovered his health he would be interned. On 10 February 1937 the home department sent the Bengal government the necessary warrant. Meanwhile the legal experts discovered that the previous "relaxed" detention had been technically illegal; and by the time they had solved the puzzle, wider political events had made Bose's detention impossible.

The election results showed sweeping Congress victories: the party had won 716 seats out of 1161 it contested (from a total of 1585), and clear majorities in six provinces. In Bengal it had obtained more seats than any other party; but the Bengal government could feel satisfied that its friends – the Muslim League, the Europeans, the independent scheduled caste groups and the Hindu upper-caste clans – had sufficient strength to preserve a suitably collaborationist government.

On a national scale the Congress was definitely moving towards acceptance of office.

The Congress Right, and the careerists who had suffered so long, were determined not to reject this, the most significant prize awarded by the Raj. The Left, led by Nehru, were opposed to this but the Right, ably marshalled by the Brahmanical skills of Rajagopalachari, manoeuvred the party into acceptance at the crucial working committee session in Delhi on 16 March 1937. On the afternoon of 17 March, while Subhas sat talking to Prabhabati in the front room of the Elgin Road house, a deputy commissioner of police walked in with a letter informing him that the order imposed on January 1932 had at last been cancelled. For the first time in nearly six years, Subhas Bose was a free man in India.

Initially, at his mother's request, Bose stayed with her at Elgin Road using the airy first-floor rooms. Almost immediately he rang Dilip, who described the moment of reunion:

> I was shocked to see how much he had thinned away. But he looked more spiritual than ever in spite of the rings of shadows under his keen eyes. He threw his arms round me and wept like a child.

As the two of them resumed their debates about life, yoga and Nirvana, Dilip realised that Subhas had changed. Prison had mellowed him, made him a gentler person. Forced back on his own resources it made him realise the virtues of humility and resignation. He was no longer the flamboyant young man quitting the ICS in a single sweeping gesture: he needed friends and help. "Only do stay with us for a while," he pleaded with Dilip when he heard of Dilip's plans to return to Aurobindo. "Don't revert too soon to your shell. You may not need us but we need you." Subhas, Dilip thought, would now try and learn to love his enemies, although with one enemy there could be no compromise, no retreat to *ashrams* and gurus. There the fight against British rule would be all the fiercer. Prison had softened him but it had not defeated him.

Bengal welcomed its son with special warmth. On 6 April 1937 Shradhananda Park was the scene of a huge meeting where 600 associations presented him with garlands of marigolds and bouquets. Bose told the crowd that he felt like a political Rip Wan Winkle and pleaded for time to pick up the threads of political life after six years of absence. He was not fit enough to resume active political work. He had to recover his health and face the prospect of doing so in the oppressive heat of a Calcutta summer. At the end of April he left the city for the cool of the hills, choosing the western Himalayan ranges. His old friends the Dharmavirs had settled in Dalhousie, a little hill station about 2,000 metres high in the Punjab, and one of the many such stations created by the Raj as summer retreats.

On 25 April Bose left Calcutta on a slow journey to the hills. He spent a few days in Allahabad, and met Gandhi, who lovingly embraced him, and then held meetings with other Congress leaders. He reached Dalhousie on 2 May, and was to remain there until 5 October. It was here, under the gaze of the Himalayas, which 20 years earlier had conjured up images of the great Hindu past, that he truly discovered his love for Emilie. Throughout his journey there he had written to her, but after he reached Dalhousie he gave expression for the first time to his true feelings. Emilie received his letter sometime in June, but the editors of Bose's *Collected Works* think it was written either in late April or early May 1937. It was written in block capitals and it said:

> I HAVE BEEN LONGING TO WRITE TO YOU FOR SOME TIME PAST - BUT YOU CAN EASILY UNDERSTAND HOW DIFFICULT IT WAS TO WRITE TO YOU ABOUT MY FEELINGS. I JUST WANT TO LET YOU KNOW NOW THAT I AM EXACTLY WHAT I WAS BEFORE, WHEN YOU KNEW ME. NOT A SINGLE DAY PASSES THAT I DO NOT THINK OF YOU. YOU ARE WITH ME ALL THE TIME. I CANNOT POSSIBLY THINK OF ANYBODY ELSE IN THIS WORLD. I AM ANXIOUS TO KNOW ABOUT YOUR THOUGHTS, PLEASE WRITE

> TO ME SOON IN YOUR OWN LANGUAGE (SIMPLE STYLE) BY AIR-MAIL SO THAT I MAY KNOW. I DO NOT KNOW WHAT I SHOULD DO IN FUTURE. I AM NOT ABLE TO DECIDE. I CANNOT TELL YOU HOW LONELY I HAVE BEEN FEELING ALL THESE MONTHS AND HOW SORROWFUL. ONLY ONE THING COULD MAKE ME HAPPY – BUT I DO NOT KNOW IF THAT IS POSSIBLE. HOWEVER I AM THINKING OF IT DAY AND NIGHT AND PRAYING TO GOD TO SHOW ME THE RIGHT PATH. EVERY TIME I HEAR THAT YOU ARE NOT WELL, I FEEL SO UNHAPPY. DO TAKE CARE OF YOUR HEALTH SO THAT I MAY FEEL SOMEWHAT RELIEVED. EVER YOURS WITH MY HEART AND SOUL.

This is clearly a love letter with a suggestion that Subhas was thinking of marriage. The previous December, in a letter to Naomi, he had asked about newspaper gossip that the then Austrian Chancellor Kurt von Schuschnigg had married secretly and this may have put the idea in his head. A visit to Europe was out of the question; although a free man, he could not be explicit in his letters. They were no longer read by the Raj but they were secretly censored: and in India privacy was impossible and friends read his letters. So he decided that when he wanted to say something affectionate he would write in German. So from then on, in the middle of a letter written in English, there would be a few lines in German which he hoped would prove too much for his Raj spies or even his friends. Occasionally he wrote entire letters in German. But not even then did Subhas Bose ever become truly passionate.

Here the contrast with Nehru is instructive. In April 1937, as Bose was writing his block capital declaration to Emilie, Nehru, then Congress President, was in the middle of his own love affair. Long before Kamala Nehru's death Jawaharlal and his wife had stopped being lovers and when she died he took a mistress. She was Padmaja Naidu, daughter of Sarojini and a niece by marriage of Nambiar. In April 1937 Nehru, in the midst of a Congress working committee session, wrote to her from Allahabad, "You move me too much....the thought of you vitalises me". The next month, as Nehru was on tour of Malaya with his daughter Indira, he wrote to Padmaja, "I famish for news of you. How I long to hold you and to look into your eyes."

Even with the soaring Himalayas to inspire him Subhas Bose could never write like this to the woman he loved. As in love so in politics. Bose's view of the developing European scene did not match the passionate feelings of Nehru. As Bose was preparing to leave Europe the Spanish civil war had broken out. This was a classic conflict between the left and right; the left sided with the Republican government against General Franco and his fascists. Nehru, when he visited Europe the following summer, was a guest of the Republican government and burnished his left-wing credentials by his enthusiastic support for their cause, speaking at public meetings under the auspices of the "Aid to Spain" committee and becoming a hero of the international left.

In a long essay for *Modern Review* published in August 1937, Bose took a more detached, almost professorial, view in analysing why Italy and Germany were intervening on behalf of Franco. He thought that a world war might come through German miscalculation, as in 1914, when Germany had not believed that Britain would fight. His various meetings with Mussolini had made him readily accept the Duce's notions of Italian military strength, which the war was to prove illusory. He concluded his fourteen page essay:

> If Franco wins, it will be a victory for Italy and Germany, and will mean the end of British hegemony in the Mediterranean and dark days ahead of France. But the Russian Colossus has often proved to be an enigma. It baffled Napoleon, the conqueror of Europe. Will it baffle Hitler?

Japan and its aggression in China engaged him. Like many Asians and in particular Indians, he admired Japan, the only Asian country that had resisted the European powers and their domination of the world. But his sympathies were with China and he hoped Japan could go on being Asia's challenge to European imperialism, but not at the expense of China. His long essay "Japan's Role in the Far East", published in September 1937, concluded:

> Japan has done great things for herself and for Asia. Her reawakening at the dawn of the present century sent a thrill throughout our Continent. Japan has shattered the white man's prestige in the Far East and has put all Western imperialist powers on the defensive - not only in the military but also in the economic sphere. She is extremely sensitive, and rightly so about her self-respect as an Asiatic race. She is determined to drive out the Western Powers from the Far East. But could not all this have been achieved without Imperialism, without dismembering the Chinese Republic, without humiliating another proud, cultured and ancient race? No, with all our admiration for Japan, where such admiration is due, our whole heart goes to China in her hour of trial, China must live, for her own sake and for humanity, Out of the ashes of this conflict she will once again rise phoenix-like as she has so often done in the past.
>
> Let us learn the lessons of this Far Eastern conflict. Standing at the threshold of a new era, let India resolve to aspire after national self-fulfilment in every direction - but not at the expense of other nations and not through the bloody path of self-aggrandisement and imperialism.

He began making more notes for his autobiography, provisionally called *Pages From My Life*. They were similar to the 1934 synopsis Seal had hawked around for the book that eventually became *The Indian Struggle*. The British police intercepted a few pages of the *Pages From My Life*, but unfortunately the file containing the intercepts has not been preserved. On 9 September Bose wrote to Mrs Woods, an Irish friend that he was likely to be the next Congress President. His doctors had advised him to stay in the hills for another two months but the Dharamavirs wanted to go to Lahore so Subhas decided to go to Kurseong and stay with Sarat. He returned to Calcutta in early October. He was not yet fully fit, but there was much to do. He had invited the Congress to hold its All India Congress Committee session due at the end of that month in Calcutta, so he had to return to the plains.

Normally in Calcutta Gandhi stayed with the rich Marwari businessmen, the Birlas, who were his financiers, but on this occasion he accepted Subhas's invitation. It marked the beginning of a short-lived rapprochement between them. Committee meetings were held there and Subhas was able to attend his first AICC session for nearly six years.

The distinguished writer Nirad Chaudhuri, who had just started work as Sarat's secretary, has provided an enthralling account of how Sarat and Subhas coped with the visit of the Mahatma. Chaudhuri, who had gone on his first holiday for a long time, was urgently summoned back by Sarat and he witnessed the extraordinary arrangements that had to be made by his household to deal with Gandhi and his retinue.

Gandhi was a vegetarian but his food had to be carefully selected. This was done by his secretary, the formidable Mahadev Desai, but he would not specify the herb or vegetable his master wanted until the morning. With the meal required by midday, it meant Sarat Bose's wife had little time to make sure that they could get the vegetable. She managed this by using the services of a nephew who was a superintendent of one of markets of the Calcutta Corporation.

Gandhi's milk had to be goat's milk, as he thought cow's milk encouraged sexual appetite, which he was always trying to control. However, the female goat had to be screened by Desai before it was milked. This meant that during Gandhi's stay there was a daily parade of about fifteen goats in the courtyard of Woodburn Park. They were examined by Desai who chose the goat whose milk would serve Gandhi. Gandhi also applied mud to his stomach and head to control his blood pressure, and the mud had to be kept in the refrigerator. Gandhi wanted to live simply and maintained that no more than three annas (old three pence) should be spent on his food each day. But in four weeks a total of three thousand rupees, nearly £300, was spent on his vast entourage. Chaudhuri also highlights Gandhi's need for money. He charged five rupees for his autograph. The way to obtain it was to put a five pound note in an autograph book: his disciples then took the money, and the great man signed the book. Gandhi's stay, as Chaudhuri has recorded, transformed Woodburn Park:

> Over the many weeks that Gandhi stayed in the house there was no getting away from the noise, the bustle and the coming and goings in that house. There were the elders themselves and their aids *(sic)*, there were the journalists there were the ever importunate visitors, and above all the crowds on the street which stood from morning to evening in thronging relays to have, as they said, Mahatmaji's *darshan*, that is, sight of him as he appeared on the balcony. And whether he appeared or not shouts of *Vande Mataran* would ring out like the chimes of Big Ben, not so plangently, however.

Opposite Sarat's house was a block of flats occupied by Anglo-Indians, the mixed race created by the English in the early years of their rule in India when they had freely intermarried and interbred with Indians. The English had long since abandoned such intimacy and kept this community at arm's length, while the Indians felt that the "Anglos", wanting to be more English than the English, were often more anti-Indian than the English themselves. These Anglo-Indians could not abide the noise and wrote abusive letters to Chaudhuri denouncing the Indians as bandicoots and wishing they would go to the devil.

The Anglo-Indians were not the only ones disturbed by Gandhi's stay with the Boses. His usual hosts, the Birlas, were not entirely happy either, and there was also tension between the Boses and the real Gandhians of Bengal who found it difficult to come to terms with Gandhi accepting the hospitality of the Boses. Gandhi also suffered a heart attack and could not be moved, nor come out and greet the crowds. This created additional work for Subhas. Like many an Indian crowd it required a person of authority to tell them that Gandhi could not appear. So Subhas had to show himself on the balcony to plead with the crowd, saying that, if they did not disperse, Gandhi would be compelled to endure the insistence and that would be harmful to him. After he finished his short speech Subhas would say, *Shanti, Shanti, Shanti*, (peace, peace, peace) and the crowds would disperse.

Jawaharlal Nehru also stayed at Woodburn Park but he was less demanding and more worried by the huge meals served by Sarat's vast kitchens.

Gandhi's stay at Woodburn Park provided the Bose brothers with many opportunities to discuss issues with the great man. He agreed with Subhas and Sarat that something ought to be done about the release of the terrorists (most of whom had renounced the gun and taken instead to Marxism). In Calcutta Gandhi appears to have finally decided that Subhas Bose should succeed Nehru as president of the Congress in 1938.

It is still not clear how this decision was reached. Congress presidents were in theory elected by the members of the All-India Congress Committee. In practice they had been chosen since the 1920s by Gandhi, in his role as the Congress "permanent president" (to borrow Nehru's phrase). Whoever he picked was automatically appointed. As we have seen, Bose had written from Dalhousie on 9 September that he was going to be the next president, which meant he had received the nod from Gandhi. Yet, on 1 October Gandhi wrote to Nehru indicating that Pattabhi Sitaramayya was his choice. Nehru's reply, if he made a formal one, has not been preserved, and we are faced with two questions. How could Bose have been so sure on 9 September? And what made Gandhi change his mind between 1 October and the Calcutta AICC meeting? J.B.Kripalani, Congress general secretary at that time and a close confidant of Gandhi, has suggested one possible answer at least to the second question. According to him, when Gandhi met Bose during the Calcutta AICC session, Bose had told him that he wanted to become Congress president but:

> Gandhiji told him that as he was unwell and had just come out of jail and was not in touch with the political affairs of the country he should wait for a year and recoup his health before he took up the strenuous work of the president of the Congress. To this Subhas Babu replied that he had been quite in touch with the affairs of the country even during his imprisonment and that if he were made President of the Congress his health would improve and he would become normal. Gandhiji then told him that if he insisted he would support his candidature.

Kripalani's testimony, however, must be treated with care. He was a bitter, vituperative critic of Bose, seeing him as one of the pack that followed Gandhi. More likely, Gandhi had decided that it was time to chain the rebel with responsibility and the irresistible attractions of power. It had worked wonderfully with Nehru. It had provided the Left with a figurehead president of its own, effectively hobbling the incumbent. Nehru had been president for two successive terms, in 1936 and 1937, just when the left was rising, and he could not, would not, advance the cause of the Left. The Left, by the same token, could not wholeheartedly attack the Congress establishment while their man was president. Besides, Bose was now a nationally known public figure. His hold over the young matched, if not exceeded, that of Nehru and his reputation as a leader of the Left nationalists was secure. Gandhi had carefully monitored his progress and noticed the growth of his influence among the peasants. The Congress's rural strength lay among sections of the landed aristocracy, who actively resented the growth of middle class and lower class peasant movements. These were particularly strong in Bihar and Andhra, and the peasant leaders from these provinces, Swami Sahajananda and Ranga, looked to Bose for encouragement and support. Ranga, who found Nehru cold and austere, believes that during his tours of the country he discovered Bose's strength and urged Gandhi to give Bose a chance. All this was helped by the prevailing political circumstances. Now that revolutionary violence was at an end, Gandhi, who believed in the British portrayal of Bose as a revolutionary leader, could sleep easy on that score; only mass movements, either Gandhi's type or some other, were viable.

Bose went some way towards satisfying Gandhi. Apart from the loving embrace he had given him on his way to Dalhousie, he used other occasions to show his devotion. On 2 October, Gandhi's birthday, he had declared that "non-violence has now permeated even those sections who were once immune to it" and that everyone should "intensify their campaign to favour non-violence".

Nevertheless, Gandhi was still not entirely sure about Subhas Bose. On 1 November 1937 he had written to Sardar Patel, "I have observed that Subhas is not at all dependable. However there is nobody but he who can be the President." On the same day Gandhi had his heart attack, which Bose called his "collapse". But sometime before that, he must have confirmed to Bose that he would be the next Congress president. However, he also advised the younger man to recover his health properly and advised him to go to Europe. It was advice that was eagerly seized on by Bose. Within days Bose wrote again to Emilie. The letter is undated but possibly written on 4 November. He informed Emilie that he would be leaving for Europe in the middle of November. He wanted to spend four or five weeks in Bad Gastein, and write another book. Emilie was not to tell anyone, except her parents about

Bose's plans. He wrote in block capitals, obviously meant as a code. But was the code meant to say he wanted to make Emilie his wife? We will never know.

Bose flew to Europe on 18 November, the day after Gandhi left Woodburn Park. He spent the Christmas of 1937 in Badgestein and it is here on 26 December 1937 that he is said to have married Emilie Schenkl. We need to qualify this because this information only emerged in 1994, 58 years later. The disclosure was made by the editors of Bose's *Selected Works* in their foreword to the edition containing the letters between Subhas and Emilie. The editors, Bose's nephew Sisir and Sisir's son Sugata, boldly say, "On 26 December 1937 Subhas Bose secretly married Emilie Schenkl." They do not give details of this secret wedding or the source for this information. Emilie was clearly the source. The revelation of the exact date of the marriage only adds another layer of mystery to a puzzling relationship. The first question is: "What kind of marriage was it?" As their daughter Anita says, it was certainly not a civil marriage. There is neither a marriage certificate, nor any report of a ceremony. Emilie was always shy about discussing the marriage. For a long time she did not disclose to anyone when they were married. In an article in *The Illustrated Weekly* in 1972 and based on extensive conversations with Emilie, Krishna Bose, Sisir Bose's wife, said they were married during the war according to Hindu rites.

However, on 11 November 1971, Emilie told the noted Indian historian B.R. Nanda, who was interviewing her as part of the oral history project of the Nehru Memorial Museum Library, that she was married in 1937. But she asked him not to include her words as part of the transcript. She repeated this claim to Leonard Gordon when he interviewed her in Vienna on 14 October 1978. To neither man did she give an exact date. Then in June 1993, with Sisir pressing her to allow him to publish the Subhas-Emilie correspondence, she appears to have provided a date for the marriage.

Anita's explanation is that Emilie was an intensely private person. When she asked her mother about her parents' marriage, Emilie would say it was none of her business. We will never be sure what form the marriage ceremony took, if there was indeed a proper ceremony.

Over the years there have been conflicting versions of the marriage ceremony. According to Abid Hasan, Bose's close assistant during the war, it was a *gandharva* ceremony of exchanging garlands, the simplest Hindu rite. But Girija Mookerjee, another co-worker in Germany at that time, claims to have seen a marriage certificate with the signature of the German Foreign Office official Adam von Trott as witness. However, as both these people were under the impression that Bose had married during the war, and neither man knew of a marriage in 1937, we have to discount their views as uninformed speculation. Some of his closest associates did not even know he was married. Nambiar, while aware of his deep attachment for Emilie, did not find out until after the war. Even if they did not have a formal marriage ceremony, there is no doubt that Subhas and Emilie lived as husband and wife (having probably first done so in Vienna sometime in 1936) nor that Subhas fathered a child. On 8 February 1943, just as he was preparing to leave Berlin for the voyage that would take him to the East, he wrote to Mejdada informing him of the marriage:

> I have married here and I have a daughter. In my absence please show my wife and daughter the love that you have given me throughout your life. May my wife and daughter complete and successfully fulfil my unfinished tasks - that is my ultimate prayer.

Despite this letter, not everyone is convinced that he had any relationship with Emilie and the doubters include some members of the extended Bose family. His nephew Dwijendranath alleged that the letter was a forgery. The marriage not only divides the Bose family but continues to outrage the more uncritical of Bose's supporters. For them the very thought of Bose marrying anyone, let along a white foreigner, was sacrelegious. After all, did he not vow not to marry until India was free? It is the accepted belief, even in certain sophisticated Indian circles, that an Indian marrying a white woman must necessarily have been duped by her wiles. Popular mythology consoles itself with the belief that the bedsitters of the West are perpetually stocked with nubile white females hiding in closets eager to trap rich but unwary Indian males. For such supporters to accept Emilie Schenkl is to believe that Bose, leader of men and putative conqueror of the British, fell to wiles that should not have defeated an undergraduate.

Bose's attitude to women lends credence to the popular theory that he was inclined towards celibacy. Yet there is nothing to suggest that he vowed never to marry till India was free. Basanti Devi was one of those who often joked about this with him: He would parry the question but never reject it. There were plenty of opportunities for him to marry in India. A handsome, attractive man, his choice was limitless, but for some reason he chose to wait for Emilie. Another factor is Indian snobbery which was expressed by Chaudhuri, who made no secret of his distaste that Bose should have married a mere secretary from a humble background when he could have had the choice of high-born Bengali women.

Prominent Indian politicians marrying foreigners was rare but not unknown. In March 1937, at about the time Subhas was declaring his love for Emilie, M.N. Roy married Ellen Gottschalk in Bombay. Ellen, a close political collaborator, had followed him to India and waited for him to emerge from a British prison. Roy's private life could not have been more different to Subhas Bose's. Patrick Haithcox has pointed out in his book *Communism and Nationalism in India: M.N. Roy and Comintern Policy 1920-39* that Roy, who spent many years abroad first as a revolutionary and then as part of the international communist movement, neither believed in monogamous marriage nor fidelity in relationships.

One other factor which possibly made Bose bind himself to Emilie, was his encroaching middle age. He had turned 40 and had told Emilie that in India a man was old at that age. He probably felt it was high time to get settled but he knew he was about to become Congress president and did not feel he could announce a marriage at that time. Roy could openly marry his foreign woman, Subhas could not. Emilie would remain a secret. So the real purpose of the trip to Europe was concealed and it was publicised as one undertaken for recuperation and rest.

Boses's journey to Europe was not without problems. Although he had avoided travelling on a British carrier and landed in Naples, it was the Italians who harassed him. Bose complained to the Italians and London soon knew all the details. A few days later the press attaché at the British embassy in Rome, had lunch with Professor Nicolo Tucci, a well known orientalist and an authority on Tibet. McClure reported back to London:

> Tucci said there had been a nice packet of trouble over that ... he [Bose] had been treated as a suspect and subjected to considerable indignity both at the Naples airport and at the Italo-Austrian frontier. It appears that at both places local police authorities looked on him as something of a Bolshevist. Bose had written an indignant letter of protest to Tucci, who had tried to calm him down and explained to the authorities who Bose was.

Tucci thought Bose might not want to come to Italy again, but while he was angry he was not about to burn his bridges there, certainly not with Mussolini. On the last day of 1937, he told Maggiore Rapicavoli, who worked for Mussolini, that the Naples incident was closed and he would like to meet Mussolini when he passed through Rome in early January. But if news of the meeting emerged, there would be trouble for him in India. In that case, he would have to deny that it ever took place. In fact he did not meet Mussolini.

By this time he had spent most of his honeymoon dictating to Emilie, converting *Pages From My Life* into an autobiography. In ten hectic days he took his story, which he called *An*

Indian Pilgrim, from his birth in Cuttack to his resignation from the ICS in 1921. He planned to cover his political years and write three concluding chapters, one philosophical, one political and one economic. But he only had time to write the philosophical one, where he stressed the importance of love in life, reflecting the change Emilie had brought.

When he arrived in London in January 1938, he showed the manuscript to Frederick Warburg of Secker & Warburg. Warburg was interested in Bose's life and aware of his developing rivalry with Nehru. He had read Nehru's autobiography and been immensely impressed. The book had also been something of a commercial success and Warburg thought a book by Bose might make a good proposition. But *An Indian Pilgrim* disappointed him. It was only about 40,000 words long, incomplete and not as well written as Nehru's book. Secker & Warburg decided not to publish, and the book was brought out, years after Bose's death, by his admirers in India.

The book was not as bad as Warburg made it out to be. True, it did not have Nehru's literary skill and ambivalent charm, but it is a piece of characteristic Bose work: clear and without any of the mystical, ambiguous flourishes that often cloud Indian writing. It is not as cogent as *The Indian Struggle* and at times reticent, but nevertheless was a pleasing account of an Indian steeped in Hinduism, struggling to come to terms with the West and it contrasted favourably with Gandhi's obsessive concern about health, bowels and food.

Bose's presence in England was the last move in the game of bluff with the British since 1933. As we have seen, Bose was under the impression that he required a formal endorsement to visit England when, in fact, all he had to do was to arrive there. Still fooled by this British bluff, he had written to the Marquis of Zetland, secretary of state for India, from Bad Gastein on 25 November. It was a polite, formal letter asking for the ban on a visit to Britain to be lifted. Zetland agreed. But, keen to preserve the fiction, Zetland asked the Foreign Office to telegraph British consuls in Austria to provide Bose with a further endorsement on his passport for the UK, but not "a general British Empire endorsement". Bose was still too dangerous to be permitted to wander at will.

Bose's arrival in London meant no relaxation in the constant police watch on him. Days before, the IPI had informed the India Office of his plans, including his proposed stay at Artillery Mansions near Victoria. New Scotland Yard filed almost daily reports of his activities in London. Bose had taken two days to reach London from Bad Gastein by train, car and ship, travelling via Salzburg, Munich, Brussels, Antwerp and Ostende. From Munich, he had sent Emilie a postcard, the first written communication between the newly weds. It was a polite note and nobody seeing it would have guessed they were married.

In Dover on 10 January 1938 Bose was met by his nephew Amiya, a student. They took the train to London's Victoria station. It was 18 years since his first visit, and this second one was to be his last. This is an important point, for in Britain Bose was the least-known of leading Indian politicians. Gandhi and his brilliantly eccentric ideas had made him a legend; Nehru had close and intimate links with the British Left. Only Stafford Cripps would get to know Bose at all well, and he evidently did not like him. Now Bose tried to make good this deficiency.

At Victoria hundreds of Indians had gathered to receive him with garlands and slogans. Most of them were students but also present was Mulk Raj Anand, the Indian novelist, whose novel *The Coolie* had been a literary success. That evening, shadowed by detectives, Bose attended a cocktail party at the Dorchester given by Captain Wentworth Day, editor of *Sporting & Dramatic.* While Bose argued that the Congress was justified in accepting office at provincial level he said that this did not mean that the demand for complete independence had been abandoned. The next day there was a reception for him at St Pancras Town Hall where some 250 people paid two shillings to hear him explain that, contrary to Raj propaganda, the Congress had not given up the struggle for freedom.

On 12 January 1938 Bose went to the East End where the Hindusthan Social Club gave him a reception in King's Hall in Commercial Road. The following day he met the Labour theorist Harold Laski and addressed a meeting of the India League panel of members of Parliament. The Conway Hall meeting on the evening of Thursday 13 January was the public focus of the visit. An IPI agent called Miss Wilford was one of the 200 people present. She confessed afterwards that circumstances did not permit her to take down Bose's speech verbatim but she managed to provide a note that ran to four a half typed pages and gave a sense of the impact Bose had on the meeting. With George Lansbury, the veteran Labour leader in the chair, and on a platform that included Indira Nehru, Pulin Seal and his nephew Amiya Nath, Bose sat through several speeches before being called upon to speak. Those who preceded him included Basil Mathews of the Royal Institute for International Affairs (who said that on his visit to India the previous year, he had not been allowed to see Bose) and Arthur Greenwood, then deputy leader of the Labour Party. After expressing his thanks for the affection he had been shown, Bose stressed that, contrary to the Raj propaganda, the Indian question had not been settled. Aware he was addressing a left-wing audience he made the point, as reported by Miss Wilford, that:

> There could be no socialism in England until India was free; democracy if it were genuine must believe that if freedom was good for some it must be right for all… He then made an exceedingly bitter attack on the Labour Party, which had let India down and had badly disillusioned Indians; for that disillusionment he was grateful to the Labour Party as it had convinced Indians that they must rely only on themselves; it was their struggle. They did not expect help from any country. They would however take gratefully any sympathy offered by friends in England and elsewhere.

Miss Wilford then provided what she called her general impression of Bose. By now, the Raj no longer saw him as a revolutionary who could be jailed with impunity. But he still remained dangerous and, however moderate, was in the Raj's eyes always seeking to inflame Indian youth against British rule. The summary gives a Raj view of Bose as he made his first and only visit as a politician to Britain, barely weeks before he became Congress President. This is what Miss Wilford reported to her bosses:

> This was a clever speech, delivered very quietly and unemotionally; the points were made effectively without any display of rhetoric and were calculated to appeal equally to the Indian and English portions of this particular audience. While eulogising Gandhi and the creed of non-violence to which Congress was vowed, he implied clearly that he had little doubt that a crisis would be forced on Congress by the Government of India, and that as a result bloodshed would almost certainly supervene. He never used the words "bloodshed" or "fighting" or "violence" in connection with the Congress but conveyed that Congress supporters should have to accept the role of martyrs; nothing that he said could be construed as an incitement to violence, but his stressing of the "martyr role" and the very restraint in his language were of a character to inflame the patriotism of an audience mostly composed of youth. He was subtly bitter all through the speech and very openly so when he attacked the Labour Party just after Greenwood had delivered the most fulsome message from the Council, in fact the wincing of the three Labour party officials on the platform was almost audible. He gave the impression that, as a man of breeding and education who had attained eminence in his own country, he was only too painfully aware of the mediocrity of the personality and speeches of those surrounding him on the platform who, such as they were, represented the best amongst his sympathisers

> in this country. On the other hand, he appeared genuinely pleased by the very rousing reception given by the many Indian students present.

The next day, 14 January, Bose met Greenwood again along with other Labour Party leaders including Clement Attlee, then leader of the Opposition, Ernest Bevin, leader of the Transport and General Workers Union, J.R. Middleton, secretary to the Labour Party and Herbert Morrison, a rising star, who would eventually become deputy leader of the Labour Party. Bose it seems did not find Attlee and Bevin either sympathetic or forthcoming.

There were meetings with Indian students both in London's Gower Street and in Cambridge and Oxford, and a lunch with Sir Walter Layton arranged by Mr Crossfield, the editor of the *News Chronicle*. Herbert Anderson of the influential Conciliation Group, other MPs such as Morgan Jones and Reginald Sorensen and Harry Pollitt of the British Communist Party also met Bose. Various other communists visited Bose at his flat in Artillery Mansions and New Scotland Yard dutifully filled their notebooks with their names. There were press conferences and interviews galore and also contacts with modern writers and Chinese groups. Everybody, as the *Manchester Guardian* later observed, was "impressed by his pleasant, quiet manner" and the "decisiveness with which he discussed Indian affairs".

The IPI, however, took comfort from the fact that Bose's visit had revealed the rifts within the Indian community. Krishna Menon, who ran the India League, used the visit to elbow out K.D. Kumaria of the Indian Swaraj League alleging Kumaria was a British agent. Menon had played a leading role in organising Bose's visit, along with Agatha Harrison (a Quaker friend of Gandhi) but IPI agents were glad to learn that Menon not think much of Bose. He was not, Menon was alleged to have said, in the same class as Nehru. The IPI felt that this news would ease the pressure on them. With Bose about to become Congress President he would be at odds with Menon and Congress publicity abroad would be less effective. As ever there were stories of Bose's connections with revolutionaries and one New Scotland Yard report said:

> A curious story regarding Bose has been heard from a man who was a very intimate friend of his. This was to the effect that Bose for a period was in the pay of the Japanese who financed the Bengal revolutionary movement.

But with one revolutionary the meeting was something the British could do nothing about. This was the encounter that probably meant more to Bose than all the other London meetings. It was with Eamon De Valera. From Bad Gastein Bose had written to Mrs Woods raising the possibility of visiting Dublin on 18 January to meet the Irish president. The Indian papers wanted a photograph of them together. Bose said he was was prepared to visit Dublin for a day. But in the event De Valera was in London to negotiate the return of the treaty ports with the British government and the two met at midnight at De Valera's hotel on Saturday 15 January 1938 IPI noted:

> The interview was at the request of the President of Eire, but this has not yet been confirmed; De Valera is at present heading a Delegation to London ... and it is possible that he wished to discuss trade questions with the President-elect of the Indian National Congress.

Bose also met Lord Zetland. He had not been keen to do so, but English friends insisted. They met for an hour and a half at Lord Halifax's Eaton Square residence on a cold January morning, and had what Zetland later described as an interview "of a very friendly character throughout". But, though Zetland was taken by Bose's "charming smile", the gap between the two men was wide: Bose could not agree that the 1935 Act was anything other than a sop. There was another very curious encounter. This was with Pamela de Bayou, the artist wife of Frederick Warburg. She had met Subhas at Conway Hall and made an immediate impression on him by saying: "I hear you do not like women. That is dreadful." As soon as that meeting was over, Subhas, Frederick Warburg and Pamela stole away to the Warburgs' London flat, and there Subhas vigorously defended himself against the charge of being a misogynist. Suddenly, to Pamela's great surprise, he said: "Come with me to India. I will put you in charge of the women's section. You can organise our women." Attractive as the idea was, Pamela could not abandon a home and a husband in England to journey to India, though she agreed to think about it. Subhas followed this up, on his return to India, with a three-page letter imploring her to come. She would be his guest and he would look after her. Nothing came of it, though to her dying day Pamela was convinced this was a declaration from Subhas' heart. She was, of course, mistaken. Pamela and Subhas never met again. Unknown to Pamela Warburg, Subhas had already pledged himself to Emilie.

This late night meeting showed how far Subhas had changed since his first visit to England in 1921. Then he had felt comfortable with only one woman, Mrs Dharmavir, and that too by seeing her as an older sister. Now he would flirt with an attractive woman, albeit harmlessly, and even give the impression of romantic possibilities.

Bose flew back to India from Croydon airport on 18 January 1938. His journey took him to Prague, where he met Dr Benes again, and then to Rome. He did not meet Mussolini but on 20 January had a long chat with Count Galeazzo Ciano, Mussolini's son-in-law who was also the Italian foreign minister. Ciano's diary recorded the meeting and reveals that, in contrast to his personal relations, Bose in political matters was always direct, at times uncomfortably so. Ciano, in turn, makes no secret of his total contempt for India and Indians:

> Bose, head of the Indian Congress, spoke to me at length of the situation of his Party. Until now there have been few projects. At the centre there is Great Britain who is in complete control. In the provinces some departments of little importance have been entrusted to the Indians. Great Britain has excellent agents in the small and large local villages, who oppress the people with the support of English troops. Program of his Party: the independence of the country. Means to achieve this: obstructionism and passive resistance. No armed conflict. They ask only two things of us: to keep Great Britain concerned about our intentions and to inform them of the general political situation, so that they can better position themselves. In turn I suggested that Bose direct his Indian sympathies towards Italy and Japan: the two countries who have most profoundly injured British prestige. He told me that he will try, but it is difficult because the Indian nation is dominated by feeling, and therefore is today favourable to China as it was towards Ethiopia. In my opinion, from my fleeting visit to India, I think that they are lifeless people without reactions, who will not attain independence unless other forces knock England down. And perhaps even then some new power will take over in India.

It was another three days before Bose arrived back in Calcutta via Naples, Athens, Basra, Karachi and Jodpur on 23 January. At Karachi airport he brushed aside questions about marriage. "I have no time to think about that." Emilie was a secret he just could not discuss. He resumed his role as the monastic nationalist. Back home, he learnt that Emilie's father had died and he sent his condolences. He also sent her money and presents: an ivory necklace, a pair of shoes, a brooch and a small box of ivory and sandalwood. But, as in the past, she was always Fraulein Schenkl. None of the letters Emilie wrote to him after their supposed marriage survive but in line with the secrecy code they had established she would still address him "Mr Bose". The relationship was so secret that not even the IPI would get a sniff of it. Bose when it came to matters of the heart could keep secrets from the British and their agents.

12
Rashtrapati

The Congress session at Haripura in early 1938 was a celebration, the first annual conference since the Congress had come to power in the provinces. Bose, who had come by train from Calcutta in a second-class compartment decorated with national flags, was accompanied by a large group of friends and relatives, and a Hindi tutor to improve his shaky grasp of the language. He received a flamboyant welcome.

It was the fifty-first session, and there were 51 gates, 51 national flags, 51 national songs and 51 white bullocks. Girls in saffron sarees (it is not clear whether there were 51 of them) escorted Bose to the president's tent. Almost overnight Haripura, a tiny Gujarat village on the banks of the river Tapti, had become a town, a kilometre in breath and three in length, with temporary roads, electricity, its own dairy, special water-works and a kitchen that catered for 100,000 people. The Ford Motor Company, realising the power of the newly installed ministers, had provided new V-8 cars for the use of the leaders. There could be no better evidence that the Congress Raj was a reality.

The high point of any Congress session was the presidential address. These were often long on rhetoric but short on substance. Bose's lengthy speech was characteristic of the man: full of matter-of-fact advice and arguments in favour of an independent India that would be a socialist state dedicated to removing the age-old ills of its people: hunger, illiteracy and disease. His trip to England and discussions with the British Left had made an impact, and he was keen to emphasise the links between colonial liberation movements and the socialist struggle in Britain. Swaraj itself was a means to the long-sought goal of a reconstructed India. In order to achieve it, a party would be required, and that could only be a post-independence Congress. It would have much to do. Population growth would have to be curbed, agriculture radically reformed, landlordism abolished, agricultural indebtedness liquidated, credit made freely available, co-operatives organised; above all there would have to be socialist planning and control. Gandhian village industries were well and good, but there could be no going back to the pre-industrial age.

Bose's down-to-earth approach is best illustrated in his answer to an old problem that had often dogged the Indian nationalists, and still continues to divide India: what should be the common language of a country so vast and diverse? English, for obvious reasons, was unacceptable. The Congress had adopted Hindi, but there had been controversy between those who wanted a Sanskritised Hindi, drawing on Hindu sources, and those who preferred Hindustani, which accommodated Urdu with its Muslim connections. The controversy embraced the script. Sanskritised Hindi was in the Devanagari script; Urdu in the Arabic. Bose had a radical, and altogether more practical, solution: Hindi in the Roman script. He had overcome his initial reluctance to use this foreign script after a visit to Turkey, a country that had adopted a Roman version of Arabic. Bose realised how useful it would be for Indians to have a language in a script used by the whole world. The Congress did nothing about it, but Bose introduced it later in his Indian National Army with great success.

Haripura saw Bose make the cover of *Time* magazine as one of the new leaders of India but his year as president was marked by fierce opposition from Patel, by suspicion and then hostility from Gandhi, and by vacillation from Nehru. Bose knew he had a job to do. There was, for instance, the need to give definite shape to the many socialist resolutions passed by the Congress. This, Bose was convinced, required state planning. During his mammoth Haripura presidential address he had sketched out his ideas for a centralised planning commission, on whose advice the state "will have to adopt a comprehensive scheme for gradually socialising our entire agricultural and industrial system in the spheres of both production and appropriation".

Planning was just the sort of practical thing to which Bose loved to apply himself and much of his presidential year was spent in setting up a Congress planning committee. In May 1938 he called a conference of Congress chief ministers in Bombay and convinced them to endorse his ideas and donate 50,000 rupees to its creation. On Gandhi's birthday in October 1938 he presided over a conference of Congress ministers of industry at Delhi, and repeated his practical vision of planning.

On 17 October, he inaugurated the committee in Bombay. He had secured the services of prominent scientists like Dr Meghnad Saha; Hari Vishnu Kamath, a man whom Bose had encouraged to resign from the ICS and join the freedom struggle, was named secretary; and Nehru was made its chairman, Bose tracking him down in Republican Spain to get him to take the job. The choice seemed ideal. Nehru had spoken eloquently of socialism and was the one prominent leader committed to planning. But some friends and relations had doubts. Nehru was a rival, and this situation, though created by Bose, would give the impression that it was Nehru who had led the way. Bose, according to a nephew who worked closely with him, retorted, "This will expose him." The anecdote needs to be treated with care, but certainly Bose's choice was generous rather than shrewd.

Nehru was not interested in detail. His forte was the visionary, often romantic view of the socialist glory to come, and he was worried about frightening the middle classes. The result was a disaster. Soon there were public recriminations between Kamath and Nehru which led to Kamath's resignation. Nehru's vague and soft-pedalling approach led to a proliferation of committees which got lost among the minutiae of planning and completely lost sight of the objective. Bose had visualised something very different: concrete, practical ideas that might have helped the Congress provincial ministers or at least goaded them into doing something. Yet it was Nehru who secured a reputation as the initiator of planning, and Bose's labours were quickly forgotten.

Bose was also aware that the Congress had degenerated into a flabby electoral machine whose supporters, as one report put it, "have no other work throughout the year except that of keeping an eye on their seat on the Congress Body". Mass consciousness had come. Crowds of 50,000 to 100,000 were common at political meetings, but the Congress did not have the "well disciplined volunteer corps" to take advantage of it. Bose's offer to remedy this state of affairs was frustrated by the fact that the Congress office was permanently located in Allahabad, 700 miles from Calcutta, and that the Congress secretary was Bose's critic Kripalani. With Kripalani keen to maintain his authority, and with the rejection of Bose's idea of moving the Congress office to Calcutta, the changes necessary to refocus the Congress away from its increasingly careerist mould never took place.

More satisfying for Subhas, was his public role as president. The president was a symbol, the man who carried the flag and took it to various parts of the country, reassuring the faithful, arousing the sceptics and gathering the uninitiated. Such meetings were the very life-blood of the mass politician. Throughout 1938, Bose toured the country. He had been doing so for more than ten years, but now the crowds were bigger, often 100,000, sometimes as many as a million. Special arrangements had to be made for his train compartments, and organisers struggled to hold back the crowds at railway stations and roadsides. Everywhere he went the routine was the same: the welcome at the station, the garlands, the speeches, the motorcade through the city or the village and the progress through improvised ranks of Congressmen (affecting a military pose to often farcical effect) to the meeting-hall. Here yet more garlands, more welcoming speeches, more references to *"Desh-ki-Neta"* (the Leader of the Nation) and cries of *"Bengal kesari ki jai"* (Long live the Bengal hero) and *"Subhas Babu zindabad"* (Long live Subhas Babu); and finally the embarrassing "thank you" speeches of the organisers.

It had not always been like this, and it would not be so in the future, but for the moment he was king, and there was something about him that was irresistible. Soli Batlivala recalls a tour to Karnataka during this period. Subhas and Jawaharlal sat in the back of the car on either side of Kamala Devi Chattopodhay, an attractive socialist feminist; Soli rode with the driver in front. For hour after hour and mile after mile they passed through the Karnataka countryside, and through every village endured the ritual of greetings from a large crowd, of garlands, speeches and requests for *darshan* (that wonderful Indian word summing up the need for favour and patronage). Soon Nehru was tired; as the trip progressed, his head began to recline against Kamala Devi's comfortable shoulder, and for the village *darshan-seekers* there was only a tired and scornful wave of his hand. Subhas, on the other hand, remained upright and erect, kept his arms and hands free of Kamala Devi, and willingly, almost happily, submitted himself to this political mechanism. Even allowing for Batlivala's hero-worshipping gloss, the anecdote has the ring of truth. The *Rashtrapati* (President) in public had to be untiring, completely dedicated and totally incorruptible by wine, women or song. It was a hard pose to keep up, but in public Bose always managed to sustain it. Despite his marriage to Emilie, in India he was Subhas the celibate.

Emilie is the only one to whom he wrote to regularly at this time. Often he would use the long train journeys to write: his favourite writing time was the 36 hours spent on the train from Bombay to Calcutta. He never discussed politics and nobody reading the letters would have discovered they were lovers. Once or twice, as in a letter written from Wardha in July 1938, just after he had met Gandhi, he wrote something emotional in German: *"Auf wiedersehen mein kleines Liebling"* (*So long my little darling*). Yet even the odd German phrases in the letters were more likely to be platonic. He would often tell Emilie of the money he was sending her, something he did regularly.

If outwardly everything was calm and there appeared to be a superficial ease with which Bose worked the Gandhi machine, there were considerable strains beneath the surface. The issue on which Bose and Gandhi nearly broke was that of the Bengal ministry. The politics of Bengal of this period would later make the partition of the province a decade later inevitable. This forms almost a case study of how the British tried to keep their hold on India, while shrewdly exploiting different religious groups in the province.

Under the 1935 Act Bengal, like other provinces in British India, was allowed to elect a Legislative Assembly. Only a small fraction of the population could vote. Under the 1919 Montagu-Chelmsford Act just 1.34 million could vote, the 1935 Act allowed 6,695 million, about 13.4 per cent of the population, to vote. But what made the elections unique, and provided an insight into the true intent of the Raj, was the way people were allowed to vote. The Assembly had 250 seats but the 7 million were not voting for this general body of members. There were all sorts of separate groups organised by race, religion and sex. The electorate was divided into thirteen groups and each group could elect a certain number of members. Only 48 of these seats could be elected by the general franchise. The general franchise could also elect 30 other members but they had to be Hindus, who were classified as depressed castes. These castes were listed in a Schedule to the Act and began calling themselves Scheduled Castes, the name by which they are now known in India. 117 seats were reserved exclusively for Muslims (only Muslims could vote for these members). Twenty-five seats were exclusively for Europeans, British citzens temporarily living in India. The British in India always classified themselves as Europeans, presenting themselves as an exclusive ethnic white community, and all their organisations were known not as British but as European. In their clubs for instance, where they excluded Indians from membership, membership was open to all other Europeans of whatever nationality. Three seats were set aside for Anglo-Indians and two for Indian Christians. Nineteen were for representatives of commerce and industry, two for the universities, two for women in general and two for Muslim women. The thirteenth, and last category, was a seat reserved for an Anglo-Indian woman.

Such a divided electorate reflected the basic British argument that India was not a single nation. In giving the Muslims such an obvious advantage, the Raj view was that they were a majority in the province and therefore deserved to be protected. However, the electoral weighting given to them was disproportionate to their size. They did not outnumber the Hindus by the margin given to them by the extra seats. Nirad Chaudhuri thinks the Muslim-Hindu ratio was 52-48 in the Muslim favour, yet the Hindus could only contest 117 seats in the 250-seat Assembly. The Raj was playing the numbers game for its own purpose. The Europeans, who were 0.0004 per cent of the population, had 10 per cent of the seats. Equally pernicious was the reservation of seats for the self styled Depressed Castes. As Chaudhuri says, "In creating a privileged electoral class of the so-called Scheduled Castes the framers of the 1935 Act disregarded the spontaneous evolution of Hindu society towards equality, and sought to perpetuate class hatred in order to serve the interests of British rule." Included in these so-called depressed castes were people like Dr Meghnad Saha, the eminent physicist, who was elected Fellow of the Royal Society in 1927, and a great Bengali linguist who presided over the Imperial Library established by Curzon. How ironic that a generation later similar measures introduced in Britain and the western world, and termed "positive discrimination", would be condemned by the very sections of society which had seen the 1935 Act as a progressive piece of legislation. Chaudhuri has no doubts what was intended:

> What was done in Bengal through the Act of 1935 was done deliberately, and I know the reason why. The disenfranchisement of the Bengali Hindus was the punishment meted out to them by that Act on behalf of the British community in India which desired it. Of all the communities in India, it was the educated and high caste Bengali Hindus whom the British sojourners hated most. The first reason for the hatred was that the nationalist movement was created by these Bengali Hindus. The hatred due to that, however, was obvious and in some ways natural, although also unintelligent. But there was another reason for this hatred which worked subconsciously for the political victimization of the Bengali Hindu, which was perverse. That was reserved for the upper-class Hindu Bengalis who devoted themselves most sincerely and with considerable success to the task of remodelling their character and outlook in the image of an ideal Englishman. Their love of English literature and the English language was the most noticeable indication of their aspiration. But to the Englishman in India all that was psychological miscegenation. So they rejected the Bengalis, who wished to bring about this transformation, with even greater determination than they showed in making an outcaste of any Englishwoman who had married an Indian.

Sarat Bose, despite being a nationalist, was in many ways the classic high caste Bengali Hindu who had tried to remodel himself as an Englishman. His speeches in the Assembly were modelled on the style of an English MP and as, Chaudhuri says, he found himself in a blind alley as a result of the elections under the Act. The elections, held between 18 and 20 January 1937, saw the Congress win 43 of the 48 open seats. Given how much the rules of the game were against it, this was a remarkable result. It had not contested the Muslim seats and the Muslim members dominated the assembly, although these were split between several parties. To emphasise how unrepresentative and odd the Assembly was, there were 25 Europeans, just 18 less than the number of Congress members, the main national party. The elections resulted in a Bengal ruled by a coalition between two Muslim parties, the Krishak Praja Party (a strong regional party with a fine-sounding radical programme), which represented the peasants and tenants, and the Muslim League, which tended to be made up of upper-class Muslims. Fazlul Huq the leader of the KPK, who became chief minister, had fought the elections on the slogan that he would provide the Muslim masses with *Dal-bhat* (rice and lentil soup), the basic diet. He was a man with whom both Subhas and Sarat felt they could do business. In May 1935 when he was recovering in the Sanatorium Rudolfinerhaus from his gall bladder operation, Subhas had written to Huq congratulating him on his election as Mayor of Calcutta and assuring him he was with him in spirit.

Before Huq formed his ministry in 1937 he had been ready to form a coalition with the Congress but the central Congress leadership was at that stage not sure it would take power in the provinces even where Congress members were in a majority, let alone in a province where Congress was in a minority. So this opportunity was lost. However some scholars working on this period are not convinced that a Huq-Congress coalition could have been formed in 1937. It seems that sometime late in 1937, as they saw how communal the Bengal ministry was, the Boses decided that they should try and get Congress into the government and make a coalition with Huq.

The finance minister of the Huq ministry was Nalini Ranjan Sarkar. He had a certain reputation in Bengal as a bounder and a lothario and a song about him and Bidhan Chandra Roy, neither of whom ever married, went thus:

> *Asashe Nalini, asashe Bidhan*
> *Kula bodura howo shabdan!*
> (Nalini and Bidhan are coming
> Women of the house beware!)

Sarkar was the one notable Hindu in the Huq ministry. He had been in the Congress and then departed. As a businessman who had no basic political philosophy he always knew on which side his bread was buttered.

In the summer of 1938 Sarat Bose, who was leader of the Congress opposition in the Assembly, failed in a no-confidence motion. This led the Bose brothers to hatch a plan with Sarkar; he was to resign creating a crisis forcing the collapse of the Huq ministry. Then the Congress could form a broad coalition with Huq at the expense of the Muslim League, its main opponent. Sarkar resisted at first but by November 1938 he was convinced. On 9 December Bose met Sarkar and the plan was agreed. The next day Bose left Calcutta for Wardha to discuss it with Gandhi. His agreement was vital if the plan was to work. On this long train journey he wrote again to Emilie, ending his letter with a rare line of love in German, "*und herzliche Liebe, mein Liebling*" (*and heartfelt love my darling*).

At Wardha, the Mahatma seemed happy with the plan for Sarkar to resign and the Congress join a coalition, even in a junior capacity. Then Sarkar changed his mind. He rushed to Wardha to explain to Gandhi that his resignation would not right. For good measure, he took with him, as Chaudhuri says, two "advocates" who were very influential with Gandhi. They were Ghanashyamdas Birla, Gandhi's main financier, and Maulana Abdul Kalam Azad who, as the most prominent Muslim nationalist in the Congress, always had the last word on any issue concerning Muslims. Gandhi dictated a letter to Bose in the presence of Sarkar, Azad and Birla, telling him he did not think it was a good idea to get Sarkar to resign and topple the ministry. "I feel ... that the best way of securing comparative purity of administration and a continuity of a settled programme and policy would be to aim at having all the reforms that we desire, carried out by the present ministry."

Bose knew that on this question he and Azad had different views. Azad felt that in provinces such as Bengal, where Muslims were in a majority, even communal Muslim ministries should not be brought down. Birla, the shrewd businessman, had judged a Muslim ministry as better for his business than a Hindu-Muslim alliance, and Sarkar, ever the chancer, clearly thought it was best to stick to what he already had.

Bose had gone to Bombay from Wardha. Gandhi did not post his letter but sent it to him by special messenger, the messenger being Birla himself. If Gandhi wanted Bose to get the message, he could not have planned it more carefully. Bose was dismayed by this apparent change of mind and expressed his intense anger at the way Gandhi had treated him. He had listened to three men, two of whom (Sarkar and Birla) were not Congressmen, as opposed to the Bose brothers who were supposed to be in charge of the Bengal Congress. "It has astonished me that me that you do not feel it is necessary even to consult me before you arrived at a decision on such a serious matter."

In the correspondence that followed, Gandhi played a skilful word game with Bose. He did not explain why he would prefer to have a pro-Muslim government - whose policies were against the secular objectives of the Congress - rather than for the Congress to share power and dilute some of the growing religious fundamentalism. Bose tried hard to convince him that that there was a great need to get the Congress in power in all provinces to enable it to present a united ultimatum to the British to leave India. Such an ultimatum would represent all of British India and over-ride any objections of the Muslim League.

Bose felt this all the more necessary because of the developing crisis in Europe. Hitler had won in Munich and was about to dismember Czechoslovakia. Bose judged that a European crisis would continue for another 12 months or so. In such a critical situation the British government could not permit a major struggle to go on in India. While Bose was convinced that Britain's problems were India's opportunities, Gandhi did not believe that international events could help India. In any event he did not think India was ready for a struggle with Britain just then. The result was that political power in Bengal did not change: Sarkar remained as finance minister and the Huq government carried on.

Bose has been criticised for both political naiveté and opportunism over the affair. Chaudhuri writes:

> That Subhas Bose should have based his calculations to create a coalition of Hindus and Muslims for the good of Bengal on the good will of so notorious an adventurer as Nalini Sarkar showed his utter incapacity to approach any political question with realism, all the more so because neither really trusted the other. Even more lacking in realism was the motive he avowed to himself and to others for this change. I cannot believe that, in trying to put an end to the Huq ministry as it was, he did not want to recover for the Hindus of Bengal a position in the government proportionate to their numbers and social and economic position. But in trying to persuade Gandhi that the aim was right he made no allusion to it.

Certainly his arguments for the alliance were contradictory, and contrasted sharply with the position of Nehru, who steadfastly opposed all such partnerships with non-Congress elements. But in the long term Bose was undoubtedly right. As one Indian historian has put it, the Krishak Praja Party's "merger with the Muslim League made the ministry almost wholly communal, and gave communalism a foothold to expand". In 1937 the Muslim League had been one of the lesser parties in Bengal; in 1947, having been in power for eight of the previous ten years, it was the most important. It played a crucial role in ensuring that India was eventually partitioned and Bengal itself divided into a predominantly Hindu West and a Pakistani (now Bangladeshi) East.

The September 1938 session of the AICC illustrated the growing tension between the Left and Right wings of the Congress. Bose had fallen sick on his way to Delhi and had to rush to get there on time. When he arrived, he found the Left and Right polarising on the question of another European war. On behalf of the Right, Rajagopalachari had moved an ambiguous resolution appealing to the good sense of the British to do the right thing by India if a war came. The Left was determined to oppose this "sloppy" resolution, and one communist leader working with the Congress, Niharendru Dutt-Mazumdar, moved an amendment. He has a precise recollection of what followed:

> In substance the amendment said, "the uncompromising struggle of India's liberation should be our cardinal policy and we must not commit the mistake that Mahatma Gandhi had made in the past" ... Bose sympathised with us but informed us that the Working Committee would not accept our amendment to Rajaji's resolution. Seventy-three of us walked out of the AICC [That night] I, along with PC Joshi and Somnath Lahiri (other communist leaders) met Bose. ... We appreciated that he had sympathised with us and we suggested that this was the moment for a proper polarisation. This was, as far as I can remember, when the idea of Bose standing for a second term was first mooted.

Gandhi was furious about the Left walkout, and when Mazumdar and the others went to see him he suggested that they should leave the Congress. Immediately afterwards, he wrote that a split might purify the party. Both sides were indeed eager to test their strength, and the 1939 Presidential election provided the ideal occasion. It was clear that Gandhi's methods, which had worked so well with Nehru, had failed with Bose. The rebel had not been chained. Bose's suspected links with the Germans may also have turned Gandhi against him. Soli Batlivala tells a delightful story of how he was once summoned to meet Bose in a Bombay flat and asked to design a suitable disguise that would enable him to fool the watching police, and meet some foreign diplomats. Soli, an old theatrical hand and well versed in revolutionary methods of deception, quickly fabricated one. He thinks Bose used it to meet Chinese diplomats.

Nothing is known of any meeting with the Chinese but in Bombay on 22 December 1938 Bose did meet Germans. With the help of an Indian businessman, N.G. Ganpuley, whom he had got to know in Germany, Bose met two representatives of the foreign organisation of the Nazi party: Dr Urchs and Dr Wulfestieg. The Germans were aware that the Indian press did not like the Nazis. As the *Hindusthan Times* had put it, India did not want to win her freedom with the help of Germany, whose "hands were reeking with violence...Freedom secured with the help of such dubious friends is not worth purchasing."

Explaining his hostility, Bose told the two Nazis that the Hitler regime must stop insulting the Indians. He cited the offending passages on India in *Mein Kampf*, Rosenborg's writings and Goering's amazing attack on Gandhi in the Daily Mail (he had called him an "anti-British Bolshevik agent in India"). Indians, said Bose, did not care for the Nazis extinguishing democracy, eliminating international and socialist ideas, nor their Jewish and racial policies and were also suspicious of Nazi foreign policy. What, asked Bose, were the foreign policy aims of the Reich? Did it plan to uphold the "ageing and tired Empire" of Britain in the event of its downfall? The two Germans could not answer, although in their message to Berlin they urged the authorities to listen to what Bose was saying. But nobody in Berlin wanted to do any such thing.

It seems the Raj's spies were listening in to this meeting and, via K.M. Munshi, a prominent supporter of Gandhi and then home minister in the Congress Ministry of Bombay Province, news of it reached Gandhi. If that is what happened, it would have reawakened his dormant fears that Bose was back on the old Bengali revolutionary-conspiratorial tightrope.

Certainly, the British government took a keen interest in both Bose's contacts with the Axis and the developing Bose-Gandhi duel. In a long, exhaustive analysis of Congress finances government officials concluded that while the big financiers like the Birlas would support Gandhi, as they had traditionally done, Bose had enough "protection money" from small businessmen to keep going.

Subhas quickly announced his candidature, knowing he would be opposed. On the train journey from Wardha to Bombay, just before he received Gandhi's letter on the Huq ministry, he had written to Emilie saying there was opposition to his re-election. His election manifesto was simple: he would fight the federation proposed under the 1935 Government of India Act. There had been talk of compromise; this should be scotched. This, he said, was the age of "the progressive sharpening of the anti-imperialist struggle in India", and in this year of destiny the Congress president should be from the Left and genuinely anti-federation. Some of the prominent leftist leaders such as Jaya Prakash Narayan supported Bose's cause, and he appeared to have assembled a working coalition. Until the election Bose and his friends held the initiative.

The Gandhians were confused about their tactics. Nehru had taken a long holiday in Europe, gone to Spain and spoken out against fascism with great eloquence. When he had returned from Europe in November 1938 Gandhi had suggested his name, but he declined and recommended Maulana Azad. Azad accepted but withdrew at the last moment, leaving, as candidate for presidency, Dr Pattabhi Sitaramayya, the relatively unknown Andhra leader. Lumbered with an unattractive candidate, the Congress right wing now tried to seize the initiative. Though Gandhi remained in the background, he authorised a statement which was issued in the name of Patel and certain other Working Committee members, declaring that the choice of president was nearly always unanimous, that in any case the office carried little or no power and that, besides, there were no issues involved: all those concerned were opposed to federation. The implication was obvious. This was really a personal fight by Bose, who was unable to control his dangerous ambition and was determined to prove that he, like Nehru, could gain a second successive term. Privately, Patel telegraphed Sarat and told him he felt Subhas's election would be harmful to the country. Subhas, nettled, replied that he was standing because there were distinct signs of compromise between the Congress Right and the British over federation. He said, "It is widely believed that there is prospect of a compromise on the Federal scheme between the right-wing of the Congress and the British government during the coming year. Consequently the right wing do not want a leftist President who may be a thorn in the way of a compromise and may put obstacles in the path of negotiations." Bose said that if the Right would accept a genuine anti-federationist like Acharya Narendra Deo then he would withdraw. This statement was issued on 25 January1939 and was to be seized on by Bose's opponents. According to Chaudhuri it was made:

> ... in the characteristic Subhas Bose manner, that is, hurriedly and impulsively, and without consultation with his brother Sarat Bose, who learned about it only the next morning from his newspaper. He at once told me that Subhas had committed a mistake. He did indeed add that what Subhas had said was true, but there was no proof. Sarat Babu was very worried about the consequences of the statement.

With the election days away, the statement did not have an immediate impact but in the weeks and months that followed Bose's opponents, as if unable to believe their luck, used it ruthlessly to undermine him. They built up a steam of moral indignation, more spurious than genuine, but then Bose had supplied them with a handy weapon. Subhas Bose at various times was doubtful he would win or that he even wanted to win. On 4 January 1939, writing from Wardha, where he had gone to see Gandhi again, he told Emilie, "Though there is a very general desire for my re-election as president, I do not think I shall be again president ... In a way, it will be good not to be president again. I shall then be more free and have more time to myself." But by the time the results were declared on 29 January 1939, Bose was sure he would win. He had secured 1,580 votes against Sitaramayya's 1,377, a narrow but clear majority, and one spread uniformly over the entire country. The next day Sitaramayya telegraphed "Hearty congratulations", and wished him "long years of health and vigour". Subhas reciprocated, but that was the last brotherly feeling in the Congress, for Gandhi had taken Bose's victory as a bitter personal blow. Two days after the elections, he issued a statement:

> I must confess that from the very beginning I was decidedly against his re-election for reasons into which I need not go. I do not subscribe to his facts or the arguments in his manifestos. ... Nevertheless, I am glad of his victory; and since I was instrumental in inducing Dr Pattabhi not to withdraw his name as a candidate when Maulana Sahib withdrew, the defeat is more mine than his. And I am nothing if I do not represent definite principles and policy. Therefore, it is plain to me that the delegates do not approve of the principles and policy for which I stand. I rejoice in this defeat.

Bose, Gandhi said, was now a president in his own right. He should form his own Working Committee and run the Congress. In any case, the Congress had become a "corrupt" organisation in that its registers contained a very large number of "bogus members". And he concluded ominously:

> After all, Subhas Babu is not an enemy of his country. He has suffered for it. In his opinion his is the most forward and boldest policy and programme. The minority can only wish it all success. If it cannot keep pace with it they must come out of the Congress. If they can, they will add to the majority. The minority may not obstruct on any account. They must abstain, when they cannot co-operate. I must remind all Congressmen that those, who being Congress-minded remain outside it by design, represent it most. Those, therefore, who feel uncomfortable in being in the Congress, may come out not in a spirit of ill will, but with the deliberate purpose of rendering more effective service.

Gandhi, in his characteristic way, had declared war. Even as Bose celebrated his victory Gandhi was meticulously preparing to destroy him. The man who could use non-violence so skilfully was to use all his political skills now to defeat the most serious challenge to his rule.

13
Defeat

For Bose the elections were a defeat for the Congress machine controlled by Patel (a view with which Gandhi agreed). Gandhi himself, Bose thought, was above the fray, or should be. So, three days after Gandhi's declaration of war, Bose hurried to genuflect:

> I do not know what sort of opinion Gandhiji has of myself. But whatever his view may be, it will always be my aim and object to try and win his confidence for the simple reason that it will be a tragic thing for me if I succeed in winning the confidence of other people but fail to win the confidence of India's greatest man.

It was hardly the declaration of a revolutionary, and at least one American scholar has seen this as an example of Bose's "good boy, bad boy" behaviour: successfully challenging authority, then trying to win its favour. The psychological explanation may be valid, but the statement also revealed a sad misunderstanding of the political situation. Bose had organised the Left in a war against the Congress Right without realising that his main enemy was not Patel but Gandhi himself. He could not win the confidence of "India's greatest man" as long as he stood where he did: he could not defeat Patel and be a friend of Gandhi. He was to pay dearly for the miscalculation. Perhaps, as some have suggested, he did not have the skills for ruthless political infighting , nor the heart. He was a superb public organiser but a poor private intriguer. And now, not having anticipated the struggle with Gandhi, he did not quite know how to fight it.

In India, and in much of the world, Gandhi is a saint. He is always Gandhiji, Mahatma, Bapu: revered Gandhi, the great-souled one, father of the nation. He is the man who never did wrong in order to achieve his political ends. For him, so the legend goes, men were just as important as the ideas they believed in, if not more so. The legend is useful and instructive, but, like most, grossly exaggerated. Gandhi was essentially a very shrewd politician who realised that religion was the easiest way to arouse the Indian people. It had been the basis on which he had constructed a national movement against the British, converting ineffectual Indian liberalism into strong, almost irresistible, Indian nationalism. It would now give him his last great victory. He may not have been, as Churchill crudely put it, "a seditious Middle Temple lawyer posing as a half-naked fakir of a type well known in the East", but he could always combine elements of his Middle Temple background with the techniques of the fakir, or mystic, for political purposes. Now, having decided to finish Bose, he did so in a masterly fashion, proving that, while presidents might come and go, he would always remain the super-president.

Gandhi had to plan his moves against Bose with great care. The Congress constitution did not provide for the removal of the president: the delegates' vote could not be reversed. But it could be thwarted. Gandhi's followers still controlled the Working Committee and the All-India Congress Committee. Without their support no president could function. He might reign, but he could not rule. It was here that Gandhi sought to avenge his defeat.

In March 1939 the Congress was to hold its annual session in Tripuri, a small rustic place near Jubbalpore in what was then called the Central Provinces. Had this been a normal year then Bose would have arrived in triumph. Worse still, he again became ill. Nirad Chaudhuri has suggested that Bose's illnesses were a psychological reaction to stress. He was invariably ill in prison and, as he faced his greatest political crisis, he succumbed to an illness that was never properly diagnosed and that led to many strange twists and turns in an already complicated story. He fell ill on 16 February, two weeks after his election triumph, and just as he was leaving Wardha after another visit to Gandhi. By the time he returned to Calcutta the illness had taken hold. His temperature would rise at noon; Bose would be racked by splitting headaches. It would reach a peak at about six pm; then he would begin to perspire profusely, and the fever would slowly subside. For hours afterwards he would lie still in his bed, ice packs pressed to his throbbing head. Occasionally the fever persisted for days; at other times, he would be normal for a day or two. The doctors' opinions varied, and it was only much later that they diagnosed it as bronchia-pneumonia with liver and intestinal infections.

During his illness, Bose was inundated with letters and packets. Astrologers and *sadhus* (holy men) sent him amulets and blessings. Well-wishers sent *ashirvadi* flowers for his recovery and the Bose women, superstitious about such things, not only touched them to his forehead so he would receive the blessing but put them under his pillow. Bose the rationalist suffered this. When a professor of Sanskrit came to see him and told him that somebody was practising *Marana Kriya*, a form of Tantra to kill him, the patient confessed that it created "an uncanny feeling within me". And in the end Bose, who hated superstition, even took to wearing amulets to ward off evil.

Bose had wanted to attend the Working Committee session at Wardha on 22 February. But the doctors warned him not to. So Bose sent Patel what he thought was an innocuous telegram:

> KINDLY SEE MY TELEGRAM TO MAHATMAJI. REGRETFULLY FEEL WORKING COMMITTEE MUST BE POSTPONED TILL CONGRESS. PLEASE CONSULT COLLEAGUES AND WIRE OPINION — SUBHAS.

This message triggered a sequence of events which were disastrous. The Congress Right argued that it demonstrated his dictatorial ambitions. The annual session at Tripuri was only a few weeks away, but – because of an obscure illness that even his own doctors could not diagnose – he would not allow the committee to transact its normal business. Patel and eleven other working committee members issued a statement drafted by Gandhi, saying that they were resigning. They were still smarting from the alleged aspersions in Bose's 25 January statement in which he had suggested that that they might compromise with the British over federation. By this time, the ban on *The Indian Struggle* with its criticisms of Gandhi and the men round him, had been lifted and was circulating in India. Bose had described Gandhi's working committee as men of "low intellectual level" who were only there because they were "blind" followers of Gandhi. Patel and his friends asked Bose to apologise for this slur. This he refused to do. Nehru also resigned, but characteristically issued a separate statement of withdrawal. This meant Subhas and Sarat found themselves alone on the working committee.

As if that were not enough, rumours circulated that his illness was feigned. This allegation was only scotched by a specially invited medical board which examined him at the Tripuri Congress. The delegates could see he was ill as he was brought on a stretcher on to the dais, where one of his nieces fanned him and another applied an ice-pack to his head. Such, however, was the bitterness between the two Congress camps that one delegate cried, "Why don't you check whether he has onions under his armpits? Onions raise the temperature!"

Already, Gandhi had clawed back some of the gains that had accrued to Bose following his election victory. Meanwhile Gandhi had successfully converted a footling political dispute in the princely Indian state of Rajkot into a major diversion, so much so that Bose was unable to meet Gandhi before Tripuri and agree on who should serve in his Working Committee. Also, just before the Tripuri session began, Gandhi declared that he had to remain in Rajkot, a thousand miles from Tripuri. and began a fast to death in order to obtain a solution to this inconsequential affair. The result, as during all the Mahatma's fasts, was that public and political attention was successfully diverted. Gandhi knew he did not have to be in Tripuri (he had enough shrewd deputies there to beat Bose) and as the Tripuri session began the carefully planned Gandhian counter-offensive now made its final push.

At a meeting of the All-India Congress Committee, preceding the open session, the Gandhians moved a resolution which regretted the aspersions cast on them and requested "the President to nominate the Working Committee in accordance with the wishes of Gandhiji". In moving the resolution, Pandi Pant compared Gandhi to Hitler, Mussolini and Lenin and asked, "We have Gandhi ... Then why should we not reap the full advantages of that factor?" Rajaji suggested trusting the Congress to Bose was like trying to cross the wide Narbada river in a leaky boat, when they had the superb craft called Gandhi. In the midst of the debate a news report was issued that, on the telephone from Rajkot, Gandhi had approved the text of the resolution. Gandhi later denied this, but that was enough to secure a narrow victory.

The open session, attended by more than 200,000 people, was Bose's first public setback. In his short presidential speech (read out by Sarat), he repeated his demand that this was the moment to submit an ultimatum to the British government over Indian independence, ending his speech with a prayer for Gandhi's good health. The voting on the resolution clearly revealed that Bose's broad-Left coalition had disintegrated. The Congress socialists, led by Jaya Prakash Narayan, abstained, unsure of either their loyalties or their own best interests. Though the followers of the former communist, Roy, stayed with Bose, the communists agonised about supporting him. They had tabled a motion that modified the Pant resolution and freed Bose. The night before the open session they met to decide their tactics should their amendment fail. While their secretary P.C. Joshi was resolutely opposed to Bose, the Bengal communists, who perhaps had an emotional identification with Bose, got their comrades to agree that should their amendment fail they would vote against the Pant resolution. The meeting had ended at 2 am, but at 6 am one of Bose's principal backers, Dutt-Mazumdar, was hurriedly awakened and told that Joshi had managed to reverse this decision. Dutt-Mazumdar recollects getting up from a sick-bed to have the reversal righted. This, he says, "led to a hysterical scene, with Joshi rolling on the floor declaring in Hindi, 'You have cut my throat'." The debate in the open session was no less emotional, with more than a hint of violence, some of it from Bose's supporters. At one stage as Nehru tried to speak some followers of Bose tried to shout him down The atmosphere in Tripuri was the most extraordinary ever seen in a Congress session. Chaudhuri did not attend. But when the Boses and their followers returned to Calcutta he heard many tales of what was said.

The most nauseating feature was the gossip, often slanderous and always mischievous which busy tongues emitted in the camp. This was due to the distrust and suspicion between the rival parties, which everyone noticed and afterwards admitted. Some of the followers of the Boses made themselves intelligence agents and carried tales to their leaders about what was being said about them by the Gandhians. A good deal must have been invention, but even when true, lost nothing in telling. What was more important the Boses believed them implicitly.

> The accounts I heard gave the impression that the tract of Central Indian jungle which for the moment had been converted into the Congress camp, buzzed like a meat market with bluebottles descending in swarms on putrescent carcases. The stench could be inhaled even in the correspondence.

In the end the Gandhians had the vote. The old magic had worked: the Congress, faced with a choice between their great-souled one and Bose, had plumped for the god they knew. Bose, sickened by the "moral squalor" of Tripuri, thought for a time of leaving politics altogether. He did not return to Calcutta but went to Jealgora near Dhanbad where one of his brothers worked to recover his health. He was convinced that Nehru had betrayed him. "Nobody," he wrote to his nephew, "has done more harm to me personally and to our cause in this crisis than Pandit Nehru. If he had been with us we would have had a majority."

Jawaharlal's ambivalence had contributed to the socialists' abstention, and in long letters, one of them running to 27 typed pages, Subhas engaged in wordy duels with Nehru. They combined the touchiness that is part of the Bengali temperament ("You take up enthusiastically every possible point against me; what could be said in my favour you ignore"), with some well-honed digs at Nehru's vacillation and "pious platitudes and frothy sentiments" about foreign affairs. Nehru, with uncharacteristic gentleness, defended himself, but not convincingly.

That Nehru and Bose were rivals is understandable. Though Nehru was nine years older, both men had risen through the nationalist movements at the same time. In Indian eyes both had the same qualities: they were young, energetic, handsome, radical, Left nationalists who conceived freedom as the beginning of sweeping socio-economic changes, and who were, as Dilip Roy later put it, "utterly inaccessible to fear that makes us falter and cringe and to meanness that makes us carp or bargain." Bose had been exasperated by Nehru's habit of abandoning well-conceived Left positions. However, since the late 1930s their relationship had prospered, and Bose, as Nehru himself acknowledged, had "treated him with utmost regard and consideration"; he had been a political elder brother to whom Bose had often turned for advice. Now, as Jawaharlal once again discovered his more primitive loyalty to Gandhi, Subhas could not conceal his hurt and disappointment.

Years later, Nehru himself would acknowledge to a British correspondent that he had let Subhas down, but said, "I did it because I have realised that, at that stage, whatever one's view might be about the way India should develop, *Gandhi was India* [the author's italics]. Anything that weakened Gandhi weakened India. So I subordinated myself to Gandhi, although I was in agreement with what Subhas was trying to do." This attitude had always characterised Nehru's political life. As Gandhi himself would put it, "We know that neither of us can do without the other for there is a heart union between us which no intellectual differences can break."

Bose had no such links, and saw Nehru's much-applauded "artistic introspection", which always enabled him to be on the winning side, as convenient hypocrisy. In this sense Bose was Western while Nehru, who was bored with Hindu rites and customs, was more genuinely Hindu. His actions conformed to the essential logic of Hindu philosophy, where almost anything can be made to mean anything else, where there can be disagreement but no final break, and where, however great the differences, there are no endings, only compromise and consensus. Bose resented Nehru's good luck, the *bhagya* that had already brought him so much glory at so little cost. He distrusted his denial of religion, and was baffled by his vacillation. He would later tell Dilip, "If he really wants to serve India through politics he must first of all make sure of his foundations. For if he doesn't take care to seek solid ground under his feet, the ground won't seek his feet either. Consequently, he will never be able to stand perpendicular anywhere."

In some ways, the rivalry between Bose and Nehru was also the classic fight between an outsider and an insider. Nehru was so much of an insider and so sure of himself that in 1937, when he was still Congress President, he did something quite remarkable. On the evening of 5 October 1937, returning from one of his trips as president, he sat down to write an article about himself, almost as an after dinner exercise. The article was written in the third person and asked the question: Was Nehru a dictator, could he became a Caesar? The answer was:

> Jawaharlal cannot become a dictator. And yet he has all the makings of a dictator in him - vast popularity, a strong will directed to a well-defined purpose, energy, pride, organisational capacity, ability, hardness and with all his love of the crowd, an intolerance of others and a certain contempt of the weak and the inefficient. His flashes of temper are well known and even when they are controlled, the curling of the lips betrays him.

Then without having it typed, or even typing it himself, he sent it to his lover Padmaja in Calcutta and asked her to pass it on to the editor of *The Modern Review*, Ramananda Chatterjee. The piece was entitled "Rashtrapati" and bylined Chanakya, the fourth century BC Indian theorist who formulated views on statecraft almost a 1,000 years before Machiavelli. The anonymous article caused a sensation. The Left was outraged and began a guessing game as to who had written it. Could it be the British? Could it be the Congress Right? Chatterjee explained that he did not know who the author was and had published it to provoke debate. Nehru eventually owned up and explained he had written the article because he did not want a third term as Congress president. This would lead, as we have seen, to Bose becoming President with Gandhi's blessings.

The point is that while Bose wrote extensively in the *Modern Review* (he even wrote a lengthy article about his illness which was full of self pity) it is inconceivable that he could have written about himself in this fashion. In Indian politics he was too much of an outsider to be confident enough to be his own critic. Nehru could afford to take such a unique position.

The Bose-Nehru relationship forms one of the most fascinating "ifs" cherished by the Indian Left. If only the two could have worked together. Like all ifs, it contains an element of wishful thinking. In the end, though both spoke for socialism, their practical interpretations of it were so different that there was an ideological divide. Though, during the war, Bose continued to make overtures to Gandhi, he never forgave Jawaharlal Nehru. Nehru, in turn, criticised Bose for his alliance with the Axis powers and vowed to fight him if he returned to India with the Japanese.

The working committee was still to be formed, and there began an exchange of letters and telegrams between Subhas and Gandhi. Bose, treating the Tripuri conference merely as a defeat that balanced his earlier victory, was wooing Gandhi, urging him to act as an arbitrator. Gandhi was unmoved. With all the skill at his command he now unleashed active non-co-operation on Bose. As in his fights with the British, the blade was coated with honey. All his letters began "My dear Subhas" and ended "love, Bapu", and he telegraphed "I suggest your coming here and living with me. I undertake to nurse you to health while we are slowly conferring." But almost simultaneously he suggested resignation: "I do not know how far you are fit to attend to national work. If you are not, I think you should adopt the only constitutional course open to you."

Like a skilled swordsman, Gandhi scored innumerable points with accurate jabs and quicksilver footwork, while Bose appeared heavy-footed. For every compromise solution Bose proposed, Gandhi had a refusal: bitterness between the old guard and the rest ran too deep, Gandhi claimed, and his involvement would be futile. Bose offered to "retire" from all official positions if Gandhi would only resume the national struggle for independence.

War, Subhas was convinced, was only a few months away, and a beleaguered Britain would not be able to resist a united Congress ultimatum of independence. Gandhi claimed his nostrils were full of "violence in the air I breathe". Even when Bose was prepared to accept all Gandhi's nominees on the Working Committee, the Mahatma could find no way of agreeing to this. He had successfully driven Bose into a corner. Even Nehru was moved to protest and he wrote to Gandhi: "To try to push him out seems to me to be an exceedingly wrong step."

Subhas Bose (standing on the right) with his friends in England in 1920 surrounded by his fellow students, lookinng the classic English graduate.

Geneva 1933: An ailing Vithalbhai Patel and Subhas Bose enjoy some sunshine on a park bench. It was to be one of their last meetings.

Bose far right, partly obscured by flowers, at the deathbed of Vithalbhai Patel at a clinic in Gland near Geneva, 1933.

Bad Gastein 1937: Bose, Gandhi cap and warm coat, poses for a picture at his favourite European spa where he began writing his unfinished autobiography. With him (left to right) are A.C.N.Nambiar, Heddy Fullop-Miller, Bose, , his nephew, Amiya, and his secretary, soon to be wife, Emilie Schenkl.

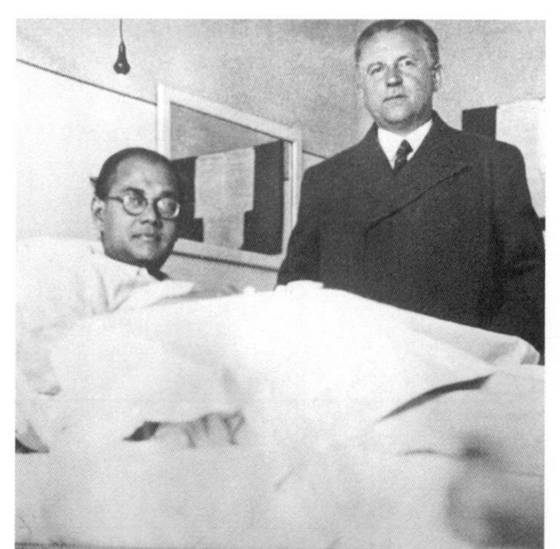

Vienna 1935. Bose, having had his gall bladder removed, recovers in a Vienna hospital. He had previously been sick for years.

January 1938: Bose on his second and last visit to England. He crossed the Channel by boat and, despite a British desire to keep him out, met friends at Victoria station.

A sick Bose being fanned by his niece Illa, surrounded by other relations, on the dais of the Tripuri Congress, March 1939.

The ancestral home in Calcutta, 38/2 Elgin Avenue from where in January 1941 Bose began his long escape from India.

Emilie in Vienna sometime in the late 1940s.

Studio poses: His mother Prabhabati, in Calcutta: she did not know of her son's marriage.

Studio poses: A picture Bose never saw: his daughter, Anita, aged ten months, in Vienna.

Like mother, like daughter: Anita and Emilie portrayed together in Vienna on Anita's 6th birthday in 1948.

Anita in a park in Vienna, the summer of 1946.

Food shortages in Europe: With Bose gone Anita's mother and gandmother had to do without in order to succour Bose's wartime child.

Bose in war-time Europe with Nambiar on the left in bow tie and Faltis on the right, next to Faltis is a German woman who had married an Indian, much to the disapproval of the Nazis.

Bose, meeting Adolf Hitler, in the fuehrer's secret headquarters in deepest Prussia.

After Subhas Bose met Hitler portraits of him dressed in European suits were in vogue in Germany.

Berlin 1942: Bose in the garden of his comfortable Berlin villa in 1942 with his Austrian friend Otto Faltis.

Bose as president of the Forward Bloc, touring Madras in January 1940. No longer in Congress he still drew huge crowds. Soon he was to escape India to secure foreign help for national liberation.

Subhas Bose, in the uniform of the Indian National Army.

Predicting victory: Bose hoists the Indian tricolour at an INA rally in Japanese-occupied East Asia in 1943.

The Wanderer car in which nephew Sisir, then a 19 year-old Medical student, drove him away from Calcutta in the middle of the night as he made his escape from India.

Bose leaves Bombay for Europe after the Raj had allowed him back for a brief visit to attend his father's funeral.

Rani of Jhansi Regiment of women formed by Bose in East Asia 1943.

Bose with Indian National Army officers, Berlin 1942.

While Gandhi's love could be, as he was to later write, soft as rose petal, it could also be harder than flint. He thought he had gained in Bose a son; now he was ready to discard him. Gandhi even rejected Tagore's advice that he should let Bose remain president. It has been argued that in this fight Subhas Bose made the mistake of treating Gandhi as an English constitutional monarch who was above the fray, while Gandhi's courtiers behaved as if they knew the divine right of kings still applied. They were also busy and there was a sideshow fight between the Gandhians and Sarat Bose, which led to many letters and showed the depth of the divide between the two camps. The bitterest part of this extraordinary correspondence concerned the alleged abuse hurled at the Boses by the Congress Right.

During Tripuri a nephew of the Boses was standing in the Gandhian camp. As they did not know who he was they spoke freely about the Boses and he claimed that he heard a senior Gandhian, the lawyer Bhulabhai Desai, call the Boses rascals. Sarat, in a long letter complaining about the Gandhians behaviour at Tripuri, mentioned this alleged incident. It led to furious denials from Desai and other Gandhians joined in. The Gandhians combined moral outrage over the accusation, with lofty sentiments telling the Boses that they were complaining merely because they had lost. In their correspondence they tried hard to paint the Boses as petulant, spoilt children who could not take defeat.

There was a brief possibility immediately after Tripuri that a face-to-face meeting between Subhas Bose and Gandhi might have solved matters. Subhas, who was ill, suggested Sarat should go and meet Gandhi in Delhi on 15 March. But Sarat, who in contrast to Subhas believed in superstition, consulted the family priest, Ashoknath Shastri, who said for a meeting to be fruitful it must be after 5 April. The meeting did not take place. Whether it would have worked is not clear, other meetings had not. Before Tripuri Nehru had advised Bose to meet Gandhi and deal with the aspersion that the Congress Right might compromise with the British. He had agreed, but then had not mentioned it again.

By the time Subhas met Gandhi, just before the Calcutta AICC session in late April 1939, only the formalities of the Gandhian victory remained to be completed. It was four months since the Presidential elections, yet Bose had failed to form his cabinet. On the first day of the session he presented his resignation. Nehru suggested a compromise but Bose, convinced all was lost, refused, and the Gandhian Rajendra Prasad assumed the Presidency. Calcutta did not take kindly to its favourite son being "robbed" of his due, and there were violent protests both at the session and in the city at large. But now Bose's friends began to cut their political coats according to the new cloth. Kiran Shankar Roy, his erstwhile machine organiser, completed his conversion to Gandhism, the communists began to distance themselves, and even the Bengal revolutionaries were abusive.

There is some merit in the criticism that for all his skills in arousing the masses Subhas Bose was not an organiser of a political party in the way of a Gandhi or even a Patel. Chaudhuri gives a trivial, if amusing, example of what he calls Bose's "unmethodical" working method. He wrote letters so late they nearly always missed the normal postal clearance. He could still get them posted if he could stamp them and have then delivered to the GPO. But then he would find he did not have the stamps. He would try and borrow stamps from his brother Sarat, who being more organised, always had spare ones. Once Sarat was not available and Subhas had to send a circular letter but he did not have the money. He managed to do so by getting credit from the clerk at the GPO. More crucially Subhas Bose never had a loyal party following. Chaudhuri writes:

> Since Subhas Bose was challenging what might be called the nationalist Establishment in India, he needed a party all the more. Yet he never had one. His following was always floating, shifting from year to year to different factions. Even his close associates did not fully trust him, and therefore were not invariably loyal. The lower ranks of the Congress nationalists gave or withheld

> their loyalty to him according to their estimate of his power to serve or harm their interests and showed the proverbial valet's disinclination to hero-worship. He was never able to knock his enemies on the head, of whose ill will he was certain. On the other hand he was paralysed all along by the factional quarrels of the professional nationalists into which he got himself enmeshed.

It should be emphasised that Chaudhuri's is the anti-view of Bose. He concluded that Sarat, his employer, was in some ways the greater Bose, certainly the straighter. While Subhas was likely to believe tales told to him, always suspecting disloyalty, and had a conspiratorial approach to politics, his brother Sarat was more honest. Three days after the session Bose announced the formation of the Forward Bloc, a party within the Congress that would bring together the warring Left and fight not Gandhi but Gandhism. Amidst this gloom there was only one bright moment. Tagore, who had written to Nehru in support of Bose's re-election as president, now hailed Subhas in rhapsodic terms as Bengal's leader; and Subhas displayed a sense of mordant wit. When Forward Bloc was suggested as the name of the new political group, Sarat asked, "But who will be the blockhead?" Subhas butted in, "Well, you know who is going to be the blockhead." It was gallows humour, suitable for what was to follow.

14
The Lonely Furrow

The next 20 months of Bose's life are the most difficult for his biographer. He fought a series of losing battles with Gandhi and the Congress establishment that finally led to his expulsion and his loss of control of the Bengal Congress. He almost single-handedly tried to build up the Forward Bloc, attracting enormous crowds wherever he went and writing fine polemical articles, but he never succeeded in creating a genuine mass party. Around him the Left splintered further. But these sad public events are easy enough to record and analyse. The parallel private events are still a mystery, or capable of so many interpretations as to make nonsense of any analysis. At some stage during this period, Bose began to plan an escape from India to Russia or somewhere in Europe to start what he would later call the "second front of the Indian Independence Movement."

It is easy to argue that Bose decided to escape as his options in India closed. This has been the conventional viewpoint, and it is the logical one. But it is more probable that the unfolding events in Europe dictated his moves. We cannot be sure. All we are left with are certain events of great anecdotal value but no definite historical merit. Bose saw the Forward Bloc as an umbrella organisation bringing together all the various Leftist groups. They would retain their individual, idiosyncratic and often conflicting identities, but they would come together for the purpose of working out a basic programme. Such an arrangement had been discussed for a long time, at least since the Haripura Congress; but few of the established Left groups were willing to join, and one of them, M.N. Roy's, was already organised as a rival body.

The Left, however, came together to form a Left Consolidation Committee, which was inaugurated at Bombay on 21 June 1939 and was a remarkably heterogeneous body. It met just before the AICC was to hold its regular meeting, where the Gandhians attacked individuals and groups starting civil disobedience without the approval of the provincial body. The Left Consolidation committee decided to organise an all-India day of protest about the AICC decision on 9 July. This achieved some success. Almost immediately the Working Committee was summoned to discuss this blatant breach of discipline. Gandhi was unrelenting, and it was he who drafted the Working Committee's resolution. It removed Bose from the presidency of the Bengal Congress Committee and banned him from holding elective office for three years. Within Bengal this sharpened the hopeless factional squabbles, which ultimately led to the suspension of the Bose-controlled provincial committee and the imposition of Gandhi's own men. While this messy battle went on Bose tried to activitate the Forward Bloc.

This involved long train journeys across India addressing meetings. In May he went to the United Provinces, in the middle of June north to Lahore and on to Peshawar, then west to Bombay and from there to south India. In Lahore, as he was in the middle of a big crowd, a pickpocket stole his money and Emilie's letters and some photographs she had sent him. Writing to Emilie about this he put in a German aside and asked her, "When will you come to India?" In July he was on his way to Jubbulpore and on 6 July on the train to Bombay, he wrote to Emilie again. He was better, but the past few months had been hard and he was thinking of taking a holiday, perhaps sometime in August or early September. This could have meant going back to Bad Gastein, the place he loved so much. But soon events overtook him, and this would be the last letter he wrote to Emilie from India.

On 3 September 1939 Bose was addressing a 200,000-strong public meeting on the Marina sea beach in Madras when somebody thrust a newspaper into his hand. The headline told the story: Britain was now at war with Germany, and India had followed. Within hours of Chamberlain's broadcast Lord Linlithgow, the Viceroy, had, without consulting a single Indian, plunged four hundred million people into a European war. For Bose, of course, this was India's golden opportunity. A Britain at war would mean a weak Britain. Never would she be more amenable to pressure. The Congress should immediately launch its final struggle for freedom. Unexpectedly invited to attend the special Working Committee meeting held at Wardha on 8 September to decide the Congress attitude to the war, Bose argued his case. Caught between Gandhi's pacifism and the lukewarm interest of others, the Congress equivocated and looked to Nehru for guidance.

The declaration of war had seen Nehru in China visiting Generalisimo Chiang Kai-shek, the ruler of nationalist China. He hurried back to India and declared, "This is not the time to bargain. We are against the rising imperialism of Germany, Italy and Japan and of the decaying imperialism of Europe." When Nehru arrived in Calcutta Bose organised demonstrations with placards declaring, "British adversity is India's opportunity."

Nehru brought to Wardha two draft resolutions. The working committee merged them, tightened up the prose and toned down his criticisms of the British, reflecting the mood in the organisation. The result was a resolution that condemned fascism and asked the British government to define its war aims. For Bose this amounted to an offer of co-operation with Britain's war effort and yet another lost opportunity. Shortly afterwards he met some of his Forward Bloc colleagues and friends from other parties in Lucknow to discuss the alternative nationalist strategy during the period of war. The meeting proved abortive. Dutt-Mazumdar and Bose travelled back to Calcutta together. On the way to the station Bose suddenly turned to Dutt-Mazumdar and asked, "Can you go underground right here and now?"

Dutt-Mazumdar, taken aback, replied, "I can, but not right away." On the train he added, "I feel I may have disappointed you by not going underground right there and then in Lucknow. But I feel *you* should go underground." Subhas was surprised, "You want me to go underground?" "Yes, you should flee the country. Sun Yat-Sen had to flee his country and go underground. Mazzini had to flee", said Dutt-Mazumdar. They sat quietly for some time as the train rattled its way towards Calcutta. Suddenly Bose said, "Don't discuss this idea with anyone else."

Dutt-Mazumdar believes that this is when Bose first started thinking of going abroad. In the summer of 1939 he had asked his nephew Amiya to take secretly to England a handwritten, signed, message to the Soviet government. Amiya recollects that Bose was convinced that the Right would do nothing and that the only way out was an armed revolution, possibly with the help of the Soviet Union. Bose had, indeed, always been favourably inclined towards the Soviets. It was the country of Lenin, the country that had produced the first people's revolution and, above all, the country that had shown how a backward agricultural society could be modernised. Soon after this, as Soviet troops marched into eastern Poland and took their share of the loot agreed with Hitler, Bose turned to Ranadive, a leading Indian communist, and said with a broad grin that he would not have minded the help of a few Russian divisions in his fight with the British.

At about this time he once again took up yoga. He had never doubted its power, and now he needed it even more. He spent long hours meditating, and occasionally he would slip out of Elgin Road to visit a yogi he admired or respected. But travel was on his mind and in October 1939 he applied to the Bengal government for a passport to go to China. The Bengal government, always glad to be rid of Bose, quickly agreed. But the government in Delhi, who already "strongly suspected" Bose of being a foreign agent, were worried about a "peripatetic revolutionary" being let loose in central Asia and seeking to foment an anti-British movement with the aid of foreign powers. Though Nehru had recently been allowed to visit China, Delhi saw no problems in answering accusations of favouritism. As one government official put it, "Nehru whatever his faults is an entirely different type from Subhas Bose"; and "a dangerous man like Subhas Bose should be under proper control under the Defence of India Act". The Bengal government began working towards this objective, one consequence of which was that Subhas Bose sought a meeting with the Viceroy.

On the morning of 10 October 1939 Bose, for the first and only time in his life, walked up to the Viceroy's House in Delhi to meet Linlithgow. No two men could have been more different or travelled more divergent routes. Linlithgow was one of the few viceroys who had acquired some knowledge of India before taking up his position. He had been chairman of the Royal Commission on Indian Agriculture between 1926 and 1928 and chairman of the Joint Select Committee on Indian Constitutional Reform in 1933. When he had first arrived as Viceroy in 1934 he had told the Indian journalist Durga Das that he wanted to make friends with the Congress as it was the only political body that stood for nationalism and promotion of self respect.

By now, he had long tired of the Indian nationalists and they of him. When Gandhi was in the middle of one of his fasts, and Churchill wondered whether Hindu doctors were secretly putting glucose in his water, Linlithgow shared Churchill's doubts and told him, "I have long known Gandhi as the world's most successful humbug." And just before he left India in 1943 Linlithgow told the Indian journalist Durga Das that India could not hope to be free for 50 years. Parliamentary democracy was new to India and it would require some six million British and European officials to make it work. Now that air-conditioning had come, he said, it would be possible for Britons to settle permanently in India, perhaps near cooler places like Dehra Dun. Nehru, in turn, summed up Linlithgow for many Indians by describing him as "heavy of body and slow of mind, solid as a rock and with almost a rock's lack of awareness." Bose had no illusions about Linlithgow but used the meeting to tell him how ruthlessly and partially censorship was being used in Bengal, that political prisoners were still in jail despite a promise to review their cases, and about the vindictive nature of the Bengal government. The Viceroy, as usual, stonewalled, though in a later telephone message his private secretary, Sir Gilbert Laithwaite, conveyed to the governor of Bengal that "the Viceroy liked him personally and the talk was quite friendly". The differences, however, were so great that there could be no progress.

Bose also used his time in Delhi to meet various Indian leaders, including Jinnah, whom he found vain, opinionated, and sure that he and he alone held the future of India in his hands. For all his activity and almost ceaseless travelling Subhas was not getting very far. But his constant battering of the Congress did have an effect. Nearly two months after war had been declared, it acted. To the Congress request that the British clarify their war aims, Linlithgow had replied that it was too early to do so. In any case, he said, it would serve no purpose. There were far too many differences among the Indian political parties, and Britain's aims in India were all set out in the preamble to the Act of 1919, the statement of dominion status of 1929, and constituted the purpose, meaning and message of the massive 1935 Act. All he would say was that Britain was fighting to resist fascist aggression. After the war it would be prepared to discuss modifications to the 1935 Act. Almost as a footnote he added that he would be willing to set up consultative committees during the war. No slap in the face could have been more resounding, and the Congress ministries in the provinces resigned. This was a victory of sorts for Bose but the Left Consolidation Committee was now in ruins.

In October 1939 the socialists had deserted it. In November, the communists had followed. And in Bengal the fight with the Gandhians reached its inevitable climax. In August the executive council of the provincial Congress committee had re-affirmed its loyalty to Bose; in October it repeated this, placed 5,000 rupees at his disposal and asked him to lead the Congress in the coming Calcutta municipal elections. On 20 December the Working Committee ousted the entire provincial committee and appointed its own ad-hoc committee. Bose became caught between the Gandhians and the Raj. The government was convinced that

Bose had backed himself into a cul-de-sac. But for a politician in such trouble he showed uncommon energy. In November the Working Committee of the Forward Bloc decided to hold an anti-compromise conference at the same time and place as the Congress's annual session. And when the Congress Working Committee called for a constituent assembly, Bose recalled Trotsky's and Lenin's attitude to the Kerensky-inspired Russian one, and Sinn Fein's contempt for Lloyd George's Irish Convention. For Bose, the Forward Bloc would play this historical role, although occasionally his own rhetoric overwhelmed him. "We can legitimately claim that today "Forward Bloc *Zindabad*" [Long live the Forward Bloc] has become a mass slogan. Its message has reached the remotest villages and has roused the sympathy and support of the masses everywhere." Before anything concrete could be achieved, the government struck. By the second week of April 1940, most of the senior Forward Bloc leaders were arrested. Bose was not touched largely because he was enjoying what Sir John Herbert, the Bengal Governor, would later call "anomalous immunity".

Herbert, a 44 year old Conservative MP of Welsh landed stock, had only the previous year been appointed. He was the third man in 1939 to become governor and his appointment was an illustration of the nepotism that marked British appointments. Herbert got the job not because he was particularly suited for it but because of his connections, having been assistant Conservative whip in the Commons and married to Lady Mary Fox-Strangways, daughter of the Earl of Ilchester. Herbert was still governor three years later and presided over the Bengal Famine of 1943, the most devastating famine to visit south Asia in the 20th century when about three and a half million people died. With the Japanese at the gates of India, and the British fearful that eastern parts of India would fall to the Japanese, his government took the decision to enforce what historians have called the scorched earth policy whereby all local transport, especially boats of all sizes and descriptions, were confiscated. This caused a huge dislocation in daily life in eastern Bengal, the main rice producing area, where river transport was the principal means of communication. Asok Mitra, who was then a young ICS officer in Dacca, has in his book *Towards Independence 1940-1947: Memoirs of an Indian Civil Servant* no doubt that this "denial policy" and the famine that resulted from it, despite a record rice harvest, was due to the bloody-mindedness of the British.

In April 1940 Herbert was still learning about Bengal and was quite puzzled by the fact that his Muslim League Bengal ministers could not arrest Bose because they feared the reaction of Bose's Muslim following. For Bose had managed in a limited sphere to do the impossible, construct a Hindu-Muslim coalition. He had done this by aligning his Forward Bloc with radical elements in the Muslim League.

There was criticism of this alliance from some Muslim nationalists and Bose had to defend himself. Bose was all the more keen on keeping doors open because by this time the Muslim League had passed its Lahore resolution, which is seen as firing the first shot for the creation of Pakistan by laying the claim for a separate country for the Muslims. It had been moved by Fazlul Huq and was passed on 24 March 1940. As Bose saw it was now even more important for there to be some dialogue between the two communities, however limited, so as to prevent a total communal breakdown.

Herbert was alarmed at the ease with which Bose worked his Hindu-Muslim coalition centred round the Muslim trio of Abdur Rahman Siddique, Mayor of Calcutta, K. Nooruddin, a member of the Dacca Nawab family, and M.A.H Ispahani, a businessman and leader of the Muslim League in the Calcutta Corporation. The governor was not even sure about the reliability of the Chief Minister, Huq, whom Subhas had consistently wooed. Even Khwaja Nazimuddin, the Home Minister, and closest to the British, feared Bose's growing Muslim support. Weeks after Bose had finally been arrested, Bengal intelligence officials would anxiously debate the possibility of Nazimuddin coming to an agreement with Subhas and enhancing his "popularity and prestige". It was, of course, a coalition at the level of elite leaders, but even then it was rare.

Bose may have surprised even himself by this feat and, quite uncharacteristically, he appears to have underestimated the consequences of his achievement, however limited. He gave no thought to what he might gain by remaining in India and working on this regional, but significant, coalition; instead he began seriously to look for people who would help him to leave India.

For some time Bose had been asking communist contacts whether they could help him get to Moscow. According to one communist source, Ram Singh Dutt, during a meeting of the Left Consolidation Committee in Bombay in April 1940, he had said he wanted to go to Moscow to interview Stalin and ask him to order the Red Army to invade India. He also made the same request of P.C Joshi who rejected it as he did not trust Bose. The man Bose finally approached was one Achhar Singh Cheena, a member of the Punjab-based pro-communist Kirti Kisan Party.

Bose had first met him in April 1939 when he was visiting the Gaya district as Congress president. At that time Cheena was in hiding as a result of the Fatehwal case. (In trying to organise a peasants' conference there had been a riot, two people were killed and Cheena was charged in relation to the killings). He sought Bose's help and Bose advised him not to give himself up to the police. In early June 1940 Bose met Cheena again. Cheena had come to visit Calcutta and stayed with Niranjan Singh Talib, editor of *Desk Darpan*, a Calcutta Sikh magazine with which Bose was very friendly. The moment Cheena arrived he was told by Talib that Bose wanted to see him urgently. The next day he went to Bose's house. Bose told him he was keen to make a secret journey to Russia to see Stalin. Could Cheena get him across the tribal areas into Afghanistan and then over the river Oxus into Russia? Cheena had already planned such a journey as he wanted instructions from Moscow on the Kirti party's war policy and on its relations with the main communist party in India. Bose gave him 200 rupees (about £20) to cover his expenses.

Cheena discussed the request with his Kirti colleagues and while some were reluctant, they decided that irrespective of whether Bose was truly a man of the left or a fascist, Moscow could sort it out and they would help him get there. A few weeks later, Bhagat Ram Talwar, a young Kirti worker in the small Pakhtun village of Ghalla Dher, received some unexpected visitors. Talwar had often scouted for the party in the tribal areas. Cheena and Ram Kishan Singh, another Kirti worker, told Talwar that they wanted him to escort "somebody" to the Soviet Union. Such journeys were quite common, but Cheena warned Talwar that they were dealing with a "very important person" The journey must be safe and they must on no account be caught.

Peshawar, near the Afghan border, would have to be the centre of operations, and the three travelled there to discuss plans. Here Talwar renewed contact with Abad Khan, a transport contractor who had often undertaken similar jobs and had a reputation for being politically conscious. For a week Abad Khan, Ram Kishan and Talwar scouted various routes and arrangements. Finally, they decided the best route would be from Peshawar through the Gandab valley to Jallalabad, one of Afghanistan's most important towns; then Bose would make a detour to see Haji Mohammad Amin at Adda Sharif, returning to Jallalabad and finally going on to Kabul, the capital. The VIP would have to stay in Peshawar for a few days in a house that belonged to another contact, and soon a house in Peshawar's Kissa Khawani Bazaar, owned by Mian Feroze Shah, was fixed up. Some time in June Cheena was informed, and he travelled to Calcutta to bring Bose. But Bose had taken a different turn.

While Cheena was making plans, Bose had continued in his increasingly futile attempts to get Gandhi and the Congress to act. Hitler's armies had launched their *blitzkrieg* on western Europe in May and within a month had overrun the Low Countries and much of France. In June 1940, Italy had entered the war as Germany's ally. Bose was now convinced that Germany would win. A golden opportunity might pass. Unless India did something, it would again be left on the sidelines.

About this time a diary kept by one Bose's principal lieutenants in the Forward Bloc (which the IPI agents subsequently read) noted: "Subhas is walking on a very slippery ground. He believes the English would lose..He is becoming desperate...Very bold programme...Perhaps he has some connection with Germany."

In mid-June Bose heard the news of the fall of Paris in Mayor Abdur Rahman Siddique's room in the Calcutta Corporation. Ispahani was there:

> I remember how Subhas' face lit up with joy. He hugged some of us and danced round the room like a merry schoolboy. To him the fall of France was his victory, the victory of his people - as with France prostrate, the day of reckoning for Britain was close at hand. He was sure that Britain could not avoid abject surrender and equally confident that the mighty empire would melt like snow on a hot day.

A few evenings later he declared, "I predict that England will accept defeat and surrender by 16 July."

It was this certainty about coming events that Bose carried to the second All-India Conference of the Forward Bloc, where on 18 June 1940 he proclaimed:

> It is for the Indian people to make an immediate demand for the transference of power to them through a Provisional National Government ... When things settle down inside India and abroad, the Provisional National Government will convene a Constitutional Assembly for framing a fully-fledged Constitution for this country.

He had nothing but contempt for those Indian politicians who were still thinking of joining with Britain in resisting the Germans: "Some of our statesmen, it seems, have been possessed with the dream of India being converted into a bastion of democratic resistance against the dictators' hordes. What a grotesque picture." At the end of the conference Bose made one last effort to convince these statesmen of his views. In Bombay he met Jinnah and Veer Savarkar, and in Wardha he met Gandhi. Jinnah saw possibilities in the war, but solely for the Muslim League, and even then in collaboration with the British. Savarkar, in the style characteristic of a blinkered Hindu nationalist, wanted more Indians to enlist in the British Indian Army to get military training, yet advised Bose to get foreign help to fight the British. Gandhi was paternal, but once again the answer was no. He could not even bring himself to bless any movement Bose might start. There was some affection between the two, but no real meeting of hearts, no real bond like that between Gandhi and Nehru. Bose and Gandhi would never meet again.

Bose returned to Calcutta in the last week of June 1940 and suddenly, almost incomprehensibly, instead of planning to leave India, announced in the *Forward Bloc* that he himself would launch *Sirajuddowla Day* (organised for 3 July by the Bengal Congress in memory of the Bengal king whose defeat by Clive had led to the establishment of the Raj) by leading a procession for the demolition of the Holwell monument, erected to honour the British dead in the Black Hole of Calcutta. Neither his friends nor his enemies could understand the reasons, and even today it is not clear why he should suddenly have been so keen to get back to a British prison - for he knew that would be the ultimate result. Tactically, it was a brilliant plan. All Indian nationalists, both Hindus and Muslims, agreed that the Black Hole was a "faked monument of shame" and, in fact, an imaginative piece of British propaganda to justify their own barbarities. For Muslims it held a special significance as "an unwarranted stain" on the memory of the last independent ruler of Bengal, as Bose described it. Yet the Bengal government had been making soothing noises about having the monument removed and later that year moved it. So why did Bose persist?

Several explanations are possible. Government intelligence sources reported that Bose was under pressure and being forced into a demonstration of political virility in the face of taunts from the Congress establishment that his political actions did not match his verbal belligerence. Calcutta revolutionaries, for some odd reason, believed he wanted to be imprisoned in order to contact his revolutionary comrades who had already been jailed. His idea was to discuss plans for escape. Dwijendranath Bose, a nephew, in a charming anecdote, told me Bose decided on this march because his escape plans had leaked. Bose would later confirm that he changed his escape plans as word of it had got out.

Early one morning Dr B.D. Dey, chief engineer of the Calcutta Corporation, arrived at Elgin Road. He was met by Dwijendranath, who took him in to see Subhas. No sooner had Dey been ushered in than he blurted out, "Subhas Babu, before you go, please make me chief executive officer." Bose, feigning surprise, asked, "Where am I going?"
Dey said, "Sardar Balder Singh told me last night that you are planning to go to Russia." Bose laughed. "Dr Dey, how many pegs [of whisky] did you have with the Sardar last night? You must be still somewhat hung over. What will I gain by leaving India? The struggle has to be waged here. In fact, I am at this very moment starting a movement to remove the Holwell monument." Dwijendranath confessed that this came as a complete surprise. "That was the first time I had heard that Uncle was going to launch the movement to remove the Holwell monument. The movement was started without any preparation and its whole motive was diversionary, but we somehow managed to run it."

So when Cheena met Talib he was told that everything had changed. The following day Bose met Cheena and confirmed this. However, Bose gave Cheena the strong impression that he had merely postponed his escape plans. Talib encouraged this view and Cheena returned to the room in Peshawar, where Bhagat Ram Talwar awaited him, to inform him of the postponement of the escape. By this time the papers were already carrying news of Bose's arrest. (Cheena for his part could not wait for Bose and decided to go on to Moscow on his own.)

On the afternoon of 2 July 1940, the day before the proposed march, Bose was having tea with Alderman B.C.Chatterji when he was arrested under Section 129 of the Defence of India Act and taken to Presidency Jail for the eleventh and last time. As so often, it was a bungled arrest, with the Viceroy annoyed that he had not been informed. As usual, too, Bose's health soon deteriorated, and his only moment of relief came when Ispahani brought greetings and news from Lala Shankarlal, an old friend and rich business backer who had just returned from abroad. Shankarlal was not allowed to see Bose, but Ispahani cheerfully conveyed his apparently innocent messages: "All friends are well and happy and are anxiously waiting to welcome you. We see no reason for you to be where you are when there is so much to be done outside." Shankarlal's friends were Bose's Japanese and other foreign contacts.

Bose had arranged Shankarlal's visit to Japan. Government sources reported that Shankarlal had met the Japanese Foreign Minister and German, Italian and Russian ambassadors, also channelling some Japanese money to the Forward Bloc. Bose had already established contacts with the Japanese in Calcutta. Dwijendranath recollects that some time in 1939, just before the annual Congress session, Japan's Vice-Foreign Minister Ohashi visited Calcutta and met Bose secretly at the Ballygunge house of a Bengali politician, S.K. Acharya, a communist. What they discussed we shall never know, since the only witness seems to have been a Bengali servant who served tea and sweets while Dwijendranath and his brother kept guard on the approach roads.

The only evidence that has ever been presented about all this was the treaty between Bose and the Japanese which Shankarlal showed K.M Munshi in 1942, claiming that it had been entered into through his own good offices. But even if the treaty is fanciful (if there *was* a treaty, why did Bose not head for Japan when he escaped, as he could have done and as the British thought he had done, instead of Russia?) the British government was convinced of his Japanese contacts. An IPI note summarised the position thus:

> When his passport application was refused and left wing quarrels began to interfere with these plans (to start an anti British agitation) Bose sent Shankarlal, secretary of the All-India Forward Bloc, to Japan in the early summer of 1940 to ascertain Axis intentions. Shankarlal returned in June 1940 after secret discussions with representatives of the Axis powers in Tokyo, much impressed with the tales of Axis invincibility and the inevitable doom of the British Empire which he heard, not a little alarmed at German claims to have powerful Islamic support stretching from the Grand Mufti of Palestine and Rashid Ali of Iraq to the pro-Amanullah elements in Afghanistan and the Faqir of Ipi and the Khaksars in India. Both the Germans and the Japanese indicated their willingness to help any movement aimed at the overthrow of British rule and also professed sympathy for further details of Subhas Bose's following. After discussions with Rash Behari Bose. Shankarlal returned with these tidings to Calcutta.

The Raj knew all about Rash Behari Bose. No relation of Subhas, he was a pre-First World War revolutionary who, had escaped from the Raj and settled in Japan. Rash Behari had tried to communicate with Subhas in 1938 urging a violent struggle but the letter was intercepted by the Raj. The government tried unsuccessfully to prosecute Shankarlal for travelling to Japan under a false passport and on 10 September 1940 Herbert, then governor of Bengal, informed Linlithgow that if all the prosecutions launched against Bose failed a warrant could be issued based on what the government knew about his relations with Japan.

Meanwhile, in Presidency Jail, Bose was seeking a way of getting out of prison. On 29 November 1940, after writing a political testament, in which he said the individual must be prepared to die if the nation was to win freedom, Bose went on a hunger strike. He would drink only water with a little salt and would not allow himself to be force-fed. A Bengal official declared:

> My personal view is that Bose's hunger strike will not be followed to such lengths as would endanger his life and that he will find some reason for calling it off when he finds it sufficiently uncomfortable. As he has been suffering for some time from overeating and insufficient exercise it seems likely that a little starvation will improve his health.

But the government was concerned. On 2 December 1940 it decided to release Bose if his condition deteriorated. Three days later doctors reported that it had indeed done so, and argued that unless he was released he might die. On the afternoon of 5 December a reluctant Herbert agreed with his cabinet's decision to release Bose unconditionally. The government was following a "cat-and-mouse" policy: the moment Bose recovered, he would be jailed. That day Subhas was taken back to his Elgin Road house in an ambulance. He was carried up to his first-floor room, which had been his father's. As always, relations, friends and sundry other visitors crowded round him. Among them was one of Sarat's sons, a young Calcutta Medical College student named Sisir. A diffident, shy young man, he had never quite established that degree of warmth and intimacy with his famous uncle that came naturally to his elder bothers and cousins. Sisir was having a post-prandial rest at Sarat's house when Subhas' personal servant came to tell him he had been summoned to the great man's bedside again. He was asked to sit on the bed right next to Bose, who asked in Bengali, "Can you do a job for me?'" Sisir, bemused, nodded his head.

The job appeared simple enough. Sisir would have to drive his uncle one night a fair distance from Calcutta, say to Burdwan. The operation would have to be quick, efficient, and quiet. Only one other person was privy to it , Sisir's cousin Illa. Subhas Bose, at 43, had finally decided that it was time to escape from India and continue the struggle from abroad.

15

"I Am Off: You Go Back"

Subhas Bose's escape from India in the winter of 1940-41 forms a significant episode in the history of Indian nationalism. For many years, little was known of it. Recently, however, a wealth of reminiscence has surfaced although fantasy and myth still persist.

Bose was now free to go where he wanted, though the Calcutta CID kept a round-the-clock watch on him. But escape from India required ingenuity and planning. India is a terrifyingly open society: everybody knows what everybody else is doing, or at least is eager to know. Bose's situation accentuated this. 38/2 Elgin Road was a joint-family house; and he was a popular politician attempting an action that was the exclusive preserve of small revolutionary cells. By this time Bose also knew that the CID had an informer in his own extended household. It was a distant cousin. Bose, it appears, gleaned this information from his CID file which he managed to read. The government files contain this report: "C.207 reports on 15th Dec. that Akbar Shah (FB) of NWFP is expected to come to Calcutta to see Subhas in a day or two in connection with the AIFB Conference to be held at Delhi on 22nd and 23rd Dec. '40."

Mian Akbar Shah's visit concealed the most vital ingredient in Bose's developing plans. These had been progressing in many hours of talks with Sisir (who was slowly taken into confidence) and followed the Cheena's scheme. Bose would travel to Peshawar, and from their friends would escort him over that curious no-government's-land, the tribal areas, to Kabul and freedom. Peshawar by train was no problem. The Delhi-Kalka Express ran from Calcutta's Howrah station every night and from Delhi the frontier mail train steamed to Peshawar. But where should Bose board the train? If he were to catch it at Howrah, the government would know that he was escaping. Eventually Asansol, one of its wayside stops in the Bengal-Bihar countryside was selected: it was near Dhanbad, where Asoke Bose lived; his house might be a useful staging post.

Mian Akbar Shah, a respectable government pleader in the small Punjab town of Nawsharra whose revolutionary instincts were now confined to maintaining close contacts with younger, more adventurous revolutionaries, readily agreed to organise the Peshawar-Kabul part of the journey. One evening, when Sisir came for his regular nocturnal chat, he was introduced to this handsome Pathan. Secret addresses, code words for communication and a suitable disguise were quickly arranged. Sisir was asked to see Akbar Shah off at Howrah. On the way Akbar Shah did some shopping at the Muslim department store Wachell Molla (a couple of pairs of pyjamas, a black fez) and "accidentally", as part of the elaborate care taken by Bose, left it in the car. Sisir completed the purchases: flannel shirts, pillows, quilts, *kabuli* sandals favoured by people of the tribal areas, copies of the Koran, a bed roll, a suitcase, an attaché case marked MZ, and a visiting card. He hid these articles in a cupboard in his house.

Now the final preparations began. A German Wanderer car was given a thorough overhaul. Sisir practised changing tyres and reconnoitred the route to Asoke's place. Akbar Shah, however, had run into unexpected difficulties with Abad Khan, who was essential in providing a guide for the journey from Peshawar to Kabul, but who was worried about being involved in the adventure. Bose was due in court on 27 January 1941, and time was running out. The deadline was quickly communicated to Akbar Shah, who once again pressed Abad Khan for a firm answer. "At last," Khan confessed afterwards, "without having made any arrangements, I told them to send for Bose". Soon Bose sent a message to Akbar Shah that he would be arriving in Peshawar by the frontier mail train on 19 January. The two had agreed a code. The telegram would read "Arrange Forward Bloc meeting" to confirm Bose was on his way.

The great escape was about to begin. Although Subhas made a point of bidding goodbye to his old guru Beni Madhav Das, he did not tell his mother Prabbavati. Convinced he had renounced the world, she afterwards begged Sarat and Bivabati to tell her where Subhas was. They could only plead helplessness. Though Prabbavati never saw nor heard from Subhas again, her faith in him remained intact. In 1943, as she lay dying, someone pictured her as queen mother to Subhas, the would-be king of India. "Don't say such things," she retorted. "I never wish, even in my dreams, that my Subhas be made a king. He always knew service to his motherland to be his life's mission. May I too always see him as a servant of his country."

Bose fixed 16 January as the day of his departure. He had already announced, and evidently convinced his extended family, that he was going into seclusion to pray and meditate. Part of his bedroom was partitioned off with screens, leaving a small aperture for the cook to serve the food. Nobody was to disturb him while he was in retreat. To make the impression complete, Bose decided to have a ritualistic family dinner. On the evening of the 16th he put on his Bengali best, silk *dhoti* and *chaddar,* and, served by his mother, ate a specially prepared meal. Then, as his family retired, Bose disappeared behind the curtains to begin his "retreat".

Only four people remained, his niece Illa and his nephews Aurobindo, Dwijendranath and Sisir, who had arrived with the car. As the other Boses went to sleep, Subhas Bose transformed himself into Mohammed Ziauddin, travelling inspector, Empire of India Life Assurance Company Limited, permanent address: Civil Lines, Jubbalpore. In place of the *dhoti* and *chaddar* came broad pyjamas, a long coat and a black fez. There was only one hitch. His normal spectacles were far too conspicuous, and he discarded them for ones he had not worn since being Mayor of Calcutta nearly a decade before. At last everything was ready. The last inquisitive family member was asleep, and at about 1.30 am Dwijendranath, on the look-out, loudly cleared his throat, which was the signal for the all-clear. Bose bid Illa a very affectionate farewell, whispering, "God bless you", and then he, Sisir and Aurobindo quietly trooped downstairs to the car. The luggage was already in the car. Soon Sisir and Subhas were on their journey.

At breakfast time they reached Bararee. Sisir dropped Subhas some 400 metres from Asoke's house and continued with the elaborate but necessary drama. He had quickly coached his elder brother in the part he had to play, and the uncle and nephew met as perfect strangers. Mohammed Ziauddin, insurance agent, looking for coalfield business among executives, met Asoke Bose, unsuspecting engineer.

Asoke had been told the outline of his uncle's plans on one of his visits to Calcutta, and played his part to perfection: He said he had to get to work; perhaps Mr Ziauddin could come back in the evening. But, said Ziauddin, he had nowhere to go. Could he wait here till Asoke came back? By all means, said Asoke. Ziauddin was introduced to Sisir, both feigning lack of interest in each other; a guest-room was fixed up, and Asoke's Muslim servant hurried to attend him. Bose rested in his room the whole day, and in the evening the theatre was resumed. Asoke and Ziauddin conversed in English; this time they discussed the best place to board the express. Asansol was the divisional headquarters of the East Indian Railways, a crowded, noisy place always guarded by a contingent of government railway police. They decided to board the train at Gomoh, a small wayside station about thirty miles from Asoke's place. Since Sisir did not know the way, Asoke offered to come along as a guide; and, since he was unwilling to leave his wife alone at night, she came to. Ziauddin was served dinner in his room, and after a polite, public, farewell he left the house, ostensibly to catch a taxi.

Half an hour later Sisir, Asoke and his wife picked Subhas up from the roadside and drove at a leisurely pace on to Gomoh. On the way they stopped in the silent Bihar countryside, and Bose told his two nephews about his plans. He was bound for Moscow and eventually Berlin. He hoped to be away by the time the court case started and all hell broke loose. For his young nephews it was an intensely poignant moment. They arrived at Gomoh just as the midnight train was due, and Subhas walked majestically over the deserted bridge, a sleepy porter lumbering behind him with his luggage; his final words were, "I am off: you go back." As Bose checked into Room 6 of the Taj Mahal Hotel in Peshawar he had every reason to feel pleased with himself. The train ride to Delhi had been uneventful, and on the frontier mail between Delhi and Peshawar he had played his role even more convincingly. At Peshawar Mian Akbar Shah had boarded the train, checked Bose was on it and followed him to the Taj Mahal hotel. He could not stay indefinitely at the hotel, so the next day Abad Khan moved him to one of the houses he had hired. That night, Akbar Shah brought along Bhagat Ram Talwar, and another Kirti worker Harmindar Singh Sodhi.

At this stage our story gets complicated for the simple reason that the people involved have provided different recollections of what happened. The Raj caught up with all the three principals involved: Abad Khan, Bhagat Ram Talwar and Sodhi. Abad Khan, imprisoned for four years for his part in Bose's escape, confessed to the police under torture to a sequence of events, which does not quite match what Talwar or Sodhi told the police. Some of the differences in recollections are trivial: more serious is how Talwar has told the story. Of all the men involved in Boses's escape only Talwar, some 35 years later, wrote a book about it. But in his book he suppressed many facts not least that he too was captured by the British and confessed to them. And in his copious description of how he took Bose out of India he does not mention that Sodhi met Bose, an omission that was significant as we shall see.

For the moment let us concentrate on Abad Khan, who was respsonsible for Bose in Peshawar. He knew he had to move Bose from the Taj Mahal Hotel but decided that his own house was not safe enough. It was very close to adjacent houses and, with Akbar Shah and the others insisting on visiting it frequently, there was always the danger of the neighbours overhearing their conversation. Then there was Mohammed Shah, a landlord friend of Akbar Shah. Abad Khan had never liked him, and was horrified when he suggested that Dr Khan Sahib, the previous Congress Chief Minister of the province, should be informed of Bose's arrival. The idea was quickly ridiculed and Abad Khan transferred Bose to another house, costlier but quieter. Here Bose was virtually under house arrest for a couple of days. Abad Khan would supply him with vegetables, meat, tea and so see that he had enough food to cook himself meals, then lock him up and then leave for the day. In the evenings he would return, to be joined by Akbar Shah, Bhagat Ram Talwar and Sodhi.

Sodhi, who had met Bose once a couple of years earlier, would later tell the police that at one of their meetings Bose asked what help Russia would give India. Sodhi, who had been to Moscow and wanted to return, replied that if India rebelled Russia would maintain the revolt. He did not think Stalin would send the Red Army to invade India, thus entering the war on the Axis side, unless conditions became much more favourable and India appealed to Russia for help. Meanwhile Russia would certainly help revolutionary propaganda and perhaps provide money.

Bose argued that with Russia and Germany virtually in alliance against the British Empire [the alliance ended in mid-1941 when Germany invaded Russia], he could not see why Stalin hesitated to invade India. Sodhi asked Bose if he was a fascist sympathiser and why he wanted to go to Russia, Bose denied he was pro-fascist and pointed to him articles in the *Forward Bloc* supporting the Russian invasion of Finland. Sodhi also asked Bose about his earlier arrangements with Cheena and Bose told him he had to change plans because Baldev Singh had got to know about it. Sodhi wanted to travel with Bose and Talwar but as neither Bose nor Sodhi spoke Pushtu it was too risky to take Sodhi. However, it was agreed he would wait Talwar's return from Kabul and go at a later date. According to Abad Khan, the longer Bose stayed cooped up in the Kabuli Gate house the more worried he became:

> One day he offered me his gold watch, but I refused to accept it. As no arrangement could be made to send him to Kabul he was growing more weary day by day. He also suspected me and told me that Akbar Shah told him that he would be sent to Kabul by some Mukaram or Muqarab Khan. He asked me who this man was, but I replied that I did not know him. I told him that my name was Abad Khan and that he should not worry. I also told him that none except God could arrest him. He was pleased to hear this.

However, Abad Khan himself was worried. The date for Bose's appearance in court was getting nearer, and he knew that once the escape was known all India would be crawling with British agents looking for him. He must be sent to Kabul as soon as possible. But, try as he would, he could not find the guide he needed. At last, on 21 January 1941, an Afghan government servant who had been an agent of Abad Khan since 1930 introduced him to a responsible Afridi guide. Early the very next day, Abad Khan hired a 1932 Chevrolet, picked up Bose and Bhagat Ram Talwar and drove through the early-morning traffic of Peshawar, past the barrier at Jamrod, towards Fort Salop. On the right side of the Fort there was a hilly track which led towards the Afridi tribal territory. Here Bose, Bhagat Ram and the Afridi guide got out of the car; Abad Khan provided Bose with some final advice, and the most physically difficult stage of Bose's journey began.

Travelling in these regions, particularly for a politician used to a sedentary life, was demanding. The route traversed a fiercely hot, stony desert with no trees, no grass; occasionally a few thorny bushes, now and again a couple of mud houses, but nearly always just a dry and arid landscape. Though it was winter, the day produced a dry intense heat totally unlike anything Bose had experienced in the Indo-Gangetic plains. He and Talwar seemed to be forever climbing and descending hills: a climb of about 130 metres, followed by a descent of some 200 metres, then another ascent. For Bose, who despite his recent illness was still a fairly heavy man, the journey was exhausting. Since he knew none of the languages of the region he played the deaf-mute uncle to Bhagat Ram Talwar's nephew, both on pilgrimage to a Muslim shrine. Within a few hours Bose felt that he had been walking for days, and was relieved only when Ram told him that they were no longer in British India. This was the land of the free tribal Pathans, who recognised no government and lived the life of their ancestors. Bose was instantly revitalised. He jumped up in the air, stamped his feet on the ground and shouted, "Here I kick George VI." He laughed, he chuckled with happiness, he spat: "Here I spit on the face of the Viceroy!" From that moment on, the journey seemed easy. By night fall they had reached the village of Pishkan Maina. Nobody knew them, or even cared who they were, yet food and hospitality were free, and even the simple meal of tea and salted maize cakes was remarkably refreshing. But the accommodation was less inviting. Twenty-five people were herded into a room without any furniture, beds or even windows, and with only a thick layer of dry grass to serve as a mattress. Often during the night Bose had to get up and go outside to get some fresh air.

The next afternoon Talwar arranged a mule for Bose, and slowly they passed the various landmarks on the way to Kabul. At 1 am on 24 January they reached their first Afghan village. But, though the trek through the tribal area had avoided the British control points, they still could not take advantage of the regular public transport to Kabul. The routes were bound to be infested with officials and spies of the Afghan government. That meant hitching lifts on trucks, which were the life-line of the Afghan economy. They were perched precariously on a truck laden with tea chests when they finally got to Jalalabad, the most important city in Afghanistan after Kabul. Now only Bundak, high up on the mountain road to Kabul, remained a possible obstacle. It contained a customs checkpoint where foreigners' papers were checked. But by the time they arrived, on another truck, it was four in the morning, the slackest period of the night. The customs guard was asleep, and Bose and Talwar quickly joined the driver in a cafe. The last hurdle had been jumped. Kabul was only thirteen miles away. They arrived at the city's Lahori Gate at mid-afternoon on 27 January 1941, just after Subhas Bose's escape from India had become public knowledge.

Ever since the morning of the 17 January, Illa had been slipping inside the screens in Subhas's room at Elgin Road and eating the food brought in by the cook. On the night of 25 January, as arranged, she had not touched it. The cook raised the alarm. Sarat had made one small change: he had decided it would be wiser if the family "discovered" Subhas had fled, rather than leaving it to the police to do so when he failed to appear in court. To make the act complete he had gone as usual to his country home at Rishra. When nephews arrived with the news he feigned perfect surprise, and skilfully taking over the main role, led the rest of the family, and indeed the country, through the ensuing intricacies. He presided over a *durbar* at 38/2 Elgin Road, sent telegrams to various parts of the country and emissaries into the byways of Calcutta. Sisir recollects:

> The police evidently took some time to wake up and did not arrive till the afternoon. They were told the set story of how uncle was living in seclusion and how his disappearance was discovered. I watched a police party going round and round the house looking for possible routes of exit at the wrong places. Uncle's personal servant noticed that uncle's European pair of shoes were missing and mentioned this to Ila. Ila promptly told him that I had given the shoes away for repairs and he appeared to accept the explanation.

Sisir visited the Kalighat temple, where a *sadhu* said that of course he had known all along that Subhas Babu would renounce the world, but that he would ask the mother-goddess in the night and see what she had to say. The *sadhu*"s confusion matched that among most of the family, among the public and in the Raj. But Sarat kept everybody on the mystic trail. When Gandhi telegraphed in surprise, "STARTLING NEWS ABOUT SUBHAS. PLEASE WIRE TRUTH. HOPE ALL WELL," Sarat told him, "CIRCUMSTANCES INDICATE RENUNCIATION". For some time no *sadhu* was safe. The police chased *sadhus* in Benares, Allahabad, the Himalayas and even in Pondicherry, and arrested some in Madras. They investigated rumours that Bose had left for Japan by ship, and as late as September 1941 were trying to run him down in Bangkok.

The escape led to both astonishment and recriminations amongst Raj officials. J.V. Janvrin, the deputy commissioner of police of Calcutta's Special Branch felt, "the whole story sounds most fantastic". The Bengal police were blamed by the Viceroy for hoodwinking them, but M.O. Carter, secretary to the governor of Bengal rejected the accusation. His note revealed the type of informers the Raj used to spy on Bose, and the problems this created:

> As regards secret information a moment's reflection will show that outsiders cannot possibly get information from inside a private house except at second or third hand through some of Subhas's relations. Such secret information if available is presumably misleading.

For the moment the stagnant and decaying political scene in India was convulsed: a major mass leader had just vanished completely.

Kabul in 1941 was little more than a glorified village. There were only about fifteen modern brick and cement buildings: the king's palace, a few apartment buildings, the embassies and consulates. The great majority lived in mud houses and for the traveller, particularly a fugitive, there was only the *serai:* a sort of cafe, where most people ate on the pavements and slept on *charpoys* or beds in a large communal hall, although there were a few private rooms. It was at a *serai* that Bhagat Ram Talwar secured a room. It provided some privacy and a couple of beds. They had to acquire bedding, fuel and some second-hand woollen garments for Bose.

Nobody expected him in Kabul, and no arrangements had been made. For well over a year he had persistently tried to contact the Russians, but without any success. At every stage they had rebuffed him. However, they had never categorically rejected him and Bose, still confident of the Russia of Lenin's revolution, was determined to unlock the door. His choice of the Kirti Party had been dictated by this consideration. Not only did they know how to get people out of India by the land route, but they also had contacts with the Soviet government. By this time Achhar Singh Cheena, unable to wait for Bose, was in Moscow and he mentioned Bose's escape plans to his Soviet contact Kozloff, a representative of the Comintern. The Russian immediately said Bose must be headed for Berlin.

Bhagat Ram Talwar was in an unenviable position. He had never been to Kabul before, knew little Persian (the language favoured in Afghanistan) and had no idea of how to contact the Russians. As Talwar would confess later, "during this period we had no contacts with that country through their embassy in Kabul or through any other source". He and Bose spent some time reconnoitring the embassy: a straightforward entry was ruled out, and eventually it was decided that Bhagat Ram Talwar would approach the officials. For three successive days the two men sat on the high walls enclosing a large open area on the right bank of the river Kabul, just opposite the embassy. Every time a Russian emerged they hastened to make contact, but without success.

The situation would have been comic, if it did not have elements of a great tragedy, and Bose decided that the only alternative was an approach to the Germans. He quickly wrote out a letter in Bengali to Sarat and an article in English on the Forward Bloc, and advised Bhagat Ram Talwar on the method to be used to contact his family in Calcutta. He had decided he would walk into the German embassy on his own. On 2 February 1941 Bose and Talwar set off for the German embassy. As it happened the walk to the German embassy took them past the Russian embassy, and on the way they saw the Russian ambassador's car immobilised in mud. It seemed a godsend and Talwar immediately approached the ambassador. "I have Subhas Bose with me and he is seeking asylum in the Soviet Union." The ambassador was suspicious. "How do I know you have Subhas Bose with you?" "Well, take a good look at him. He is standing next to me dressed as an Afghan national. In any case, it can be checked with photographs that have been published." The ambassador looked at Bose for a long time. Was this a British plot? He had grave suspicions that the British had allowed Bose to escape in order to create trouble between Russia and Afghanistan. In any case, he could not act without instructions from Moscow. As Bhagat Ram watched in dismay, the ambassador looked away and the car drove off. The Russian connection had failed.

After a detour they approached the German embassy, which proved much more receptive. The cover story Bose had prepared was not required, and as Bose approached the gate the sentry opened it and allowed him in. He was met by a delighted young officer who had been reading about his escape, and who took him to Hans Pilger, the long-serving German ambassador. Pilger had met Bose on one of his visits to the German Foreign Office, and was just as pleased to see him. However, he was nervous and worried. It was rash of Bose to have come to see him like this, he said. Kabul was crawling with agents of the Afghan and British governments. When Bose replied that this was all the more reason why he should be sheltered at the embassy until he could be given a safe escort out, Pilger became even more nervous. There were far too many Afghans working at the embassy, and nobody knew how many of them were spies. He would immediately contact Berlin, and was hopeful of a favourable reply; but Bose should not come to the embassy, he should keep in touch with a Herr Thomas of Siemens. The arrangements would take time. The Afghan government conducted very strict border checks, and there was very little traffic across the border. Soon after Bose left, Pilger contacted the Italian and Russian ambassadors, and telegraphed to Berlin the Russian suspicion that it was all a British plot.

Meanwhile, Bose and Talwar were condemned to a precarious existence in the *serai.* They had already spent six days there, far too many for travellers stopping at a place meant for itinerant drivers of mules and horses. They made a curious pair: one older, heavier in build and pretending to be deaf and dumb; the other younger and fitter — both wandering about Kabul all day and returning to the *serai* in the evening. They looked suspiciously like agents waiting for a contact, or smugglers.

One Afghan government spy had been watching them very closely. The evening before they were to meet Herr Thomas he confronted them, wanting answers to a whole series of questions. Who were they? What were they doing here? How long were they going to stay? Bhagat Ram Talwar, through a judicious mixture of piteous explanation (his uncle was deaf and dumb, had come for treatment in Kabul and was waiting to get into hospital) and an appropriate bribe, saw him off. But he would be back.

The next day Herr Thomas had no answers to their increasingly urgent questions. Berlin was glad that Bose had escaped, but arrangements for safe conduct were still being made. Would Bose please come back and see him after another three days for a message and instructions from Berlin? The pattern of their stay in Kabul was now set. Every three days a meeting with Herr Thomas, who would smile affably and offer financial help (which they refused) but no firm commitment.

The spy reappeared on the next day. He could not understand why it should be so difficult to get hospital space. He was convinced they were smugglers, and insisted they come to the police station. When Bhagat Ram Talwar increased the bribe he left, but this was only a temporary reprieve. He appeared again the following day, and Bose had to reluctantly part with his gold wristwatch, a gift from his father. Talwar went to see Uttam Chand, a former comrade of his and, in the face of some reluctance, persuaded him to give them accommodation.

The move meant that, for the first time since he had left Peshawar 16 days earlier, Bose could enjoy homely comforts: a warm, heated room well covered in the central Asian fashion with carpets and mattresses, the chance to change his filthy *salwar* and shirt, a bath, and Bengali music on the radio. But the man who lived on the floor below recognised him, and fled the next morning with his family. There were, he told another friend, evil spirits in the house and he could no longer stay there. Uttam Chand was convinced he had gone to the Afghan government. Although Bhagat Ram was less apprehensive, they decided to move back to a *serat,* this time to a slightly classier one generally used by truck drivers. However, Bose's delicate digestion could no longer cope with the rich Pathan food, and he was racked with serious dysentery and severe abdominal pains. The *serai* was the last place for proper care and attention but, as they dared not risk a return to Uttam Chand's house, they had to improvise. Bhagat Ram described Bose's symptoms to Uttam Chand who communicated them to a local doctor, obtained medicines and arranged for proper food.

By this time Uttam Chand had taken over Bhagat Ram Talwar's duties of liaising with Herr Thomas, though the Siemens man could offer little joy. The Reich Foreign Ministry had taken its time to consider Pilger's report, and it was only under pressure from the Italians (who had not been formally approached by Bose) that they bustled into action. The two Axis governments had jointly approached the Russians to allow Bose through their territory. Herr Thomas later told Bhagat Ram Talwar that Japan had pitched in as well, and described the issue as "as important as Lenin's crossing over to Russia with the help of the German government" The request had been made in mid-February 1941 but the Russians had made no response. Their suspicions remained intact. However, Bose was convinced that the Soviet Union would have him, if only he could get through. He was bitter about the fact that the Kirti Party had sent him a guide who had no contacts, and decided it was time he made his own arrangements to travel to the border areas and enter the Soviet Union across the river Oxus. Here again Uttam Chand seemed to have the answers. One of his many contacts was a certain Yakub. An escaped murderer, he lived on the border, having conveniently married into a family of dacoits and smugglers. Cautiously, Bhagat Ram Talwar opened negotiations with Yakub. He knew such men had no loyalties except to the highest bidder, and that he would have to be careful. Yakub was quite enthusiastic and a tentative programme was drawn up. It was decided to leave on the morning of 23 February.

Bose had written to Pilger about his plans, and the afternoon before the departure Bhagat Ram Talwar paid what he thought would be his last courtesy call on Herr Thomas. But now at last a chink of light appeared through the mystifying Axis darkness. Thomas persuaded a reluctant Bhagat Ram Talwar to visit the Italian legation, and there he was met by a concerned and interested man named Pietro Quaroni. Quaroni was probably the most perceptive of the Axis diplomats. Having pressured his own government to help out on the visa problem, he was now determined to have Bose for the Axis. As his later report to his government put it:

> In the past we have spent big sums of money, for instance, on the press propaganda in the two Americas, with the results we can see today. Here one could work on a much more solid terrain. If what is being attempted should work out even in part probably several months of war, human lives, millions' worth of materials will be saved. Our enemies in all their wars, the present one included, have always largely used the "revolutionary" weapon with success: why should we not learn from our enemies?

It was dangerous, Quaroni told Talwar, to proceed to the Soviet border on one's own. The Axis governments were doing their best and were quite hopeful. When Talwar mentioned that the journey was already arranged, Quaroni asked him to fix a meeting with Bose. For a long time Bhagat Ram Talwar, Bose and Uttam Chand discussed Quaroni's proposal. To abandon Yakub now seemed unwise. After weeks of inactivity, they seemed at last to be getting somewhere; but, of course, if the Axis really delivered, their chances were much better. And a journey to Berlin or Rome did not eventually rule out Moscow. "I want you," Bose told them, "to drive any such ideas out of your heads. My absolute preference is for Moscow. Only it will be easier to go to Moscow from Berlin or Rome than from here."

Bose had also to consider that Moscow had already rejected him. What guarantee was there that he would be accepted in Yakub's company at the Oxus? The same evening Bose met Pietro Quaroni and talked so far into the night that Quaroni invited him to stay on at the legation. It was the first of many meetings, during the course of which Bose for the first time expressed his views on the coming struggle. A government of Free India should be set up in Europe, he argued. Having obtained a guarantee of the freedom, integrity and independence of India from the Axis powers, it would immediately begin a special radio campaign beamed exclusively to India and it would try to foment revolution there. The help given would, of course, be in the form of a repayable loan, and Bose for his part would broadcast only once he was convinced of the Axis' good faith. Quaroni later reported:

> According to Bose, India is morally ripe for the revolution; what is lacking is the courage to take the first step: the great obstacles to action are on the one side the lack of faith in their own capabilities and on the other the blind persuasion of British excessive power. He says that if 50,000 men, Italian, German or Japanese, could reach the frontiers of India, the Indian army would desert, the masses would uprise and the end of the English domination could be achieved in a very short time. ... Bose is of the opinion that the main obstacle to the possibilities of a revolution in India is the great fear of England.

Quaroni had already come to the same conclusion. Kabul, they agreed, should be the centre of Bose's organisation in India, and Quaroni urged Bose to ask his followers to turn to sabotage. Bose, who had not thought of it, agreed to get his revolutionary followers to consider it. At the end of these discussions Quaroni was fairly bubbling with enthusiasm, and he reported to his minister in Rome:

> If in June, 1940, that is at the time when the defeat of England seemed certain, we had had a ready organisation like the one Bose proposes now it might have been possible. Political and military India is a cornerstone of the British Empire. Last year's chance is gone but a similar one could come this year also. One should be ready to take full advantage of it. To put up this organisation money will be required, probably not a little of it.

About Bose he had no doubts:

> Bose is a type that we all know from his works and his actions. Intelligent, able, full of passion; and without doubt the most realistic, maybe the only realist among the Indian national leaders. ... What he says about the Indian situation tallies with what one can make out of the very censored Indian press which is a sign that his statements do not sin of optimism and this is a thing in his favour.

Things seemed to be moving in the direction Bose wanted them to; now he ordered suits for himself and bought shoes, some travel and toilet articles and a suitcase. The Germans and the Italians were trying three different plans: a transit visa through Russia, a diplomatic courier who would arrive in Kabul and be replaced on the return journey by Bose, and possible travel through Iran and Syria. The courier plan looked the best bet and Quaroni advised Bose that they expected someone soon. By this time the British legation in Kabul knew from one of their spies that Bose was in town but after some debate decided not to ask the Afghans to arrest him. They were not sure the Afghans would agree and it might also compromise their source. The British minister in Kabul asked Delhi whether he should do something about Bose. London was consulted and Peel at the India Office, wrote to Sir Olaf Caroe, who was then Foreign Secretary to the Government of India, that no action should be taken "for fear of compromising a source."

On 3 March 1941 the Soviet government, after a month of Axis soundings in Moscow, informed Count Werner von der Schulenberg, the German ambassador there, that they were ready to grant a transit visa to Bose. Finally, on the afternoon of 15 March, as Bose was in the middle of his tea, a message arrived that couriers had come and Bose must be ready to leave on the 18th. There were more photographs, more shopping and a final affectionate farewell for Uttam Chand and his children, whom Bose had come to love. It was decided that Bhagat Ram Talwar, working under the name Rehmat Khan, would be the main link between Bose and India, the messages being routed through the Italians and the Germans.

Three days later a large car drew up. It contained a Dr Wagner who was a German engineer, an Italian courier and a driver. Bose was now Orlando Mazzotta, an Italian diplomat with an Italian passport whose registered number was 64932. In the cold Afghan air with the dawn yet to come, Bose bid Bhagat Ram Talwar an affectionate farewell ("he became so sentimental," Talwar recollects, "that he could not say a word to me while parting") and set off. Compared to his recent journeys this was bliss: a leisurely, dignified car ride to the Russian border, then the train through the historic Asian cities of Bokhara and Samarkand, to Moscow.

Moscow at this stage was physically untouched by war. It had watched Hitler devastate the west and, as an ally of Hitler, picked up its own robbers' swag, gobbling up the eastern half of Poland. But it was a tense city. Although in March 1941 there was no public sign of the imminent end of the Nazi-Soviet pact, behind the scenes a lot was going. Just as Bose arrived, German experts were visiting Soviet aircraft factories as part of the pact which allowed each country to exchange information. Inside the Kremlin, there was concern about other German moves, and nervousness about Hitler's motives. Hitler had started to move into the Balkans and just before Bose arrived German reconnaissance aircraft loaded with cameras and primed with film began to make systematic aerial survey of Soviet frontier districts and the middle interior of the country. The Soviet generals noted this with some alarm and Stalin started taking an interest in war games involving attacks on the Soviet Union.

Bose would not have known of all this. And we can imagine with what anticipation he stepped on the platform of the main Moscow railway station. Here at last he had arrived in the capital of the country he had always wanted to visit. And how ironic this visit was. He had been knocking at the Soviet's door for nearly a decade but every time he had asked to enter in his own name he had been rebuffed. Now, posing as an Italian, the door was suddenly thrown open. Bose must have been pleased by his initial welcome at the station. He was received in style and with great hospitality. The Soviets treated him as if he was a visiting dignitary, providing him an escort from the railway station to the German embassy, where he met Ambassador von der Schulenberg. But all attempts by Bose to meet Soviet officials failed. The Soviets were determined to rebuff any plans Bose had to meet Soviet leaders and were very evasive when he even raised the question of contacts.

It is likely that at this moment Cheena was in Moscow talking to Kozloff about Indian politics and Bose. Cheena had told Kozloff how Bose had given him money to help arrange his trip. Kozloff's response was it was just as well Cheena had not brought Bose with him. It would have led to unwanted international complications. Kozloff also added that it was curious Bose should want to visit Russia as Lala Shankarlal "was flirting with the Japanese government".

Cheena was both surprised and impressed by the fact that Kozloff knew Shankarlal's name and this may suggest that the British who, as we have seen, knew all about this, had tipped of the Russians. The British were courting the Russians, feeding them information, including warnings of Nazi attack. Within weeks Churchill was to alert Stalin that Hitler had moved large forces to the east, and the British may also have told the Soviets about Bose and his contacts in Japan.

As we now know, Hitler had already made up his mind to invade the Soviet Union. The only question was when he would start Operation Barbarossa. Schulenburg had kept reassuring Hitler that Russia posed no threat but Hitler disregarded this. Schulenburg was to learn about the invasion plans a few weeks later when he followed Bose to Berlin on his leave. Bose's meeting with Schulenburg had a significance. Like so many German diplomats, he was part of the old pre-Nazi world of Germany, people who were nationalists but not maniacs. In Berlin Bose was soon to meet many more like him. Like Schulenburg, they were to be strung up by the Nazis following the failed bomb plot against Hitler in July 1944.

Bose had barely a few hours in Moscow. On the evening of 31 March he was escorted back to the railway station and took the train to Berlin arriving there on the afternoon of 2 April 1941. The Germans were more hospitable than the Russians. By now Quaroni had concluded:

> Two things are necessary to make revolution — men and money. We do not have the men to start a revolution in India, but luck has put them in our hands. No matter how difficult Germany's and our monetary situation is, the money that this movement requires is certainly not lacking. It is only a question of valuing the pros and cons and to decide on the risk.

The Germans did not follow through on Quaroni's advice however. Subhas knew that at least one person would be overjoyed to see him, Emilie. The next day, he persuaded the German Foreign Office to send her a telegram. It read: "Bose is now in Berlin and asks you if possible to come here immediately." He also wrote her a letter, the first in nine months, saying, "You will be surprised to get this letter from me and even more surprised to know that I am writing this from Berlin." He told his wife Berlin would be his headquarters. He could not go to Vienna just yet, so she should come to him. Since Emilie's mother and sister did not know she was married to Subhas or, even in love with him, his summons to her was still couched in terms of secretarial help: "It is possible that I may require a secretary here. If so, can you come? Will your mother and sister agree to it?" Bose also insisted she keep a secret. He was no longer Subhas Bose, but Orlando Mazzotta. "So when you write you will have to address me as Orlando Mazzotta. Please treat as strictly confidential the fact that I have come here. You may however tell your mother and sister, provided they do not speak to anybody else."

Bose enjoyed his first and only taste of conjugal life as an Italian and living far from India, in war-time Berlin.

Part Five

CHALO! *DELHI!*

The time has come when I can openly tell the whole world, including our enemies, as to how it is proposed to bring about the national liberation. Indians outside India, particularly Indians in east Asia, are going to organise a fighting force which will be powerful enough to attack the British Army in India. When we do so, a revolution will break out, not only among the civil population at home, but also among the Indian Army which is now standing under the British flag. When the British government is thus attacked from both sides — from inside India and from outside – it will collapse, and the Indian people will then regain their liberty. According to my plan it is not even necessary to bother about the attitude of the Axis powers towards India. If Indians outside and inside India will do their duty, it is possible for the Indian people to throw the British out of India and liberate 388 millions of their countrymen.

Speech at a mass rally at the Padang
in front of the municipal offices,
Singapore, 9 July 1943

16

The Good Germans And The Bad Indians?

On 1 May 1942 Subhas Chandra Bose broadcast from Berlin. After declaring that he was not an apologist for the Axis, he continued:

> Friends, I have laughed whenever I have heard Britain's paid propagandists calling me an enemy agent. I need no credentials when I speak to my own people. My whole life, which has been one long consistent and continuous record of uncompromising struggle against British imperialism, is the best guarantee of my bona fides. ... All my life I have been a servant of India and till the last hours of my life, I shall remain one. My allegiance and my loyalty have ever been and will ever be to India and India alone, no matter in which part of the world I may live at any given time.

In other broadcasts and public statements he would ask whether it was just conceivable that the Axis powers had deceived him, only to conclude that, if the British politicians, "universally admitted" to be the "cleverest and the most cunning" in the world, had been unable to deceive him no other politicians in the world could hope to succeed. This in essence formed Bose's justification for his decision to work with the Nazis and then with the Japanese.

Within a week of the fall of Paris in June 1940, he had, in a signed editorial in Forward Bloc, speculated about the division of spoils between Germany and Russia, and with extraordinary accuracy predicted the likely geographical demarcations. Bose was convinced that Germany would want a free hand on the continent except in the Balkans, and that Italy would impose its will in the Mediterranean. The Balkans and the Middle East would be Russia's, all would share Africa, and Japan's help might be enlisted to carve up the British Empire. As Bose was making his predictions, Joachim von Ribbentrop, Hitler's Foreign Minister, was trying to get the Soviet Union to join the Axis. But where, Bose wondered, would such a robbers' feast leave India?

This likely share-out between the conquering powers greatly worried Bose, and was one of the reasons he later gave his European associates for his decision to leave India. He was convinced that Jinnah was preparing to partition the country and, crucially, he believed that at least one important Indian leader should be present at the peace negotiations at the end of the war; he predicted that the vanquished (Britain) would bargain with the victor (Germany), but not totally surrender.

Bose had read the history of the First World War thoroughly, and knew that one of Britain's successes at Versailles had been that no representative Indian leader had raised the banner of revolt there. The various Indian overseas efforts had been the work of exiled Indians, out of touch with conditions in India, and Britain had easily brushed them aside.

As it developed around him, Bose failed to denounce wartime Nazism. He never took the broader view that the Nazi evil arose from the evil he fought: imperialism. Nazism was equally a product of racism, if in a more virulent form. He did not see this or, even if he did, he did not think it was his business to say so. This dangerous myopia resulted naturally from his obsession with the good of India. Everything was directed to this supreme national aim. In this Bose was not unique; his behaviour was characteristically Indian. George Orwell wondered during the war whether any Indian could be a reliable anti-fascist. Bose had long ago decided, "My enemy's enemy is my friend."

This should have made his arrival in Germany a sensation. During the First World War, Germany had been an active and welcome centre for Indians opposed to the Raj. But, on Hitler's rise to power, Indians were quickly made aware that they were not welcome in Germany. By the time Bose arrived there were only some 39 Indians registered in the Reich, most of them students or working in industry and commerce, and none of them political activists. For the German government India was just a useful landmass with which to bargain in its negotiations with Japan and the Soviet Union.

On 27 September 1940 a tripartite pact had been signed by Germany, Japan and Italy, and India had been assigned to the Russian sphere of influence. Japan had been gravely perturbed by the Nazi-Soviet pact of August 1939. A section of the Japanese army was strongly anti-Soviet and had long been insisting on a "strike north" war against Russia as part of Japan's imperial plans. The opposing "strike south" faction of the armed forces wanted to attack Britain in east Asia and America in the Pacific. They gained power in October 1940 and Japan's relations with the Soviet Union improved. India appeared to both Germany and Japan as a tempting bait to offer the Soviet Union. It would still leave many other countries free for German and Japanese "New Order" plans. But during his decisive visit to Germany in November 1940, Vyacheslav Molotov, the Russian foreign minister had been more concerned with Russia's traditional spheres of influence in Europe and was openly sceptical of German aims and policies. Hitler, who had at last met his match as a negotiator, was furious. He had, of course, already decided that Germany must attack Russia.

In the complex scheming that went on between the four totalitarian countries, India was often assigned different roles. On 6 January 1940 General Alfred Jodl, chief of the Oberkommando Des Heeres (OKH) operations staff, had prepared a paper arguing for joint German-Soviet action in Afghanistan and India. These plans developed and by 30 June 1940 Jodl had provided for direct action against India and Afghanistan.

The Germans had in fact been active in Afghanistan since the end of the First World War. With Soviet help they had tried to restore the deposed King Amanullah, a progressive monarch influenced both by the Russian Revolution and Kemal Ataturk's rise in Turkey. Amanullah wanted co-education, a secular state with rights for women, free elections, Turkish-style changes in dress and development of industry. But the Islamic clergy resisted his plans and he also incurred the wrath of the British. He had not only inflicted a defeat on them in 1919, securing Afghanistan's borders with British India, but his progressive ideas had worried the Raj's political agents who feared that the tribes on their side of the border, still living in a largely medieval Islamic world, might take a liking to such western ideas. In 1928-29 a British-sponsored tribal revolt finally forced him to abdicate and he went into exile in Italy in the 1930s, dying there in 1960. Bose was keen to help Amanullah regain this throne and told the Germans he would be welcomed back by 90 per cent of the Afghans. But the scheme to aid Amanullah had come to grief in the complex rivalry between the foreign-policy bureau of the Nazi party, the government officials at Wilhelmstrasse (the Foreign Ministry), and the Abwehr (the secret service). One strategist planned to use the tribes of the northwest frontier to harass the British, and the troublesome Faqir of Ipi was lavishly financed (at one stage at the rate of £10,000 per month) to tie down British troops.

Afghanistan, in turn, had its own designs on parts of India, and was willing to join Germany provided she got a piece of India and a guarantee that the Soviet Union would respect Afghan territory. All these plans crashed against one rock: Adolf Hitler. For Hitler the British and their empire were the epitome of all that was noble and glorious in the achievements of the Nordic races. He believed that the Ukraine and the steppes of Poland and Russia would see the establishment of a German Raj to match the British Raj. Before the war he had often offered to guarantee the British Empire and during the war he renewed this proposal several times. Hitler never gave up his hope that the British would make peace and in January 1941, even after British planes had bombed Berlin, there were plans for a new British Embassy there. Marie 'Missie' Vasslitchikov, the daughter of a Russian prince, who spent the war years in Germany, wrote in her diary, "Can they really believe England will give in eventually?" But despite the fact that Bose meant little to the Führer, his arrival was electrifying news for the "petty county squires" of Wilhelmstrasse, as Hitler described the diplomats.

Bose arrived in Berlin on 2 April 1941. The next day he met the director of the political department, Dr Ernst von Woermann, a colourless but efficient man who had been deputy head of the German Embassy in London in 1936 and assumed his present post in 1938. Like many in the German Foreign Office he had no liking for Nazism and had only recently become a party member. Bose quickly developed his arguments. He wanted to set up an Indian government-in-exile, as the Poles and others had done in London; he would require certain promises from the Axis powers, and they must be prepared to help with propaganda, instigate uprisings in India and eventually invade the country. All that was required to free India, Bose argued, were 100,000 men with modern equipment.

Woermann, however, was not interested. "I maintained a purely non-committal attitude on this point," he recorded later. This stonewalling soon became the standard German response to Bose's plans and ideas throughout his years in Germany: "We shall have to consider; we shall have to wait and see" and finally, "The Fuehrer knows best: he will decide". On other matters Woermann was more helpful. Bose was provided with small sums of money from the Foreign Ministry's personnel department, and his long-term finance was planned. Right from the beginning Bose made it clear that while Germany would have to provide money, "this will be in the form of a loan to the Free Indian Government established in Europe. At the end of the War, when an independent Government is set up in India, the loan will be repaid in full."

Since the Afghan government did not know of his stay in Kabul it was decided that the route of his escape would not be disclosed, but Woermann wanted Bose's arrival to be announced publicly the following week with appropriate ceremony. Bose in turn told Woermann that he hoped to submit his programme in the next few days. Six days later Bose submitted his first memorandum to the German government. In Europe he wanted a "Free Indian" government to be set up, and a treaty signed governing its relationship with the Axis powers. If the Axis won, Bose was prepared to provide them with "special facilities" in India. He also wanted Free Indian government legations established in friendly countries, intensive propaganda through the radio and, above all, practical help for India-arms, agents, etc., sent through Afghanistan and the tribal areas.

Almost ten months before Japan entered the war, he visualised a Japanese victory. It was an extraordinary prediction:

> The overthrow of British power in India can, in its last stages, be materially assisted by Japanese foreign policy in the Far East. If Japan decides on expansion south-wards it will lead to an open clash with Great Britain. If war then breaks out it appears more certain that the East Indies and the Far Eastern squadrons of the British navy will, under the present circumstances, be no match for the Japanese navy and even if America comes to the rescue of the British navy, a Japanese victory could still be hoped for. A defeat of the British navy in the Far East, including the smashing up of the Singapore base, will automatically weaken British military strength and prestige in India. India is, therefore,

intensely interested in the developments in the Far East. And since Japanese expansion southwards necessitates a prior agreement between the Soviet Union and Japan, India is greatly interested in a pact which will, on the one hand, expedite a settlement of the China affair and will, on the other, enable Japan to move more freely and confidently towards the South.

The Germans reacted cautiously. Woermann minuted this very perceptive reaction:

1) Compliance with Bose's plan would mean that we would announce the liberation of India from English rule as a war aim. It is doubtful whether the moment has arrived for doing this in an official form.
2) The establishment of a Free Indian government in Berlin, under Bose's leadership, would mean that we make a certain political group, namely, the leftist Forward Bloc, the exponent of India. This group is in opposition to other recognised Indian leaders such as Gandhi and Pandit Nehru. There would hardly be any direct government benefit, whereas this would meet with an unfavourable response in large parts of India.

Woermann had also found other flaws in Bose's arguments. In their first interview Bose had said 100,000 modern soldiers would deal with the 70,000-strong British component of the Indian Army. The Indian component of the Army by this stage would have totalled nearly 300,000. Bose argued they would instantly revolt. The following week Bose reduced the strength of the force required to face the British in India to half, 50,000 men, without explanation. Worse, he wanted quite illogically to remain incognito as His Excellency Orlando Mazzotta. Who had ever heard, the Germans asked scornfully, of His Excellency Orlando Mazzotta, travelling on an Italian passport, heading a Free Indian government in Berlin? Bose did not want to disclose his identity because, as Woermann noted, if the Germans accepted his government-in-exile plans he would, "remain in Germany during the war and carry on his fight from here". But if they did not, "he intended to go to the Indian border and fight from there". In that case, disclosing that he had been to Germany would be a grave disadvantage.

On 29 April 1941 Bose met Ribbentrop at the Hotel Imperial in Vienna. Ribbentrop was a man with weak, watery, eyes, one kidney (the other was taken out as doctors tried to save his life after he was struck down by tuberculosis), who found it difficult to concentrate and suffered from bouts of depression. Outwardly, the 48 year old German was elegant in appearance, fluent in French and English and hard working but not well regarded in Germany. German diplomats despised him with Count Otto von Bismark, speaking for many, saying, "He is such an imbecile that he is a freak of nature." Hitler's old Nazi colleagues also hated him. Hermann Goring often tried to remove him as Foreign Minister. Joseph Goebbels said of them, "He bought his name, he married his money and swindled his way into office"

The reference to the name was that, while born Ulrich Frederich Willy Joachim Ribbentrop, he acquired the title "von" denoting nobility in Germany when, as a 32 year old, he was adopted by a distant relation, a 62-year old spinster called Gertrud Charlotte von Ribbentrop. In return Ribbentrop agreed to pay her a pension, although he quickly reneged on this deal. But it meant he could call himself Joachim von Ribbentrop, which was very important to him. Having made his money as a wine and spirits merchant, he had wormed his way into Hitler's favour only in the 1930s when his Berlin house in Dahlem hosted various meetings that enabled Hitler to come to power. Through much of the 30s Hitler gave him various jobs including ambassador to Britain, but it was only in 1938 that Hitler made him foreign minister, replacing Constantin Freiherr von Neurath, the pre-Nazi foreign minister.

Bose knew none of this and thought he was meeting an important foreign minister of then the most powerful state in the world. He discovered a man who had modelled himself on his master Hitler, and was at his Nazi bombastic worst: the war was all but won, England was finished, the Fuehrer had often tried to make peace with Britain on the terms of "let Germany rule Europe and we will let you have your empire"... "In her arrogance and stupidity, however, England had rejected the Führer's hand". When Bose said that Indians feared that, though the English might accept defeat, they would try to regain lost terrain, particularly India, Ribbentrop replied, "the English had gone too far and it would all be over with them this time". Ribbentrop warned Bose not to antagonise Gandhi and was non-committal when Bose reassured him that, contrary to British propaganda, the country would not fall apart if the British left, that it contained a well-developed political organisation – his own – that the moment for action had come.

On the wider political questions Ribbentrop had little to offer. Disruptive activities were fine, but a declaration of Indian independence guaranteed by the Axis was different. Even when Bose argued that Indian prisoners of war being captured in increasing numbers in north Africa could be used as a strike force Ribbentrop refused to rise to the bait. Ribbentrop was more interested in telling him about the Fuehrer's great plans for Europe.

Perhaps the most interesting exchange between the two men took place when Ribbentrop asked Bose about how India felt towards Germany. "Bose answered that he wanted to admit in all frankness that feeling against the National Socialists and the fascists had been rather strong in India. For the English and the communist propaganda had upheld the thesis that National Socialism and fascism were striving to dominate the other races. The foreign minister interjected at this point that National Socialism merely advocated racial purity, but not its own rule over other races. Racial purity was also valued in India and conformed moreover, to the laws of nature."

Though Ribbentrop avoided political commitments, he was generous with money. Within a few days, he sanctioned one million reichmarks for propaganda against the Raj, granted Bose a personal allowance of 12,000 reichmarks and found him quarters in Berlin. But he still remained Orlando Mazzotta. It was too soon to reveal his identity.

Back in Berlin on 3 May 1941, Bose presented Woermann with a "supplementary memorandum". By May 1941 Rommel was sweeping through North Africa and, even as Bose wrote, he heard over the radio of fighting in Iraq between the British and the Iraqis. A month earlier, the very day Bose had arrived in Berlin, Rashid Ali al-Gilani a nationalist, pro Axis politician had led a coup toppling the pro-British Regent Prince Abdullah. Britain had granted Iraq independence in 1932 but had a treaty, which secured its oil pipelines to Haifa and allowed it to operate RAF bases in the country. It now sent Indian troops into Basra. Rashid appealed to the Germans and after some effort Ribbentrop persuaded Hitler to aid the Iraqis. The British soon made Rashid flee and won an important victory, but the use of Indian troops in Iraq emphasised to Bose how for more than 200 years Britain had relied on Indian soldiers to maintain its empire.

Bose recognised that setting up a Free India government-in-exile would be difficult and dropped the idea, but felt that a declaration on India was a must. "I therefore request: that an early pronouncement be made regarding the freedom of India and the Arab countries." Germany must help revolts in these countries; attack India, the heart of the British Empire, overthrow the pro-British Afghan government; and help the Iraqi government. If all this were done, Germany would have a string of friendly countries "from North Africa on the one side and right up to Japan in the Far East." This would become all the more important if Germany were in conflict with Turkey or the Soviet Union. If Germany did not secure her ties with the oriental countries but still went to war with the Soviet Union, "Germany will probably lose the sympathy of the oriental countries which she has gained because of her fight against British imperialism".

Not that Bose wanted Germany to fight the Soviet Union. The Soviet-German pact was still the linchpin of his strategy. "For the success of the task of exterminating British power and influence from the countries of the near and the Middle East, it is desirable that the status-quo between Germany and the Soviet Union should be maintained."

With this memorandum Bose was able to prise open the German official door a little more. On 10 May, Woermann noted that Hitler had cleared a declaration on India. It would be issued within eight or ten days, and Bose would be consulted. By 19 May a draft declaration was floating around. It was not quite what Bose had wanted, but it seemed a first step. It remained, however, the last. The draft endlessly kicked around in Wilhelmstrasse; words were added, words were subtracted, words were changed, but it was never issued. Hitler would never agree to its release, not even when Mussolini pressed him. On 24 May Woermann informed Bose that it would have to be postponed. But, Woermann added, the Germans would help him set up a Free India office to be centrally operated from Berlin.

During his two years in Germany, Bose would every now and again be asked to join some plan dreamt up by the Abwehr and the Foreign Office. On 7 November 1941 Bose went to the Abwehr to be part of a proposed India-Arab committee and to meet Fawzi al-Kawakji, an ex-Iraqi officer and the only relatively successful Arab guerrilla commander. The meeting had come a few weeks after Hitler had accepted three Alpine divisions from Mussolini which were to be employed in the Caucasus and had talked of using them against India. Inspired by this the Germans toyed with the idea of organising a general uprising in India and in those Arab countries garrisoned by Indian troops to help Rome's drive to Suez and beyond. But before the meeting could discuss any military matters Bose made it clear that Germany must declare her war aims for India. The officials knew where Hitler stood on this and so the scheme foundered.

That meeting and many others showed how determined Bose was to maintain his independence in wartime Germany. However, life with the Nazis for Orlando Mazzotta could never be simple: Bose was always confronted by the master-race outlook. It was only after Foreign Office representations that he was addressed as "Your Excellency" and given the status of a notable, and a guest of the government. Even this was due to a very lucky break, for Bose had landed among Germans, many of whom were fervent anti-Nazis.

Some three months before Bose had arrived in Germany, while he was still in Kabul, the German Foreign Office, seeking to exploit Britain's problems in India, had on its own begun to think about India. Some of the officials believed Germany was not doing enough. Bose's arrival intensified these feelings, and the Germans responded by first forming the *Arbeitskreis Indien* (India Working Group), which a few months after his arrival was enlarged into the Special India Department. It came under the charge of State Secretary Wilhelm Keppler. His only qualification for the job was that he was an old Nazi party hack and Hitler's financial adviser. (He had helped set up the meeting between Hitler and Franz von Papen, the former chancellor in January 1933, which had enabled the Nazis to form the electoral pact that brought Hitler to power.) He worshipped Hitler and would tell one English visitor that the Fuehrer had a private line to God the Father.

By the summer of 1941 the India Working Group possessed the nucleus of an organisation — but, more crucially, the department included among others, Adam von Trott zu Solz, Dr Alexander Werth, and Franz Josef Furtwangler. They were all dedicated anti-Nazis trying to remove Hitler; none more so than Adam von Trott who was horribly murdered by the Nazis following the failure of the July 1944 plot to kill Hitler.

Trott's life was the supreme example of a person working for Nazi Germany who was not even remotely a Nazi. He is the classic "good German" who fought and died so that Germany and a decent Europe might live. Indeed one English biography of him is entitled *A Good German*. After the war, the German socialist Frederick Stampler wrote, "Everything about Trott must have filled this new tyranny with fury; the aristocrat versus the vulgarian, the

Christian versus the heathen, the respecter of religious liberty versus the suppressor of freedom of belief, the German versus the despoiler of Germany, the Socialist versus the betrayer who abused and violated the name of socialism."

Trott had been a Rhodes scholar at Balliol in Oxford in the 1930s, making many friends particularly with men who would become prominent in the Labour party. He got close to Stafford Cripps who during the war defended Trott against charges by his Cabinet colleague Anthony Eden that he was a dishonest man. In Oxford he had also become very friendly with Humayan Kabir who would later became a minister in independent India. When Gandhi visited Balliol, Trott had met him, been photographed with him and treasured his memory of that occasion. Trott had no fondness for the British Empire and would tell his many English friends that the pink blobs on the map would have to go. Life for Trott could never have been easy. It was often dangerous balancing his outward support for the regime against his secret plots to overthrow it. So in theory Bose could not have found a more ideal good German with whom to team up.

But almost from the beginning Trott did not like Bose. Always a complex person, he sympathised with Bose's aims but did not warm to the man. In August 1941, three months after he had first met Bose, he wrote to his wife Clarita, "he is highly gifted but, despite everything, on a human level we remain definitely cool. It is as if every time we have to start again at the beginning." The following week Trott wrote, "I am beginning to be indispensable to him, the fundamental beliefs are too negative for a rewarding relationship." On 14 August 1941, clearly fed up, he wrote to Clarita, "The office work drives me to distraction."

Trott so disliked Bose that he told one of his colleagues a story about Bose's alleged personal behaviour, which is entirely out of character for Bose and impossible to credit as true. We shall examine this story later. Trott could not abide Bose's fixation about removing the British from India while choosing to turn a blind eye to the greater evil of Nazism. Trott hardly helped matters by refusing to reveal his real feelings to Bose. He did not take Bose into his confidence and tell him that he was really playing a double game: a Nazi official who was using his position to undermine the regime. Bose and the whole India Department was in reality a wonderful cover story for Trott as he plotted the downfall of the Nazis. Ostensibly, the India Department was meant to be attacking the British, or at least their worst excesses, at their weakest point: their occupation of India. Indeed as one of Trott's biographers, Giles MacDonogh says, "Trott's advocacy of attacks on Britain's Achilles heel in India was one of his major claims to fame."

The arrival of Bose was a godsend for Trott, as the department now got lavish money from the German Foreign Office. Trott had access to all of it, and a free hand to work against the Nazis while being financed by them. He could hire his friends who were sympathetic to resisting Hitler. He could also use the Free India mission to freely travel in Germany and around Europe, visiting neutral countries where he could contact British and other western powers in order to convince them that there was a German resistance to Hitler. Indeed, just weeks before the July 1944 Stauffenberg bomb plot against Hitler, Trott used the excuse of Free India business to go to Holland and contact the Dutch resistance in an effort to make the Allies believe that they could do business with the plotters. It raises, as MacDonogh, says, "the question of how Trott could exploit this British weakness (in India) while at the same time professing a love of Britain and her people."

It is somewhat ironic that when Trott first met Bose, it was the Indian who had the false identity of Mazzotta, necessary to escape the British. Trott never carried a false passport but in working for the Nazis he always had to profess false beliefs. By the time the world finally knew his true loyalties his plan to rescue Germany from Hitler was doomed. Yet despite paying the highest price, even after his death many in Britain refused to believe Trott was really committed to the destruction of Nazis, and this remains the great tragedy of his life. Trott, as MacDonogh says, was often buttoned up, sinking into a discreet persona, which after years of

Nazi rule had become second nature for him. If Trott found Bose buttoned up as well, we can only speculate what might have happened had he unburdened himself to Bose! Both men had an eclectic mind; both were interested in Hegel (Trott wrote a thesis on him at the age of 21). Trott had studied Eastern religions and when he was in China in 1937 he tried to create a political system which would find a common denominator between Eastern and Western ideas. There is no evidence that in their various meetings Bose and Trott ever strayed into such wide-ranging discussions; more the pity.

Bose, who liked Trott, did not sense the hostility the German felt towards him and was surprised that when he finally left Germany, Adam von Trott did not come to bid him goodbye. In contrast to Trott, Alexander Werth, Trott's main assistant, had professed his anti-Nazism more openly. Werth, who had a Jewish stepfather, had spent some time in *Colombiahaus*, one of the Nazi SS's torture chambers in Berlin-Tempelhof. He had survived to leave for England with his stepfather. There he qualified and practised as a lawyer and played host to Trott before returning to Germany just before the war.

Trott's other main assistant was Franz Josef Furtwangler, a trade unionist and Social Democrat. Fairly early on in their relationship Bose and Furtwangler disagreed about tactics. Furtwangler advised him not to identify with the Nazi regime. While Bose had no intention of doing this, he could not abide Furtwangler's sermons on how he should handle India. The German told him he should not bring his disagreements with Gandhi and Nehru to Germany, all such conflicts should be put aside. Bose, says Furtwangler, closed up like "a cuttle fish." But even Furtwangler had to acknowledge how difficult life was for Bose in Nazi Germany. Although he judged the Indian's two years in war-time Germany very harshly as tragicomic, he concluded, "but I should not like to maintain that this was entirely his fault. The atmosphere of the National Socialist psychopathic tyranny with its intrigues and prattling chaos was for him a permanent strain on his nerves."

The group that Trott had built up was certainly the most extraordinary that could have possibly assembled under official Nazi German patronage. For a start, they did not have a conventional office. Housed in foreign missions, empty following the start of the war. They worked in offices, which were more like homes, with elaborate bathrooms and kitchens. We get a flavour of Trott's "India Office" from the diaries of Missie Vassiltchikov who had been recruited to work for Trott just as Bose was on his way to Kabul:

> Adam Trott has installed me temporarily in a kind of research institute attached to his India Office, as his bosses might get wary were we not only to hold similar political views, but also to work together. My immediate chief is an elderly woman journalist (Frau Freda Kretschmar) who is a specialist in Indian affairs. Adam seems to hope that once I know more about the work I will eventually influence her in a way useful to him, but I fear he overrates my capacities. Adam has one room; then comes an office for me and two secretaries; then another large room for Alex Werth and a man called Hans Ritcher, whom everybody calls 'Judgie' and then there is a tiny hole in the wall with a Herr Wolf (known to all 'Wolfchen'). And Lore Wolf, his secretary. Wolfhen is often slightly tipsy but he is intelligent and nice [Downstairs in the converted garage worked Missie's sister and other officials]... Office hours are, however, most irregular. We are supposed to start after 9 am and work till about 6 p.m. But at lunchtime the bosses evaporate; so do we, although this is not officially allowed. The gentlemen hardly ever return before 4 p.m. or even later. We have therefore to catch up afterwards and sometimes go on until ten.

Missie Vassiltchikov did translations and book reviews and also took dictation in German, but made many grammatical mistakes. If Missie's portrayal of Trott is accurate he could not have been more unlike the archetypal German. He was a very disorganised worker, hated routine and liked, as Missie puts it, to "retire to more Olympian heights and not be bothered by red tape." When Missie complained, his secretary said, "Herr von Trott is a genius and you can't possibly demand that a genius is tidy as well."

With Ribbentrop happy to guide the Special India Department via an annual teleprinter message from his special train in Westphalia, Trott and his team had plenty of time to play at being geniuses. It was in this world that Bose had landed in the spring of 1941. One of the problems we face in assessing it is that we do not have Bose's side of the story and some of the participants who survived the war adapted their story to suit their audience. Werth was a classic example of this Many years after the war, when Sisir Bose started his Netaji Research Bureau in Calcutta to perpetuate the memory of his uncle, Werth became an honoured guest at the Bureau where he lectured and wrote books. Here he had much to say about Bose the political leader usually in fulsome praise and nothing about the private man. But before that in Germany, he had told Trott's wife scathing stories of Bose's private life during the war, which present a very different picture of Bose.

For all the material comforts that Trott and Werth provided they could not make policy and by the end of May 1941, Bose was disillusioned by the response to his lengthy and eloquent presentation of the Indian case. Werth began to detect "extreme agitation". Just then Mussolini invited Bose to Italy.

Despite the help given by Quaroni and the Italian legation in Kabul, Mussolini had been unaware of Bose's presence. He only came to know of it through sheer chance. On May 11, in one of the most amazing incidents of the war, which to this day remains shrouded in mystery. Rudolf Hess, Hitler's deputy, flew to Britain. He landed in Scotland with a crazy plan that he could make peace between Britain and Germany. Hitler was shocked and Ribbentrop had to hurriedly fly to Rome to try and explain to Mussolini what was going on. The meeting by all accounts was very bizarre. Ribbentrop had no explanation and throughout the meeting Bismarck, the Counsellor of the German Embassy, kept kicking the leg of Ciano's secretary every time Ribbentrop made an absurd statement. After he had waved goodbye to Ribbentrop at Rome airport Bismarck told the Italians, "Let's hope they all crash and break their necks but not here, we'll have unpleasant work to do."

It was during this meeting that Ribbentrop let slip that Bose was in Berlin. However, he was extremely reluctant to let him go to Rome. Bose's identity and presence in Berlin were still a secret and Italy was well known as a sieve which could seldom retain political secrets. Also, the thought that Mussolini would receive Bose before Hitler was not comforting. But eventually Ribbentrop agreed, and on 29 May Bose flew to Rome.

Bose had two meetings with Count Galeazzo Ciano, the Italian Foreign Minister and Mussolini's son-in-law on 6 and on 29 June. After the first meeting Ciano noted in his diary:

> He would like the Axis to make a statement about the independence of India, but in Berlin his proposals have been received with much reserve. Nor must we be compromised, especially because the value of this young man is not clear. Past experience has yielded rather modest results. (The actual words Ciano used were guesto giovanotto which has also been translated as upstart but young man is the one preferred by the latest volume of Ciano's diaries.)

But for all his doubts about Bose, Ciano would not let him out of his sight and kept him virtually under house arrest. In between his two meetings with Bose Ciano went to Venice to effectively take instructions from Ribbentrop who told him a declaration on Free India would be premature. For Bose the Rome visit was important for two other reasons. In Rome on 22 June 1941 Bose heard news that destroyed one of the linchpins of his strategy. Hitler had invaded Russia. Now there was little point in returning to Berlin, and he decided to travel to Vienna. On 17 July he returned to Berlin, met Woermann, and told him:

> The Soviets had been popular in India especially among the intellectuals from whom the leaders are drawn. It is believed in India that the Soviet Union is an anti-imperialist power and would therefore be an Indian ally against England. In the German-Russian war the sympathies of the Indian people were clearly with Russia because the Indian people felt definitely that Germany was the aggressor and was for India, therefore, another dangerous imperialist power.

In Nazi Germany nobody dared say such things, not even privately to government officials. But, as the Germans had already realised, Bose was not a sycophant. The German diplomats in Rome had become well aware of this and reported to Woermann that while Bose had a "first rate personality" he was difficult and probably best kept in mothballs in a neutral country, such as Switzerland, till a favourable moment in the war arrived. But Woermann was not keen, the Swiss authorities refused to have anything to do with the idea and Bose, in any case, would certainly have rejected it. He was not the type, like Aga Khan III, to spend the war in cushy Switzerland. Woermann, however, thought some brainwashing on Soviet Union was in order. He minuted: "It is clear from his statement that Bose being far from Berlin is strongly influenced by the Soviet thesis on the question of the German-Russian conflict; it will therefore be our first task to put him right in this respect." It was a task in which the Germans were destined to fail.

A few days later a German writer, Dr Giselher Wirsing, who was also tutoring him in German, visited Bose in his Berlin hotel and found him sitting cross-legged in front of a large world map, wrapped in thought.... "I sat quietly next to him and could easily read his thoughts. A few days ago Hitler had begun the campaign against Soviet Russia". Bose finally broke the silence and said, "That won't be good."

Right through the war Bose steadfastly refused to join any Nazi condemnation of the Soviet Union. He appears to have got round this by never referring to the Russians in his broadcasts, as George Orwell shrewdly noted. However, the German invasion of Russia would have dramatic consequences for Bose's plans for developing anti-British underground links in India and he was often unaware of these consequences.

The trip to Rome had not improved Bose's position in Germany, and hospitality could also bring humiliation. In Rome, as Woermann had instructed the German embassy, Bose had been provided with funds, and Trott had helped him buy much-needed clothes. But when the accounts were submitted Keppler questioned every Reichsmark spent and Bose was once again reminded of his precarious status in Germany. And with Germans still not doing anything on the one question that "greatly excited" Bose - a declaration on Free Indi - Bose could still console himself that they seemed eager to do something by way of propaganda.

A few days after Bose met Ribbentrop, the German Foreign Minister had inquired about radio propaganda to India. By 5 May an official of the *Rundfunkstelle*, the German Foreign Office broadcasting bureau, had drawn up an elaborate eight-page plan. India, the official concluded, had over 120,000 wireless sets, 30,000 of them shortwave and mostly owned by people who were strongly nationalistic and pro-German. The broadcasts should be aimed at them and be in Hindustani, Bengali, Telugu and Tamil, most of the major Indian languages. Ribbentrop himself was in favour of Bose's idea of clandestine medium-wave broadcasting from the tribal areas of the North-West Frontier Province, or even from Kabul Radio, which had been constructed with German help. Not that they were short of radio stations in the East, Bangkok, Saigon, and even Chunking were possible places, and in Shanghai there was a short-wave German radio whose power was soon to be increased from one to five kilowatts. Perhaps the most interesting idea was to set up a "black" transmitter in the Dutch station of Huizen and pretend the broadcasts were being made from India.

Ribbentrop knew that radio propaganda by itself could not bring about rebellion but it could foment discontent - and that was a start.

The Rome visit also raised another issue for the Germans: whom could they get to spy on Bose? Bismarck had noticed that Bose was accompanied by a German woman and made what he thought was a helpful suggestion to Berlin: Why not use the woman to spy on Bose. The woman was, of course, Emilie Schenkl and a horrified Berlin quickly put Bismarck right. Bismarck was not the first German to think of using Emilie as a spy. According to Emilie's daughter Anita, the Germans wanted her to join the Foreign Office but she refused, as she felt an official position might mean having to report on Subhas to the Germans. Before Bose had arrived in Berlin Emilie had started working for the Vienna Postal Services and when she went to Berlin, she took a sabbatical from the job.

Emilie had come to Berlin in April, possibly brought there by Otto Faltis, Bose's old friend from Vienna. Subhas and Emilie initially stayed in some of the grand hotels of Berlin. For a time it was the Excelsior the neo-baroque building much-loved by Greta Garbo, who murmured, "I want to be alone" into one of its pillars. It is said Bose left this hotel after a Nazi called Kellner refused to call him His Excellency, which upset him. They also stayed at the Esplanade, a grand hotel. Bose then moved to perhaps the grandest of them all, the Kaiserhoff, an elegant sandstone building and the first grand hotel built in the city. Bismarck had used it for the Berlin Conference of 1878, and Hitler had used its top floor as his temporary base in the 1930s.

Berlin was not quite the strutting capital of the Reich it had been when the war had started 18-months earlier. Then, after the fall of Poland, the film *Feuertaufe* (Baptism of Fire) showing scenes of the brutal destruction of Warsaw by the Luftwaffe, had been greeted with hoots of joy in the cinemas of Berlin, and a young German officer walking down the streets had told Howard Smith, an American journalist, "We shall never be beaten." This faith in ultimate victory was still there when Bose arrived, two months before the invasion of Russia, but Bose could see that Berlin had experienced air raids and been forced to take precautions. Netting covered Hitler's five-mile East-West axis running from the Havel to the Spree, which pointed like an arrow to the heart of government quarters. The netting was placed on two miles of specially erected steel poles to camouflage this axis. Attempts were made to hide other avenues from Allied bombers. When Bose finally got his Free India Centre he walked everyday under what looked, said one Berliner, like "an enormous, overgrown, green circus marquee." This was because the whole length of the Charlottenburger Chaussee from the Brandenburg Gate through the Tiergarten, the Berlin Park near which the Free India office was located, was covered with a canopy of camouflage netting laced with strips of green cloth and false tree tops.

In other parts of the city, like the Adolf-Hitler–Platz, dummy buildings were erected to confuse the bombers. The sparkling Goddess of Victory at the centre of the avenue, Siegessaule, was draped in netting, and the buxom goddess stripped and painted a dull brown. Huge antiaircraft guns were placed on main buildings including the Reichstag. Then there was the heavy presence of the Gestapo, and announcements that anyone committing a crime during the blackout would be executed. In the first month of the raids, a man who had snatched a woman's purse and another who had stolen coal were beheaded. After the raids, the Gestapo would use political prisoners to defuse unexploded bombs. There were also bossy air raid wardens who warned of showing any light during blackouts. One Berlin poster had Death riding a plane and tossing a bomb in a building that had shown a light. But, despite this, or perhaps because of it, as Alexandra Richie points out in her book Faust Metropolis, *A History of Berlin*, Berliners never developed the spirit which marked London during the Blitz".

In the summer of 1941 the villa the Germans had earmarked for Bose was ready. It was the former residence of the American military attaché at 6-7 Sophientstrasse. A red brick, luxurious house with a sitting room and dining room on the ground floor, and bedrooms with ensuite bathrooms on the first, it also had a large garden and was situated in the fashionable Charlottenburg area For the next two years it would be his home, the centre of Indian nationalist activity, and the only period in his life when he would live with Emilie as man and wife.

Subhas and Emilie lived there in some style. He had a chauffeur-driven car, and was provided with food and fuel that was not available to ordinary Germans. Emilie clearly enjoyed the facilities, and liked soaking herself in the bath every day. This only stopped when she got a skin complaint and the doctor told her she must not bathe so often. The Boses also had a staff in the shape of a husband and wife team called the Beduns. These servants lived in a little cottage in the garden, but also used the small attic at the top of the villa. Herr Bedun took care of the garden and acted as manservant for Bose, converting to waiter when Bose entertained. Fraulein Bedun did the cooking and the housework.

Herr Bedun clearly was in awe of "His Excellency Bose". Even with the special allowances given to Bose, it was not that easy to get tomatoes, and on one occasion Herr Bedun approached Emilie and said, "Would you please ask His Excellency if I could plant some tomatoes?"Emilie looked at him witheringly, and replied, "I do not have to ask His Excellency. Go ahead and plant some tomatoes."

Bose clearly liked the Beduns. When their daughter got married, he gave permission for her wedding party to be held at the villa. There were occasional visitors in the evenings, and dinner parties. One visitor he particularly liked was Ghulam Siddiq Khan, a former foreign minister of Afghanistan. Ghulam Siddiq had lived in Germany since 1930 and was a strong supporter of ex-King Amanullah. When Bose arrived in Berlin Ghulam Siddiq was working on a joint plan with the Russians to restore the king, and after June 1941 he worked on this plan with the Germans and the Italians. Bose frequently urged the Germans to break off relations with the Afghan government, and set up a government-in-exile in Berlin headed by Ghulam Siddiq. He felt this could lead to him setting up a similar one for India. The two men spent many an evening discussing plans.

Bose's social circle also included perhaps the most curious British subject in the Reich. This was William Joyce, American by birth, and Irish by upbringing. Joyce spent the war broadcasting on Radio Berlin in a programme aimed at Britain called *Germany Calling*. Dubbed "Lord Haw Haw" by the British papers, his strident pro-Nazi broadcasts caused such anger that after the war Joyce became the last man in Britain to be hanged for treason. An anti-Semite, he was such a racist that in 1938 in London he had refused to teach coloured students. In Berlin he often played chess with Bose, and the Nazis made him change a book he had written because they felt it would upset Subhas.

Every so often Bose complained of lack of energy. Dr. A.Q Faroqi, an Indian Muslim who became his doctor, gave him injections of glucose, which sometimes caused a bad reaction.

We have one contemporary portrait of Bose's life style in Berlin, dating from the spring of 1942. Luigi Barzini, the Italian journalist, had lunch with him in his villa. Barzini was served in the European manner, European food, and wine by a waiter in white gloves, presumably Herr Bedun. Barzini was much taken by Bose, seeing him as a Buddha of Asiatic nobility. He wrote of his "kind of smiling expression, high forehead,finely drawn mouth, altogether a feeling of superior intelligence, (a) certain ingenuity, a grace of exaggerated adolescence. You could almost take him for a European were it not for the bronze colour of the skin".

By the time he met Barzini, Bose had given up his Italian identity of Mazzotta. Having had an Italian identity for a year, Bose had shed some of his Indian taboos. An Italian who did not drink did not seem natural, so Bose had become a modest drinker. Also, having lectured Emilie for years to give up smoking, he took to cigarettes, becoming a chain smoker. Even so he never stopped trying to persuade Emilie to give up smoking, although by using the special allowances given to him he also procured cigarettes for her.

In other ways life for Subhas did not change. He still preferred to work late at night, rarely surfacing before eleven in the morning, despite Emilie's preferrence for more regular hours. In the afternoons he went to the Free India Centre, generally walking the half mile to the villa near Tiergarten. Emilie accompanied him, and Subhas enjoyed walking back late at night. With crime not a worry, the nights without bombing allowed husband and wife to take a pleasant stroll.

Emilie also kept up the job that had first brought her to Subhas, taking dictation as Bose brought the story of the nationalist struggle up to date, writing two more chapters for *The Indian Struggle.*

We have seen how, as Rangakakababu, uncle to Sarat's children, he had been a great playmate, playing hide and seek with them and chasing them up and down stairs in Sarat's Woodburn Park house. Now Emilie replaced the children. He would often chase her around the house, up and down the stairs and round the garden. This was a more relaxed Bose in comparison to the stern, unbending, image he had always presented. One Indian in Berlin attributed the more relaxed Bose to the Allied bombs falling on Berlin. This was the first time Bose had experienced bombings and, according to this theory, the tension made him shed some of his inhibitions.

It may also have cemented the relationship between Subhas and Emilie. Many years later Emilie would tell her daughter Anita that the couple often had quarrels over political issues. Emilie did not care for Subhas's left wing views. She was very conservative and rather fond of Hitler, while Subhas never concealed his dislike of the Fuehrer and would talk mockingly of "your Hitler". On one occasion, the discussion got so heated that Emilie was ready to pack her bags and leave. This may seem an unlikely story but the fact that Emilie, while loving Subhas, did not worship him uncritically as an Indian woman might have done, was probably a factor in the bond that developed between the two.

Subhas did feel some guilt about living with Emilie and two years later in Burma, as he faced defeat at the hands of the British, he provided a glimpse of his inner turmoil to a colleague. The colleague was Lakshmi Swaminathan, an Indian doctor he had recruited to his ranks. Late one night after dinner he told him, "I have done something that I don't know whether the people in India will be able to understand ". He then unburdened himself of the relationship with Emilie, something he had not done to anyone else. Subhas told Lakshmi it was Emilie who was keener on the marriage and Subhas had at last relented. "Do you think people in India will understand?" Lakshmi reassured him that he had done nothing wrong and had not left her stranded. Lakshmi's recollection of the conversation is not precise and Peter Fay, the American author of a book on the INA, who was told this story by Lakshmi, narrates it in such a manner that it has a certain dream-like quality. But it is clear Subhas felt troubled and worried about his life with Emilie.

Although Emilie helped Subhas loosen the hitherto repressed sexual side of his life, the reserve he felt towards women never quite disappeared. Back in Vienna in the 1930s, Heddy Fullop-Miller had once taken a fancy to Subhas, come back to his flat and demanded he kiss her. Subhas, taken aback, had gallantly kissed her hand saying, "But Madam you are like a mother to me". In India such a remark would be considered a compliment and Subhas could not fathom why Fullop-Miller was affronted.

One day, as Subhas walked in the garden of the villa, a women suddenly confronted him. It seems that despite the attempts to keep his presence a secret, it had leaked and had been much discussed among some students at a Berlin Institute, which specialised in Oriental studies. One of the girl students decided to find out and scaled the walls of the villa. Like that moment with Heddy Fullop-Miller, Subhas was unnerved, summoned Emilie and asked her to deal with the intruder.

Emilie's presence with him in Berlin was bound to be controversial. Apart from the racial aspect of a white woman cohabiting with an Indian in Nazi Germany, albeit one posing as an Italian, there was the class factor and this brought out the snobbery in Trott and Werth.

They could not abide her. Indeed Emilie may have been another reason why Trott did not like Bose. As a German aristocrat, he found this lower middle-class Viennese woman beneath him. This first emerged when Trott and Werth helped furnish the villa for Bose. Werth later recorded how they went about it:

> Trott and I ourselves brought the furniture together and we took an exceptionally malicious pleasure in making Fraulein Schenkl's bedroom as ugly as possible. She was the typical product of the Second World War, the baggage in fact of any war. She got permanently on our nerves with her risible desires which we, and later Bose, had to satisfy with such regularity. As a result of Indian sensitivity in personal affairs, and especially in erotic matters, we had to take care that in all things the wishes of the Fraulein Schenkl be fulfilled from the first month of their Berlin existence. What we took amiss, though never let on to them, was the fact that they were well aware of too, that we were in no position to refuse.

Trott quite scandalously also told Werth that Bose was not averse to visiting bars where he could find drink and women. After the war Werth would tell Trott's widow Clarita that her husband told him:

> Whenever for instance Bose went into a bar , where there were women, he did so with the greatest pleasure, becoming the later it got, ever more taciturn and aristocratic in his bearing. Finally he became so grand that we could without insulting him make our way home. As for the rest, 'the singers fall courteously silent.

This seems very unlikely. The man who would respond to a woman asking to be kissed by kissing her hand, and who when confronted by a strange woman in his garden would summon his wife, could not, even in the extraordinary situation of war-time Berlin, change so much. The only explanation for this is that Werth, who wrote this after he had spent some time in a Soviet Gulag, an experience that broke him, was trying to write in a manner to please Clarita. Like her husband, she could not abide Bose.

Werth wrote this memoir in 1957 when Clarita, seeking to rehabilitate her husband's name, had gathered *Berichtas* reports from various people who knew him. This would form part of the raw material for the biography on Trott that David Astor, a close English friend of Trott, organised, hiring Christopher Sykes to write the book, *Troubled Loyalty*. Interestingly, despite the fact that Sykes detested Bose, he did not use this part of Werth's *Berichta* in his book.

The German Foreign Office never gave up on attempts to plant a Mata Hari on Bose and having failed with Emilie turned to Missie's boss Freda Kretschmar. She was meant to spy on Subhas and keep a watch on Emilie as well. Kretschmar, like Trott and Werth, did not care for Emilie being very snobbish about her and calling her Bose's "personal companion" whose effect on Bose was bad. Was there perhaps some sexual jealousy involved here? Anita recalls being told by her mother that many women in Vienna fancied Subhas Bose. We do not know if Fraulein Kretschmar did, but there was to be an interesting twist to the Kretschmar story, involving another Indian, at the end of the war.

We also do not know of the alleged "bad effect" Emilie had on Subhas. Indians who worked with Bose have given contradictory explanations. Some said she had no impact, but two Indian men asked to oversee the Indian Legion complained that Emilie knew more about the organisation then they did. The only time Emilie intervened was clearly beneficial and an occasion that Kretschmar should have welcomed. Some time in 1942 Emilie was approached by Eva Maria, a German from Breslau in Silesia. She was studying textiles in Berlin and had fallen in love with her fellow student, Brajlal Mukerjee, the son of the great Indian artist D.L. Mukerjee. The Nazis told her to end the relationship as it was not allowed under Nazi racial laws and also warned her not to tell any Indian. Eva Maria shrewdly decided to tell Emilie, fully aware who her consort was. Emilie told Subhas and he intervened with the Germans. We do not know in what way he intervened but it clearly worked. In February 1943, as Subhas Bose was on his way to the Far East, Eva Maria got married to Brajlal and then after the war spent 51 years in India and produced two children.

Not that having his own villa meant the petty hassles of Nazi bureaucracy ceased. Almost a year after he moved into the villa, he was complaining to the Germans for suggesting he could not speak English and, in a letter to Emilie written on 26 October 1942, he asked her to check phone bills that did not belong to him. He then told her that he had pointed out to the Germans, "I can speak English". By this time Bose was beginning to discover, there was not in reality a German government. What mattered at any given time was what Hitler thought. And now in July 1941, as his forces advanced at breathtaking speed into Russia, Hitler in his table talks to his cronies saw a future German Empire in eastern Europe. He spoke admiringly about the British and how they ruled this vast country of 400 million brown people with so few British administrators. This prompted Ribbentrop to change his plans about even starting the Indian propaganda.

On 11 August 1941, Bose had a meeting with the Abwehr and the Foreign Office where plans for subersive action in Afghanistan and the North West Frontier were discussed. Bose made it clear it would be futile without a declaration on India by the Axis and three days later he wrote a anguished letter to Ribbentrop stating that many in India were thinking the Axis would not help India gain freedom, so it would be better "to make peace with Britain in the best terms possible." In the absence of a declaration he warned, "*The march of the German troops towards the East will be regarded as the approach not a friend but of an enemy.*" He underlined this sentence hoping to hurry the Germans, but it did not work.

With nothing to do in Berlin, Bose went on a tour of the continent with Emilie, visiting Brussels and Paris, trying to recruit Indians for his Free India Centre. He ended up in Bad Gastein, a favourite place, where he spent much of September and October.

Bose returned to Berlin in late October to find the situation had changed thanks to the Italians. They had quickened the pace, and the Germans had followed. On 4 October 1941 the Italian Foreign Ministry informed the German embassy that it had allocated a floor of a Foreign Ministry building to set up what came to be called the "Centre India", headed by a Muslim, one Mohammed Iqbal Shedai. This forms perhaps one of the least-known aspects of German and Italian wartime efforts to aid Indian revolutionaries, and undoubtedly the most curious. Little is known about Shedai except what has been gleaned from Italian and German documents. Born in 1898, a year after Bose, he had been involved in communist activities in his youth. He had spent sometime with M.N. Roy in Moscow and was expelled from France in 1938. He then decided to work under the tutelage of Mussolini who, acting as the self-proclaimed protector of all followers of Islam, was happy to become his patron.

During the following year Shedai's activities rivalled those of Bose, and the two men had a stormy, controversial relationship. Bose saw in Shedai the personification of the growing Muslim separatist tendency, which he had feared ever since his last meeting with Jinnah in India. Shedai's Azad Hindustan organisation consisted entirely of Muslims, including a relative of the Grand Mufti of Jerusalem and a former Foreign Minister of Afghanistan, close to ex-King Amanullah. Himalay Radio, which now began broadcasting from Rome (pretending to broadcast from India), vituperatively denounced Gandhi and Nehru and increasingly argued a separatist "Pakistan" line. Shedai could not have been more different from Bose. He was a gregarious man who liked wine and women, and had established quite a rapport with the outgoing Italians. Shedai also wrote curious letters: once to the Japanese consul in Rome confessing, "I am lazy". He also wrote to the German consul, "From six in the morning till five in the evening, I am busy and in the evening my head does not work".

Bose did not think Shedai was suited for serious political action but he did try to work with him. In August 1941 on his trip to Paris, he had lunch with Shedia and Werth at the Tour d'Argent. The two men also had lunch with Pierre Laval, the Vichy French Prime Minister. Bose wanted to take Shedai back to Berlin to help with the broadcasts to India. But when Shedai visited Germany in September, he criticised much of the German work, blaming it on "His Excellency Mazzotta" and his "dictatorial" ambitions. Anxious to promote his own cause, Shedai missed no opportunity to attack Bose. He was scathing about the way the Indian prisoners of war (POWs) were being treated in the Annaberg training camp near Dresden in Saxony; and, when Bose and Trott tried to persuade him to come and work in Berlin, he set his own conditions. He wanted an Axis declaration on Free India, Rome's permission to transfer his activities, and a joint "Italo-German-Indian Committee". Bose, who thought committee work was democratic in structure and would produce only waffle, shot the idea down. Shedai was unable even to present the idea to the Germans, and refused to leave Rome. However, with the Italians keen to participate in the India act, he was able to prosper — but only for a time. At the risk of getting ahead of ourselves, we must give here a brief summary of how Shedai's career ended.

By the summer of 1942 he had persuaded the Italians to revive the Amici dell' India, Friends of India, and publish a magazine called *Italia e India.* In May 1942, as Shedai was doing this, he invited Bose to the opening ceremony. Bose went to Rome but did not attend. However, he met Shedai and used the occasion, as we shall see, to meet Mussolini and Ciano and other Italians such as the Secretary of State Prunas, his old friend Professor Tucci, Amanullah the ex-King of Afghanistan, the Grand Mufti of Jerusalem and the Iraqi Rashid el Gilani.

Shedai was also able to act in the military sphere, using the idea Bose had given Ribbentrop at their April 1941 meeting in Vienna. The Italians had captured the first Indian POWs to fall into Axis hands during their north African campaign, and by 1 June 1942 Shedai had enlisted forty volunteers from various Italian POW camps. In July, with two of his most able volunteers, he went on a tour of camps in north Africa and recruited a few hundred more. By August 1942 the Centro Militare India, as the Italian-Indian war effort was called, could boast two companies of volunteers under an Italian commander, Major Avrea. Originally the Italian plan seems to have been to assemble fifty to eighty Indian POWs and to select about twenty of them for sabotage activities in India. By October 1942, there were 250 of them in Torre Muara, north Africa, and a further fifty were receiving parachute training. The Italians were learning quickly from the German example; but in November 1942 it all came to an end. Rumours swept the Torre Muara camp that the Indians were about to be sent back to Libya to help deal with Allied landings there, and on 9 November the camp mutinied. Shedai was completely discredited and the Centro Militare was dissolved. Bose, who had often warned the Italians about Shedai's amateurish efforts, felt completely vindicated.

Little is known of what happened to Shedai after that; but from the beginning the Italian effort had unwittingly succeeded in goading the Germans into action. Soon after the Italians set up their Centro India, Trott visited Rome to discover their plans. He came back with an agreement wherein both sides agreed to co-ordinate their Indian activities, though this, like all Axis agreements, was rarely implemented. At this stage Bose's organisation in Berlin was known as "Stab Mazzotta", Organisation Mazzotta. During September and October, it took shape as the Free India Centre. On 30 October 1941 the Free India Centre, Zentral-stelle Freie Indien, was opened at 10 Lichtensteinallee in the Tiergarten, and three days later Bose formally opened it.

By this time many of Bose's pet schemes had taken shape. For years Indian nationalists had squabbled about the right greeting to be used amongst themselves, the appropriate national anthem, the common language – and had disagreed along caste, religious and sectarian lines. In that Berlin suburb Bose got everybody to accept *Jai Hind* (Hail to India) as the national greeting, *Jana Gana Mana*, Tagore's song for India, as the national anthem, and Hindustani written in Roman script as the national language. Of these innovations, the first two would be adopted after 1947 by a free India. One other decision was taken. Bose was no longer Bose but *Netaji* (leader, or, as the Germans often interpreted it, Fuehrer). Later Sivaram, a member of Bose's propaganda team in south east Asia, said that he deliberately cultivated this title. Some have seen this as Bose giving himself airs. Werth in his Bericht would write that, "Bose liked to be called "Excellency and in the end extended this to Trott and me when there were others present".

Bose did not seek the title of Netaji. It was conferred upon him by the small band of Indians in Germany, in keeping with the Indian tradition where great men are always given honoured titles. Tagore was Gurudeva (Great Teacher), Gandhi was Bapu (Father), Patel was Sardar (Leader) and Subhas's own guru Das was Desbhandu (Friend of the Nation). The Indians had discussed long and hard what they should call Bose. The original title proposed was *Hamare Neta* (our leader) which became "Netaji."

Bose was still using the assumed name of Mazzotta when, in the spring of 1941 he began recruiting Indians to his cause. One of them was Abid Hasan, an electrical engineer. Hasan thinks he was the second Indian Bose recruited. He had been asked by another Indian called N.G. Swami to meet an Italian gentleman, and his experiences illustrated Bose's techniques. Hasan, from a rich Nawabi family of Hyderabad, was already politically aware. On his visits to India he had attended Congress meetings and during the non-co-operation movement even landed in jail. But in Germany he was part of a microscopic Indian community, unaware of his compatriots' existence and just intent on carrying on with his work. The meeting with Bose changed all that. "At our first meeting," he recalls, "we spoke for about an hour. And he devoted himself completely to me. I had to recount everything from my birth onwards. He asked me, for instance, why I had taken electrical engineering, was I fond of mathematics and all that. There was nothing about what he was going to do, what he had done. It was only about me, my family, what my father had done, whether I had taken any part in political activity. He was really surprised that I had. This was his secret. He showed such great personal interest." At the end of it Hasan required little persuasion: he would remain one of Bose's most devoted followers. Slowly Bose built up his team. Bewildered by the succession of European events and unable to comprehend how they could help India, these Indians, as Girija Mookerjee recalls, "fell under Subhas' charm". It was a personal bond and one they willingly maintained for the rest of their lives.

Their first task was to organise the programmes for the *Azad Hind*, Free India radio, which began broadcasting within days of the Centre's opening. Initially the programme was simple: forty-five minutes consisting of a talk by Bose, who was still His Excellency Orlando Mazzotta, and some news. Soon there were at times some thirty-five Indians working at the Centre, and Bose had begun to tell them of his other plan: an *Azad Hind Fauz* - a Free India Army.

He drew, Hasan recalls, the necessary historical parallels. Ireland had raised a revolutionary army, but when she had declared independence no important power had backed her. The United States had won her freedom because France, a leading nation, had aided her. Along with military strength, there had to be foreign political help. For the handful of men gathered round him this was a sensation. They had never heard anything like it before. Hasan's senses "told him it was absolute rot and nonsense this fellow was speaking". There were never more than ten or twelve followers at such gatherings, some twenty-thirty Indians in Germany, some fifty in all occupied Europe . Yet "here was a man who was talking of having an army of thousands and a diplomatic corps of hundreds. But somehow or other so great was his personality that you believed him. Every one of us believed in this fantasy."

About this time a German army officer, Lt-Col. Soldtman, interrogated a first group of 1,000 Indian soldiers and thirty-seven officers at the Italian POW camp at Derna, and reported that they were strongly anti-British. The SS were eager to organise them but, despite German requests, the Italians refused to hand them over, claiming that they needed them for their own immediate propaganda activities. Other attempts followed, including one to recruit Pushtu-speaking Indian POWs. By June 1941, however, Indian POWs had begun to assemble at Annaberg near Dresden, in Saxony. They had come from various places: the camp at Lamsdorf in Silesia and the larger, almost cage-like camps in Cyrenaica.

On 16 October 1941 Ribbentrop himself revived the idea of using Indian POWs for "broadcasting purposes in case of a possible advance into the Caucasus, into Iran, etc." He wanted everything to be "fully ready for action in about two months". And money was no problem. As the Foreign Office note concluded, "In so far as funds were needed for this he was willing to make them available". Ribbentrop's views were meant for Hitler, who "unambiguously" recommended the setting-up of an Indian Legion. But again the Italians intervened. A summit conference between the Free India Centre and the Italian Ufficio India in Berlin in December 1941 had agreed that work on the formation of the Indian Legion should start immediately; an infantry battalion was to be raised and all training was to take place under German command. But the Italians were tardy in releasing the Indian POWs to the Germans, a delay which led ultimately to the Shedai explosion and, despite Hitler, the OKW continued to treat the whole exercise as an experiment, as Trott bitterly minuted.

The Germans had a lot to learn about Indian soldiers and the conditioning they had received under centuries of British rule. The British had not only split the Indians into martial and non-martial races, but also made sure that the Army was divided into watertight religious and caste compartments. The British did not, as Indian nationalists alleged, create these divisions, they merely maintained and strengthened them to support their claim that Indians were too divided to be ever able to govern themselves. So, in the Indian Army every platoon had a Muslim, Hindu and Sikh section, which never mixed. The different communities had their own greetings. When Bose first said Indians needed a common greeting, Hasan, who had an impish sense of fun, suggested, "Hello", which Bose found far from funny. Then Hasan came up with *Jai Hind* and it became the unifying greeting to symbolise the unity of the new India Bose was seeking to build.

Food was another problem. In Annaberg there were complaints about food and the disregard of caste habits. The Hindus, of course, did not eat beef and the Muslims did not eat pork. But more than that there was the problem created by *halal*, the Muslim religious injunction of slaughtering animals in a particular fashion. In the British Indian Army, as the different Indians never mixed, this did not matter since there were separate kitchens and mess facilities. Now in Europe they ate together and the different slaughtering methods led to some troops getting larger pieces of meat than others. Eventually these problems were solved, but Hasan and others had to work hard, and the complexities of Indian life often defeated the Germans.

Later, German investigators researching the attitudes of Indian POWs in north Africa discovered that the British policy of isolating them from politics had worked wonderfully well: the soldiers were indeed apolitical, as their British masters wanted, more interested in the Vedas than political literature. Asked why they were fighting Germany, they replied it was because "the present lord of India" wished it; they had joined the army to avoid hunger. It was only the swastika on the investigator's uniform that brought any response and that from the Hindus for whom it is an ancient Hindu religious symbol (although the Nazis had reversed its shape). Worse, though the Germans had separated the Indians from their British officers, they had not segregated the men from the NCOs, who had a long history of active collaboration with the British.

When Bose visited the Annaberg camp in December 1941 he met with hostility and anger. Carefully coached by the NCOs, the men refused to listen to him. But Bose was persistent, and the next day, in personal interviews, some of the anger melted. The men were curious about ranks, pay, loss of British benefits and possible new enticements from the Germans. To all this, Bose's reply was the same. This is for India. This is not a mercenary army like the British Army: you are fighting for a cause. But, as ever, he was a good listener, and many went away convinced of his sincerity and his cause. On his return to Berlin Bose decided to separate the NCOs from the men and send Swami and Hasan, to the camps. For recruitment various methods were used. It was found that the most effective were the traditional ones: more money, more food, Red Cross parcels and access to women.

The Red Cross parcels play a curious part in this story. Quite unwittingly, the British helped the formation of the Legion but they also created tensions with the Germans. The British, worried that their Indian solders might defect, made sure through neutral countries that they received their mail and Red Cross parcels with food and clothing from England, Canada and the United States. The British knew some of their Indian POWs had joined the Legion but while the war lasted did not know who had and who had not.

One German soldier, envious of the Red Cross bounty, wrote:

> Every fortnight they get a three-pound parcel from the English Red Cross with rice, cigarettes and chocolates, tins of wheat flour and other first class stuff. As against this the real value of troops is nothing. They are handled with kid gloves. If a hard word is said to them they remind one that here they are volunteers and only German soldiers for propaganda purposes.

Milan Hauner, the great historian of this period, wrote:

> According to almost unanimous statements made by captured German members of the Indian units, without the parcels the Legion would have had to have been disbanded. Not only were these parcels the chief means of keeping the men content but they used them extensively and quite successfully to attract the favours of local women. Not surprisingly these parcels were also used as bribes within the Legion and many German officers kept their own families and girlfriends supplied with these extra rations.

Not all German members of the Legion benefited and those that did not were angry. One German soldier complained about these "romantic fellows with turbans, thick beards and plaits" who got all the goodies. But for all the German girl friends the Red Cross parcels provided, sex still remained a problem for the Legion. Ultimately, writes Hauner, in Holland in the summer of 1943 brothels were set up for the Indians.

There is no proof that violence was ever used in recruitment, and in the end around 4,000 of the 15,000 POWs joined the Legion, only a handful of whom were officers. Two camps were set up. One at Regenwurm near Mesertiz in the Frankfurt/Oder district was a *Sonderkommando*, a special elite unit, which had 90 trainees. A second larger camp at Frankenberg, which then moved to Koenigsbruck in Saxony had about 3,000 men. Recruitment here inched up during 1942. On 15 September 1942 Bose, after a visit to Koenigsbruck, wrote to Emilie saying the numbers were 740. In a letter written to her, probably the following month, the numbers had gone up to 1100. After long deliberations the Frankenberg unit came under the overall command of General Friedrich Fromm, commander in chief of the Home Army. The other camp came under the overall control of Admiral Wilhelm Canaris, head of the Abwehr, the German counter intelligence service. Both men were later implicated in the Stauffenberg bomb plot and executed. Just as Bose had fallen into anti-Nazi hands of the German Foreign Office, so the Indian Legion was the ultimate responsibility of the very officers who were plotting to remove Hitler.

If recruitment to the Indian Legion was not easy, then the one Indian Bose desperately wanted in Berlin was proving just as elusive. First there was the problem of finding him, then persuading him to come and work for Bose. The person Bose sought was Nambiar. Almost as soon as he had arrived in Germany he had asked Emilie about him. Nambiar had tried hard to keep out of the clutches of the Germans. When Hitler occupied Czechoslovakia, Nambiar had escaped via Zurich to England, then moved to Paris. When France fell, he moved around the south of France, which was then under the control of Vichy France. He was in Foix with his French girlfriend Mademoiselle de Saussure, living at the home of Swami Siddeshwarananda of the Ramakrishna Mission, when, in the third week of August 1941 Dr Oesterreich of the German Embassy in Paris visited him and said Bose wanted to see him.

He went to Paris where he lunched with Shedai and Werth. At the lunch Bose said little. Next day he told him of his plans, describing how India was ripe for revolution, and that this was a great opportunity to work with the Axis against the British. Nambiar wanted a free India but did not like the idea of working with the Nazis, and resisted Bose's blandishments for nearly six months. It was not until January 1942 that he finally arrived in Berlin; even then Werth had to go to France to bring him there. He was accompanied by another Indian, Girija Mookerjee. By then he felt he could not refuse Bose, and was convinced the British would lose the war. Mookerjee, like Nambiar, was an anti-Nazi Indian nationalist. He had lived most of the 1930s in England, and at one stage been repatriated back to India as a destitute person. But he had only got as far as Italy where he had sold his steamship ticket and stayed on in Europe. He had come to know Nambiar in Prague where he worked for Professor Lesny and had just escaped as the Nazis arrived. When Nambiar came to London in 1939 he visited him. At the start of the war, he was a correspondent for the *Hindustan Times* in Paris, and when the Nazis arrived, he was jailed. Released from jail in March 1941, he had just re-established contacts with Nambiar when the call from Bose came. In one of the many ironic twists of the war, being British subjects resident in Vichy France, they received 1,750 francs each month as financial assistance provided by the British through the American consulate in Vichy.

Mookerjee provides the further twist to this story of the Indians recruited by Bose in war time Germany. As he worked for the Free India Centre, as a broadcaster and script writer, he got to know Freda Kretschmar. They became lovers and when the European war ended IPI, which had kept a careful watch on Mookerjeee since his student days in England in the 30s, reported that he was joining her in Baden Baden to move back to France.

In January 1942 Nambiar and Mookerjee arrived in Berlin just in time to celebrate Bose's forty fifth birthday at his villa. They lunched with Bose and then attended the tea party Emilie had organised. Bose made a speech, administered the free India oath and they signed the visitors book. Nambiar and Mookerjee stayed on for dinner and Nambiar could see the enthusiasm Bose had generated in this small group. The next day Bose took them to the Free India Centre and announced Nambiar as his deputy. Two days later on 26 January the Indians celebrated independence day at the Kaiserhof Hotel. Four hundred guests including diplomats were present, but Bose was not there. He had told Nambiar that it was not yet time to shed the identity of Mazzotta, "he preferred to wait for an occasion when his appearance would be more dramatic" He knew it could not be far away. The long winter of 1941, which had been a hard one for him in Berlin, was coming to an end.

The previous months had seen no progress on the Free India declaration and, as Bose was still shrouded in the disguise of Mazzotta, he could do nothing about the campaign against him in the British press. On 10 November 1941 Eric Conran-Smith, secretary of the Home Department of the government of India had told the Indian Council of State that Bose had "gone over to the enemy" and had signed a pact with the Axis designed to lead to the invasion of India.

This marked the start of a tremendous propaganda offensive against Bose by the British press, which had so far been speculating in which *ashram* he was hiding and how he had escaped. They termed him "Bose the quisling", a theme that the right wing papers like the *Daily Express* and the *Evening News* maintained till well into the 1960s. The *Daily Mail,* with a photograph of Bose under the caption "Indian turns traitor", announced: "Indian Quisling No. 1 Flees to Hitler". The *Daily Express* carried a photograph of Bose in a long overcoat and Gandhi cap talking to a German guard at a Berlin zoo in 1934, and the heading: "Indian leader plans invasion 5th Column"; while for the *Empire News* it was "Chandra Bose Haw-Haw". "Subhas Chandra Bose, India's Quisling No. 1, is to become the Indian 'Lord Haw-Haw' broadcasting from Berlin," an article that was a mixture of half truths and pure invention.

Bose could do nothing about these lies, for he was still incognito, and he was unable even to get an audience with Ribbentrop. With German armies at the gate of Moscow, they were sure of victory in the east, and a declaration on Free India could be seen as a ploy to try and get England to accept terms. If, after Russia's collapse, England still refused to accept terms then the declaration could be made. About this time Alfred Rosenberg showed Hitler a paper on how the British controlled India, a document Hitler found interesting as a model for the rule of Russia. Bose is said to have vowed never to see Ribbentrop again but Trott persuaded him to write once more to the foreign minister. He helped with the draft, an effort that Trott was very proud off. It worked, although the invitation was hardly gracious.

On 29 November 1941, a messenger arrived at Bose's villa at midnight and Subhas was forced to get up from his bed and go to the Wilhelmstrasse. The midnight hour spent with Ribbentrop was dismal. After thanking the German government for its help and hospitality, Bose showed him the British press cuttings and said it was necessary to make a reply "so that his followers would not defect". He also raised a problem that had been bothering him ever since Hitler had come to power: the derogatory references to Indians in *Mein Kampf.* These, he said, "had been exploited in an unfavourable sense by English propaganda. It was by far the most important thing to let the Indian people know what the Führer thought about India because the Indian people did not know either Germany or the views held there."

Ribbentrop was more interested in haranguing Bose about his own world view. The time was still not opportune for the declaration on India: "German policy did not think much of declarations with no force behind them, because it was possible that the opposite effect from the one desired could occur." Look at Iraq and Syria, warned Ribbentrop. They had both been lost to Germany. India was not quite the same but "there, too, however, one should proceed cautiously and only say something concrete when a success was in view, for example when German troops had crossed the Caucasus."

Only one thing was certain: England would be destroyed and her empire would fall. When Bose, who doubted whether Hitler was quite sincerely ill-disposed to England, asked if this was the Führer's view, Ribbentrop replied that "the Führer believed in the final defeat of England." The only thing Ribbentrop offered Bose was a possible meeting with Hitler, who had met the Grand Mufti of Jerusalem the day before, despite the fact that he had arrived in Berlin much later than Bose. Bose must have felt like giving up. What changed his mood was news from the East.

In October 1941 Colonel Yamamoto Bin, Japanese military attaché in Berlin, received a telegram from the Imperial Japanese headquarters instructing him to "make a direct observation of a man named Bose and report". Japan, feverishly preparing for war, had just started taking an interest in India and Bose. But with Bose under the personal "protection" of the German Foreign Ministry, Yamamoto could make no headway. It required the personal intervention of the Japanese ambassador, Lieutenant-General Hiroshi Oshima, for the Germans to allow the Japanese to meet him. They met in late October 1941 and Bose, who had attempted to contact the Japanese himself, made an impassioned plea for Indian independence. India had long looked to Japan for guidance and light. Japan's victory over Russia in 1905 had marked the regeneration of Asia after a long slumber, and now she must help India awaken to light and freedom. Yamamoto and Oshima were impressed, and soon Bose became a frequent and welcome visitor to their embassy. After Japan attacked the United States at Pearl Harbour in December 1941, and progressed triumphantly through the Far East, Bose congratulated Oshima and Yamamoto and posed the question: When could he return east?

In truth, India had not figured much in Japan's plans. In 1940 when Japan's intended Asian empire, the Greater East Asia Co-Prosperity Sphere was defined, India was not part of it. The Indo-Burmese frontier was to be the western limit of Japan's conquests. Japan had wanted to reserve India as a bait to get the Russians to join the Tripartite Pact joining Germany, Italy and Japan. Just before Pearl Harbour, a war ministry paper had outlined a Japanese empire from the Arctic to the Antarctic and from the west coast of India to the eastern islands of the Caribbean Sea, but during the detailed plans these ideas were quickly buried. There were indeed some ideologues in Tokyo who imagined a vast Japanese empire that included India. The Scientific Research Institute for Total War planned a Central Government for Ceylon, which would include the coastal strip of India starting just north of Goa. In another plan the empire would be made up of three concentric circles with India in one circle, as an independent country, but with a government far removed from ideas of liberalism and self-determination. These ideas, however, never became official government policy.

Japan's interest was concentrated on regions considered vital for the survival of her empire: Hong Kong, Indo-China, the Philippines, Malaya, Singapore, the Dutch East Indies and Burma, with a neutral Thailand, and a possible expansion into Australia and New Zealand, but not India. Japan had to fight Britain, and that involved fighting Indian troops in British pay. Japanese planners appreciated the need for subversion, resulting in Army headquarters'planning which led to a major Japanese involvement in the sub-continent. These moves took time to mature, and were delayed inevitably by the suspicion and jealousy with which the Axis partners viewed each other. The question of whether Bose should be transferred to East Asia was also entangled with the quest for an Axis declaration on India. The whole matter started a game between the Axis powers that would take nearly a year to resolve. The Japanese expressed an interest in issuing a declaration on India, using Rome as a conduit to reach Berlin. The Italians proposed a conference which opened in Berlin on 7 December, the day Japan unleashed ther war in Asia Bose attended, Shedai came from Rome. There was talk of a joint Italian-German policy, but it achieved nothing. Two months later Shedai would try to get the Japanese interested in his ideas. Had they nibbled Bose might have been in trouble, but the Japanese did not even bother to reply.

Bose met Oshima on 17 December and Woermann the following day urging them to both issue a declaration and transfer him to the east. In the weeks and months that followed the Germans and the Japanese adopted contradictory positions at various times. Ribbentrop approved the idea of Bose going to east Asia and pressed Oshima for a Axis declaration on India but the Japanese were dubious about the declaration saying they must wait until their troops were nearer India. While Ribbentrop vetoed a call by Indian nationalists in east Asia to send Bose there, the Japanese pressed for an Axis declaration. Hitler wanted nothing to do with it. He still saw India as a corner stone of the British empire. As this game was played out, Japan's relentless conquest of British colonies created its own logic, and was the cue for Bose to finally shed his Italian guise. He had danced a jig when Paris fell, seeing this as the foretaste of the coming fall of Britain and the liberation of India. He viewed the fall of Singapore on 15 February 1942 as the death-knell of the dominance the Europeans had exercised over the Asians for almost two centuries. From now on a handful of whites could no longer continue to rule millions of brown people founded on white supremacist racial idea. Singapore had turned that idea on its head. Although defended by 139,000 troops, Malaya and Singapore had fallen to fewer than 65,000 invading Japanese. The fall of Singapore was a momentous occasion for India, and indeed for all Asians fighting European domination. Bose made the most of the moment.

On 19 February 1942, Bose wrote to Woermann saying that he was now prepared to reveal his real identity. He had waited for a year for the Axis to make clear its policy. Now he could wait no more.He could not allow this historic opportunity to go to waste. Bose had heard General Tojo's speech in the Japanese House of Peers marking the capture of Singapore. Amidst the usual rhetoric there was a pointed note which, as Hauner has rightly said, sounded like a head master lecturing a child.Tojo told Indians to get out of"the spell of Britain's power and propaganda" and not waste "this God-sent opportunity".

There were other reasons for Bose moving east. Japan's incredible advances had prompted the British,despite Churchill's opposition, to try and make a deal with the Indian nationalists.Just as Singapore was falling Generalissimo Chiang Kai-shek and his wife went to India. Ignoring furious protests by Churchill, Chiang Kai-shek insisted on visiting Gandhi. While he wanted India to join with China in the fight against Japan, he also wanted Britain to give "real political power to the people of India." Bose's immediate plan was to broadcast over German, Italian and Japanese radio stations. While the Italians readily agreed, it took Ribbentrop more than a week to get Japanese agreement. Finally on 27 February, more than a year after leaving Calcutta, Bose broke cover and for the first time broadcast openly over Azad Hind Radio. India's moment of liberation had come:

> For about a year I have waited in silence and patience for the march of events and now that the hour has struck, I have come forward to speak. The fall of Singapore means the collapse of the British Empire, and the end of the iniquitous regime which it has symbolised and the dawn of a new era in Indian history.

Bose's statement was broadcast and re-broadcast several times over Axis radios from Berlin, from Rome and from Tokyo. Goebbels was suitably impressed. He recorded in his diary: "Bose's appeal has made a deep impression on world public opinion.The crisis in India can no longer be denied" — though he recognised that nothing tangible would emerge until the Japanese gained some more victories.

Bose's presence in Berlin was still not revealed. Goebbels intervened at the last minute to stop it.As he noted in his diary,"For the present it is a good thing to have Bose functioning from an anonymous centre.There will always come some proper moment for us to reveal that he is in our midst...They still don't know in London where Bose really is. I shall see to it that he continues to remain camouflaged. He is to be uncovered only after he has been received by the Fuehrer."

On 26 February 1942, Bose attended a meeting organised by Colonel Erwin Lahousen, of the Abwehr, between the Abwehr and Japanese military representatives. He submitted an ambitious eleven-point proposal for co-ordinated Axis propaganda: Rangoon should become the centre of Indian propaganda, Bose himself should go there. Burma, he was convinced, would be set free by the Japanese, and this would have a tonic effect on India. Indian nationalists should invite Axis powers to India in order to prevent anti-Axis uprisings, and Japan should advance into India accompanied by Indian volunteers. Bose's men would be instructed to start sabotage activities. The end result would be the perfect scenario: the Germans would advance through the Caucasus, the Japanese Navy would seize the coastal cities of Chittagong, Calcutta, Madras, Karachi and Bombay, and India would be free. The Germans still did appear keen on a Free India declaration. On 22 February a new draft appeared, and while Bose was presenting his ideas Trott was drawing up a detailed day-by-day programme.This started with a public statement by Bose, followed by a meeting with Hitler and then by the declaration. Italy quickly agreed. But despite repeated requests by

Ribbentrop, Japan made no positive response, either on the declaration or the plans for India. On 28 February Bose broadcast again. On 1 March Goebbels recorded in his diary:

> We have succeeded in prevailing upon the Indian nationalist leader Bose to issue an imposing declaration of war against England. It will be published most prominently in the German press and commented upon. In that way we shall now begin our official fight on behalf of India, even though we don't as yet say it openly.

In the face of the Japanese refusal to divulge their plans for India the German efforts died a natural death: the declaration was once again buried and, when Bose asked for free leave to proceed to the East, Ribbentrop brusquely turned him down.

Bue at this very moment in Britain Bose and his efforts in Germany were already making an impact on official policy.

The Raj was increasingly alarmed by Bose's activities and the relentless Japanese advance. Just before Pearl Harbour, politics in India had seemed dead. Azad, the Congress president, emerging from prison, felt, as he wrote, "a sense of humiliation we seemed to be the victims of circumstances, and not the masters of our destiny!" The Congress was no nearer its goal of freedom. But as Japan advanced the Congress Right was once again willing to talk to the British. The Raj released the Congress leaders from prison and at a meeting in Bardoli, between 23 and 30 December 1941, Rajagopalachari and Azad were able to persuade the working committee to offer to co-operate in any resistance against the Japanese in return for freedom. This encouraged the most prominent Indian collaborators to send a message to Churchill, then in America, calling for a fresh initiative to solve the "Indian problem."

Churchill and Amery struggled to come up with an answer that would look progressive yet preserve British rule. Although Churchill and Roosevelt had proclaimed the Atlantic Charter in August 1941, pledging freedom to all peoples as the war goal of the Allies, Churchill in a House of Commons speech had made it clear that this did not apply to "India, Burma and other parts of the British Empire", only " the states and nations now under Nazi yoke". From Delhi Linlithgow was giving Downing Street his usual advice: sit tight, do nothing — we are the rulers, we must rule. Curiously, the Viceroy's main reason for his characteristic conclusion was his fear of Bose's activities. The crucial paragraph of his telegram of 21 January 1942 read:

> Further transfer of power would give marked encouragement to quisling activities. Recent report from military authorities in Eastern India is to the effect that there is a large and dangerous potential 5th column in Bengal, Assam, Bihar and Orissa. And that indeed potential of pro-enemy sympathy and activity in Eastern India is enormous. Sarat Bose[who, as we shall see, had been jailed] has been a lesson. The activities of U Saw and Tin Tut [senior civil servants occupying responsible positions] are another and grave one. I know that we are frequently urged to do something 'to touch the heart of India' and our sympathies naturally lean in that direction. But Cabinet will agree with me that India and Burma have no natural association with the empire, from which they are alien by race, history and religion, and for which as such neither of them have any natural affection, and both are in the empire because they are conquered countries which have been brought there by force, kept there by our controls, and which hitherto it has suited to remain under our protection.

It was a revealing paragraph. Linlithgow was admitting to a colossal failure by the Raj. The highest British representative in India was confessing that after two centuries of British rule there was nothing that tied Indians to the British except British power. Now that British might was being destroyed by an Asian power, and Japan was proving that claims of European superiority were nonsense, the entire structure of the Raj was in danger. The repercussions were immediately felt. Attlee, who had been pressing for progress on India, calling for a statement of policy or a promise of future constitutional action, was aghast. Churchill, of course, had often declared that he had "not become His Majesty's First Minister to preside over the liquidation of the British Empire"; but events had forced his hand. Early in 1942 Roosevelt told close friends that he thought India was lost to the Japanese, and Churchill himself told King George VI that Burma, Ceylon, Calcutta, Madras and part of Australia might fall. The War Cabinet now preferred to listen to Attlee, who was convinced that the viceroy was a disaster, and that until something was done India would fall to the Japanese, and Bose.

On 19 February 1942, four days after the fall of Singapore, Stafford Cripps and Attlee moved. Cripps, recently back in London from Moscow where he had been considered a great success as ambassador, entered the War Cabinet, and Attlee set about drafting the proposals which Cripps took to India. These were substantially the same proposals as the so-called August offer made in August 1940 by Amery. Both promised India the right to frame its constitution after the war in return for immediate co-operation during the war. Cripps went further in saying that after India became a dominion, "immediately after the cessation of hostilities" the new Indian Union would have the right to leave the British Empire. However, any province of British India or an Indian princely state could abstain from joining the Indian Union, acknowledging that the India thus created might not be the whole land mass. During the war there would be no changes. The viceroy's executive council would have an Indian majority, but key posts such as commander-in-chief, home affairs, finance and external affairs would be in European hands.

Despite this turn of events, Bose still felt unhappy. While Cripps flew eastwards, Bose left Berlin for Bad Gastein, frustrated, angry and at a loss as to what to do. Once again the Germans had promised much but delivered little. When in mid-March an official arrived to ask him to return to Berlin Bose lambasted the Germans. They could not, he said, be serious about Indian independence. They kept on postponing a declaration of policy, and they had not even helped in the recruitment of the Indian Legion. Perhaps the whole Indian show was part of an effort to reach a sort of compromise with the British. After all, Bose had heard the Japanese speculating that the Nazis would never let him go in case he became a useful bargaining piece in any negotiations with the British. The visitor suggested a meeting with the Fuehrer; which, it was hoped, would entice Bose back to Berlin. Bose continued to sulk in Bad Gastein until, after much persuasion by Trott, he returned to Berlin and began broadcasting to Indians about the Cripps mission.

The Cripps proposals were not as great an advance as the British government made out. In fact, as Amery pointed out to a disturbed Linlithgow, who was horrified at the idea of a mission from England and happy when it ended in failure, it was a holding operation: a limited exercise that would appease many people yet give nothing away. Neither, however, had realised what the personal effect of Cripps would be. At his first meeting with Maulana Azad, the Congress president, Cripps assured him that the expanded Executive Council would consist only of Indian members, and would in fact function like the British Cabinet. The viceroy would be a titular head, and the secretary of state for India reduced to the role played by the Dominion secretary in relation to white dominions such as Australia and New Zealand. Cripps was promising more than he could deliver: a horrified Linlithgow threatened to resign, Amery and Churchill rebuked Cripps, and Azad and the Congress soon realised that the British were once again asking for co-operation during the war in return for 'jam tomorrow'. Debate continues as to who was actually responsible for the talks breaking down. Nehru's official biographer, Sarvepalli Gopal, blames Cripps, while Cripps, to his dying day, believed that it was Gandhi who sabotaged his plans.

It was on Gandhi that Bose's activities and broadcasts had had their biggest impact.

Azad, to his shock, discovered that while Gandhi still had no clear idea about the war, he was doubtful of an Allied victory; and, as he noted in *India Wins Freedom*:

> Subhas Bose's escape to Germany had made a great impression on Gandhi. He had not formerly approved many of Bose's actions but now I found a change in his outlook. Many of his remarks convinced me that he admired the courage and resourcefulness Bose had displayed in making his escape from India. His admiration for Subhas Bose unconsciously coloured his view about the whole war situation.

Gandhi was also a keen listener to Bose's broadcasts. He asked Ranga whether he had listened to Bose and said, "He sounds very happy and very active, and he is doing his work."

The failed Cripps mission set Bose's adrenalin flowing again. In a series of broadcasts, he denounced Cripps and the Indians who were now seeking a compromise with the British. The British Empire was breaking up anyway: "It will soon disappear from the face of the earth and consequently, even if Britain were to offer to India terms that are far more conciliatory than the British proposals, there is no meaning in entering into a compromise with such a power." And if Britain by some chance won the war, how could the Indians enforce the guarantee? Had the collaborators forgotten, he asked, that ever since 1927 the Congress had year after year declared that it would have nothing to do with a British war? In 1939 the Congress had expelled M.N. Roy for suggesting co-operation with the British. Yet the very same leaders were going back on their words. "We are, therefore, waiting, " Bose added, bitingly, " to see what disciplinary action will be taken against these gentlemen," men who all their political lives called themselves faithful followers of Gandhi.

The Germans claimed that these broadcasts had an immense impact, Goebbels noting in his diary that "Bose's propaganda conducted and guided from here is gradually getting on the nerves of the British." The modern British view is that their effects were negligible, although certainly a great many people in India listened to him.

There was a convincing testimony of Gandhi's sympathies when, in the middle of Cripps' mission, news came that Bose had died in a plane crash. Though Bose was broadcasting openly from Berlin it was still not known where he really was and many believed the report that he had perished in an aircraft carrying some Indian nationalists to Tokyo. While Bose in Berlin fretted that he could not convey the correct news to his family, Gandhi consoled Bose's mother. "The whole nation mourns with you the death of your brave son. I share your sorrow to the full. May God give you courage to bear this unexpected loss."

Nehru, who would soon say publicly, " I shall also fight Mr Subhas Bose and his party along with Japan if he comes to India. Mr Bose acted very wrongly though in good faith", was most upset about this message. Gandhi, referring to Nehru's reaction, sorrowfully told Ranga later that "Some people did not like it." Cripps was appalled. Many in India had mourned Bose's death, but for a man like Gandhi – a believer in non-violence – to do so was, for Cripps, the final proof that the British could never work with that old man. Gandhi, he concluded, was determined to prevent a compromise.

What Cripps did not know was that, Bose apart, there was another man in Berlin who was hoping for his failure. This was Adolf Hitler. India figured quite often in his table talks around this time. On 3 March 1942 he said, " If the English give India back her liberty, within 20 years India will have lost her liberty again". The Fuehrer despised Cripps, a drawing room Bolshevik who lived like a monk. Given the choice Hitler preferred Churchill. Churchill was older and drank and smoked excessively, but would have preserved the Empire and not given India independence. "Cripps gaining control would mean the end of the Empire," said Hitler. As the Japanese had advanced to India's border, Hitler felt unhappy about the decline of the white man, and spoken of giving the British 20 divisions to "help throw back the yellow men." On 27 March 1942 his table talk recorded him saying, "The Indian world has already been so disturbed by the presence of the Japanese on its frontiers, and by the fall of Singapore, that the man of compromise, Nehru, has been eclipsed by Bose".

As if to underline how confused Nazi policy was on India, Ribbentrop saw Cripps' failure as Churchill's greatest defeat. His reasoning was that there was now a profound domestic crisis in India and a very favourable Axis military position providing an opportunity for a joint Axis declaration on India. The Japanese were now interested, Mussolini supported it and Ribbentrop urged it on Hitler. Hitler had always been worried that any such declaration would not please "peace-favouring circles in Britain" who would see it as a German attempt to prise India away from the British Empire which he still wanted to guarantee. But Ribbentrop argued that the failure of the Cripps Mission would force those "peace-favouring circles in Britain" to sue for peace to prevent the Axis from implementing the declaration.

The failure of the Cripps mission marked a watershed for both the Congress and Bose. The Congress, and Gandhi in particular, were now convinced that there could be no future in negotiations with the British, while Bose increasingly turned to Japan. Japan's attempts to organise her own group of Indians had by now progressed further than Germany's. Her amazing conquest of the British colonies had produced tens of thousands of Indian POWs and also many prospective Indian leaders.

Two Army officers of very different backgrounds had played a crucial role in this. One was a Japanese major called Iwaichi Fujiwara, an idealistic intelligence official. Fujiwara was that rare exception; a Japanese who truly wanted to act as a liberator. His notes written in 1941-42 urged Japan to "eschew a Machiavellian policy and, standing on the basis of freedom and equality, assist with all our strength the attainment of Indian independence." Three days before Pearl Harbour he had concluded a deal in Bangkok with Pritam Singh, a Sikh who organised the Independent League of India. The agreement specified that Japan would help India gain freedom but not ask for any concessions in free India. In return Indians in East Asia, regardless of caste or creed, would join Singh's organisation and Pritam Singh would help Fujiwara subvert the loyalty of the Indian soldiers fighting for the British. One of these soldiers was a 33 year old Sikh captain in the 1st Battalion of the 14th Punjab Regiment, Mohan Singh (no relation of Pritam Singh).

On the morning of 15 December, the day after Britain had surrendered in that part of northern Malaya in a small place called Alor Star, Mohan Singh met Pritam and Fujiwara. His conversion from the apolitical Indian solder to a revolutionary appears to have been sparked by his shrewd sense that Britain's defeat was India's opportunity. On the last day of 1941, while Pritam Singh watched, Mohan Singh signed an agreement with Fujiwara to help form a "liberation army" of Indians from prisoners of war. Indians, it was emphasised, would be in charge of this army and the Indian Independence League.

Yet this was an agreement at a local level. There existed neither an Imperial Japanese policy on India nor agreement amongst the Indians, many of whom were suspicious of the Japanese and had no desire to see them replace the British as their masters. However all of them were agreed that they wanted Subhas Bose brought from Germany to lead the Army. Mohan Singh had said this to Fujiwara, who passed this on to his superiors.

This was not easy for the Japanese, who had a 'Bose' of their own. His name was Rash Behari Bose. He was no relation of Subhas and was actually an Indian revolutionary from the pre-First World War period. In 1912 he had masterminded a plot to kill Lord Hardinge as the then viceroy rode on an elephant while making a state entry into Delhi. The bomb did not damage Hardinge, except by showering him with gramophone needles, but some of his staff were killed. Rash Behari escaped and after that continued to evade the pursuing British. In 1915 he set a date for an uprising against the British, seeking to suborn British Indian troops for this purpose. The date was 21 February 1915, but a British spy leaked the plans and Rash Behari just managed to escape. He eventually fled to Japan where he became friendly with Sun Yat-Sen, the great Chinese leader, who introduced him to Toyama Mitsuru, the leader of the Kokuryu-kai, the Black Dragon Society, a militant Japanese group that believed in Asia for the Asians. He married the daughter of a Japanese restaurant owner, who gave him two children and by the time Japan entered the Second World War he had been a Japanese citizen for almost two decades. So as Japan's thoughts turned to India they turned to him to organise a conference of Indian nationalists in Tokyo at the end of March 1942.

The basic division between the Indians was between the soldiers, who had suddenly become politicised, and civilians who had lived for decades in Malaya and Singapore, many of them as lawyers educated in the British colonial system. Among the latter group were some who were suspicious of Japan's intentions and saw Rash Behari Bose as a Japanese puppet. This included Pritam Singh and Swami Satyananda Puri, who Subhas Bose had sought to recruit as his agent in East Asia. These two were most vocal in their distrust of the Japanese and wanted Subhas as leader. They intended to make this clear at Tokyo but on their way to the conference their plane crashed leading to misleading news that Subhas Bose had been killed. The night before he died in the plane crash, Swami had told German diplomats in Shanghai how much he distrusted the Japanese. His death left the field clear for Rash Behari Bose.

But Rash Behari Bose did not have it all his own way and through the summer of 1942 there were other conferences of Indians where strong opposition to him was expressed. One in June 1942 in Bangkok passed 35 resolutions to ensure the Japanese would allow Indians to run their own organisation, called for Subhas Bose to be returned to Asia, and declared its allegiance to the principles of the Indian National Congress. Fujiwara urged Tokyo to work with these Indians, but Tojo cabled back, " There is a limit to letting the Indians get their own way." Rash Behari Bose, aware of how distrustful some Indians were of the Japanese, did not let his colleagues see the Tokyo reply, explaining that it was being translated. Tokyo, in turn, watched what the Congress was doing in India and debated as to whether they should support Subhas Bose or the Congress. It took them some time to decide to support Subhas Bose. First they had to consider the older Bose. How would he react to another, more famous leader being brought over to lead the movement? Finally a Japanese official invited Rash Behari to his office and put the question. "In that case," replied Rash Behari modestly, "I would step down."

On 17 April 1942 the Japanese Cabinet decided to "use Subhas Chandra Bose according to present policy and concomitant with the development of the situation of the 10 January decision." On that day it had been decided that Japan would stimulate anti-British propaganda in India and "invite [Bose] to Tokyo and judge his utility value from the standpoint of this policy. At the same time we shall inform him of Japan's national power and the enthusiasm of all Japan for assisting India's independence."

Bose's move to the east was still many months away, but this decision revived Japanese interest in a joint Axis declaration on India. The familiar game was resumed, though this was to be the final round. On 11 April 1942 the Japanese, for the first time, sent their Axis partners a draft declaration on India and the Arab peoples. The Wilhelmstrasse was not impressed: the draft was "too journalistic and little concrete"; while the Italians were worried that the reference to "Arabic peoples" might affect their colonies in that part of Africa under Arab influence. Despite this, they were keen on a declaration, and the German Foreign Office produced yet another draft. This, together with the Japanese one, was presented by Ribbentrop to Hitler on 16 April with a strong recommendation for acceptance. Knowing his Fuehrer, Ribbentrop argued that such a declaration would be welcomed by "peace-favouring circles in Britain", a misconception that Hitler harboured. Hitler was still not convinced, and the next day rejected it. He saw "no point in adhering to such a declaration just when the Japanese want it." Japan's astonishingly rapid progress had revived all his old fears about "the yellow peril'", and when Hitler met Mussolini on 29 April 1942 at Klessheim Castle in Salzburg he used this argument to sweep away Mussolini's pleas in favour of the declaration.

Bose made one more attempt to obtain some sort of statement, and on 4 May, he used the occasion of his visit to Rome for the Schedai activities, to meet Ciano. Ciano noted in his diary:

> I receive Bose, head of the Hindu nationalists. He is unhappy upon learning that the declaration in favour of independence for India has been postponed *sine die*. He believes that in this way we are acting in favour of Japan, which will move on its own account without considering the interests of the Axis. He now thinks the British domination of India is coming to an end. British forces are small and Indian troops have no desire to fight. Naturally, we must take these declarations by Bose for what they are, because is trying to bring grist to his mill.

The next day Bose met Mussolini and for all Ciano's hostility, Bose found Mussolini more receptive. Ciano's diary records:

> I go with Bose to see the Duce. A long conference without any new developments, except the fact that Mussolini allowed himself to be persuaded by the arguments put forth by Bose to obtain a tripartite declaration in favour of Indian independence. He has cabled the Germans proposing, contrary to the Salzburg decisions, proceeding at once with the declaration. I feel Hitler will not agree to it very willingly.

Ciano was right. Hitler would not agree to a declaration. He was,however, considerably upset that Mussolini had seen Bose before he had. On his return to Berlin, Bose was surprised to be told that Hitler would now meet him.

The Bose-Hitler meeting has generated historical controversy as to when it actually took place. The eleventh volume of *Netaji Collected Works* states that it was on 28 May 1942 in the Reich Chancellory in Berlin. But this author has accepted the authority of Milan Hauner, who explains that the date of 29 May was given out by the German Press Agency as a result of the desire to coordinate the announcement with the Japanese and the Italians. Hauner has no doubt it took place on 27 May at Hitler's headquarters in east Prussia.

On that day in 1942 Bose flew to Rastenburg in East Prussia, now part of Poland, where Hitler had built special headquarters, known as the Wolf's Lair, shortly before the start of his Russian campaign. Set in the deep Prussian forest, it was meant to defend Hitler from enemy bombing or parachute landings, although in the event none came. Every effort was made to make the headquarters look inconspicuous. Even the little rail station, where Hitler's train was always kept waiting under steam, had no name on the platform, just the codename Gorlitz. And even from this station it was not possible to see the headquarters, which lay in forest paths beyond checkpoints protected by guards and marked as a restricted area. As Bose landed at Rastenburg, he saw nothing of the headquarters and only realised he was there when his car drove up at the first checkpoint. Then he saw bunkers camouflaged in grey and green, with 15-ft thick walls of reinforced concrete, squatting in the wood like primeval monsters.

Dr Paul Otto Schmidt, the German Foreign Office interpreter who often took foreign visitors there, was present during the Bose meeting. He sets the scene:

> The quarters occupied by Hitler and his military staff were in the heart of the forest, miles from any human habitation. They consisted of comfortable

> hutments, built partly of stone, with wood panelling inside, and were furnished quite simply and in fairly good taste....Anyone coming from the sunny expanses of the surrounding countryside to this encampment in the gloomy East Prussian forest found the atmosphere oppressive. The electric light in Hitler's rooms often had to be on all day. Hitler himself seldom went out-as though even the dim light of the forest was too bright for him-and his entourage only rarely emerged from the dark wood. .. I could well appreciate the oppressiveness of this twilit atmosphere at Headquarters...and always breathed a sigh of relief as I escorted foreign visitors away from the dark forest.... Low corridors , like galleries in a coal mine, ran through these montagnes synthetiques. The rooms were very small and one felt cramped in them, and the dampness from this mass of concrete, artificial light and the perpetual buzzing of ventilating machinery increased one's sense of unreality. It was in this milieu that Hitler, growing daily paler and more puffy, received his foreign visitors. The general effect was of the lair of a legendary evil spirit. Observers less grimly inclined felt themselves to be in film studio. A witty colleague once said to me,'The wood used in the Hansel and Gretel films we've just finished will be taken down tomorrow, and the day after tomorrow we'll start shooting Anthony and Cleopatra; the pyramids are up already.

Bose arrived in heavy, humid summer heat, when there was an infestation of Mosquitoes. This was so bad that some of Hitler's men, despite wearing long leather boots and thick uniforms, also went around with mosquito nets on. Bose first met Ribbentrop, who apologised for not replying to his three letters and warned him not to fly to Japan using the Italian aircraft that Mussolini had offered him, but to take the submarine instead.

In the afternoon Bose finally, met Hitler, 13 months after arriving in Germany. The only picture of the meeting shows Bose in a double breasted suit of the type he liked wearing in Berlin. It is not clear if he was wearing a bow tie which he had also taken to in Berlin. Hitler wore the grey military coat he had donned on the day war had been declared, and which he had vowed not to take off until victory. There is thin, almost whimsical, smile on Hitler's face, and the Swastika emblem is prominent on his chest. But while Schmidt is to Bose's left, as he shakes Hitler's hand, there is no sign of the two other men at the meeting. They were Ribbentrop and Walter Hewel. Hewel had briefly shared Hitler's Landsberg imprisonment in 1923, and then had become a planter in Java. He was now being used as an English expert by Ribbentrop. The photograph is dimly lit, emphasising the gloomy surroundings and matching the mood of this awful meeting.

Neither Bose nor Hitler expressed their real feelings, and both indulged in a fair bit of play acting. Bose gave no hint of his distrust for Hitler, while Hitler gave no indication of his previously expressed contempt for Indians, nor his vision of the British Empire being a model for the German one his armies were creating. Bose found Hitler had recovered from the Russian winter of 1941, when his armies failed to take Moscow and suffered their first defeat. In Salzburg, just a month earlier, Ciano had felt this had taken its toll, and noticed grey hairs on Hitler for the first time. But by the time of the Bose meeting the Germans had won a great victory at Kharkov, with Hitler taking the credit. The start of the battle had been dismal for the Germans. The Russians had surprised them, German generals wanted to withdraw, but Hitler insisted they kept their nerve. There would be no withdrawal. By 22 May it was the Russians who were encircled, with 239,000 Russians taken prisoners and 1,240 tanks captured or destroyed. On the day before the meeting, Rommel had also launched his attack in north Africa, which he hoped would take the German forces to Cairo. The Japanese were still victorous, and Axis fortunes were at their height. Never again would things look so good for them.

Bose was well aware that Hitler rarely gave anyone a chance to talk. He had heard that when Hitler met Mussolini in Salzburg, he had spoken uninterruptedly for an hour and a half. So Bose had decided on a clever opening gambit. As the notes by Schmidt, show, he greeted Hitler "as an old revolutionary," thanking him for the "honour" of meeting him. "The day would forever remain as historical date in his life," he said. Then he thanked Hitler for the help Germany had given him but emphasised that the "actual war of independence had to be fought by India herself. " Yes, he said, the need to get closer to India and use Japanese military help meant he had to go east, but Germany would still remain important. Germany, hoped Bose, would continue to give moral and diplomatic support, so that India would not have to depend solely on Japan. The most surprising moment came when Bose asked the Fuehrer, "as an old and experienced revolutionary" to advise him on the basic principles of revolution.

Hitler must have been surprised to be addressed as an old revolutionary, a phrase he had not heard since the beer hall days. He now saw himself as a soldier, and, ignoring Bose's invitation to opine on revolution, began to lecture Bose on what he saw were the military realities. It was one of his characteristic monologues: part history, part folklore, and much dangerous nonsense. In Schmidt's seven-page printed report, Bose's remarks take just over a page, probably five minutes of conversation. Hitler's words occupied nearly all the rest of the hour or so of the meeting. As a soldier, said Hitler, he never promised what he could not deliver and warned Bose that he "should not forget that the power of a country could only be exercised within the range of its sword." Germany was far away from India, and could do nothing at the moment. But if Germany, like Japan, could get near India then "he (the Fuehrer) would have requested Bose to stay with him, march into India with the German troops and subsequently kindle the revolution against the British". Hitler realised Bose had to leave for Asia, but warned him to take care to work out a safe journey, since he was "too important a personality to let his life be endangered" by an experiment such as flying to Tokyo from Rome. As far as India was concerned, his instincts convinced him that it would take India "one hundred to two hundred years" to become a nation, as it had taken Germany. When Bose boldly interrupted to question the racial slurs on Indians in *Mein Kampf,* Hitler lost some of his fluency, and justified his utterances by saying that weak subject nations could not "build up a united front against the oppressors". In any case, he had had to say those things, in order to discourage passive resistance in Germany from developing along the Indian pattern "which in any case was a completely wrong doctrine".

The meeting ended with Hitler wishing Bose well in his travel plans. But for all this outward goodwill, it had been a disastrous meeting. Bose would later tell friends how impossible the German leader was: a Teutonic version of the Faqir of Ipi, with whom one could not hold a coherent discussion for even a few minutes. But the meeting made Bose a public figure in Germany. It was after leaving Hitler that he held his first press conference, more than 14 months after his arrival in Berlin, and he was to feature increasingly in the German press. The Raj took careful note of this publicity and was worried by Bose's attempts to have the slurs on India in *Mein Kampf* removed. IPI agents in Stockholm reassured them that Bose had approached Martin Bormann, Hitler's deputy, and was unsuccessful in having these passages removed.

Some of the shrewder British newspapers noted that not all Bose's remarks pleased the Germans, particularly a reference to the war lasting a "very long time, possibly several years" This part of his statement was not published in German newspapers. It was not the only restriction Bose faced. Since shortly after his arrival, all his telephone calls had been monitored. The Gestapo watched him closely. Yamamoto gained the impression he was guarded by a "tiger cub". and Bose was wary of communicating even with friends. He and Emilie often walked in the garden when they wanted a private conversation.

But in areas where the Special India Department had greater control, Bose was allowed more freedom. Werth has told us that the radio broadcasts were not censored, although Bose's open letter to Cripps was amended by Ribbentrop. By the summer of 1942 both the Free India Centre and the radio propaganda were at their height, with three radio stations operating. Cripps and his failure stimulated Bose to start two more radio stations. One of these was called "National Congress," which, he told Nambiar, would win over Gandhi to his methods. The third "Azad Muslim" was intended to counter the activities of the Muslim League. Bose was keen that the stations should sound to listeners in India that they were being broadcast from India. Nambiar was not convinced, as it was the same station, and on so few frequencies that most would not be deceived.

Bose's German work was now almost all propaganda. He spent much of the summer of 1942 writing broadcasts, arguing that England would lose the war, and that Indian independence could not coexist with British imperialism. India had to take its destiny in its own hands. The 45-minute broadcasts had lengthened to three hours. There were a variety of languages, ranging from English through Tamil and Telugu to Marathi, and a simple diet of talks was supplemented by Indian music recorded from the BBC. The talks ranged from weekly military reviews, and survey of events to commentaries. An *Azad Hind* magazine had been started, and about 3000 copies of it were printed. While Bose was using the name of Mazzotta, he contributed articles signed with the initials O.M. or used the initials of other staff members.

On 12 June 1942, at his first press conference, he told the world that," I regard myself as a servant of the Indian nation and my present task is to lead the fight for India's independence. But as soon as India is free it will be the duty of the Indian people to decide what form of government they should desire and who should guide the future Indian state". He did mention he had his own ideas, but he spent much time in Berlin working on them. He had studied many types of government, but rejected a Westminster form of democracy for India, insisting that firm state control and centralised planning would be an essential ingredient. He even envisaged a "protection force" to be trained by the German Gestapo. Nambiar says Bose wanted some men trained in police work, others in the German Navy and Air Force or the labour organisation. A group was eventually sent off for police training. This involved six months conventional training , then working with the SS, although they were not given German uniforms in case they decided their police powers. Bose was said later by Nambiar to have had great faith in German training, and later put in a request for the police group to be sent east.

Bose also spent some of the spring and summer of 1942 travelling in German-occupied Europe. In April 1942, with Trott and Nambiar, he went to Prague to meet Reichprotektor Reinhard Heydrich , the man who was, possibly, the architect of the Final Solution. The evil Heydrich, later assassinated by Czech partisans, fascinated Trott. In June, seeking recruits for the Free India Centre, they went together to Belgium and France where Bose met General Arthur Falkenhausen and Arthur Seyss-Inquart. In Paris on 11 June 1942 Bose opened the Free India Centre there, and had a second meeting with Pierre Laval. Bose used the occasion to discuss Axis war aims in India, North Africa, the Mediterranean, Afghanistan and North Africa. Laval argued that whoever won the war both France and India would emerge as free nations. Bose intervened to say, "Were the British to come to France again you would not be able to maintain your optimistic prognosis." Bose then asked the Vichy prime minister about the future of French North Africa, and wondered whether the Germans would alter the *status quo*. Laval was not sure, and Bose said, "I too have my worries about Berlin, I still don't know how correctly it will deal with India after the war." Trott and Nambiar were silent witnesses to these extraordinarily frank comments, ones rare in the Nazi world.

From 14 to 16 July Bose visited Heinrich Himmler at his SS headquarters. Himmler's foreign policy expert Walter Schellenberg was to say of Subhas, "Bose's outstanding intelligence and his mastery of modern propaganda methods made a deep impression on Himmler, and we were therefore considering whether we should not shift our support to him." This was apparently a reference to Himmler's Far East agent Sidi Khan, but the move did not happen.

Bose's best and most spectacular efforts were directed towards the Indian Legion. Problems had continued to dog the Legion. Nambiar has summed them up:

> I often met the commanders of the two groups (Walter) Harbich of the Abwehr and Major Krappe. Harbich was Bose's favourite. Before Legion started it had been planned to send Harbich and Lenz to Afghanistan. Harbich looked like a Pathan and could easily have passed for one but did not know appropriate language. Lenz, working with Uzbecks at Messeritz knew a number of frontier languages.

The Legion's numbers at Meseritz did not increase as much as those at Frankenberg owing to special training imposed by the Germans. The Indian soldiers thought they had special rights: some of the German officers and the NCOs did not understand Indian mentality and used abusive language. Some of the Indian non-combatants could not stand the training, and the Indian POWs were anxious for quick promotion. In July 1942 when the Legion moved to Königsbrück accommodation and training had improved. With German successes in the war more POWs were attracted and regimental strength was reached by January 1943. Nambiar says:

> Bose had never been actually opposed to the idea of the Legion being used for other purposes then fighting the British. I remember him once thinking of employing the Legion in North Africa when Rommel's drive on Alexandria was in progress, as he wanted to associate the Legion with it. At that time he was trying to pay a visit to North Africa himself but was opposed by both Germans and Italians. The proposal was also not well received by Rommel's HQ for military reasons; the Legion would be more of a hindrance than a help. However Krappe and his adjutant Lt. Kutscher went to North Africa and watched operations to gain experience.

Bose rejected plans to transfer the Legion to Greece for training on the grounds the recruits were too raw to be so far away from the influence of the Free India Centre. He also squashed plans to send it to Czechoslovakia. But the Legion did serve as a useful propaganda unit, and in north Africa, in one fortnight in the summer of 1942, the Afrika Korps reported 47 desertions from the retreating British Indian Army. The numbers were not significant, but for Bose they were psychologically important. The British Indian Army was slowly becoming politicised. It was in this direction that he now bent all his energies. With recruitment of volunteers in Germany proving slow, Bose increasingly travelled to Italy to talk to and persuade Indian POWs. Girija Mookerjee observed his efforts:

> I saw how the whole audience was coming under his spell and how they were listening...When he had finished...they had acquired new life, new animation, and new excitement. Most had come out of sheer curiosity. Dozens now asked to be enrolled.
>
> Standing very erect under a tree, this is what he would often tell the POWs:
>
> The English are like the dead snake which the people are afraid of even after its death. There is no doubt that the British have lost this battle...The problem is how to take charge of our country...We are young and we have a sense of

> self-respect. We shall take freedom by the strength of our arms. Freedom is never given, it is taken.

His listeners were peasants, far from home, in unfamiliar, confusing surroundings and full of doubts about what was happening. 1942 was a grim year for the Allies, a year of constant defeat. For many, a Bose speech was the revelation on the road to Damascus. They made this personal pledge: "*Hukam Netajika bajana padega*" –"We shall have to carry out the orders of Netaji." In October 1942, the first Legion battalion paraded in front of Bose and other guests including Yamamoto (who took pictures of the event). Their expansion had meant they were now on the Wehrmacht payroll and had to take a loyalty oath to Hitler. Five hundred Legionaries under Lt-Col. Kurt Krappe declared:

> I swear by God this holy oath that I will obey the leader of the German State and Adolf Hitler as Commander of the German Armed Forces in the fight for freedom of India in which fight the leader is Subhas Chandra Bose and that as a brave soldier I am willing to lay down my life for this oath.

Bose always made sure that he dressed in distinctive Indian clothes for such occasions. Normally he wore suits. There is a photograph of him taken in 1942, when, accompanied by Trott and Nambiar, he visited Himmler's headquarters. He is wearing a suit and looks anonymous. But when inspecting the Legion, he wore what is now Indian national costume: the long Indian tunic buttoned at the neck and a black Gandhi cap on his head. He stood out in the crowd of Germans in their military uniforms. Bose presented to the Legionaries the tricolour of green, white and saffron of the Indian National Congress with a picture of a springing tiger superimposed on it. He told them, "Your names will be written in golden letters in the history of Free India: every martyr in this holy war will have a monument there. I shall lead the army when we march to India together." Yet even as he spoke he knew he would never lead this army to India. Japan increasingly beckoned him, and the Legion was now a footnote in his story.

Back in Berlin, Bose renewed his efforts to find a way to return to Asia. Despite the Japanese government's decision to invite him, and the agreement in June 1942 between Ribbentrop and Oshima about his transfer, Tokyo had still made no firm moves. On 23 July Bose wrote to Ribbentrop, "In view of the internal developments in India, I would like to be in the Far East in the first week of August, if possible." It was another uncanny Bose prediction. Though Ribbentrop agreed, he could do nothing. When India erupted in anti-British violence during August 1942 Bose was still in Germany, with only the radio to encourage his cause.

Indian nationalist historians have presented the "Quit India" struggle of 1942 as a brilliant movement which very nearly won the war against the British. It was, like all nationalist agitations, a genuinely popular one; but, far from being successful, it was wretchedly led and devised. In fact its leaders were arrested even before it could be launched. That it continued very nearly into the summer of 1943 only revealed the depth of nationalist sentiment, a revelation that surprised both the British and Indian leaders. It was Gandhi's last campaign, and one that exposed the inadequacy of his planning and his dependence on "inner light." Gandhi, as we have seen, had been impressed by Bose's activities, and by mid-1942, he was convinced that the Allies would lose the war. He was also certain that Japan had no evil designs on India and that, if the British left, it would not invade. Nehru was still opposed to any hint that India was not with the Allies in the struggle against the Axis, but, as so often, Gandhi knew India better.

The Indians, far from being pro-Allied, were vehemently anti-British, and if anything they welcomed Japanese victories. They knew all about the belief in racial superiority of the Europeans that underpinned the Raj, and the British government's racially discriminatory behaviour – for example its desertion of its Indian and Chinese subjects in Malaya in the face of Japanese invasion – had deepened this distrust. Many echoed Gandhi's statement "I am so sick of slavery that I am even prepared to take the risk of anarchy."

By May 1942 Gandhi had begun preparing resolutions for the Congress expressing such views; opposition from Azad in particular and Nehru (to an extent) modified them. But when the working committee met between 5 and 14 July 1942, it formulated the policy that came to be known as the "Quit India" resolution. Britain should leave India, it demanded, though Gandhi was now willing to sign an immediate defence pact with the Allies to safe-guard India from Axis aggression. Having made this call for war, Gandhi made no plans to pursue it. Naively, he assumed that the British government would allow him to function, and to scheme for revolution. But as soon as the Congress rumblings became evident, the War Cabinet in London instructed Linlithgow to deport Gandhi to Aden, and the other members of the working committee to Nyasaland. A warship stood by off Bombay for this purpose, but the viceroy rejected the deportations but agreed on severe repression.

On the evening of 8 August 1942 the AICC met in Bombay and passed the Quit India resolution by an overwhelming majority. In the early hours of the next morning the British government unleashed its carefully prepared counter offensive. Gandhi, Nehru, Azad and many others, down to the lowest level of Congress leadership, were arrested. India was placed under virtual military control. In spite of this the movement continued, a remarkable testimony to the strength of nationalist feeling. Underground radio stations operated for some months afterwards, and there were many successful guerrilla movements; 318 police stations were burnt, 945 post offices raided and 59 trains derailed. It required all the armed might of the British in India to crush the biggest threat to their rule since 1857, although, as Linlithgow wrote to Churchill, the gravity of the situation was concealed for reasons of military security. The Raj used 57 infantry battalions and 35,000 men to keep India under control. The Whipping Act was re-introduced, and over 66,000 people were arrested. In 538 instances the troops had to open fire, on six occasions rebel territories were bombed from the air, Tiger Moths were used to keep open communications and, at one stage Bihar was cut off from Bengal and Assam. By November 1942, 1,028 people had been killed and 3,215 injured. On 20 March 1943, Major-General Rob Lockhart, military secretary in the India Office, was to write in a secret note that, "for the duration of the war, and probably for sometime after, India must be considered as an occupied and hostile country".

It was the autumn of 1943 before the British crushed the revolt. But Gandhi had not succeeded in forcing them to quit India. It marked a colossal personal defeat for him, and he never recovered his political touch. For Bose in Berlin it was frustrating. He had predicted, almost to the day, the start of the revolt. (On 4 August, Trott wrote to another German official that Bose was expecting a major crisis after the AICC. meeting.) But he could do little to help except to broadcast to India.

Gandhi had responded to his calls three years too late, but at least the fight had begun. But words were not enough. In hindsight it is clear that had the Japanese been able to coordinate their Indian strategy with the August revolt, things might have turned out differently. But the Japanese thought Gandhi had been premature, and they were still reluctant to transfer Bose to Asia. There were also technical problems: the Germans, Italians and Japanese, aware of their fading control in the air and over the sea, could not agree how best to transport him.

In June 1942, the Italians had agreed to fly Bose non-stop from Rhodes to Rangoon, possible as they had just completed a similar flight. The Germans thought this too dangerous. On 23 July, Ribbentrop told Tokyo the sea route was better, but although a Japanese submarine arrived in the French port of L'Orient in Brittany, the Imperial Navy refused to use it to transport Bose, explaining it was there for other purposes. In August, the Italians again made an aircraft ready, but the Japanese vetoed its use, arguing the aircraft would have to use Soviet air space. Japan, not yet at war with the Soviet Union, did not want to risk this. By mid-

October yet another flight was arranged. Bose handed over charge of the Free India Centre to Nambiar, had a farewell meeting with Ribbentrop on 14 October, and prepared to fly from Rome the next day.

But, as the Germans feared, the Italians had been unable to keep the news secret. On 12 October the *Daily Sketch* in London reported that Bose was leaving for the East. The flight was promptly cancelled. Another month went by. There was almost an action replay: another journey to Rome, another cancellation. These repeated disappointments had begun to affect Bose. Associates who had always found him cool, collected and patient now feared his temper. He was uneasy, unable to concentrate on work and full of nerves. His health had also broken down. By this time Emilie had left Berlin. She was carrying Anita, and the couple decided that the birth should be in Vienna. Not even Nambiar knew he was married, and the appearance of a child would have been embarrassing. In the third week of October Bose visited Bratislava, and then went to see Emilie in Vienna. This was their first separation since he had arrived in Europe the previous year, and he often wrote her letters which reflected happy domesticity. He also made sure she had food coupons and cigarettes. In December that year, he returned to Vienna to spend his first and only Christmas with Emilie, and their new-born child. In January 1943 Bose left for Paris to make sure the Free India Centre was working well, and then returned to hear the news for which he had waited so long. Tokyo had finally decided to accept him.

The first Indian National Army, led by Mohan Singh had been dissolved as a result of differences between Indians and the Japanese. Mohan Singh was under arrest, and Tokyo had now agreed that Bose would leave by a German U-boat which would then rendezvous with a Japanese submarine somewhere in the Indian ocean. The Germans agreed the plan. Publicly it was still business as usual. Bose celebrated Indian independence day on 26 January with over 800 guests in Haus der Flieger and two days later spoke to the Legion. He did talk of going away, but gave the impression he might go east to the Russian front. Two days later, a group of German naval officers came to the villa to brief him on the voyage, and to carry out a through medical examination. In December he had suffered from influenza, and also had a bad reaction to some glucose injections. Emilie, leaving Anita behind with her mother and sister in Vienna, had returned to Berlin to bid him goodbye. Just before he left, he gave her a letter in Bengali to Sarat telling his brother of their marriage and of the birth of Anita on 29 November 1942 in Vienna.

On 5 February 1943, the Japanese decided with the Germans on the rendezvous point of the submarines near Madagascar. Bose had originally wanted to take Swami, Mookerjee and Hasan , but was told he could take only one companion, and he chose Hasan. Hasan thought he was going to Greece, and started studying Greek. It was only when he arrived at Kiel railway station on 7 February and saw Nambiar, Keppler and Werth that he realised this was to be a very different journey. Emilie was not there, but this was to maintain the deception that Bose was only on a short journey. She stayed at the villa for sometime before Nambiar moved in.

One man's absence from Kiel station was a shock to Bose. Adam Von Trott was not there, and Nambiar, who liked the Trotts but knew how the German felt about Bose, later told him, "You must be glad to see the back of him.."

On the morning of 8 February 1943 Bose and Hasan sailed from Kiel in *U-180* with Commander Werner Musenberg in charge. Hasan had been thrilled by the idea of travelling in a submarine, but the moment he entered the U-boat his spirits sank. They were quartered in a small dark corner, and there was no escape from the all-pervasive odor of diesel oil. He later said:

> The fumes permeated everything, the bread we ate looked as if it was soaked in diesel oil, the blankets seemed drenched with it and our corner was so small

> that if you stood erect you got in the way of somebody or other. It was really a small recess, the corner of a passage that was the officers' mess. People ate off the table there, part of the space was used by surgeons to perform their operations and there were navigational charts and instruments dotted round the place. Netaji was allowed a corner of about 2ft by 3ft. Fortunately we were still in German waters and allowed to come on the bridge.

Once Bose had got used to the fumes and the food, Hasan's last illusions were removed: "I thought I would be getting three months of good rest, but as soon as Netaji had settled in he started working." For the 93 days the journey lasted, Bose sketched out his plans for liberating India.

17

The Man Called Silver And The Bose Conspiracy

On 12 March 1943, as Bose's U-boat, having made its wide sweep through the Atlantic, headed for the Cape of Good Hope and its rendezvous with the Japanese submarine, there was a meeting in Bletchley of the three most important branches of British intelligence. Gathered in the Nissan huts there were officials of IPI, the Indian Political Intelligence, SIS. the secret intelligent service and MI5, Britain's counter intelligence. Bletchley in Buckinghamshire was the natural meeting place for these men, as it was the war-time centre of British intelligence and the headquarters of "Ultra", the intelligence produced by code-breakers who used primitive computers to break German codes and read all their wireless messages. The Americans had their own equivalent, Magic, which was reading Japanese codes and had known about Pearl Harbour even before the attack. The Allies were thus aware of the Axis powers' plans, and Bose's voyage involving two enemy submarines would have been known.

The Bletchley meeting had been called to evaluate the intelligence on Bose, and to decide what should be done about him. No British documents from this meeting have ever been released, but some years ago a Russian historian discovered in the Soviet archives a Top Secret document summarizing it. It was entitled: "Report of the Soviet Agent to the Governing Body of British Intelligence." The document is fascinating. It provides further and final confirmation of one of the most remarkable stories of the war. As Bose sought to foment rebellion against the British in India, he also unwittingly helped create an agent who proved to be one of the most amazing double, if not quadruple, agents of the the Second World War. He started off working for the Italians and the Germans, then worked for the Russians, and finally for the British.

From late in 1942 this man came under the control in Delhi of a Scot called Peter Fleming, the brother of Ian Fleming, foreign manager of *The Sunday Times*, and later to become creator of the fictional character James Bond, agent 007. Peter Fleming was head of GSI.(d) or D Division, and his forte was counter-intelligence, feeding false information to the Germans and the Japanese. Fleming operated a small network of secret agents and this is how Fleming's biographer Duff Hart-Davis describes them:

> Many of these were double agents—that is, they had first been hired by the Japanese or by the Germans and were ostensibly still working for them, although in fact they had switched their allegiance to the Allies. Easily the best of Peter's double-agents was a man known as "Silver" – a Hindu called Bhagat Ram (or sometimes Kishan Chand) who appeared to be giving such devoted service to the Axis powers that during the war he was warded the Iron Cross, Germany's highest military decoration. Silver did indeed perform services for the Germans and the Japanese, among them to smuggle the revolutionary leader Subhas Chandras Bose out of India into Afghanistan, and thence to Europe. But Silver's main allegiance was to Russia, and he served the British only because they were allies of the Soviet Union.

Duff Hart-Davis has summed up Bhagat Ram brilliantly. Since his biography was written a great deal of material has emerged, not least Bhagat Ram's own war-time confession to the British. Long kept a secret, it gives us a very full picture of the man who helped Bose escape, and pretended to be his secret agent in India, but really served Bose's enemies and all through the war fed Bose some choice fiction, most of it concocted by the British. Bose was, of course, blissfully unaware of this, as were the Germans and the Italians. What is even more remarkable is that when, in the 1970s, the Netaji Research Bureau started to publish material on Bose and his war-time activities, Bhagat Ram Talwar went to its seminars to retail his story, and then wrote his own book. His writings can now be seen for what they are: self serving words, copious in trivial detail but often misleading and fictitious. Even 30 years after the end of the war Bhagat Ram Talwar did not and could not publicly confess all that he had done. Now, 60 years later, the incredible story of Silver and his impact on Bose can be told.

When we last saw Bhagat Ram Talwar it was March 1941 in Kabul, and he had just bid goodbye to a very emotional Bose as he drove off with the German Herr Wenger for the Russian border. During one of his discussions with the Germans and the Italians in Kabul, Bose had told them that Bhagat Ram Talwar would be his secretary and linkman with India. He gave Talwar some letters, one for Sarat written in Bengali and one in English for Sardul Singh Caveeshar, the leader of the Forward Bloc in Punjab. They were marked as coming from "somewhere in Europe". Bose also told him to see Bakshi in Calcutta.

The Italians gave Talwar money for travel, and on his return to Lahore he met Mian Akbar Shah, who bitterly complained that Bose had tricked them by saying he wanted to go to Moscow but had gone to Berlin instead. Talwar tried to defend Bose, saying the Russians had not helped in refusing to see him. There was some discussion by the Kirti leaders as to whether they should still help Bose. On ideological grounds they did not want to, but they liked the money provided by the Italians and decided the Bose letters should be delivered. Caveeshar, however, refused to accept them. He was worried that British agents were watching him, and claimed the letters were not in Bose's handwriting.

Talwar then set off for Calcutta accompanied by Mohinder Singh Sodhi. Sodhi and Talwar met Sarat at his home in Calcutta where they were given 150 Rupees. It had been agreed that Talwar would return to Kabul with two reliable men – one of them from among Bose's revolutionary supporters in Bengal – and have him trained in sabotage techniques and wireless work. The man chosen for this purpose was Santimoy Ganguli, one of Bose's Bengali revolutionary supporters. Sodhi was the other person accompanying Talwar back to Kabul. The trio did not work harmoniously. According to Ganguli, Sodhi considered himself superior to Talwar, having been to various parts of the world including Moscow. He told Ganguli that one of his motives for getting out of India was he was wanted on a murder charge.

Tawlar, Sodhi and Ganguli reached Kabul on May 1. There was some delay before they could establish contact with the Italians. Eventually they did, meeting Quaroni at the summer place in Pagham outside Kabul. Quaroni spent an hour teaching Ganguli how to apply dynamite sticks with a fuse for blowing up bridges, railways stations and buildings. He suggested they blow up Attock Bridge, the great bridge that guarded the frontiers of British India. He also told them that castor oil could be mixed with aviation fuel at RAF aerodromes. Talwar and Sodhi were worried about staying in a *serai* and the Italians offered to shift them to a private home They found there a message from Bose telling them he had reached Berlin, was negotiating with the Axis leaders on Indian freedom, and was also in touch with Indian POWs. Sodhi made a pitch for money, telling the Italians that if they paid well they could achieve big results. It was agreed that Talwar and Ganguli would return to India while Sodhi stayed behind in Kabul. The Italians were again generous, giving Talwar around 20,000 Afghan rupees which amounted to 4,000 Indian rupees, about £310.

By this time the Germans had sent to Kabul a special agent for Indian work. In one of his messages Bose had told Talwar about him, and before Bhagat Ram Talwar left Kabul he met him. He was Carl Rudolf Rasmuss, a former German trade commissioner in Calcutta, who could speak broken Bengali. Rasmuss had a long talk with Talwar, and told him Bose wanted Bhagat Ram and Sodhi to act as his eyes and ears in the tribal areas, working in close cooperation with the Faqir of Ipi. Rassmuss also gave Talwar a photograph of him shaking hands with the Nepalese commander-in-chief who, said the German, was a good man and would help anybody who carried his photograph.

Sodhi needed a place to stay in Kabul. Uttam Chand rented living quarters above his shop and the Italians happily paid for it. Meanwhile Talwar and Ganguli returned to India, Ganguli to put his newly acquired sabotage knowledge to use, while Talwar promised to come back with reports of what Bose's party was doing in India. The pair arrived back in Lahore on 21 June 1941, the same day that the Germans armies attacked Russia. The German invasion changed the nature of the war for communists all round the world. Until then the communists, taking their lead from the Soviet Union, had characterised it as an imperialist war; but now it was a people's war. Bhagat Ram Talwar and the Kirti party took the same view, but they were like children out of touch with their parents. They did not know what to do. They had no contact with the Russians, and desperately wanted instructions from Moscow. With the home of communism under attack from the fascists, should they still deal with the Axis representatives in Kabul?

The honourable and simple, solution would have been at this stage to end all contact with Rasmuss and the Italians. But the Kirti liked the German and Italian money. Talwar had brought 5,000 Afghan rupees from Rasmuss, 20,000 from the Italians. They decided that for the time being they would hide the fact that Bose was in Berlin and feed him misleading information.

In August 1941 Talwar returned to Kabul with a memo for Bose prepared in the name of the All-India Revolutionary Committee The memo was the work of Gucharan Singh Sainsra, who worked for the newspaper *Hindi Milap* and had a reputation as a literary figure. He was the first person Talwar had consulted in May when he returned to Kabul after his trip with Bose. Sainsra liked to write fiction and among his friends it was said he worked "underground" on the literary front. Now he produced a totally fictitious work claiming great success on behalf of Bose's revolutionary followers. Talwar showed the report to Sodhi who was impressed by its fantasy of strikes and anti-war activities, amongst Indian troops.

The sting in this tail was at the end. It concluded that the work of maintaining an anti-British front in India was very difficult and required a lot of money, 80,000 Indian rupees (£6200) were needed. The Italians liked what they read but not the request for money. They gave some, promised more, and also presented Talwar with a box of detonators, which Talwar soon ditched.

Talwar arrived in Kabul to learn that Sodhi had finally managed to contact the Russians. While Talwar had been away in India, playing Santa Claus with the money given to him by the Axis and concocting fiction for Bose, Sodhi was driven to near desperation by his failure to establish contact with Moscow. Finally, three days before the German invasion of Russia he decided the only thing to do was to go directly to the Russian legation. In Afghan clothes he might not get pass the guards, so he bought a second-hand suit, tie, collar and hat and dressed like a European. Thus attired he went up to the guards at the Legation, told them he had come from the British Legation and was let in. Inside he met a Russian official. He told him he had been to Moscow where he had been known as Sherwan and that he wanted to return. The Russian promised to report to Moscow and let Sodhi know.

Three days later came news of the invasion, Sodhi heard it on the wireless at Uttam Chand's house. He went back to the Russians. Now the Russians told him the war situation made travel impossible and advised him to go back to India. Talwar used Sodhi to contact the Russians who advised them that one of their Kirti comrades was on his way back from Moscow with instructions. But what, asked these two Indian communists, should they do about Bose? Ditch him? No, said the Russians, maintain contact, there is no harm but there must be no interference in the British war effort.

Reassured by this Russian guidance, Talwar and Sodhi met Rasmuss, who told them that the Germans had taken over from the Italians as their main point of Axis contact. As far as the Germans were concerned the whole thing was far too delicate and expensive for the Italians, although there was also some worry about Quaroni's wife being a Russian. Rasmuss wanted the names of all Bose's party workers in India and he also spoke of getting Bose's Bengal workers to contact the German legation in Bangkok. Rasmuss offered to sent two Germans with them to India to train them in sabotage and wireless work but the Indians declined this offer, explaining that two Europeans would be hard to conceal. It was about this time that two Germans sent to the Faqir of Ipi were shot by the Afghans. Rasmuss agreed it was not such a good idea. But he was again generous with money, giving Talwar $5,500.

Around the end of July 1941 Sodhi, Talwar and a third Indian, who Bhagat Ram had brought with him on this trip, left Kabul for the Punjab. In India the Kirti party did not know what to do about Bose. Soon after Sodhi and Talwar returned to Lahore, sometime in mid-August, there was a critical meeting of the Kirti leaders to discuss relations with Bose. The Germans were devastating their beloved Soviet Union, so how could they maintain contact with the Germans and Bose, whom they now saw as a traitor? Some thought all contact should be ended but the money was useful and they consoled themselves with the thought the Russians knew what they were doing.

Sodhi was sent to Bombay to cash the dollar notes Rasmuss had given him while Talwar journeyed to Calcutta. There as he would later tell his British interrogators, he met Ganguli and told him Kirti would only work with Bose's men if they agreed to sign the communist pledge. They could not agree to this and Ganguli took him to meet Sarat Bose. According to what he later told his British interrogators this is what happened:

> Sarat explained that he was not concerned in any political differences...questioned Bhagat Ram as to Subhas's present whereabouts. He had apparently not heard previously of his arrival in Berlin He told Bhagat Ram he was sorry Subhas had not gone to Moscow and then enquired what the Kirti group were proposing to do as regards the Kabul contact now that Subhas had joined the Axis. Sarat tried to convince Bhagat Ram that the Axis had no inimical intentions toward India and their quarrel was only with the British. Sarat also wanted to know if the Punjab communists had any independent connection with Russia, to which Bhagat Ram replied No The meeting ended inconclusively and Bhagat Ram did not see Sarat Bose again.

Indeed he did not see anybody from Bose's camp again. This was also his last meeting with Ganguli who journeyed to Lahore thrice but never met Bhagat Ram Talwar again. He was always told he was working in the tribal areas. What we see here is a first glimpse of Bhagat Ram Talwar's emergence as a double agent. This double life began to assume a more formidable shape as the war progressed. In September 1941 there was another meeting in Lahore. Sodhi had come back from Bombay flushed with rupees, having converted the dollars into 18,400 Rupees, about £1400. Two thousand rupees were given to Bhagat Ram, who bought two battery receiving sets to take back to Kabul. He also had with him another fictitious report, no doubt prepared by the fiction master Sainsra, to show to Rasmuss for onward transmission to Bose in Berlin.

The moment Talwar got to Kabul he contacted the Russians. At the Soviet Legation he met three Russian diplomats, who were pleased with his work and stressed he must maintain his contacts with Rasmuss. The Russians, at the onset of their epic struggle with the Germans, wanted to find out as much as they could about German plans and Rasmuss was a wonderful source. They fairly grilled Bhagat Ram Talwar to make sure he was prepared for the risks of being a double agent. Talwar assured them he was and so were his party workers in India. In order to pull off the deception, he was told to stop pretending to be a communist.

When Bhagat Ram met Rasmuss he spun his tale with some conviction, fanciful stories of the Forward Bloc organising anti-British movements including the planting of cells inside the Indian Army, and preparing for large scale strikes to stop war production. The Sainsra fiction of an underground organisation called the Indian National Revolutionary Committee was also revealed. Berlin wanted Talwar to be trained on portable wireless sets. Rasmuss wanted a small set to go to the tribes, and a large one kept in Uttam Chand's house. Bhagat Ram handed the small set to the Russians and it was never seen again, although the Germans did eventually recover the larger set.

In Berlin, blissfully unaware that Talwar had become a double agent, Bose asked that two Bengalis be sent across Burma to Bangkok where they should get in touch with Satyananda Puri and his assistant Nandy. They were to use the password "Elephant". Satyananda would then arrange a meeting with a German agent called von Plessento. As regards money, said Bose, an approach should be made to the manager of the Calcutta National Bank which had a branch in Bangkok so that money deposited in Bangkok could be withdrawn in Calcutta. Bose also wanted Forward Bloc contacts in the Indian Army fighting with the British in Libya to be given the password "Silver Moon". If captured by the Germans or the Italians they should give this password and would be treated as friends. Berlin was keen that Forward Bloc men be sent to the Persian Gulf, Ceylon and Burma and asked Talwar to bring two men to Kabul for training in cipher work and sabotage.

Bhagat Ram Talwar returned to India in November 1941 with 800 gold sovereigns and £14,625 in mixed English pound notes. (Interestingly when Sodhi met him a day or two later he was told Bhagat Ram had brought back 498 gold sovereigns and 2500 mixed Bank of England currency notes, money which Sodhi despite a visit to Bombay had difficulty in changing into rupees.) The Kirti leaders had no desire to do any of Bose's bidding but they liked the money too much and were happy to dream up further nonsense for him.

By January 1942 Talwar was back in Kabul with another fanciful report for Bose. When he showed it to the Russians, they expressed alarm. They did not want the Germans to know about British troop movements in India and the dispositions of the forces. Bhagat Ram had to reassure them that, fiction was carefully mixed with fact, all the verifiable information was from published sources and only the troop figures were made up. Rasmuss, assuming all this was genuine, was delighted, as was Witzel, a German military intelligence officer.

While Talwar was in Kabul, Bose began a series of broadcasts from Berlin beamed to India, speaking of agents being parachuted into India. The British carefully monitored them and the first of these from Azad Hind Radio was heard in London at 5.30 pm on 28 April 1942. The British record of that broadcast reads as follows: "You are now going to hear a very important announcement issued by our leader, Subhas Chandra Bose. Our Leader, Subhas Chandra Bose has issued the following statement, which we would beg our listeners to broadcast throughout India. The statement begins:

> After a great deal of careful preparation, we have decided to establish closer contact between our comrades living outside India and those comrades who are living at home. For this purpose we are going to use a modern and up to date instrument. We are going to make two experiments and watch the results. After these experiments we can decide our future plans. On 3 May, the first batch of our comrades will be sent to India by plane and according to our calculations they will reach their destination in India in the early hours of the morning of the 4 May, between two o'clock and three o'clock. After dropping the parachutists the aeroplane will return at once. We are purposely not giving out

> the exact place of arrival, because our enemies will then attempt to arrest our comrades. We know quite well that our comrades who are making this hazardous journey will be killed at once if they fall into the hands of our enemies. We request our co-workers, friends and sympathisers, everywhere in India, to look out for aeroplanes and parachutes in the early hours of the morning of the 4 May between two and three o'clock. As soon as they see the parachutes, they should kindly give all possible help to the parachutist comrades, give them shelter. Moreover, the article to be carried by the parachutist should be hidden in a safe place. When all this is done, the parachutes should be either buried under the earth or set fire to, so that there may not be any trace of them. In no case should they be burnt at night, because fire may attract enemy agents to the place. If all goes well on the 4 May, then the second aeroplane will reach India on the 8 May, in the early hours of the morning, between two and three o'clock. It is not necessary for our comrades and friends in India to light any lamps as a signal, because that has already been arranged by our agents in India at the exact place where the aeroplane will arrive.

There was a second broadcast by Bose at 5 pm on 7 May 1942 which the British again monitored:

> I announced on the 28 April and the 2 May from this station that we wished to send some reliable co-workers to India by plane, with equipment. I announce to you now that the first batch landed safely at the appointed place, but owing to the mistake of some people in India they were not fully successful. The people of India warned the enemy agents by showing more light than was necessary. The agents immediately began to investigate and our members had to destroy their equipment. However, our members are safe and alive, as no agent was able to detect them. The parachutes, according to the instructions, were destroyed. The only regret is that we lost the equipment, which our members took with them. According to our plans our second plane will arrive in India on the 8 May between two and three am. We ask our agent to show only the amount of light specified in our instructions. If they act according to the instructions given then we hope to succeed on the 8 May. I ask our agent, friends and sympathisers to look out for the parachutists on the 8 May between now and three am, and be prepared to help them in every way. They must be careful and must not make mistakes this time.

Finally, just after 8 pm on 22 May, Bose made a third broadcast on parachute landings in India:

> We are glad to inform our countrymen that the second attempt made by Azad Hind on the 8 May to establish contact with our comrades at home, was successful. We are grateful to our noble friend (............Kaysar?) whose assistance was of very great help. But for this assistance the experiment of the 8 May might have ended in failure. However, the two aeroplane flight on the 4 May and on the 8 May have enabled our comrades to gain valuable experience, which will be of great use on subsequent occasions. We hope, in view of this experience, it will not be necessary in future to publicly announce any aeroplane flight to India, since such announcements give information to our enemies as well. We shall, however, make one further request of our friends and

> sympathisers in every part of India. It is possible that when our comrades fly to India in future they may not have time to dispose of the parachutes after landing, because they must hurriedly escape with their luggage. Consequently, if anybody comes across a parachute lying on the ground, he should not make any fuss about it, but should quietly burn or bury it.

The Germans were keen to land men in the tribal areas in their efforts to help the Faqir of Ipi. In April 1942 when Rasmuss met Talwar his two-page summary of the latest instructions from Berlin had much emphasis on these landing.
Bhagat Ram was asked:

(1) To prepare a parallel Forward Bloc administration to be set up in the name of Azad Hindustan in enemy occupied areas as soon as India was invaded. All volunteer organisations to obtain secret arms and to hold themselves in readiness meanwhile. They should be told that a large "Indian Army" was being trained in Berlin from among Prisoners of War and German internees who would come to liberate India. Simultaneous preparations were necessary among the tribes so that large scale tribal risings would coincide with internal revolt and an Axis invasion. The Faqir of Ipi would give the lead to the tribes. Meanwhile stocks of secret petrol and bombs should be arranged in India and tribal territory. Landing grounds should be prepared in tribal territory where German parachute troops could be dropped from the air. Propaganda should be widely spread urging Indians to resign from the Army and civil employment as the defeat of Britain was imminent, and adding that those who did not do so before India was attacked would be treated as enemies by the invading Axis troops. For this purpose lists of pro-British Indians were to be prepared and held in readiness. Intensive propaganda against the British scorched earth policy was also very essential.
(2) To form guerrilla bands of deserters from the Army who should be trained to operate behind the British lines when the Germans attacked from the North-West and the Japanese from the East.
(3) To persuade as many Indians as possible meanwhile to desert with their arms and to carry out an intensive whispering campaign spreading defeatism and calling on government officials to resign.
(4) To undermine confidence in British currency combined with a propaganda campaign enumerating Axis victories in Russia.
(5) To encourage slowing down tactics in factories but not to sabotage any big industries.

Meanwhile Bose wanted any German or Italian prisoners of war who escaped to be given refuge in tribal territory. He asked for figures of military deserters, how many of them had deserted with their arms, and where they were now hiding. Also what proportion of the Indian Army was likely to remain loyal when the Japanese invaded the east of India, and whether the Forward Bloc contacts in Burma and Ceylon had achieved any success yet. Wherever there were Sikh troops Bose wanted Sikh agents to be used among them. He was also interested in the wider political questions such as the position of Nehru and other Congress leaders following the breakdown of the Cripps negotiations, the reactions in Bengal to the Forward Bloc ministers and the present whereabouts of a number of Bose's political supporters in Bengal.

Very dutifully Talwar handed the typed summary of these instructions to the Russians, making handwritten notes for himself (which were recovered by the British at the time of his arrest). Rasmuss wanted him to go back to India as soon as possible but the Russians preferred him to wait a few days as they were expecting an important official from Moscow. This official was the man in charge of Soviet Asiatic Intelligence. Before the German invasion he had been directing Russian intelligence in Europe. He spoke German, and several other European languages, but no English or Hindustani. Three members of the Russian Legation accompanied Bhagat Ram Talwar to this meeting, with one acting as interpreter. It turned out to be a long meeting. The Russian officer wanted to hear the whole of Talwar's story, his early communist connections and how he helped Bose escape. The questioning which began at 7pm continued until 5 am the next morning, interrupted only for food and brandy. Talwar was to have three meetings with the Russians during the course of which he told them everything Rasmuss had told him. The details delighted them and it was clear the Germans completely trusted Talwar. For the Russians this was a priceless discovery in the midst of war: an Indian who had free access to their enemy. They told Talwar he must continue his Axis contacts and obtain as much information as possible, particularly in relation to German plans in Afghanistan and the Middle East.

However, the Russians were worried Talwar might overplay his hand and they warned him to be on his guard against letting the Germans have any suspicion that he was betraying them. The risks were great: he had no contact with Bose's followers in India, was not following the instructions he was being sent from Berlin and was instead feeding Bose fiction.

The Russians had one nagging doubt about Talwar. His communist convictions were strong and they were confident he would never betray Russia, the motherland of communism, but might he help the Japanese? Although the Russians were not at war with Japan his Russian minders reminded him there was no difference between the Germans and the Japanese war plans. They were one and the same enemy. Uttam Chand was present at one of the meetings and the Russian official impressed on him his responsibility in keeping Bhagat Ram Talwar's true role secret. Uttam Chand was to be the only Indian in Kabul who knew of Bhagat Ram Talwar's connections with the Russians. By this time the pattern of such visits was set. Bhagat Ram's first and last stops in Kabul were always the Russians. He would get instructions from them before he met the Germans, and before he departed for India he would tell them everything he had learnt from the Germans. On this visit just before he was ready to leave Kabul he saw Rasmuss and collected money: 500 gold sovereigns and one lakh (100,000 Afghani rupees) and immediately afterwards told the Russians about this meeting. For them the arrangement could not be sweeter. Not only was their enemy funding their own man but they did not have to pay him anything.

In Kabul there was a moment when Rasmuss might have smelt a rat. News came that Sodhi and two others had been arrested by the British. The other two names meant nothing to Rasmuss, but he knew Sodhi and he asked Talwar about his arrest. Was it the same Sodhi he had met? Would he betray secrets? Talwar assured him he was an old revolutionary and would not betray anything. As it happens at that very moment, as IPI noted, Sodhi had "begun to talk freely" to the British. He had been arrested at a wayside railway station near Delhi. Caught unawares by the British he confessed everything. Sodhi's arrest formed another chapter in what IPI was now calling the "Bose conspiracy" and they were delighted by what they discovered. In an IPI note to Silver, the head of department, an official commented:

> The main conclusions to be derived from Sodhi's disclosures regarding the Bose conspiracy is that, at any rate so far as Kabul, the N.W. frontier and the northern part of India are concerned, there is no cause for anxiety. Sodhi and the Kirti group joined Bose's proposed Axis scheming more or less by accident and soon found that they offered generous prospects for party funds. The proposal which they put forward to cause trouble in India found favour in Kabul beyond their intrinsic merits and were well paid for...The statement of Harmindar Singh

> Sodhi has considerable propaganda value and I suggest this aspect of the matter be brought to the notice of the Government of India. The world at large, perhaps more than the Nazis themselves, should be interested to know that large sums of Nazi money had been paid to further the grandiose schemes of Subhas Bose which turned out to be nothing more than paper schemes drafted by Indian communists with their tongues in their cheeks who saw an easy way to make money.

By August 1942 IPI calculated that the Italians and the Germans between them had paid Bhagat Ram £8,700, a colossal sum for India then. The note on Sodhi was dated 24 March, 1942 and it speculated that, "the full story of this scheming, however, it not likely to be told until Bhagat Ram of Galladher (alias Rahmat Khan, Bose's so-called secretary) is arrested and discloses all he knows". Bhagat Ram Talwar was in Kabul when this assessment was being made but the British did not have to wait long to catch him. Unknown to the British, Talwar himself was now keen to be put in touch with them.

Talwar left Kabul on 22 May arriving back in Lahore on 1 June, 1942. He was not very well, suffering from fever and liver trouble. It was only on 2 August that he left Lahore to return to Kabul for the sixth and last time prior to his arrest. He arrived in Kabul on 13 August. On arrival, he learnt that Uttam Chand had been arrested and sent back to Peshawar. He accordingly stayed in a serai and was unable to make his usual contact with the Russians, as Uttam Chand's shop was the contact point. However he eventually managed to meet two of the Russians in the bazaar and at another meeting Talwar showed them the further report he had brought back from India for the Axis. (The British later found a copy of this report among his papers.)

He explained to the Russians that Witzel had particularly asked for military information, which neither he nor Sainsra knew much about and which they therefore had to invent. The Russians read the report and said that it should show greater numbers of Indian troops to impress the Axis with the strength of Indian defences. Similarly, as regards aircraft, tanks and mechanised equipment, the Russians wanted higher figures shown, in order to convince the Axis that whatever may have been the case in Burma and Malaya, India was a different proposition. Talwar altered his figures accordingly.

It was now that he confessed to the Russians that it was impossible to keep on generating such fiction. The political side of his reports was easy, he could cope with that. But he knew nothing of military matters and to go on feeding the Germans military fiction was very difficult. He suggested that the Russians should get in touch with the British authorities and provide him with the required bogus information so that his contact with Axis could continue without risk. The Russians said they were already considering this, and that it was being dealt with in Moscow.

The next day, 24 August, Talwar met Rasmuss and Witzel and handed over his report. Rasmuss said he had tried to plead Uttam Chand's case with the Afghan authorities but had failed. He correctly guessed that the arrest had been brought about through British intervention. Others working for the Axis had also been arrested. With Uttam Chand gone, Bhagat Ram had nowhere to live, so the Germans took him back to their Legation. He stayed there for the next three days while they cross-examined him on his report. The report was then sent by wireless to Berlin, and Talwar was told to arrange his own accommodation pending a reply from Berlin. He took a flat in Baber on the outskirts of Kabul, which he rented from an Afghan police official, paying three months' advance rent. The Germans paid for the flat as they had paid for so much else.

Rarely in the history of spying has there been such an extraordinary situation. Here was an Indian portraying himself as a nationalist seeking to end British rule in India and ostensibly helping the Indian leader in Germany foment anti-British rebellion. But in reality his heart and soul was with Russia. He now saw Bose as a traitor. In the midst of a total war between Germany and Russia, while staying in a Kabul flat paid for by the Germans, he kept up his secret contacts with the Russians. So through the late summer of 1942 Talwar trotted back between the Germans (whose money he took) and the Russians whose communist beliefs he had accepted. When he went to see Rasmuss on yet another visit he was given a list of requirements by Berlin in the tribal territory. Berlin wanted Talwar to prepare a landing place where a small number of German parachutists could be dropped by night. It was proposed that eight or nine German technicians would be dropped. Among this party would be a few Indians who had been specially trained in Germany. Talwar assured them these arrangements could be made, but it would be impossible to keep the presence of Europeans secret in tribal territory and the British authorities would come to hear of it. Berlin wanted the parachutists to be hidden in a house in tribal territory, and insisted that some such arrangement should be made. They had a series of detailed questions about India. Was aluminium manufactured there? What weapons and other war equipment were being manufactured at the Tata Iron Works? Are tank engines being manufactured in India or are they imported? How many lorries, truck, and armoured car assembly plants exist in India and in what places? What sort of goods were the Eastern Supply Group Council providing for the war effort? Berlin also wanted details of aeroplane factories, and whether aeroplane engines and spare parts were being made or imported. The previous instructions were repeated. There must be an intensified and year-round programme of sabotaging railway lines and other communications, done under cover of the Congress movement.

Berlin also wanted to know what the immediate reactions were in India to Rommel's advance into Egypt. What were the latest military movements of American and Allied troops in Iran, Iraq and Syria? What supplies were being sent from India to Russia along the Quetta-Zahidan railway? Was the Quetta-Kandahar-Tarmiz railway open to military transport? Sabotage of this railway was important.

Bose ordered the Forward Bloc to cooperate with the Faqir of Ipi and other tribal leaders, and that Talwar should comply with Berlin's latest instructions about tribal territory. Propaganda was necessary amongst the tribes based on Azad Hindustan propaganda and stressing the material gains the tribes would win through Axis victory. A Forward Bloc-Ipi Pact would encourage the other tribes. It was also important to establish immediate contact with the Japanese via Rangoon. Bose wanted to know what contacts had been established in Ceylon, and what the Forward Bloc was doing there. His message added that two Indian Legions had been formed in Berlin from among prisoners of war and other internees, and that he himself had been assisting in instructing them. Bose was also keen to find out what had become of the two Forward Bloc ministers in the Bengal cabinet. As Berlin asked the questions Talwar passed them over to the Russians, always on the same day.

The Second World War was to produce many remarkable spies, not least the German Richard Sorge, who spied for the Russians from Tokyo and warned them of the German invasion before he was caught and hanged by the Japanese. But Bhagat Ram Talwar must be regarded as one of the most successful agents in the history of espionage.

Delighted as the Russians were with the gullibility of the Germans they wanted more. With the approach of autumn and the change of seasons, Moscow was sure Axis war plans would also change. It was imperative to find out what these plans were. Bhagat Ram Talwar was told he must stay in Kabul to discover them. There was another reason why the Russians wanted Talwar to linger in Kabul, although they did not tell him this reason. By this time the Russians were already involved in intricate negotiations with the British about him and Bose. Since June 1942, when Bose had gone public in Berlin following his meeting with Hitler, the Indian government's intelligence service was convinced he would try and make his way east. They now knew the details of his journey in fleeing India, and they debated how best to make sure the Russians did not allow him a passage through Moscow again, posing perhaps as a

Japanese diplomat making his way back to Tokyo.

In June 1942 IPI and India Office exchanged notes about how the Foreign Office should approach Moscow. On 18 June IPI speculated on three routes Bose might use to return to Asia and said it was keeping a watch on all of them. One route could be via Spain, Portugal or North Africa to South America and thence by sea to Japan. They concluded this was unlikely, as communications between South America and Japan were difficult. Another route could be via Turkey, the Russian-controlled areas of Iran and thence to Kabul, where he would be taken in charge by the German Legation and moved across Assam's frontier into Burma and Siam. Unlikely again, concluded IPI, as he did not speak the languages in these parts of the world and would require guides in Iran.

Perhaps Bose could be disguised as a Japanese courier and travel across Turkey and Russia. "This route" concluded IPI, "offers the least line of resistance and would appear to be the most likely". But how could they warn the Russians? The Foreign Office wanted to tell the Soviets how Bose had travelled on an Italian passport and got a Soviet visa but the India Office did not want this divulged. The Foreign Office felt the Soviets could be expected to keep a secret. But the India Office said, "One point is if we tell the Soviet government they would scratch their heads to wonder where we got his information and might infer that we maintain an organisation in Soviet territory".

In the end a "Most Secret" telegram was sent on 22 June 1942 to the British Ambassador in Moscow. He was told that while London had no definite information of how Bose might travel east "it seems likely that he will try to travel across Russia, and possibly via Turkey or Afghanistan". It stressed his pro-fascist views and stated that it was "of considerable importance to the Allied cause that Bose should not succeed in his plan". The British ambassador was told: "Please take matter up urgently with Soviet authorities preferably with M. Molotov himself and request that all possible steps should be taken to watch for and detain Bose. It is of greatest importance that our knowledge of Bose's intentions should not reach enemy and more especially the Japanese." The note ended with this advice: "Please burn after perusal."

Molotov had recently visited Britain and the British were certain he appreciated the need for shielding "Indian production from Axis intrigues." Just as the British were making their approaches to Moscow about Bose, the Russians were approaching London about Bhagat Ram Talwar. IPI's note of 29 August, 1942 stated, "Actually since then the Russians have themselves come forward asking us to collaborate in 'running' various Indian sources of information in Kabul which apparently they had been doing for some time, until they found that we had either arrested them or otherwise put them out of action".

But the problem here, as the IPI noted, was: "I gather there has been a slight hitch over this: the Russians want us to collaborate in Moscow and not in Kabul which we had asked them do." The British agreed to this. Their end in Moscow was controlled by Colonel G. A. Hill who had been part of Bruce Lockhart's mission to the Soviet Union in 1918 when, inspired by Churchill, the British and other western European countries tried to strangle the newly-born Bolshevik regime. His Russian counterpart in Moscow was one Colonel A.P. Osipov, an NKVD subversive expert. Osipov ran Bhagat Ram Talwar in Kabul using a Russian called Captain Allekherdov who was known in the Afghan capital as "Zaman".

While all this was going on the British were also wondering what they should tell the Afghan government and what propaganda use they might make of the Bose consipiracy. Ever since Sodhi's arrest and confession the British had debated as to whether they should inform the Afghan government of the intrigues by Axis diplomats in Kabul.

In the end the British concluded they did not want the Axis diplomats thrown out of Kabul but instead "pumped" for information. Only a limited amount would be told to the Afghans as this might get back to the Russians. When a note on Sodhi was prepared for the Afghan government Sodhi was referred to by his code name of Muhammad Khan, "principally because it may be seen by the Russian Ambassador". The decision was to keep quiet and use Bhagat Ram Talwar as a British agent as well.

It was October 1942, before all this finally came together and by then Talwar had persuaded Rasmuss he could not go to the tribal areas and would be much better off returning to India, which of course is what the Russians wanted him to do. Just before leaving Kabul on October 25 Talwar had one final meeting with the Russians. The Russians told him that his position had been discussed with the British authorities in Moscow. If on his return to India he should be arrested he should at once explain matters to a British officer, and ask that GHQ Delhi be informed of his arrest. All the time he should insist that the British keep his arrest strictly secret.

The Russians also told Talwar to get in touch with the Communist Party on his return to India and arrange with them for two reliable contacts to be sent to Burma using the password "Silver Moon" to play the same double game with the Japanese that he had successfully been doing with the Germans. Rasmuss had previously told Talwar that Berlin had changed the password to "Rising Moon". Talwar objected to this on the grounds that the old password "Silver Moon" had already been given to the two men, who he claimed were already in Burma. It would therefore be unwise to change the password. Of course no such men had been sent; this was another of Bhagat Ram's fictions but such was his hold over Rasmuss that this request was seen as just the sort of thing a shrewd agent would say. At Rasmuss's insistence Berlin confirmed use of the old password "Silver Moon".

As regards meeting the Communist Party leaders in India, the Russians gave him no definite instructions but said that its leaders in Bombay were in touch with the British and that Bhagat Ram should proceed to Bombay and see P.C Joshi, the general secretary. He had not previously met Joshi, but knew his photograph and had also read one or two copies of the *People's War*. The British were later to speculate as to why the Russians were keen for Talwar to contact them, and IPI concluded that "the Russians' appeal to the English aren't clear. Partially it seems to me they were driven by a wish to use this case against the Germans, besides they understood that they would need the English cooperation; Utamchand's arrest influenced them. They aimed at setting him free."

The Russians had some plan to send Uttam Chand back to Kabul and use him as an agent. The British-Russian exchange of information was not always smooth. When the Russians asked the British for information about the Far East and the British told them they didn't have this kind of information, the Russians were extremely displeased.

Talwar had planned to return to Kabul in December. On 29 November he and Sainsra were concocting another of their reports on political and military matters for Bose when the CID raided Sainsra's house and arrested Talwar, Sainsra and two women.

The moment the CID walked into the house Talwar followed faithfully the script the Soviets had given him. The arrests were done by the Raj's Indian policemen. Talwar refused to tell them anything and demanded he be taken to the British officer who was in overall charge. He then disclosed his real identity, asked that his arrest be kept secret and that the GHQ in Delhi should be informed. He was taken to Lahore Fort where he voluntarily made a detailed statement explaining all the papers found on him. He also revealed the two German codes he carried and the money the Germans had paid him. He told the British he was "prepared to go back to Kabul and continue his contact with the Axis, reporting details to the Russians in Kabul and to the British "if and when he returns to India." He also told them that apart from Uttam Chand nobody knew of his contacts with the Russian, although the higher reaches of both the Kirti and the main communist party of India did.

After he had given his lengthy statement, the British cross-examined him and Bhagat Ram Talwar now revealed his true feelings about Bose. Long after Indian independence, he would speak eloquently at a Netaji seminar of Bose's patriotism. In December 1942 this is what he had to say about Bose:

> He now regards Subhas Bose as a traitor to his cause and having deliberately betrayed those who helped him. He is thoroughly glad therefore that he has been able to pay him back in the same coin. He has no sympathy with the present Congress movement which he regards as only serving enemy interests. From his conversations with Ramuss and Co he does not believe the Congress Party in India have any direct connections with the Axis or at any specific item of the Civil Disobedience campaign has Axis inspiration behind it except indirectly. He admits that his own contacts with the Axis in Kabul developed purely fortuitously as a result of Bose's journeys and Bose having subsequently nominated him as his link with India. He is absolutely confident the Axis in Kabul have no other Indian agent working for them in India, and no independent means from Kabul of checking up on his completely non-existence contacts with "Bose's organization" in India.

Bhagat Ram Talwar was soon free and back in Kabul. He did tell Rasmuss about his arrest but spun him another yarn. He told him what even the IPI was to describe as an " unreal version". This was that he had been arrested with 60 people in Peshawar after accomplishing a successful diversion but because of "some negligence" he managed to escape. The gullible Rasmuss believed this story, dazzled by another Talwar fantasy. But his arrest marked an important change. From this point until the end of the war all the information Bhagat Ram Talwar took to Rasmuss came from Peter Fleming's D Division. Since the British-Russian collaboration worked through Moscow the Russians passed Talwar's information to Hill in Moscow and this, in turn, came back to the British in India.

For Talwar this must have been heaven. He could not keep away from Kabul, having fallen in love with his life of a double agent (named Silver by D Division). He no longer had to worry about inventing fictions for the Germans. Fleming's biographer has a telling description of the many journeys Bhagat Ram made:

> He made regular trips there from Delhi, taking with him comprehensive intelligence reports which he pretended he had put together himself from his network of agents and which he handed over to the German or Italian legation in the Afghan capital. In fact, almost all his information was supplied by D Division, who were able to monitor the radio traffic that went out from Kabul to Berlin and Tokyo and so could check how much of their own material was reaching enemy headquarters. With care and stealth they gradually enhanced Silver's reputation by feeding him with such information of higher and higher priority, and the Germans eventually judged him so valuable that they sent him an extra powerful radio set so that he himself could transmit directly to the headquarters of the Abwehr (intelligence service) in Berlin. At one stage Silver appeared to be doomed for an Afghan who knew him well spotted him in Delhi in the company of British service personnel. D Division suggested strongly that it would be wise for him not to return to Kabul thinking that if he did he would certainly be liquidated; but he insisted on going back. Silence fell for nearly five months; the British heard that Silver had indeed met the Afghan again, but when the man asked him to dinner he had poisoned his host by slipping a dose of chopped-up tiger whiskers into his curry.

While all this was going on in Kabul, what was happening on the other side of India, in Bengal and with the Japanese? When they caught up with Talwar the British had cross-examined him on this and he had assured them that there were no agents there. He was right, but that did not mean Bose's men were not actively seeking to contact the Japanese. In April 1941 the Japanese consul-general in Calcutta telegraphed Yosuke Matsuoka, the foreign minister in Tokyo:

> We should secretly transport large quantities of weapons and substantially increase the actual strength of the Forward Bloc. But even then the long awaited moment of independence and the expulsion of British imperialism will only come through their own soldiers' attack and a genuine popular movement. At the same time on our part we must, at least, contact Bose and his party.

Contact was made in a somewhat "curiously roundabout and haphazard manner" as an IPI memo of August 1942 concluded, devoting several pages to the contacts between the Japanese and Bose's men in Calcutta. This contact was initially the work of Dwijendranath Bose, who the IPI described as Bose's "favourite nephew". He had formed a secret revolutionary group called the All-India Youth League, which IPI described as " a secret wing of the Forward Bloc, as well as a personal organisation in the hands of the Bose family".

In the spring of 1941 Dwijendranath Bose had distributed leaflets saying assistance from abroad would be coming as a result of Subhas Bose's secret mission and all Forward Bloc supporters should hold themselves in readiness. About this time certain Sikh political extremists came to Calcutta and met Niranjan Singh Talib. They wanted his assistance in establishing contact with Usman Khan whose real name was Hari Singh, a Sikh revolutionary living in Shanghai. Hari Singh had said he could supply them with Japanese arms. A meeting between the Sikh extremists and Kagiama, the Japanese Vice-Consul in Calcutta, was held in March 1941. But while Kagiama could not arrange for a Sikh to go and meet Hari Singh, he expressed general sympathy with Subhas Bose and his movement.

Meanwhile Dwijen had approached the Japanese consulate, asking for help in the name of Subhas Bose's movement. By this time. Kagiama had been replaced by Okazaki. Dwijen sent him various youth league leaflets and pro-Japanese posters. Okazaki was interested, but wanted to meet a representative leader. Dwijen decided that this could only be his uncle, Sarat Bose. This led to several meetings of the Japanese with Sarat. His son Sisir has described how these meetings took place through the summer of 1941, some of them at Sarat's country home in Rishra. At times the consul-general brought his wife with him to provide the veneer of a social occasion, but the priority was serious business. Maps of Bengal and the North-West Frontier province were examined , and the Japanese conveyed messages from Subhas received via Berlin and Tokyo. The British were privy to all this and soon after Japan entered the war Sarat Bose was arrested, just as he was about to become a minister in the Bengal government. The British believed his desire to become a minister was to prevent his arrest. He spent the rest of the war in jail.

Subhas Bose's arrival in Japan would see more agents enter India. Fleming was delighted to hear that he was in the Far East . Intelligence is a game and spy masters, be they friends or opponents, develop a respect for their enemies. From afar Fleming had observed and admired Bose. Before Bose's return east Fleming had tired of the Japanese. They were willing to swallow the most incredulous tales, but they were slow witted. With Bose it was different. Fleming's biographer says:

> D Division were delighted by Bose's arrival in the Japanese camp....now they hoped his wide experience of clandestine activity would greatly increase the receptivity of the Japanese intelligence services, as Peter, himself, put it they looked forward to dealing with a sophisticated adversary who could be relied on as Japanese could not to see the point of the information they gave him.

Bose had been followed to the East by Swami who became his spy chief. Swami managed to land quite a few agents in India,but while this increased the stakes for Fleming's D Division the overall result for Bose was no different to what he had achieved via the Germans in Kabul. Some were double agents almost from the start, others became willing double agents when they got to India. Nobody like Talwar emerged, although there was one remarkable man who Fleming's Division called "Owl". An Indian peasant in his late twenties called Adjudya Das, Owl was an infantry private in the British Indian Army, and had been taken prisoner by the Japanese. He joined Bose's Indian National Army and was parachuted back to India with a Japanese radio set and other items of interest. He was asked to report troop movements and bomb damage. But, says Fleming's biographer:

> No sooner had he landed, however, than he reported to the nearest police station with his radio and asked what he could do. D Division took over control of his set and used him to play back to the Japanese from Calcutta. Before long his own cautious reports began to whet the appetite of the Japanese and they started asking more detailed questions to which Peter's team was only too happy to supply answers.

Many other agents did the same and there can be little doubt that for all the efforts of Bose and his men the British won this intelligence game easily, adding the wider and more important triumphs that Ultra and Magic gave the Allies.

We are, however, jumping ahead of our story. Let us return to that meeting in Bletchley on 12 March. At the time Bose was in a German submarine.Through Ultra the British knew its location, and British intelligence officials consider the options. The secret Russian report noted:

> The most serious fact in our situation is that Bose is on the way to Japan in the German submarine.They suppose if he gets to Japan he'll be able to contact his own Indian party, Forward BLOC , *and first of all he'll find out that the colossal organization of Bhagatt Ram doesn't exist, the whole thing is a pure blackmail.* The Admiralty wants to withdraw him when the Japanese boat takes him from the submarine. It's a very good plan, especially if it comes into being because Bhagat Ram's organization will be safe and the Germans will be able to boss the latter without Bose.

It is clear that if they had decided to do so they could have picked Bose up. But they did not. Why? We cannot say. About this time the American's using Magic had been breaking Japanese codes for some time helping them to turn the scales at the Battle of the Coral Sea in May 1942 and at Midway the following month. In 1943 the Americans decided to assassinate Admiral Isoroku Yamamoto, the great Japanese naval commander, who had plotted the Pearl Harbor attack and subsequent sea triumphs for the Japanese. They knew of a flight he was taking which would provide the ideal opportunity. Roosevelt, who had to give consent for such an individual action, approved and the plan was successfully carried out while Bose was on the high seas. Had they picked up Bose the secret of Ultra or Magic or both might have been revealed to the Germans and the Japanese. Britain probably decided that was too big a risk. In terms of wining the war in the Pacific killing Yamamoto was a much higher priority than exterminating Bose.

18
Netaji

On 26 April 1943 the Japanese submarine *1-29*, under the command of Commander Juichi Isu, arrived in the Mozambique Channel, near that haven of neutral Portuguese territory. Six days earlier, amidst tight security, she had left the Malayan port of Penang, ostensibly on a routine mission hunting enemy shipping. Locals, many of them Indians, had been intrigued to see as senior an officer as Captain Mesao Teraoka , a submarine flotilla commander, on board. He effectively took charge of the boat and they were convinced something was afoot when they learnt that the ship's cooks had been busy buying up spices for Indian curries. Long before the *1-29* arrived in Portuguese waters rumours had circulated throughout Penang that the man they had long heard about was about to arrive. It was only when the submarine reached its destination that Captain Teraoka told his crew their mission: to pick-up Subhas Bose. The *1-29* had arrived at the rendezvous spot about ten hours ahead of schedule. There is some dispute as to where the exact spot was. The best guess is that it was 400 miles south south-west of Madagascar.

It was late in the day before the Japanese spied the German U-boat. In the enveloping darkness, a transfer was impossible, and both submarines were under orders to maintain strict radio silence. There could be no conversation between them. Sunrise on 27 April brought fresh problems: the seas were now so rough that the two vessels could not get near each another. All they could do was circle each other and wait for the weather to break. But their luck held: no enemy planes or ships arrived. In the evening, as the sun was about to set, the Japanese officers saw two men jump overboard from the German vessel and swim towards them. Quickly hauled on board by the Japanese, they turned out to be a German officer and a signals man. The reason for their dare devilry was quickly made clear. The U-boat was low on fuel and could not carry on any longer.

As day dawned on 28 April the sea was still rough, but it was decided that the exchange had to take place. The two Germans, on a rubber raft, dragged a strong manila hemp rope back to their boat; Bose and Hasan boarded the raft, clung to the rope and were hauled towards the *1-29*. Bose could not have timed his arrival better, because the next day the Japanese were due to celebrate the emperor's birthday with sake; and as the submarine began its return voyage Bose was plied with Japanese-cooked curries. The transition from the unpalatable German diet was a great relief, but Bose was not yet used to four meals a day. When the Japanese kept insisting, he asked, "Do we have to eat again, Captain Teraoka?"

The Japanese high command still did not know what to do with Bose, and feared that their deteriorating war position would not permit them to go ahead with Bose's plan for a march on India. Bose was soon to become aware of the problems in the Co-Prosperity Sphere. After his arrival in Sabang in Sumatra (the *1-29* had been diverted there, Penang being considered dangerous because of rumours), Japanese officials were concerned that he should rest and recuperate before plans were made. When Bose replied that he had had all the rest he needed, they smiled politely but said nothing. In Sabang, he was met by his old Berlin friend Colonel Yamamoto, who had returned to Japan at the end of 1942 on the land route via Turkey and Russia, and now headed the Indo-Japanese liaison group known as the Hikari Kikan.

Bose's journey from Sumatra to Tokyo took five days, illustrating the difficulty of travel in the Co-Prosperity Sphere. A few days after he arrived all Japan mourned the death of

Admiral IsorokuYamamoto. The country was clearly on the defensive: Guadalcanal was lost, and American submarines were savaging Japan's shipping. German defeats in Stalingrad and north Africa, too, had turned the tide against the Axis. Subhas had arrived at the wrong time and Prime Minister Hideki Tojo, struggling with his problems, could see no reason why he should receive the Indian.

At Tokyo's Imperial Palace Hotel Bose's quarters were sumptuous, and a stream of Japanese dignitaries, including the Navy minister and the foreign minister, called on him; but for three weeks Tojo kept him waiting. Hasan, however, believes that the wait was engineered by Bose and suited him, as it enabled him to get to know the Japanese leadership before he met the prime minister. Among those he met was Lieut-General Seizo Arisue, chief of military intelligence.

Tojo finally met Bose on 10 June 1943. Not knowing what to expect, Bose began the discussion quietly, but soon launched into a passionate argument for liberating India. Tojo, used to dealing with sycophants, particularly among non-Japanese, was so taken by this that all his coolness seemed to vanish, and he suggested a second, longer, meeting. This took place four days later, with Tojo flanked by his foreign minister, Shigemitsu Mamoru, and his chief-of-staff, General Sugiyama. When Tojo had finished outlining Japan's strategy, Bose asked, "Have you, sir, considered the question of sending the Japanese Army into India for the liberation campaign if it is deemed necessary?" Bose had raised the same question with Sugiyama earlier, suggesting a march to Chittagong, but for Tojo this was a revolutionary proposal. His response was to prevaricate. But after Bose had left, Tojo was reported to have turned to Shigemitsu and declared, "He is a great Indian, fully qualified to command the INA. [Indian National Army]." Shigemitsu had already come to the same conclusion. By this time Subhas had met Rash Behari Bose, who confirmed that he was waiting for his younger namesake to take over.

Two days later Bose was invited to the Japanese Parliament to listen to Tojo declare that he fully sympathised with Indian efforts to free her, and would give all possible assistance. On 19 June Bose held his first press conference in Japan, and over 60 Japanese and foreign newsmen gathered to hear him assert, "The enemy that has drawn the sword must be fought with the sword. Civil disobedience must develop into armed struggle. And only when the Indian people receive the baptism of fire on a large scale, will they qualify for their freedom."

His credentials, he said, were not in doubt: he had escaped in response to Indian needs, and all he was doing now was in accordance with the Indian people's deepest convictions. True, Japan had earlier been considered an aggressor in China – he himself had condemned her – but this was a new Japan: a country that had re-awakened Asia by her victory over Russia in 1905, and one whose cultural ties with India went back twenty centuries. The new Japan had pledged her might to India's fight for freedom. There could be no going back.

On 27 June 1943 Bose left Tokyo for Singapore, arriving there on 2 July He had decided not to visit China and Manchukuo. As if in recognition of his new role he did not travel under the pseudonym of Mazzotta (or even Matsuda, the Japanese version of his pseudonym). For the first time since leaving India he used his own name. For a whole week he received a delirious welcome from the Indian community. His most dramatic moment, certainly the most satisfying, was when he inspected the Indian National Army in Singapore.

Bose had been due to arrive at Kallang, near Singapore's city centre, but when his plane landed at Seletar there was a furious rush by Indians and Japanese to meet him. Mohammed Zaman Kiani, who had been in the British Indian Army, and became commander-in-chief of the INA, described in his memoir how Bose was driven by road to Kallang to inspect an INA guard of honour and was absolutely captivated when he saw the soldiers .Two days later Subhas formally took charge of the Indian independence movement in east Asia. Over 2,000 people witnessed and ratified the proceedings. Rash Behari Bose made a gracious handover, "You might now ask me what I did in Tokyo for our cause and what present I have brought for you. Well, I have brought you this present…from now on Subhas

Chandra Bose is your president, your leader in the fight for India's independence…and I am confident that under his leadership you will march on to battle and victory."

Then Bose delivered the first of his classic east Asia speeches. Whatever happened in the war, he said, the British Empire was doomed; but she would continue to tighten her grip on India. She might make face-saving compromises, but she would never relinquish India. Indian freedom would only be achieved when Indians abroad combined with Indians at home. The events that followed Gandhi's call to the British to 'Quit India' in August 1942 had shown that India had moved from passive non-violence to active resistance. Now all that was required was for Indians abroad to organise and start a second front. For this, help from Japan and the Axis powers was necessary. Bose said that some might doubt the sincerity of the Axis powers. Were they doing India a favour? They, for their own purposes, wanted to destroy Britain's influence. As for sincerity, the best proof was he himself. All his life he had fought the British: their prisons, their governing class, their cunning and deceit. They had failed to corrupt him: how could the Japanese or the Germans succeed in a few months?

Bose turned his attention to the fighting army that would spearhead the revolutionary war. The INA was renamed the *Azad Hind Fauj* (Free India Army) and as it paraded in front of the Municipal Buildings in Singapore he addressed "the soldiers of liberation." He had often dreamt of organising such an army, and in Germany had spent many hours planning and working for it. When he had arrived in Singapore, he had not been able to take his eyes off the guard of honour assembled to greet him. Bose knew its officers and men were already his. He pledged himself to them.

On 5 July Bose reviewed the INA, telling them their cry from now on must be *Chalo Delhi,* Onwards to Delhi: "If you follow me...I shall lead you to victory and freedom. It does not matter who among us will live to see India free. It is enough that India shall be free and that we shall give our all to make her free." The next day Tojo gave the army his approval. The diary of important events of the INA (in 1943) records what happened:

> At 11.20 hrs - Premiere General Hideki Tojo accompanied by a large number of Japanese officers arrived. Srijut(a term of respect) Subhas Chandra Bose went forward to receive them. As Premier General Tojo came out of the car, both Srijut Subhas Chandra Bose and Premier General Tojo laughingly shook their hands. This created a great pleasure in the mind of everybody. This was the symbol of showing more relationship among Indian and Nippon.

The military display confirmed Tojo's excellent opinion of Bose. Even Field-Marshal Count Terauchi, commander of the Japanese forces in southeast Asia, who had already met Bose, was impressed, and when Tojo met Terauchi later, the two men agreed that here was a leader of "great calibre". On 9 July, Bose and Tojo were together again, and in the central plaza of Singapore more than 60,000 Indians – nearly all the Indians in Singapore – gathered to express their support. In Tokyo, when Japanese newsmen had asked him if he had plans for Indian liberation, Bose had replied, "Naturally there is a plan and the plan is being worked out." Now he revealed it. A Provisional Government of Free India would be set up; it would own the allegiance of all the Indians in east Asia. "Total mobilisation for a total war" would be the cry. He wanted 30 million dollars and 300,000 soldiers, an army that would be powerful enough to attack the British Army in India. "When we do so, a revolution will break out, not only among the civil population at home but also among the Indian Army which is now standing under the British flag."

Hugh Toye, the British intelligence officer who interrogated the INA after the war, is right in questioning Bose's belief that he only had to arrive outside Jericho for the walls to collapse. But as often with Bose, there was symbolism here. For the first time a truly national Indian leader had raised a banner of armed revolt. Not even the Revolt of 1857, which Bose often presented as the First War of Independence, had India produced a single leader who appealed to the entire country. To the soldiers of the INA Bose combined the direct vision of a commanding officer with a remarkable knowledge of world affairs; for the officers his technical knowledge and grasp of military matters were a revelation, and his personal warmth and friendliness touching. Officers were always welcome at his home; often he would play badminton with them and offer them his own clothes. In an Indian society where leaders behaved like gods he was a mere mortal. So if an officer came to his home for a meal and needed a wash he held out the soap or towel for him, a simple gesture that had a big impact. For the civilians, used to timid politicians, here was a politician who knew the working of politics, had fought the best in India, had conferred with Hitler, Mussolini and Tojo, and yet spoke a language readily understood by all.

He was helped by his style. By now he had quickly discarded his flowing silk suits – he had arrived in Singapore in one of them – in favour of a military uniform: khaki tunic, forage cap and knee-length military boots, which he wore even in the hottest weather. Whenever he travelled he demanded all the rights and privileges of a head of state. On his road journeys in Malaya, for instance, he insisted on a full ceremonial escort: Japanese military jeeps mounted with sub-machine guns, a fleet of cars, and motorcycle outriders. On his travels to Thailand, Burma and elsewhere he took an entourage of a couple of ADCs, a physician, a valet, an orderly and a personal secretary.

Megalomania? Perhaps. But the Indians in east Asia were immigrants; a minority were rich, but all of them suffered from the classic insecurity of immigrants. Though many kept abreast of Indian politics, they had no deep knowledge, no genuine awareness of Indian affairs. Bose felt they had to be made politically conscious if he was to further his grandiose plans. Pomp and ceremony were essential for this process. Bose knew that before the Indians could be aroused they had first to be convinced that Indians were inferior to none. They had lived all their lives in an alien country, dominated first by the British and now by the Japanese, and made to feel inferior to both.

In this connection Sivaram, the Indian journalist soon drawn into Bose's publicity team, tells an interesting story of how the title "Netaji" took hold among Indians, Malays and Chinese in east Asia. When Rash Behari Bose was preparing to hand over to Subhas he had thought of christening him *Deshsevak* (Servant of the Nation), an interesting variation on the name given to Das, Subhas' guru, who was *Deshbandhu* (Friend of the Nation). But soon after Bose arrived in east Asia, Hasan told Sivaram that Bose would like Indians there to address him as "Netaji". Hasan told Sivaram, "The role of India's Füehrer is just what Subhas Chandra Bose will fill." Sivaram and Ayer, later Bose's information minister, discussed the title. Ayer was doubtful about it, but Sivaram, seized with the idea, saw the opportunity for an interesting exercise in scientific propaganda. In what he described later as "a quiet and subtle way" he introduced the prefix Netaji to Subhas Chandra Bose's name in the news and comments carried by the newspapers of the Indian Independence League, the Japanese-sponsored body for east Asian Indians. 'Netaji' had arrived. Subhas Bose, like Mahatma Gandhi, had acquired a title which would always be associated with him. In India today, to call him Subhas Bose is to reveal one's political opinion of him.

Certainly there were excesses. Many of those who actively opposed the INA were imprisoned, and others were turned over to the Japanese, by whom they were tortured. Many Indian soldiers were killed by the Japanese in hideous circumstances, although there is nothing to suggest that Bose knew about the tortures. But it is true that Bose showed no mercy to deserters and saboteurs, insisting upon stern punishments.

Netaji sometimes allowed the emotions of the crowd to overrule his better judgement. In September 1943 Bose and Ayer were driving to one of the many mass rallies in Singapore. Suddenly he turned to Ayer and said, "I am going to say that the INA will stand on Indian soil before the year is out." Ayer, who was privy to most things, was stunned: had the Japanese approved? Had there been some special arrangements with Tojo to make Bose so confident? But Subhas merely smiled and said it would turn out all right. More than 50,000 Indians packed into a vast Singapore park to hear Bose at his best, and just before the end he made his announcement. Ayer could feel the ground shaking under his feet as the audience leaped in the air and cheered for two minutes.

The Japanese liaison officers present were also stunned, but in a very different way. His concluding promise was not in the original draft and, as the Indians celebrated, the officers tried to get Japanese newspapermen to kill the story. That evening they told Ayer and Sivaram, who were arranging the broadcasts to India, that the concluding portion of Netaji's speech could not go to air. Ayer and Sivaram telephoned him, and Bose made the broadcast himself, repeating his promise.

Late that night Bose, Ayer and Sivaram returned to Bose's house for their usual late night political chat. Sivaram, due to leave for Burma, was eager to know the plans that had prompted Bose's promise. At last Bose simply said, "Oh, it was such a huge crowd, and I felt towards the end of the speech that it was expecting something from me, something more than what I had already said."

Symbolism, of course, was always an essential element of Bose's appeal. He believed the British were the masters of spin, claiming to run the greatest and most benevolent empire in history. He wanted to use their tactics to make Indians believe that he and his revolutionary movement was more powerful than it was. Bose's INA was, of course, the second INA. As we have seen the first one had disintegrated under the weight of Japan's racial and imperial arrogance, from Indian suspicions of Japanese plans, and, above all, from the inability of the heterogeneous Indians to work together. Its disintegration had ruined much of the work of Fujiwara. By the time Bose arrived to take over the reformed INA, the Japanese had locked up Mohan Singh, the original commander. After some persuasion from some of Singh's erstwhile colleagues, who were now working for Bose, the two men met.

Just after Christmas 1943, Bose went to Singapore's notorious Changi Prison and met Mohan Singh. During the two hour meeting Bose told Singh, using the Hindi term "Bulana," that he had intended to summon him. Singh, defending himself, made no secret of his now very anti-Japanese views:

> For himself he had seen enough of the Japanese to realise that the greatest disservice he could do his country would be to introduce them into it. He felt that Japanese entry into India would only make of that country another China, even if the British were defeated and that the dissolution of the INA must inevitably make them think twice about attempting to do so.

This summary comes from report No 1007 to the Combined Services Detailed Interrogation Centre by Hugh Toye. It was made in November 1945, as part of Toye's job as the British Intelligence Officer interrogating INA prisoners. Toye wrote it after he had interrogated Singh in Pearl, another Singapore prison. Singh is identified as H/1050 and Toye, who had begun to form a better appreciation of Bose, concluded:

> H/1050 talks of Bose very much as Pompey might have spoken of Caesar. Bose made a success of something in which H/1050 had failed. Bose, adroit politician as he was, thought H/1050's failure had been due to a loss of temper, and greatly angered H/1050 by not appearing to understand the purity of his aims. For this reason H/1050, who once thought of Bose as a sincere patriot, now calls him an unscrupulous adventurer whose only motive was lust for power. Personal glory and the glamour attached to the position of Fuehrer, which once were able to sway H/1050 himself, were in his view the forces which drove Bose. He

does not recognise that Bose, too, in his way stood up to the Japanese and he regards him as a collaborator and a traitor totally insensitive to the lofty ideals of freedom which he himself followed.

Many years later when Singh came to write his memoirs in independent India, he did not call Bose a traitor or a collaborator. But he did not present him in a good light and alleged that though Bose promised to free him, he made no attempt to do so, possibly because he was not sure that Mohan Singh would support him (the Sikh had declared his over-riding loyalty to Nehru). The Bose-Singh meeting ended abruptly as Bose had to return to his Singapore residence before the blackout. Bose promised to call again but did not do so. Bose did, however, get Singh moved to a healthier prison in Sumatra and had his conditions improved. Nearly nine months after this meeting Bose had to encounter the political ghost of Singh. As he was visiting Maymo in Burma in September 1944, someone in the crowd shouted out *"Mohan Singh Zindabad"*. Bose told the man that he "could not release Mohan Singh as his views on the running of the INA greatly differed from his." In any case, the men of the second INA did not want Singh. Bose ignored the first INA as if it were a bad dream, and concentrated on turning the second one into a living reality.

By this time, Bose had already formed a very different relationship with Singh's Japanese mentor, Major Fujiwara. Bose had met him for the first time a few months earlier, on 26 August 1943, in the company of Major General Todai Kunomura, chief of staff of the 15th Japanese Army. The contrast in the settings of the two meetings was vivid. The meeting with Fujiwara took place in Bose's residence in Kallang in Singapore, a beachfront house set in spacious grounds, its neatly trimmed lawn brilliant with bright red and yellow cannas and roses. For the visit water had been sprinkled at the entrance, a gesture that touched Fujiwara. He was sad that Mohan Singh was sitting in prison but was overwhelmed by the personality of Bose. Forty years later in his war memoirs F.Kikan (which stands for Fujiwara Kikan, meaning Fujiwara Liaison Group), Fujiwara recalled:

> A tall man in military uniform, looking very dignified and noble, stepped out of the line towards me...I knew that he was Netaji Bose. He was effusive in his greeting as if welcoming an old friend. In his appearance I saw the nobleness of a philosopher, steely will, passionate fighting spirit, and great wisdom and refinement. At first glance, he appeared to me a man of extraordinary ability...Netaji Bose exchanged greetings with Gen. Kunomura first. Then he walked towards me and shook hands firmly. As he gave me a cordial look of profound appreciation and his voice spoke my name, I felt his warmth running through my body like an electric wave. He embraced me and invited me to sit on a sofa as if he would carry me there. My old INA officers gathering around us watched me with deep emotion. When everyone was seated Netaji spoke highly of me. I was very much touched, especially when he showed his deep compassion and high esteem and appreciation for my friends, Pritam and Gen. Mohan.

This was a shrewd move by Bose who was aware of how close Fujiwara had been to Mohan Singh. Fujiwara recorded what Bose said:

> Major Fujiwara, I have been anxiously waiting for this opportunity to meet you since I was in Berlin (he must have been acquainted with my name through communication from Pritam). I am really glad to see you. I have heard about your distinguished contributions to the INA. from Gen. Mohan (he seemed to have met Gen Mohan in exile and heard about the INA. from its founding), IIL and INA. comrades, Lieut. Kunizuka [former F Kikan member and the Hikari

> Kikan interpreter], and Senda.. Pritam, Gen. Mohan, and you are the founding fathers of the INA., a revolutionary army that we have been unable to organize but you have formed and handed it to me. I wish to express my appreciation to you on behalf of the Indian people. I regret that Gen. Mohan is not able to honour us with his presence today. I think highly, however, of the objectives and achievements of Pritam and Gen. Mohan and appreciate them very much.

Unlike Mohan Singh, Fujiwara came to worship Bose and thought he was the closest an Indian came to being a Japanese *samurai.*

Soon after his arrival in Singapore Bose had wanted to expand the strength of the INA from 13,000 to 50,000 and eventually to 3 million. The Japanese were aghast. They could at best equip about 30,000 and then only with light arms. During his visit to Singapore, Tojo refused to commit himself to this expansion, and half-jokingly suggested that the "disorderly crowd" (meaning the existing INA) should be controlled. The official Japanese history of the country's involvement with Bose suggests that poor translation prevented Bose from appreciating the drift of Tojo's argument, and that he harboured the mistaken impression that local Japanese officials were thwarting Tokyo's will. Bose felt that a large army was necessary not so much for fighting as for the psychological effect it would have on the British:

> In India the British Army boasts of its military strength "10 times" more than its actual strength. Indians believe this and are being influenced by it. Now, I follow the British Army's example, and would like to propagate that the Provisional Government of India has more than "30 divisions". At any rate, I would first like to create units which may be called divisions and fill in the required number of soldiers as quickly as possible.

It was on this pipe dream as much as anything else that he based his strategy. As he would tell Ayer and Sivaram almost nightly, "Propaganda must be bumptious to be really effective. We must always be thinking up new things to hold the interest of the people."

Indians were not the only ones affected by Bose. Soon after his Singapore investiture Bose embarked on a series of journeys: to Bangkok, Saigon and Rangoon. Everywhere he went he was ceremoniously received. To the leaders of these countries he seemed the embodiment of a nascent and welcome Asian nationalism. The Thai prime minister Marshal Luant Pibulsonggram, struggling with his own problems of collaborating with the Japanese, was initially reluctant to receive him, but when he did so he was immediately captivated. He later told his associates, "If you want to know what personality is, look at Subhas Bose."

Burma was on the border of India and for Bose the visit there was emotional. Now he was going to Rangoon not as a prisoner of the British but as a free man. He visited the tomb of Bahadur Shah, the last Mughal Emperor exiled by Britain to the Burmese capital. On 29 July, when he reached Rangoon, 100,000 gathered at and around Mingaladon airport to welcome him. Significantly, Bose developed a tremendous rapport with Ba Maw, head of the new Burmese government. Soon after Bose arrived Ba Maw asked him, "What are you going to do next?" Bose stared at him for some time as if he did not understand the question, then replied, "Why, fight, of course." Over the next two years the two men came into closer contact. It was not always easy. For Burmese leaders struggling to come to terms with Japanese-style independence whereby the Japanese retained control of all the important affairs of state, and Burma was still effectively occupied by the Japanese Army, Bose and the INA introduced a troublesome dimension. All Indians in Burma were subject to the Provisional Government of Free India formed by Bose, and he mobilised the resources of some of the richest Indians still carrying on business there.

Nearly 150,000 Indians had fled when the Japanese entered Rangoon, and a third of them died on the long retreat to India. Despite considerable friction between Indians and Burmese at lower levels, Bose's friendship with Ba Maw and other leaders remained intact. The two agreed at their first meeting that Britain was their main enemy, and that, whatever happened, the Burmese and the Indians would not fight each other. Although the fluctuations of war threatened this understanding, particularly when a section of the Burmese Army revolted against the Japanese, Bose never allowed the INA to be turned against the Burmese. In fact, throughout those years, Burma was remarkably free of the anti-Indian riots that had marred Indo-Burmese relations under British rule.

By this time the British, while trying to ensure nobody in India knew what Bose was doing, had provided him with an unexpected propaganda weapon. This was the great Bengal Famine in the summer of 1943. Famines were hardly unknown in India, and during British rule there had been many. Mike Davies has chronicled these disasters in *Late Victorian Holocaust,*showing how millions died of starvation during the Raj. He calls them El Nino Famines, famines where the impact of nature was made worse by the policies followed by the Raj. By contrast, the Bengal Famine that began in the summer of 1943 was man-made, the worst in south Asia in the 20th century, killing three and a half million people. The dreadful incompetence of Raj officials, compounded by the local Bengal government, then wholly controlled by the Muslim League, had produced heart-rending misery. People were so desperate for food that they begged not so much for rice, but for the water in which it is cooked, that Bengalis call "fana." This had some nutrituional value, just to stave off hunger. The streets of Calcutta were clogged with skeletal people. There were many Raj officials who thought that some of the beggars might have been shamming. Instead of taking responsibility they blamed Indian traders for hoarding. Churchill was not sympathetic to the plight of the starving Indians, arguing that feeding them would mean feeding the Congress. So indifferent was the Raj to the disaster that even as sympathetic an observer of the British Raj as today's historian Lawrence James, who is always trying to see the good the British did, admits the incompetence of the administration and points to the racism that shaped the attitude of the War Cabinet in London:

> Linlithgow, Wavell and Amery had to persuade a far from sympathetic War Cabinet that India's need were so great and so urgent that already scarce shipping had to be diverted from such vital wartime duties as the transport of men and ammunition. It was a hard and heart-breaking task, made worse by the interference of Churchill's courtier and adviser, Lord Cherwell, who held all non-white races in contempt and imagined himself an expert on India affairs. Wavell rated him "a fraud and a menace" which was a good judgement as any on Cherwell's talents and value.

As it happens, Wavell, who had become viceroy in 1943, was more sympathetic to the plight of the Indians than his predecessor, the leaden Linlithgow, who could not even find time to visit Bengal during the famine. For Bose the famine was another indictment of British rule and in August 1943, he offered to ship to India 100,000 tons of rice as a gift from the Indians in East Asia. Wavell rejected the offer, providing more grist to Bose's attacks on the Raj.

Setting up a Provisional Government had been Bose's main objective since his return to Asia. Tojo had agreed to it "in principle" at their meetings in Tokyo, and had again endorsed it when he visited Singapore in July. But not all Japanese officials agreed with Tojo. To the lower ranks of the Japanese Army in Singapore it made no sense: it was a government without territory, without citizens and without any authority. Even Tojo and his Cabinet regarded it as a part of Japan's aggressive propaganda towards India. On 9 October 1943 the Supreme Military Headquarters of Japan decided that if Bose did set up such a government, it would be recognised, but not in a formal diplomatic sense: there would be no exchange of diplomatic personnel, no administration of territory. Finally, on 21 October 1943, Bose inaugurated his government. He realised that he did not have enough men of the right calibre; most of those who surrounded him were ordinary individuals made extraordinary by circumstances. Ayer suggested that Bose have a Cabinet of one, with all matters apart from war and foreign affairs in the charge of departmental secretaries till such time as suitable candidiates emerged. Bose would have none of it. It would be seen as dictatorship. In the end he appointed four Cabinet ministers; there were also eight military and eight civilian representatives, and he appointed himself head of state, prime minister, minister of war and minister of foreign affairs.

Two nights before the government was announced Bose sat down to write the proclamation. Hasan says Bose dictated it but Ayer has a very different and more vivid recollection:

> He took hold of a bunch of quarter sheets of blank paper, took a pencil in hand, and started writing. ... He did not lift his eyes from the paper in front of him, silently handed to me the first page as soon as he finished it, and I walked out of the room and sat at the typewriter...He never even once wanted to see any of the earlier pages that he had written. ... In the entire script there was not one word corrected or scored out, and the punctuation was complete.

When Ayer finally presented the typed 1,500-word proclamation, Bose did not change a comma. It was the manifesto of the nationalist movement, and Subhas Bose required no prompting to write it. On the afternoon of 21 October 1943 the proclamation was read out at a packed Cathay cinema in Singapore. Then Bose took the oath of allegiance, breaking down in tears halfway through:

> In the name of God, I take this sacred oath that to liberate India and the thirty-eight crores of my countrymen [388 millions] I, Subhas Chandra Bose, will continue the sacred war of freedom till the last breath of my life. ... I shall remain always a servant of India and to look after the welfare of thirty-eight crores of Indian brothers and sisters shall be my highest duty.

At midnight on 23 October the government, in its first act, declared war on Britain and the United States. There was some opposition to declaring war on America, but Bose easily overrode the objection, a development that set the pattern for all Cabinet meetings that usually lasted well into the night. Bose's decision was final.

The same day Japan recognised the Provisional Government. By 19 November 1943 eight other countries, including Germany, Italy, China, Manchukuo (now Manchuria), Burma, Thailand, Croatia and the Philippines had also recognised it, and Eamon de Valera had sent a personal message of congratulation from Dublin. Not everybody was convinced, but for the great majority of Indians, Bose and his government were the only points of assurance in the uncertain world. Even the British would acknowledge this. Within days of Japan's surrender a secret Raj memo declared:

> Bose's influence over the INA is very considerable... it affects all races, castes and communities almost equally strongly. They regard him with deep admiration, respect and confidence as a sincere patriot, as an able leader without peer among the overseas Indian community, as the organiser of India's first 'National Army', as the protector of his countrymen under Japanese occupation, and as one who successfully dealt with the Japanese and was accorded by them greater respect and power than most other leaders in the same position.

One of Bose's remarkable innovations was the formation of the women's regiment called the Rani of Jhansi regiment, named after the heroine of the 1857 rebellion. During the submarine trip, Bose had talked to Hasan of forming such a regiment. In Singapore, he found the ideal woman to lead it. She was Lakshmi Swaminathan. Her father had been an British-trained criminal lawyer and a leading member of the bar in Madras. Her mother, Ammu, a devoted follower of Gandhi, had taken Lakshmi to the 1928 Congress Session in Calcutta and thought that Bose, strutting around in his military uniform, was an "upstart". Love had brought Lakshmi to Singapore. With a failed marriage behind her, she had fallen in love with a classmate, who she identifies only as 'K', a fellow doctor. Lakshmi followed him to Singapore in June 1940. On 19th February 1942, she had been at the meeting in Farrer Park, which launched the first INA, dazzling Fujiwara with her "regal" looks. Later one evening in the summer of 1943 Bose summoned her to his Singapore residence, and asked her to take charge of a women's regiment. Lakshmi would later tell Peter Ward Fay of that encounter:

> He was charming, I was very, very impressed. I don't think I have ever been so impressed by another person as I was by him. He asked me whether I would be willing to take up the job he had in mind. "'What I am asking of you is not a small thing" he said. "Just now we are in Singapore. But don't think I want to have this women's regiment simply as a showpiece. After training you people I intend to send you to Burma. You'll have to fight in the jungles of Burma. And it won't be easy there, because the Allied forces are gathering strength. So think it over very carefully. I want you to be absolutely sure this is something you want to do."

Her decision to accept Bose meant a parting of the ways with 'K'. She also drifted away from her mentor K.P Keshava Menon, a Kerala barrister who had come to Malaya in 1927 and been an active supporter of Gandhi's movements. He took part in the first INA, but then fell out with the Japanese and would have nothing to do with Bose. He argued that Bose's strategy meant substituting the Japanese for the British as masters, and if India had to be a colonial country he would much prefer the British. He would later make very sceptical remarks about Bose, asking that while he might be "the head of the movement, was everything all right with his head?" In November 1944, after being questioned for four months by Kempei Tai, the Japanese secret police, Menon was sentenced to six years rigorous imprisonment.

Bose's decision to invite Lakshmi to head the Rani of Jhansi regiment not only gave her a new life and a challenge but also led her to the great love of her life. This was Prem Kumar Sahgal. A captain in the 2/10 Baluch Regiment of the British Indian Army, he had fought in the Malaya campaign with distinction before surrendering with the other British forces in Singapore. He then joined the INA, becoming Bose's military secretary and eventually commanded his own regiment in the 2nd INA division in March-May 1945. The Lakshmi-Prem relationship was to be the great romance of the INA, although Lakshmi and Prem did not marry until they returned to India after the war.

Bose's purpose in forming the Rani of Jhansi regiment was as a means of re-shaping Indian society. Reba Sen was a 16-year-old in Rangoon at that time. Her father worked in the Burmese Government Medical Service, had looked after Ba Maw but had decided not to leave Burma when the British retreated following their defeat by the Japanese. He became Bose's physician and when Reba joined the Rani of Jhansi regiment asked Bose why he wanted to set up the regiment. She reflected:

> Netaji told my father that he did not expect the women to fight but one of the main problems with India was the lack of discipline. If the women got disciplined as a result of military training then as mothers they would produce

children who were more disciplined and this would have a good impact on future generations of Indians.

Reba was part of a group of about 200 or 250 women who in 1943 started their military training at the Kamayut Camp about 20 miles from Rangoon. The barracks constructed of bamboo would be their home for a year and a half, until Bose and his INA withdrew from Burma in 1945. They were allowed home only on Sundays. For the rest of the week they received military training identical to that of the British Indian Army, with commands being shouted in Hindustani. The women were taught how to use a rifle, a revolver and Bren and Sten guns as well as undertaking bayonet practice. Mornings began with what was called *Kuch Gawaz* which was mainly drill and square bashing. Over the week these women, ranging from students such as Reba and her younger sister, to 30-year old housewives, were trained in military life. This included a 20-mile route march once a week carrying a heavy pack and rifle. It was a spartan existence. Initially the food was good, but later it became very basic, just rice and some vegetables. After the day's training the only amusements were the ones the women could organise amongst themselves. The Japanese did not allow radios in the barracks, but Reba's father had held on to his old radio and kept in touch with affairs.

What all these women had in common was a devotion to Bose. Few Indians who met him could fail to be impressed by him. Reba had a vivid illustration of this when her transport broke down and Netaji provided the women with a meal. It was a Sunday evening and she and other girls were going back to camp in a *tonga* – a horse drawn carriage. The wheels broke and the girls were stranded. They realised that they were quite near Bose's house in Rangoon, a two storey building close to Lake Victoria and the university, and half way to the training camp. They decided to ask for help, but the sentries on guard would not admit them. Bose, hearing the noise, appeared on the upstairs veranda, and told the sentries to let them in, then suggested they dined with him. Reba recalls:

> We ate the same food that he did and it was touching to see that there were no distinction between the leader and the troops. I noticed that there was a box containing betel nut mixture and Netaji was very fond of it. When he realised we liked it he asked us to take it and laid on transport for us to go to the camp.

The main task of the women was often to provide sentry duty for the various meetings addressed by Bose. At one such meeting there was pelting rain but the women remained in their positions ramrod straight. Bose pointed to this and asked, "Did these women fall from heaven? They are also Indian women". This was his answer to those Indians in East Asia who did not think their daughters were strong enough to undergo military training.

Rangoon was one of two homes Bose had in East Asia during his two years there, Singapore being the other. Here his seaside bungalow provided a more beautiful physical setting than either of his homes in Woodburn Park or Berlin. The house had grounds where he could play badminton most evenings. Although Sarat had owned a dog and Subhas liked dogs there was no dog in the Singapore bungalow. There were cats but Subhas hated them.

Posing as an Italian when in Europe had changed Bose's habits. Subhas had become a chain smoker, and drank a little. But in many other ways he was unchanged. Even in wartime Singapore he rose late and breakfasted in his bedroom-cum office, which had a roll-top desk at which he worked. War-time Singapore could not match the opulence of Sarat's home, and breakfast was nothing like as lavish as at Woodburn Park: just a couple of hard-boiled eggs and several cups of tea. Tea was a constant, as was chewing supari, a mixture of betelnut, cardamom and cloves. His day really began when he smoked his first cigarette at around 8 am. After that he was rarely without a cigarette, smoking as many as 40 a day depending on his workload. He would smoke the cigarette to the last butt, which meant his fingers were often scorched.

But he never smoked in bed. He did not want to and nor could he, for he slept under a mosquito net with the ceiling fan going all night. The thoroughness with which he smoked was matched in other things such as when taking medicine. Ayer, his information minister, who often visited his Singapore house, recalled:

> A few mornings he took some Ayurvedic (ancient Indian) medicine in honey. If he happened to be in his room when he was taking the medicine I was a fascinated observer. He hated clumsiness, he had a tiny flat, oval shaped black stones mortar of the type used by vaido (indian pharmacist), with a three-inch pestle to match. After washing both his hands with soap he would carefully put the powder in the mortar and pour a few drops of honey on top of it, then grind it slowly for sometime until the whole thing became a shiny brownish paste. Then lap up the paste direct from the mortar, scrape every bit of the paste from the tip of the pestle with the right middle finger, and lick it carefully and enjoy it like a child eating jam.

Lunch was simple: plain boiled rice, thin dal, vegetables, some dahi (curds), and a banana ending up with coffee. After lunch Bose had a smoke and slept for a little while. Then he would receive callers until nearly dusk. After that, as long as the light lasted there would be a game of badminton, followed by bath. Here is Ayer again:

> After a bath, Netaji would come down for dinner about 8 pm. This was a more leisurely meal, which Netaji would eat very well and enjoy every morsel of. At least two helpings if fish was really good, plenty of pooris with dal, followed by a plateful of rice with curry, one more helping of rice if the curry was very good, followed by some sweets. Netaji would not touch it if it was custard, for fear of adding to his weight; if was any other sweet, just a bit to see how it tasted. Coffee would go round. Then we could tell how soon or late Netaji wished to go to bed that night. Once in a way, Netaji used to turn in very early, meaning, of course, about 11-0 p.m. He would not touch coffee those nights. Then we knew. He would smoke a cigarette or two, chat with one of us for a few minutes in a semi-sleepy way, then get up and go to his bedroom. If he took one cup of coffee, he had decided to go to bed about midnight or 1-0 a.m. Two cups, then he wanted to sit up till 2-0 or 3-0 a.m. If he ordered more coffee to be sent up to his room sometimes after dinner, then it was to be practically an all night affair.

One practise he never abandoned. In bed, before falling asleep, he read religious or political books.

19

The Toast Of Japan

On 5 November 1943 the Greater East Asia Conference opened in Tokyo. The Allies had publicised widely the historic importance of the periodic gatherings of Roosevelt and Churchill in Casablanca, Tehran, and other exotic places. Lt-Gen. Seizo Arisue had toured Japanese-occupied Asia earlier during the year and discovered, to his surprise, that not many people believed that the Co-Prosperity Sphere was a Japanese philanthropic enterprise, in fact quite the reverse. He suggested to Prime Minister Tojo that a properly organised international conference be held, preferably in Bandung in Java, so as to convince people that Japan was not the aggressor the Allies pictured her to be. Initially Tojo had been lukewarm to the idea, but, as Japan's military position deteriorated, and with it Tojo's fortunes, he decided he needed a propaganda boost. The conference was a disaster.

The choice of Tokyo as the venue instead of Bandung was unwise. (Eleven years later men who now led a truly free Asia were to meet in Bandung) The leaders Tojo hosted in Tokyo were political pygmies, and 18 days later Roosevelt, Churchill and Chiang Kai-Shek were able to meet in Cairo and had no trouble burying the Tokyo conference in an avalanche of high-sounding declarations about fighting Axis tyranny on behalf of democracy.

Out of the Tokyo publicity disaster, Subhas emerged as the only star. The group photograph taken after the conference showed Tojo in the middle surrounded by the assembled leaders, and Bose was to be seen standing a little apart. Both at and after the conference he stood out. Since he could not commit India to the Japanese Co-Prosperity Sphere he chose to be an observer, not a delegate. When he spoke he said that he believed in Japan's promises, that this was indeed a conference of liberated nations meeting as equals, and India's fortunes would rise or fall with those of Japan. "If our allies were to go down, there will be no hope for India to be free for at least a hundred years." But whatever happened the struggle would go on. The speech was an outstanding success. Many of the delegates were moved, and Ba Maw was almost ecstatic. Tojo concluded the conference by declaring the Japanese would hand over the Andaman and Nicobar islands to the Indian Provisional Government. For the next week Subhas was the toast of Japan. He was asked to address a public meeting. This was an almost unprecedented invitation, since few foreigners were allowed to address Japanese audiences. There followed by a series of meetings with various officials, including an audience with Emperor Hirohito.

On 18 November 1943 Bose left Tokyo, taking the long route back to Singapore. There were triumphant receptions in Nanking, Shanghai, and Manila, where Jose P. Laurel, the Filipino president installed by the Japanese, gave him a lavish reception. He also visited Saigon. Everywhere he went the aura and the glow created at the Greater East Asia Conference preceded him.

Reinforcing his image as a world statesman Bose had his own plane, a present from Tojo. But the pilot and crew were Japanese, and when Bose had suggested that perhaps an Indian pilot and crew would be most suitable, Tojo had softly said, "My pilot will look after your safety. And who knows whether your pilot may fly in the wrong direction?" Just to make sure that no such mishaps occurred, Tojo attached two Hindustani-speaking Japanese to the crew, who no doubt easily monitored Bose's conversations. However, when the 11-seater plane arrived wearing large Rising-Sun emblems, Bose ordered that the INA's tricolour with a leaping tiger at its centre be painted on either side of the aircraft's nose.

During his stay in Japanese-controlled China, Bose made radio appeals to Chiang Kai-Shek from both Nanking and Shanghai asking him to make an honourable peace with Japan. He had clearly changed his tune with regard to Japan and its aggression in China. Now he claimed Japan had changed, and wanted a genuine partnership, a claim he may not have believed. He could hardly say anything else, although American intelligence agents closely monitored Bose's visits to Nanking and Shanghai speculated that he might be considering switching sides and coming over to the Allies. The Americans were always worried that their corrupt Chiang Kai-shek, might defect to the Japanese, but Bose never contemplated switching sides himself, despite sensing that Japan was losing the war.

Okawa Shumeii, the ultra-nationalist Japanese philosopher, asked him what he would do if Germany were defeated. "We fight on," replied Bose, "and if necessary join the Soviet Union." Okawa got the impression that Bose was beginning to realise that Japan could not win the war and had started to distance himself from Japan's cause. It was a significant pointer to Bose's future actions.

In the last days of 1943 the battle with Britain that Bose had long planned began to take shape. It is an accepted myth, propagated by some British writers, that in 1944 the Japanese launched an invasion to conquer India. During the war British Intelligence reported that the Japanese were planning a "full-scale invasion of India." Since the war there have been many books describing Japan's incredible gamble to seize India. But the Japanese were never so ambitious. Lieutenant Colonel (later Sir John) Figgess, who consulted the surviving Japanese commanders, told the Historical Section of the Cabinet Office on 26 June 1948, that:

> The Japanese High Command did not seriously contemplate an invasion of India by land in 1944. They did, however, hope to inflict such serious defeat on the British Indian forces that Subhas Chandra Bose would be able to lead his Indian National Army unopposed into India and thus achieve a virtually bloodless conquest.

Even Bose did not visualise a swift march to Delhi. Both he and the Japanese were working along more complex lines. Bose visualised the INA establishing a foothold in India from where his revolutionary army could steadily advance. At least they might create a position whereby, whatever the outcome of the war, a free Indian state of some size would survive. They had in mind the sort of entity that President Sukarno had established in Indonesia in 1945.

For the Japanese, the campaign in India was the product of years of planning, and much discussion and disagreement. The Japanese had begun to prepare for a thrust into India as soon as they had conquered Burma in May 1942. In December that year, three British-Indian divisions had attempted to seize Akyab island on the Arakan coast, but had been easily halted. It was not until February 1943 that fighting in Burma came alive. In that month Britain's Orde Wingate had launched Operation Loincloth. In this a British infantry brigade, lightly equipped and specially trained, had penetrated the Chindwin river area, operated behind Japanese lines for two months, temporarily cut the Mandalay to Myitkyina railway line, and killed many Japanese. In military terms it meant little, but for the first time British troops had taken the offensive against the Japanese, and the British press soon built Wingate up as a great "man of destiny". Lt-Gen. Renya Mutaguchi was outraged. This aggressive, irascible general, who had engineered the Marco Polo Bridge incident, which had led to the war with China in 1937, began mapping out an advance to India. By June 1943 he had evolved a plan: two divisions would make a determined thrust along the Sittaung-Palal-Imphal route, trap and break the British, and finally take Imphal in the mountainous regions of the Burma-India frontier. The whole thing would be over in three weeks.

Bose's plan was different. He had pressed Sugiyama at their first meeting to launch an attack through Chittagong on the coast far to the south. The fall of this East Bengal port would simply be the catalyst for the INA: for the British would be thrown into disorder, and Bengal would form a ready and welcome base for revolutionary activities. It was about this time that Ian Stephens, then editor of *The Statesman* in Calcutta told a dinner party that, were the Japanese to parachute Bose on to the *maidan*, some 90 per cent of the city's inhabitants would rush to join him. Stephens' guests were not amused, but this was also Bose's assumption.

For the Japanese, however, Chittagong was strategically impossible: the supply problems would be horrendous. As a port it would be exposed to attacks from both air and sea, two sectors in which Japanese strength was rapidly diminishing.

Bose's incredible success with the east Asian Indians had removed one crucial doubt. Indians, or at least some of them, would welcome Japanese action in India. There was no need to worry about hostile reactions from the Congress leaders. In August, soon after Bose's return from his whirlwind tour, two Japanese officers called on him. Both the visit and what they had to say surprised and delighted him. The Japanese Army was preparing an offensive in Imphal and the INA. would be actively involved.

By September 1943 everything seemed ready for the offensive that was to start as soon as the monsoon ended. In April the Japanese had created the Burmese Area Army, under Lt-Gen. Kawabe Masakazu, and Mutaguchi was made commander of the 15th Army, answerable to Kawabe. It was a strong team. Both men had worked together before and understood each other. In June, the Burma Area Army held map manoeuvres and decided to scale down some of Mutaguchi's more optimistic plans. He had wanted a thrust far into India by September and build a defensive line along the Brahmaputra river, linking with Dimapur and Shillong on the Assam plains. The others decided that a line along the mountain range west of the Imphal plains would be more defensible. By September Kawabe had received instructions from the Southern Army to prepare for an offensive in October.

But in Tokyo Tojo refused to fire the starting pistol. There were problems. The required infantry strength had not been built up, and Japanese air power was inadequate. October passed; there were more plans, more map manoeuvres and more losses of temper by Mutaguchi, who had already sacked one of his chiefs of staff. There was still no word from Tokyo, until December 1943, when representations to Tojo persuaded the Japanese leader to sanction the offensive.

On 7 January 1944 the Imperial General Headquarters issued the formal orders "to capture strategic areas near Imphal and in north-eastern India, for the defence of Burma". It was another two months before the campaign would begin, but the Japanese and the INA were on their way. The same day, Bose shifted his headquarters to Rangoon, a move that followed complex negotiations with Japanese commanders, most of whom would have been happy if Bose had kept as far from the front as possible. The newly independent government of Burma – despite Bose's friendship with its leaders – was also apprehensive about his move to Rangoon.

Yet when he landed at Rangoon the ceremonies were punctiliously observed and the entire Burmese Cabinet assembled to receive him. For Bose his arrival climaxed a series of triumphant celebrations, including a visit to Port Blair in the Andaman Islands just before the end of 1943.

Bose had arrived in the islands from Bangkok, where he had made a state visit and had been feted by the Thai government. In Bangkok he told Lieut. Colonel Loganadhan, who was already in his cabinet, that he would be the first chief Indian commissioner of the islands. When Bose arrived on the Andamans on 29 December 1943 he was received by the resident Japanese admiral and stayed in the former home of the British chief commissioner. He renamed the Andamans and Nicobars the *Shahid* (Martyr) and *Swaraj* (Independent) Islands respectively, and made as much of his visit as the Japanese would allow. Bose realised, however, that their transfer to his government meant little. The islands were strategically important to the Japanese Navy, which had agreed to Tojo's order only very reluctantly. The Japanese admiral who received Bose pointed out that the transfer ceremonies were a propaganda exercise. Nothing of real value would be in Loganadhan's hands – at the most some departments of civil administration. Later Loganadhan complained to Bose how the Japanese had made his whole existence redundant; the only department in his charge was education.

Certainly he could do nothing about the brutal Japanese occupation, the main burden of which fell on the educated Indians. British submarines often visited the waters around the islands, and the Japanese Navy grew paranoid about spies. Their treatment of those they suspected was horrific. By September 1944 55 Indians had been executed and 33 imprisoned as British spies, and some were forced to watch their wifes and children being tortured before their very eyes.

One Indian author, N. Iqbal Singh in his *The Andaman Story*, has accused Bose of being naïve about the Japanese and their methods. In December 1944, a year after the so-called Indian takeover of the islands Loganadhan came back to Singapore, sick in heart and body, and was not replaced. But even having nominal charge of the island was an emotional moment for Bose and it fulfilled his rash promise that his people would stand on Indian soil by the end of 1943.

By January 1944 there were accepted problems with the Indian National Army. It was, as Bose had admitted, deficient in many respects, and there was no agreement with the Japanese about how best to use it. When Bose had arrived in east Asia it had numbered about 12,000 men. His calls for more men and his visits to POW camps had netted a further 2,000, but still not enough to raise a second division, for the majority of captured Indian soldiers remained loyal to the Raj. After Count Terauchi had agreed to use the INA in the Imphal operations, a "Subhas Brigade" was formed from men of the 1st Division. It had no artillery, no mortars and no wireless or telephonic equipment. Its machine-guns had few belts, magazines or even spare parts, and medical arrangements were farcical. There were only five medical officers, and they had limited medical supplies and no surgical instruments to look after 3,000 men. "There was also a great shortage of clothing and boots," recalls Shah Nawaz Khan. "Some of the soldiers had to do jungle warfare training barefooted in the most impenetrable and poisonous insect-infested tropical forests of Malaya." But some supplies were bought with Indian civilian money, and in November 1943 the Subhas Brigade was considered sufficiently trained to move to Rangoon.

Sugiyama had agreed to recognise the INA as an allied army, but that still left niggling questions, such as its status, unresolved. When an INA officer met a Japanese officer, who should salute first? The question had led to fighting between the Japanese and Indian officers, and eventually it was decided that officers of the two armies would salute each other simultaneously. Then there was the question of military law. All other armies recognised as allies by the Japanese – Nanking Army, the Manchurian Army, the Burmese Army – accepted Japanese military law. Bose would have none of this. The official Japanese history of those years recalls:

> Bose passionately contended the Japanese military police were hateful and the Indian people and the Indian Army feared them equally. He refused to let them exercise any power over Indian soldiers and Indian people. At last after prolonged negotiations he agreed that they might exercise extremely restricted powers under extremely necessary defensive situations ... The Japanese also agreed that even these restricted powers would not be exercised by low-grade gendarmerie.

Bose's biggest fight with General Kawabe, however, centred round the precise role of the INA in the Imphal operations. Each Japanese division involved in the fighting was to have attached to it small INA propaganda and espionage units, known as *Bahadur* (Fearless) groups, and Kawabe wanted the Subhas Brigade to be similarly split up and attached to the larger Japanese formations. To accept such a supine position would be to strike at the very basis on which Bose had built his appeal. Bose told Kawabe, "The first drop of blood to be shed on Indian soil should be that of the INA." For hours the two men argued. Eventually Kawabe agreed that the Subhas Brigade would not be split into units smaller than battalions. (Later the three battalions were given specific tasks: the first was to form part of the Japanese force operating against the 81st West African Division in the Kaladan Valley, the other two were to guard the routes over the Chin Hills.) But to Kawabe the idea of the INA as a spearhead was absurd. The INA numbered 8,000, whereas the Japanese were putting 230,000 on the field.

The two men met often during the Imphal operations, and developed a warm, deeply felt understanding: Kawabe respected Bose and felt a sense of responsibility towards the INA. When the campaign turned into a disaster he often shielded the worst news from Bose. However, Bose's relations with the Japanese government's civilian representatives were not so cordial. Yamamoto, Bose was convinced, was not always acting as an intermediary should. In January 1944, Tokyo decided to replace him by General Isoda Saburo, but the relationship never recovered. In March 1944 there were two flashpoints. They concerned the formation of the Azad Hind Bank, and the chairmanship of the Indo-Japanese War Co-operation Council that would function in India after the success of the Imphal operation. Both issues gave rise to conferences that lasted hours. But by now Bose was used to the Japanese technique. In Ayer's words:

> The Japanese were rather slow of speech both in the original and in the interpretation. On top of that they would go on repeating what they said, totally ignoring all arguments to counter their assertions or opinions. I had an impression that the Japanese deliberately employed this elephantine method just to drive the other party to the point of utter exhaustion.

Bose kept his temper under check, and he was always patient: if the Japanese had come prepared for a two-hour conference, he was ready to go on for another hour, leisurely chain-smoking. Then, just as the Japanese were preparing to leave, he would pick up a sheet of paper and say: "Just a few small matters." The Japanese would sit down again, thinking it would take only a few minutes more, only to find themselves involved in a full-scale discussion.

For three days the Japanese argued against the formation of the National Bank of Azad Hind. It was not feasible and top bankers had said so. Bose produced rich Indians who were ready to provide the capital and even write their investment off. It would cater to Indian business that other banks could not tap. But the Burmese would never agree , countered the Japanese. Their own state Bank of Burma was doing poorly, and a successful Indian bank would once again make them feel dominated by an Indian immigrant business class. Bose replied that the Burmese had agreed to the formation of the bank. At last the Japanese conceded. The bank was eventually set up with a capital equivalent to 5 million rupees.

The discussions regarding the chairmanship of the Indo-Japanese War Co-operation Council were even more emotional, and foundered altogether over the question of whether the chairman should be Japanese or Indian. Bose knew that if the Japanese double-crossed him in India, he had no physical sanctions. His only weapons were the moral fervour and dedication of the INA. So, from the beginning, he was keen to impress the Japanese with his spirit of independence. When a new Japanese commander-in-chief arrived in Rangoon, Bose insisted that the man call on him first; only then would Bose pay a return visit. In his situation, form was as important as substance. If everything else failed, Bose would threaten to complain directly to Tojo or Sugiyama in Tokyo or, at times, threaten to withdraw from the movement, raise his own suicide squad of 500 men and march to the front. It was almost a replica of the Japanese tradition of total dedication, and it never failed to impress the Japanese. The official Japanese historian recorded: "His intense sense of equality and independence made him argue stoutly and vehemently against anything that encroached on Indian independence."

But for all his belief that rich Indians would support the Azad Hind Bank, Bose was struggling with the east Asian Indian businessmen. He had always made it clear that India's fight for freedom must be financed by the Indians. The money he took from the Germans and Japanese were a loan that he intended to pay back. Bose and his army had great need of money. By October 1943 the monthly expenses amounted to 1 million local dollars , about £116,700. The need for money would increase as more recruitment and other projects began. Bose did not want to depend on Japanese help for more than military essentials. If this was to be an Indian effort, Indians must provide the money, and in Malaya and Burma there were many men rich enough to do that. Initially money flowed in – five million local dollars were collected between July and October 1943. But then Bose came up against the hard-nosed attitude of the successful Indian business community, which often promised much but delivered little.

Bose had quickly assessed the worth of many Indian businesses in Malaya and Burma. As a result of Bose's movement, they were protected by the Japanese and thriving, so they should contribute. Bose had set a collection target of ten per cent of Indian assets, and started off being mild and persuasive. But the hardened immigrant businessmen were immune to such persuasion; some thought of changing their nationality, others made promises they never meant to keep, and all looked anxiously over their shoulders, hoping the British would come back. Bose now revealed the sterner side of his nature. On 17 October 1943 he said: "I shall wait for one or two more weeks and I shall see and after that all the steps that I have to take in the name of India I shall take." By 25 October he was asserting, "Legally speaking there is no private property when a country is in a state of war ... Your lives and your property do not now belong to you; they belong to India and India alone." The speech worked. Within the next two days 20 million Malayan dollars were collected. But the income was still too spasmodic for Bose's plans. Boards of management for raising funds were set up, to which Indians were obliged to declare their assets. From 1944 ten to 25 per cent of the rich Indians' wealth was collected. Board letters stated, "I am ordered to return your present cheque for one hundred dollars and to demand from you payment of your arrears amounting to three thousand dollars within one week ... Failure to do so will result in your being called up here to answer for your action". These letters became common, and were followed by arrests of slack payers. A Hikari Kikan (Japanese liaison group) document found in Bangkok after the war records:

> At the time of his recent state visit to Siam, Bose presented to the Kempei Tai (secret police) a list of names of persons whose arrest he specifically requested and a total of ten persons have accordingly been arrested in three round ups.

Some of these men were tortured and the British later recorded the case of of Noor Mohamed who was jailed from 13 January to 26 July 1945, and emerged so emaciated that his own daughter could not recognise him. Bose believed that the greater good, the liberation of India, justified such methods.

The Japanese operations in Burma in 1944 consisted of two campaigns, each in a different sector: one in Arakan, launched in February, was a holding operation, and the second, launched a month later in the Imphal-Kohima area, was the main campaign. Burma is separated from India by the Chin Hills, an extension of the Himalayas, though their saw-toothed, heavily-forested ridges are not as high. The terrain consisted of thick jungle, innumerable streams that with the onset of the monsoons became raging rivers, and jungle paths and trails just sufficient for the occasional traveller and the jungle inhabitants. The terrain was so difficult that until 1942 there was not even a proper railway connecting Burma with India, and most travel took place along the rivers. By 1944 the British, the Americans and Japanese had constructed roads wide enough to carry military supplies, yet the terrors of the jungle remained: malaria, that could claim more men than the actual fighting, various forms of jungle disease, particularly the terrible Naga sore, and a state of mind called "jungle happiness" in which men became listless, preferring the jungle to crowds and cities, and often unloosed artillery bombardments in the belief that a sniper had been sighted.

Imphal was the capital of the state of Manipur, which separates Assam from Burma. Three thousand feet high (a thousand metres), it is a plateau surrounded by high mountains. In 1944 its access to Assam and India lay through the small rail-head of Dimapur, whence a single-track railway meandered down to the plains. Dimapur was connected to Imphal via the steep Kohima road. Today, a lot has changed and Imphal and Kohima are capitals of separate states within India, but the best means of communication between Bengal and the two towns is still by plane. By the time the Japanese poured across the Chin Hills, the British, using the near-slave labour coolie force of the feudal tea-planters, had vastly improved the Kohima road, but even then it would prove inadequate and in the end air support was to be the crucial factor. Allied air strength was overwhelming.

Arakan, a coastal plain about 150 miles (230km) long and 50 miles (80km) wide, lies outside the mountain range that forms the Indo-Burmese border. Though parts of the plains are cultivated, much of it is covered in jungle, and the monsoons there, as in Imphal, were an experience few forgot. In both areas the rains began in May and lasted until September, bending everything to their will. The jungle became greener, roads were washed away, tracks became mud and rivers became torrents of flood-water. Not far from Imphal is Cheerapunje, the wettest spot on earth, with a rainfall of 400 inches in a year. The only difference between the two areas was that Arakan was more pleasant during the summer: in Imphal summer temperatures of 120 degrees Fahrenheit were not uncommon. These impossible conditions affected both armies, and dictated their actions.

On 15 January 1944 General Tadashi Hanaya, the Japanese Army commander in Arakan, ordered Major-General Tohutaro Sakurai, commander of the 55th Division, to launch the Arakan diversion. The division had been organised into three task forces, each named after its commanders – the Tanabashi force, the Kobe force and the Doi force. Each of them had a 200-strong Bahadur unit of the INA specialising in propaganda, sabotage and subversion. The Japanese objectives were to engage the two British Indian Army divisions, the 5th and the 7th, divert British reserves from Imphal to the Arakan, and inflict heavy casualties on the British. It was a daunting task. Sakurai had not only to defeat the British but to do so quickly enough to use their supplies for his own needs: he was carrying only seven days' rations.

The campaign began brilliantly, thanks to Major L.S. Mishra, the INA commander in Arakan. His Bahadur unit successfully seized a vital British outpost manned by British Indian soldiers. On 4 February 1944 the Tanabashi and Kobe forces took Taung Bazar, swept round the Ngakyedauk Pass, trapping the 7th British Indian Division. On the morning of 7 February the headquarters of the 7th at Laung Chaung were attacked. The Japanese advance had been so swift that the divisional commander, General Frank Messervy, was still in his pyjamas when they arrived. He managed to escape, but supplies had to be abandoned, and some of the Japanese soldiers had an excellent breakfast in the officers' mess. Hanaya had planned to annihilate the 7th Indian Division by 11 February, using the tactics that had worked so brilliantly during the Malaya and Singapore campaigns: seal it off, and then, as it tried to break out, cut it to pieces. But, contrary to Japanese expectations, the British chose to stand and fight, rather than to run away as they had done so often in the past. Moreover, with Japan's air force unable to intervene in strength, the British were able to keep up an almost continuous stream of air supplies.

By mid-February superior British air and ground strength had begun to turn the tide: it was now the Japanese who were encircled. By March both Delhi and Churchill were claiming a great jungle victory. The Japanese had suffered over 5,000 casualties, Sakurai's armies had begun to retreat back to Burma and almost for the first time the Japanese soldiers were surrendering. Yet it was not as grand a success as the British painted it. It had taken five divisions and an enormous airlift to hold off 12,000 men, the British suffered 8,500 casualties, and Lt-General William Slim, the British commander, had committed his reserves to the diversion. It was this last news that Mutaguchi had been waiting for.

Bose had already been discussing aspects of the Imphal campaign with Japanese commanders. On 24 January 1944 Colonel (later Lieutenant-General) Tadasu Katakura, chief of general staff of the Burma Area Army, met Bose and revealed that the Japanese intended to bomb Calcutta. Bose was appalled, and succeeded in convincing the Japanese that the political losses would far outweigh any military gains. Other plans, however, were approved. A few days later Kawabe summoned Shah Nawaz Khan and told him that the Subhas Brigade would be the first INA troops to see action. The Japanese were putting them on trial; they would be subject to the severest tests, and if Indian arms were to liberate India his men must come through victorious. For days before the brigade left for the front Bose was constantly with them, and on 3 February 3,000 soldiers stood in full military kit to hear a final rousing appeal from him.

It seemed everything was going well. In mid-February Bose had dinner with Mutaguchi and Fujiwara. The general could not have been more confident. Not only the plains of Imphal but the plains of the Brahmaputra and the road to Delhi were there for the taking. Bose was overjoyed. "If the Japanese Army succeeds in the Imphal invasion and pushes the INA forward in the Assam plain, the Indian people, as well as the officers and men in the British-Indian Army will respond to the INA." That night Bose invited Fujiwara back to his house, and into the early hours of the morning sketched out his military plans and his political hopes. He was already thinking of how the Provisional government would administer the liberated areas. Soon after his arrival in Singapore Bose had estimated that it would take 12 months after the INA set foot in India to liberate the whole country. To further this he had set up a Reconstruction College, where an Indian ex-magistrate trained the future administrators and civil servants of Free India. They were to be helped by a new revolutionary party with an ideology and a programme. It would first administer the liberated areas and then, like the Nazi Party in Germany, run the country.

By now his plans were complete: as areas were liberated they would come under the Provisional government and be constituted into provinces or states. If two liberated areas were not contiguous, separate administrations would be set up, though the existing boundaries of the states of British India would be maintained. Each province would be ruled by a governor, assisted by a governor's secretariat and an advisory council. The governor's secretariat would be in charge of several departments, ranging from internal affairs to finance, law, and public enlightenment, which covered internal propaganda – theatre, cinemas, literature, the press – external propaganda and education. The advisory council would consist of 50 people, half of whom would be civilians. The village would be the smallest administrative unit; ten of them would comprise a *dasgoan* (village union), ten dasgoans a *sarkl* (circle), and the progression would continue through districts and up to provinces or states. Special Indian currency notes and Provisional government stamps were printed, and detailed instructions given for the reception of British Indian Army soldiers captured in Burma.

A.N. Sarkar, legal advisor to the Provisional government, was charged with drawing up what was called a Unification Plan for India. Sarkar, a magistrate from Bengal who had come to visit his relatives in Malaya and got caught up in the war, produced a scheme that distilled all Bose's political ideas. It embraced socialist reconstruction and tight state control. There would be regulations about dress – khaki shirt and trousers for work, white shirt and trousers for leisure – and food: a spoon and fork for eating, and if fingers wer used, only three of them were to be utilised. Industrial progress would be through strict state planning. In a free India Japanese firms would not be allowed to operate, though for the present the Japanese Army would have to help with food and medicines, and with seed for growing and reaping crops. As far as maintaining the currency was concerned, Bose formed a monetarist policy:

> When inflation of currency does appear, we will have to adopt additional measures which have a deflating effect by taking off from the market surplus currency, that is currency which is not covered by goods and services and which is really the cause of inflation.

To achieve this, there would be special taxes on immovable property, higher income tax, and taxes on amusements, narcotics, tobacco and state lotteries. So, as the Imphal operations began, Bose set the Free India government in motion. Mutaguchi had said that there would be no Japanese military administration in the liberated areas, and on 16 March Bose named Lt-Col. A.C. Chatterji, who had been busy collecting funds, as "Chief Administrator of Occupied Territories". The INA carried a proclamation addressed to the brothers and sisters in India calling for their co-operation; however, this also listed ten hostile acts which would merit execution or severe punishment. On 4 April, with the fighting already a month old, Bose issued his second proclamation:

> The Provisional Government of Azad Hind (Free India) is the only lawful government of the Indian people. The Provisional Government calls upon the Indian people in the liberated areas to render all assistance and co-operation to the Indian National Army and to the civilian officials appointed by the Provisional Government.

The early reports were all encouraging and Mutaguchi had no doubts about the outcome. He had set up his headquarters in the hill town of Maymyo in central Burma, nearer India, and he confidently told Japanese war correspondents:

> I am firmly convinced that my three divisions will reduce Imphal in one month. In order that they can march fast, they carry the lightest possible equipment and food enough for three weeks. Ah, they will get everything from British supplies and dumps. Boys! See you again in Imphal at the celebration of the Emperor's birthday on 29 April.

Mutaguichi's Army comprised three Japanese divisions: the 15th, the 31st and 33rd. Two INA battalions and two Bahadur espionage and propaganda units were attached to them, and two more INA. regiments joined the fighting in April and May. Mutaguchi had had his problems organising the task force. Only the 33rd was really acclimatised to Burmese conditions. The 31st, which arrived just before D-Day, had been cobbled together from a regiment which had been virtually destroyed in an entirely different sort of war with the Americans in Guadalcanal, while the 15th was delayed in Thailand, where the local Japanese command had encountered many problems, and arrived so late that a fuming Mutaguchi had to postpone the start of the operation. On 8 March 1944, the 33rd started, and on 15 March the other two divisions followed.

As in the Arakan, the plan was simple and everything depended on speed. The 31st was to cross the Chindwin at the northernmost point of the operations, capture Kohima and then move south towards Imphal to help the 33rd, the main striking force, while the 15th would cross the Chindwin lower down and complete the encirclement of Imphal. As with the Arakan campaign, the advance was swift. By early April the 15th and the 31st divisions had covered more than 150 miles, and were already fighting on Indian soil. The 31st had made swift progress towards Kohima, and on 6 April Japanese radio confidently claimed that Kohima had fallen. There is conflict between Japanese and British military records about the fate of Kohima. Japanese historians assert that Kohima did fall to their army; the British only concede that Kohima underwent a severe siege and that certain parts after ferocious fighting were occupied.

For the Japanese victory seemed certain. The fall of Imphal was only a matter of choosing a date; though the Indians favoured 21 April, commemorating the day the Provisional government had been formed, the Japanese opted for the 29 April, as it was the Emperor's birthday. In their eagerness to claim victory, the Japanese released one photograph which showed, they said, a group of INA soldiers entering a Manipur village carrying a photograph of Netaji and being enthusiastically greeted by villagers. The *Azad Hind* newspapers gratefully published the photograph, but an alert reader recognised it as a lane in the Bukit Timah area of Singapore, and the INA soldiers as cadets in the middle of training.

However, the Japanese commanders had made two crucial mistakes. As early as 26 March the 33rd Division had successfully bottled up the British 17th Indian Division in a narrow valley surrounded by towering mountains. But the Japanese 215th Regiment, blocking the exit, was under heavy pressure, and Lt-Gen. Yanagida ordered them to evacuate a strategic ridge which formed part of the blockade. The relieved British poured out, and Mutaguchi and Yanagida exchanged furious cables. Yanagida wanted the whole operation re-examined, but Mutaguchi – never a man to control his temper – ordered Yanagida to pursue the enemy immediately. He eventually did but by then a week had been lost.

At Dimapur there had been an even more serious miscalculation. This was the only rail-head connecting Assam with Bengal and the British source of supplies and reinforcements. At the beginning of April it was virtually undefended, for General Slim did not have enough men to protect it properly, and feared an attack. The sudden appearance of the 31st at the gates of Kohima had thrown the British into considerable confusion. Had Lt-Gen. Kenryo Sato, the commander of the 31st, masked Kohima with a detachment and thrust violently towards Dimapur, the main supply lines of the British would have been cut. But he did not. Slim had time to recover, and would later thank Sato for not being more imaginative, a quality a great commander needs and which Slim, of course, had in abundance. Speed and surprise, two Japanese assets, were lost.

But whatever Sato's failures, the tide of war had already turned against the Axis. Imphal mirrored this Allied resurgence. 155,000 British forces faced a combined Japanese-INA. strength of between 95,000 and 96,000. (the Americans calculated the lower figure, the British the higher) At Imphal the Japanese could muster only 61,000 troops against the 90,000 fielded by the Allies, and in the air they were hopelessly outnumbered. Soon after the Imphal operations started the Japanese Burma command had been forced to divert virtually all its air strength to the Pacific, and Lt-Gen. Noburu Tazoe, commander of the 5th Airborne Division in Burma, pleaded with Mutaguchi and Kawabe to stop the campaign. In contrast the British and Americans flew in reinforcements and supplies constantly.

The troops had left Burma with three weeks' rations, and once Mutaguchi's "Imphal-in-a-month" deadline had come and gone the Japanese were on the defensive. Even as they advanced, Allied planes roamed their rear areas at will, destroying roads, disrupting communications and inducing that sense of inferiority that can be fatal in battle. By the end of April all divisions were frantically cabling headquarters about their problems. Battle-strength had depleted by 40 per cent, there were no anti-tank weapons and food and supplies had run out. As Sato put it: "The 15th Army Headquarters (Mutaguchi) sent me orders, but no food or ammunition."

Sato's doubts were shared by some in Tokyo's Imperial General Headquarters. But Tojo, who was fighting for his political future, made precarious because of Japan's worsening war situation, felt a successful Imphal operation would provide some diversion. So the battle continued, described by Slim in his memoirs as "swaying back and forth through great stretches of wild country; one day its focal point was a hill named on no map, the next day a miserable unpronounceable village 100 miles away. Columns, brigades, divisions marched and counter-marched, met in bloody clashes, and reeled apart, weaving confused patterns hard to unravel."

By this time the monsoon was already more than a month old, having started early and with great force. The inadequate Japanese supply lines had almost disappeared, and soldiers were surviving on rice mixed with jungle grass. Withdrawal was not a word a Japanese commander could utter lightly, and Kawabe, for his part, had promised to commit double suicide with Bose if the operation failed.

Finally at the end of June, when yet another thrust towards Imphal had failed, Mutaguchi recommended a withdrawal to the Chindwin. Though Kawabe rebuked him, he did forward the request to Tokyo.

On 8 July 1944 Tojo ordered the retreat. By then, disaster had overtaken both the Japanese and the Indians with them. The total INA involvement in the Imphal operation was never more than 8,000 men, and for the Japanese commanders the INA was only an untried guerrilla army. Shah Nawaz pictured its predicament well in his report to Bose in April:

> When this regiment was raised, I, as well as every single soldier of this regiment, were [sic] of the conviction that we shall form the spearhead of the advance into India, or we shall be among the very first troops to enter into Indian territory. . . . When we actually arrived at the front line, the type of duty that was given to us was: (a) road-making or preparing, (b) repairing bridges, (c) extinguishing jungle fires, (d) driving bullock carts carrying rations for the Japanese troops. . . . duties of a labour battalion.

By April 1944, men of the regiment were living on jungle flowers and grass. In mid-May Shah Nawaz was suddenly told that his regiment would at last see some fighting. Palel had fallen, Imphal was about to fall and he was ordered into the Kohima sector in support of the Japanese 31st Division. It meant a route march of hundreds of miles through the Chin Hills and the Kabaw valley – some of the roughest terrain in an area where no terrain was easy – to Ukhrul, near Kohima. By the time Shah Nawaz and his men reached Ukhrul, the 31st was retreating and the Indians were soon marching back to Tamu, and eventually, in early June, to the Burma side of the Chindwin. Many had died, some had deserted; only Shah Nawaz and his staff officers had got beyond Ukhrul, and then only for reconnaissance.

Even more tragic was the story of the main force of the INA 1st Division, the only other unit to see action. Soldiers had reached Rangoon from Malaya in March and Bose had easily persuaded Kawabe to attach them to the Yamamoto detachment fighting in the main Palel-Imphal sector. The division, under the overall command of Colonel Mohammed Zaman Kiani, was split up into a Gandhi Brigade, commanded by his cousin Lieutenant-Colonel Inayat Jan Kiani, and an Azad Brigade under Lieutenant-Colonel Gulzara Singh. In mid-April the Kianis were told by the Japanese to advance with all possible speed to Palel. It was too late, said the Japanese, to take part in the battle for Imphal: it had fallen or would fall in a few hours, but they could participate in the celebrations that would follow. Speed was of the essence if they wanted to do that, and there was no need for heavy equipment. So the Gandhi Brigade abandoned all its heavy baggage, machine-guns and even hand-grenades, and the men, anticipating the joy of standing on Indian soil, marched off, each with with a blanket, a rifle and 50 rounds of ammunition.

When they reached the battle area, they found that Imphal had not fallen, that the captured British supplies there did not exist, and that they were required to attack Palel with nothing more than their faith in their revolutionary arms. They fought bravely, but it was suicidal: the British occupied the best ground and were massively entrenched. The Gandhi Brigade suffered terribly. Many in the regiment were ill (particularly the civilian recruits from Malaya and Singapore) and the men had not eaten for three days, but seven times on the night of the 2nd they attacked the Palel aerodrome: every time they were beaten back with heavy casualties. By 4 May, their fighting strength gone, they withdrew to Khanjol, their base. The brigade, and the Yamamoto detachment, held out in this sector in the most appalling conditions for another 80 days.

The Azad Brigade, though it did the best fighting of the entire INA 1st Division stood up better. However, it did not reach the front till the end of May, when the situation was already hopeless, and by mid-July, like the Japanese, it had to retreat to Burma.

British authors writing on the campaign have mocked the INA, outraged by the idea that any Indian could have taken up arms against the benevolent British rule. General Sir Francis Tuker writes of how the Indians of the British Army were so much better than the Indians of Bose, a Bengali babu .Slim even refused to call them the INA, referring to them derisively as "Jiffs", Japanese-influenced forces. But after the war the Intelligence Department of the Indian government in an assessment of the INA wrote:

> A measure of courage cannot be denied to the leaders of INA front-line units...they faced up to British equipment, tanks, guns, and aircraft with rifles and bullock carts and empty stomachs.

In late June Kawabe had met Bose and told him of the decision to withdraw. But Bose still displayed robust confidence:

> We will not repent even if the advance of our revolutionary army to attain independence is completely defeated. Increase in casualties, cessation of supplies, and famine are not reason enough to stop marching. Even if the whole army becomes only spirit, we will not stop advancing towards our homeland

During the conversation Bose offered him the Rani of Jhansi Regiment, the one composed entirely of women, but Kawabe did not react. In his public statements Bose still kept up a defiant front. More decorations were announced, special days in honour of heroes were commemorated and the Imphal defeat was seen as a tactical retreat, the better to prepare for a future round.The INA had defeated the enemy in "every battle", and only unexpected heavy rains had washed away the chances of certain success in Imphal. Bose said:

> As soon as all our preparations are complete, we shall launch a mighty offensive against our enemies once again. With the superior fighting qualities, dauntless courage and unshakeable devotion to duty of our officers and men, victory shall surely be ours.

Was this perhaps the moment, as his critics have alleged, that Bose lost touch with reality? Fighting with an army of spirit, offering to throw women, who till recently had been housewives, into battle, refusing to acknowledge that Imphal was a disaster? Shortly after the end of the war Fujiwara, after praising many of Bose's qualities, wrote:

> The standard of his operational tactics was, it must be said with regret, low. He was inclined to be unrealistic. For instance, without being familiar with the actual fighting power of the INA., he was always demanding it to be employed

> in a separate and decisive operation on the Imphal front and, in July 1944, when the tide of battle had turned and the Japanese Army had retreated, he urged that although the Japanese might retreat, the INA should continue to confront the Allies until their aim was attained. He was temperamental and had strong likes and dislikes. ... It cannot be said he possessed much magnanimity or very much tolerance for the opinion of others.

Admittedly Fujiwara wrote this when a prisoner of the British, unsure of his fate, but certainly Bose's reading of the war situation was dreadful. From Berlin he had declared that what mattered were not the sea battles over fuel and supplies, but the land wars; later he would dismiss the invasion of Italy and the landings at Normandy as of no consequence, and right until the moment of Japan's surrender he never publicly renounced his faith in a Japanese victory.

But hindsight is easy and, as far as Imphal was concerned, the reasons Bose gave for the defeat – failure to take Imphal before the monsoons began, and lack of air support – have been confirmed in the historical perspective. Besides, his words must be judged in the light of his over riding concern: military victory was only part of the immense psychological and political victory he was seeking. A few thousand Englishmen ruled a country of millions, supremely confident that Indians could never envisage a British defeat. It was this attitude that Bose was seeking to destroy: success at Imphal would have meant that Indians, for the first time, would have seen Britain beaten on the soil of their motherland. And even the official British history of the war against Japan conceded that Imphal's fall might have led to "a revolt in Bengal and Bihar against British rule in India which might well have been on a far greater scale than the riots of 1942."

After Imphal, it was all the more necessary to keep up the fighting talk. The east Asians Bose had organised had been immigrants only a short time ago: their politicisation was recent, their revolutionary fervour capable of sudden change. To concede defeat would mean the end. So, as Bose toured north Burma in September 1944, visiting what remained of the INA front line, he sought to rekindle his fighters' revolutionary instincts. But the men told him terrible stories. Some had committed suicide in preference to more dreadful route marches, and those who had survived faced wretchedly inadequate hospitals. Bose found patients with faces distorted and swollen by beri-beri and untreated gunshot wounds that had turned septic; in Maymo a single nurse looked after 85 patients.

Worse still was the psychological defeat his men had suffered. His whole campaign had been based on the premise that when the INA confronted the Indian mercenary army of the British, the latter would not fight. Mercenary would meet revolutionary, be converted and become a revolutionary himself. Instead, the revolutionary had reverted to his comfortable mercenary status. INA soldiers took to looting from local tribes. From early1944 the British-Indian divisions had fought with high morale; they were to form two-thirds of the strength of Slim's 14th Army which reconquered Burma.

For all their jibes about the INA being a puppet army and a collection of JIFC (Japanese-Inspired Fifth-Column) activists, the British had prepared meticulously for the day when their Indian soldiers faced the INA. Some time in 1943 a counter-propaganda unit was set up in the newly created South East Asian Command. It concentrated on psychological warfare. From the beginning of 1944 it carried out intensive campaigns via leaflets, weekly news sheets in Japanese, Burmese and Indian languages, and of course, broadcasts. During the Imphal operations all this was reinforced by the liberal air-dropping of safe-conduct passes signed by General Sir Claude Auchinleck, commander-in-chief of the Indian Army, promising "excellent food, clothing and medical attention" and, instant forgiveness "if you tell our military or non-military officers all that is true as you come to them".

Also, all details about the INA were kept from the Indians. The INA was constantly portrayed as ignorant dupes of a bestial, cruel race, and Bose as a quisling out to impose his own rule under Japanese tutelage. Many of the British loved to refer to Bose as a fat Bengali *babu* who, by the British division of Indians into martial and non-martial peoples, was genetically not equipped to lead an army. There was strict censorship of news about INA participation in the Imphal operations.

Not surprisingly, the British told their Indian men nothing of Bose's nationalist arguments, aware that this would dent their own indoctrination. This was so successful that 715 INA soldiers deserted. Bose never really recovered from this shock. On his return to Rangoon, he rounded on some officers: they were lazy, more concerned with their own luxuries than the welfare of their men; it was, he said with some justification, their lack of leadership that had brought about this catastrophe. He asked other officers what should be done? Should each soldier be given the power to shoot anyone who wanted to desert? No, replied the officers, but in the weeks and months ahead this desperate remedy appealed more and more to Bose.

Did Bose, personally, also feel vulnerable? It was around this time he had a late night conversation with Lakshmi when he unburdened himself on his relationship with Emilie.At that stage nobody in East Asia, barring Hasan, knew about Emilie. It shows how much pressure Bose was under that he chose to confide in Lakshmi, thinking that, as one Indian woman experienced in the ways of men and with a failed marriage behind her, she would understand.

His thoughts also turned towards finding an alternative to Japan to help in his liberation struggle. Despite his expresssed belief in an eventual Japanese victory, Bose looked to the only other power which could possibly help him: the Soviet Union. Some time before the Imphal retreat began, Bose had dined with Vice-Admiral Kan-ei Chudo, commander of the Japanese naval forces in Burma. The vice-admiral had already written off the Imphal adventure, but wondered if Bose might consider another assault on India, this time from the Russian side of the border in central Asia. "The Soviet Union now has a non-aggression pact with Japan. If you are so inclined, I shall be pleased to do everything, even to personally escorting you to Samarkand or Tashkent." In all the vicissitudes of the war, the Soviet Union was one country Bose had never criticised. He sat silent for a few minutes, then asked Chudo to get it endorsed from Tokyo. A month later, Yamamoto made much the same suggestion, and Bose again showed interest. But Tokyo, hopeful of using the Soviets to mediate with the Allies, showed no interest.

Soon, however, Bose himself had a chance to pursue the idea. Following the fall of Saipan to the Americans, Tojo resigned and was replaced as prime minister by Kuniaki Koiso. Bose immediately sent him a telegram promising full support in the war effort and offered 50 million yen to meet the expenses of manufacturing weapons for Japan's army and navy. On 9 October 1944 Koiso invited Bose to Tokyo. He arrived there on 15 November, and it was agreed the Japanese would provide for 35,000 troops and Bose a further 15,000. Bose also wanted free access to forward areas during the next round of the fighting. Japanese failure to allow this, he argued, had been one of the causes of the Imphal debacle.

Perhaps his most important achievement was to negotiate a loan agreement with the Japanese. Whatever money the Japanese lent the Indians would be repaid when India was free. The Japanese were impressed with the stress Bose put on this point. Before his visit, he had been told of Japanese government plans to honour him with the Order of the Rising Sun. To the horror of the Japanese he declined. Until India was free he could not accept a foreign order. His efforts to contact the Russians, however, left the Japanese even more perturbed. They gave him no help, and so Bose tried contacting the Russians direct. One night, returning to his hotel, he quickly wrote a note for the Russian ambassador and asked one of his assistants to take it to him. A few hours later, the assistant returned dejected: the ambassador had not even bothered to receive him, and his secretary had returned the letter unopened.

Japanese cities were now being bombed by the US Air Force as never before, and Bose was realistic enough to know that Japan had lost the war. But in his speeches he gave no hint of his felings. He addressed the students of Tokyo University, sketching out his vision of a modern, industrialised India and talking of the synthesis of communism and fascism. If that last idea was indefensible, in his speeches he also directly addressed the Americans and, as Toye insightfully points out, sketched out a formidable defence of his decision to ally himself to the Japanese. Bose said:

> I want to tell my American friends that Asia is now surging with revolutionary fervour from one end to the other..... We are men as much as you are. We want our freedom and we shall have it by any means. You had an opportunity of helping us, but you did not do so. Now Japan is offering us help and we have plunged into the struggle alongside of her. It is not Japan that we are helping by waging war on you and on our mortal enemy - England. We are helping ourselves, we are helping Asia...

In essence Bose argued that before Japan entered the war in 1941, the European powers had no plans to give their Asian colonies freedom. Even the Americans, who always loudly proclaimed their anti-colonialism, had a colony in Philippines. Japan's entry into the war had changed Asia forever. It is noteworthy that some British writers with no time for Bose, like the military historian A.J Barker, implicitly accept this. As Barker wrote in *The March On Delhi:* "Indian freedom was probably assured by the events of 1942 when Japan destroyed the mystique of white supremacy in the Far East".

Bose returned to Burma in late November 1944, faced with the problem of keeping his movement together. The Indian Independence League was now in disrepair. Recruitment in Singapore had fallen from nearly 10,000 in April to a little more than 500 in November. Indian merchants, always reluctant to pay their dues, were now confident that if they delayed the British would arrive. Collections in Malaya, which in April had totalled $2 million were by November only a little over $600,000. Large amounts were outstanding in Singapore although, when Netaji's birthday was celebrated, he was, much to his distaste, weighed in gold, and jewellery of almost one and a half times his weight was collected.

Fund-raising, however, could make no difference to the wider conflict. In the last three months of 1944, the Japanese had been steadily pushed back to the banks of the Irrawaddy River. On 3 December the British had landed on Akyab, which Bose had once considered a staging post on the way to Chittagong. A few days before the birthday celebrations, the 25th British Indian Division had landed in the Maybom peninsula. By mid-January the Japanese were struggling to hold on to their defences on the Irrawaddy river. Here the rebuilt INA was planning its second campaign. Some of the lessons of Imphal had been learnt. The new soldiers had been kept away from the survivors and freshly indoctrinated with tales of INA heroism. Company commanders had been told to examine and report on the men's spiritual fitness. Yet, even before the INA had joined this fresh battle orders had been issued against desertion.

The INA was holding a 12-mile(20km) sector south of Nyaungu; but until they could consolidate their position the entire front lay wide open. On 14 January the British crossed the Irrawaddy 50 miles north of Mandalay. The Japanese assumed that this was the main line of advance and concentrated their forces there. In fact Slim's real destinations were Nyaungu and then Meiktila, and even before the INA commander, Major G.S. Dhillon, could establish himself, the British struck. By 16 February they had captured Nyaungu and Pagan, and the INA could only join the Japanese in barring the way to Meiktila.

Two days after Nyaungu fell Bose left Rangoon for the front. On 20 February 1945 he arrived in Meiktila. Neither the Japanese nor the Indians knew quite what was happening. All along the front, heavy fighting was raging. The British had taken Mandalay and now threatened Meiktila, which was the rail and road communications nerve centre of the Japanese Army in Burma. Its fall would mean the virtual end of Japanese resistance on the road to Rangoon. Bose's assistants pleaded with him to leave Meiktila, but he would not hear of it. The Japanese and the INA had a stronghold on Mount Popa, and Bose was determined to go there. Eventually, Shah Nawaz persuaded Bose to stay at Meiktila while he himself investigated the situation. He returned on 25 February and that night, in an open field brilliantly lit by moonlight, a furious argument erupted.

Bose said he wanted the INA to die fighting like heroes. The Axis might be beaten, but the INA must leave behind a legend of bravery and heroism that would make Indians proud, and inspire them to further action. As they were talking, a Japanese officer arrived and informed them that a powerful British armoured column had broken through the defences near Pyinbun and was advancing on Taungtha, only 40 miles (about 70km) north of where they were. There were no Japanese troops between Taungtha and Meiktila, and 40 miles for the tank of a powerfully supported armoured column was just a two hour journey. Bose should leave at once for Pyinmana, where there were stronger defences. For Bose, who had repeatedly asked his men to give their blood, this was anathema. Now, more than ever, he was determined to go to Popa. Shah Nawaz tried to reason with him and at last lost his temper, but could not shake Bose. Eventually, with the help of some of Bose's entourage, he devised a delaying plan: a letter needed by Bose took hours to be typed, Bose's driver started muttering about engine trouble, and soon it was daylight and no travel was conceivable.

Bose was persuaded to rest in a hut for a few hours, and a Japanese official accompanying him went to get information. He returned with grim tidings. A British mechanised brigade had arrived at Mahlaing, only ten miles away. Not only was Popa probably isolated, but Meiktila itself was doomed and the Rangoon road probably blocked. Bose faced a choice of being trapped in Meiktila or taking his chance and fighting his way back to Pyinmana.

He decided to fight his way back. The only transport available was a small car that could at best accommodate four people. Bose, his doctor Colonel Raju, Shah Nawaz and Major Takahashi, the Japanese official, got in. Shah Nawaz filled the car with grenades and ammunition, the Japanese rode on the footboard with a loaded machine gun in hand, Raju sat next to the driver clutching two hand-grenades and Bose, a machine gun in his lap, sat in the back. It was a journey that seemed to last a lifetime. At the small Indian village of Indo they missed, by a few minutes British fighter planes machine-gunning the place. They hid in a cactus hedge near the village, but a suspicious Burmese spotted them; and they retreated to thick jungle a mile away. Within minutes British planes started circling the cactus hedge. Like fugitives they survived the day in the jungle, living on grain that Shah Nawaz had fetched from a field nearby.

Finally Bose managed to reach Pyinmana on 27 February. The next day he called together the INA commanders and the Japanese. During the retreat, his men had seen him resting in a hammock fixed to the trees, reading a book. Now he told them he had been re-reading the history of the Irish independence struggle.

> Though all the determined fighters of that freedom were killed, their spirit continued to live seventy or eighty years. Today we see Irish independence as a fact before our very eyes. I am greatly inspired by that example. If the present situation continues it is difficult for Burma also to foresee its future. Therefore, here at this place I shall fight leading the 1st Division and die. Being sure that the spirit of independence will live among Indians I shall wage the last decisive battle here.

The Japanese were horrified. Shah Nawaz and Mohammed Zaman Kiani were more respectful, and, after they had promised that they would defend Pyinmana to the last man, Bose was persuaded to leave for Rangoon. Before he did, he organised a new X Regiment, cobbled together from the remnants of the 1st Division. This was ordered to hold a defensive position at Yezin, a few miles north of Pyinmana.

Bose had barely settled back in Rangoon when his worst fears were confirmed. Four senior staff officers of the INA unit at Mount Popa had deserted, and the British were already airdropping leaflets signed by them urging their comrades to follow their example. The old fears that had haunted him ever since the defeat at Imphal returned. Popa was a personal failure.Perhaps, if he had followed his own instincts and had gone there, this would not have happened. For days he stayed in his Rangoon bungalow, brooding and seeing no one, and having his meals sent to his room. When, finally, he emerged he was outwardly calm, but desperation marked his actions. Nearly 5,000 INA officers and ranks were assembled in Rangoon and harangued for over four hours, anti-traitor days were ordered to be celebrated in all camps and prizes given for the best dramas. Finally, in two special orders of the day, Bose announced that soldiers now had the right to shoot any officer who looked like deserting.

Through his actions several commanders were relieved of their duties, and others were arrested, but this only put a short-term stop to defeatist talk in Rangoon. The men who had deserted were some of the finest soldiers, who had fought courageously and with determination. Troops they had left behind doubted the purpose of fighting on. Sahgal, who had noted that discipline and morale had lapsed and that soldiers had wandered round giving his position away, analysed the men's feelings:

> Turkey's alignment alongside the anti-Axis powers has had a very adverse effect on certain Muslim officers....The officers feel that by fighting against powers that are allied with the Turks, they are being disloyal to Islam...There is a general feeling among the officers and men of the unit that it was useless to continue fighting against the enemy, so superior in numbers and armaments, and helped by the traitors, who had gone over to his side. A majority of these officers, under normal circumstances, would never have done anything treacherous, but finding themselves so overwhelmed, they did not have the moral strength to continue the struggle and decided to save themselves by going over to the enemy.

Shah Nawaz's diary for April and May, too, records the dismal picture:

> April 2: This day started with unpleasant shocks. Signal Officer No.2. Regiment deserted. Captain Mohammed Hussain and his Adjutant deserted from No.4. Regiment. Went and met Col. Sahgal at 0200 hours. Learnt that his trusted officers were deserting.
> April 4: He (Sahgal) reported that most of the men including battalion commander Jhajeen Shah have deserted. Only approximately one coy is left of that Bn. Men have taken away their arms with them. Our men fought bravely, but soon after the attack they started walking over. It appears they have had enough.
> May 5: 0700 hours. The discipline and morale of troops have deteriorated, no control, officers are leaving the men.
> May 7: 0800 hours. After travelling all night reached a village ten miles south of Taikchi. Discipline and morale of troops is completely gone. One soldier fired at Col. Dhillon but luckily missed. He was put away.

Some INA units fought bravely. Captain Bagri with about 100 men, equipped with grenades and bottles of petrol, charged at British tanks and perished. A group of 98 men under

Lt. Gian Singh Bisht, armed with rifles and two anti-tank mines, engaged a British motorised infantry column of 13 tanks, 11 armoured cars and ten trucks: hand-to-hand fighting ensued and all the men were killed. These were isolated incidents. Nothing could stop the British advance, and the position was worsened by the decision of the Burmese forces to revolt against the Japanese. Aung San, the defence minister, who led the revolt, and had been in touch with British agents, advised Bose that the INA should do the same. Bose, aware that the Indians in Malaya would pay a heavy price if he did, refused. However, he pledged never to allow the INA to be used against Aung San's men.

On 20 April, the eve of the British capture of Pyinmana, Bose turned down the Japanese commander-in-chief Kimura's request for a withdrawal. He would stay on in Rangoon with his full Cabinet and fight to the last. Nor would he allow Kimura to withdraw. But hours of furious discussions followed, in which his Cabinet insisted that he withdraw. It was senseless falling into British hands when the war was still raging and there was the possibility of fighting again. On 23 April news came through that British armour had thrust beyond Pyinmana. Nothing stood between them and Rangoon.

Bose began to make his final arrangements. He installed Major-General Loganadhan as his deputy in charge of the INA in Rangoon. Loganadhan, with 7,000 men, arranged the transfer formalities; and, in contrast to the chaos that had ensued when the British withdrew in 1942, there was an orderly assumption of power by the re-conquering British when they took Rangoon on 4 May 1945. Four days later the Germans surrendered to the Allies bringing the war in Europe to an end.

Just before he left, Bose went to see Reba Sen and her family. The previous month her camp had been disbanded, Bose telling the girls to go home but promising that he would come back. That night he left a few possessions with Reba's father asking that they be given to his brother Sarat. They consisted of a fine Japanese vase given him by Tojo, and a jade box from Mussolini. Both were later handed over to Sarat. In a sense Subhas Bose was suggesting that he was embarking on a journey from which he might never return.

On the night of 24 April Bose, accompanied by most of his government and three major-generals, left in a convoy of four cars and 12 lorries. The journey was to bring out the best in him. It was a clear, moonlit night, and as they slowly drove towards Pegu they could see fires raging all round them as the Japanese, who had started evacuating a day earlier, burnt their files and records. The convoy, camouflaged by branches and leaves, had barely been an hour on the Rangoon to Pegu road, when the first of many British air attacks forced it to take shelter. That set the pattern for the retreat. Pegu was an inferno. The Japanese had set fire to ammunition dumps there, and the day after the Bose convoy passed through, the British arrived. Air attacks made daylight travel during the day impossible, and at night the roads were clogged with Japanese trucks and soldiers struggling with heavy packs. Until they reached and crossed the Sittang, where the Japanese had mustered defences, there were constant fears of British tanks appearing behind them.

By the time they reached the Waw river in the early hours of 26 April the convoy had lost a group of trucks that had taken the dirt road, and been mired in the mud. Bose had miraculous escapes. He emerged unhurt after his car skidded into a ditch about eight feet deep, and was twice strafed – once while shaving at a wayside shelter, and later in an open paddy field. On both occasions, looking supremely nonchalant, he had calmly lit cigarettes and brushed aside his companions' fears. Captain Mrs Janaki Thevar, one of the commanders of the Rani of Jhansi Regiment, found him red-eyed and glad to have endless cups of tea, but anxious and worried about the safety of his convoy. When General Isoda came up to him at the Waw and suggested he cross first, Bose exploded, "Go to hell! I will not cross over till all the girls have gone across first." With no bridges across the Waw, the girls had no choice but to wade across, holding their rifles above their heads. Nobody drowned, but it was a near thing.

The next night's crossing of the Sittang was even more hazardous. By then the convoy had lost all its trucks, either to air attacks or to the mud. Only Bose's car had survived; and as the Japanese had blown up the bridge, there was only a small ferry to take them across the river. With the convoy having no transport, the journey from Sittang to Moulmein became a long, weary route march. Bose led the column carrying, like everybody else, his own pack. When Janaki Thevar persuaded Bose to take off his boots and change his socks, she found his feet covered with blisters. Moulmein was still 30 away, but Bose refused Japanese offers of a special car. When General Isoda came back with transport, Bose shouted, "Do you think I am Ba Maw of Burma, that I will leave my men and run for safety? I have told you repeatedly that I will not go unless my men have gone ahead."

He had promised to be with his men in sunshine and sorrow, joy and suffering, and now that they were passing through the hell of jungle retreat, he could not abandon them. If he left them, the Japanese, concerned with getting their own men to safety, might leave them stranded. Bose kept a careful check on their well-being. Were the sick being looked after? Was there enough food? Could the water of this or that village be safely drunk?

On 3 May Bose and his party reached Moulmein where there was decent accommodation, proper food and rail arrangements to move on to Bangkok. The Japanese placed a train at Bose's disposal and arranged for goods wagons to take the other members of the INA. Halting during the day, and travelling only at night the train reached Bangkok on 14 May. Despite the wretchedness of the journey, Bose had brought his men and women through: only one man was killed, though all his government records were lost.

This retreat also confronted Bose with one of the worst atrocities of the war in Asia, the use by the Japanese of their prisoners and conscript native workers in near slave conditions to build the Burma-Siam Railway. During his journey to Bangkok Bose passed the camp at Tarsao, two thirds of the way along the railway and was spotted by British prisoners working on the railway. Robert Hardie in *The Burma-Siam Railway* notes, "30 May 1945 people from the camp at Tarsao report that Subhas Bose was there for a few days on his way over to Thailand from Burma".

The story of the Second World War has often been recounted and almost exclusively through Western eyes. *The Bridge on the River Kwai,* both the book and the movie, is a classic example of this. It describes how the Europeans suffered at the hands of the Japanese, but ghastly as this was, the cruelties the Japanese inflicted upon their fellow Asians were much worse. Diseases such as cholera had taken the lives of thousands of Asian troops, and most of the labourers were denied medical attention and adequate food. This aspect of it has never made it to the big screen. Hugh Toye has written perhaps the best analysis:

> During this journey, if not on his visit to Nompradok where he had seen the INA anti-aircraft gunners protecting the end of the Burma-Siam railway almost a year earlier, the plight of Tamil slave-workers on the railway must have come to his attention. The atrocities suffered by the European prisoners of war sent up from Singapore to work on this railway are well known; out of a total of 61,000 employed, 16,000 were murdered or worked to death, and some of the Japanese concerned were tried and sentenced as war criminals after the war. But labourers from the rubber estates in Malaya had been transported by the thousand for a fate worse, far worse, than that of the European prisoners. Tamil refugees were arriving in considerable numbers in Northern Malaya at the end of 1944 and the Malaya League opened relief camps at Alor Star to house them. Doubtless at Bose's instance, the Ramakrishna Mission in Singapore had sent its deputy head, Brahmachariar Kailasam, to enquire on the spot, and he had prepared a report which Bose was only to see in Singapore in June 1945. Bose and Raghavan raised the matter with the Japanese who admitted that 120,000

Tamil labourers had been taken from Malaya and that only 40,000 had survived. Raghavan estimated that 60,000 had been taken from Burma and that only 20,000 had survived.

As Bose and his men slogged their way out of Burma news came from Europe that Hitler had killed himself in his Berlin bunker. Two days before Mussolini had been strung up by his own people. Bose pondered what to do. By this time the British, always keen to find out what Bose was up to, had managed to recruit a spy from Bose's camp. His code number was 1189 and he reported back to London:

> S.C. Bose and his party leaving Rangoon on 24 April 1945 reached Bangkok on 14 may. The party, at the time of leaving Rangoon, had in its possession gold, gold ornaments and diamonds contained in 4 boxes of varying sizes ranging between 9"x9"x4" and 6"x4"x2". An additional quantity of gold was purchased on the way at Moulmein to the extent of RS 700,000 drawn by S.C. Bose from Yokohama Specie Bank, Moulmein Branch. While at Bangkok several meetings of the Cabinet Minister of the PGI(Provisional Government of India) were held between 18 May to 14 June, the object of which was to decide as to the future course of action so far as the existence of the PGI was concerned. No decision could be arrived at as S.C. Bose had to leave for Singapore in order to carry out his propaganda over the radio against the acceptance of "Wavell Proposal "(suggesting a constitutional settlement in India). In course of these meetings Lt Col (Maj Gen) Chatterjee suggested that a nucleus of the PGI should be shifted to Yunnan Province in order to contact the Communists who had more influence in that part of China, and through their help to contact the Soviet authorities in Siberia. At the same time it was thought desirable to leave behind certain Cabinet Ministers and high-ranking INA Officers to carry on the fight with HQ at Bangkok and Singapore. The following were the officers present in these meetings;
> (1). S.C. Bose
> (2). Lt Col (Maj Gen) Bhonsle
> (3). Lt Col (Maj Gen) Chatterjee
> (4). Lt Col (Maj Gen) Kiani
> (5). Capt (Col) Gulzara Singh
> (6). Iyer
> (7). A.M. Sahai
> (8). A.N. Sarkar
> (9). Isar Singh, Gen Secretary IIL Bangkok
> (10) Parma Nand
> (11). D.M. Khan
> (12). Deb Nath Das
> (13). Karim Ghani (also attended the last meeting)
> After the 2nd meeting (exact dates not remembered) Kiani left for Singapore to arrange the accommodation for the Rani of Jhansi girls numbering about 120 who were at that time at Bangkok. At about the same time Chatterjee, Iyer and A.M. Sahai left for Saigon - Chatterjee to establish the site for the PGI, Iyer for broadcasting work and Sahai on a special mission at Hanoi not known to B1189.

B1189 was Major-General Bhonsle, Bose's trusted lieutenant.
Bangkok was no longer the city Bose had so often ceremonially visited. The Thai

government was urgently re-appraising its status with the Japanese, and none too happy about sheltering Bose and the INA. The League in east Asia was now bitterly divided and virtually run down because of lack of funds. Bose, staying in a house vacated by a prominent Indian businessman, held regular meetings with his Cabinet and tried to revive the League organisation. After much persuasion, the Thai government consented to a loan, though not as much *baht* as Bose wanted. The League issued more threatening letters to recalcitrant Indians, and both in Singapore and Kuala Lumpur there were arrests of those who defaulted or who promised much but gave little. Ministers and officials were sent to various capitals to collect money, and to provide other possible centres of retreat should things not work out in Bangkok. Bose remained in the Thai capital, concentrating on mounting a propaganda offensive in India and on making contact with the Soviets.

But a plot had been discovered by the Japanese among his senior ministers in Rangoon. A minister of state for propaganda, Karim Gani, mentioned in the intelligence report by B 1189, had been arrested, as had the head of Bose's secret service, and accused of organising a secret society with the intention of contacting the British. There were other problems. Bose had ordered the INA 3rd Division, the only one still intact, to fight with the Japanese in defence of Malaya. Most of its officers were old British Indian Army hands ,while the majority of the men were recruits from Malaya. They were faced with the prospect of aligning themselves with Japanese forces that were increasingly resented in Malaya and Singapore, and of defending a country in which the Indians had no interest. While they fought for India with the help of the Japanese, the local Malays, Chinese and other ethnic communities had helped and supported them. Now that they were virtually under Japanese command they found they were despised as part of the Japanese occupation forces, with inevitable consequences. Anti-Japanese units of Chinese guerrillas were being organised by the Allies, and these resented the seemingly total identification of the INA with the Japanese. Some of Bose's ministers and advisers were also having doubts about his all-out propaganda efforts denouncing any compromise settlement in India. Talks about this had started soon after the end of the war with Germany. In June 1945 most leaders of the Congress, such as Nehru and Azad, were released, and the viceroy, Lord Wavell, invited various Indian parties to a conference in Simla for another attempt at "a constitutional settlement" in India. The conference, held between June and July 1945, was another total failure, and only proved that Jinnah's Muslim League had a veto over any peaceful settlement of the so-called "Indian problem". Bose, who knew Jinnah's methods, was not surprised.

During the previous year's negotiations between Gandhi and Jinnah, Bose, in his broadcasts, had warned the Mahatma of the consequences of conceding an equal negotiating position to the Muslim League. Simla confirmed his fears. Interestingly, Bose had clung to his belief that, in India, Gandhi was still paramount. He said that only two men mattered, himself and Gandhi. Soon after the Mahatma was released from prison in 1944 Bose broadcast a special message to him, asking for his blessing and concluding by christening him "Father of the Nation,"a name that stuck. As the Raj and the Congress appeared to edge closer to settlement, Bose began almost nightly broadcasts, imploring, arguing and pleading with political India not to compromise with the British.

The Congress leaders were regularly accusing him of being a Japanese puppet, and, as the chances of compromise brightened, Bose made sharp retorts to Nehru and Azad, challenging them to call a full session of the Congress and test their strength. Self-interest played a part in these speeches. If the Simla conference had succeeded, Bose's efforts could have been nullified, his claim to speak for an enslaved India critically damaged. The speeches, of course, followed the line Bose had consistently argued since 1941: a country could win independence only by force of arms. Compromise with the Muslim League would only strengthen this reactionary, obstructive body and help the British divide and ruin India. They also reveal an acute international mind. Bose sensed that the post-war world would be socialist or at least strongly inclined towards social-democratic systems. He was convinced that Labour would emerge stronger after the 1945 elections and might even win. This prediction was made when few in the British Labour movement had such euphoria. Within weeks of Germany's fall Bose had begun to sketch out with remarkable prescience the political map of post-war Europe:

> I firmly adhere to what I have consistently said in the past - namely, that the collapse of Germany will be the signal for the outbreak of acute conflict between the Soviets and the Anglo-Americans. The whole world knows that the war aims of Soviet Russia are different from those of the Anglo-Americans. The Soviet government knows that the defeat of Germany has been due first and foremost to the heroism, tenacity and sacrifice of the people and armed forces of the Soviet Union. Consequently, the Soviet government, being conscious of its own strength, will never give in to the Anglo-American powers the post-war reconstruction of Europe...neither Britain nor the United States of America, who are capitalist-imperialist countries, can produce a plan of social reconstruction which will be acceptable to the nations of Europe. Consequently, we come to the conclusion that there is no other alternative for the nations of Europe than to give trial to the experiments that have proved to be eminently successful within the Soviet Union...If there is one man in Europe who holds in his hands the destinies of the European nations for the next few decades, that man is Marshal Stalin. The whole world and, above all, Europe, will therefore follow with breathless anxiety the moves of the Soviet Union in the days to come.

In May 1945 such a forecast of the split in the Allies was remarkably bold. It is not surprising that Bose became increasingly convinced that the Soviet Union could be his only possible ally in the fight against Britain. He speculated about moving to north China or Manchuria, and contacting the Russians from there. On 18 June Lieutenant-Colonel Takakura, an officer at the Imperial Headquarters in Tokyo, visited Bose at his Bangkok residence and held a long discussion. The Japanese wanted Bose to move his headquarters to Saigon and place the INA under the command of the Southern Army of Japan. Bose refused. Instead he wanted to be allowed to establish a "safe-deposit" government in Manchuria. His plan if Japanese resistance collapsed was to seek Russian help which would be much easier from Manchuria. But the Japanese, who had steadfastly refused to allow him access to the Soviets, saw Bose's moves as a gross betrayal. Takakura was outraged and asked if Bose was losing faith in Japan? A meeting ended at 3 am with Bose agreeing to move to Saigon once all his troops were there, but he would not agree to let the INA fight the Chinese. He also decided to strengthen the Indian Independence League in Shanghai and other places in China to provide him points of contact with Soviet diplomats.

All these plans were turned upside-down on the night of 10 August 1945. At about midnight Bose learned that the USSR had declared war on Japan. Soviet forces were advancing into Manchuria. His plans to contact the Soviets seemed doomed. What made it worse was that Bose was effectively cut off from the world. Since the last week in July he had been in Seremban, having gone there to deal with a serious mutiny at the INA training centre. This proved to be a minor matter although, as Ayer presents the story, it was a difficult situation for Bose. A senior officer had defected to the enemy, using a Chinese girl as the decoy. The Japanese wanted the Chinese girl arrested and handed over, and told Bose that as she was not an Indian he had no jurisdiction. But, says Ayer, Bose knew she would be tortured and agonised over it.

By this time the communist guerrillas that had been fighting the Japanese for years were becoming bolder, and the Japanese wanted the INA commander to turn on them. With

Bose's support, he refused to do so. It was while he was in the middle of this imbroglio that news came of a Russian attack on Japan. Bose heard it via a telephone call from Kuala Lumpur. His initial reaction was that it did not matter. He refused to accept the advice of Kiani to return to Singapore and ignored three telegrams from the Japanese to hurry straight on to Saigon. The Hikari Kikan had presented a comprehensive picture of the fast changing war situation, but Bose ignored it.

The way Ayer presents the story Bose appeared to have been in a cocoon at this time. The only explanation for this is that Bose was so isolated from the world that he did not appreciate how quickly events had moved on. He had gone to Seremban in a hurry, and had not intended to be there for more than a day or so. The former British guest house in which he was staying did not have a short wave radio. So when Russia attacked he had to send Ayer to Kuala Lumpur to get agency news reports. Lack of proper access to news may also explain why Bose appears to have entirely missed the significance of another sensational event that had taken place four days before Stalin launched the Red Army against Japan.

This was on 6 August 6 1945, when the American B-29 bomber *Enola Gay* dropped an atom bomb on the Japanese city of Hiroshima. The Americans followed this with a second bomb on Nagasaki, two days later. There is no evidence in the memoirs of Bose's entourage that they were aware of the existence of the atom bombs, let alone appreciated the enormity of what the Americans had done. Ayer does not mention it and says of the days between the end of July and 10 August, "Nothing very sensational happened until the night of 10th of August, 1945." To be fair to Bose and his entourage not many people grasped the enormous significance of the atom bombs. Hugh Toye was in a *bivi* tent in Calcutta's Maidan, in several inches of water, when he heard the Americans had dropped a large bomb and dismissed it as just another war-time wonder weapon.

The Japanese knew very well what the American atom bombs meant and began to sue for peace.

Bose heard this news at 2 am on the morning of 13 August 1945, again not directly from the radio, as did most of the world, but from a small delegation from Singapore which drove to Seremban to tell him personally. On the morning of 12 August a BBC broadcast made it clear that it was only a matter of time before Japan surrendered: "The next word on surrender lies with Japan". The Japanese envoy in the Swiss capital had been given the Allied terms, which demanded, of course, unconditional surrender, and the Emperor had met Shigenori Togo, the Foreign Minister. Time difference meant the BBC broadcast was heard in Singapore around tea time. One of the listeners was Bose's stenographer whose short-hand notes were brought to Bose by IIL officials in the early hours of 13 August, 1945.

When they arrived Bose was in his bedroom, wearing a half sleeve vest but still in his top boots and breeches. Overhead there was a single bright electric lamp and a fan to cool the warm night air. Bose motioned the men to pull up chairs round him and asked, "Well, what is the news you have brought?"

One of them said, "Sir, I am sorry to say that Japan has surrendered!" (This was not the case: surrender came two days later). Bose said nothing, except "Um", and then smiling, said '"So, that is that. Now, what next?" For Bose's advisers, it was the end of the world. But Bose reassured them: "Well, don't you see?" he asked. "We are the only people who have not surrendered." Ayer has left us a vivid portrayal of the small hours of the morning in this little Malayan town as Bose wrestled with the calamity:

> It was nearly 4.30am. He was still in his top boots and breeches and his half-sleeved undervest. He paced up and down or a few minutes, then said, "It is rather warm here, come on let us go and sit on the verandah" Out on the veranda a chill breeze was blowing and it was draughty where he went and sat at the corner of the veranda where some cane-chairs had been placed. I sat

> opposite to him. The light was dim compared with that in the room. Still I could see his face very clearly. He looked undoubtedly grave and was silent for a while as was usual with him on serious occasions. He spoke almost in a whisper. "Now we have got to think out what shall we do." When I looked at the watch it was nearing 5 am and I said to him "Sir, do you know it is five in the morning, don't you think you ought to have a little rest before we start early in the morning on a twelve hour non-stop drive to Singapore?". The man's humour even at that eerie hour was irrepressible. He said, '"Oh, it doesn't matter. We shall have plenty of rest from tomorrow!" and he smiled broadly.

Bose knew he had to maintain a cheerful front. His life had been full of ups and downs but the men he had gathered round him in east Asia had no such experience and their morale must be maintained. After barely an hour's sleep, he was on his way back to Singapore early the next morning. The drive took most of the day, and was not easy. It had to be in a convoy – an armed guard in a lorry leading Bose's car followed by another car – as there were fears from attacks by communist guerrillas. Bose tried to lighten the mood as much as he could. The car following him was packed with bananas which were scarce in Singapore but plentiful in Seremban. Whenever the convoy stopped, Bose joked that it would be better to give the bananas away than have the sun finish them.

As soon as he was back in his beach house, Subhas plunged into three days of intense talks with his ministers and advisers. Publicly he issued a special order of the day trying to scotch rumours that Japan had surrendered; privately all options were considered. On the afternoon of 14 August Bose had a tooth extracted and, ignoring the dentist's advice to stay in bed, he went to see a play on the life of the Rani of Jhansi put on by the women of that regiment. It was written by P.N Oak, ADC to Major General J K Bhonsle. At the open-air theatre 3,000 officers and men enjoyed this stirring patriotic Indian play. It was the last time Bose was to be seen at such a large public open-air gathering.

Halfway through the performance something equally dramatic happened. Sarkar, a lawyer and a member of the Provisional government, unexpectedly arrived from Bangkok, and drove straight from the airport to the theatre. Bose asked him to sit next to him and give him the latest news. That evening Sarkar joined Bose for dinner and sat in on the ongoing conference of his advisors and ministers. Ayer records:

> Before Sarkar turned up on the scene it had been more or less decided that Netaji would stay on in Singapore with all the Ministers present there and face the British when they eventually landed on the island. This decision was arrived at after a good deal of very frank discussion of the advisability or otherwise of Netaji's staying on in Singapore and being taken prisoner by the British. All these discussions took place in Netaji's presence and he also spoke frankly but in a very impersonal way.... The consensus of opinion among the members of the Cabinet was that Netaji must not be taken prisoner by the British. Single-handedly Netaji opposed this idea. He said that he should remain with his army in Singapore and face the British His view prevailed for the time being..... Meanwhile, as I said earlier, Sarkar turned up on the scene and a very important talk followed that night. After listening to what Sarkar had to say, Netaji showed a slight inclination to reconsider his own decision about staying on in Singapore.

Ayer does not say what Sarkar reported. Bose was certainly open to persuasion. In Rangoon he had been persuaded by his Cabinet to leave and not surrender. In Singapore before the theatre performance Bose and his ministers had joked about what would happen once the British arrived and when Bose would surely again experience the inside of a Raj jail. They debated where the British would try Bose, in East Asia or India? One minister suggested that if the British sentenced him to death for waging war against Britain it would mark the death knell of the British Empire.Then suddenly Sarkar arrived, and he began to change his mind.

Could it be that Sarkar, the legal man, had told Bose he would be treated as a war criminal? Just six days earlier, on 8 August, a six-week conference of Allied lawyers in London had concluded with the decision to hold a war crimes trial of the Axis leaders. The United States had always been keen on such a trial, as was the Soviet Union, but not the British. As late as 12 April 1945, two weeks before Germany's surrender, the British Cabinet had decided that there was no need for a trial. All Nazis should be considered as outlaws and summarily shot. It was at the London conference that the British finally accepted the idea of an international tribunal, and agreed its procedures.

But Nazi Germany was a state, and the crime for which the Nazis were eventually tried in Nuremberg was of waging aggressive wars. Bose could hardly be accused of that. The British could have tried him for treason, but this would have been a spurious charge. Could they have just shot him out of hand? Bose, by now, must have known the fate that had befallen the Europeans who had collaborated with the Axis, and how Mussolini had been hanged by Italian partisans. Did Sarkar brief him on the London conference and its implications for him? We do not know. What we do know is there was some very confidential talk in some British circles about shooting Bose the moment they captured him, although this was never official policy. In the end, as we shall see, there was an Indian trial of Bose's men, which had the kind of impact on Indian opinion that Bose's ministers thought might result from a trial of their leader.

On the afternoon of 15 August Tokyo radio formally announced its acceptance of the surrender. The Japanese for the first time heard the voice of their Emperor who in, perhaps, the most dramatic understatement of the war, said the situation had not worked out to Japan's advantage.

Bose did not want to be humiliated by the British and he told Kiani he had no desire to fall into British hands again. He wanted Kiani to lead INA guerrillas into the Malayan jungle. Kiani, sensibly, refused, arguing that this would only invite reprisals against Indians in Malaya. The war, Kiani told Bose, was over and the INA must surrender. When Bose tried to argue the revolutionary thesis Kiani protested that while Bose could think like a revolutionary who never surrendered, he as a soldier could not.

Before leaving Singapore Bose had to attend to one matter of detail . He saw Colonel John Stracey, and approved of the plans for a memorial to the INA fallen. One of the first things the British did was to demolish it, although many years later in a Singapore free of British rule a memorial to Bose and the INA did go up.

Then Bose left Singapore on the journey from which he never returned.

Part Six
THE MYTH AND THE *LEGEND*

Though the crushed jewels drop and fade The artist's labour will not cease, And of the ruins shall be made, some yet. more lovely masterpiece.

A.E *(an Irish poet in one of Subhas Bose's favourite poems)*

20

What If He Had Returned?

It is 23 January 2004, and crowds all over India are celebrating the birthday of Subhas Bose. Politicians who have never known him, and many who fought him when he was alive, garland his statues, invoke his name and urge their audiences to follow his example. More than 60 years after his death Bose has become a myth: the alternative hero of the Indian struggle for freedom. Banners at these meetings tell their own story. *Subhas Bose 1897-2004.* Subhas Bose is not dead. One day he will return and rescue India.

The legends and the myths have been a long time in the making, and they express a deeper Indian unease. Had he lived and returned to India after the Second World War, would he have shaped a country far more successful than the one wrought by his rivals and successors? Would we have seen an India united, strong and fearless? Bose became a legend in his own lifetime, but his transformation into a myth fit to rank with those mentioned in the ancient Hindu classics came after his death through forces he had himself tried to harness for his cause. They were catalysed through the British decision to hold a symbolic trial of certain INA men in the Red Fort of Delhi.

At the end of the war the INA was scattered all over east Asia. As its personnel were finally shipped back to India they found the country ignorant of their existence and firmly under British control. "Not a dog barked as they flew us back," was how one officer later recalled the journey home.

Within days of Japan's defeat, the British began considering the INA problem. London had left it for Delhi to decide, but Delhi was deeply divided and needed to be convinced that Bose was in fact dead. On 24 August, the day after the official death notice, Wavell recorded in his diary: "I wonder if the Japanese announcement of Subhas Chandra Bose's death in an air crash is true, I suspect it very much, it is just what would be given out if he meant to go underground." He asked his home member, Sir R.F. Mudie, to prepare a note for the trial of Bose and the INA.

Even within the extended definition of "war criminal" Mudie could find nothing that could be said to include Bose. His advisers were deeply worried about the consequences of a trial, and the Home department note he sent to Wavell acknowledged the difficulties of handling Bose. Interrogation of the INA and the other Indians in East Asia had established that, contrary to British propaganda, Bose was regarded not as a puppet of the Japanese but as a great hero. He had dealt with the Japanese as an equal, and had created India's first national army. Then there was his undoubted prestige and status in India, particularly in Bengal, where he "ranks little, if anything, below Gandhi as an all-India figure."

After listing the various measures that could be taken to deal with Bose, the report discussed their drawbacks. Public pressure would not allow him to be hanged in India; the Burma government was unlikely to want to try him there; trials in Singapore or elsewhere would create just as many problems. A quick military execution was a solution, but that could hardly be defended, and the military might read it as a subterfuge to avoid the independence issue which would figure in a civil trial. Imprisoning him would only lead to agitation for his release. The report concluded:

> In many ways the easiest course would be to leave him where he is and not ask

> for his release. He might,of course, in certain circumstances be welcomed by the Russians.This course would raise fewest immediate political difficulties but the security authorities consider that in certain circumstances his presence in Russia would be so dangerous as to rule it out altogether.

By November 1946 and after several investigations the British concluded that while there might be a ten per cent chance Bose might still be alive, there was not much else they could do about it. The 25,000 1NA prisoners being repatriated to India presented very different problems. Senior British Army commanders were convinced that the INA were 'traitors' and their officers a "rabble", and that, if the integrity and the discipline of the British Indian Army were to be maintained, they should be severely punished. Some preferred kangaroo courts and quick executions. But the higher echelons of the Raj were not entirely convinced that this was the right policy; in any case, it was not possible to execute 25,000 men secretly. A few were executed, but for the great majority a more selective policy was implemented. They were classified into "whites" – those who had joined the INA with the intention of re-joining the British. Then there were the "greys", those who had been misled by Bose and the Japanese. and finally the "blacks," those who had fervently believed in the cause.The whites were to be restored to their former positions in the army, the greys were to be tried, dismissed and released; only the blacks were to bear the full brunt of British punishment. They were beyond redemption, and Auchinleck was convinced that when their full story emerged the Indian public would be horrified.

Former INA soldiers were already housed in camps set up in Delhi's Red Fort, and this, it was decided, would be an excellent place for a trial. The Fort was ideally situated for press and media coverage. On 5 November 1945 the trial of Shah Nawaz Khan, Prem Kumar Sahgal and Gurbaksh Singh Dhillon began. Dhillon was charged with murder, Shah Nawaz and Sahgal with abetting murder: all three were charged with "waging war against His Majesty the King, Emperor of India". The trials lasted till 31 December, and proved to be a sensation, though not in the way Claude Auchinleck wished.

The war had not brought Indian independence any nearer, and the British mistook the political quiet for approval. But almost nine months after the end of the hostilities, when the British in Delhi held their victory celebrations, the Indians went wild with fury: the old Delhi town hall was partly gutted, Indians dressed in European clothes were attacked, parading troops were booed and the police had to open fire in order to restore order. The INA and Bose had created a potentially revolutionary situation: one on which the political parties were eager to build for their own platforms, none more so than the Congress.

The Congress had suffered a double defeat during the war: it had gained little through either negotiations or mass struggle, and now it was a case of "the Congress proposes, the Muslim League disposes". In these circumstances, the Congress soon realised the potential of the fervour behind the INA, and it quickly adopted resolutions both approving of their actions and pledging it to defend them at the trial. A party dedicated to non-violence was at last beginning to realise the usefulness of violence.

Even Jinnah urged the government to treat the INA prisoners with leniency. By now the Indian press, freed from wartime censorship, was full of stories and legends of the INA and Bose. 'Jai Hind' had replaced all other greetings between Indians, and Bose's photographs, invariably in INA uniform, graced a million *pan* shops.

The defence was led by Bhulabhai Desai, who in the past had been a bitter critic of Bose. By the time of his own death, a few months after the trial, he was as great a champion of Netaji as any. The trial became, as Nehru said, a dramatic version of that old contest, England versus India: the legal niceties vanished and even the personalities of defendants were obscured. For Indians it was not only illegal but a slur on Indian nationalism; the victors were disposing of the vanquished in the very place where the latter had planned to hold their victory parade. Besides, the three accused – Shah Nawaz was a Muslim, Sahgal a Hindu and Dhillon a Sikh – represented all the major communities of India. Auchinleck may have hoped that would stress the communal nature of Indian politics – always Britain's strongest point; but for Indians it demonstrated that the INA was indeed a national army: that Bose had indeed succeeded in uniting Muslims, Hindus and Sikhs for a common cause.

The defence based its argument on the host of precedents, old and new, which supported the right of subject countries to fight for their freedom. But, for all Desai's eloquence, as far as the court-martial was concerned he was arguing a lost cause, one they were incapable of appreciating, let alone accepting. The predictable verdict was that all three officers were guilty of waging war against the King. Dhillon and Sahgal were acquitted of the charge of murder and abetting murder; Shah Nawaz was found guilty of abetting murder. All three were sentenced to transportation for life, cashiering and forfeiture of arrears of pay and allowances.

However, the British military authorities had become painfully aware of the consequences of the trial. Even before it had opened, "INA days" had been organised in various parts of the country. The day the proceedings got underway the police had to open fire on a protesting crowd at Madura in south India. Then, as the trial proceeded, the Red Fort itself was besieged; more than a hundred were killed or injured by police firing. Between 21 and 26 November 1945 Calcutta was strike-bound. In a rare gesture of communal amity, Hindus and Muslims, their trucks flying both Congress and Muslim League flags, jointly took over the city, attacking American and British military establishments and shouting the slogans of freedom and nationalism coined by Bose. Some 49 military vehicles were destroyed and 97 damaged, and about 200 military personnel injured: 32 Indians lost their lives and 200 were wounded. The violence soon spread along the Gangetic plain to Patna, Allahabad and Benares, and eventually places as far apart as Karachi and Bombay were affected.

Claude Auchinleck was no longer the confident commander-in-chief who had ordered the trial, and even as it was proceeding he wrote to the Viceroy expressing his doubts:

> I know from my long experience of Indian troops how hard it is even for the best and most sympathetic British officer to gauge the inner feelings of the Indian soldier, and history supports me in this view. I do not think any senior British officer today knows what is the real feeling among the Indian ranks regarding the 'INA'. I myself feel, from my own instinct largely, but also from the information I have had from various sources, that there is a growing feeling of sympathy for the 'INA' and an increasing tendency to disregard the brutalities committed by some of its members as well as the forswearing by all of them of their original allegiance. It is impossible to apply our standards of ethics to this problem or to shape our policy as we would, had the 'INA' been of our own race.

Not wanting to be caught napping again, Auchinleck set up a special organisation in his military headquarters "to find out the real feelings of Indian ranks on this subject". He also decided that no more INA personnel would be tried on the major charge of waging war against the King, and that only those who had committed "acts of gross brutality" would be brought before the courts – at most between 20 and 50 men. Later Mason, joint secretary in the war department of the government of India, declared that the INA's "patriotic motive would be taken at its face value and its members would be treated as though prisoners of war".

A week before the trial ended, the Viceroy empowered Auchinleck to commute sentences of death or transportation for life, and when Auchinleck came to confirm the sentences of the three men, he only agreed to the verdict of cashiering and forfeiture of pay: the transportation decision was quashed and, taking into account 'the prevailing circumstances', the men were set free. Shah Nawaz, Sahgal and Dhillon were welcomed like the heroes of a conquering army and their tales were carried back to the remotest villages of India to be told, retold and eventually mythologized. For a time the INA seemed to have become India - even for Gandhi. Now, in his weekly *Harijan* column, he invariably referred to Bose as Netaji, and conceded that "the hypnotism of the INA has cast its spell upon us. Netaji's name is one to conjure with. His patriotism is second-to-none (I use the present tense intentionally). His bravery shines through all his actions." He, too, believed Netaji was alive.

The British, however, continued with the selective trials, and on 4 February 1946 Captain Abdul Rashid was sentenced to seven years' imprisonment for certain acts of brutality. Rashid was a Muslim, and now the Muslim League came into the picture. For four days between 11 and 14 February, the streets of Calcutta, Bombay and Delhi witnessed unique political demonstrations in which Hindus and Muslims forgot their differences and came together to fight the INA's battles. Four days of strict martial law were required to bring Calcutta back to normal; by then nearly 50 were dead and over 500 injured. In January, too, some 5,200 Royal Indian Air Force personnel had gone on strike to protest over their conditions and as an expression of sympathy for the INA. cause. And on 18 February a revolt began on HMS *Talwar,* a training ship of the Indian navy moored off Bombay. By nightfall on the 20th virtually the whole of the Royal Indian Navy was in open rebellion: seventy-eight ships in the various ports of India – Bombay, Karachi, Madras, Vizagapatnam, Calcutta and Cochin, and even in the Andamans – and nearly all the shore establishments had hauled down the Union Jack. Only ten ships and two shore establishments still remained with the British. Other units of the armed forces were quickly affected. Between 22 and 25 February the RIAF in Bombay and Madras went on strike and on the 27th Indian soldiers in Jabalpur followed. In Bombay and Karachi, the main naval centres, ratings were able to generate impressive mass support. In Karachi gun battles had ensued, which continued for two days before heavy British reinforcements finally defeated the men. In Bombay there had been what even the British-owned *Times of India* was forced to call "mass uprising ... in sympathy with the naval mutiny . . . unparalleled in the city's history". The communists and the Congress Left had called for sympathy strikes and over 600,000 workers from the textile mills of Bombay had responded. For almost three days, they had fought running, unequal battles with British troops in the streets and lanes of Bombay. The British had tanks and machine-guns, the workers had improvised weapons and even at times stones from dug-up roads. But for a few days some of Bombay's teeming working-class slums had become "no-go areas", and the British had had to call in white troops to quell the uprising. In the end 270 had died and 1,300 had been injured (the government's official figures were lower: 187 and 1,002).

Undoubtedly a revolutionary situation had been created. But now, suddenly, the ratings found there were no leaders. They knew their navy but they had been horribly wrong about the Indian political parties. The naval ratings had virtually given the politicians a whole unit of the British Indian armed forces; they had even started calling it the Indian National Navy. For the politicians, however, this was too alarming a prospect. Jinnah advised the men to go back and assured them that, if they did so, he would use constitutional means to remedy their complaints of bad food and service conditions. The Congress leaders were plainly frightened by the prospect of leading a revolution; Nehru came to Bombay and deplored the revolt. And as the ratings wondered what might have happened if there had been a leader prepared to lead them – Bose perhaps – the British re-took their ships.

But if the Indian politicians had no use for revolutionary situations, the Labour government had been quick to understand the implications. On 4 December 1945 Herbert Morrison announced in the House of Commons that a ten-member parliamentary delegation would visit India to study the situation. The five-week visit took place in January and February 1946 and, by the end of it, nearly all the visiting MPs were convinced that India was in a dangerous state. The February disturbances convinced Attlee that the imperial tide had at last ebbed. India could be held by force of arms for a few years more, but the cost for a Britain devastated by war would be too high. The British government announced in February 1946 that a Cabinet mission of three ministers would visit India. That mission, in fact, failed in its purpose. The situation required another intervention by Attlee. It was his speech in the House of Commons on 20 February 1947, when he pledged the British government to transfer power to Indian hands, if necessary as two separate nations, "not later than June 1948", that finally led to the emergence of the two nations of India and Pakistan on 15 August 1947.

That such a situation existed owed much to Subhas Bose. He did not precisely visualise the extent of the post-war turmoil. In his wildest dreams he could not have matched the fervour the INA trials produced. But he had told his men in Burma to fraternise with the Indians in the British Indian Army, and until the end he was confident that if Indians kept up their resolve Britain, in an increasingly hostile post-war world, would have to concede independence.

True, his army did not parade as victors in the Red Fort, but the INA trials proved that his belief in a revolutionary consciousness was grounded in a deeper understanding of the Indian people than his enemies had credited him, or even his most fervent friends believed in. The vision had been genuine. He just did not have the means, while alive, to translate it into a reality. Even Dilip, so sceptical of worldly struggles, recognised that the romance of Bose's INA had finally breached the dyke that separated Indians from the other army maintained to enslave them.

Through 1946 and 1947, as Indian leaders bartered with the British and among themselves to produce a divided India, they appeared to be constantly looking over their shoulders to reassure themselves that Bose's ghost was not going to appear, like Hamlet's father, turning into flesh and blood. The years of struggle had wearied them, they did not have the stomach for another fight, and they were relieved to get what crumbs they could from the imperial table. When the Congress finally accepted the partition plan Nehru had only this consolation to offer for the sudden abandonment of a lifetime's principles:

> But of one thing I am convinced, that ultimately there will be a united and strong India. We have often to go through the valley of the shadow before we reach the sunlit mountain tops."

Had Bose not died but returned to India after the war he might well have prevented the tragedy that partition produced. He would not have been a tired politician ready to accept office under any terms. Bose's often repeated warning that the Congress would pay dearly for the "acceptance of office mentality" was historically acute. It came in the late thirties when the Congress was struggling to cope with the consequences of the 1935 Government of India Act and the blandishments it offered. In the 1936 elections, the Congress reaped the rewards of nearly two decades of unceasing mass struggle against the British and totally vanquished the Muslim League. But by 1945, after a decade of negotiations and some power sharing with the British, the Congress was reduced to the level of the Muslim League; just another group, albeit powerful, seeking the rewards of office. And by placing such faith in the negotiating chamber the Congress had played into the hands of Jinnah, the master lawyer and negotiator. As Bose had foreseen, the Congress had thrown away the trump card of its power, mass struggle, for the dubious delights of the round table.

But could Indians have lived with Bose? An extreme man, he produced extreme reactions: total adulation or permanent rejection. Certainly, the India of Bose would have been very different from the India of Nehru. Bose had often said that India needed at least 20 years of iron dictatorial rule, and he would most certainly have rejected the type of parliamentary democracy that has developed.

Surely, Bose's rule would have degenerated into autocracy, like that of Mrs Gandhi between 1975 and 1977? Though the analogy is not quite accurate, for Mrs Gandhi's rule degenerated long before the events of June 1975, Bose's critics pointed for conclusive evidence to his behaviour in Germany and with the Japanese during the Second World War. In a climate that brooked no dissent and where the leader was always right, he too came to believe that he could do no wrong. Part of the possible reason for this change of personality, if there was a change, may lie in the fact that at that stage, particularly in south-east Asia, he found himself like a king without any worthwhile courtiers. The people who surrounded him there were political innocents, thrust into the wider world by events beyond their control. They could only applaud, never interject. Bose was, as the official Japanese history puts it, "a bright morning star amidst them".

There is also evidence that suggests Bose was not quite the dictator a simple reading of his speeches makes him out to be. There was an authoritarian streak in him, but his actions often belied his dictatorial postures. In 1939, as Congress president, he behaved in his fight with Gandhi less like an autocrat and more like a negotiator who had won one round, and expected to reap some benefit. Throughout his political career, he was always loyal to colleagues, even at the risk of damaging his own chances: hardly the mark of a man of iron.

Almost alone among Indian leaders, Bose offered solutions that were both visionary and practical. Nehru's socialism may have been more rounded, rigorously logical, and free of Bose's celebrated eclecticism. But its strain of romanticism divorced it from the realities of India, and the Nehru years resulted, almost inevitably, in a country with the most progressive socialist legislation outside the old Soviet bloc which happily allowed the most unbridled capitalism to grow and flourish on a feudal structure that had changed little, if at all, since the British days. The cynicism this produced has bitten so deep that every government since has had to struggle against it, and no combination in Indian politics looks likely to counteract the years of wasted opportunities and lost hopes.

Bose had the capacity to inspire total love and dedication, and produce gold from dross. He was hated by many, but those he touched loved him with an almost overpowering sense of completeness. And this, combined with his rigorous, matter-of-fact manner and an instinctive feel for ancient Indian loyalties, might well have produced the revolution that India needed and still lacks.

Like Turkey's Kemal Atatürk, a man he admired, Bose might well have produced a nation at once new, yet full of old virtues. This is best illustrated in his enlightened approach to women: he was not one for making strident feminist statements, but even on the submarine taking him from Germany to Japan, he was telling Abid Hasan of the need to get Indian women to join the INA. He described how they would have to abandon their beloved sarees in order to do so. He did get many immigrant women to join the INA, demonstrating that Indian feminism could be happily blended with the exigency of war.

The ideological development that Bose sought has never materialised. Like all national liberation movements, the independent Congress was a coalition of business seeking to oust British capital, of rural landowners confident that native rulers would do more for them than alien ones, of various interest groups, and of socialists aware that the Congress was the only party capable of furthering their ideas. Gandhi did suggest that the Congress should disband after independence, but this was clearly impossible: self-interest, if nothing else, ruled it out. Today almost all the major political groups in India – communists, socialists, free-enterprise capitalists, Gandhian socialists – trace their ancestry to the Congress; only the right-wing Hindu BJP, can claim a different parentage.

The most valid criticism of Bose is related to the nature of the nationalist movement itself. For Bose's faults – and there were many – were inevitable in a nationalist fighting a colonial power that both fanned nationalism, and denied its legitimate expression. The Raj, as Marx penetratingly observed, did unwittingly bring modern ideas into India, but the nationalist reaction it produced in India was distorted by the British presence.

In many ways the most dramatic impact Bose might have had on a free India could have been on foreign relations where his rival Nehru fashioned a foreign policy that can now be seen to be a disaster. As we have seen, in 1939, in one of his long letters to Nehru, Bose ridiculed Nehru's love for frothy, pious, sentiments when it came to foreign affairs. Nehru rebutted the charge, but in independent India, Nehru's non-aligned policy was often dictated by just such frothy, pious sentiments, and the legacy he has left behind has proved a heavy drag.

This is most noticeable in Kashmir where Nehru choose to go to the United Nations when a resolution on the ground might have been possible, and, certainly much more beneficial. Similar mushy sentiments dictated his China policy until it fell apart so dramatically in 1962 with China's invasion of India's border regions. Neither Kashmir nor India's border dispute with China have been resolved, and continue to have an enormous impact on Indian domestic policy, not least the need to maintain a huge defence force.

On both Kashmir and China Nehru was guided by Mountbatten who Nehru chose as free India's first viceroy. How much a part his love for Edwina, Mountbatten's wife, played in this we do not know, but the decision proved both sentimental and wrongheaded. It was Mountbatten who pushed Nehru to take the UN route to solve the Kashmir situation. The situation on the ground was complicated by the fact that the commanders of both the Indian and Pakistan forces were actually British. Their decisions were dictated by the interests of the old colonial power. In what must be a unique situation in modern warfare, the newly independent Indian and Pakistani armies fought each other, while the British commanders of the two armies often spoke by telephone warning each other of the actions their subordinates were planning! On China Nehru relied on Mountbatten's military expertise that the Chinese could not possibly attack over the eastern Himalayas. They did just that, routed the Indians, and Nehru never recovered.

Bose would never have agreed to an Englishman staying on as viceroy after independence Nor given his hard-headed approach to issues would he have allowed foreign policy to became almost an adjunct of high sounding moralising as it did under Nehru. Non-aligned was made into a creed which could not be questioned. This was so even years after Nehru's death when it was clear it had long outlived its usefulness. The result was that Indian policy makers failed to recognise that the United States was fast becoming the dominant world power, and that it would be useful for India to shed its useless non-aligned policy. Bose might have pined for the Soviet Union through the 1930s but his realism would have made him see where the force lay.

But if Bose was a realist, was he not also an opportunist? How else can we explain his war-time alliance with the Axis? Though he bravely maintained his independence from both the Germans and the Japanese – itself no mean feat – he deliberately avoided the wider implications of their awful philosophies. However, his argument that foreign help was required in order to drive the British out was justified by the events of 1945-6, and has been the bedrock of nearly all successful national-liberation movements since the war. In this, at least, Bose was probably far ahead of his time. In our age, when a national-liberation movement's acceptance of foreign help from all and sundry is a common fact of life, the idea may seem of no great significance. In the early forties, for a subjugated non-white race even to think of any such thing was revolutionary indeed.

Western historians assessing Bose clearly find his war-time alliance impossible to comprehend. Gerhard L. Weinberg, the German born American historian, writing the massive Cambridge University *A World At Arms*, a global history of the Second World War, devotes some space to Bose and takes great pleasure in mocking him and his ideas. Unusually in a history of World War II Bose features on the first page of the book, which also sets the tone for Weinberg's assessment of him. He begins with the words on the memorial the British built after the battle of Kohima honouring their dead and asking future generations to remember,

"For your tomorrow we gave our today". Then Weinberg tells his readers that the British in Kohima were opposed by "some Indians who believed that the Japanese treated the people of their colonial empire, such as the Koreans, far better than the British treated theirs."

How ridiculous, suggests Weinberg, could anything be more foolish or deluded? In practice neither Bose nor the men who fought for him in the INA had any illusions about the Japanese. Bose never believed the Japanese would be better than the British. His view was that it did not matter what the Japanese were like, he was using the Japanese to do something the Indians had failed to achieve throughout British rule – raise an army to fight the British. This is, after all, what George Washington, founder of Weinberg's adopted country,did, accepting the help of the *ancien* regime of France. Did Washington ask questions about the benevolence of the regime in France? It was soon to be overthrown in the French revolution, and condemned as the scourge of mankind! Washington, like Bose, felt it was none of his business what the French monarchy was like. For him French assistance was very useful. In the crucial battle ofYorktown there were more French than Americans fighting the British.

Elsewhere in his book Weinberg shows his grasp of Indian history to be so shaky that he comes across more as a pamphleteer than a historian, as evidenced from his nonsensical charge that Bose's violent ways lead to a worsening of the communal situation. Given this, it would perhaps be too much to expect him to appreciate the Indian compulsions, shared by the great majority of the non-white world, that guided Bose. For Bose seeking the help of the Japanese was better than being a slave of the British. India, he felt, would somehow sort it out with the Japanese.

A hypothetical question often asked is what would have happened had Bose not escaped from India in 1941? The answer is that he would certainly have spent the war years in jail. Rather than being at the mercy of the British, the activist in Bose wanted to initiate action of his own. He opted to escape to take advantage of world events. His choice of friends was unwise, but since the Soviets took no interest, he had little choice.

Any evaluation of Bose's war-time alliances must take into account two other factors. One is that while the war was generally a fight between freedom and slavery, the governments claiming to represent freedom also had their own slaves and not everyone fighting on freedom's side was interested in this freedom versus slavery question. If Bose's war-time decisions were faulty, there were other war time leaders on freedom's side who also had their dark sides. There are, for example, Churchill's views on India and Indians. Even such an admiring historian of Churchill as Andrew Roberts candidly admits that when it came to Indians Churchill was a racist, who thought they were inferior and incapable of ruling themselves. Franklin D Roosevelt, the other great war time leader, wanted a free India, but commanded an Army that was racially segregated. Indeed one of his commanders spoke of the need for racial segregation in terms that could have been written by Hitler.

Secondly the simplistic "goodies versus baddies" analysis breaks down completely when you turn to Asia during the Second World War. We all know who the Asian "baddies" were. They were, of course, the Japanese, the allies of Bose. Even now you only have to visit Korea and China to realise how hated the Japanese remain for their colonial rule in that part of the world. But who were the Asian "goodies"? There are not too many names that can be flourished. There was one "good" Asian leader who was highly rated – Chiang Kai-shek, feted as the great hope of Asia, the man who symbolised the fight for freedom on that continent. He can be seen in all those pictures of war-time conferences sitting next to Roosevelt, Churchill and Stalin. His influence was immense, so much so that when it came to post-war peacekeeping China got equal status with the United States, Soviet Union, Britain and France, and became a permanent member of the United Nations. But can it really be argued that this man, probably the most venal and corrupt politician China has produced in its long history, was a good Asian? And how did the Americans treat the one Asian who fought the Japanese, but wanted freedom for his country from the French?. They demonised him and bombed his country. He was, of course, Ho Chi Minh.

Bose's wartime vision was that Indians had a wonderful opportunity to fight for freedom , a freedom won without a real war was in his view meaningless. "It is our duty," Bose told his INA, "to pay for our liberty with our own blood. The freedom that we shall win, through our sacrifice and exertions, we shall be able to preserve with our own strength."

Indians disillusioned with the progress made by independent India have turned to these words for an explanation of what went wrong. Freedom came too easily. And so over the years Bose has become the symbol and the voice of that alternative struggle for Indian freedom. Though it contributed significantly, it did not manage to seize power from the British.

Even more than Gandhi, Subhas Bose remains the one leader who Indians hope will re-appear to rescue them from the mess that others have created. Perhaps, as Sisir Bose said, this feeling can only be understood in psychological terms. It reflects the fundamental frustration generated by the events of August 1947 – a frustration that Santimoy Ganguli, Bose's one-time associate, felt even as he witnessed the celebrations around him. On 15 August 1947 Ganguli stood at the junction of Lower Circular Road and Lansdowne Road in central Calcutta. All around him crowds were shouting, "Jai Hind!" Strangers were embracing one another. Young people atop lorries and buses were waving Indian flags and crying, "Inquilab Zindabad!"(Long Live Revolution) Suddenly Ganguli felt a hand grip his shoulder. He turned round to stare into the face of a notorious CID officer from Elysium Row. The officer was beaming and shaking Ganguli violently. He said, "Cheer up! What's the matter? Don't you know what day it is? Today we have become brothers!"

Ganguli smiled weakly, and gave a silent nod; but to this day he does not know how he managed to restrain his tears. Nothing had changed. Power had been transferred, and suddenly the jailer and the jailed had become one. This was not the freedom he had fought for. It was only 25-years later, when some of the brightest youths of Bengal answered the call of Mao that Ganguli's heavy heart lifted. The Indian revolution he had fought for, which his leader had so eloquently championed, might still have a successful conclusion.

That hope was to prove as false as many others. The result is that Indians are left still hankering for a leader like Bose, a hankering made worse by the fact that – in the face of all evidence – many still refuse to believe he died in 1945. This refusal has lead to a curious kind of politics in independent India, and done much to damage the reputation of Bose and to prevent a proper assessment of the man.

Postscript:

STORY WITHOUT *END*

The problem with the Subhas Bose story is that for some peculiarly Indian reasons it has no finality. It is now nearly 60 years since that August day in 1945 when Subhas whispered his last words in a Japanese Military hospital. Even so millions of his countrymen refuse to believe that he died, and at the time of writing a former Supreme Court justice of India is sitting in an office in Calcutta enquiring into his death.

Leonard Gordon, the American historian, who has researched extensively into Sarat and Subhas Bose has written, "The Boses now live in the historical imagination of their countrymen." Unfortunately far too many Indians can only come to terms with Subhas Bose through a fictional imagination of what happened to him after 1945. In 2000 one Indian novelist even pictured Subhas Bose in the Russian Gulag. The result is instead of making an assessment of who Bose was, and what he stood for, the constant emphasis in India is on what happened to him after 18 August 1945 and questioning whether he is still alive. So Bose, the most rational and straight talking of Indian politicians, has become a mystery and an enigma.

To an extent Bose contributed to this, especially in the way he kept his marriage secret. There is no disputing the fact that he lived with Emilie as man and wife, producing a child. But there is no evidence of a marriage certificate, and it was only as late as 1994 through his nephew Sisir – who must have been told this by Emilie– that the exact date of the marriage, 26 December 1937, became known. Bose lived for a further eight years, but did not tell his closest relatives that he had married, although a few who worked with him during the war did discover the truth. So it was not until three years after his death that people knew he was married. How this came about is an interesting story in itself.

Emilie received three letters from Subhas after he left Kiel in the German U-boat in 1943. These letters came either by submarine, or via the Axis diplomatic bag, which also brought Bose's messages to Nambiar on the Indian legion . Sometime in late 1945, or early 1946, with Vienna under the occupation of the Allies, Emilie and Anita received a visit from some British soldiers. In the group was a Sikh, and Emilie turned on him and asked, "Are you not too ashamed to betray your country?" The embarrassment on the Sikh's face showed that Emilie had scored a point. The British were keen to find out more about Subhas's wife, and they returned soon after. On this occasion Emilie was not at home, and her sister, confused and befuddled, allowed them to take away the letters Subhas had written from East Asia. Emilie later tried to retrieve them, but was not successful.

The loss of the letters was only a minor problem. Her bigger worry was trying to raise Anita, who by then was three and a half, in Vienna, a city devastated by war. Anita, of course, has no recollection of her father, but she has a vivid memory of Emilie making her pray every night for his safe return. One of Anita's great wishes was to have a sister and she often asked her mother for one. But what will father say? Emilie would ask. Anita always replied, "I am sure father will not mind."

Sometime later, Emilie decided to contact Sarat. She wrote to him in Calcutta enclosing a photocopy of Subhas's letter of 1943 to his Mejda informing him of his marriage. Despite several reminders she had no reply, but it seems the letters never reached Sarat. Then, according to Anita, quite by chance contact was established.

Nehru, probably through Nambiar, learnt that Subhas had left a child in Europe and told Sarat. This made Sarat get in touch with Emilie, and finally the Bose family in Calcutta found out about the marriage. Sarat wrote to her some time in 1948, and then flew to Europe with his wife and children to meet her. But there was still an element of mystery. Roma, Sarat's daughter, described to Leonard Gordon how Sarat made this trip mysterious. When the family reached Prague Sarat summoned his children and told them, "We're going to meet someone in Vienna". Roma asked, "Rangakakababu?" (Subhas Bose) "No", Sarat replied, "not him, but his wife and daughter. They were married late in 1941 and I have come to see them. It is the purpose of my visit."

It is noteworthy that Sarat was under the impression the marriage was in 1941 when, as we now know, it took place in 1937, an indication that part of the marriage mystery was still to be unravelled. By this time, there had already been contact with friends and some family members. Aurobindo, another nephew of Subhas, had visited Emilie and Anita in Vienna, and sometime in 1947 Subhas's old friend Nathalal Parikh called on them. Parikh was very concerned about Emilie's financial condition and asked if she needed money. Emilie, who worked in the post office, assured him she was well provided for, but said that she needed a watch. Anita has a vivid memory of Parikh taking off the wristwatch and giving it to her mother.

Life in post war Vienna was hard. This was the Vienna that is brilliantly portrayed in Graham Greene's *The Third Man*. Food was scarce, racketeering rife, and life often a lottery. There was a brief period one winter when Anita could not leave home because she had no shoes. She had outgrown the pair she had. In the summer Emilie had cut off the toes of the shoes that were too smnall thereby turning them into slippers, but they were not suitable for a central European winter. Nehru and Patel arranged some financial assistance for Emilie, and then Sarat suggested they should move to India. There was a plot of land next to his house and he planned to build a house there, and to provide a separate flat for Emilie and Anita. Sarat was well aware that she would need privacy, and wanted to recreate the European style of life to which she was accustomed. But then Sarat died, and with him the plans. Emilie never visited her husband's country and in latter years would say to those who asked why this was so that she could not have stood the heat.

By the time Anita visited India she was 19 and it was 1961. The visit, organised and financed by the Bose family, received extensive media coverage in India, where she spent a few days with Nehru, breakfasting regularly with her father's old political rival. The arrival of Anita also revealed the deep divisions within the family about Bose's marriage. While Sarat Bose and his children accepted Emilie and Anita as members of the Bose clan, others refused to do so. And there are followers of Bose who, to this day, do not believe he married, let alone married a European.

As this marriage mystery was unravelling, the deeper riddle of Bose's death was taking hold in the imagination of some Indians.

H.V Kamath provided the starting point for this controversy in December 1945, four months after the air crash. This is how Reuter reported the story:

> **SUBHAS BOSE STILL PLANS FREE INDIA.**
> Burdwan, Bengal Friday – Subhas Chandra Bose, Indian nationalist leader reported by Tokyo last August to have been killed in an air crash, is not only alive but "prosecuting a plan to make India free," Mr H V Kamath, one of his followers, said today.
>
> Mr Kamath, a former member of the Indian civil service who resigned to become a leader of Bose's extreme left "Forward bloc" party, declared two days ago that "from information made available to him" Bose was still alive.
>
> Today, in a public speech, he reiterated his assertion, and observed that "the

> British Empire is now between two ghosts – the ghost of Hitler in Europe and the ghost of Bose in Asia.
>
> Mr Kamath announced that all members of the "forward bloc" – at present an illegal body – have decided to join the Indian National Congress party. Subhas Bose was founder under Japanese auspices of the "provisional government of India" whose Indian National Army" operated with the Japanese during the war." – Reuter

Kamath never explained where he got his information from and how reliable it was. In retrospect it is clear he declared Bose was alive to keep the Forward Bloc going, but this provided the cue for various people to begin to doubt that Bose had died in the plane crash and to report seeing him alive and well in India and overseas in places which included China and the Soviet Union. Sarat initially nursed doubts, but was eventually convinced his brother had died. Gandhi also had doubts but they were resolved when he met Habibur Rehman and Ayer.

However, there have always been people ready to report sightings and raise more doubts. All this excited the interest of the Raj. The director of the Intelligence Bureau in Delhi visited London, met officials of the IPI and, "mentioned the receipt from various places in India of information to the effect that Subhas Bose was alive in Russia. In some cases circumstantial details have been added. Consequentially he is not more than 90 per cent sure that Subhas is dead. He recognises, the possibility, that the Russians are circulating the story for reasons of their own. For we know that they did this in at least one instance in Persia."

Until this stage Lord Mounbatten, Supreme Allied Commander in South East Asia, had not doubted that Bose had died, but now he thought there should be an investigation. On 16 May 1946 SACSEA headquarters in Singapore sent a message to the British mission in Tokyo to ascertain whether Bose really died in the air crash. A thorough investigation was carried out by Lt Colonel John G. Figges. He began with the belief there might be something in the theory that Bose had faked the crash, and interviewed as many people as he could find with who had first hand knowledge of what happened to Bose. Those he interviewed included Lt Colonel Shiro Nonogaki, who was a passenger on the plane and drew a sketch showing the position of the crew and the passengers. He told Figges that three engineers, the wirelesss operator, Major Takizawa and Lt General Shidie died while W.O. Aoyagi the pilot, Major Kono and Bose were seriously burned, and Rehman and Lt Colonel Sakai had less serious injuries. Bose was more seriously injured because he "was sitting next to the petrol tank and owing to the cold had just previously donned a rather tight-fitting type of jacket which could not be easily removed after the crash when Bose was lying on the ground in flames"

Lt Colonel Sakai another passenger confirmed Nonogaki's testimony. He recovered from the crash and travelled with Rehman to Tokyo carrying the box containing Bose's ashes.

Lt Colonel Shibuya Masanori, an officer on the staff of the Taiwan Army headquarters in Taipei did not see Bose at any time, but was called to discuss the possibility of taking Bose's body to Tokyo. This was dismissed as impractical and he was cremated, with Lt Colonel Shibuya issuing orders for the cremation.

Lt Colonel Takamiya Hiroji of Kempei, the Japanese secret police, who was attached to the Taiwan Army Headquarters said he had been ordered to go to the hospital and inquire about Bose's condition. He told Figges he found him conscious but weak, and was told by the doctor "that there was little hope for Bose and that he was sinking fast". He did not see Bose's body after death. Lt Colonel Miura Tatsuo, a staff officer of the 8th Hikoshidan of the Taiwan Army staff, told Figges he did not see Bose either dead or alive but received the first report of the accident from the local airfield company commander. He carried out the investigation into the crash. Figges concluded, "This investigation by the way appears to have been very cursory but the explanation offered being that all the staffs in Taihoku(the Japanese name for Taipei) were in turmoil as a result of the sudden ending of the war".Figges's most detailed examination was of Sub-Lt Tsuruta Toyoshi who was a doctor on duty in the Nammon Ward of the Taipei Military Hospital the afternoon that Bose's plane crashed. He attended to Bose from the time he was admitted until his death about four hours later.

There was some discussion about embalming the body, but Tsuruta said he was not sure he could do it and issued the death certificate saying death was due to "heart failure resulting from multiple burns and shock."

Figges wanted to know how could Tsuruta be sure it was Bose. "Tsuruta stated that there was of course no documentary evidence since all the clothes and personal papers were destroyed before the patient arrived in his ward but it was a matter of common knowledge that Bose was in the aircraft and there could not possibly be any error in identity".

Figges spent much time trying to find Aoyagi the pilot. He had heard conflicting reports of his fate and eventually managed to establish that Aoyagi had survived in the hospital until 29 September when he finally succumbed to his multiple injuries. Aoyagi had been posthumously promoted to 2nd Lieutenant and Figges saw the death certificate signed by Medical Officer Koike Tetsuo of the Japanese Army dated 29 September, 1945. Figges had no doubts Bose was dead and on 25 July 1946 he sent a four page statement entitled "Report on the Death of Subhas Chandra Bose". Figges concluded:

> As a result of series of interrogations of individuals named in the following paragraphs it is confirmed as certain that S. C Bose died in a Taihoku Military Hospital (Nammon Ward) some time between 1900 and 2000 hours local time on 18 August 1945.The cause of death was heart failure resulting from multiple burns and shock. All the persons named below were interrogated at different times but the several accounts of the event agree both in substance and detail at all points where the knowledge of the subjects could have been deemed to be based on common experience. The possibility of a pre-arranged fabrication must be excluded since most of the individuals concerned had no opportunity to contact one another prior to interrogation.

This was conclusive, but a few months later, on 19 October 1946, another British interrogator, Alfred Turner, went to Stanley prison in Hong Kong and took a statement from Taneyoshi Yoshimi. Yoshimi said, "I Taneyoshi Yoshimi Captain Medical of the Imperial Japanese Army, at present at Stanley Gaol, Hong Kong, having observed a statement in a Japanese newspaper, requesting information regarding the death of Chandra Bose, wish of my free will to place any knowledge I have of this matter at the disposal of Authorities requiring it.To the best of my ability and memory I hear (sic) state the events surrounding the death of Chandra Bose."Yoshimi then went on to describe how to tried to save Bose's life in the statement we have already quoted.

For the British this was the end of their investigations and they believed that Bose was dead. Unfortunately these British reports remained secret and classified for many years and in India the myth of Bose being alive became a very active industry.

By this time Nehru, Patel and others were part of the interim government that was preparing India for independence. There were a series of debates in the Council of State in which the subject of Bose's death cropped up. The questions and answers have all been faithfully recorded by the Indian *Hansard* and serve to confirm that the government knew little more than had been reported. Speculation that Bose might still be alive were, however, fuelled by exchanges like this:

Sardar Mangal Singh:
A few days ago the Honourable Leader of the House made a statement that Netaji Subhas Chandra Bose is dead. Is that the view of the Government of India or his personal view?
The Honourable Sardar Vallabhbhai Patel:
The Government of India have no view either way.
Maulana Zafar Ali Khan:
When that view is challenged by a person in the responsible position of Sardar Sardul Singh Caveeshar who said "Pundit Nehru's statement does not satisfy us", we want this House to be informed whether Subhas Chandra Bose is dead or alive actually?
The Honourable Sardar Val1abhbhai Patel:
As I have said, not only myself but,the House will be very glad if it turns out to be true that he is alive. But it is for Sardar Sardul Singh Caveeshar to give any informatjon he may have to the Government of India.
Mr. Ahmed E. H. Jaffer:
(a) Will the Honourable the Home. Member please state whether Government have any definite evidence that Subhas Chandra Bose is alive?
(b) Have Governent's attention been drawn to the announcement by the President of the Forward Bloc that Mr. Bose is about to announce his arrival in Delhi at an early date?
(c) Is it a fact that the present Interim, Government propose to keep a Cabinet seat vacant for Mr. Bose
(d) Have Government received any communication from Mr. Bose during the last few weeks?
(e) Do Government propose to place any information on the subject before this House?
The Honourable SardarVallabhbhal Patel:
(a) No.
(b) Yes
(c) The question of finding a place for Mr Bose will arise only if he makes an appearance
(d) No
(e) Government have no information to place before the House.
Mr Ahmed E.H. Jaffer:
Is it a fact that if he turns up he is going to be appointed Defence Member?
Mr. President:
Order, order. Next question.

And so on.

What is fascinating is that these debates, just as India was gaining independence, set the pattern for persistent questions about the whereabouts of Bose. In one form or another the same questions have been repeated over and over again throughout the last 60 years. There also seems no end to the inquiries. About every 20 years the Indian gvernment has one.

The first was in 1956, known as the Netaji Inquiry committee or also the Shah Nawaz Committee after the chairman Shah Nawaz Khan. Suresh Bose, Subhas's medical brother was a member as was S.N Maitra from the ICS. Its members gathered evidence between April to July 1956, visiting India, Japan, Thailand and Japan, but, for some reason, not Taiwan. They interviewed Rehman, other survivors and Dr Yoshimi. The evidence they gave was that Bose had died in the crash. There were minor differences in the detail of their recollections, but given 11 years had passed that was hardly surprising. However, Suresh Bose refused to accept this and published a 181 page Dissentient report which, in effect, argued that there were two conspiracies. There was a conspiracy on the part of Nehru to make people believe Bose had died in the crash, and there had been a real conspiracy between Bose, Rehman and the Japanese to concoct a crash story in order to allow Bose to escape. Suresh had no doubt that his brother was still alive. He dismissed eye witness accounts of the crash on the basis that if two of them had had minor differences of detail in their recollections, then their entire testimony was suspect.

Twenty years later in 1970 the Bose enquiry game resumed but with a slight difference. The Shaw Nawaz enquiry had not been a judicial commission. It was time to have one. Headed by a retired Chief Justice of the Punjab High Court, G D Khosla, it carefully weighed the evidence showing how the eye witness accounts of the crash were very credible, and that the fantasy theories of Bose's survival were just that – pure fantasy. Its unambiguous conclusion was that Bose had died as a result of the air crash.

Neither inquiry convinced those who wanted to believe Bose was still alive. Periodically through the 1960s and 1970s meetings were called saying Bose was about to reappear. For some time in the 1960s, a sadhu of the Shaulmari Ashram in north Bengal was widely believed to be Bose, despite denials by the sadhu himself and the absence of any similarity of appeareance between the two men.

One person who did much to keep alive the myth that Bose could not have died was an Indian politician and onetime MP, Professor-Samar Guha. He published a book called *Netaji: Dead or Alive?* He also pressed the Indian government to coax the Soviets to unlock their Gulag and release Bose. Guha was certainly inventive, and in the late 1970s published a photograph in a newspaper purporting to be a recent one of Subhas Bose. The picture turned out to be the head of Subhas pasted on the body of his brother Sarat.

As the turbulent 20th century drew to a close another inquiry was announced. On 14 May 1999 a retired justice of the Supreme Court, Manoj Kumar Mukerjee, was asked to inquire:

(a) Whether Netaji Subhas Chandra Bose is dead or alive;
(b) If he is dead, whether he died in the plane crash as alleged
(c) Whether the ashes in the Japanese temple are ashes of Netaji
(d) Whether he has died in any other manner at any other place and if so when and how
(e) If he is alive in respect of his whereabouts.

The notification issued by the Indian Home Ministry establishing the commission had a preamble suggesting there was no need for further inquiries. The government accepted that both the Shaw Nawaz Khan committee and the Khosla commission had " come to the conclusion that Netaji Subhas Chandra Bose met his death in an air crash." Despite this it felt "there is a widespread feeling among the people that the issue of finding the truth about Netaji's death still remains."

Justice Mukerjee was soon provided with a staff, and an office just behind the headquarters of the Calcutta Corporation that Bose so loved. It bears all the hallmarks of Indian government bureaucracy at work, with the commission staff, like the judge, all retired government officers enjoying a comfortable sinecure.

By early 2004 the Mukerjee commission had held 25 sittings, examined 112 witnesses and collected 203 exhibits. Occasionally, as in the examination of Lakshmi Sahgal in June 2001 , the commission has travelled to take evidence, in that instance to Kanpur but generally the sessions are held in Mahajati Sadan, the building Bose conceived.

It was here, in February 2004, that I had the opportunity to witness the commission at work. The hearing that day was meant to examine five witnesses, but not one of them turned up. However in the style familiar to India a crowd gathered outside the building, and remained there long after everyone had gone giving this the air of yet another Indian tamasha. At first they viewed me and my English wife with suspicion. Then they discovered that I was an author inquiring into Bose, and jumped to the conclusion I had some fantastic new information about Bose's whereabouts. They were saddened to discover this was not the case.

Upstairs the hall where witnesses would have been examined remained empty. A cardboard cut out of Bose in INA uniform urging his men forward looked rather forlorn. In an adjoining room Justice Mukerjee was holding court to the media.

Almost four years after the commission had been set up Justice Mukerjee estimated he had completed 85 per cent of its task. Some of his work had involved dealing with a claim that an ascetic in Faisalabad known as Gumnami Baba, who had since died, may have been Bose. A nephew of Bose had moved a writ petition in the High Court urging that various documents and books of this Baba should be preserved and examined to see if he was indeed Bose. One of the Baba's books was a tome called *Himalayan Blunder*, which discusses Indian-Sino relations and the 1962 war with China. Gumnami Baba, it seems, had made handwritten comments along the margins of the book, and some of Bose's followers claimed his handwriting matched that of Bose. Mukerjee had this handwriting examined by three handwriting experts, but he told me their findings were sealed.

DNA samples of the Baba had also been taken and attempts were being made to match them up with surviving members of the Bose family. Unfortunately, according to Justice Mukerjee, the United States preoccupation with Iraq meant American laboratories, seen as best equipped to deal with such DNA analysis, were not readily available..

One of the relations who had provided a blood sample for the DNA match was Subrata Bose, a nephew of Subhas and now a prominent politician in Bengal. He was also one of the five witnesses who failed to materialise that day in Calcutta. This was particularly disappointing. The previous evening I had heard him speak at a meeting of the Asiatic Society, where he had explained how he would be happy to have his blood sample tested for DNA to match that with the Baba, but would not allow it to be matched with any DNA samples from elsewhere. and certainly not with the ashes of Subhas in Japan.

Subrata Bose also hinted at dark goings on in the manner in which the Mukerjee Commission had organised its visit to the Tokyo temple where Bose's ashes are kept. Subrata Bose had travelled with the commission to the temple in Tokyo only to find it was closed. How could the Indian embassy, which had organised the visit, not been aware that the temple was shut on that day, asked Subrata, his tone implying some deep conspiracy?

Subsequently in the presence of Indian diplomats the urn containing the Ashes had been opened and remains of bones near the jaw had been found. The Commission, said Justice Mukerjee, was looking to have this verified for DNA.

One supreme irony of investigations into Bose's death has been that many of those who refuse to believe he died following the air crash end up in England hoping furiously that the archives of the old enemy will provide some clue to help them prove either that Subhas is still alive or at least that he did not die as a result of the aircrash. So it was that in the summer of 2001 Justice Mukerjee visited Britain, and went to the Wheatley home of Hugh Toye to take evidence. He also searched archives in Broadlands, where the Mountbatten papers are kept, archives in Oxford and the British Library in London, where the IPI files are now kept, We have already quoted from these but there is one document, a letter dated 7 August1946 that has not been released. This is how its non-disclosure to the public is recorded in the IPI files:

PUBLIC RECORD OFFICE
Group: P&J India Office
Class: Box60

Piece: 1115/24 (1937/47)

Following document(s) retained in the Department of origin under section 3 (4) of the Public Records Act, 1958

Letter 7/8/46 No4018

So is this letter the key to the so-called Bose mystery? The British authorities refusal to release it is now the focal point for those who believe that Bose is still alive. When Justice Mukerjee visited London he used the good offices of the Indian High Commission to press the authorities to release this document. A meeting was arranged with officials of the record and historical department of the Foreign Office. Justice Mukerjee was told that this document had not been released "for reasons of personal sensitivity." The Foreign Office will not elaborate on this, but I understand that what this means is that this letter, written by an individual, had some remarks about Bose and his personal life, possibly a reference to his child. The letter is not believed to be flattering to Bose. It was shown to a member of the Bose family, and he had agreed that it would not be appropriate for it to be released. The letter does not have any bearing on, or contain any information on Bose's death. But for those in India who relish the conspiracy theory, and cannot believe that Bose died as a result of the plane crash, the fact a letter has been withheld is a further reason to flog this very dead horse.

Justice Mukerjee was assured by the British officials that they have no documents dealing with Bose that are still classified, and that all material relating to him is in the public domain. However the judge is still not satisfied and told me, "But though it may not relate directly to his death there may be circumstantial evidence which may be relevant, and which should be made available."

Much of the commission's work has been taken up with speculation that Bose may have reached Russia after all. Dr Purabi Roy, an academic who knows Russia well, and is the wife of Kalyan Roy, the son of Bose's old colleague, Kiran Shankar Roy, has been the most forceful advocate of this theory. She has given evidence to the commission on three occasions, citing several possible Russian sources which she believes could prove Bose was in the Soviet Union some time in 1946. She also alleges that she was thwarted in her pursuit of this material by both the Russians and the Indians.

On 23 November 2000 Dr Roy was questioned by Justice Mukerjee as to whether she had any information as to whether Bose reached the Soviet Union. Her answer was: "The point is very significant. Not a single person I had interviewed ever said categorically that alleged disappearance of Netaji Subhas Chandra Bose had nothing to do with USSR or that Subhas Chandra Bose was not in the USSR. Not a single person could rule out that question."

When Justice Mukerjee asked her to point out the classified documents which proved that Bose was in the Soviet Union up to October 1946 Dr Roy said:

> It is difficult to say which are the classified documents. If the documents are classified we cannot even have an access to the document or the checklist thereof. Certain classified documents were perused by Mr A Kolesnikov in his official capacity. He only informed that there was a definite document showing that Voroishilov, Vyschinskii, Mikoyan, Molotov discussed about Subhas Chandra Bose – whether he would be allowed to stay in the Soviet Union or whether they will have to deal with him otherwise. On that basis Mr Kolesnikov informed Shri Chitta Bose about stay of Subhas Chandra Bose in the USSR in 1946.

All this greatly excited the commission and those Indians who want to believe Bose did not die in the crash. But while interesting it is no more than hearsay. The affidavit and evidence Dr Roy has presented to the commission is nowhere close to anything that can be considered as proof, and nothing like as rigorous as the investigation Figges made less than a year after the crash.

If we are to believe that the crash story was a hoax and a cover for Bose to disappear then we have to accept an even more implausible theory. This is that in the midst of Japan's greatest crisis following the dropping of atomic bombs on two of its cities, Bose somehow managed to fashion an extraordinary story of deception which involved scores of people spread over several countries, some of whom had never met each other. As we have seen Figges did consider this possibility, but then after meeting the Japanese witnesses ruled it out.

Let us go back briefly to Vietnam and 17 August 1945. We know that Bose was in Saigon on that date, and we have a photograph of him getting off the plane. We also know this was a time of utter chaos, Japan had just surrendered, did not know what to do, Bose had to work very hard to persuade the Japanese to give him a seat on a plane, the bomber codenamed Sally. He eventually managed two seats, one for him, one for Rehman, leaving people like Ayer and Hasan behind

The Sally took off from Saigon with Bose, Rehman and some Japanese including Colonel Shidei on board. It arrives in Tourane in Indo-China, modern da Da Nang, where he spends the night of 17 August. Early the next morning he heads for Taipei. There is plenty of evidence to support all this. The detail of the arrival and departures is beyond dispute.

So if the conspiracy theory is to be believed and if we are to consider that the crash in Taipei was a fake conceived by Bose to cover his disappearance, we have to discover what happened to the plane. Did it just vanish? It was certainly never seen again. This, in many ways, would be an even bigger mystery. Also what happened to Shidei, the senior most Japanese on the plane and the other Japanese including the pilot ? We know what Figges found out. The families of these men have never disputed that they died in or as a result of the crash. Those who say the crash did not happen must explain how Rehman got his burns, and how he sustained other injuries, which he carried for the rest of his life and displayed to Gandhi? If they argue that Rehman, out of loyalty to Bose, faked injuries, then we must assume that Shidei and the other Japanese also disappeared with Bose and ended up in the Gulag, for they have certainly not been seen since 18 August 1945?

Further, if we assume that there was a plane crash in Taipei but that Bose was not on board the aircraft then the question that needs asking is at what point did he disappear?. Was it in Tourane in Vietnam? Or somewhere between Tourane and Taipei? And how would this have helped him get to the Soviet Union? The proof in favour of the crash fatality is voluminous, while there is not a single shred of evidence to indicate how, where and when he got in touch with the Russians, and somehow reached the Gulag.

The pity of it is that it does not help us bring the story of Bose to a proper conclusion and frustrates efforts to make an assessment of his achievements, not even 107 years after his birth, and 60 years after his death. Subhas Bose must be a seen as a man of his times, who was also ahead of his times. There can be no doubting his love for his country and his immense dedication and spirit of sacrifice.

In 1921 he could so easily have chosen a life of comfort. He had qualified for the ICS, his father believed India would have some form of self-government within ten years. What could be more comfortable then serve the foreign masters for a decade then take over? Many Indians of a similar background to Bose made that choice and although they had to wait for 26 years, not 10 as Janakinath thought, for the British to haul down their flag, the Indian Civil Service that the Raj had created to administer their empire became the Indian Administrative Service of free India and the old ICS wallahs switched masters and flourished.

But Bose was a man of self-respect, honour and principle. He could not accept that just because he was born an Indian and not a European, he was a lesser human being. Recall the paternalism and racism that was part of the climate of the time. When Bose took this decision not to join the ICS Lytton was governor of Bengal. As we have seen, Lytton praised the Indian collaborator Mullick as the finest kind of Indian. And why? Because Mullick's highest ideal was for an Indian to try to be as good as an Englishman. Mullick thought if the Indians worked hard enough and accepted everything the Raj said, then they could aspire to equal the race that believed it had a divine right to rule India. Bose rejected this racial belief in the master race, and believed that he was the equal of any man. An accident of birth had created him a brown man and he should not be considered inferior. If Britons could be free and decide their own destiny, then so should Indians. In the 1920s this was quite a revolutionary thought and the British quickly realised how revolutionary Bose was.

The British also saw that here was an opponent, unlike most other Raj opponents, who was clever, capable and if not checked likely to damage to the Raj. That is why their treatment of Bose was always different from most other Indian nationalists including Nehru.

It was also Bose, along with Nehru and a few others, who for the first time began to make Indians believe that they had the right to demand complete freedom from any association with the British Empire. Again for the early 1930s this was a revolutionary demand. At that point in time very few Indian nationalists believed they could aspire to complete freedom from the British. All they wanted was to be treated in the same way as the other white dominions of the British Empire.

Here is it interesting to note how late the call for freedom was made by Indian nationalists. Bose pushed Gandhi into it only in 1929. And even then, as Motilal Nehru told the Raj, if the British were prepared to give the Indians any form of dominion status, they would accept it and try hard do prove that Indians could be the equal of the British and eventually capable of running their own affairs. It is remarkable how moderate these Indians were, how keen to curry favour with the British and how easily the British might have been able to satisfy them.

The years 1930 to 1931 were, in retrospect, the crucial period. Raj historians have argued long and hard as to whether the British withdrew from India too quickly in 1947. This is a nonsensical argument. By then the British were in no position to make choices, for they were pushed by events beyond their control. The war had drained their resources, and earlier Japanese victories had demolished the myth of the racial superiority of the white man.

In India the British missed the bus at the beginning of the 1930s. This was the time when Westminster was formalising the independence already granted to the white dominions of Australia, New Zealand and South Africa. However these dominions were, as Birkenhead said, daughters of Britain, people of British race and blood. Such people could aspire to equality,whereas the Indians could not. Bose understood this well enough,but other Indian leaders still laboured under the impression that there would come a time when the British would finally accept that the brown man could be their equal.

How much race influenced British political thinking can be seen in relation to Ireland. As the white dominions became independent so did Ireland, Britain's oldest colony. Ireland's struggle for independence, starting with the demand for Home Rule was a feature of 19th century British politics. But it was only in the 1920s that British politicians – particularly those on the right, who had always been opposed to Home Rule for Ireland let alone independence – were able to make the leap and realise that the Irish had to be free. The fact that Ireland was a white country clearly played a big part in this, whereas India not being white just could not be conceived as a country capable of ruling itself.

It is interesting to note that Birkenhead's otherwise very perceptive biographer John Campbell is clearly puzzled by this. He describes how Birkenhead, having opposed Irish independence, then supported it leading to the creation of the Irish Free State in 1921. Campbell writes," He was always terribly clear-minded. Had his human sympathy been engaged, as it had been by Collins and Griffith(Irish Republican leaders) in the very similar

Irish situation, he might have been able to close his eyes, as he had in 1921, to constitutional anomalies for the sake of progress. But he was not. He surveyed India entirely with his intellect: his only emotions were exasperation and mounting contempt."

It is interesting to look back at the debates in the British Parliament in the1930s as the Statute of Westminster, which formalised the status of the white dominions, was being debated. Even Stafford Cripps, who later became a champion of India, said that while he hoped at some future date India would be self-governing, he still saw it as part of the Empire. An India free outside the Empire had not entered the minds of even those Englishman who could engage with Indians on a human level, as Cripps undoubtedly did. Nobody thought of full scale independence for India on the American style.

Bose saw India gaining independence from Britain more in the way the Americans and the Irish had done. His vision was a conference between India and Britain to discuss when and how Britain would leave India in the same way that the Treaty of 1921 led to the creation of the Irish Free State. Maybe Bose made too much of the Irish model. After the Treaty of 1921 it required many years of negotiations before modern Ireland emerged. Even after De Valera had got the treaty ports back in 1938, when, as we have seen, he met Bose in London, Ireland still had this curious connection to the Crown. This meant that when it sent ambassadors abroad they were sent in the name of the British monarch. During the war, although Ireland was neutral and had an embassy in Berlin, there was no Irish ambassador, as George VI could hardly have written to Hitler asking him to accept the Irish ambassador on his behalf.

Perhaps had Bose occasionally compromised he might have been more succesful. Certainly he made a mistake in not surrendering to the British in Singapore. His last adventure seeking the Russians was ill-advised and ended disastrously. But even if his end was an unhappy one he had achieved much. His patriotism, his spirit, his belief that India had the right to be a free, proud country and his many practical ideas to take the country forward all ought to be cherished. Bose made mistakes, but for all his mistakes he was one of the most remarkable men to emerge from India in the 20th century and ought to be honoured for that.

Indians do honour him now, of course, not only unofficially but also officially with his centenary celebrations marking the formal rehabilitation by the Indian government. In January 2004, on the occasion of his 107th birthday, India's Ministry of Information and Broadcasting published an advertisement in India's major newspapers showing Bose in INA uniform, quoting his words on freedom and declaring that this cry of "Delhi Chalo", "still calls, still rings in our ears, still inspires us, still guides us, still reminds us of the colossal sacrifice for freedom."

But as Amitav Ghosh, the Indian novelist whose father fought with the British Indian Army against Bose's INA, and whose novel *The Glass Palace* is a beautiful study of the conflict of loyalties British rule produced, has written, "the official celebrations served only to reinforce the ambivalence of his memory.". It is an ambivalence that Ashish Nandy, a psychoanalyst and a leading Indian thinker has given expression to. He says, "Bose is one of the most tragic figures in Indian history. He was a nationalist, but his categories were mostly western. Bose was a very torn person. He represents everything that we are afraid of in ourselves".

Indians need to come to terms with this. One simple way of resolving that contradiction in a practical manner would be for Indians to move on from endlessly and fruitlessly debating whether he died in Taipei or not on 18 August, 1945, and bring back his ashes from the temple in Tokyo. This could be the cue for making use of his legacy to develop the modern free India Bose lived and died for.

Bibliography
And Other Sources

This book is based on research in the archives kept at various libraries and government record offices around the world, supplemented by personal interviews with various individuals, including Subhas Bose's only surviving daughter Anita Pfaff (née Bose). In recent years the files of the Raj's MI5 have been opened, releasing fascinating new information on Bose. In addition, I have consulted the various government records that have been published in book form and also other books and articles relevant to my work.

Archival Material

India Office Library and Records, British Library, London
Private Papers: Lord Brabourne, MSS.EUR.F.97; Sir Harry Haig, MSS.EUR.F.115; Sir Maurice Hallett, MSS.EUR.E.251; Lord Linlithgow, MSS.EUR.F.125; Lord Zetland, MSS.EUR.D.609.

Other records
Files of the Bengal Governor's Secretariat: R/3/2; Records of the Public and Judicial Department: file L/P&J/7/792 brings together valuable material relating to Bose's tussles with the Raj between 1927 and 1934.

Indian Political Intelligence
In consequence of the development of Indian anarchist activities in England in 1909, the India Office suggested (after consultation with Scotland Yard and the Government of India) that an officer of the Indian Police should be placed on deputation in England. The organisation he headed was first called the India Political Intelligence Office but the name finally decided for this organisation in 1921 was Indian Political Intelligence or IPI. This was the Raj's MI5.
The IPI's documents were opened to the public in the late 1990s. They cover the period 1913 to 1947. There are five files on Bose: L/P&J/12/214-218. Also files on two of his close wartime assistants: A.C.N. Nambiar: L/P&J/12/73, and Girija Mookerjee: L/P&J/12/446.
Public Record Office, Kew, London
WO (War Office) 208.

Foreign and Commonwealth Office Library, London
Microfilm copies of captured records of Auswartiges Amt, particularly: serial 41: German Embassy, Rome, 'Bose, India's Independence 1941'; serial 195: State Secretary, 'India 1941-3'; serial 1292: Office of State Secretary Keppler, 'India (Organisation in France 1942-4)'; serial 1313: Office of State Secretary Keppler, 'India - Propaganda in Germany 1941-3'; serial 1313: Office of State Secretary Keppler, 'India - Political reports 1942-3'; serials Fl-20: Reich Foreign Minister's Secretariat, 'Record of conversations between Joachim von Ribbentrop and Bose 1941-2'.

Government of Japan
Records in the keeping of the Chief of the Reference Room, Diplomatic Record Office.
Diaries of Japanese Military Officers in Second World War, Japanese Foreign Ministry.

Russian Archives
Report of the Soviet Agent to the Governing Body of British Intelligence (copy kindly supplied by Milan Hauner).

Indian Archives
Nehru Memorial Museum and Library, Delhi:
Private Papers: Dharmavir, S.S. Caveeshar; J.N. Nehru; Rajendra Prasad; Vithalbhai Patel; B.P. Singh Roy; B.C. Roy; M.N. Roy; Nalini Ranjan Sarkar; Promode Sengupta.
The Files of the All-India Congress Committee 1927-47: The Congress was often banned by the Raj, its files and records seized by the police; what remains is necessarily incomplete, yet useful and, at times, a quite fascinating insight into the organisation of this remarkable political party.

National Archives of India, Delhi
Private Papers: Bholanath Roy Collection; Kommerzialrat Otto Faltis Collection (including photographs); Mrs Woods Collection (including photographs).

Other records
Certain documents relating to the Indian Independence League.

Official records
The records of the government of India - particularly the files of the Home Department in the political series 1921-45.

West Bengal State Archives, Calcutta
The records, alas, are not well maintained here - and such is the paranoia about secrecy that any notes made from the files have to be submitted to the authorities for approval before they can be taken away. The most useful information is contained in the Home Department's Political Series (1921-45); some in the Revenue Series.

West Bengal Legislative Secretariat, Calcutta
Proceedings of the Bengal Legislative Council (1921-39).

Calcutta Corporation Library
Copies of the *Calcutta Municipal Gazette.*

Protestant European School, Cuttack (now called Stewart's School)
The school records contain a certain amount of information regarding Subhas Bose's early scholastic career.

Published Records

Over the years, governments have also published previously secret documents in book form. The ones I found most useful were:

The Transfer of Power 1942-7, ed. P.N.S. Mansergh, 12 vols, HMSO, 1970-1983.
Speeches and Documents on the Indian Constitution 1921-7, ed. M. Gwyer and A. Appadorai, 2 vols, London, 1957.
Documents on German Foreign Policy 1918-45, Series D, vols 12-13 (1 February 1941 to 11 December 1941) (English Series).
Akten zur Deutschen Auswartiges Politik 1918-45, Series E, vols 1-4 (German Language Series).

Confidential government publications
Periodically the intelligence reports that the Raj's officials had gathered were published in book form - rarely more than a hundred copies and with the circulation limited to the top officials. After Indian independence, these books have been re-issued for a wider audience by Indian publishers. The relevant ones are:
Ker, James Campbell: *Political Trouble in India 1907-17* (compiled 1917).
Petrie, David: *Communism in India 1924-27* (compiled 1933).
Kaye, Sir Cecil: *Communism in India 1919-24* (compiled 1926); *Terrorism in India 1917-36* (compiled 1937).
Hale, H.W.: *Political Trouble in India 1917-37.*

Interviews
Dr G. Adhikari; Satya Ranjan Bakshi; Bina Bhowmick (née Das); Anita Pfaff (née Bose); Dwijendranath Bose; Sailesh Bose; Narain Chakraborthy; Pratap Chunder Chunder; Madhan Mohan Das; Gour Dutta; Santimoy Ganguli; Arun Chandra Guha; Abid Hasan; V.B. Karnik; J.B. Kripalani; Somnath Lahiri; Uttam Chand Malhotra; Niharendru Dutt-Mazumdar; B.T. Ranadive; N.G. Ranga; Dr Radhanath Rath; Kalyan Roy (son of Kiran Shankar Roy); Bhagat Ram Talwar (correspondence only); Hugh Toye.

Oral transcription list at NML
Mrs S.C. Bose; Satish Das Gupta; Nellie Sengupta; Dr Sampurnananda.

Radio Broadcasts
Excerpts from short-wave radio, Tokyo, and other affiliated stations, December 1941 to 1 September 1944, compiled by Research and Analysis Branch, Office of Strategic Services, Honolulu (copy supplied to me by K.K. Ghosh).

Newspapers
Advance, Calcutta; *Amrita Bazar Patrika,* Calcutta; *Azad Hind* (published from Berlin in 1942–4); *Bharat* and *Krishak,* Bengali weeklies of Calcutta; *Bombay Chronicle,* Bombay; *Calcutta Municipal Gazette,* Calcutta; *Englishman,* Calcutta; *Forward,* Calcutta; *Hindusthan Standard,* Calcutta; *Hindusthan Times,* Delhi; *Illustrated Weekly of India,* Bombay and Delhi; *Independent India,* Delhi; *Indian Express,* Bombay; *Liberty,* Calcutta; *Modern Review,* Calcutta; *The Nation,* Calcutta; *The Oracle,* Calcutta; *Presidency College Magazine,* Calcutta; *Scottish Churches College Magazine,* Calcutta; *Statesman,* Calcutta; *The Times,* London; *Syonan Times* (as the *Singapore Times* was renamed during the Japanese occupation, 1942–5); *Times of India,* Bombay.

The Subhas Bose Collection

What follows are books containing letters, speeches, articles and autobiographical writings by Subhas Bose during his lifetime. In the last 20 years, the Calcutta-based Netaji Research Bureau has published his *Collected Works* in 12 volumes.

Bose, Subhas Chandra, *Through Congress Eyes,* Allahabad, 1938.
La Lotta dell'India 1920-1934, Firenze, 1942.
Famous Speeches and Letters of Subhas Chandra Bose, Lahore, 1946.
Impressions in Life, Lahore, 1947.
Important Speeches and Letters of Subhas Chandra Bose, Lahore, 1947.
Netaji Speaks to the Nation 1928-1945, Lahore, 1946.
An Indian Pilgrim: 1897-1920, Calcutta, 1948.
The Indian Struggle 1920-34, Calcutta, 1948.
The Mission of Life, Calcutta, 1953.
An Indian Pilgrim: An Unfinished Autobiography and Collected Letters 1897-1921, Calcutta, 1962.
Selected Speeches of S.C. Bose (reprint), Delhi, 1962.
The Indian Struggle 1920-42, Calcutta, 1964.
Correspondence 1924-32, Calcutta, 1967.
Fundamental Questions of Indian Revolution, Calcutta, 1970.
Crossroads, 2nd edn, Calcutta, 1981.
Netaji Collected Works (edited initially by Sisir Bose and then jointly with his son Sugata Bose):
Volume 1: *An Indian Pilgrim and Letters 1897-1921,* Calcutta, 1980.
Volume 2: *The Indian Struggle 1920-42,* Calcutta, 1981.
Volume 3: *Correspondence 1922-26,* Calcutta, 1981.
Volume 4: *Correspondence 1926-32,* Calcutta, 1982.
Volume 5: *Statements, Speeches, Prison Notes and Boycott of British Goods 1923-29,* Calcutta, 1985.
Volume 6: *Correspondence, Statements, and Speeches 1929-32,* Calcutta, 1987.
Volume 7: *Letters to Emilie Schenkl 1934-1942,* Calcutta, 1994.

Volume 8: *India's Ambassador Abroad: Letters, Articles, Speeches and Statements 1933-37,* Calcutta, 1994.
Volume 9: *Congress President: Speeches, Articles and Letters, January 1938-May 1939,* Calcutta, 1995.
Volume 10: *The Alternative Leadership 1939-41,* Calcutta, 1998.
Volume 11: *Azad Hind: Speeches and Articles, 1941-43,* Calcutta, 2002.
Volume 12: *Chalo Delhi: Speeches and Articles, 1943-45,* Calcutta, 2004.

In addition to this, the Bureau publishes every year *The Oracle*, a journal recording speeches made during the annual birthday celebrations of Subhas Bose on 23 January.

Other Books and Articles

A list of all the books relevant to this topic would require a bibliography almost as big as this book. What follows is fairly selective.

Adhikari, G. (ed.) *Documents of the History of the Communist Party of India. Vol. I: 1917-1922; Vol. II: 1923-1925; Vol. III: A 1926, B 1927, C 1928.* Delhi, 1971-82.
Ahmad, Muzaffar, *The Communist Party of India and Its Formation Abroad,* Calcutta, 1962.
Ahmed, Rafiuddin, *The Bengal Muslims 1871-1906,* Delhi, 1981.
Ahmed, Sufia, *Muslim Community in Bengal 1884-1912,* Dacca, 1974.
Akbar, M.J., *Nehru -The Making of India,* London, 1988.
Ali, Tariq, *The Nehrus and the Gandhis: An Indian Dynasty,* London, 1985.
Allen, Charles, *The Buddha and the Sahibs*, London, 2002.
Allen, Louis, *Sittang: The Last Battle,* London, 1973.
The End of the War in Asia, London, 1976.
Argov, Daniel, *Moderates and Extremists in the Indian Nationalist Movement 1883-1920,* Bombay, 1967.
Arun (ed.) *Testament of Subhas Chandra Bose,* Delhi, 1946.
Ayer, S. A., *The Indian Independence Movement in East Asia* (Netaji Oration 1961), Calcutta, 1961.
The Story of the I.N.A., Delhi, 1972.
Unto Him a Witness; The Story of Netaji Subhas Chandra Bose in East Asia, Bombay, 1951.
Azad, Maulana, *India Wins Freedom,* Delhi, 1976 (reprint).
Aziz, K.K. (ed.) *Muslim under Congress Rule 1937 – 1939: A Documentary Record,* 2 vols, Islamabad, 1978.
Ba, Maw, *Breakthrough in Burma: Memoirs of a Revolution, 1939-46,* London, 1968.
Banerjea, Surendranath, *A Nation in Making,* Bombay, 1963.
Banerji, Nripendra Chandra, *At the Crossroads,* 2nd edn, Calcutta, 1974.
Barker, A.J., *The March on Delhi,* London, 1963.
Barnett, Correlli, *The Collapse of British Power,* Gloucester, 1984.
Basu, Apama, *The Growth of Education and Political Development in India 1898-1920,* Delhi, 1974.
Batlivala, S.S. and Jhaveri V.K. (eds) *JAI HIND: The Diary of a Rebel Daughter of India with the Rani of jhansi Regiment,* Bombay, 1945.
Bazaz, Prem Nath, *The Role of the Bhagavad Gita in Indian History,* Delhi, 1975.
Beamish, John, *Burma Drop,* London, 1958.
Bergamini, David, *Japan's Imperial Conspiracy,* New York, 1971.
Beschloss, Michael, *The Conquerors,* London, 2002.
Bhagat, K.P., *A Decade of Indo-British Relations in 1937-47,* Bombay, 1959.
Bhagavan, Manu, *Sovereign Spheres,* Delhi, 2003.
Bharati, A., *The Ochre Robe,* London, 1961.
Bhargava, Moti Lal and Americk Singh Gill, *Indian National Army – Secret Service,* Delhi, 1988.
Bhattacharya, J.N., *Hindu Castes and Sects,* Calcutta, 1973.
Bhattacharyya, Buddhadeva, *et al.*, *Satyagrahas in Bengal 1921-39,*Calcutta, 1977.

Bhattacharyya, Buddhadeva (ed.) *Freedom Struggle and Anushilan Samiti*, Calcutta, 1979.
Bhuyan, Arun, *The Quit India Movement*, Delhi, 1975.
Birla, G.D., *In the Shadow of the Mahatma: A Personal Memoir,* Bombay, 1953.
Bloch, Michael, *Ribbentrop,* London, 1993.
Bondurant, Joan V., *The Conquest of Violence*, Princeton, 1958.
Borra, Ranjan, 'Subhas Chandra Bose - After Three Decades', *Asian Affairs,* May/June 1975.
Bose, Arun Coomer, *Indian Revolutionaries Abroad, 1905-1922*, Patna,1971.
Bose, Ashok. K., *Subhas Chandra Bose and Calcutta Corporation,* Calcutta,1997.
Bose, Asoke, *My Uncle Netaji,* Calcutta, 1977.
Bose, Buddhadeva, *An Acre of Green Grass*, Calcutta, 1948.
Bose, Krishna, 'Important Women in Netaji's Life', *Illustrated Weekly of India,* 13.8.72 and 30.8.72.
Netaji: A Biography for the Young, Delhi, 1995.
Bose, Nirmal Kumar, *Studies in Gandhism,* 4th edn, Ahmedabad, 1972.
Modern Bengal, Calcutta, 1959.
My Days With Gandhi, Calcutta, 1953.
Problems of Indian Nationalism, Calcutta, 1969.
Bose, Pradip, *Growing up in India*, Calcutta, 1953.
Bose, Sarat Chandra, *I Warned My Countrymen,* Calcutta, 1968.
Bose, Sisir K. (ed.) *The Great Escape,* Calcutta, 1975.
A Beacon Across Asia, Delhi, 1973.
Netaji and India's Freedom, Calcutta,1975.
A Pictorial Biography (edited with Birendra nath Sinha Netaji), Calcutta, 1979.
The Voice of Sarat Chandra Bose, Calcutta, 1979.
Remembering My Father: A Centenary Tribute, Calcutta, 1989.
'Ten Historic Netaji Documents', *The Oracle,* Netaji Centenary Number, January 1997.
Bose, Sugata, *Agrarian Bengal,* Cambridge, 1986.
Bose, Suresh Chandra, *Dissentient Report,* Calcutta, 1958.
Brackman, Arnold, *The Other Nuremberg,* London, 1989.
Braund, Harold, *Distinctly, I Remember: A Personal Story of Burma,* Victoria, 1972.
Brecher, Michael, *Nehru: A Political Biography,* London, 1959.
Briffault, Robert, *Breakdown: The Collapse of Traditional Civilization,* 2nd edn, New York, 1935.
Bright, J.S. (ed.) *Important Speeches and Writings of S.C. Bose,* Lahore, 1946.
Subhas Bose and His Ideas, Lahore, 1946.
Broomfield, J.H., *Elite Conflict in a Plural Society: Twentieth-Century Bengal,* Berkeley, 1968.
Brown, E.A., *Eminent Indians,* Calcutta, 1946.
Brown, Judith, *Gandhi's Rise to Power: Indian Politics 1915-22,* London, 1972.
Gandhi and Civil Disobedience, London, 1977.
Nehru: A Political Life, London, 2003.
Bullock, Alan, *Hitler and Stalin Parallel Lives*, London, 1993.
Bush, Barald, *U-Boats at War (Wo War der U-Boat Krieg?),* New York, 1955.
Cady, John F., *A History of Modern Burma*, Ithaca, 1958.
Calvocoressi, Peter and Wint, Guy, *Total War*, London, 1979.
Campbell, John F.E., *Smith First Earl of Birkenhead,* London, 1983.
Campbell-Johnson, A., *Mission with Mountbatten,* Bombay, 1951.
Casey, Lord, *Personal Experience 1939-1946,* London, 1962.
Cashman, Richard I., *The Myth of the Lokamanya: Tilak and Mass Politics in Maharashtra,* Berkeley, 1975.
Chadha, Yogesh, *Rediscovering Gandhi,* London, 1997.
Chagla, M.C., *Roses in December*, Bombay, 1973.
Chakrabarty, Saroj, *My Years with Dr B.C. Roy*, Calcutta, 1982.
Chakravarty, D.R. and Chaudhuri, B.P., *Leftist Leaders of India,* Calcutta, 1947.
Chand, Uttam, *When Bose Was Ziauddin,* Delhi, 1946.
Chandra, Bipan, 'Elements of Continuity and Change in Early Nationalist Activity', *Indian History Congress Proceedings,* 1972.

Nationalism and Colonialism in Modern India, Delhi, 1979.
The Rise and Growth of Economic Nationalism in India, Delhi, 1966.
Chatterjee, Dilip Kumar, *C.R. Das and Indian National Movement*, Calcutta, 1965.
Chatterjee, Manini, *The Chittagong Uprising 1930-34,* Delhi, 1999.
Chatterjee, Partha, *A Princely Imposter,* Delhi, 2002.
Chatterji, A.C., *India's Struggle for Freedom,* Calcutta, 1947.
Chatterji, Bhola, *Aspects of Bengal Politics in the Early 1930s,* Calcutta, 1969.
Chatterji, D.K., *C.R. Das and the Indian National Movement,* Calcutta, 1965.
Chatterji, Jogesh Chandra, *Indian Revolutionaries in Conference,* Calcutta, n.d.
In Search of Freedom, Calcutta, 1967.
Chatterji, Rakhahri (ed.) *Politics in West Bengal*, Calcutta, 1985.
Chattopadhyay, G., *Communism and Bengal's Freedom Movement,* Vol. I: Delhi, 1970.
'The Almost Revolution, A Case Study of India in February 1946', in *Essays in Honour of Prof. S.C. Sarkar*, Delhi, 1976.
Bengal Electoral Politics and Freedom Struggle 1862-1947, Delhi, 1984.
Chattopadhyay, K.P., 'Subhas at Cambridge', *The Loka-Sevak*, Netaji, January 23, 1954.
Chaudhuri, Kali Prasanna, *Netaji and India,* Shillong, 1956.
Chaudhuri, Nirad, 'Subhas Chandra Bose: His Legacy and Legend', *Pacific Affairs*, XXVI, 4, December 1953.
The Autobiography of an Unknown Indian (reprint), Bombay, 1976.
Continent of Circe, Bombay, 1966.
'Subhas Chandra Bose', *The Illustrated Weekly of India*, LXXVI, 38, 18.9.55.
Thy Hand, Great Anarch! London, 1987.
Chopra, P.N. (ed.) *Quit India Movement: British Secret Report*, Faridabad, 1976.
Choudhary, Sukbhir, *Peasants' and Workers' Movement in India 1905-1929*, Delhi, 1971.
Chowdhuri, S.R., *The Leftist Movement in India 1917-47,* Calcutta, 1977.
Churchill, Winston, S., *The Second World War,* 6 vols, London, 1948-53.
Ciano, G., *The Complete Unabridged Diaries of Count Galeazzo Ciano*, 1937-43, edited by Robert Miller and Stanislao G. Pugilese, London, 2002.
Clarke, Peter, *The Cripps Version,* London, 2002.
Cohen, Stephen P., *The Indian Army: Its Contribution to the Development of a Nation,* Berkeley, 1971.
Cole, J.A., *Lord Haw-Haw-and William Joyce,* London, 1964.
Collins, L. and Lapierre, D., *Freedom at Midnight,* Delhi, 1976.
Mountbatten and the Partition of India, March 22-August 15 1947, London, 1982.
Connell, J., *Auchinleck,* London, 1959.
Cooke, Colin, *The Life of Richard Stafford Cripps,* London, 1957.
Corr, G.H., *The War of the Springing Tigers,* London, 1975.
Coupland, Reginald, *The Constitutional Problem in India* (3 parts), London, 1942-3,1945.
Cronin, Richard P., *British Policy and Administration in Bengal*, Calcutta, 1977.
Das, Chittaranjan, *The Way to Swaraj,* Madras, 1923.
India for Indians, Madras, 1921.
Songs of the Sea, Collected in Aurobindo Ghosh's Poems and Plays, Vol. II, Pondicherry, 1942.
Das, Durga, *India from Curzon to Nehru and After,* New York, 1970.
Das, Durga (ed.) *Sardar Patel's Correspondence 1945-50,* 5 vols, Ahmedabad, 1972.
Das, Sitanshu, *Subhas: A Political Biography,* Delhi, 2001.
Das, S.A. and Subbaiah, K.B., *Chalo Delhi: An Historical Account of the Indian Independence Movement in East Asia,* Kuala Lumpur, 1946.
Dasgupta, Hemendra Nath, *Subhas Chandra,* Calcutta, 1946.
Deshbandhu, Chitta Ranjan Das, Delhi, 1960.
Dasgupta, Sivaprasad, *Atlas of Fight for Freedom by Subhas Chandra Bose,* Calcutta, 1947.
Datta Gupta, Sobhanlal, *Comintern, India and the Colonial Question*, 1920-37, Calcutta, 1980.
Datta, Sudhindranth, *The World of Twilight,* Calcutta, 1970.
Davis, Marvin, *Rank and Rivalry: The Politics of Inequality in Rural West Bengal*, New York, 1983.
Davis, Mike, *Late Victorian Holocausts*, London, 2001.

De, Amalendu, *Roots of Separatism in Nineteenth Century Bengal*, Calcutta, 1974.
De, Biswanath (ed.) *Subhas Smriti (Remembering Subhas)*, Calcutta, 1975.
Desai, A.R., *Social Background of Indian Nationalism,* Bombay, 1966.
Peasant Struggles in India (ed.), Bombay, 1979.
Desai, Bhulabhai, J., *I.N.A. Defence - Subject People's Right to Fight for Freedom,* Bombay, 1960.
Desai, V.H. (ed.) *Saga of Azad Hind,* Hyderabad, n.d.
Deva, A.N., *Socialism and The National Revolution,* Calcutta, 1946.
Dewey, Clive, *Anglo-Indian Attitudes, The Mind of the Indian Civil Service,* London, 1993.
Dhar, N., *Vedanta and Bengal Renaissance,* Calcutta, 1977.
Dikshit, Sheila, Natwar-Singh, K., Parthasarathi, G., Sharada-Prasad, H.Y., Gopal, S., Kumar, Ravinder (eds) *Jwawharlal Nehru, Centenary Volume*, Delhi, 1989.
Draper, Alfred, *Amritsar, The Massacre that Ended the Raj*, London, 1981.
Dawns Like Thunder, The Retreat from Burma 1942, London, 1987.
Durlab, Singh (ed.) *Netaji Speaks to the Nation,* Lahore, 1946.
Durrani, Mahmood Khan, *The Sixth Column,* London, 1955.
Dutt, B.C., *Mutiny of the Innocents,* Bombay, 1971.
Dutt, Rajani Palme, *India Today* (reprint), Bombay, 1970.
World Politics 1918-1936, New York, 1936.
Dutt, Romesh Chunder, *Three Years in Europe 1868 to 1971, With an Account of Subsequent Visits to Europe in 1886 and 1893,* Calcutta, 1896.
Dutt, Roy B.N. (ed.) *Sir N.N. Sircar's Speeches and Pamphlets,* Calcutta, 1934.
Dwivedy, Surendranath, *The Quest for Socialism*, Delhi, 1984.
Edwardes, Michael, *The Last Years of British Rule,* London, 1963.
Elenjimittam, A., *The Hero of Hindustan,* Calcutta, 1947.
Elphick, Peter, *Singapore, the Pregnable Fortress*, London, 1995.
Elsbree, Willard H., *Japan's Role in Southeast Asian Nationalist Movements 1940 to 1945*, New York, 1953.
Erikson, Erik H., *Gandhi's Truth*, New York,1969.
Evans, Sir Geoffrey and Brett-James, Anthony, *Imphal: A Flower on Lofty Heights,* London, 1962.
Fay, Peter Ward, *The Forgotten Army*, Ann Arbor, 1991
Fest, Joachim C., *Hitler*, New York, 1975.
The Face of the Third Reich, New York,1970.
Frank, Katherine, *Indira Nehru Gandhi,* London, 2001.
French, Patrick, *Liberty or Death,* London, 1997.
Fischer, L., *A Week with Gandhi,* London, 1943.
Fuchs, Stephen, *Rebellious Prophets*, Bombay, 1965.
Fujiwara, Iwaichi, F., *Kikan*, Hong Kong, 1983.
Gallagher, J. *et al.*, *Locality, Province and Nation,* Cambridge, 1973.
Gandhi, Mohandas K., *The Collected Works of Mahatma Gandhi,* 88 vols, Delhi, 1958-1983.
Gandhi, Sonia, *Two Alone Two Together, Letters between Indira Gandhi and Jawaharlal Nehru, 1940-1964*, Vol. II, London, 1992.
Ganpuley, N.G., *Netaji in Germany: A Little-Known Chapter,* Bombay,1959.
Gaube, K.L., *Famous and Historic Trials,* Lahore, 1946.
Ghose, Aurobindo, *The Doctrine of Passive Resistance,* 2nd edn, Pondicherry, 1952.
Ghose, Kali Charan, *The Footprints on the Road to Indian Independence,* Calcutta, 1975.
Ghosh, Ajoy, *Articles and Speeches*, Moscow, 1962.
Ghosh, Amitav, 'India's Untold War of Independence' in *The New Yorker's* Special Fiction Issue June 23 & 30,1997.
The Glass Palace, London, 2000.
Ghosh, J.N., *Netaji Subhas Chandra,* Calcutta, 1946.
Ghosh, K.C., *The Roll of Honour: Anecdotes of Indian Martyrs,* Calcutta, 1965.
Ghosh, K.K., *The Indian National Army: Second Front of Indian Independence Movement,* Meerut, 1969.
Ghosh, Moni, *Our Struggle*, Calcutta, 1957.
Ghosh, Sudhir, *Gandhi's Emissary*, London, 1967.

Giani, K.S., *Indian Independence Movement in East Asia,* Lahore, 1947.
Gilmour, David, *The Long Recessional, the Imperial Life of Rudyard Kipling,* London, 2002.
Glendevon, Lord, *The Viceroy at Bay,* London, 1971.
Goebbels, J., *Diaries,* edited by L.P. Lochner, London, 1948.
Goel, Sita Ram, *Netaji and the C.P.I.,* Calcutta, 1955.
Gopal, Ram, *Indian Muslims, A Political History (1858-1947),* Bombay, 1959.
Gopal, S., *Jawaharlal Nehru: A Biography,* Vol.1, Bombay, 1976.
Gordon, L.A., *Bengal: The Nationalist Movement 1876-1940,* Delhi, 1974.
Brothers Against the Raj, Delhi, 1990.
Goswami, T.C., *Footprints of Liberty,* Delhi, 1971.
Government of India, *Netaji Inquiry Committee Report,* India, 1956.
Government of India, *Report of the One-Man Commission of Inquiry into the Disappearance of Netaji Subhas Chandra Bose,* Delhi, 1974.
Government of India, *Sedition Committee Report,* Calcutta, 1918.
Greenough, Paul R., *Prosperity and Misery in Modern Bengal: The Famine of 1943-44*, New York, 1982.
Grigg, John, *The Young Lloyd George*, London, 1990.
Guha, Arun, *First Spark of Revolution,* Delhi, 1971.
Guha, Ranajit (ed.) *Subaltern Studies III.* Ed., Delhi, 1984.
Guha, Samar, *Netaji - Dead or Alive?* Delhi, 1978.
Gupta, Amit Kumar (ed.) *Myth and Reality: The Struggle for Freedom in India, 1945-47*, Delhi, 1976.
Gupta, Atulchandra (ed.) *Studies in the Bengal Renaissance*, Calcutta, 1958.
Gupta, Partha Sarathi, *Imperialism and the British Labour Movement,* London, 1975.
Power, Politics and the People, Delhi, 2001.
Haithcox, John Patrick, *Communism and Nationalism in India: M.N. Roy and Comintern Policy 1920-39,* Princeton, 1971.
Hale, H.W., *Political Trouble in India 1917-37*, Allahabad, 1971.
Harbich, Walter and Werth, Alexander, *Netaji in Germany*, Calcutta, 1970.
Hardas, Balashastri, *Armed Struggle for Freedom,* Poona, 1958.
Hardy, P., *The Muslims of British India*, Cambridge, 1972.
Hart, B.H. Liddell, *History of the Second World War,* 2 vols, London, 1972.
Hart-Davis, Duff, *Peter Fleming: A Biography,* London, 1974.
Hartog, Rudolf, *The Sign of the Tiger,* Delhi, 2001.
Hasan, Mushirul, 'Communalism in Indian Politics: A Study of the Nehru Report', *The Indian Historical Review,* IV, No. 2, January 1978.
Hashim, Abul, *In Retrospection,* Dacca, 1974.
Hassell, U. von, *Diaries 1938-1944,* London, 1948.
Hauner, Milan, *India in Axis Strategy*, Stuttgart, 1981.
Hay, Stephen N., *Asian Ideas of East and West*, Cambridge, 1970.
Hayashida, T., *Netaji Subhas Chandra Bose: His Great Struggle and Martyrdom,* Bombay, 1970.
History of the Showa Emperor (in Japanese), Vols 8-10, Tokyo, 1969 and 1970.
Hitler, Adolph, *Mein Kampf*, London, 1970.
Table Talk 1941-44, edited by Hugh Trevor-Roper, London, 1953.
Hodson, H.V., *The Great Divide: Britain-India-Pakistan*, London, 1969.
Hoffman, Peter, *The History of the German Resistance 1933-1945*, Cambridge, 1977.
German Resistance to Hitler, Cambridge, 1988.
Stauffenberg, Cambridge, 1995.
Howard, Michael, *British Intelligence in the Second World War,* Vol.V, London, 1990.
Hutchins, Francis G., *Spontaneous Revolution*, Delhi, 1971.
Huq, Fazlul, *Bengal Today*, Calcutta, 1944.
Ienaga, Saburo, *The Pacific War*, New York, 1978.
Imam Zafar (ed.) *Muslim in India,* Delhi, 1972.
Irving, David, *Hitler's War,* London, 1979.
Isherwood, Christopher, *Ramakrishna and his Disciples*, New York, 1965.
Islam, Kazi Nasrul, *The Rebel and Other Poems,* trans. Delhi, 1974.

Islam, Mustafa Nurul, *Bengali Muslim Public Opinion as Reflecting the Bengali Press 1901-1930*, Dacca, 1973.

Ispahani, M.A.H., *Qaid-e-Azam Jinnah as I Knew Him*, Karachi, 1967.

Jalal, Ayesha, *The Sole Spokesman: Jinnah, the Muslim League and the Demand for Pakistan*, Cambridge, 1985.

James, Lawrence, *Raj, The Making and Unmaking of British India*, London, 1997.

Jayakar, M.R., *The Story of My Life,* Vol. 1, New York, 1958.

Jhaveri, K.V. (ed.) *Freedom's Battle*, Bombay, 1947.

Jog, N.G., *In Freedom's Quest: Life of Netaji Subhas Chandra Bose,* Delhi, 1969.

Jones, F.C. and Barton,P., *The Far East 1942-6,* London, 1955.

Jungle, Traudl, *Until the Final Hour,* London, 2003.

Kabir, Humayun, *Muslim Politics 1906-47*, Calcutta,1969.

Kamath, H.V., *Netaji 1937-40: Prelude to the Final Struggle* (Netaji Oration 1963), Calcutta, 1964.

Karnik,V.B., *Indian Trade Unions*, 2nd edn, Bombay, 1966.

Kaul, Gautam, *Cinema and the Indian Freedom Struggle,* Delhi,1998.

Kaushik, P.D., *The Congress Ideology and Programme 1920-47,* Bombay, 1964.

Kaye, Sir Cecil, *Communism in India 1919-24*, Calcutta, 1971.

Keay, John, *The Honourable East India Company,* London, 1991.

A History of India, London, 2000.

Keer, Dhanajay, *Savarkar and his Times*, Bombay, 1950.

Kennedy, Paul, *The Rise and Fall of the Great Powers*, London, 1988.

Kenny, Mary, *Germany Calling,* London, 2003.

Ker, James Campbell, *Political Trouble in India 1907-17,* Delhi, 1973.

Keyes, Charles P., *The Golden Peninsula*, New York, 1977.

Khan, Shah Nawaz, *My Memories of the I.N.A. and its Netaji,* Delhi, 1946.

The I.N.A. Heroes, Lahore, 1947.

Netaji Inquiry Committee Report, Delhi, 1956.

Khare, N.B., *My Political Memoirs or Autobiography,* Nagpur, 1959.

Khosla, G.D., *Last Days of Netaji,* Delhi, 1974.

Kiani, Mohammad Zaman, *India's Freedom Struggle and The Great INA,* Delhi, 1994.

Kipling, Rudyard, *Selected Prose and Poetry of Rudyard Kipling*, New York, 1937.

Kirby, S.Woodburn, *The War Against Japan. Vol. III: The Decisive Battles,* London, 1965; *Vol. IV: Reconquest of Burma,* London, 1961.

Singapore: The Chain of Disaster, London, 1971.

Kohn, Hans, *A History of Nationalism in the East*, New York, 1929.

Krasa, Miloslav, *Looking towards India: A Study in East-West Contact*, Prague, 1969.

Kripalani, J.B., *Gandhi, His Life and Thoughts,* Delhi, 1970.

Kripalani, Krishna, *Rabindranath Tagore*, London, 1962.

Krishna, Gopal, 'The Development of the Indian National Congress as a Mass Organization, 1918-1923', *The Journal of Asian Studies,* XXV, No. 3, May 1966, pp. 413-30.

Kumar, Ravinder (ed.) *Essays on Gandhian Politics*, London, 1971.

Kurti, Kitty, *Subhas Chandra Bose as I Knew Him,* Calcutta, 1966.

Lahiri, Amar, *Said Subhas Bose,* Calcutta, 1947.

Laushey, D.M., *Bengal Terrorism and Marxist Left,* Calcutta, 1975.

Lavalle, Eduard M., 'Confrontation within a Confrontation: Subhas C. Bose and the 1928 Strike', in *Bengal in the Nineteenth and Twentieth Centuries* (ed.) John R. McLane, East Lansing, 1975.

Leach, Edmund and Mukerjee, S.N. (eds) *Elites in South Asia,* Cambridge, 1970.

Lebra, Joyce C., *Jungle Alliance,* Singapore, 1971.

Japan's Greater East Asia Co-Prosperity Sphere in World War II: Selected Readings and Documents (ed.), Kuala Lumpur, 1975.

Japanese-Trained Armies in Southeast Asia, Hong Kong, 1977.

Leifer, W., *India and the Germans,* Bombay, 1971.

Leitz, C., *Nazi Germany and Neutral Europe,* Manchester, 2000.

Lewin, Ronald, *The American Magic*, New York, 1982.

Lewin, R., *Slim: The Standard-Bearer,* London, 1976.

Lohia, Rammanohar, *Guilty Men of India's Partition*, Allahabad, 1960.
Low, D.A. (ed.) *Soundings in Modern South Asian History,* London, 1968.
Lion Rampant, London, 1973.
Congress and the Raj, London, 1977.
Lytton, Earl of, *Pundits and Elephants,* Bombay, 1963.
MacDonogh, Giles, *A Good German: Adam von Trott zu Solz*, London, 1989.
McLane, John R., *Indian Nationalism and the Early Congress*, Princeton, 1977.
Macmillan, Harold, *Tides of Fortune,* London, 1969.
McPherson, Kenneth, *The Muslim Microcosm: Calcutta 1918-1935*, Wiesbaden, 1974.
MacMunn, G.F., *The Armies of India* (first published 1911), reprinted Delhi, 2002.
Majumdar, A.K., *Advent of Independence,* Bombay, 1963.
Majumdar, Niranjan (ed.) *The Statesman: An Anthology*, Calcutta, 1975.
Majumdar, R.C., *History of the Freedom Movement in India* (3 vols), Calcutta, 1962, 1963.
Majumdar, S.K., *Evolution of Netaji: The Warrior Prophet of India* (Netaji Oration 1969), Calcutta, 1969.
Malhotra, Uttam Chand, *When Bose was Ziauddin,* Delhi, 1945.
Markovits, Claude, *Indian Business and Nationalist Politics 1931-1939*, Cambridge, 1985.
Masani, Minoo, *Bliss Was It in That Dawn,* Delhi, 1977.
Maser, Werner, *Hitler,* London, 1973.
Mason, Philip, *A Matter of Honour: An Account of The Indian Army, its Officers and Men,* London, 1974.
The Men who Ruled India, London, 1985.
Masters, John, *The Road Past Mandalay,* London, 1961.
Mehotra, S.R., *India and the Commonwealth, 1885-29,* Delhi, 1965.
The Emergence of the Indian National Congress, Delhi, 1971.
Menon, Narayan, *On to Delhi,* Singapore, 1944.
On With the Fight, Singapore, 1944.
Blood Bath, Singapore, 1944.
Menon, V.P., *The Transfer of Power in India,* Madras, 1968.
Meskill, Johanna Menzel, *Hitler and Japan: The Hollow Alliance*, New York, 1966.
Minault, Gail, *The Khilafat Movement,* Delhi, 1982.
Mishra, D.P., *Living an Era,* Vol. I, Delhi, 1975.
Misra, B.B., *The Indian Middle Classes,* London, 1961.
Mitra, H.N. (ed.) *The Indian Annual Register: 1919-1924,* Calcutta, published annually.
Mitra, Nripendera Nath (ed.) *The Indian Annual Register: 1925-1947*, Calcutta, published annually.
Momen, Humaira, *Muslim Politics in Bengal*, Dacca, 1972.
Montagu, Edwin, *An Indian Diary,* London, 1930.
Mookerjee, Girija, *Netaji, the Great Resistance Leader* (Netaji Oration 1965), Calcutta, 1966.
This Europe, Calcutta, 1950.
'International Image of Subhas Bose', *Indian Express,* 23.1.67.
Builders of Modern India, Delhi, 1956.
Mookerjee, N., *Netaji: Through German Lenses,* Calcutta, 1974.
Mookerjee, Shyama Prasad, *Awake Hindustan!* Calcutta, believed before 1944.
Moon, Penderel, *Divide and Quit,* London, 1961.
Gandhi and Modern India, London, 1968.
Moore, Barrington, Jr, *The Social Origins of Dictatorship and Democracy*, Boston, 1966.
Moore, R.J., *Liberalism and Indian Politics 1872-1922,* London, 1966.
Churchill, Cripps, and India 1939-1945, Oxford, 1979.
The Crisis of Indian Unity 1917-40, London, 1974.
Escape from Empire: The Attlee Government and the Indian Problem, Oxford, 1983.
Moraes, F., *Witness to an Era,* Delhi, 1976.
Mosley, L., *The Last Days of the British Raj,* London, 1961.
Mussolini's Shadow. The Double Life of Count Galeazzo Ciano, New Haven, 1999.

Muggeridge, Malcolm (ed.) *Ciano's Diplomatic Papers 1939-43,* London, 1948.
Chronicles of Wasted Time: Vol. II, London, 1981.
Mukherjee, Hiran, *Nehru: The Gentle Colossus,* Calcutta, 1964.
Gandhi: A Study (2nd edn), Delhi, 1960.
Bow of Burning Gold, Delhi, 1977.
Mukherjee, Uma, *Two Great Indian Revolutionaries,* Calcutta, 1966.
Nair, A.M., *An Indian Freedom Fighter in Japan*, Bombay, 1982.
Nair, Kusum, *The Story of the I.N.A.,* Bombay, 1946.
Nanda, B.R., *Mahatma Gandhi*, London, 1958.
The Nehrus, London, 1962.
Socialism in India (ed.) Delhi, 1972.
Narayan, Jaya Prakash, *Towards Struggle,* Bombay, 1946.
Narendra, Deva, *Socialism and the National Revolution,* Bombay, 1946.
Nehru, Jawaharlal, *Soviet Russia*, Allahabad, 1928.
An Autobiography, Bombay, 1962.
Discovery of India, Delhi (6th impression), 1988.
A Bunch of Old Letters, Bombay, 1960.
Selected Works, 15 vols, Delhi, 1972-82.
Selected Works, 31 vols, second series, Delhi, 1984-2002.
Norman, D., *Nehru: The First Sixty Years,* 2 vols, London, 1965.
O'Malley, L.S.S., *History of Bengal, Bihar and Orissa under British Rule*, Calcutta, 1925.
Oshawa, J.G., *Two Great Indians in Japan: Rash Behari Bose and Subhas Chandra Bose,* Calcutta, 1954.
Overstreet, Gene D. and Windmiller, Marshall, *Communism in India*, Berkeley, 1959.
Palta, K.R., *My Adventures with the I.N.A.,* Lahore, 1946.
Pandey, B.N., *Nehru,* London, 1976.
Pandey, B.N. (ed.) *The Indian Nationalist Movement 1885-1947: Select Documents*, London, 1979.
Parikh, N.D., *Sardar Vallabhbhai Patel,* Vol. II, Ahmedabad, 1956.
Patel, Vallabhbhai, *Sandar Patel's Correspondence 1945-50,* 10 vols, Ahmedabad, 1972-4.
Pennington, William, *Pick Up Your Parrots and Monkeys*, London, 2003.
Philips, C.H., Singh, H.L. and Pandey, B.N. (eds) *The Evolution of India and Pakistan 1858-1947*, London, 1962.
Philips, C.H. and Wainwright, M.D., *The Partition of India: Policies and Perspectives 1935-47,* London, 1970.
Prabhu, R.K. and Ravindra, Kelekar (eds) *Truth Called Them Differently (Tagore-Gandhi Controversy),* Ahmedabad, 1961.
Prasad, B., *Changing Modes of Indian National Movement,* Delhi, 1966.
Prasad, Rajendra, *Autobiography,* Delhi, 1957.
Punjabi, Kewal L., *Indomitable Sardar: A Political Biography of Sardar Vallabhbhai Patel,* Bombay, 1962.
Pyarelal, *Mahatma Gandhi, the Last Phase,* Ahmedabad, 1956-8.
Platoon Lectures of the I.N.A., Singapore, 1943.
Rab, A.S.M. Abdur, *A.K. Fazlul Huq*, Lahore, n.d.
Rai, Chowdhuri Satyabrata, *Leftist Movements in India 1917-47*, Calcutta, 1977.
Rai, Ganpat (ed.) *Famous Speeches and Letters of Subhas Chandra Bose,* Lahore, 1946.
Ram, Moti (ed.) *Two Historic Trials in Red Fort,* Delhi, 1946.
Ranga, N.G., *Distinguished Acquaintances,* Vol. II, Delhi, 1976.
Fight for Freedom, Delhi, 1968.
Rao, B.S., *India's Freedom Movement,* Delhi, 1972.
Rao, T.S., *Netaji: Where Art Thou?* Bombay, 1958.
Rath, R., *The Story of Freedom Movement in Orissa States,* n.d.
Rawal, Ram Singh, *The l.N.A. Saga,* Allahabad, 1946.
Ray, Prithwas Chandra, *The Life and Times of C.R.Das*, Calcutta/Oxford, 1927.
Ray, Rajat, *Urban Roots of Indian Nationalism*, Delhi, 1979.
Ray, Rajat Kanta, *Social Conflict and Political Unrest in Bengal 1875-1927*, Delhi, 1984.
Ray, SvipTakss, *Bharaterbaiplabiksangrameritihas (History of the Indian Revolutionary Struggle)*, Calcutta, 1955.

Read, Anthony and Fisher, David, *Berlin, The Biography of a City,* London, 1994.
Reid, Sir Robert, *Years of Change in Bengal and Assam,* London, 1966.
Reuth, Ralf Georg, *Goebbels,* London, 1993.
Revri, Chamanlal, *The Indian Trade Union Movement,* Delhi, 1972.
Ribbentrop, Joachim von, *The Ribbentrop Memoirs,* London, 1954.
Richie, Alexandra, *Faust's Metropolis: A History of Berlin,* London, 1999.
Rolland, Romain, *The Life of Ramakrishna,* Vol. I, Calcutta, 1914.
The Life of Vivekananda and the Universal Gospel, Calcutta, 1931.
Index Journal (1945-1943), Paris, 1960.
Ronaldshay, Earl of (Marquis of Zetland), *Essayez,* London, 1956.
Ross, Alan, *The Emissary, G.D.Birla, Gandhi and Independence,* London, 1986.
Roth, Radhanath (ed.) *Rash Behari Basu and His Struggle for India's Independence,* Calcutta, 1963.
Roy, Bidhan and Chandra, *Towards a Prosperous India: Speeches and Writers,* Calcutta, 1964.
Roy, Dilip Kumar, *Netaji - The Man: Reminiscences,* Bombay, 1966.
The Subhas I Knew, Bombay, 1946.
Roy, M.N., *India in Transition,* Geneva, 1922.
Fascism, Calcutta, 1938.
I.N.A. and the August Revolution, Calcutta, 1946.
Memoirs, Delhi, 1964.
A Political Biography, Bombay, 1978.
Roy, P.C., *Subhas Chandra,* Calcutta, 1929.
Roy, S. (ed.) *Communism in India -1935-45,* Calcutta, 1976.
Royle, Trevor, *The Last Days of the Raj,* London, 1989.
Rumbold, Sir Algernon, *Watershed in India 1914-22,* London, 1979.
Rushby, Kevin, *Children of Kali,* London, 2002.
Safrani, Abid Hasan and Thivy, John A., *The Men from Imphal,* Calcutta, 1971.
Safrani, Abid Hasan, 'A Soldier Remembers', *The Oracle,* Calcutta, Vol. VI, no. 1, Jan. 1984, pp.24-65; Vol. VII, no. 1, Jan. 1985, pp.17-29.
Saggi, P.D., *Nation's Homage: Life and Work of Subhas Bose,* Bombay, n.d.
Saha, Surendra Mohan, *Ideology of Netaji: Thesis of All-India Forward Bloc,* Calcutta, 1949.
Sahgal, Lakshmi, *The Role of Women in the Azad Hind Movement* (Netaji Oration 1964), Calcutta, 1965.
Sahgal, P.K., *The Indian National Army* (Netaji Oration 1966), Calcutta,1967.
Sarat Chandra Bose Commemoration Volume, Calcutta, 1982.
Sareen, T.T. (ed.) *Select Documents on Indian National Army,* Delhi, 1988.
Japan and the Indian National Army, Delhi, 1986.
Sarkar, Sumit, *Swadeshi Movement in Bengal 1903-8,* Delhi, 1973.
Modern India 1885-1947, Delhi, 1983.
'The Logic of Gandhian Nationalism: Civil Disobedience and the Gandhi-Irwin Pact (1930-1931)', *Indian Historical Review,* ffl.No. 1, pp.114-46.
Sarkar, Tanika, 'The First Phase of Civil Disobedience in Bengal, 1930-31', *Indian Historical Review,* IV, No. 1, pp.75-95.
Sayeed, Khalid B., *Pakistan, The Formative Phase 1857-1948,* London, 1968.
Schmidt, Paul, *Hitler's Interpreter,* London, 1950.
Seal, Anil, *The Emergence of Indian Nationalism; Competition and Collaboration in later 19th Century,* Cambridge, 1968.
Sen, Shila, *Muslim Politics in Bengal, 1937-47,* Delhi, 1976.
Sen, Sukomal, *Working Class of India,* Calcutta, 1977.
Sen, Gupta and Subodh, Chandra, *India Wrests Freedom,* Calcutta, 1982.
Sengupta, B.K., *India's Man of Destiny,* Calcutta, n.d.
Sengupta, Padmini, *Deshapriya Jatindra Mohan Sengupta,* Delhi, 1968.
Seth, Hiralal, *Subhas Bose, Is He Fascist?* Lahore, 1943.
Shah, Harin, *Gallant End of Netaji,* Delhi, 1956.
Sharma, S.R., *Netaji, His Life and Work,* Agra, 1948.
Shaw, James, *The March Out,* London, 1953.
Singh, Durlab, *Formation and Growth of the Indian National Army,* Lahore, 1946.

Famous Letters and Ultimatums to the British Government (ed.), Lahore, 1944.
Netaji Speaks to the Nation (ed.), Lahore, 1946.
The Rebel President, Lahore, 1942.
Singh, Gurchan, *Singa, The Lion of Malaya*, Kula Lumur, n.d.
Singh, Mangat, Burbachan, *The Tiger Strikes,* Ludhiana, 1986.
Singh, Mohan, *Leaves from my Diary,* Lahore, 1946.
Soldiers' Contributions to Indian Independence, Delhi, 1975.
Singh, N. Iqbal, *The Andaman Story*, Delhi, 1978.
Singhal, D.P., *A History of the Indian People*, London, 1983.
Sinha, L.P., *The Left Wing in India*, Muzaffarpur, 1965.
Sinha, Pradip, *Nineteenth Century Bengal: Aspects of Social History*, Calcutta, 1965.
Calcutta in Urban History, Calcutta, 1978.
Sinha, Probodh Chandra, *Sir Asutosh Mookherjee*, Calcutta, 1928.
Sinha, Surajit (ed.) *Cultural Profile of Calcutta*, Calcutta, 1972.
Sitaramayya, Pattabhi, *History of the Indian National Congress,* 2 vols, Bombay, 1935, 1947.
Sivaram, M., *The Road to Delhi,* Tokyo, 1967.
'If Subhas Were Alive', *Sunday Standard,* 2.1.66.
Skidelsky, Robert, *Maynard Keynes,* Vol. 1, London, 1983.
Slim, Field-Marshal Sir William, *Defeat into Victory,* London, 1956.
Smith, Denis Mack, *Mussolini, A Biography*, London, 1983.
Mussolini's Roman Empire, London, 1977.
Snow, Philip, *The Fall of Hong Kong,* London, 2003.
Sokthankar, Y.N., 'The Subhas We Knew At Cambridge', *Indian Express,* 24.1.70, 26.1.70, 28.1.70.
Sopan, *Netaji Subhas Chandra Bose, His Life and Work,* Bombay, 1946.
Spratt, Philip, *Blowing Up India,* Calcutta, 1955.
Subuhey, S., *Netaji Speaks,* Bombay, 1946.
Suda, J.P., *The Indian National Movement,* 1969.
Sykes, Christopher, *Troubled Loyalty: A Biography of Adam von Trott,* London, 1968.
Tagore, Rabindranath, *Lectures and Addresses,* London, 1962.
Letters from Russia, Calcutta, 1960.
Rabindra Racanabali (*Collected Works of Rabindra Nath Tagore*), 14 vols, Calcutta, 1961.
'Indian students and Western teachers', *Modern Review,* April 1916.
Talwar, B.R., *The Talwars of Pathan Land and Subhas Chandra's Great Escape,* Delhi, 1976.
Tamhankar (ed.) *On to Delhi,* Bombay, 1946.
Tendulkar, D.G., *The Mahatma,* Vols 1-8, Delhi, 1960-63.
Thivy, John A., *A Short Sketch of the Indian Independence Movement in East Asia,* Calcutta, n.d.
Thomas, K.P., *Dr B.C. Roy,* Calcutta, 1955.
Tinker, H., *Reorientations,* London, 1965.
Toland, John, *The Rising Sun*, New York, 1971.
Tomlinson, B.R., *Experiment with Freedom*, Oxford, 1967.
The Indian National Congress and the Raj, London, 1976.
Toye, Hugh, *The Springing Tiger: A Study of a Revolutionary* (reprint), Bombay, 1974. (An expanded version of this book is now awaiting publication and Hugh Toye kindly lent it to me as he also lent Subhas Pasha, his unpublished manuscript now in St Anthony's College, Oxford.)
Tripathi, Amles, *The Extremist Challenge,* Calcutta, 1967.
Tuchman, Barbara, *Stilwell and the American Experience in China 1911-1945,* London, 1970.
Tuker, Sir Francis, *While Memory Serves: The Story of the Last Two Years of British Rule in India,* London, 1950.
Vassiltchikov, Marie (Missie), *Berlin Diaries 1940-1945,* London, 1985.
Vivekananda, Swami, *Lectures from Colombo to Almora* (9th edn), Calcutta, 1964.
Voigt, Johannes, *India in the Second World War,* Delhi, 1987.
Volkogonov, Dmitri, *Stalin,* London, 1991.

Vyas, M.R., *The Azad Hind Movement in Europe* (Netaji Oration, 1962), Calcutta, 1963.
Passage through a Turbulent Era, Bombay, 1982.
Wadud, Kazi Abdul, *Creative Bengal,* Calcutta, 1949.
Ward, Andrew, *Our Bones are Scattered,* London, 1996.
Wavell, Lord, *The Viceroy's Journal,* London, 1973.
Weinberg, Gerhard L., *A World at Arms,* Cambridge, 1994.
Germany, Hitler and World War II, Cambridge, 1995.
Weiner, Myron (ed.) *Party Politics in India*, Princeton, 1957.
State Politics in India, Princeton, 1968.
Weizsacker, Ernst von, *Memoirs,* London, 1951.
Werth, Alexander and Harbich, Walter, *Netaji in Germany,* Calcutta, 1970.
Wheeler-Bennett, John W. and Anderson, John, *Viscount Waverley*, London, 1962.
Williamson, Sir Horace, *Communism in India,* Calcutta, 1976.
Wirsings, Giselher, *Indien – Asiens Seiche Jahre,* Düsseldorf, 1968.
Wolpert, Stanley, *Tilak and Gokhale: Revolution and Reform in the Making of Modern India,* Berkeley, 1962.
Jinnah of Pakistan, Karachi, 1989.
Woodruff, R., *The Men Who Ruled India,* 2 vols, London, 1953.
Yule, Henry and Burnell, A.C., *Hobson-Jobson,* Delhi, 1986.
Zaidi, Z.H. (ed.) *M.A. Jinnah-Ispahani Correspondence 1936-1948,* Karachi, 1976.
Ziegler, Philip, *Mountbatten*, London, 1985.

Books - Bengali:
Ahmad, Abul Mansur, *Amaar dekha rajnitir panchar (Fifty Years of Politics as I Saw It),* 3rd edn, Dacca, 1975.
Bagchi, Moni, *Deshnayak Subhas Chandra,* Calcutta, 1965.
Bhattacharya, Prakash, *Netaji-o-Quisling Prasanga,* Calcutta, 1975.
Bose, Krishna, *Itihaser Sandhane,* Calcutta, 1973.
Bose, Shyamal, *Subhas Ghare Fere Nai,* Calcutta, 1973.
Bose, Sisir, *Kumar Mahanishkratman*, Calcutta, 1975.
Dey, Bishwanath, *Subhas Smiriti,* Calcutta, 1970.
Dey, Sailesh, *Ami Subhas Balcchi,* Calcutta, 1968.
Ghosh, Sudhanshi Ranjan, *Sabar Priya Subhas,* Calcutta, 1970.
Majumdar, Nepal, *Rabindranath-o-Subhas Chandra,* Calcutta, 1973.
Sarkar, Hemant K., *Subhaser Sange Baro Bachhar 1912-24,* Calcutta, 1946.
Sri Avijit, *Taihoku Theke Bharate* (revised edn), Calcutta, 1975.

Chapter Source Notes

Prologue: Journey into the Unknown

Interviews with Hugh Toye over several meetings between 2002 and 2004 and S.A. Ayer in summer 1977 (also his *Unto Him a Witness*).
War Office Document WO 208 /3812 in the PRO.
Indian Political Intelligence File L/P&J/12/217 in IOR.
Report into the death of Subhas Bose by Lt Colonel J.G.Figgess, 25 July 1946 (kindly supplied by Hugh Toye).
'Subhas Chandra Bose and Japan': an official document prepared by Asian Bureau Ministry of Foreign Affairs Government of Japan, August 1956, published in *Netaji and India's Freedom.*
Netaji Inquiry, *Committee Report*, Government of India, 1956.
Report of the One-Man Commission of Inquiry into the Disappearance of Netaji Subhas Chandra Bose, Government of India, 1974.
Suresh Chandra Bose's *Dissentient Report.*
Harin Shah's *Gallant End of Netaji.*
Samar Guha's *Netaji Dead or Alive?*
Sisir Bose and Alexander Werth edited *A Beacon Across Asia.*

Sarat Bose Diary quoted in Gordon's *Brothers against the Raj.*
Tatsuo Hayashida's *Netaji Subhas Chandra Bose: His Great Struggle and Martyrdom.*

PART ONE: THE REBEL AND THE BHADRALOKS

1 - Muscular Hinduism

A photocopy of Jankinath's diary entry hangs on one of the walls in the room where Subhas was born. The Bengali sayings are part of the folklore of the province.
Interviews with Dwijendranath Bose, Calcutta, August/September 1977; Dr Radhanath Rath Cuttack, August 1977, Madan Mohan Das, a classmate of Subhas, and Bina Bhowmick, daughter of Beni Madhav Das in Calcutta, October 1977.
Indian Political Intelligence File L/P&J/12/217 in IOR.
Subhas Bose's *An Indian Pilgrim* (1965 edn) and *Netaji Collected Works* Vols 1 and 5.
Swami Vivekananda's *Lectures from Colombo to Almora.*
Hemanta Sarkar's *Subhaser Sange Baro Bacchar.*
M.J. Akbar's *Nehru.*
Tariq Ali's *The Nehrus and the Gandhis.*
James Campbell Ker's *Political Trouble in India 1907-17.*
Sumit Sarkar's *Swadeshi Movement in Bengal 1903-1908.*

2 - The Rebellion

The Bholanath Roy Collection NAI.
Dharmavir Papers, Jawaharlal Nehru Memorial Library, Delhi.
Dilip Roy's *The Subhas I Knew.*
Subhas Bose's *An Indian Pilgrim* and *Netaji Collected Works* Vol. 1.
Sisir Bose (ed.) *Netaji and India's Freedom.*
Bholanath Roy's *Oaten Incident 1916.*
Leonard Gordon's *Bengal* and *Brothers Against the Raj.*

PART TWO: THE MYSTICAL HERO

3 - At Last: The Guru

Bholanath Roy Collection (NAI).
Amrita Bazar Patrika (ABP) 17.9.22, 20.9.22, 3.4.23, 4.6.23, 6.6.23 and 25.1.38. *Forward* 24.3.24.
IPI File no. L/P&J/12/214 (IOR).
Subhas Bose's *The Indian Struggle 1920-34* (all references are to 1948 edition except where specified) and *Netaji Collected Works,* Vols 2 and 3.
Hemanta Sarkar's *Subhaser Sange Baro Bacchar.*
R.K.Prabhu and Ravindra Kelekar (eds) *Truth Called them Differently (Tagore-Gandhi Controversy).*
Hemendra Das Gupta's *Subhas Chandra.*
Bishwanath Dey's *Subhas Smiriti.*
Upendra Nath Bannerjee's *Subhas in Masik Basumati.*
Judith Brown's *Gandhi's Rise to Power: Indian Politics 1915-22; Gandhi and Civil Disobedience* and *Nehru A Political Life.*
Ashok Bose's *Subhas Chandra Bose and Calcutta Corporation.*
Alfred Draper's *Amritsar: The Massacre That Ended the Raj.*
M.J.Akbar's *Nehru the Making of India.*
Tariq Ali's *The Nehrus and the Gandhis.*
Nirad Chaudhuri's *Thy Hand Great Anarch!*
R.J. Moore's *The Crisis of Indian Unity.*
Christopher Sykes's *Troubled Loyalty.*
Sir Algernon Rumbold's *Watershed in India 1914-22.*
Gail Minault's *The Khilafat Movement.*
Leonard Gordon's *Bengal* and *Brothers against the Raj.*

4 - The Man

Interviews with Abid Hasan in Hyderabad in June 1978, V.B. Karnik in Bombay in June 1978, Satya Ranjan Bakshi in Calcutta in summer 1978 and several interviews with Anita Pfaff (née Bose) through the summer/autumn 2003 and spring 2004. Also Dwijendranath Bose.
Subhas Bose's *Kon Pathe* (the enlarged Bengal edn of *Crossroads*) and *Crossroads* (the English edition).
Dilip Roy's *The Subhas I Knew.*
S.A. Ayer's *Unto Him a Witness.*
Nirad Chaudhuri's *Thy Hand Great Anarch!*
Hari Vishnu Kamath in the *Sunday Standard*, 13.12.64.
Ram Sharma edited *Netaji, His Life and Work.*
Leopold Fisher's observations in 'The Great White Swami', *Overseas Hindusthan Weekly*, 5.2.81.
Bishwanath Dey's *Subhas Smiriti.*

5 - Enter Revolutionaries

History Sheet of Subhas Chandra Bose in IPI file no. L/P&J/12/214, IOR.
'Connection of Revolutionists with the Swarajya Party' in File no. 399/11/1924, Home Poll, NAI.
File no. 61/1924, section 5, Home Poll, NAI.
File no. 379/11/1924, Home Poll, NAI.
File no. 379/1/Poll of 1924 and K.W. Home Poll, NAI.
File no. 308/1924, Home Poll, NAI.
File no. 10/68/1927, Home Poll, NAI.
Interviews with Satya Ranjan Bakshi and Arun Chandra Guha.
Subhas Bose's *The Indian Struggle 1920-34; Correspondence 1924-32* and *Netaji Collected Works,* Vol. 3.
Dilip Roy's *The Subhas I Knew.*
John Campbell's *F.E. Smith.*
Partha Sarathi Gupta's *Imperialism and the British Labour Movement.*
Arun Channdra Guha's *Aurobindo and Jugantar.*

6 - Guru Lost

File no. 29/XIV/25, Home Poll, NAI.
File no. 80-III, Home Poll of 1926, NAI.
File no. 65/X VII 1926, Home Poll, NAI.
File no. 104 & K.W./1927, Home Poll, NAI, including Bengal government's telegram P no. 2755-X of 11.4.27.
Subhas Bose's *The Indian Struggle 1920-34; Correspondence* and *Netaji Collected Works,* Vols 3, 4 and 5.
Leonard Gordon's *Bengal* and *Brothers Against the Raj.*

7 - The Reluctant Heir

File no. G. 57 (III) 1926 AICC Papers, Nehru Memorial Library (NML), Delhi.
ABP, 13.11.27.
M.A.H. Ispahani in *Illustrated Weekly of India*, September 1975.
Subhas Bose's *Correspondence*; *Mission of Life* and *Netaji Collected Works,* Vols 3, 4 and 5.
Nirad Chaudhuri's *Continent of Circe* and *Thy Hand Great Anarch!*
John Campbell's *F.E. Smith.*
Partha Sarathi Gupta's *Imperialism and the British Labour Movement.*
Mushirul Hasan's *Communalism in Indian Politics: A Study of the Nehru Report.*
Ashok Bose's *Subhas Chandra Bose and Calcutta Corporation.*
R.J. Moore's *The Crisis of Indian Unity.*
Gail Minault's *The Khilafat Movement.*
Judith Brown's *Gandhi's Rise to Power: Indian Politics 1915-22; Gandhi and Civil Disobedience* and *Nehru A Political Life.*
Leonard Gordon's *Bengal* and *Brothers Against the Raj.*

8 - The Many Fronted War
File no. 179/1929, Home Poll, NAI.
File no. 112/1930, Home Poll, NAI.
File no. 65/1930.
File no. 257/VII/1930, Home Poll, NAI.
File no. 38/1931, Home Poll, NAI.
File no. 155/1931, Home Poll, NAI.
File no. 672 serial 1-4, Home Poll, West Bengal State Archives.
File no. 101/31, Home Poll, West Bengal State Archives.
File no. P-6 1927-31(PTI) AICC Papers, NML.
File no. G25/506 of 1934-35 AICC Papers, NML.
ABP, 26.12.28, 3.5.28, 4.5.28, 19.8.30, 20.8.30, 14.4.31, 23.4.31, 28.4.31, 4.6.31, 18.9.31, 4.10.31, 12.11.31, 13.11.31.
Subhas Bose's *The Indian Struggle 1920-34; Netaji Speaks to the Nation* and *Netaji's Collected Works*, Vols 4, 5 and 6.
Netaji Birthday Supplement of the *Calcutta Municipal Gazette*, 24.1.1970.
Nirad Chaudhuri's *The Continent of Circe;* Article in *Illustrated Weekly* 18.9.55 and *Thy Hand Great Anarch!*
Asoke Bose's *My Uncle Netaji.*
Hemendra Dasgupta's *Subhas Chandra.*
M.J.Akbar's *Nehru: The Making of India.*
Tariq Ali's *The Nehrus and the Gandhis.*
Ashok Bose's *Subhas Chandra Bose and Calcutta Corporation.*
R.J. Moore's *The Crisis of Indian Unity.*
Pattabhi Sitaramayya's *A History of the Indian National Congress*, Vol. 1 (1885-1935).
D.A. Low's *Congress and the Raj.*
Judith Brown's *Gandhi's Rise to Power: Indian Politics 1915-22; Gandhi and Civil Disobedience* and *Nehru: A Political Life.*
Leonard Gordon's *Bengal* and *Brothers Against the Raj.*

9 - Re-enter Revolution
File no. 163/1931, Home Poll, NAI.
File no. 31/XXVII/1932, Home Poll, NAI.
File no. 31/XXVII/1932, Home Poll, NAI.
File no. 31/34/1932, Home Poll, NAI.
File no. 31/103/1932, Home Poll, NAI.
Interviews with Satya Ranjan Bakshi and Arun Chandra Guha.
ABP, 23.12.31, 3.1.32, 24.2.33, 2.3.33, 2.3.33.
Arun Channdra Guha's *Aurobindo and Jugantar.*
Dilip Roy's *The Subhas I Knew.*
Nirad Chaudhuri's *The Continent of Circe* and *Thy Hand Great Anarch!*
Manini Chatterjee's *The Chittagong Uprising.*

PART THREE: EXILE

10 - The Ambassador With a Cause
Interviews with V.B. Kamik, Bombay, June 1978 and Anita Bose.
IPI File nos L/P&J/12/214, 215 and 216 and File nos L/P&J/12/73 and 446, all in IOR.
P&J 1208 (L/P&J/7/792) IOR.
P&J 930 (L/P&J/7/792) IOR.
P&J 1589/33 (L/P&J/7/792) IOR.
P&J 2530/33 (L/P&J/7/792) IOR.
P&J 1885 (L/P&J/7/792) IOR.
P&J 2745 (L/P&J/7/792) IOR.
P&J 4263 (L/P&J/7/792) IOR.

P&J 4246 (L/P&J/7/792) IOR.
P&J 4247 (L/P&J/7/792) IOR.
P&J 4289 (L/P&J/7/792) IOR.
File no. 35/11/1933, Home Poll, NAI.
File no. 31/103/33, Home Poll, NAI.
File no. 44/56/1934, Home Poll, NAI.
File no. 44/56/34, Home Poll, NAI.
File no. 35/8/34, Home Poll, NAI.
File no. 44/56/34, Home Poll, NAI.
Woods Collection, Vols I and II, NAI.
Nehru Collection, Part I, Vol. VIII, NML.
ABP, 18.4.33, 10.5.33, 24.5.33, 25.5.33, 18.7.33, 14.3.34, 3.3.34, 14.6.34, 31.7.34, 11.1.35, 16.6.35, 17.3.36.
Subhas Bose's *Impressions in Life; Fundamental Questions of Indian Revolution* and *Netaji Collected Works,* Vols 7 and 8.
Dilip Roy's *The Subhas I Knew.*
Asoke Bose's *My Uncle Netaji.*
Jawaharlal Nehru's *A Bunch of Old Letters.*
Walter Leifer's *India and the Germans.*
Hitler's *Mein Kampf.*
Anthony Eden's *Facing the Dictators.*
Kirkpatrick's *The Inner Circle.*
Rosenberg's *Myths of the Twentieth Century.*
Kitty Kurti's *Subhas Chandra Bose As I Knew Him.*
Sisir Bose and Alexander Werth's *A Beacon Across Asia.*
Alfred Tymaeur in the *Saturday Evening Post,* 11.3.44.
Leonard Gordon's *Brothers Against the Raj.*

PART FOUR: THE EMBATTLED LEADER

11 - Subhas in Love

Interviews with N.G. Ranga in Delhi on 28.6.78, Pamela de Bouvey and Frederick Warburg in London, October 1978, Anita Pfaff and J.B. Knpalani.
Woods Collection NAI.
MSS. EUR.D.609/9 Zetland Papers IOR.
IPI File nos L/P&J/12/214, 215 and 216.
File no. F27/40/36, Home Poll, NAI.
File no. F44/26/KW, Home Poll, NAI.
File no. 41/18/37, Home Poll.
File no. G-25/1936, AICC Papers, NML.
File no. 44/13/1937, Home Poll, NAI.
File no. 28/16/38, Home Poll, NAI.
Return Showing the Results of Election in India (1937), Cmnd 5589.
ABP, 25.1.38.
Subhas Bose's *The Indian Struggle 1920-34; Through Congress Eyes;* 'Europe - Today and Tomorrow', *Modern Review,* September 1937; 'Japan's Role in the Far East', *Modern Review,* October 1937 and *Netaji Collected Works,* Vols 7 and 8.
Jawaharlal Nehru's *A Bunch of Old Letters.*
N.G.Ranga's *Distinguished Acquaintances.*
Asoke Bose's *My Uncle Netaji.*
Nirad Chaudhuri's *Thy Hand Great Anarch!*
S. Gopal's *Jawaharlal Nehru,* Vol. I.
R. J. Moore's 'British Policy and the Indian Problem 1936-40', in *The Partition of India: Policies and Perspectives 1935-47.*
Dilip Roy's *The Subhas I Knew.*
George Orwell's *Collected Essays and Journalism.*

Katherine Frank's *Indira Nehru Gandhi.*
Leonard Gordon's *Brothers Against the Raj.*

12 - Rashtrapati

Interviews with Niharendru Dutt-Mazumdar, Calcutta, June and July 1977, Soli Batlivala, Bombay, June 1978, and Dwijendranath Bose.
IPI File nos L/P&J/12/214, 215 and 216.
File no. 4/14 A/40, Home Poll, NAI.
Nehru Collection, Part I, Vol. IX, NML.
File no. 39 of 1938 AICC Papers, NML.
ABP, 22.1.39, 28.1.39, 30.1.39, 31.1.39, 1.2.39, 129.
Subhas Bose's *Crossroads; Through Congress Eyes* and *Netaji Collected Works,* Vols 7 and 9.
Jawaharlal Nehru's *A Bunch of Old Letters.*
Nirad Chaudhuri's *Thy Hand Great Anarch!*
B. R. Tomlinson's *The Indian National Congress and the Raj 1929-42.*
Milan Hauner's *India in the Axis Strategy.*
N.G. Ganpuley's *Netaji in Germany.*
Pattabhi Sitaramayya's *A History of the Indian National Congress,* Vol. II.
Frank Moraes' *Witness to an Era.*

13 - Defeat

Interviews with B.T. Ranadive, Calcutta, 24.1.78, Somnath Lahiri, Santimoy Ganguli, Narain Chakraborthy, Kalyan Roy, son of Kiran Shankar Roy (all in Calcutta in 1977 and 1978), also Dwijendranath Bose, Niharendru, Dutt-Mazumdar and Soli Batlivala.
Nehru Collection, NML.
IPI File nos L/P&J/12/214-217, IOR.
R/3/2/61, IOR.
File no. G 20/111, AICC Papers, NML.
ABP, 4.2.39, 14.5.39, 4.5.39, 9.5.39.
Subhas Bose's article 'My Strange Illness', *The Modern Review,* April 1939; *Crossroads* and *Netaji Collected Works,* Vol. 10.
Nirad Chaudhuri's 'Subhas Chandra Bose', *Illustrated Weekly,* 18.9.55 and *Thy Hand Great Anarch!*
Asoke Bose's *My Uncle Netaji.*
Pattabhi Sitaramayya's *A History of the Indian National Congress,* Vol. II.
Mitra, *Indian Annual Register* 1939.
Jawaharlal Nehru's *A Bunch of Old Letters.*
Dilip Roy's *The Subhas I Knew.*
Hugh Toye's *The Springing Tiger* (unpublished revised edition).
Taya Zenkin's *Reporting India.*
S. Gopal's *Jawaharlal Nehru,* Vol. I.
Tendulkar's *Mahatma,* Vol. 5.
Hiran Mukerjee's *Nehru: The Gentle Colossus.*
Mohit Sen's *The Indian Revolution.*
Leonard Gordon's *Bengal* and *Brothers Against the Raj.*
Sharma's *Netaji: His Life and Work.*

14 - The Lonely Furrow

Interviews with Dutt-Mazumdar, Dwijendranath Bose, Lahiri, Ranadive and Ranga.
Nehru Collection Part I, Vol. VII, NML.
Rajendra Prasad Collection (on microfilm), NML.
M.N. Roy Papers, NML.
File no. 645/1939, AICC Papers, NML.
File no. 28/79/39, Home Poll, NAI.
File no. 95/4/40, Home Poll, NAI.
File no. 149/40, Home Poll, NAI.

IPI File nos L/P&J/12/214, 215 and 216.
R/3/2/15, IOR.
R/3/2/25, IOR.
R/3/2/16, IOR.
R/3/2/17, IOR.
R/3/2/21, IOR.
MSS. EUR F 125/40, Linlithgow Papers, IOR.
Hindusthan Times, 7.7.40.
V.B. Karnik's *M.N. Roy: A Political Biography.*
Haithcox's *Communism and Nationalism in India.*
B.R. Tomlinson's *The Indian National Congress.*
Subhas Bose's articles in *Forward Bloc* between 28.10.39 and 25.11.39 and on 6.1.40, 20.1.40, 15.6.40; *Crossroads; The Indian Struggle 1920-42* (1964 edn) and *Netaji Collected Works,* Vol. 10.
Jawaharlal Nehru's *A Bunch of Old Letters.*
Bhagat Ram Talwar's *The Talwars of Pathan Land* and *Subhas Chandra's Great Escape.*
M.A.H. Ispahani in the *Illustrated Weekly*, September 1975.
N.G. Ranga's *Distinguished Acquaintances.*
Sisir Bose edited *Netaji and India's Freedom.*
Bishwanath Dey's *Subhas Smiriti.*
A.K. Majumdar's *Advent of Independence.*
Hemendra Das Gupta's *Subhas Chandra.*

15 - "I Am Off: You Go Back"

Interviews with Santimoy Ganguli (several meetings in May and August 1977 and in February 1978), Dwijendranath Bose, Bina Bhowmick, Uttam Chand and correspondence with Bhagat Ram Talwar.
Serial 195 - Documents of State Secretary, 'India 1941-3', part of captured German documents at Foreign and Commonwealth Office (FCO), London.
IPI File nos L/P&J/216-218 in particular 'The Bose Conspiracy Case', IOR.
R/3/2/18, IOR.
R/3/2/20 and R/3/2/21, IOR.
File no. WO 208/773 containing the Confession of Bhagat Ram Talwar to the British PRO, Kew.
File no. 44/25/44, Home Poll, NAI.
File no. 149/40, Home Poll, NAI.
Sisir Bose's *The Great Escape* and *Netaji and India's Freedom* (ed.).
Asoke Bose's *My Uncle Netaji.*
Dilip Roy's *The Subhas I Knew*, p. 192.
Bhagat Ram Talwar's *The Talwars of Pathan Land* and *Subhas Chandra's Great Escape.*
Uttam Chand Malhotra's *When Bose Was Ziauddin.*
Subhas Bose's *The Indian Struggle 1920-1942.*
Milan Hauner's *India in Axis Strategy.*
Paul Leverkuehn's *Der geheime Nachrichtendienst der deutschen Wehrmacht in Kriege,* Frankfurt, 1957.

PART FIVE: CHALO! DELHI!

16 - The Good Germans and The Bad Indians?

Interviews with G. Adhikari in Delhi on 28.6.78, Abid Hasan, Ganguly, Batlivala and Anita Pfaff.
IPI File no. L/P & J/12/218, IOR.
IPI File no. L/P&J/12/73 and 446, IOR.
Interrogation of Nambiar (copy kindly supplied by Hugh Toye), IOR.
Promode Sengupta Papers, NML.
Otto Faltis Collection, NAI.

File no. 44/25/44, Home Poll, NAI.
File no. F44/32, Home Poll, NAI.
Serial 41, serial 195, and Fl-20, G57 Serial 1314 item 4, 6 and 11 FCO.
Documents of German Foreign Policy (DGFP), D/XII, no. 300, no. 323, no. 425, no. 511, no. 561 and no. 598; DGFP, D/XIII no. 120, no. 379, no. 404, no. 468, no. 521, no. 515.
Alexander Werth's *Bericht to Clarita von Trott* (in German, kindly supplied and translated for me by Giles MacDonogh); *Ciano's Diary 1937-43; The Goebbels Diaries* and *Transfer of Power,* Vols I and II.
Subhas Bose's *India Calling; Selected Speeches of Subhas Chandra Bose;* Editorial in *Forward Bloc,* 15.6.40; *Crossroads; The Indian Struggle* 1920-42 and *Netaji Collected Works,* Vols 2 and 11.
Milan Hauner's *India in Axis Strategy.*
A.C. Nambiar's foreword to *Netaji in Germany.*
Girija Mookerjee's *Netaji: The Great Resistance Leader* (Netaji Research Bureau Bulletin 7/1966) and 'International Image of Subhas Bose' in the *Indian Express,* 23.1.67.
Giselher Wirsings's *Indien – Asiens Seiche Jahre.*
George Orwell's introduction to *Talking to India.*
M.R.Vyas, *The Azad Hind Movement in Europe* (Netaji Research Bureau Bulletin, 1963).
Rudolf Hartog's *The Sign of the Tiger.*
Ram Goel's *Netaji and the CPI.*
People's War 19.7. 42, 3.9.42 and 26.9.43.
Talwar's *The Talwars of Pathan Land* and *Subhas Chandra Bose's Great Escape.*
N.G.Ganpuley's *Netaji in Germany.*
Marie 'Missie' Vassiltchikov's *Berlin Diaries 1940-1945.*
Alexander Richie's *Faust's Metropolis: A History of Berlin.*
Michael Besschloss's *The Conquerors.*
Sisir Bose and Alexander Werth's *A Beacon Across Asia* and *Netaji and India's Freedom.*
Michael Bloch's *Ribbentrop.*
David Irving's *Hitler's War.*
Giles MacDonough's *A Good German.*
Christopher Sykes's *Troubled Loyalty.*
Joyce Lebra's *Jungle Alliance: Japan and the Indian National Army.*
Maulana Azad's *India Wins Freedom.*
K.K.Ghosh's *The Indian National Army.*
J.W.Wheeler-Bennett's *King George VI.*
W.D. Hassett's *Off the Record with FDR.*
William Shirer's *The Rise and Fall of the Third Reich.*
S.Gopal's *Jawaharlal Nehru,* Vol. I.
Mary Kenny's *Germany Calling.*
J.A. Cole's *Lord Haw-Haw-and William Joyce.*
Leonard Gordon's *Brothers Against the Raj.*
Note: The Bose Hitler meeting has generated historical controversy as to when it actually took place. The eleventh volume of *Netaji Collected Works* says that it was on 29 May 1942 in the Reich Chancellory in Berlin. But I have accepted the authority of Milan Hauner who explains that the date of 29 May given out by the German Press Agency was as a result of the desire to co-ordinate announcements with the Japanese and Italians. Hauner has no doubts it was on 27 May at Hitler's headquarters in East Prussia (see Hauner pages 484-487).

17 - The Man Called Silver And The Bose Conspiracy

Report of the Soviet Agent to the Governing Body of British Intelligence (in Soviet archives, copy kindly supplied by Milan Hauner).
IPI File, The Bose Conspiracy, File no. L/P&J/12/218, IOR.
File no.WO 208/773 PRO Kew (This includes Bhagat Ram Talwar's confession to the British plus other reports on Talwar's activities, instructions from Bose and the Germans, British CID reports and amounts of money paid by the Axis to Talwar.)
Milan Hauner's *India in the Axis Strategy.*
Michael Howard's *British Intelligence in the Second World War.*

Duff Hart Davis's *Peter Fleming.*
Interview with Hugh Toye and his revised unpublished edition of *The Springing Tiger.*

18 - Netaji

IPI File L/P&J/12/218, IOR.
File no. WO 208 PRO.
Interview with Supriya Sengupta in London, December 2003. Correspondence with J.A.E. Heard, head of British counter-propaganda unit in south east Asia.
'Plans for Administration of Conquered Areas in India', on microfilm at the General Services Administration, National Archives and Record Services, Washington.
Transfer of Power, Vol. VI.
The War Against Japan, Vol. III.
Subhas Bose's broadcasts on Rangoon Radio on 6.7.44 and Singapore Radio on 25.5.45.
Subhas Bose's *Selected Speeches; India Calling* and *Netaji Collected Works,* Vol. 12.
Fujiwara Essays SEATIC *Historical Bulletin* no. 240, Singapore, 9.7.46.
Iwaichi Fujiwara's *F. Kikan.*
Sisir Bose and Alexander Werth's *A Beacon Across Asia* (eds) and *Netaji and India's Freedom* (eds).
M. Sivaram's *The Road to Delhi.*
Sopan's *Netaji Subhas Chandra Bose: His Life and Work.*
Shah Nawaz Khan's *My Memories of the I.N.A. and its Netaji.*
Ayer's *Unto Him a Witness.*
Mohan Singh's *My Contribution to India's Independence.*
Ba Maw's *Breakthrough in Burma: Memoirs of a Revolution 1939-46.*
Milan Hauner's *India in the Axis Strategy.*
Ian Stephen's *Monsoon Morning.*
Hugh Toye's *The Springing Tiger* (revised unpublished edition).
Field Marshal William Slim's *Defeat into Victory.*
Louis Allen's *The End of the War in Asia.*
Moti Ram's *Two Historic Trials in Red Fort.*
Peter Fay's *The Forgotten Army.*

PART SIX: THE MYTH AND THE LEGEND

19 - What If He Had Returned?

Interview with Santimoy Ganguli.
Wavell's *The Viceroy's Journal.*
Suresh Bose's *Dissentient Report.*
Samar Guha's *Netaji - Dead or Alive?*
K.K. Ghosh's *Indian National Army.*
Gautam Chattopadhyay's *The Almost Revolution.*
B.C. Dutt's *Mutiny of the Innocents.*

20 - The Story without End

IPI File L/P&J/12/217, IOR.
Report into the death of Subhas Bose by Lt Col. J.G.Figgess, 25 July 1946.
Interviews with officials of the Record and Historical Department of the Foreign Office and India House in London, summer 2003, Justice Mukerjee, Dr Purabi Roy and Subrata Bose in Calcutta, February 2004 and Hugh Toye and Anita Pfaff.
Transcripts of evidence given to Mukerjee commission by various witnesses between 15 July 2000 and 27 November 2003.
Leonard Gordon's *Brothers Against the Raj.*

Books by Mihir Bose

History and Biography:
Michael Grade: Screening the Image
False Messiah: The Life and Times of Terry Venables
Memons
The Aga Khans

Business:
The crash: The 1987-88 world market slump
A new money crisis: a children's guide to money
Are you covered? An insurance guide
Fraud - the growth industry of the 1980s
How to invest in a Bear Market

Cricket:
Keith Miller: A Cricketing Biography
All in a Day: Great Moments in Cup Cricket
A Maidan View: The Magic of Indian cricket
Cricket Voices (interviews with players, officials, spectators etc)
A History of Indian cricket (Winner of the 1990 Cricket Society Literary Award)

Football:
Behind Closed Doors: Dreams and Nightmares at Spurs.
Manchester Unlimited: The Rise and Rise of Manchester United.

General Sport:
Sporting Colours: Sport and Politics in South Africa
(runner-up in William Hill Sports Book of the Year, 1994)
Sporting Babylon

Race and Sport:
The Sporting Alien